MW00535419

THE COMSTOCKS OF CORNELL

Portrait of the Comstocks painted by Professor Olaf Brauner, summer 1920.

THE COMSTOCKS OF CORNELL —THE DEFINITIVE AUTOBIOGRAPHY

ANNA BOTSFORD COMSTOCK

EDITED BY KAREN PENDERS ST. CLAIR

COMSTOCK PUBLISHING ASSOCIATES
AN IMPRINT OF CORNELL UNIVERSITY PRESS
Ithaca and London

First published 2020 by Cornell University Press

Printed in the United States of America

Library of Congress Cataloging-in-Publication Data

Names: Comstock, Anna Botsford, 1854–1930 author. | Penders St. Clair, Karen, editor.
Title: The Comstocks of Cornell—the definitive autobiography / Anna Botsford Comstock ; edited by Karen Penders St. Clair.
Description: Ithaca [New York] : Comstock Publishing Associates, an imprint of Cornell University Press 2020. | Includes bibliographical references and index.
Identifiers: LCCN 2019020876 (print) | LCCN 2019980589 (ebook) | ISBN 9781501716270 (cloth) | ISBN 9781501716287 (epub) | ISBN 9781501716294 (pdf)
Subjects: LCSH: Comstock, John Henry, 1849–1931. | Comstock, Anna Botsford, 1854–1930. | Cornell University—Faculty—Biography. | Entomologists—New York (State)—Ithaca—Biography. | College teachers—New York (State)—Ithaca—Biography. | Women wood-engravers—New York (State)—Ithaca—Biography.
Classification: LCC QL31.C65 C66 2020 (print) | LCC QL31.C65 (ebook) | DDC 595.7092 [B]—dc23
LC record available at https://lccn.loc.gov/2019020876
LC ebook record available at https://lccn.loc.gov/2019980589

This book is dedicated to the archivists and librarians of the Carl A. Kroch Library, Division of Rare and Manuscript Collections of Cornell University (2012–2017) who supported me in research and in friendship during this restoration project. An archivist preserves the voices of the past and allows these ephemeral narratives to speak their truths. These reverberations resonate for the rest of us and give a contextual connection to our past.

To the voice of Anna Botsford Comstock—written, preserved, and waiting. We may finally hear you as you had intended.

Dedication in the 1953 edition of *The Comstocks of Cornell.*

"This book is dedicated to fellow entomologists, to other scientists, and to the students and friends of Mr. and Mrs. Comstock, in the spirit of the gracious tribute paid to them by Cornell University students in the dedication of their historical yearbook, *The 1929 Cornellian.*

To

John Henry Comstock

and to

Anna Botsford Comstock

Partners in science, as in life,
By all revered as Scholars, Teachers, Writers,
And dear to many a student generation by reason
Of their open home and helpful hearts,
We dedicate this volume."

Anna Botsford Comstock, to thy name we sing
As we sit 'round the campfire each night.
And gladly in chorus our voices shall ring
As o'er us the heavens shine bright.
And the work that you've done, we will still carry on
With a will that is lasting and true,
'Neath the hills and the trees, by the lake that you loved
We will always remember you.

The lyrics sung for decades around a campfire by Girl Scouts camping on Cayuga Lake, Ithaca, New York, at Comstock Lodge. Liberty Hyde Bailey bequeathed the land to the Scouts, during Comstock's lifetime, for continued nature learning. She was grateful to him beyond the measure of words. Lyrics remembered by former Girl Scout, and nature enthusiast, Ann Brittain.

Contents

Acknowledgments

A book of this magnitude does not come together without incurring acknowledgments. From archival librarians to academics, from family to friends, I wish to thank you all with a humble heart and profound gratefulness. My appreciation is not diminished for those of you who are not specifically listed. In particular are:

The 2012–2017 staff of the Carl A. Kroch Library, Division of Rare and Manuscript Collections at Cornell University: Anne Carson, Tabitha Cary, Jude Corina, Evan Earle, Marcie Farwell, Erin Faulder, Connie Finnerty, Heather Furnas, Lance Heidig, Eileen Keating, Eisha Neely, Laura Linke, Freddie Lowe, Cheryl Rowland, Patrick Steven, Theo Wolf, and Hilary Dorsch Wong for their insight, patience, and humor as they handed me Box 8 time and time again. All images in the book were also provided courtesy of the Kroch Library, Division of Rare and Manuscript Collections.

To my husband, Kevin St. Clair, our daughters (Haley, Maris, Riley, Jordan, and Casey) with their families, and my parents, Les and MaryAnn Penders, my love and gratitude for your endurance, patience, and cheerleading.

To Kitty Liu, Meagan Dermody, Karen Laun, Candace Akins, and Cornell University Press for understanding my vision and wanting to bring this project to fruition.

To my dear friends Diane Kilts and Betty McKnight, as well as Randy and Amy Wayne, Erica Anderson, Bob Dirig, Bruce Britain, and Marty Schlabach for their personal and professional support over the past several years.

To Benjamin Stevens for German translation and to Theo Wolf for assistance in research for the French translation.

Finally, a special note of acknowledgment and thankfulness to Edward D. Cobb, research support specialist and historian for the School of Integrated Plant Science (Plant Biology section) at Cornell University, for his penchant for history, his interest and unwavering support of my work, and sincere genuineness. One could not have a better friend and colleague.

For the Reader

As editor of the twenty-first-century edition of *Comstocks of Cornell*, I have minimized my personal imprint on Mrs. Comstock's autobiography. My goal has been to preserve as much of her voice and personality as possible in her finished typescript since she wrote it ninety years ago. My edits, items I did not touch, and Mrs. Comstock's writing style are explained as follows:

- The paragraphing style of this book is Mrs. Comstock's, and she wrote in the present-tense, first-person point-of-view. The 1953 edition grouped her paragraphs and changed her tense to the second- and third-person points of view.
- Mrs. Comstock's language in her manuscript connects the timeline of her life, whereas the omissions and alterations of her language in the 1953 book chopped the connections. The alterations to phraseology were so prolific that context, tense, and voice of the manuscript were changed from Mrs. Comstock's to that of Glenn Herrick. The omission of emotional adjectives and substance minimized the impact of the storytelling capacity of Mrs. Comstock's memoir. She wrote as if she were sitting next to you and telling her story. Yet the sense of this intimacy was lost in the Herrick edits.
- Mrs. Comstock referred to her diaries as the template for her book. She wrote of her and her husband's day-to-day life and habits. In her publications, their lives were recorded and remembered with an emotional pleasure that is palpable through her writing and reminiscences. Unfortunately, these original diaries have not been recovered and are presumed to have been destroyed.
- The language of the 1953 edition differs from Mrs. Comstock's own verbiage. For example, we read on manuscript page 7–26: "He *told us plain truths* about our *inefficiency and lack of skill, but told them so sweetly* and *so* tactfully that we felt honored rather than disgraced." Compare this same sentence to the 1953 edition, page 153: "He

criticized our work so kindly and tactfully that we felt honored rather than disgraced."

- I have corrected little of Mrs. Comstock's language. I did correct blatant typographical errors (for example, she routinely misspelled the word "magnificent").
- I did not correct spelling if the word or phrase was colloquial to the time period, such as "Cryptogamic Botany, "non-plussed, "cosily," and "lustre."
- Nor did I correct Mrs. Comstock's writing pattern. For example, Mrs. Comstock would split words in ways we might not today: "Chicken-pox," "far-away," "high-strung," "room-mate."
- Mrs. Comstock did not regularly call her husband by his first name, as was written in the 1953 edition. The original editors substituted "Harry" for "Mr. Comstock" more often than not. In her manuscript, Mrs. Comstock refers to her husband, in the formal, almost eight hundred times, compared to the informal first name at forty-two times. This name replacement by Herrick and colleagues removed the formality of Mrs. Comstock's language and the respect she held for her husband in his academic position.
- Square brackets [ ] are placed around words that I or a previous editor clarified, primarily to explain state abbreviations, academic organizations, nicknames Mrs. Comstock used, or to reinstate initials in names that had been removed.
- Scripted brackets { } appear for sections of the manuscript that were initially omitted from the 1953 publication and that now have been returned to their place in this book. Through discussions with the publisher and myself, we came to an agreement that such a demarcation of the omitted text would interfere minimally with the reading experience of the reinstated material and would allow the reader to compare and contrast what are essentially two different books from one copy of the original manuscript.
- Parentheses ( ) are Mrs. Comstock's comments to herself as she typed her manuscript.
- Many of the sentences are transposed in the 1953 edition from the manuscript. The information relayed is unchanged and the essence of the meaning is comparable. The transposed sentences created some confusion for me as I compared the manuscript to the printed book.

—KSt.

74

5-24

I had been invited to an afternoon tea at the home of Mrs. Prentiss. The Prentisses had also been married that summer and had built a home on the Campus. I had worked hard all the morning and thought I had my house in order when I went out. Mrs. Prentiss, a woman older than myself and of much experience, was an exquisite housekeeper; she had furnished her home tastefully and with the aid of two maids kept it in beautiful order. I admired vastly the daintiness of the appointments in her home; when I came back to our house and opened the front door, I discovered that I had forgotten to dust the stairs before I went, and the sight of them was too much for me. I sat down on the lower step and wept, for it taught me that a housekeeper may try her best and yet fail to do everything just as it should be done. Moreover, the experience caused me, through the later years, to treat my maids with consideration. That year of housekeeping taught me to deal leniently with the human hazard in housework and to that lesson mainly I owe the fact that people who have worked for me have always cheerfully done their best.

Although our house was isolated and far from town, a grocer's wagon came twice a day, a meat wagon once, and the milk wagon morning and night. Of course we were economical, for our first ambition was to pay off the mortgage on our home. Professor Russell came to call one day and rapped vigorously with his knuckles on our front door. When we opened the door, he

Photograph of page 5–24 of the Comstock-manuscript.

Editor's Commentary

This book is the autobiography written by naturalist educator Anna Botsford Comstock and is also about her husband, the entomologist John Henry Comstock, during their tenure at Cornell University in its foundation years. The manuscript, which Mrs. Comstock had typed in preparation for publication, is based on her diaries during the zenith of their professional careers in their respective fields of study and on her personal reminiscences during the last years of their lives. The abstract statement for my doctoral thesis sums up the impetus for my years of research on the Comstock manuscript:

> Anna Botsford Comstock contributed significantly to fostering imagination in nature study education at the turn of the 20th century. Through the process of restoring the 'Comstocks of Cornell'-manuscript for historical accuracy and completeness, Comstock's genuine voice is revealed thereby emphasizing her written legacy in both scientific and Cornell University history.[1]

That research uncovered discrepancies between this document and the 1953 edition of *The Comstocks of Cornell*. The 1953 edition of *The Comstocks of Cornell* has been regarded with veneration as the definitive biography of John Henry and Anna Botsford Comstock by researchers since its publication. The first document in the original order of the book's publication was the little-known Comstock manuscript, typed by Mrs. Comstock, which served as the 1953 book's template. *The Comstocks of Cornell* (1953) was altered from its source, becoming a biographical book with third- and fourth-generation information, which was only a shadow of the autobiographical document that Mrs. Comstock wrote. The importance of my dissertation and its parallel archival research was to bring the egregious actions to light and to restore the voice of Mrs. Comstock to her own autobiography as definitively as

1. St. Clair, Karen Penders, *Finding Anna: The Archival Search for Anna Botsford Comstock* (2017). https://doi.org/10.7298/X44X55ZB.

possible. The significance of this book is that it resonates with the genuine voice of Mrs. Comstock. By using first- and second-generation material, touched only marginally by this editor, this book is as near to Comstock's original written piece as could be obtained.

For more than thirty years, Professor and Mrs. Comstock directly influenced the personal expression and professional imagination of their students. The collegiate lives of dozens of young men and women were enriched by their alliance with the Comstocks, and the Comstocks' influence also spread to their department colleagues during their tenure at Cornell.

Long after Mrs. Comstock had been awarded accolades for her wood-carving artistry in the illustrations of her husband's entomological work, and while she continued the development of her own nature study curriculum, Comstock sat down to write her and John Henry's biography. As Mrs. Comstock's widely acclaimed *Handbook of Nature Study* (1911) gained acceptance and popularity, however, other obligations pulled her from the autobiographical manuscript, and the document was put away until such time that Mrs. Comstock could devote herself fully to its completion.

The work on her autobiographical manuscript was picked up again around 1928, in the last years of Mrs. Comstock's life. During this time, Professor Comstock, an invalid from several strokes, could not speak or walk. Mrs. Comstock had been debilitated by cardiac problems for many years, and her strong frame weakened as cancer began its insidious unraveling of whatever good health remained. A determination to finish her work on the book, and the sense of urgency she must have felt as she labored over it, are palpable through the pages of the manuscript.

When Mrs. Comstock completed the manuscript, she did not have a title for her book. The task of editing, printing, and subsequently naming her book fell to the hands of others in the decades to follow. As probate and protocol dictated, after the death of Professor Comstock (six months following his wife) their collective effects and papers were ultimately bequeathed to Glenn Washington Herrick (1870–1965), their closest living relative, and to their attorney, George H. "Jim" Russell. The original 760-page autobiographical document was among the possessions bequeathed to these executors of the Comstock estate in February 1931.

Glenn Washington Herrick was a second cousin to Mrs. Comstock on her father's side. He said of his cousin that to everyone she always spoke beautifully and quietly. Those who knew her valued her friendship, her loveliness, and her sense of wonder of the world, which resonated through the grateful hearts she touched. It was at her urging that Herrick petitioned to attend Cornell University. Herrick was a student at Cornell University from 1892–1896 and followed in the footsteps of John Henry Comstock by studying in the department of entomology. He would say of his undergraduate years that the men who most impressed him were John Henry Comstock and Liberty Hyde Bailey for he was gratified to work with them and admired them completely. Herrick's passion for his own work stemmed from his devotion to his mentor, John Henry Comstock, a man he described as a natural teacher, quiet, kindly, and one who loved cigars.[2]

After graduation, Herrick was a biology professor at the State College of Mississippi, Starkville, for several years, and then briefly taught entomology at the Agricultural and Mechanical College of Texas, College Station. He returned to Cornell in 1909 as professor of economical entomology for the Department of Entomology and Limnology.[3] Those who knew Herrick characterized him as friendly, sincere, and a bit naïve. Herrick's teaching was described as animated and clear, his religious convictions strong, and his hospitality an enjoyment. He wrote many bulletins and papers on insect control that were considered good and inspiring, but not groundbreaking to the degree of his peers' accomplishments. Herrick, who was a lifelong accumulator of information, was bored after his retirement from Cornell University in 1935. He would occupy himself with projects that he hoped would give him a small boost of satisfaction, if not attention. Herrick carefully studied the newspaper in his retirement, saving every news clipping or document of interest to him, as it served as a valuable gateway to the world for him. Herrick preserved the corrected pages of his own articles and of those written about him. He kept original illustrations he rendered, the travel brochures from every place he visited across the United States (and into Canada), and ledger booklets of household expenses from 1917 to 1963. In the early 1950s, the fastidious Professor Herrick, rooted in a pattern of monotony, returned to a passion project he had tabled twelve years earlier. He still held the autobiographical manuscript of Mrs. Comstock, and he still desired to publish it, but this time under his own name. That the manuscript should fall to one who was painfully inclined to detail was fortuitous; however, Herrick's enthusiasm may have worked against him as he endeavored to share this last offering from the Comstocks. Herrick's devotion was admirable to one Comstock, but at the sacrifice of the voice of the other.

---

2. St. Clair, *Finding Anna*, p. 89.

3. From the Memorial Statement for Professor Glenn Washington Herrick who died in 1965. The memorial statements cited in this book were prepared by the Office of the Dean of the University Faculty of Cornell University to honor its faculty for their service to the university. https://ecommons.cornell.edu/handle/1813/19056.

As we follow the history of the Comstock manuscript and its publication, the enormity of the value of the document was not lost on Herrick. In 1937, he originally sought the manuscript's publication with guidance from a core of close intimates of the Comstocks. He did so through an exchange of twenty-one letters from the fall of 1937 until the following summer of 1938. Herrick took counsel from two Cornell emeritus professors, Simon Henry Gage (1851–1944) and George Lincoln Burr (1857–1938); or rather, he pushed for their opinion of and support for publication of the manuscript. In August 1937, Herrick wrote to Gage, then President of the Comstock Publishing Company, that he believed Mrs. Comstock's manuscript would make a "very interesting book" and was "a fine narrative" of both Comstocks. Herrick also believed that such a biographical book as this would have "wide remunerative value" and suggested two titles to Gage:

> Our Years Together as Teachers, Scientists and Writers: an Autobiography of John Henry Comstock and Anna Botsford Comstock, or
>
> A Life Program Together as Teachers, Scientists and Writers: an Autobiography etc.[4]

Herrick's plans were met with succinct objections by Professor Burr, a notable Cornell historian in his own right. In a letter to Herrick, dated April 1938, Burr questioned the historical significance of corrupting someone else's manuscript, especially after their death, and of the changes Herrick proposed to make, and had already made, to the document. Professor Gage, a close personal friend of both Professor and Mrs. Comstock, was significantly concerned about the Comstocks being personally presented in a diminished point of view. The manuscript was then passed from Simon Gage and George Burr to the critical eye of Woodford Patterson (1870–1948), editor of the *Cornell Alumni News* and secretary of the university. Patterson culled large sections from the document with a purple wax pencil. Patterson believed that the Comstock manuscript was too personal and trite for scholars of the Comstocks' character. He believed a book produced from such a manuscript would devalue the contributions both Comstocks made to their individual fields of study.

Patterson's terse review of Mrs. Comstock's autobiography halted any further discussion of publication with Herrick by the board of the Comstock Publishing Company. Shortly after receiving Patterson's letter of July 19, 1938, and the assessment contained within, Simon Gage met personally

---

4. St. Clair, *Finding Anna*, pp. 96–97.

with Glenn Herrick to persuade Herrick to curb his enthusiasm for publishing Mrs. Comstock's manuscript. Gage proposed that creating a marginal biography that emphasized the accomplishments of John Henry Comstock would be more appropriate to the Comstock legacy. Gage added that Mrs. Comstock's professional legacy was secondary to that of her husband's. Herrick wholeheartedly agreed with Gage; however, privately he was also more inclined toward establishing his name in the time line of the Comstocks' biography. Twelve years after this fateful meeting, Herrick's decision to send the document to print regardless of Gage's opinion was equal to Patterson's culling within the Comstock manuscript.

As mentioned above, when Herrick re-opened his files in the early 1950s to work on the manuscript, he did so with all previous detractors to his project being deceased. With such key participants (Gage, Burr, and Patterson) silenced, Herrick had the literary freedom for the final dissection of the Comstock manuscript. The worthiness of Herrick's publication efforts collapse when one realizes that he was the one who corrupted the *Comstocks of Cornell* in every plausible way the others had hoped to preserve of the Comstocks' legacy—the historical, the personal, and the academic. At any time during these early phases of the second publication attempt of the Comstock book, Herrick could have reset the marginalized document back to its near 1937 format, which he had enthusiastically tried to sell to Gage, Burr, and others. Yet, years later, he remained swayed by Woodford Patterson's critique against Mrs. Comstock's memoirs, particularly as Herrick believed Professor Comstock may have been diminished, and as such, he kept Patterson's expunctions.

Whatever essential core of Mrs. Comstock's persona remained after Patterson's culling was further altered by Herrick's over-enthusiastic admiration for Professor Comstock. Herrick removed the emotional grit of the attachments Mrs. Comstock held to objects, people, or situations significant to her throughout their lives. The personal anecdotes, emotional adjectives, historical Cornell University persona, and truly, any statement of detraction—or declination of Mr. Comstock that Herrick perceived as damaging to the deceased entomologist's career by Mrs. Comstock—was omitted by his critical hand. Herrick's severe edits and omissions created for posterity a third- and fourth-generation document that diminishes the stature of Mrs. Comstock's university status as a professor's wife, the legacy of her work and professorship, and her intentions to preserve their lives equally. The ramifications of such a personal sense of hubris on the part of Herrick created a book that is not a piece of fiction but is also not entirely genuine when compared to its manuscript. Herrick changed the first-person narrative of Mrs. Comstock to a third-person narrative with him as the voice of the Comstocks.

The only printed edition of *The Comstocks of Cornell* has served as a reference for many books and publications since its debut. As a historical reference piece of the beginnings of Cornell University, and of the lives of the Comstocks, the book represented a window into a particularly poignant time of Cornell's history as told with a singular voice from that time: Mrs. Comstock's. The recension of large portions of Comstock's memoirs of her and her husband's personal and professional life together is not unique or unusual, nor singular in its occurrence. Written documentation that has been altered in such a way is a continual critical talking point among rhetoric and archival researchers. The altering of facts, recollections, and point of view in the recording of history is so prevalent through time that to discover an example where these instances are *not* adulterated would be the true find.

The document that is Anna Botsford Comstock's autobiographical manuscript is preserved in the Division of Rare and Manuscript Collections at the Carl A. Kroch Library within Cornell University. What remains of the document today is 712 pages in length, forty-six pages less than what Woodford Patterson reported receiving in 1938. The Comstock manuscript is composed of twenty chapters, denoted by Roman numerals, by both Mrs. Comstock and myself, for continuity. The shortest chapters are I and XIX at twenty-six pages each; the longest manuscript chapter is IV, at sixty-six pages, and concerns Anna Botsford's family history, childhood, and youth up to her admission to Cornell University. For comparison, in the 1953 edition of the book, Anna Comstock's early life is recorded in thirty-five pages, with the longest chapter in the book, regarding John Henry Comstock, his childhood, youth, and his work, at fifty-two pages.

Manuscript Chapters XV (35 pages), XVI (33 pages), XVII (55 pages), XVIII (47 pages), XIX (26 pages), and XX (34 pages) total to 230 pages of the manuscript and were all omitted from the 1953 edition of the book. This figure does not include the many paragraphs, several pages, and other chapters also removed from the manuscript.

Chapter XIV is missing and per Herrick in a note he left at the front of Chapter XV: "Chapter XIV: I cannot account for it."[5] The parallel chapter in the 1953 edition, Chapter 15, is titled "Cornell's New Quarters for Entomology and Nature Study." This chapter is duplicated in this book as it was printed in the 1953 edition. Important in this chapter is the chronological range of 1908–1912 during which time Mrs. Comstock relays how

5. John Henry and Anna Botsford Comstock papers, #21-23-25. Division of Rare and Manuscript Collections, Cornell University Library.

she conceived of the idea of, and prints, her magnum opus, *The Handbook of Nature Study*. It is within the time frame of this chapter that the Comstocks bought, and sold, the land called The Pinnacle, which would later be the site of the rhododendron and azalea collection on Comstock Knoll at the Cornell Botanic Garden. In this chapter is when they purchased the property that would become their last permanent home and the future site of Comstock Publishing Company. In this chapter, Mr. Comstock finished the manuscript for *The Spider Book*, and John Walton Spencer, nature study educator in partnership with Mrs. Comstock, who was known fondly as "Uncle John" by thousands of nature-enthusiastic children, succumbed of unknown causes in Ithaca, New York. The death of Spencer is significant because his loss brought the end of an era in nature education, not only in his home state of New York but also nationwide given that his work reached thousands of children. We can only surmise what might have been omitted from this chapter.

Another significant artifact of the 1953 edition is the choppy chronological order of the book's format. For example, Chapter 16 splits the year 1912 (a leftover remnant from Chapter 15 described above) and continues through to 1914. Several prominent events in the Comstocks' personal and professional lives occurred during these years that Mrs. Comstock would have unabashedly described, or at the very least commented upon, although she may have been silenced for her candor. Such events include the surprising retirement of Liberty Hyde Bailey as dean of the College of Agriculture at Cornell in June 1913. Not six months later, in December 1913, Professor Comstock resigned his Cornell professorship to take effect almost immediately, at the end of the year. Alice McCloskey, also at Cornell as a prominent nature study educator in her own right, became an associate in rural education and edited the Rural School Leaflets. The following year, 1914, McCloskey was promoted to assistant professor, as was Mrs. Comstock. McCloskey, however, is demoted to "Mrs. Comstock's assistant" in the 1953 edition and is mentioned only the one time. My point here is that Mrs. Comstock gave credit to her peers where credit was due, which is evident in her manuscript, but not in the 1953 edition of the book. Further research on my part yielded that the two women were dissimilar on many levels. Comstock was considered a scholar, artist, and scientist. McCloskey was considered frank and sincere, yet maybe less educated. Perhaps Herrick knew of this contention and opted for the latter's removal? Other nature educators mentioned in Mrs. Comstock's manuscript were omitted from the book, including Julia Rogers and Ada Georgia. Mary Rogers Miller is mentioned once in the book in a footnote referencing her husband. All of these women made significant contributions to nature literature and nature education in the disciplines of their interests. Today they are among the specters lost by judicious omission.

Not everything was crossed off in the manuscript, however; some of the initially untouched text in the manuscript was also *not* included in the book. This led to careful reading and comparison on my part between the manuscript and the 1953 edition to recapture what (or who) was lost, to re-introduce emotional descriptors and colloquial language, and to ensure accuracy and completeness. All 712 pages (except for Chapter XIV as mentioned above) of Mrs. Comstock's manuscript have been restored completely in this book.

The 1953 edition of *The Comstocks of Cornell* is 267 pages in length, also divided into twenty chapters; however, the last chapter is only four paragraphs in length. Some changes were made by Herrick for diplomacy, or what we today call "political correctness," particularly regarding slavery, religion, or university politics. Details lost in the 1953 edition include those of early Ithaca, New York; early Cornell University milestones; and pioneering personalities, visitors, and alumni of Cornell University across several departments. As mentioned previously, the choppiness in the chronology of the book comes from the omission of great portions of (or entire) chapters spliced together with the remnants. A sobering example of such a schism occurs at page 229 of the 1953 edition: Mrs. Comstock's infamous *Handbook of Nature Study* is first mentioned here, and shockingly, there remains only forty-two pages in the biography for the discussion of the final twenty-five years of the Comstocks' lives!

This 1953 edition has served as a single important source to describe the collective history and background information of both Professor and Mrs. Comstock, their colleagues, and Cornell University. The ramifications of Herrick's actions have affected more than sixty years of researchers and educators. Anna Comstock's voice is one worth recovering from her original manuscript because she tells the history of her husband's entomological work and her nature-study work at the turn of the 20th century. The anecdotes she provides give a strength of precedence to the work we do today in agricultural, entomological, and horticultural extension work, as well as nature education and public garden initiatives. The extent to which Comstock is still referenced today in these disciplines legitimizes the strength of historical relevance of her memoirs. Knowing both John Henry and Anna Comstock through their complete biography, and autobiography, helps us to rediscover their efforts, the efforts of their colleagues, and opens us to listen to their collective legacy.

Karen Penders St. Clair
Ithaca, New York

THE COMSTOCKS OF CORNELL

John Henry Comstock, n.d.

Chapter I

The Boyhood of John Henry Comstock, 1849–1865

Professor Comstock contributed his own recollections to this chapter by dictating them to his wife. Anna Comstock refers to John Henry Comstock as "Henry" in the early chapters of her manuscript, when she wrote of his childhood, and until they become a married couple in her Chapter V. Thereafter, Comstock refers to him as "Mr. Comstock" throughout the manuscript. Two exceptions in her manuscript to this etiquette are the instances where she, herself, annotates a personal conversation with him, or that of her parents, Mr. and Mrs. Botsford, when he is informally called "Harry." This protocol was not used for the 1953 edition. Words, sentences, or sections omitted from the 1953 edition appear here in scripted brackets { }. —KSt.

{For a hundred years of her history, the push of enterprise has been westward in America. To us today it is quite inconceivable that a century ago New England seemed to be suffering from overpopulation. A host of pioneers pushed out into the wilds of New York State and the more daring ones were going even as far as Illinois, Michigan and Wisconsin. Always the vigorous and ambitious had found their limitations in the old civilization unbearable, and with faces turned eagerly toward the setting sun they pressed on to untold hardships and greater opportunity.}

It was in the year 1848 that an ambitious pair fared westward from Stephentown, New York, {a town that almost touches} the borders of Massachusetts {and is therefore truly of New England in its characteristics}. Here

Daniel Allen had reared a large family that was destined to scatter to the uttermost limits of America. His youngest daughter, Susan Allen, {had fallen in love with and} married Ebenezer Comstock, who had come from Massachusetts to teach school and give lessons in singing in the neighborhood of Stephentown {in 1847}. Immediately after their marriage they bade farewell to family and friends and migrated bravely to {Janesville,} Wisconsin.

Little enough do we know of Ebenezer Comstock, except that he was ambitious, an excellent singer, and that through his own efforts he had obtained the means of studying for the better part of two years at Williams College. He was several years older than his bride and the Comstock genealogy makes him a direct descendant of Samuel Comstock, a Quaker who settled in Providence, R.I., before 1648. Of {his wife}, Susan, we know much, for she lived a long, brave life; and because of certain heroic qualities in her, we may well believe a tradition that her Allen ancestors were relative of the redoubtable Ethan. She was a sweet-tempered, gay girl, with a love for finery, which her husband also secretly liked, although his religious convictions were against the pomp and vanities of the world. There is, in an old chest in our garrett, a beautiful velvet waistcoat, a dumb witness that Ebenezer liked personal adornment for himself. In fact, the few things we have left of him indicate a man of fastidious personal tastes.

Ebenezer had saved a little money and with it he purchased a farm in the year 1848. Today the lands which formerly comprised the farm lie within the city limits of Janesville. Unfortunately the major portion of the purchase price of the farm remained unpaid in the form of a mortgage. But here in their new surroundings the pair found friendly neighbors and happiness in creating a home in pioneer fashion. Here, on February 24, 1849, their son, John Henry, was born.

In this same year gold was discovered in California, and dreams of riches drove everything reasonable from the minds of men. Little wonder that the contagious excitement captured the adventurous spirit of Ebenezer Comstock. The possibilities of future wealth were discussed by Ebenezer and Susan, with always a thought of the future of their little son. At last the arrangement was made. A man was to work the farm and keep up payments on the mortgage for three years, which was the limit of time Ebenezer planned to be gone; so he purchased his outfit, bade a hopeful farewell to wife and child—for who could doubt his return, possessed of wealth, in three short years?—joined a train of covered wagons and started on the long journey, while the wife settled down to the care of her baby and the farm.

But alas for high hopes and future plans! The emigrant train consisted of two hundred men and some women and children. In those days little was known of preventive medicine, and before the journey was fairly begun cholera broke out in the ill-fated community. At once the party divided for the sake of safety. Ebenezer Comstock was one of twenty healthy, stalwart members who separated themselves from the others and pushed on. But somewhere along the River Platte the scourge overtook them, and of the twenty only two escaped and went on. It was not until many years later that one of those two sent back word of the death of Ebenezer, and of the place where it had occurred.

Meanwhile misfortune had overtaken Susan Comstock. The man left in charge of the farm was not efficient and did not make enough money to meet the payments due on the mortgage. Then the poor wife discovered that she was in the hands of a scheming money-lender, who made a business of selling farms and foreclosing as soon as the law allowed. Cheated out of her property, she sold her household goods and with her year-old son started eastward, to rejoin her people. She spent a year at Milton, Wisconsin, with her sister and brother-in-law, Mr. and Mrs. Nelson Carr. These two, however, were soon to be drawn westward by the charm of Eldorado. The next year Susan Comstock spent at Pierpont and Conneaut, Ohio, in each place finding a situation as housekeeper where she could care for her child and earn some money; and finally, when Henry was four years old, she reached her own people in the State of New York.

There are but few stories of Henry's babyhood extant. He was of a nervous temperament and very active—characteristics that lasted throughout his life. I once said to his Aunt Hannah, "He must have been a little terror," to which she answered: "On the contrary, he was a very obedient child and very easy to manage. He needed to be kept busy and I gave him a little tin pail which he spent hours in filling with chips and bringing into the house. I never saw a better child." There was one incident, however, that remained in the mind of his mother and aunt as long as they lived. One Sunday morning they dressed Henry in white and put him in the bedroom, closing the door for safety while the others were donning church apparel. When they were ready they went for the child, but he was not to be found. A window that opened on the piazza had been raised, so little that it did not seem possible that even the child's head could have been squeezed through. A frantic search ended in amazement when Henry was found sitting in the pig trough, feeding the pigs and looking much like one of them. They were late to church that day.

Henry's earliest recollection was of being held in some one's arms and hearing some one say, "We are out of sight of land." This must have occurred during a journey on the Great Lakes from Milton, Wisconsin, to Ohio.

Susan was independent and ambitious and soon found a place as housekeeper for a merchant of the Powell in Troy, New York. Mr. Powell was a widower with a small daughter, Mary; and, barring the uncertainty of the fate of her husband, Susan and Henry were happy in this new home. In fact,

Susan had the faculty of making a home even where she was only a temporary sojourner. But again adversity overtook her. She became ill and for two years was unable to do anything for the support of her child. She was taken to a hospital, the Marshall Infirmary, and by some fate not quite explainable the little boy was put in an orphan asylum, for the time being. Alas for the children in orphanages in the benighted days when the contract for food for the inmates was given to the lowest bidder! Mr. Comstock's recollections of this experience give a graphic picture of the conditions:

> "My memory is somewhat vague. I thought there were about three hundred children there, but am not sure. A few things stand out clearly. At night we slept in a large room which, I think, was an attic, immediately under the roof. The beds were double and were arranged around the sides of the room. I do not know whether there was more than one sleeping room for boys or how many of us were in this room—perhaps forty or fifty. There were recesses in the sides of the room, perhaps leading to dormer windows. The boys occupying these used to hang bedclothes in front, and have a circus behind this curtain after the attendants were gone. We were all invited to the circus. The only toilet facility accessible to us at night was a large vessel in the center of the room. Many of the children suffered from ophthalmia [*sic*] and one of the regular occurrences was the lining up of the children and administering to each an eye-wash. The attendants were invariably kind to us.
>
> "Several long tables were in the dining room at which we stood when we ate and were served by several young women. Fare was scanty. For breakfast we had a liquid called chocolate and a half-slice of bread. I do not remember so much about the mid-day meal, except that frequently, if not always, it consisted of a dish of vegetable soup. I did not care for carrots, the boy who was my neighbor at table did not like turnips, so we used to exchange the few pieces of these in our soup.
>
> "The evening meal was not served in the dining room, but was brought up to the assembly room in large dishpans and consisted of a half-slice of bread over which there had been spread molasses. On Sunday we marched to church and on return were served with a meal, the big element of which, I remember, was a piece of boiled beef for each child.
>
> "The one bright memory I have of my stay in this asylum is of the following incident: It was a rule that if anything was lacking at a child's place at the table, nothing was to be said about it until the close of the meal. One morning there was no bread at my basin of chocolate and I was forced to stand fasting through what seemed to me an interminable

meal. After the children had left the dining room, I went down to the serving table at one end and told of the oversight to one of the attendants, at which she took up a loaf of bread and cut me a slice across the entire loaf. This full slice of bread seemed more sumptuous than any banquet of which I have partaken in my later years.

"One day I was called to the reception room where I found an old uncle of my mother who had come to see me. He made a short call and went away, but I have been told that he said to his wife on reaching home, "Polly, they are starving Susan's boy and we must take him out of the asylum." Soon I was brought to his home, to what seemed to me a heaven of plenty."

Uncle Daniel lived on a mountain, and this impressed the small boy very much. It was here that Henry had his first schooling; it must have been when he was five years old. He remembers the old-fashioned schoolhouse with the writing desk placed along the side of the room and a backless bench below it. The big scholars sat with their legs on one side of the bench when writing, then swung them over to the other side to face the teacher when reciting. One other thing he remembers was a great rock, probably a boulder, near the schoolhouse, on which the children played; it was an awesome rock, because printed in it were hollows shaped like a foot and a hand, and the children firmly believed that these prints had been made by Satan himself.

Henry was to stay with his uncle only until his mother might become able to care for him. Mrs. Comstock had a sympathetic, winning nature; and partly because of this natural aptitude, and perhaps partly because of the contacts made during her long illness in the infirmary, she decided to become a nurse. Of course this was before the day of trained nurses. Her decision made it necessary for her to find a home in which Henry could be cared for while she was serving in her new profession. At this juncture Susan's elder brother, John Allen, who was a Freewill Baptist minister with a parish in North Scriba [*sic*], New York, wrote to her offering to take the lad for the winter. The offer was gratefully accepted and the boy remained for more than two years a member of his uncle's family. The memory of this period was not a happy one. Aunt Alma, the wife of John Allen, was a saintly woman, who was very kind to the child, but Uncle John, being a minister, was around the house most of the time and took the disciplining of Henry very seriously. With the good old fashioned theory that a boy can be whipped out of all error, he dealt "according to his lights" with the lad. His letters to his sister always assured her that Henry was a good boy and that he was sent regularly to school and was learning fast. But Henry had the misfortune to stammer in his speech and Uncle John undertook to break him of the habit by corporal punishment, a measure scarcely suited to the temperament of a highly nervous and sensitive child. Henry's nervousness was also the cause of further whippings, for he was required to wash dishes in a stone sink and was punished every time he broke a dish. His Aunt Alma, however, had taught him to write, so that now, in his eighth year, he could write his mother a letter:

"November 14, 1856

My dear mother:

I thought I would write you a few words and let you know how I am. It is vacation now and Aunt is learning me how to write, so when school commences I can write in school. I shall have a new fourth reader before school commences; the price of the reader is 68 cents. Tell Grandma that I am sorry that she has been sick so long. Tel Judson and Jane that I will like to see them very much. Sarah Jane has got so she can run all around. I should think that grandpa would feel very bad to have grandma sick so long.

From your son Henry Comstock"

The Sarah Jane whose "running around" Henry mentions in his letter was the baby daughter of Uncle John, and it was really through her that his stay at his uncle's terminated. Evidently the lad's stammering was a sore affliction to Uncle John, for he wrote to his sister:

> "I like Henry very well with the exception of his stuttering, which is quite annoying, and my little girl will mimic him every time she hears him, which gives me many painful feelings. I try to stop him when I am in hearing and then, usually, he talks quite straight. I am sorry it is so. I would not have Sarah get into that habit—not for any money. I will keep him till Spring and will do my best to break him of it, and if I cannot succeed I would rather he would go."

The boy's well-to-do aunt, Mrs. Nelson Carr, who now lived in Rosa, California, wrote to Uncle John asking about Henry with a view to adopting him. The reply was that he stammered and would never amount to anything and that they had best not consider the matter, which makes it clear that there was no love lost between Uncle John and his nephew, but although Henry disliked his uncle, he was always devoted to his Aunt Alma. Uncle

John certainly never understood how his harshness cut to the soul the high-strung boy in his charge. On the contrary, he always felt that he had done a great deal for Henry, and after the latter had a home of his own made him a visit which, owing to my influence with my husband, was quite amicable. I remember him as an imposing man, big, with white hair, and evincing still the indomitable will that essayed by brute force to crush out the stammer from a little boy's speech.

Susan Comstock, owing to her success as a nurse, had been able to pay for the keep of her boy and had clothed him. From time to time Henry dutifully acknowledged the money and the clothing sent by his mother:

"December 1856

Dear Mother,

I received the money that you sent me and got my boots and received the clothes you sent me and am very thankful for them. I am going to school Monday and I hope to see you before long. Excuse this short letter from your son

Henry Comstock."

When John Allen received a call to another church he left Henry in the family of a neighbor, Henry Green. These people were {very} kind to the boy. It was inconvenient, however, for them to keep him during the winter of 1858, and they, in turn, found a place for him in the family of Timothy Donohue, whose members also were {very} kind to the little stranger under their roof. The Donohues had previously lived in Oswego and they continued to attend church there, driving in from Scriba. This impressed Henry {greatly}. He writes to his mother: "I go to Sunday School every Sunday. There are 70 scholars . . . I go to meeting at the Episcopal church." His memory of his stay with the Donohues was pleasant, although the family was very poor and their fare very plain. He remembered that his lunch for school consisted of bread with only a piece of salt pork between the slices. He was ashamed to {display this in the presence of} let the other children see it and always ate his lunch in the woodshed. However scanty his fare at the Donohues, it was as good as the family had, and he was not dissatisfied.

The next summer he went back to the Greens. It is now that we begin to get evidence of his longing {and homesickness} for his mother, which was to be the undercurrent of his life for the coming years. But he realized that she was doing the best she could and he never complained. In May, 1859,

Mrs. Green adds the following postscript to a letter which Henry had just written his mother:

"Henry writes a few lines with a broken heart to his mother and with tears in his eyes." It is interesting in the light of this information to read Henry's letter:

> "My dear mother: I take my pen in hand to write a few lines to let you know how I am well and like to live with Mr. Green. Mrs. Green sends her respects to you and she says that I am a good boy. She says she wants you to write to her. Mr. Green has had a letter from Uncle John stating that they are all well excepting Sarah has had the chicken-pox. Excuse this short letter."

Not one word in this staunch missive indicated to the far-away mother that he was broken-hearted because he could not see her.

Henry was evidently a very delicate child and the wonder is that he lived at all. Almost every letter from Mr. and Mrs. Green to his mother speaks of his health as "improving" or tells of some illness. But there is one constant message in these letters, as in those of his Aunt Alma, "Henry is a good boy." The reiteration is reassuring when we consider that he was also quick-tempered, {and that he was exceedingly} active, nervous, and high-strung. He always "moved like a flash," as has been said of him hundreds of times.

In the summer of 1860, when he was eleven years old, Henry took a hand in his own destiny. His longing to see his mother seemed about to be realized. He had made arrangements to go with a man to Schenectady, where Mrs. Comstock was then living. The journey began with high hopes, but {unfortunately an unexpected down-pour} a heavy rain had torn out a bridge on the railroad and both passengers were obliged to return to their homes. His heart almost breaking, the disappointed boy trudged homeward along the hot, dusty road. Suffering with thirst, he stopped at a {friendly} farmhouse to rest and get a drink. A kindly, {motherly old lady} woman met him at the door and invited him to sit down on the porch. She sensed at once a troubled child and by dint of easy questioning drew forth the story of his young life. It touched her motherly instincts {deeply} and she called to her husband, to whom the story was repeated. These two {individual} persons, Captain Lewis Turner and his wife Rebecca, were then and there to begin their role as foster parents of this lonely child. Before the story was fairly told Captain Turner, encouraged by the unmistakable sympathy of Rebecca, had made up his mind to offer the boy a home. He told Henry that he needed a boy to help him about the place, for his own sons were all grown and gone from home. But the boy was torn with his desire to see his mother, and in any case he felt that he must consult the Greens before making a decision. The Greens were wise people in their common judgments. They assured Henry that this would be a fine place for him and that he would do well to accept the offer, especially since the railroad might not be repaired for a long time and no one knew when he might be able to reach his mother. So the boy went back to the Turners' and {together} he and the Captain made the bargain. He was to have his board and clothes and three months of winter schooling; in return he was to do whatever work Captain Turner wished. He was to come for the summer on trial, and if both parties liked the arrangement he was to continue. In the new home of which he thus became an inmate he formed ties of affection that remained strong for a lifetime.

Captain Turner {was a remarkable man. He} had served for years on the Great Lakes as a master of schooners, which in those days engaged in the grain and lumber trade with the ports of Lake Michigan and Lake Superior. There was a large fleet of these boats and during the winters the harbor of Oswego was full of them. Oswego was a very important city in those days because it was the port farthest east. Its wharves were extensive and a row of great grain elevators lined the east shore of the Oswego River.

Navigating a sailing ship on the Great Lakes is a highly specialized calling. No experience on salt water prepares a man for it. During the summer the waters may be smooth and the winds gentle, but in the spring and fall it requires great knowledge and skill to keep the ships off the dangerous shores; indeed, many a vessel has gone down in the midst of the turmoil even of open waters.

Captain Turner was capable, fearless, and honest. He had retired from sailing because of age and lameness. It was in 1882 that I first saw {Captain Turner} him. He was still a handsome man with features clear-cut and with silvery hair; although then eighty or more years old, he was still an impressive personality, vigorous and original in thought and expression.

Not less interesting was Rebecca, the wife of Captain Turner. She was born in the Mohawk Valley of Dutch parents and spoke Dutch fluently all her life. Her personality was strong and vivid and her heart warm. She was a good housekeeper, a famous cook, and a woman of fine sentiment, judging from the contents of her many letters to Henry's mother. They were written in a fine, old-fashioned hand and were sweet and comforting, and withal newsy and entertaining. Her sense of humor cropped out in the superscription of her letters from "Hurricane Hall." Between the pranks of her sailor sons when they were at home in the winter with nothing to do and the stentorian commands of her {Captain} husband the Turner home was {certainly} a breezy place.

There were three sons in the Turner family. The eldest was Joel, who was already captain of a ship. Henry, unmarried, was the next who with the advent of the Comstock boy made two Henrys in the family, a source of some confusion. This was obviated by calling the smaller boy Hank, or more often Hankey. Lucian, the youngest boy, was about eighteen and he too was a sailor. His home name was "Whig". Of course all these boys were at home winters, when the lakes were frozen. All of them gave the little stranger welcome, made playthings for him, and treated him in a most kindly and friendly way. He returned the affection with a devotion such as only a lonely boy could give. Although he was taken at first on trial the matter was soon settled. The following letter is the first one written by Henry to his mother concerning his new home:

"April 18, 1860

"Dear Mother:

"I take my pen in hand to let you know how I am. I am well and hope you are. I was fortunate enough to find a place to live this summer, a mile from Scriba Corners, at Captain Lewis Turner's. I like to live here very much and I would like to have you come here this summer to see me. Excuse this short letter.

"From your son, Henry Comstock".

In his next letter he tells something of his duties at the Turners': "You wanted to know in your letter what I do here. I get up in the morning and get the cows and I milk one cow and feed the chickens and pigs and the little turkeys and the calf. I asked Mr. Turner if he thought he would keep me this winter and he said he didn't know anything to the contrary. I would like to see you very much".

It is interesting, through Mrs. Turner's letters to Mrs. Comstock, to trace the growth of the reciprocal understanding and affection between Henry and the Turners. Mrs. Turner's first letter gives a picture of the boy's life with them that first summer.

"Scriba, April 21, 1860.

"Mrs. Comstock

"Dear Madam:

"Permit me to address a few lines to you; although a stranger to me you are the mother of "Little Henry" as we call him, whom circumstances have thrown under my care. I will try to do the best I can for him—We like your

Henry very much and I think he is suited; he seems quite happy playing with his ships and other toys. He has four ships chasing each other on a pole like a windmill and when the wind blows they get wrecked quite often and he displays much skill in repairing them. He is very sensitive, and he often speaks of you and reads your letters over and over. I wish you would come and see him.

"Yours respectfully,

"Mrs. R. A. Turner"

The next letter shows that Mrs. Turner's motherly sympathy had fathomed the misery of the boy's heart and his homesickness for his mother. She writes:

"Scriba, N.Y.

"August 30, 1860.

"Mrs. Comstock,

"Dear Madam:

"I think it about time that you heard from your child. I tried to get him to write, but he said he did not know what to write. I told him what to write several times, but he would cry and say he could not. I do not know what has come over the child, but I think his heart pains to see his mother.

"I told him he must write and gave him materials and left him alone in the dining room. In about two hours I went in and found him crying as if his heart would break. You will see the first page blotted with his tears. I wish you would write immediately and let me know when you will come.

"Please accept my best wishes,

"Rebecca A. Turner."

In response to these letters Mrs. Comstock promised to come as soon as she could leave the patient she was caring for. She did so, and her visit was of infinite comfort to the boy. He slept with his mother and was loved and cuddled to his heart's content. But when she had to leave the parting was very hard. Mrs. Turner wrote:

> "I pity the poor child from my heart. Yesterday morning I heard him crying and tried to comfort him but he said 'I can't help it. I woke up and went to kiss my mother and she was not there this morning.' I heard him crying again before daylight this morning. Mr. Turner was up as usual and so I called Hankey to come and get into bed with me.

> He put his arms around my neck and kissed me and I told him I would be his mother and love him all I could. He said, 'I know it, but I am lonesome'. You don't know how much that child loves you and you have great reason to bless God for such a child . . . He has his book tonight and is very cheerful; he is to have a sleigh and learn to skate and I will do all I can to make him happy."

The loneliness of the boy and his pathetic longing for his mother struck a deep chord of sympathy in Mrs. Turner's heart and she received the child into a corner of her affections on an equality with her own sons. Ever after the foregoing incident, she was "Ma Becky" to him, and Captain Turner soon became "Pa Lewis", terms of affection which were continued to the end of their days.

The life at Hurricane Hall was interesting. During the summers Henry was alone with Captain and Mrs. Turner, but when the sons came home in the winter life became more exciting. Captain Turner always had on the farm a yearling bull, and one of the regular "circus" performances of the Turner boys was to "break the bull" as soon as the first sleighing occurred. With an improvised harness, the boys would quietly hitch the bull to a stone-boat while they were safely in the barn with all of the doors shut. Then the door was opened and there was a war-whoop, with the frightened bull tearing forth in a frantic effort to get away from the monstrous thing to which he was tied. The boys would ride on the boat when they could catch it right-side-up, but those moments were rare. Most of their efforts were spent in keeping out of the way of the skipping, bobbing boat and within capturing distance of the crazy bull. When the animal had run until he was tired out, the stone-boat was lifted around and the beast was headed for home. After a few lessons of this kind the animal would become docile and amenable to command; then, of course, the sport was over.

The next year after Mrs. Comstock's visit Joel Turner, "Captain Joe", was married and there was a daughter in the house until a home nearby was prepared. Henry soon became fond of "Maggie", the new sister, and they remained staunch friends during her long, sad widowhood. Joel Turner was a strong, fine man with marked ability, evinced by the fact that he was made captain of a schooner while very young. He was still a young man when one fall his ship was caught in a terrific gale and went down with all on board, not a man surviving to tell of the catastrophe. The one mute witness to mark the wreck was a drifting yawl which had belonged to the ship. It was just another tragedy of the sea, leaving in its wake a young widow with five small children.

Henry Turner's marriage occurred some years after Henry Comstock's advent into the family. His wife was a {charming}, witty and interesting woman and she proved to be an important factor in Henry's life. She was a reader and Henry's ally in political discussions; the Turners were all Democrats, but Henry, owing to his views regarding slavery, was a "red hot" Republican. He remained firm in his belief despite the constant influence of this family for which he cared so sincerely. He has often said that he would have been "pretty lonesome" in his stand if it had not been for "Mate", as Mrs. Henry Turner was called in the family.

The youngest son, Lucian Turner, married early and lived near at hand. After many years he abandoned the life of a sailor and, as fate would have it, spent his last years in Ithaca, where he had a position with the Ithaca Trust Company, a place in which his absolute honesty and reliabilty were important factors. The oldest son, dead before Henry Comstock joined the family, had also been a sailor same to the conditions of the family. It was late fall and his ship was making its last trip, when a terrible sleet and snow storm swept over the lake; the waves were high and the rigging was covered with ice. Lewis Turner, although a mere lad, was the only man of the crew who could be trusted at the wheel, and there he stood without relief for forty-eight hours. He brought his ship into port, but the strain brought on pneumonia resulting in tuberculosis, which ran its course rapidly.

It was characteristic of Captain Lewis Turner that he lived up to his exact promise to the boy. Henry was given his winter schooling, and on no occasion, however great the need of his help, was he allowed to miss one day at school. On the other hand, no matter how slack the work on the farm, he was never permitted to go to school in the summer.

Letters from Mrs. Turner to Mrs. Comstock often mentioned the fact that Henry was "learning fast". However, he had great difficulty with his spelling. He has often said, "I could learn to spell all right if the words of the English language were spelled as they sound". In his letters to his mother the words were usually spelled correctly, but he says that this was due to his constant consultation of his spelling book. His handwriting in the first letter to his mother was plain and bore many of the characteristics of his hand in his later years. A letter to his mother when he was fourteen gives an interesting account of his work on the farm and of his thrifty habits:

> "Ma Becky and Pa Lewis have gone visiting and Mate has gone to see her little brother and I am alone. We expect the boys home in a week and we have our fall work done and I am ready to go to school, which commences next week. We have raised four hundred bushels of corn, one hundred bushels of potatoes and a great many apples. I wish you were here to help eat them. We made eight barrels of cider besides many cider apples we sold. I have a turkey to sell that I raised. Pa Lewis

has given me a lamb and is going to winter it for me. I have got the pay for my blackberries, which was ten shillings and six cents. Wasn't that a good day's work; 21 quarts at 6 cents a quart? I did not put any money in the bank. I am trapping for mink and muskrat. A good mink skin is worth from 3 to 6 dollars and a muskrat is worth 25 cents. I have got two muskrat skins. I am going to gather butternuts next week. I picked up a quart of beechnuts one day and I gave them to the old woman that knit me a pair of socks. I have knit a pair of suspenders and have commenced a stocking. It is getting late and I must go to bed, for I get up at daylight to go to my traps. Goodbye for the present."

It seems Mrs. Comstock made as frequent visits to the Turners as was possible. Mrs. Henry Turner has told me that her visits were most welcome. There was a certain blitheness of manner in Susan Comstock that pleased people and was of great value to her patients. Mrs. Turner said: "She was such good company that we liked to have her come and stay as long as possible. She always brought us the latest fashions and helped us make or remodel out dresses in attractive ways. She had the knack of always looking handsomely dressed herself because she knew the value of lace collars, undersleeves, and ribbons and could make an ordinary dress look 'dressy'".

During these days of boyhood Henry found two school friends related to the Turner family who were his constant companions—Sarah Turner, a niece of Captain Turner, and Ida Bachelor, a niece of Mrs. Turner. He played with them and studied with them and they were important factors in his young life and happiness. There was always time between duties on the farm for a wholesome lot of play, and the children were allowed the freedom of it. There was a charming woodlot nearby with a brook running through it in which they spent many happy hours. Henry naturally loved everything out-of-doors, except snakes and "walking-sticks."[1] Long after he became an entomologist and accustomed to handling all sorts of insects, he always hesitated a moment before seizing a "walking-stick". These uncanny insects with their long, stick-like bodies and long, slender legs always gave him a moment of repulsion.

One day, when playing near a stream with some boys from the next village, the question of swimming came up. The boys asked, "Can you swim, Comstock?" Ashamed to own his lack of knowledge of this sport he replied, "Of course I can swim," and plunged bravely into the stream. By sheer force of will power he paddled across the deepest part to the far bank. "Oh, you

---

1. A "walking-stick" is a member of the grasshopper family. It has a long, slender, stick-like body with long slender legs." —original handwritten footnote by G. W. Herrick.

swim dog-fashion", jeered the boys. Happy to have escaped from drowning, he retorted, "Yes, that's the way *I* swim". It was not long, however, before he had overcome all occasion for reproach of this kind.

Henry longed for a violin, for it appealed to him as the best of all musical instruments. Undoubtedly, the boy had inherited a love for music from his father, and through out his long life good music was a source of much pleasure for him. Of course a violin was completely beyond his reach, but his mind dwelt upon it so much that he often dreamed he owned one, only to awaken to disappointment, and a keen sense of loss. He remained throughout his life partial to the music of this wonderful instrument.

There were two graces in Hurricane Hall, [clean] orderly housekeeping and excellent cooking that exerted an unconscious but wholesome influence on this boy whose previous years had been spent under such irregular conditions and among such untoward circumstances. His love of the beautiful was nourished by the appeal of the woodlands, fields, and streams through which he roamed with constant delight and growing appreciation of nature. Ma Becky sympathized with his love of the out-of-doors and often accompanied him on excursions for the gathering of wild flowers and of the golden cowslips for dinner "greens".

He was much in the habit of talking to himself as an outward expression of a busy, imaginative mind. May Turner has told me that she used to watch him bringing in milk from the stable. He carried it in two [long] deep pails, and while muttering to himself was quite oblivious of the high step at the kitchen door, against which the bottoms of the pails inevitably bumped. The resulting splash, however, always brought his mind back to earthly matters.

Thus passed his boyhood, now that he had found a home which welcomed him and welcomed his mother when she could spare the time for a visit. His schooling was limited to the three months in the winter, and he made the most of it. He was clothed comfortably, and it was no small task to keep him mended, he was so very active. Mrs. Turner used to say as she worked patiently patching his trousers, "Hankey, when you buy your own clothes you will be more careful of them", but this was a false prophecy, as I can attest.

In 1861 the Civil War came on. Henry was greatly affected by it. He was nearly twelve years old then, [but] and he wrote his letters on a sheet of paper with a colored print of the American flag in the corner with the inscription under it: "if any one attempts to haul down the American flag, shoot him on the spot". Two years later he tried to enlist but was ruled out because of his youth and small stature.

John Henry Comstock, n.d.

Chapter II

A Sailor and a Scholar

Mr. Comstock's recollections continue into Chapter II. "Hankey" is the correct spelling throughout the manuscript. Both mothers used this form in their letters to each other about the young Henry Comstock. In the 1953 edition, the editors spelled it as "Hanky." An anecdote of Mr. Comstock's religious convictions, removed from the 1953 edition, appears in this section. —KSt.

In March, 1865, occurred an event that had a profound influence upon the relations of Susan Comstock and her son. She had a patient who desired her services on a journey to California; it was a temptation she could not withstand. She had never heard a word from or about her husband since he had left her for California seventeen years before, and she had a feeble hope that, were she in California, she might be able to solve the mystery. Her brother-in-law and sister, Mr. and Mrs. Nelson Carr, were living in Santa Rosa and had often urged her and Henry to come to California. She decided to go and made the journey with her patient by boat, crossing the Isthmus by train.

Henry took the news bravely and encouraged her to go; he says in a letter to his mother: "I am glad you have a good chance to go to California and I will do the best I can until I can go too". Living as he did among sailors, it was natural that he should turn to sailing as the most available means of earning money; but he was a slender youth, often ill from malaria contracted, perhaps, in his babyhood, and Ma Becky knew he could not go as a common sailor before the mast. With her usual tact and good judgement she proposed to teach Henry to cook so that he could have a "berth" as steward, a job better suited to his physical condition. He was an apt pupil and Ma Becky was an excellent teacher. Before the season opened in the spring he was well grounded in Ma Becky's art of good cooking.

His first experience was on a small lumber vessel plying between Oswego, N.Y. and Kingston, Canada. His wages were ten dollars a month. Of his experiences on this boat he has written the following account:

> "The first year that I sailed I was on a small French Canadian schooner, "Queen of the Bay", which traded between the Bay of Quinte and Oswego. The crew consisted of the captain, the mate, two foremast hands, and the cook; I was the cook. Although the members of the crew could speak English, the language of the ship was the patois of the French Canadians. I made no effort to learn this, for I soon divined the significance of certain expressions that were frequently used in an emphatic manner. One of these was *Sacre' musdaw.*[1] This was frequently addressed to me; and I recognized its import, although I did not know and have not yet learned the English equivalent of these two words.
>
> "Naturally my social intercourse with my shipmates was quite limited, which doubtless was fortunate. But I took an interest in the details of the management of the craft. I learned to steer a trick, to stow the gaff topsails, and to do various other things that did not pertain to my duties in the galley. I was not without resources, however, for I had a few books with me, and I bought an accordion. This instrument was probably more comfort to me than to my associates; for I knew nothing about music and have no musical ability. The chief resource of my comrades on board was a game of chance played with cards. This was always resorted to when the men had been paid off; and it invariably resulted in the wages of the foremast hands finding their way into the pockets of the captain and mate.
>
> "In port my shipmates found other sources of enjoyment; and owing to the shortness of our trips, we were in port often. I never went ashore with them, and do not know what they did there; but frequently their condition on their return gave evidence of the principal [sic] thing that they had been doing, the drinking of strong liquors. They were all in this condition one morning in Sackett's Harbor, when they came aboard, after spending the entire night ashore. We were to go from

1. This may be a phonetic spelling of *sacre'maudit*, meaning "bad blood," or something seen as impure. —KSt.

> Sackett's Harbor to Kingston and some one suggested that, as the wind was fair, we might sail through the canal that then traversed Wolf Island, instead of making the longer trip around one end of the island. We made sail and reached the canal shortly. Soon we came to a bridge across the canal and a horn was blown to signal the keeper to swing the bridge. But the old woman on duty would not open the bridge until she had received the toll. There was nothing to do but to run the boat on to the shore, which was done, the operation being accomplished by many *Sacre' musdaws*. After the fee had been paid the boat was poled off the bank with much trouble by the inefficient crew and we passed through the bridge. I was asked to take the wheel, which I gladly did, as it was sport for me to keep the boat on its course between the banks of the canal. About this time the captain went below; and a little later, when I glanced down the companion-way, I saw he was lying in his berth in a drunken stupor. One after another the mate and the two men followed his example; and I found myself alone guiding the ship over a course that I had never before traversed. This seemed a simple matter; for the wind was fair, the sails properly set, and I had only to keep the boat from running onto either bank of the canal. All went well until I found the canal opening into a lake, on which we were soon sailing. Evidently the thing to be done was to cross this lake and to enter the other section of the canal that connects it with the open water on the Kingston side of the island. I endeavored to see some indication of where the entrance to this canal was, but could discover none. Finally, I selected a point on the opposite shore that I thought might be the entrance and headed the boat for it. Before reaching this point the boat stopped moving and a glance over the side showed that she had been run into the mud of a marsh. It was evident that my role as a navigator had been played. I lowered the sails and waited for the crew to sober up. When the captain began to curse, as he discovered what had happened, the mate rebuked him and said, "The boy was not to blame".

At the end of the first season of sailing, Henry had twenty dollars in his pocket after he had bought his clothing for the coming year, and with this surplus he started home. But at Cape Vincent some one gave him a counterfeit ten-dollar bill and it was a sorrowful boy who arrived at Hurricane Hall with just a half of his saving with which to buy his books and meet extra winter expenses.

However, he started to school with the prevalent idea at his age of have "a good time". But when he entered the school room he saw a diminutive woman hardly reaching to his shoulder; and he was disgusted because he felt it wouldn't be fair to "raise Cain" with such a little teacher. She came to him and looked over his books and asked him why he had an arithmetic different from that of the other pupils; he explained that he had "figured" through five arithmetics and the only way to get anything new was to find a new kind of arithmetic. She exclaimed, "Why, you should take up algebra and stop studying arithmetic". It was the first time in his life that even a thought of higher education had dawned on his mind. He had seen on the back pages of one of his arithmetics an advertisement of an algebra by the same author and he wondered vaguely what it might be like, but never thought that it might be something for him to study. He was excited at the alluring prospect of a new study and walked to Oswego, five miles and back, that day to buy an algebra.

A new world then opened to the boy, and that devoted teacher, Miss Eleanor Dickinson, taught him his algebra after school hours, for she had so many classes with her sixty or more pupils that she felt she could not take the time during regular hours to teach an advanced subject. To her influence Henry always attributed his ambition for an education. She worked faithfully with him and at the end of the winter told him that he ought now to go to some seminary where he could study advanced subjects and prepare for college. He had become thoroughly imbued with the desire for a college education and gave his whole thought and energy to his work in school. Ma Becky writes of him to his mother at this time:

> "Hankey studies all he can, more I think that he ought to for his health. Poor child, he is so anxious to learn, and if he has his health he will succeed. Susy, he is almost as big as Whig[2] and he grows handsomer every day. I think you will be proud of him when you see him."

The following summer was a happy one for Henry, since he sailed with Joel Turner on the schooner "Thornton". This was a most prosperous and pleasant season. Joel Turner was captain, Henry Turner was mate, Lucian Turner sailed before the mast, and Henry Comstock was the steward. Henry was promised $25 per month, and more if matters turned out well. He writes his mother, May 17, 1866:

> "I commenced work the 16th of April. I like it well, but it keeps me at work all the time. I do not get any time to study, unless I do it evenings, and then I am too tired and go to bed. I will finish my letter at Bay City. We had a rough night, It blew very hard but we came through

2. "Whig" is Lucian Turner, the youngest of the Turner sons. —KSt.

all right. We passed a schooner yesterday that was capsized; we think it happened that night. It looked hard to see her lying on her side, not knowing how many poor men perished on her. Capt. Joel says he will give me a dollar a day on this trip."

In a later letter, he tells his mother how much he will save and what he will do with some of his money. He will pay Pa Lewis and Ma Becky something in gratitude for their kindness to him, buy enough clothes to last him through the year and save from $150 to $200 for his winter term in some seminary. He ends by assuring her, that "I can send you money instead of your sending it to me".

He never got over being homesick for his mother. He writes her on August 24th from Lake Erie:

"I thought I would write you, although it is so rough that I can hardly write. I was so glad to get your letter. I look forward to the time when we can be together again. How we will enjoy ourselves. Oh, how I want to see you! I look at your photograph but it isn't mother!

"Mother, I have been thinking how it would be if, when I go to California, if I should, instead of taking a steamboat, get a berth on some ship as steward and go around the Horn. It would take more than five or six months and I would get pay for it, instead of its costing me two or three hundred dollars.

"I have got a healthy family to cook for and they have good appetites. I have baked up five barrels of flour since I came aboard the Thornton this spring. Today I have been baking bread, huckleberry pies, green apple pies and gingerbread this afternoon, and rough weather at that".

In a later letter he gives his bill of fare:

"For dinner I had roast mutton, boiled potatoes, turnips and onions and pickled beets, bread and butter, and duff for desert [*sic*]. I guess you do not know what duff is, for it is a sailor's dish. It is a kind of pudding boiled in a tin form and eaten with a sweet sauce. I have been patching my clothes this afternoon and must now go and knead my bread and get supper."

Henry was always friendly and making friends. He writes in October:

"We were in the Welland Canal over Sunday. I got acquainted with a boy there who keeps a grocery store and he is only four months older than I. His name is Hugh Keefer. He asked me to come up to his house Sunday and we had dinner and supper together at 3 on board ship, I went afterwards to the house. It is a nice place with a nice yard with flowers in it and I had a pleasant visit with them. In the evening Hugh, his mother, two sisters, two cousins and myself went to church and heard a good sermon. The text was in the 21st chapter of Revelations, part of the first verse, "and there was no more sea". He spoke of the sea dividing nations and friends in this world, but in the other world there will be no more sea to part friends".

At the end of this, his second summer of sailing, he writes to his mother:

"I had a nice time on the lake this fall. We had some rough weather, but came out all right. Captain Joel gave me $350 for my summer work, which was nearly $50 a month. Then, after the Thornton laid up, I made a trip on another schooner at $2.50 per day. I worked 13 days, which amounted to $32.50, making in all $382.50 for my summer work, out of which I have bought enough clothing to last me about a year and have $175 in cash, which will be enough to keep me in school this winter and $100 left in the spring. Then, if I have good luck next summer, I can save enough to keep me in school a whole year, which will cost about $350 for clothes and all."

An experience of Henry's on the Thornton which he describes in his own words is of interest:

"In the fall of 1866 the schooner Thornton, on which I had sailed through the season, laid up in Milwaukee. As I was about to start home by rail I had a chance to ship as steward on a schooner that was about to sail for Oswego. As this gave me a chance to go without expense and at the same time to add to my summer's earnings, I gladly accepted it. I hurriedly got a stock of provisions aboard and she sailed at once. We had been out of port only a few hours when we encountered a gale of wind from the west, which soon drove us nearly to the east shore of the lake. Then followed a battle with the winds and waves that I shall never forget.

"For three days and nights we endeavored to beat our way out into the lake; but, although we headed out, the schooner made so little headway that our course was nearly parallel with the shore, which was constantly in sight; and the certain knowledge that, if the schooner were driven upon this shore, there would be little hope of any one being able to get from it through the breakers to safety, made our condition seem desperate.

"During these three days we were first driven far toward the north end of the lake, where a projecting headland made it necessary for us to put about and work our way south. We kept on tack for a long distance, and then put about again and worked our way north.

"The trying nature of these three days was greatly aggravated by the fact that the captain lost his nerve. I remember one afternoon, when the schooner was pitching violently, he walked up and down the quarterdeck, clinging to the rail and saying repeatedly, 'Wood and iron cannot stand this long.' I think that his fear might have made some of the crew more anxious; but several of them expressed freely to me their disgust with the performance.

"I should say, however, that this was the only experience of the kind that I had during my sailing days. The captains of the sailing vessels of that period were, as a class, remarkably brave; they were accustomed to danger, and when it came they met it calmly.

"The attitude of the several members of the crew during this gale differed greatly. Some were unusually quiet and others unusually profane. One evening the men were trying to eat supper, which I had cooked with great difficulty, owing to the pitching of the schooner; they were seated about, on the floor of the cabin, braced in corners and elsewhere to keep from being thrown about. I was attempting to serve them without spilling the food and remarked petulantly, 'I hope we shall be in smoother water before breakfast', to which one of the men replied, 'We shall be in hell peddling matches before that time'. Then the meal was continued in silence.

"Among the incidents of this experience that are indelibly fixed in my memory is the following: No one on board undressed for bed during the storm. At night I lay down on a couch that was in the captain's stateroom. There was a small dog on board and when I lay down he would come and snuggle close to me, and each time when the schooner would shake itself free from a big wave he would tremble in abject terror.

"The performing of my duties during the three days of storm was attended by many difficulties: it was essential that the meals should be ample and served on time; and instead of merely a cold lunch set out for midnight, as was the usual practice, I served hot coffee with the lunch. It was not easy to make coffee on a stove that was oscillating through an arc of ninety degrees; but by partly filling my largest coffee kettle and securely lashing it to the stove the feat was accomplished.

"Most of the dishes ordinarily cooked on top of the stove were cooked in the oven, with the door securely fastened. But the most serious problem that I met was the making of bread. When getting the supplies for the trip in Milwaukee I did not think of yeast, and as I could find none on board it was necessary to resort to making of salt-rising bread. I set emptyings [homemade yeast] promptly, but before it was time for them to rise we encountered the gale, and the constant motion of the vessel prevented their rising. I was forced, therefore, to make biscuits and other substitutes for bread. The second day I tried again and with the same result. More substitutes for bread had to be made.

"On the morning of the third day a brilliant idea occurred to me. I set the emptyings in a tin pail and suspended the pail from the ceiling of the galley, above the stove, where it was kept warm. The suspended pail preserved the vertical position in spite of the pitching and rolling of the vessel, so that the emptyings were undisturbed and 'raised' splendidly. The sponging of the bread was equally successful; and in due time a fine array of loaves was placed under the stove to rise; they came up in fine shape, ready to be put in the oven, when I was interrupted.

"The captain came to the companion-way and asked me where the ax was. On my telling him that it was at the woodpile near the foremast, he asked me to get it and bring it into the cabin where it could be quickly found in case the schooner should become dismasted and it should be necessary to cut the stays and set the masts adrift to prevent their pounding the ship to pieces.

"I started for the ax, but when I was about midship a great wave came over the rail and swept me across the deck and nearly over the rail. Just as I was about to be swept overboard, I seized hold of a rope, the reef-tackle down-haul, which extended beneath the fore boom, and clung to it until the water ran off the deck. I then secured the ax and started back in a somewhat excited condition. I had reached the narrow space between the cabin and the rail of the ship, when the mainsail split. We were still trying to beat our way into the lake, and were sailing as nearly head to the wind as possible. As soon as the mainsail was split the great pressure on the forward sails swung the vessel around into the trough of the sea, where it rolled violently; the vessel rolled over so far that the masts were parallel with the surface of the water. I saw the feet of the man at the wheel slip from the now vertical deck and the man hung suspended from the spokes of the wheel. I was in a comparatively safe position in the narrow space between the cabin and the rail of the ship and had thrown my arm about a timber-head. Suddenly I thought myself sitting by the stove in Ma Becky's kitchen at Scriba, where it was warm and comfortable. I had never had a dream

> that was more real than this illusion. The only explanation that I can offer of this occurrence is that I was scared out of my wits.
>
> "My illusory visit home was a short one, and I returned to an active half-hour's work. The foresail was dropped immediately in order to balance the pressure on the two masts, the mainsail was mended as soon as possible, and then with both foresail and mainsail set we resumed our course.
>
> "I then went below and, passing through the main cabin, reached the doorway of the galley. There a sight met my eyes that produced in me the most severe fit of anger I have ever experienced. The beautiful bread that I had left ready to put in the oven had slid back and forth over the floor of the galley and all that was left was a coating of white dough on the floor. I said not a word, but jumped up and down in speechless rage. That was the end of my emotions; all fear had vanished and I quietly got down on my knees and scraped the dough from the floor."

The winter of 1866–67 found Henry in Mexico Academy and very much delighted with the experience. He writes his mother,

> "I am at school at last! I have one of the nicest rooms in the Academy; it is on the second floor, a corner room, 18 x 20 feet. It has three large windows, from which may be had a fine view of the country around. My roommate and I have been fixing the room so that it looks a good deal better. We have bought new curtains for the windows, a wood box, and a good many such things. I have bought a new table and chairs, table spread, lamp, etc.
>
> "My studies for the term are reading, grammar, algebra, arithmetic, chemistry, and Latin. We have good teachers here. One of them called in to see me since I began this letter; he said that we kept our room in the best order that he had seen since he has been here."

The winter at Mexico Academy was a new experience for the boy in many ways. Mexico is a small village about fifteen miles east of Oswego. It has one main street and was dominated at the time by the academy building set in the midst of a grove. The building had schoolrooms below and dormitories above for boys who were non-residents. The Academy was co-educational; the girls found places to live in town and the boys boarded in town. There were about 150 pupils, largely local residents. Henry made the acquaintance here of an attractive, gay set of young people, and he entered into this society with zest.

His term at Mexico Academy ended in February and evidently Henry did some thinking. His cash had suffered unexpected inroads from livery bills and "oyster suppers" and he made up his mind to change schools, and be a little careful about becoming part of a gay social set in the new place. This was the first time in his life that he had had plenty of money and it is a satisfaction to find him at last enjoying some of the pleasures of youth. He may have looked upon his vanishing bank-account ruefully, but surely Fate smiled at him indulgently for this spirit of real boyish recklessness.

However, he had some cash left, as is shown by a letter written to his mother on the letter-head of "Falley Seminary", March 30, 1867. This page bears the engraving of a dignified brick building of colonial type and below it the names of J. P. Griffin, A. M., Principal, Rev. J. J. Brown, Vice-Principal. Henry states the case lucidly:

> "There have been some changes since I wrote you last. I finished the term at Mexico Academy, then went home for two weeks vacation; I had heard so much said about this Seminary that, having two or three weeks leisure time before navigation opens, I thought I would try and see how I like it. Then the next fall I will go to the one I like best. This is a boarding school. It is in Fulton, a pleasant village situated on the Oswego river about twelve miles from Oswego.
>
> "I think I can do better here than in Mexico, for here they are more thorough and a graduate from this school can enter college easier than from almost any other around here. You see, mother, I am bound to go through college and have a profession. I don't know what it will be, but I guess it will be Law. I have a long road before me, I realize, two years of hard study before I can enter college and four years in college and one in a law school. But when I am through I will be a man, and will know something."

Then he adds a great piece of news, that he is to sail with Captain Monroe Turner on a brig, "one of the largest ships that floats fresh water. She trades between Buffalo and Chicago, and she is so large she cannot go through the Welland Canal. I think I can earn enough next summer to keep me in school a year."

But alas for his hopes! He writes again, June 3, 1867, from the schooner, "Forest Queen", Ogdensburg:

> "I was taken with the fever on April 10 at Fulton and was sick ten days before I could get home. Professor Griffin and his wife were very kind to me. I went to Pa Lewis's and stayed 38 days. I had a chill

every day for six weeks and had to try two doctors before the chills were broken up.

"I was so sick I lost the berth with Captain Monroe Turner. I tried to get another cook's berth when I got well, but could not, so I shipped on this schooner as a sailor-man. I worked one day at that, when the steward was paid off and the Captain wanted to get another. I thought it would be easier to cook than to work on deck, so I told him I was a cook and he gave me the berth.

"Oh mother, how I wish I were through school, so that I could come to California. It doesn't seem as if I could stay through college; but we can enjoy ourselves all the more when I do come. You would rather I should stay a year or two longer and come with a good education, would you not?

"You said in your letter you wished I were a Good Templar. I am. I joined the Lodge and have taken both degrees and served as Worthy Deputy Marshal. You will see my name in one of the papers I sent you. I signed a pledge last winter not to use tobacco in any form, chewing, smoking or snuffing. I like the order of Free Masons and I think I will join when I am old enough."

This was surely a sad summer for the sailor lad. The first of August he wrote from the schooner "Corsican": The schooner Forest Queen sank July 18. We were loaded with ashes, taking them from Toronto to Oswego. When about a half-mile out the captain discovered the schooner was sinking. He had a tug tow us where the water was not deep, so that when she was at the bottom the water was level with her decks, filling her hold and cabin. We got all our things off from her before she filled. We worked five days unloading her. I did not have to work as hard as the rest. The captain let me work as second engineer on one of the steam pumps, but we had to work from two in the morning until nine in the evening. Then I shipped on this schooner and am now going to Milwaukee."

Despite his bad luck, he saved enough money to enable him to attend Falley Seminary that winter. In November an important occurrence changed the trend of his own life as well as that of his mother. The news came of her marriage to Mr. John Dowell, a mine owner and hotel keeper in Forbestown, California, a town well up on the flank of the Sierras. At that time placer mining was a profitable business, and the widow, wearied of buffeting the vicissitudes attending the profession of nursing, and having heard of the death of Ebenezer Comstock, yielded to the pleading of her own heart in favor of a man of pleasing personality. She married "well" according to the news of the event sent by her sister, Mrs. Nelson Carr, of Santa Rosa, California, at whose home the ceremony took place.

It must have been a severe shock to Henry when he learned of his mother's marriage, for it had been his dream to be with her and care for her as soon as possible, and he had planned to go to California the next year. However, he met the situation with reason and consideration, and his mother was given no inkling of his {deep} disappointment. He writes her rather stiltedly:

> "It is with mingled feelings of surprise, pleasure and regret that I sit down to write this letter. I cannot help being surprised at an event that has occurred so unexpectedly to me, but it is with feelings of pleasure that I think of you as having a companion upon whose arm you can lean in confidence and love.
>
> "It also affords me great pleasure to think that although I am doomed to be absent from you, you have one with whom to pass the time and thus keep you from being lonely. I shall feel easier and not worry so much about you, but it is with feelings of regret that I think of staying here; but it may be all for the best."

Enclosed with this letter was one to Mr. Dowell, an evident labor of composition, rather cold in its beginning but soon sincere and cordial:

> "It seems strange for me to say father, for you will be the only father I have ever known. My own father died when I was too young to remember him, and I look forward with pleasure to the time when we shall meet. I have to study late and early to get my lessons. My studies are all good sound ones and a fellow has to work to master them. They are Latin, Greek, and Geometry. I like Geometry; anything in mathematics is easy for me but Latin and Greek make me work hard. Besides this I have to write a composition one week and speak a declamation the next week, and so on through the term. I am also a member of a literary society and have to debate in that every Friday night.
>
> "I have a very pleasant room; it is a corner one, so it has a good view in two directions. It has been newly papered and grained, so it looks as neat as a parlor. We do not study in our school rooms as they do in common schools, but every two students have a room to themselves."

Falley Seminary was typical of those remarkable schools which provided secondary education far and wide through New England and New York and the new western states during the middle years of the 19th century. The teachers were well trained and were excellent drill-masters. The classics had precedence, yet some attention was paid to the sciences and great effort was made to stimulate the ambition of the pupils for higher education. Music and art were also {made much of.}

These schools were co-educational. In Falley Seminary the girls' dormitories were at one end of the building, the boys' at the other end, and the class rooms between. Music and art were supposed to be largely {peculiar} to the "female department", but girls were welcomed in the Latin and Greek classes and boys were encouraged to study music, drawing and painting.

Public High Schools {may have driven these old seminaries out}, but they have never really taken their place. They stood for personal care of the pupils, a {personal} responsibility for their morals and tastes, and great severity of training {in the "solid" studies}. Henry Comstock has often {stated} that never {in his life} did he receive the drill in any study that Principal Griffin gave him in Latin. Henry never studied Latin or Greek after he left Falley Seminary, and the training he received there in those languages was a strong staff on which he leaned {through his many years of work as a man of science.}

He did not {inform} his mother {of the fact} that, owing to the disastrous summer, he swept the halls and {rang the bell for change of classes} in payment for his room rent and tuition {at Falley this year.}

{An amusing and very} characteristic incident occurred connected with his duties as bell-ringer. He was obliged to ring the bell for rising and retiring. He rang the retiring bell at ten P. M. One night he was very tired, {but it still lacked} a quarter to ten, so he threw himself upon the bed and fell asleep; he awoke with a start, feeling sure that he had slept but fifteen minutes {at the most,} and immediately went and rang the bell. He had barely got back to his room when the Principal was pounding on his door and demanding why he was ringing the bell at two o'clock in the morning.

All his life Henry had this habit of falling asleep when he was tired and of waking up and going on with his work as if nothing had happened. After he entered Cornell, a student {crossing Cascadilla bridge} found him lying on his back on the parapet, fast asleep. He had stretched himself out {for a moment} to look at the stars and listen to the rush of the water sixty feet below him and had promptly fallen asleep.

{It was during} the winter of 1868 that Henry's stepfather gave him an urgent invitation to come to California and make his home with him and offered to defray the expenses of the journey. This inclined Henry to go especially as his health was not very good and he hoped that change of climate might help him. But, unwilling to sacrifice his education, he began to look up schools and colleges in California. The State University {of California} had not yet been established. The only college he could find was the Catholic College of Santa Clara in San Jose, and he sent for a prospectus. The course of study was too classical and too theological to fit his plans. Many years later, when he was a professor at Stanford University, he made a pilgrimage to the college at Santa Clara and had a very delightful afternoon with an {old father} who showed him the treasures of the college and who was vastly interested that his guest had thought of being a student there.

So Henry decided not to go to California. He writes his mother later:

> "If I should come to California, I am afraid that I should not go through college, in the first place I do not think the colleges are so good as in the Eastern States, and besides I couldn't find anything to do in California that I could make as much money at as I can to stay here and to sail summers."

This summer of 1868 Henry sailed on the schooner "A. Ford". He writes April 27: "I am getting $1.50 per day now and I have a good deal of leisure time. I have my books aboard and when I have time I study them. I have a good captain."

A letter from Mrs. Turner to Henry's mother in July gives a sympathetic account of Henry. She says:

> "Our Hankey was home for the Fourth and we had a good visit. I gave him a beautiful bouquet and I have made him a hanging basket with cypress and trailing vines to hang in his cabin so he can have something from home when he is on the lake, he is so fond of flowers.
>
> "Susy, you don't know what a treasure he is—he is my child as well as yours. He is such a dear good boy. I love him more every year. I don't know what I shall do without him and Pa Lewis thinks so much of him too! You don't know how he as twined himself around my heart! The principal of the Academy calls him one of his gems. {All I can say is that he is another Ishmael Worth;} if he lives he will be a self-made man, one of nature's noblemen and, dear sister, he will always be Little Hankey to me, the child of my care."

An interesting incident occurred when Henry first shipped on the schooner "A. Ford." He came aboard and left his satchel and overcoat in the cabin while he went off on an errand. The captain's wife was on guard and she noticed a book in the overcoat pocket, and, thinking she would see what sort of a book the new steward was reading, she found it to be a Bible, one that had been given at Christmas by his {little} teacher, Eleanor Dickinson. The Captain's wife concluded that the young man was of the right sort. Later that season his ship suffered in a peculiar wreck, which he describes as follows:

> "Late in the fall of [1868] I was steward on the schooner, A. Ford, which was carrying a cargo of wheat from Milwaukee to Oswego. We were on our way through the Welland Canal when the catastrophe about to be described occurred.
>
> "We were in the lock at Allentown, which was the highest lock of the old canal; if I remember correctly, it lifted the vessel 14 feet. The lock had been emptied, but the lower gates were still closed. The crew were in the cabin at breakfast, having taken the opportunity to eat while the lock was being emptied. As in all lake schooners of that period, the cabin was in the rear end of the vessel and largely below the level of the deck; and, as we were bound down the canal, the cabin where the crew was eating was only a few feet from the upper gates of the lock.
>
> "In the level above the lock there was a steamboat, one of the Northern Navigation Companies propellers, which was getting ready to take the lock after we had passed out and the lock had been filled. The propeller had been run up close to the lock gates, when the signal was given to back hard, with the intention of stopping the boat in this position; but, instead of backing hard the engineer by mistake sent the boat ahead hard, with the result that it crashed through the lock gates and dropped fourteen feet upon us.
>
> "Our first intimation of what was taking place was a crash followed by the bisecting of the stern of our vessel by the bow of the propeller, which came within a few feet of the breakfast table. I remember distinctly the rush that was made immediately by all hands for the deck. A crew never turned out more promptly than did this one.
>
> "As the propeller was tightly wedged between the broken lock gates, the water did not pour upon us from the upper level, but it passed freely under the propeller into the lock; and, when I reach the dock, our schooner was being tossed up and down on the torrent that was rushing beneath us. I remember that I ran and seized hold of the mainmast stays in order to keep on my feet and stood looking up, expecting that the topmast would be shaken down. Very soon the hawsers that held the schooner in place in the lock were broken, and she was driven against the lower gates; this resulted in the destruction of the lower gates and the smashing of the bow of the schooner. The torrent of water carried the schooner out of the lock and down the canal about

five hundred feet, where she sank, a helpless wreck, both stern and bow being crushed.

"A serious result of this affair was the stopping of the navigation through the canal for two weeks; and, as it occurred at the busiest time of the year, when the wheat crop was being shipped east and freights were high, the financial loss was great. More than two hundred schooners were held waiting above the lock before it was repaired.

"This was not my only shipwreck experience; but, occurring as it did on a quiet morning, upon a narrow ribbon of water flowing through a country landscape, and being the one in which I was in the greatest danger, I regard it as the most remarkable of my nautical experiences."

The fall of 1868 saw Henry back in Falley Seminary for two terms, which finished his preparation for college. He writes from the seminary in February, 1869:

> "Mother, what profession do you think I had best study for? I have thought a great deal about medicine but have not yet decided. I want to go where I can do the most good in the world. I do not think I have a call for the ministry and fear if I should undertake it I should not succeed. I have recently connected myself with the Methodist Episcopal church on probation and am striving to lead the life of a true Christian."

This reveals something of the religious nature of the boy. He had persisted during childhood in going to Sunday School without much encouragement from his surroundings. At Falley Seminary, as in all other schools of its class, there was a great pressure put upon the students to embrace religion. There were weekly prayer meetings and compulsory attendance at church. Those pupils already gathered into the fold were encouraged to plead with and exhort those who had not yet "experienced religion". This experiencing religion was a stumbling block for Henry and caused him {great} spiritual anguish. No sudden light shone upon his path, no ecstasies swept over his soul. The {very} best he could do was to earnestly try to follow the precepts of Christ and {live a moral and} upright life, which was considered a very arid method of experiencing religion in those days. Nevertheless, the church accepted him as a probationer.

{To two causes} Henry has always attributed his escaping the pitfalls that beset the path of a sailor boy. First, he saw vice at its worst, with no glamour about it; his natural refinement and fastidiousness made the life in the dens and dives along the water fronts revolting. {Vice was unveiled to him at the start and its "hideous mien" repelled him. Second, his deeply religious nature which, captained by reason, made him believe that sinning, because of assured forgiveness, was poor business.}

{The following experience illustrates his early religious fiber:

One summer, when sailing from one of the ports, three women were taken on board. Of course they were women of the streets and two of them had acquaintances among the sailors. One of them was left on deck in the evening with Henry. She seemed to him rather refined and too good for the life she was evidently leading; in a sudden surge of boyish chivalry he made an appeal to her to live differently. Although he was inspired by Christ's example in dealing with the woman of Samaria, he did not talk religion to the girl, for he felt she would not respond; he simply begged her to turn over a new leaf, and she, greatly affected, promised. She asked him about his life and he told her of his ambition to go to college and how he was saving his money for his education.}

{Three or four years after this, during the last summer he sailed, he received a note from her asking him to call on her in Chicago when he should be in port and giving her address. He went with some hope and many misgivings. He found her in a home furnished with taste and refinement. She told him sorrowfully that she had tried to break away from her old life, but found her path blocked by her past, and that the best she could do was to keep this house of assignment; at the same time she had been "living straight" herself. Then she told him she had a reason for sending for him. She drew forth a purse filled with money and told him she had been saving it to help him through college, that he should take it and never see or hear from her again, and that it had been a great comfort to her to save this money.}

{Henry was dumbfounded and of course told her he could not take it, at which she threw herself on her knees at his feet crying, "You won't take it because of the way it was earned", and sobbed as if her heart were broken. He tried to explain to her that he couldn't let any woman support him, no matter what she did, not even if she were rich and had money to throw away, that the right sort of man did not take money from women, and that he was deeply grateful to her for her kindness and would never forget it. He left her and never heard of her or saw her again, but the incident made a great impression upon the boy, and made him many years later very much in sympathy with efforts to save women from prostitution.}

{Surely a religiousness that would lead a boy unscathed through such an experience as this is worthy of respect, although Henry mournfully regarded himself as not "blessed with grace".}

In July he finished his course at Falley Seminary rather unexpectedly. He found languages very difficult {as he did to the end of his life}, although by persistent effort he mastered several so that he could read scientific works in them. {On the other hand}, he was fascinated by all the natural sciences and cared much for mathematics. He had expected to take a classical course in college because the science courses in the colleges of that day were weak. He had one more year of preparation before he could go to college and as yet he had not chosen one.

During the last term at Falley a visiting clergyman, addressing the weekly meeting, rather incidentally but fervently said: "I hope that no man here expects to go to that godless institution Cornell University, which has finished its first year with a great ball."

{Now,} dancing was no temptation to Henry, for he did not learn to dance until he reached middle life. But he was always of an investigating turn of mind, and there was something in this sweeping denunciation of an institution of learning that aroused his curiosity. So he sent for a catalogue. Strange to say, his most intimate friend at Cornell University, {Professor} Simon H. Gage, attending a Methodist Seminary at Charlotteville, New York, also first heard of Cornell in a prayer-meeting and through a similar stricture, with the same effect upon him as upon Henry. Denunciation is often a very effective way of advertising. From the catalogues both found that the courses in science at Cornell were most attractive. Thanks to a great educator, Andrew D. White, an institution had been founded where there was no caste in studies. All the more broad-minded does this seem when one considers that Mr. White had graduated from a classical course in Yale, where, at the time, the graduates of her scientific school were regarded with aloofness.

The more Henry studied the catalogue the more he became convinced that Cornell was his college. He had already had enough Latin and Greek to enter this wonderful school of science in which Agassiz was to teach, and moreover he would thus save a year of time.

However, when he broke the news to his Principal Griffin, he was severely reprimanded. "You are a Methodist and you should go to a Methodist college," was the last word of the master. It must have been a bitter disappointment to {Professor} Griffin, and he probably considered it equivalent to sending Henry to perdition to have him go to a {college that was not under direct control of a religious sect.}

When the day of his departure came, Henry went to bid good-bye to Principal and Mrs. Griffin. The lady {met him and} was kind in her farewell, but Mr. Griffin would not see him. This was a hard blow to the boy when he was leaving this school which had been so dear to him; after he {turned the first corner} and was out of sight he sat down beside the road and wept{, for he was cut to the heart by this experience}.

It was many years afterwards when he saw Principal Griffin again. Henry was a professor at Cornell University and was giving a lecture {before some society} in Syracuse. Mr. Griffin, then a feeble old man, came to hear the lecture and {told Henry that it was the first time he had come out for months to attend a lecture, for his health was broken. He had been profoundly hurt by the decision of the boy for whom he cared so much, but} time had mellowed his outlook and reconciled him to the career of his pupil.

{The die was cast and} Henry had chosen the right institution for the development of his talents and powers. Little did he dream when he entered Cornell that he would spend sixty years there instead of four.

There was always a dramatic quality in every crisis in Henry Comstock's life. {Fate donned her mask before she trod the stage for Comstock and spoke the words that changed the tenor of his life}; this is well illustrated by the incident that made him choose entomology as the science above all others to which he wished to give his life {and energies}.

He had studied the Botany of the Great Lakes until he was fairly familiar with the flowering plants. In his Wood's *Botany* he found {in the back part a little space given to} the cryptogams and {that aroused his ambition} to get possession of an adequate book on the non-flowering plants. Whenever his schooner was in port in a large city, he visited book-stores in quest of such a volume, but had no success. One day in Buffalo, he went into a shop and asked for a book on Cryptogamic [*sic*] Botany. The clerk {dazed by the sound of such a} scientific term, looked non-plussed {at first; but he was a man of resources}, and said to Henry: "Come with me, here on these shelves are all the science books we have. Look them over for yourself"{, an invitation eagerly accepted}. There was no botany of flowerless plants there, but there was another book that caught and fixed his attention—Harris' *Insects Injurious to Vegetation*, a most admirable book on entomology. {Thaddeus W. Harris, "The father of economic entomology in America" studied medicine, practiced a brief interval and then became librarian of Harvard University. He continued his interest in entomology and published many papers on economic species of insects in addition to the foregoing book.[3] It was superbly illustrated with many wood engravings by Henry Marsh, which made the volume a classic in the history of that art. It also contained {many} eight

3. Economic entomology is the study of entomological species that cause particular damage to agriculture and hence can cause economic losses to farmers (or help save crops from invaders) as opposed to studying entomology for the sheer wonder of the creatures themselves, in all their life stages, and environmental interactions.

colored {lithographic} steel plates by J. H. Richard, all to illustrate a text that is a model of lucidity {and simplicity}. Henry was breathless over the discovery of this book, for he had not known that there was such a science as entomology. He {asked the price of the book and} found it to be ten dollars. That was too much for a sailor lad, saving money to go through college, so he ruefully went back to his ship to get supper for the men. But he could think of nothing else save that wonderful book, and that night he could scarcely sleep from thinking of it.

The next morning, as soon as breakfast was out of the way, he drew ten dollars of his pay from the captain and hurried to the bookshop with a terrible fear {in his heart} that someone else had bought the book meanwhile. But it was there and it became his own, and he went walking on air back to the schooner, which was being loaded with coal; the dust pervaded everything, so he covered the book with paper and handled it with care so that no smudge could deface it, and he began to study it with an intensity of interest that absorbed every moment of his spare time. {He remembers learning} the Orders of Insects, with the book propped up before him while he was washing dishes. And from that time on he knew that what he desired most of all was to become an entomologist. But of course he could not make money enough to live in that way! He could earn his living by being a doctor or a teacher, but the study of insects should be his chief interest in science.

A few years later, Professor Comstock made the following notation on the fly-leaf of this book: "I purchased this book for ten dollars in Buffalo, N. Y., July 2, 1870. I think it was the first Entomological work I ever saw. Before seeing it I had never given Entomology a serious thought; from the time that I bought it I felt that I should like to make the study of insects my life's work.—J. H. C., Nov. 19, 1876."

In the fall of 1869 Henry entered Cornell. This Institution had had one successful year of existence and it had one building completed—Morrill Hall. Saving that building, set in a field on a hill above Ithaca, there was little to indicate the present Campus. Ezra Cornell, the founder of the University, had expressed his breadth of view regarding an institution of learning in his {famous} words, "I would found an institution where any person may find instruction in any study." He also had a great sympathy for {the poor} youth who {wished} an education and had no money. Therefore a part of his plan was to give students work on the farm and buildings in order to help them earn their way.

Robert Simpson, a Scriba friend, had come to Cornell with Comstock and the two planned to room together. No dormitories were available except the 'Cascadilla Place', a water-cure establishment which had been converted into an apartment house for professors and their families and for a few students. So the boys found a room in the town. Henry had brought with him equipment for boarding himself, but his landlady would have none of it, and he had to make other arrangements. However, it was not for long, his sailing in the Saginaw region that summer had filled him with malaria, and his stay at Cornell was only five weeks; he went home discouraged, shaking with ague every day.

A stay {at the Scriba home} during the fall enabled him to subdue this dread disease, and, in the winter, he writes his mother: "I went to Ma Becky and lay idle all the fall, and then I took charge of the school in the steam sawmill district, which is about one and one half miles from home. I boarded at home all winter, walking to and from school; when I had finished the time I had been engaged to teach, the school district hired me for two weeks more, so you can see that I gave satisfaction."

This was a large school of perhaps sixty pupils. Henry found three kinds of textbooks in arithmetic in use. Knowing the aversion of parents to purchasing new books covering the same ground, he hit upon the plan of urging the pupils forward and promoting them to new books. He saw to it that these were of a kind to bring his parallel classes together, in this way he aroused pride instead of friction. He conceived the idea of making the pupils evolve their own rules in arithmetic. This greatly pleased the commissioners.

678

Colburn G.

Dec E. Algebra 4.4 — Physiology 3 — Eng Lit 2 — French 3½

Comstock J. H.

Dec E. Algebra — Physiology 4¾ — Eng Lit 3 — French 3.6 — Vet Surg 4½

Apr Geom 4 — Phys. Sk 5 — 3 — 3.3 — Comp Anat LP. 4h 5

3° T. — Bot 4 — 3½ — 3 — L.P.

1871—2

Dec E

Apr E — Geology 4½ — Comp Anat 5 8 LP — Entomology 5, 8 LP — Essay

3° T E Trig 3¾ — 4 — Zool 3½ — LP

1872-3

Dec E — Psychology 3- — Rht 4½ — Rht 3¼ — German 3½ — French 3 — Comp Anat L.P. 5, 4h

Apr E Pol Eco 3¾ — 3 — 3.8 — Zool 4½ — 4.8 LP

3° T E — Sp Bot 4½ — 3½ — 3.3 — 5.5 — Sp Geol 5 — Zool LP 10 5

1873—4

Dec E — Ch LP 3 2½ 4.6 — Physics 3¾ — Entomology 10 5

Apr E Ast 4¼ — 3½ — Physics 3¾ — 10 5

3° T — 4½ — 10 5

Page 678 of the Registrar's book indicating John Henry Comstock's academic record.

Chapter III

Undergraduate Days at Cornell, 1870–1874

This chapter about John Henry Comstock's life, as with Chapter I and Chapter II, was virtually untouched by Herrick et al. in their 1953 edition. Removed from the chapter are paragraphs particular to Mr. Comstock's family and comments by David Starr Jordan, later President of Stanford University, about Comstock's early years at Cornell with his budding entomological interests.

{A half-sister of Henry Comstock, Margaret Dowell, was born on February 1, 1870. He rejoiced for the sake of his mother, who had been so separated from her first-born, and who now would have the happiness of watching her developing child with all the associations dear to a mother. A fine, strong personality had entered the world, although for many years she was merely a dream child to her brother.}

In the summer of 1870, Henry sailed on the schooner "Delos de Wolf" with Captain Litz, he carefully saved his wages, and in September, he again entered Cornell University, this time to stay.

His Scriba friend, Robert Simpson, came with him and the two rented the basement of a house owned by Frank Cornell, son of the founder of the University. It was a large, pleasant house, {on the edge of a stream}, on Dryden Road, opposite Dwyer's pond. Here the two boys boarded themselves. Henry, mindful of the speed with which cash on hand evaporates in college, sought work and found it in the construction of McGraw Hall.

At this time there was only one college building, Morrill Hall, finished. White Hall was enclosed but unfinished and the foundation of McGraw was laid. There was also a large wooden building, nearly where Goldwin Smith Hall now stands, which housed Chemistry, and the Veterinary Department; several other departments crowded in where there was standing-room. The University also owned Cascadilla Place, intended as a water-cure but converted into an apartment house and dormitory for professor and students. The administration office and faculty room were also in Cascadilla.

The city of Ithaca, its beautiful elms shading {the aristocratic old} colonial houses {that graced its quiet streets, had been built decorously and cosily at the bottom of} the valley at the south end of Lake Cayuga, {a few daring houses had essayed climbing the hill for a little distance}. Seneca and Buffalo streets were fringed with houses up to Spring Street, now Schuyler Place, but beyond this were only a scattering of dwellings. The {old} Schuyler homestead now a part of the University Infirmary, was noticeable for its ample grounds and its air of retirement behind attractive plantings of shrubbery.

There was a house or two on Eddy Street and a farm house or two on College Avenue (then Heustis [*sic*] Street). Some students found rooms in these isolated houses and a few were taken into Cascadilla Place. The end sections of Morrill Hall were dormitories and White Hall was to be similarly constructed. But most students found places to live in the village and walked to the University by devious unpaved paths, the favorite being the one through the {picturesque old} cemetery.

There was no afternoon work in the laboratories that was in the least compulsory. There were no evening entertainments on the Campus. All lectures of a popular or general character were given during evenings in Library Hall, an auditorium in the Cornell Library Building. The Woodford Orations and the Commencement exercises were held in this hall until the Armory was built. Many were the noted men who lectured there: Agassiz, Bret Harte, Bayard Taylor, Edward A. Freeman, James Russell Lowell, George W. Curtis, and Mark Twain.

Henry applied for work to Elijah Cornell, who was a brother of Ezra Cornell and also the builder in charge of the erection of McGraw Hall. "Very well," said Elijah Cornell, "you may roll that stone". It was a very large stone, much too heavy for a slight boy like Henry to lift; but nothing daunted—he went at it with vim, pushing and tugging as hard as ever he could, finally rolling the stone over. Then Mr. Cornell sent two men to help move it to the gangway, and said to Henry:

"You can take a hod and carry up the brick".

"Is that three-cornered thing a hod?" asked Henry.

"Yes, that three-cornered thing is a hod," answered Mr. Cornell, amused.

So Henry filled his hod with bricks and toiled manfully up to the places where they were being used. After about half an hour Mr. Cornell put him at an easier task and one that lasted during the construction of the entire building. Evidently Mr. Cornell wished to convince himself of the grit of the boy and was satisfied. The stone which he was asked to move interested Henry and he noted that it was placed by the keystone of the arch of a window, above the west door of the north wing of McGraw. In after years he often went around to say "Howdy" to the stone that started him at Cornell. The walls of McGraw were up to the second story. The stones for further construction were brought on a car to a platform where {the boys stood}; the car was pulled up on an inclined plane by horse power in the basement. It was the boys' business to unload the stones from the car so that the workmen could get them. For this they received fifteen cents an hour. It was hard work {while they were at it}, but there were waits of ten minutes between cars which they promptly utilized for study. Mr. Cornell noted this with approval. One day when they had completed their studying and put their books away, he called out to them, "Get your books, boys, get your books." Henry was always an admirer of Elijah Cornell, who was sturdy and strong of personality, and American to the backbone in the best sense of the word. Henry had noticed that the workmen pronounced his name as if spelled "Corn'll" and asked about it. "Our name was always pronounced Corn-'ll until some of us got to be high-toned, and now it is pronounced "Cor-*nell*", {was his dry answer}. It is interesting to note that Professor Comstock lectured to classes for thirty years, from a rostrum on the very site of this platform on which he stood handling stones for the walls of McGraw.

Thus Henry worked and studied and with his room-mate boarded himself. {Of course} he had the advantage over the other boys of knowing how to cook; but, between working and studying, the cooking was naturally much neglected and was a good deal of a bore, since it was only incidental and not a business.

At Christmas he went home, but he found {Hurricane Hall} changed. The children were away, and Pa Lewis, whose {ordinary conversation in the tone of a captain commanding a ship} had helped to name the place "Hurricane Hall," had become strangely quiet. He had stopped using sea oaths, a purely decorative profanity to such an extent that Henry remarked to his mother, "I should not be surprised if he became a Christian yet". Ma Becky too, was not very well; and she too noted all these changes. In a letter to Mrs. Dowell she says:

> "The Captain is so different; you know his whims. Well, he has gotten over the most of them. Henry and I often talk about it. This old Hurricane Hall that used to be so full of life and joyousness is quite lonely now except for the little sunbeam grandchildren that often stray in to cheer us and to lighten it up. You know old Hurricane Hall has always stretched its long arms to all who would take shelter under its roof. But nearly all those that used to fill it have left and gone out into the world to do for themselves,—{some in one way, and some in other ways}. Even my foster child, my little Hankey, has gone."

However, this Christmas homecoming of the foster child brought to Hurricane Hall some of its old activities. Let Ma Becky tell the story in a letter to Henry's mother:

> "Hankey wrote me as he was coming home to spend the holidays; so I wrote him to fetch his big trunk empty. He and Squire Simpson's son room together. One cooks one week and the other the next. Robert Simpson brought his trunk home empty too. Now I will tell you what we put in Henry's trunk. Maggie[1] boiled {a piece} of corned beef and baked a shoulder of fresh pork and added a can of pears, a berry pie and {some} pickles. Mate[2] baked four mince pies, a fruit cake and a chicken, and gave a bottle of catsup,{and} I made him a fruit cake and a sponge cake, a pan of fried-cakes, a big milk pan full of molasses cookies, {and another} of sugar cookies, a lot of tarts, {a bowl} of jelly, six pounds of sausages, {and as much} head cheese, {some} pickled pigs' feet, {a loaf of} bread, {a can of} lard, {five pounds of} butter, two cans of berries, {two cans of} cider apple sauce, potted chicken, {a big piece of} pork, a nice big pillow, two dish towels, {a pair of new} socks, and Mate gave him {a pair of} socks too and Maggie a towel.
>
> Hankey said: "Ma Becky, I don't believe there is another such trunk going to {school} this morning. Pa Lewis wanted the trunk to hold more, but when he helped put it in the sleigh he thought it was heavy enough."

1. Mrs. Joel Turner, wife of JHC's older foster brother.
2. Mrs. Henry Turner, wife of JHC's younger foster brother.

On his return to the University in January, 1871, with this famous trunk, something happened which was to influence profoundly his {future} life. He announces the event in a letter to his mother: "Professor Wilder has chosen me as his assistant, so I think I shall be able to pay my expenses while staying here. Is not that grand?" Indeed it was grand, {for more so than} he dreamed, for he was thus to come under the direct {and intimate} influence of a scientific investigator of high rank and {at the same time of} charming and stimulating personality.

Dr. Burt G. Wilder had been a pupil of Agassiz. He had charge of Zoology and Physiology in Cornell and was a brilliant teacher {with an inspiring influence upon his special students. Dr. Wilder} had been a surgeon in the army during the Civil War, {although very young for such important work}. He had expected to devote his life to medicine, but was diverted to Cornell through Agassiz's influence and recommendation. He wrote the following account of the beginning of Henry's apprentice-ship as his assistant:

> "At the opening of the University in the fall of 1868, the equipment for illustrating my courses in physiology and zoology comprised the purchased French and English charts and the Auzoux papier mache models of human organs and typical animals.[3] These were in lecture rooms on the second and fourth floors of Morrill Hall. Professor Jeffries Wyman, my Harvard teacher, sent us {a lot of the} parts of skeletons of various animals; and during the first two years these, together with specimens preserved in alcohol, collected in the vicinity or sent to us, were gathered confusedly in an ill-lighted basement room. For the care of the room and its contents I depended upon the irregular assistance of students not especially interested in Natural History. While contemplating with dismay the boxes, bottles, jars and earthen crocks, and wondering how, for the presentable and useful arrangement of their contents time could be spared from instruction and preparation for it, as if in answer to my prayer, suddenly there appeared a brown-haired, blue-eyed youth, a little older than the average freshman, with an expression both serious and alert. He introduced himself as John Henry Comstock, newly admitted, wishing to become a naturalist, and willing to help himself by work. His aspect and desires appealed to me. Few words were needed for him to appreciate the conditions and their remedies. He hung up his coat, found water and utensils, and attacked the situation like an

3. When studying as a medical student in Paris, Thomas Jerome Auzoux (1797–1880) created inexpensive biological models from a secret papier-mâché mixture of paper, glue, cork, and clay.

inspired anthropomorphic squirrel, bringing order out of chaos in a surprisingly brief period. The promptness, discrimination and energy displayed in this first humble task characterized his service in the higher positions to which he was advanced, and have been emulated by his successors Simon Henry Gage, Pierre Augustine Fish, and Grant Sherman Hopkins. I shall always be grateful for the opportunity of contributing toward the success as teachers and investigators of these four representative early Cornellians."

Henry was still dreaming of studying medicine and was, therefore, greatly interested in the work in Dr. Wilder's laboratory. {In addition to his} earning fifteen cents an hour, he was learning how a laboratory of science was managed and was associating with a man whom he soon came to love and honor.

He {tells} his mother that he will now be able to earn enough to pay expenses with an opportunity during vacations to earn extra money for his clothes. Later, he informs her that he had {been baptized and had not only} joined the Methodist Episcopal Church but had become a "Master mason in good standing." He also announced with {great} pride that "Our president has gone to San Domingo as a member of the United States Commission." The honors and responsibilities conferred upon the Hon. Andrew D. White, {then head} of Cornell University, was a matter of personal pride to every student {in those days}.

The summer of 1871 found Henry in Ithaca working on McGraw Hall and saving his money for the coming year, despite his longing to accept Ma Becky's invitation to spend the summer with her. It was inevitable from {his previous way of life and} his democracy of spirit that he should make {the acquaintance of} the laborers working on McGraw and should establish relations with them, {some of which lasted throughout life. Edward McNally}, one of these, was afterwards coachman to President Adams and to President Schurman to whom we were next-door neighbors. {All of his life, Edward was a friend and admirer of Comstock.} Once, {in after life, when he had stood near and} watched Mr. Comstock perform some mechanical operation {in the garden} with skill and dexterity, he exclaimed: "It's a {great} pity, Mr. Comstock, that yez be a professor. Yez might have been something else for half the money."

In the fall of 1871, {for reasons of economy,} Henry took a room in Morrill Hall, where he boarded himself and managed to live on his small earnings. He spent every available moment in Dr. Wilder's laboratory. Somewhere he contracted typhoid fever. There was no hospital in Ithaca {until many years later,} so there was no place where a student could be cared for except in his room and there were no nurses to be had. It was then that Dr. Wilder showed himself a philanthropist as well as a physician. He and his lovely wife with their child were living in a few rooms in Cascadilla, for there were not enough rooms anywhere in those days to accommodate the professors' families. They gave a room, the doctor's study, to the sick boy and saw to it that he had the best care possible {at the time. His} fellow students took turns in nursing him; {and much of the burden was assumed by} Robert Leavitt, {who earned the everlasting gratitude of the patient.} In later years, a student's guild {was established which received voluntary contributions to} a fund for caring for sick students. Comstock was treasurer {of this organization for many years.}

By December he had recovered from {the long run of} the fever, but was given an opportunity of spending two weeks at the Turner home at Scriba before returning to his work at the University. He writes his mother:

> "I found during my sickness that I had a good many friends in Ithaca. Professor and Mrs. Wilder have proven themselves to be true friends to me and I feel as though I could never repay them. I am with Professor Wilder the greater part of the time. I work four hours a day for him and do the greater part of my studying in his private laboratory. He is one of the best lecturers in the University."

At this time, Henry was attending lectures in Geology by Professor Charles Frederick Hartt and in Comparative Neurology by Dr. Wilder. He was also reading a French play under Professor William C. Russel and all the while studying Entomology by himself because no professor of Entomology had yet been appointed.

Of these three able men, Doctor Wilder was Henry's special patron saint, always at hand to help and {suggest ways and means} and give encouragement. The other two came to have great influence upon his life and ideals. Professor Russel, afterwards Vice-President of the University, {was from the first} one of Henry's inspiring and helpful friends.

Charles Frederick Hartt {was one of the most brilliant men ever connected with Cornell University.} He was an admirable lecturer, a musician, an artist, and a linguist, as well as a geologist, and had the power of linking his students to him in bonds of loyalty and devotion. It was under Professor Hartt that Henry received his first instruction in invertebrate zoology. In 1874 Hartt left the University to become Director of the Imperial Geological Survey of Brazil. He took with him a company of brilliant young men, among them were John C. Branner, {Richard Rathbun, and Orville A. Derby. Unfortunately,} Hartt {became a victim of} yellow fever and met an untimely death.

Henry had chosen Cornell primarily because the University catalogue informed him that a professor of Entomology would be appointed, and his chief interest was in this science. But at the end of a winter term, in the spring of 1872, a crisis came in Henry's finances. "I have known lots of fellows, "he often said, "who left college because of lack of money; but once when I tried to leave college I did not have enough money to get out of town; so I stayed and things happened so that I continued to stay."

What happened he described to his mother in a letter June 1872, as follows:

> "At the beginning of this term it was found that the professor of Entomology would not be able to be here this year, so I was asked to deliver a course of lectures on Economic Entomology in his stead, which I have done.[4] I gave the last lecture Tuesday. I like lecturing very much. My class was made up of such nice fellows, most of them further advanced in other studies than I am. In fact, nearly all of them graduate this year. But they had not studied Entomology so I was not afraid to go before them to lecture."

{David Starr Jordan, one of these, says, "In those far-off days, Comstock taught me all I know and most that I have forgotten of insects and insect life, while I taught him the names and habits of the flowers of Western New York."}

At the exercises in connection with the presentation of the Comstock Memorial Library Fund in 1914, a letter from Dr. Jordan {for the occasion} was read by Mrs. Ruby G. Smith. In it, Dr. Jordan related this {delightful} anecdote regarding Comstock, {which apparently happened during} his sophomore year:

> "Now after forty-four years, I may freely tell a story which, so far as I know, has never been told before. In those days, it was believed that prizes were a help to scholarship. This is a fallacy. A prize may help a scholar sometimes, but not scholarship. That is forever its own reward. Old notions of education withered on every side under the clear gaze of our epoch-making young President,[5] but this one fallacy slipped by unnoticed.

---

4. Footnote on page 3-11-A of manuscript, and pages 42 to 43 in the 1953 book:

"The incident was recorded as follows by the Secretary of the General Faculty of the University:

'A petition of thirteen students was made to the Natural History Faculty of Cornell University requesting that 'permission and facilities be given to J. H. Comstock to deliver a course of ten or twelve lectures during the present Trimester upon Insects Injurious to Vegetation' and also asking that 'attendance upon the lectures and an examination satisfactory to the Professor of Zoology be allowed to count as one hour per week; and that regular participation in the field work be allowed to count for the other hour of the two assigned to Entomology in the Spring Trimester of the 2nd year of the 4-year course in Agriculture.'

"This petition bore the following signatures and endorsements: Herbert E. Copeland, E. R. Copeland, J. A. Thompson, F. P. Hoag, David S. Jordan, M. C. Johnston, W. R. Lazenby, G. E. Foster, P. M. Chadwick, W. H. Schumacker, Thomas W. Jaycox, C. Y. Lacy, R. W. Corwin. Forward approved by the Natural History Faculty. Burt G. Wilder, Dean.

"At a meeting of the Faculty held April 5, 1872, The accompanying application was granted. W. T. Hewett, Secretary."

5. Andrew D. White.

And thus it happened that a class in Zoology of the Invertebrates was assigned a prize of fifty dollars. The committee in charge decided that three students showed like merit and that the prize should be divided equally among them. These three were Simonds, a geologist, now Professor in the University of Texas; Comstock, a chaser of butterflies, and myself, who passed in those days as a botanist. Simonds had made the neatest and most accurate drawings, so it was said. Jordan had written the best examination paper, and Comstock seemed to know the most about the subject.

Unknown to Comstock, in view of his dire need, Jordan and Simonds {withdrew} their claims so that the whole award went to the one who seemed to know most of the subject."

At the suggestion of Dr. Wilder, Henry spent the summer of 1872 in Cambridge, Mass., in the Museum of Comparative Zoology, under the special tutelage of Dr. H. A. Hagen who, {at the time,} had charge of the entomological collections of the Museum. Dr. Hagen, {who was} an authority on the Neuroptera,[6] had been brought from Germany on the initiative of Agassiz, and although he gave no lectures in Harvard at that time, he received this student of Entomology with enthusiasm and gave him a series of memorable lectures which proved a lasting source of inspiration {to this young instructor. In after years,} Professor Comstock related this wonderful experience:

"It was a very warm summer. Dr. Hagen would come into his room, where I had usually preceded him and was at work, take off his coat and vest and hang them on a hook behind the door; then he would light his pipe, which had a long flexible stem, sit down at the table, place the bowl of the pipe on the floor at his side and after a few puffs to make sure that the tobacco was burning well, would say, 'Now you kom und I vill you tell some dings vat I know.' He used a sheet of paper and pencil in lieu of a blackboard; I sat facing him at the small table and took notes. These introductory rites took place every morning with almost no variation, and preceded lectures which dealt very largely with the morphology of insects. They were superbly clear and well organized and my notes on them were of very great use many years later, when I gave lectures on this subject in Cornell University."

6. Footnote added by G. W. Herrick: "A large group of insects with varied habits but in general with many-veined (nerved) wings. —Editor." The insect genus is not consistently underlined by Mrs. Comstock, nor consistently italicized in the 1953 edition. —KSt.

Henry felt justified in borrowing money from this summer's instruction, something he had never done before. He had asked {that fine old man,} Squire Simpson of Scriba, the father of his early room-mate at Cornell, for a loan of fifty dollars, and it was granted. {But} fifty dollars was not a great sum with which to meet expenses at [Harvard] for a summer. {However,} he had a free room in a temporary building called Zoological Hall, and lived as cheaply as possible. When he found his money dwindling, he told Dr. Hagen that he could not stay very much longer but did not tell him why. The Doctor divined the cause and asked him to take his dinners with Mrs. Hagen and himself, which he gladly did, and thus came under the influence of a {sweet and} gracious lady and a charming home.

In the autumn of 1872 {new and quite} unexpected fortunes came to Henry. He was doing janitor work in South University dormitory (Morrill Hall) {where he cared for the room among others} of Myron Stolp, {who was at that time acting as} Master of the Chimes. Stolp was to leave college in June and he advised Henry to apply for the position. Henry went at it in his usual thoroughgoing way; he took music lessons on the piano industriously until he could read music and then applied for the job, which was granted him. This was a good move financially because it gave a room, heated, lighted, and cared for, and, {in addition,} board at Cascadilla. At that time Henry was rooming with George Berry, a classmate. {Since} Berry was something of a musician, Henry offered him a partnership, this was a good arrangement, since it gave each more liberty. {Later,} Berry developed into an expert chime-master.

The chime, given by Miss Jennie McGraw, afterwards Mrs. Willard Fiske, was housed in a wooden campanile situated where the library now stands. {It was a beautiful chime} of ten bells, to which Mrs. Andrew D. White had added the large one.

When McGraw Hall was built, the bell tower was constructed purposely for these chimes, and in the summer of 1872, they were moved from the old campanile to their new quarters. Henry and his partner were given a room in the bell tower, opening off the large museum room on the second story; for a study and the room above for a bedroom. Thus they were very near the chimes. Board at Cascadilla cost $4 a week and Henry asked the treasurer if the University would give the $4 instead of the board. This was granted. So the partners boarded themselves, the two of them for the $4, and felt very rich and luxurious. Henry confided to his mother that everyone says they have the most beautiful room in the University because it has windows on its three sides, {offering magnificent} views.

One of the advantages which Henry experienced through this appointment was a friendly acquaintance with Miss Jennie McGraw, who often came to see the chimes and the boys. She was {greatly} interested in their {rewriting} tunes for the chimes; so they worked at this industriously, preparing {several hundred}. Her favorite was "Robin Adair", and never in the long years since her death, has that melody been rung on the chimes without bringing to one man the sweet remembrance of a beautiful and noble woman. "Robin Adair" was rung, at Mr. Comstock's request, on the day of his retirement from active work in the University.

In the spring of 1873, an event occurred in the life of Henry which really determined his career. {David Starr Jordan in his, "The Days of a Man", gives a succinct account of this event. In speaking of Comstock, Dr. Jordan says, "In his tireless enthusiasm for Entomology, he gave special lessons to a group of three or four, Copeland and myself among the number. Afterwards thirteen of us sent a petition to the faculty asking that these private lessons be recognized as university work. Our request being granted, Comstock was made an instructor in Entomology". Henry, at this time only a sophomore,} was so successful with this course of lectures and {so happy in the work} that he determined to forsake medicine and to follow the profession of teaching while going on with his studies in science. {In a happy mood,} Henry wrote his mother in May,

> "I am very happy tonight and I thought I would write and tell you about it. Yesterday, at a meeting of the Board of Trustees of this University, I was elected Instructor in Entomology. This will be a fine position for me. It will not interfere with my studies, so I shall be able to keep on with my classes as before. My work will consist of a course of lectures in the spring term, private instruction in my laboratory, and care of a collection of insects. I shall spend the summer vacation in the field making collections and studying the habits of insects. My salary will be for the first year five hundred dollars, which is enough to support me nicely here."

In Henry's room at this time, was a small case containing eight drawers, on each of which was painted the name of an order of insects. This was the beginning of his collection, and it is doubtful if even the sight of his hundreds of boxes of specimens in later years afforded him the pleasure and pride that he derived from this poor little cabinet. He expected in time to have each drawer full and to this end he spent his {very} limited leisure in collecting.

One day he was peeling the bark of a dead pine tree near the Cascadilla bridge, collecting beetles, when President White coming along {spied him and, without stopping to note that the tree was dead, called out in great indignation:} "Young man, what are you doing there, ruining that tree?"

"Hunting grubs, sir! The tree is dead", was the {scared} reply. Then followed {an explanatory} conversation which was the beginning a {life}-long friendship.

President White's most remarkable quality, the sign and seal of his genius, was his vision in the various fields of thought and education. His training had not been in the sciences and yet, by far more than most scientists, saw what a part their work was to play in the development of the world. Thus it was that he, in those days of beginnings, was the sympathetic helper and the inspiration of every man teaching science in Cornell. It was his vision that planned for the teaching of Economic Entomology at Cornell {from the first}, although at that time this science was scarcely {here and had received very little attention from the educational institutions.}

As soon as {Henry} was appointed Instructor in Entomology, Mr.[7] White became an enthusiastic aid to the boy. He had the then very new idea that the relation of birds to insects was important, and encouraged {Henry} to get a shot-gun and kill some of the common birds and examine their stomachs to identify their food. Shooting had never been in Henry's line; but {nothing daunted}, he borrowed a gun and went at it.

{At that time} President White had a house servant, a {fellow} named Isaac, {the longest, lankiest, most} carroty-haired, and loose-jointed {man ever set up by capricious nature}. The first day Henry used the gun, he went down into Cascadilla Gorge and began hunting {for birds}. He {finally saw one} in a tree, aimed hastily, and {shot}. A howl {of pain and rage, such as could have come from no bird}, greeted his first essay at Economic Entomology and {before Henry's stupefied gaze} Isaac appeared on the bank above him, shaking his fist and dancing weirdly, {like an animated jumping jack}. Henry had not killed a bird, but he had {potted} Isaac. {Explanation on the part of the hunter was met with wrath on the part of Isaac, whose leg was smarting from a load of bird shot. Later,} Dr. White told Henry {gently and} tactfully {that owing to the configuration of the Ithaca landscape, perhaps the bird hunting had best be abandoned.}

During this year Henry came more under the influence of William Channing Russel, who was then the Vice-President of the University. {Professor} Russel was a striking figure, large, with iron-gray hair {that was like a lion's mane}, and with bushy eyebrows through which shone {the keenest and

7. "Dr." in the 1953 edition. —KSt.

kindliest} eyes, a man of thought and of great powers, deeply interested in humanity, especially {interested} in the welfare of {Cornell} students, and yet the brusque manners {that} hid from {the general} student {vision} his kindly soul and warm heart. In those days a man often taught {many and} diverse subjects in the University, and {although} Professor Russel taught French, his strength as a lecturer was in Roman History. He made it real and alive with issues to set {us} thinking. The {boys} called him "The Old Roman"{, which was a rather fitting sobriquet}.

In {the year} 1873, Felix Adler came to lecture at Cornell for one term. He was young, attractive, and brilliant, and was regarded as a radical {then} although his views would seem conservative now. He was dreaming of a future of helpfulness to mankind and this dream he has lived to see realized in his great ethical movement. His class room was thronged by enthusiastic young men, who thought for themselves and enjoyed the daring leadership of the "Young Eagle", as they affectionately called him. {While he was here a} Sunday afternoon class organized for social betterment met in Professor Russel's study at his house on Seneca Street.

Henry was among the members to this class and enjoyed it {greatly. Finally,} Dr. Adler suggested that their efforts should not be limited to talking about things, but that they should do something, and it was {suggested} that they start a {working-man's} reading room. {This was done:} a room was found in the Ithaca Calendar Clock Company's building at the corner of State and Albany Streets, and was furnished by contributions; members of the class shared in the duty of keeping it open evenings and all went well until college closed in June, when Henry found himself the only one left in the class to take care of the room for the summer.

That summer he worked industriously, especially in the orchards on West Hill in Ithaca. But, however {hard he worked} during the day, he {must spend his tired} evenings in the reading room until the last loiterer departed and then {he must climb the hill to his room}. He kept the reading room open all summer and turned it over to the class in the fall; but some of the best workers had graduated {and the} others felt they could not spare the time to keep it up, and it was abandoned.

{It was} in July of 1873 that Henry met the greatest loss he had {ever experienced}, the death of his beloved Ma Becky. He spent three weeks caring for her during the Christmas holidays and visited her in the spring and again in July. {She suffered greatly and on July 14th died as she had lived, peacefully and unafraid. Henry writes his mother:

> "Yesterday I received a telegram saying Ma Becky was dead. I rode all night and reached here this morning. Ma Becky died happy and her

life went out like the light of a lamp when it is exhausted. She is lying on the parlor sofa and looks really beautiful. I send you a flower from her bouquet, her last; you know how she loved flowers. I cannot write more now."}

Not one of her own devoted children mourned her loss or has kept her enshrined in more tender memory than has the son of her adoption. He truly loved Captain Turner and went to see him afterwards whenever he could, but for him as for the others the heart went out of Hurricane Hall when the mother died.

{It was} in June 1873, that Henry made a pilgrimage to Dr. Asa Fitch, {for years} State Entomologist of New York, a man whose really remarkable work on the habits of insects had been published in the State Reports, where it was read by no one except a few entomologists.

Henry found him in a stately old home in Salem.[8] He had been a practicing physician and, according to the custom of the doctors of that day, he had a small office building {in one corner of} his yard. This he had used for a museum for his collections. He received Henry genially, showed him every attention {and tried to tell [him] what he wanted to know. Mrs. Fitch was also very cordial and showed Henry the gold medal bestowed upon her husband by a scientific society. The doctor was not very explicit as to his methods of work. Henry asked, "How shall I go to work to study insects?" and the doctor answered, "The way to do is to sit down and study an insect."}

During the fall of 1873 it seemed best for Dr. Wilder to arrange to be away for a part of the winter term, giving lectures before medical students at Bowdoin College. To enable him to do this, it was arranged that Henry should give the lectures in Invertebrate Zoology before Dr. Wilder's class of freshmen. He {writes}: "Today, the first day of the winter term, I begin a course of lectures before a class of 150 students. I did not know of it until a few days ago and am very busy preparing for it".

He was not only busy, but anxious. This class was {always more or less} unruly, because it was the only class where the freshmen met in a body, and they were subject to attack from sophomores in passing in and out of the lower halls of McGraw. This kept the class more or less excited and turbulent.

When {the day came and} the class assembled {there appeared before them a quiet, unassuming boy-teacher} who told them he was going to try

8. New York.

to do his best for them and could not promise anything more. {When the occasion came for} their first clapping of hands and the cheering {which usually led to more violent demonstration}, he simply lifted his hand for quiet, and then told the students he could not do his best if they cheered, and asked them not to do it again, and they never did, until the end of the lecture, when they cheered so heartily {that it was a source of comfort and not perturbation to their teacher.}

{It must have been during the year 1872 that} Henry became a member of the Delta Upsilon Fraternity, where he made many life long and congenial friends—David Starr Jordan, John C. Branner, W. R. Dudley, J. T. Newman, S. H. Gage, Edward L. Nichols, {and Leland O. Howard, who were all undergraduate members with him.} The fraternity had rooms in the Cornell Library Building. Since it was a non-secret fraternity, {it had the advantage of being able to use its chapter room and anteroom for receptions of guests at evening entertainments. "The Delta U Quarterlies" was the name of the informal dances given by the fraternity each year, they were delightful functions, eagerly enjoyed by those fortunate enough to be invited.}

{While Henry attended the quarterlies occasionally in the role of host, he did not dance, never having been disposed to cultivate this amusement. However,} the life in Delta Upsilon was a potent factor in developing him socially, while the associations formed in the group played an important part in his later life.

He {writes on} April 26, 1873: "I was very busy this term. Besides my studies I have a good many special students in my laboratory and I lecture twice every week." The laboratory referred to is the room in the McGraw tower opening off the second gallery of the museum. It was fitted up simply and the teaching was, {of course}, elementary; but it was here that L. O. Howard and {several} others began their study of Entomology. {Later,} the room in McGraw tower off the main floor of the museum, {formerly the study of Comstock and Berry,} was made the entomological laboratory, and it was there that this new department began its real growth. This was a light room, though small, and had the advantage of being near the lecture room which Dr. Wilder shared with Comstock.

At first the entomological laboratory was without a microscope, {for this was} a very expensive piece of apparatus in those days. Mr. John Stanton Gould, an eminent non-resident lecturer in Agriculture, took a great interest in the entomological laboratory and gave {to it} his {personal} microscope. In later years Mr. Comstock always entertained a warm feeling for Romeyn Berry because he was Mr. Gould's grandson.

Entomological books were few, and another rare gift came in the form of Edwards' *Butterflies*,[9] a work {beautifully illustrated} in color, issued in parts {and expensive}, the gift of the Hon. Henry B. Lord, that scholarly man whose friendship shed a benign lustre on the University for more than forty years. Mr. Lord was {self-educated} but truly educated. Besides reading Greek with a joy and freedom known to few classical students he was a botanist with wide knowledge of plant species. Through his interest in botany he became interested in butterflies, and subscribed for {this great work; and then, realizing the small equipment} of the new laboratory he generously gave it where it was needed.

Henry's collecting soon crowded all the cabinets at his disposal and he did not know what to do. President White {made a call one day}, as he often did, and Henry {confided to} him his perplexity. There was no University money to be had then, but President White did what he often was moved to do in those days,—put his hand into his own pocket and gave money for the cases.

It was early in the year 1874 {that a piece of} good fortune came to Henry. At that time Ithaca was the home of B. G. Jayne, {a man of much reputation as} a special agent of the U. S. Treasury Department, {acting as a detective of custom-house frauds.} Mr. and Mrs. Jayne had a beautiful home on University Avenue, where they lived with their two small children; Mr. Jayne had to be away much of the time and he asked {Frank Carpenter, who was his special friend,} to find a student who was {steady and} reliable, who could stay in the house with Mrs. Jayne and the children at night for protection and company. {Carpenter proposed Comstock for the place; he gladly} accepted and he passed {some} happy months with this fine and considerate family.

In June 1874, Henry graduated with his class of seventy. The class had entered about 300 strong, {but many had fallen by the wayside.} However, despite illness, a broken arm, and self-support, {received} his diploma {with the rest}. He regarded it with pride and joy and it proved the only degree he ever received {in his life, that of B. S.} He would gladly have studied for advanced degrees, but his work always rested heavily upon him that he never had time to go to another institution to study. {Moreover, he was so early a member of the Cornell Faculty that} he could not get an advanced degree at that institution, which gives no degrees to its professors. {In later life it fell to his lot} to give many courses and to conduct the examinations of many a Doctor of Science.

---

9. William H. Edwards, *The Butterflies of North America*. Philadelphia Entomological Society, 1868.

There were so few women at Cornell {in those days}, that they were noticeable at lectures; but one came as a visitor to many lectures who would have been noticeable anywhere. {Her name was} Benchley, and {she certainly was a progressive woman.} She believed in dress reform and wore bloomers—{not the kind called by that name now, but the original costume,} which consisted of a short full skirt falling just below the knee and wide-legged pantaloons {of the same material} that reached to the feet. I {remember well how she looked with her rather} striking face, lined with character, framed by her short gray curls, and crowned with a {little} lace cap. {Her figure was lost in the bloomer costume, but her hands were} always {busy with} knitting while she listened to {the words of} scientist or philosopher.

{She was an enterprising woman in ways other than in dress.} In those days, {if one wished} to go from town to the University, {he had} to walk or to hire a carriage {and pay} a dollar and a half. {As the University grew,} Mrs. Benchley, {who lived out on Dryden Road beyond the University and} resented this, {and she} established a bus line between {the two and} the University, {the bus ran every hour and} the fare was ten cents. {How} many of us cherish her in grateful memory for that practical philanthropy!

Commenting on undergraduate life at Cornell to his step-father, Henry {says}: "College life is very different here from what it is at most colleges. Here the men are more earnest. A great part of the students are poor men who are working their way through. Consequently we do not perform as many boyish pranks as they do at other colleges."

The scientific {association} of Peoria, Ill., had arranged for a school of Botany and Zoology to be held {in that place} during the summer of 1875. Dr. Wilder was to teach the Zoology and Professor Alphonse Wood {the} Botany; and through Dr. Wilder {Mr. Comstock} was invited to teach {the} Entomology. {The reason for teaching Entomology in this particular summer school was because there lived in Peoria a Miss Emily Smith, afterwards a student at Leipzig University under Leuckart. She was one of the most important members of the Peoria Scientific Association, ad as she was interested in insects, she wished instruction in this field.}

{Mr. Comstock} was {greatly} elated over this invitation; not so much because of the money, as to be asked to teach with Dr. Wilder and Professor Wood. When he was a sailor boy on the Great Lakes he had studied the plants of the shores with the help of his Wood's *Botany*, which was his constant companion and next to his Harris' *Insects* his most loved book. So {now} it was a rare privilege to {meet its} author and {a rare honor} to be his colleague.

{Miss Smith was a girl of remarkable force of character and determination. She showed her determination by entering Leipzig University several years later, for further study of Zoology. She was a fellow-student there with George Lincoln Burr, who afterwards became professor of medieval history at Cornell and one of our most intimate friends.}

The fall of 1875 was a happy one for {Mr. Comstock}. His work was going well, he had an interesting class in his laboratory, and he was {intoxicated} by the wonders of creation that he was always discovering. He writes to his mother:

> "Many of my friends here wanted me to study medicine, but I felt that I could do as much good in the world as a naturalist as if I were a physician, and I enjoyed Natural History so much. My work is so pleasant to me that the days are always too short. How I wish, mother, I could be with you and take you for walks in the fields. I could show you many things that are strange and beautiful."

These words held the keynote to his teaching and to his attitude toward his work. He felt so keenly the wonder {of it all} that he carried the classes with him in the tide of his own earnest enthusiasm.

Anna Botsford, circa 1875.

Chapter IV

Anna Botsford Comstock—Childhood and Girlhood

This chapter is the longest in Mrs. Comstock's manuscript, and here she tells the story of her family and heritage. For the 1953 publication, this chapter was divided in two (Chapter 4 and Chapter 5). Mrs. Comstock's voice was altered in the 1953 publication, with rearranged sentence structure that omitted connecting prepositions and left out her descriptors. For example, Comstock's descriptions of her childhood home flow from one room into another as she gives the reader a tour while she is mentally walking through the house. This change of voice between the 1953 publication and Comstock's manuscript continues throughout the volume. Another interesting point in her style of writing is that Mrs. Comstock used marginalia in her early works. Marginalia are notes on the side margin of the page of a document, which appear in this particular chapter when Comstock introduces a new topic. This chapter in her manuscript is the only one that has marginalia for she seemed to abandon the technique in subsequent chapters. The paragraphing and punctuation follow Mrs. Comstock's style.

My earliest memories are of the log house in which I was born. {It was at the edge of an orchard, some distance from the street, and the path to the door was set on either side with rose bushes and peonies. The entrance was through a porch which had at one side a pantry and milk room. The first floor of the house consisted of one spacious room which was really palatial as compared with apartments in our cities of today. At one end of the room was a kitchen stove, a dish-cupboard painted blue, and a cherry fall-leaf table which was spread for meals; this end of the room was kitchen and dining-room. The middle was the sitting room, with an inviting lounge at one side, a cherry bureau and stand on the other, rockers and other chairs, cushioned for comfort, in between, a rag carpet covered the floor. The other end of the room was for beds. In either corner was a four-poster feather bed, hung with white curtains above and white valances below. The curtains were looped back, showing snowy coverlets and pillows. The floor was carpeted, and the space between the beds could be added to the sitting-room when needed. When the company came to stay all night, they retired behind their bed's curtains to undress and dress, and we did likewise.} However, I slept in a trundle-bed, which, during the day, was rolled under the bed in which my parents slept.

{At the far end of the room,} between the beds, was a wide casement window, beyond which a great cinnamon rose-bush {flourished and} bloomed. White fringed curtains at the window so enhanced the view of the pink roses that the picture always remained in my memory.

{Below} the window, {standing side by side}, were two green chests, their fronts white and ornate with initials and flowers in gay colors. One of these belonged to my father and the other to my mother. Each had {at one end} a till and a drawer {below it} for letters and papers, {and they were} receptacles of mystery to me, who seldom was allowed to look while the contents were examined. White linen, fringed covers were spread over the chests and on them were our small store of books and {various} boxes for hats or other apparel, each covered with white fringed doilies.

The walls and ceilings of the room were plastered and papered in light colors. On the wall hung some old color prints framed—"Robert Burns and His Highland Mary", "Washington on a White Horse".

In 1854, the southwestern counties of New York State were in the post-pioneer stage of development. My grandfather, Daniel Botsford, had moved his family with ox-teams from Bristol, Connecticut, to Otto, Cattaraugus Co., New York, in 1823. He was a {direct} descendant of Henry Botsford, who settled in Milford, Connecticut, in 1639. His wife, Polly Foote Botsford, was a {direct} descendant of Nathaniel Foote, who settled in Wethersfield, Connecticut, in 1640.

My maternal grandfather, Job Irish, and his wife, Anna Southard Irish, had moved with their family, also by ox teams, from Danby, Vermont, to Collins, Erie County, {at an earlier period, probably} about 1815. They were Quakers, my grandfather a direct descendant of Joseph Irish, who came to America soon after William Penn had settled in Dutchess County, New York, but later with his eight sons migrated to Rutland, Vermont. His sons were persecuted by both the Colonials and British during the {War of the Revolution} because they refused to fight. One of my grandfather's uncles was shot down in his own doorway by a rascal in ambush. His home was in a clearing in the forest; his wife buried her husband with her own hands and with her four small children went through the wilderness to Rutland.

Both my grandmothers died before I was born, but I remember my grandfathers {very well}. Grandfather Irish was a quiet, dignified man whom I loved dearly. He wore a broad-brimmed, pale-gray beaver hat and walked with a cane, for he was partially blind. In meeting and at funerals he wore his hat during the services, according to Quaker habit.

Grandfather Botsford was active, rather nervous and somewhat deaf. He had been a soldier in the War of 1812 and had the traditional Yankee hatred of all things British. He was an ardent Methodist, a Whig, and later a violent Republican. He {was a constant} reader of newspapers and enjoyed political argument. The {madder he and} his opponent became, the keener his enjoyment. {He was} industrious and honest and brought up his family in the fear of God and the rod. He had taught school and was an excellent penman.

My father, who was five years old when the family moved from Connecticut, remembered that he was afraid to go after the cows {in the beaver-meadows because, by the time the cows were} in this yard, the wolves in the woods behind them were howling. He {was very much afraid}, but his father made him get the cows just the same. When he was fourteen years old and was allowed to carry a gun, he lost all fear.

Grandfather and grandmother [Botsford] put {great} religious pressure on their children, each, when reaching the age of fourteen, was given a Bible which must be read from cover to cover, and then was expected to "profess religion" and join the Methodist church. This worked well with the four elder children, but my father, was not made of malleable stuff. He read the Bible through (I now have the copy, bound in tooled leather) and declared it was interesting history and nothing more. {They} labored with him and prayed with him, and at him. They scolded and they persecuted him, all to no avail. {Worst of all,} his younger sister Urania and brother Wiley joined him in this rebellion. Probably as an aftermath of this experience, my father and Uncle Wiley became Democrats. Political discussion at our family gatherings was often so hot that my Quaker mother left the room {in disgust and dismay}.

My father bought his time of his father after he was sixteen and worked for neighbors, clearing land and farming during the day and taking the daughters of his employers to dances and to singing or spelling schools {nights}. There was no caste in pioneer society. The hired help were sons and daughters of neighbors who were land-owners and of equal rank, but who had children to spare.

There {had been} winter schooling in a log schoolhouse, where my father learned to read and write well, and mastered enough arithmetic for business and enough geography to make him intelligent in world affairs.

People have told me that both my father and Uncle Wiley were handsome youths, {well formed}, with {very} black hair and heavy eyebrows, {very} blue eyes and red cheeks. My {earliest} memories of my father were of a powerful personality, in whom I took much pride, {and of} whom I stood in awe and fear, and yet {whom} I loved. I remember as of yesterday his appearance when he started off for "general training", for he was enlisted in the State Militia. He wore a dark blue suit, a wide red sash {around his waist}, leggings topped with red points, a red and white cockade on his hat; he sat very straight on his horse, and, to me, he was all that was gorgeous and grand. He {was a reader of} newspapers and a thinker concerning political questions; he knew the record of every important Senator and Congressman and State Legislator. He hated slavery, {but he also had a Northerner's prejudice against negroes and did not like contact with them}. He thought the Government should have bought the slaves and freed them. He regarded the Civil War as a conflict brought on by extremists North and South, and which might have been avoided had the leaders been moderate and reasonable; it was a horror to him {all his life}. He was {absolutely} honest {and upright} in business affairs and was kind-hearted and generous to the unfortunate. He liked to work and was skilled in {each of} the varied industries of the farm. He was witty and had a keen sense of humor; he was also sarcastic and pessimistic.

My mother was my father's complete complement. She, too, was a pioneer's child. One of her earliest memories was of losing her pet lamb when the wolves {broke into the sheepfold and} killed twenty-six sheep in one night. Her mother, {whose loss she mourned all her life,} was thrown from a horse when on an errand of mercy to a sick neighbor, and died {as a result,} leaving a family of five: my mother, the next to the youngest, was nine years old. People who knew my grandmother, for whom I was named, spoke of her as a large, handsome woman possessed of a kind heart and a spirit of helpfulness. {After} two years my grandfather married again, a {Canadian} widow, {who was a harsh mother and stepmother. She} treated her own daughter as cruelly as she did my mother and her sisters, with the result that they slipped away as early as possible and worked for the neighbors, {to get away from the discomfort}.

Mother loved her school in the old log schoolhouse. She loved beauty and poetry. Her {old} English Reader, rich in the essays and resounding poetry of the 17th and 18th centuries was a joy to her all her life. She read the prose and learned the poetry. Through her Quaker ancestry, she had lost all sense of music and could not sing; so she used to put me to sleep by reciting poetry; then and there she implanted in me a love of rhythm and rhyme. {She had one teacher, Leman Pitcher, whom she adored. He taught her something of botany and also of astronomy; she must have been a favorite, for he wrote an "acrostic" with her name which she treasured all her life.}

She had a passionate love for beauty in nature. My hours of great happiness were when she could go into the fields and woods with me. She taught me the popular names of sixty or more {common} flowers; {she taught me} a dozen constellations, an asset for enjoyment in after-years. Her delight over the beauty of a fern, or a sunset, or a flower made me appreciate them too. This love of nature lasted throughout her life. {I remember how,} one evening after she was eighty, she stood at the window watching the sunset, and turning to me, her face glowing, said, "Anna, heaven may be a happier place than the earth, but it cannot be more beautiful."

Mother had a {sweet,} sunny disposition {and was optimistic; she} believed that everyone meant to do right. She refused to listen to critical gossip; and the acme of her condemnation when some one had {smashed} the Decalogue[1] was, "I fear he doesn't live consistently." She was born into the Hicksite Society of Friends and always clung to her Quaker principles. She and my father were always in accord, {since the} Hicksites were quite unorthodox. However, mother was not troubled by creeds. {In later years,} her meeting changed to orthodox and she attended it with the same serenity of spirit as when in her own society.

She enjoyed work and was quick and executive in all her undertakings. She was an excellent and resourceful cook and a neat, orderly housekeeper. Moreover, she had the faculty for making a room look inviting and "homey". {Her "parlor," with its white curtains, comfortable lounge, cushioned rockers, and cheerful pictures was a room which invited the guest to cosy comfort.} She was an expert cheese maker, her products always bringing top prices. She could spin flax and weave linen. {I still have a piece of her linen of beautiful,} intricate pattern. She was an expert spinner of wool and could knit stockings in the dark. {She could also weave woolen cloth.} She was an exquisite needlewoman; her hemming was a work of art, so delicate and so even were the stitches. She was strong of body, blithe of spirit, courageous, capable, fearless, peace-loving, and self-sacrificing. {In appearance,} she was not tall and was rather stout in her early years. She had wavy black hair, violet eyes {that were very} expressive. She was quick in movement and observing. She enjoyed fun, but had small sense of humor. She was an excellent nurse and deemed it no hardship, after working all day, to sit up at night with a sick

1. In Judaism and Christianity, the ten injunctions relating to morality and worship, known commonly as "The Ten Commandments." —KSt.

neighbor; {in fact}, she {always} helped in care for the sick within a radius of three or four miles of her home. Invalids {used to say} that her presence brought cheer, comfort and healing.

My father and mother had both been married before they married each other and were childless {by these earlier unions}. My father had married a schoolmate, Hannah Bartlett, {and had bought land, cut the forest off part of it, and built a log house and barn.} Here he had lived six years when his young wife died of tuberculosis.

My mother, when sixteen, had married Harlan King, {a man ten years older than she}. He was an invalid for years and the two lived at the home of his father. Mother loved the King family and was beloved in return. Harlan King {lived} twelve years after their marriage, {and after his death} mother stayed with his people until she married my father.

These earlier marriages complicated my relationships {and} greatly enriched my life. The Kings and the Bartletts were interesting people {and both were interested in this second marriage}. Both families visited us often and made much of me; I supposed they were my own relatives and always called them so. Much has been said against second marriages, but I, being a product of one, have my own ideas. {These} former conjugal partners were spoken of {frequently in my presence} with affection and reverence. {I placed flowers upon the graves of each whenever I visited the cemeteries}, and always felt that these two belonged to me. My father was devoted to mother's mother-in-law, Grandmother King, and invited her to live with us. She was a reader and thinker and he found her stimulating as well as charming. He {also} loved {two of} her children, {Alvin and Marietta}, as much as he loved his own brothers and sisters. {On the other side,} Grandmother Bartlett, a formal, dignified old lady, whom I visited occasionally, was so fond of me that she willed me her gold beads and pink china, although she had {plenty of} her own granddaughters {who longed for these treasures. Moreover,} the Bartletts, brothers and sisters, were highly esteemed by mother, and one of the sisters, Aunt Sylvia Moore, a widow and homeless, lived with us for seventeen years. Little wonder I grew up with a conviction that second marriages need in no way detract from the love and loyalty belonging to the first.

Owing to the generous attitude of my mother and father, our home was an asylum for the unfortunate. I can remember hardly a period when we did not have some one with us who was in need of physical support or spiritual and moral comfort. Sometimes it was a child needing care, but most often older folk, like my mother's stepmother, who chose to live with mother rather than with her own daughter, although she had been so harsh that my mother had left home when she was twelve. To my parents, a home was a sacred trust to be used for the benefit of humanity, although they would {have been the last} to state the matter in such a way. They simply did what to them seemed right toward those who were less fortunate than themselves. {However,} their example in this respect, made a deep impression upon me, and, {as far as I have been able}, I have always looked upon my own home as a blessing to be shared and not to be regarded selfishly; {and in this attitude my husband always gave me willing support.}

We left the log cabin, when I was about three years old, for a story-and-a-half frame house, a short distance away, {set in} the edge of a primeval forest. This was more commodious, {as there was} a parlor, a dining-room, a kitchen, and two bedrooms on the first floor, and bedrooms in the low-ceiled chambers. There was a front piazza with seats at each end. {Soon afterwards} a cheese-house was erected, a few yards away. {This consisted} of a room for the vat and presses {and another room perhaps thirty feet long and half as wide.} The floor of this large room was painted yellow, and the walls were plastered white; there were white shades at the windows, and on rows of benches were cheeses, each weighing thirty to forty pounds, trim and shining yellow, each on its board; it was a room of beauty and neatness and order. Between the cheese-house and the farmhouse was the pump.

The barns were on the opposite side of the road, and were designated "the cow barn" and "the horse barn"; each of them gave ample room for storing hay and grain, and each was a fascinating place in which to play.

Until after the Civil War, we were largely a self-providing family. We raised wheat and corn, which were ground in the village mill to serve as our own bread-stuff. We raised our own vegetables and potatoes and apples, burying them in earth-covered pits to keep them fresh {for winter use} after those in the cellar had been eaten. We had sheep and spun our own yarn, but hired it woven into cloth {for winter wear}. We made enough maple sugar to last us the year round. We killed our own meat—cattle, pigs, and sheep; cured {our own} hams, salted {our} pork and corned, or dried, our beef. We {also} had plenty of hens and eggs. We bought tea, coffee, spices, white sugar, salt; cotton cloth, and calico and delaines {for dresses[2]}; thread, needles, pins, boots and shoes, and on rare occasions silk for a dress for Mother. For every-day wear for Father, wool from our sheep was made into "full cloth" at the village woolen mill and a tailoress came with her goose[3] and made him the suit. Mother spun the yarn and colored it for our blankets and coverlets. Now and

2. Delaine is a high-quality lightweight fabric of wool or wool-cotton blend. —KSt.

3. A heavy clothing iron heated on top of a wood stove. —KSt.

then she wove rag carpets {for our floors}. The chief source of our income was the cheese, although {often} my father also "broke steers." He was an adept at training oxen {to perfect obedience and he always} received high prices for them. We always had oxen on the farm to supplement the horses.

{The farm was a busy place from early spring until November.} Father was a progressive farmer and was among the first to buy a mower and other machinery. He knew the right ways of doing things and his farm was always good to look at. {All} the stock was well fed and showed excellent care, the fences were kept up, the barns were {swept every day in summer after the cows were in pasture, and in winter} the cattle were well bedded. He was implacable toward Canada-thistles and white daisies. Many a time I was sent up into the meadow to pull up a daisy plant, which I had to bring back and destroy.

Though on a farm, we were {by no means} isolated. {As I look back now I realize anew that} we had neighbors of a high type, both intellectually and morally. {They were} people of intelligence and had eager minds. They read all the books available, {either bought or borrowed}. They all read newspapers and were conversant with all public interests and questions. Our nearest neighbors took Harper's Magazine from the first number issued. Our community was up-to-date on all the issues afloat and {they all}—Phrenology, Spiritualism, Water-Cure, Transcendentalism, and especially Abolitionism—impinged upon us and we {in turn} impinged upon them.

The women found time for visiting about the neighborhood during the summer and autumn, and in the winter there were frequent evening {parties. These were often} dances, for the empty cheese-houses proved most satisfactory ballrooms. On such occasions the main refreshments were paid for by all and usually consisted of {canned oysters, made into} soup, and crackers, pies, cake, cheese, and pickles were contributed largely by the hostess. These gatherings were gay and helped much to keep up the neighborly morale. {I think} there was always someone in our circle who played the violin and who cheerfully donated his services {to the dancers on these occasions.} My father was a skillful and graceful dancer. In those old square dances {I am sure} he had a dozen different fancy steps for "coming down the middle"; I remember I was very proud of him.

Our school was an important factor in our home. {The rural schoolhouse} was set on a high hill; it was a frame building which had taken the place of a log house built by pioneers, who believed education the cornerstone of our national structure. The schoolhouse {was about a half mile from our home and} was on one corner of our farm. We had three months of school in the winter, usually taught by a man, {as the} "big boys" from the farm were free to attend school at that season. We had three months of school in the summer, invariably taught by a woman as only the younger children attended this session. {The rule of our district was that} the teacher {should} "board around", staying a week at a time with each family. {However,} our house was so near that my mother and father always welcomed the teachers {to stay with us} whenever they chose. This resulted, in many instances, in making the teacher a member of the family and added {greatly} to the interest of our evenings, especially in the winter. {I remember that} one ambitious young man read aloud to my parents *Timothy Titcomb's Letters* and a {volume} on popular astronomy. {As I remember them,} our teachers were superior and interesting young men and women, and I {adored} them almost without exception.

Of great interest to me, too, were the peddlers that sold goods in the rural districts. As we were half-way between villages ten miles apart, and they usually arrived about supper time, they were always welcomed and entertained free of charge; {and they were, on the whole, a decent lot}. Among my favorites was "The Old Scotchman," {as we called him}, who sold {table} linen {and towels}. He dressed in Scotch style {with bare knees} and wore a tam-o'-shanter. {His charm for me was} his love of children, {one evidence of which was} a ticking-bag full of delicious, small candies, {from which he extracted} a handful for me. {When} I saw him coming {from afar} I would run to meet him. Another favorite was a tin peddler who came with a horse and covered wagon. He was handsome and interesting, full of fun, and could have made a success on the vaudeville stage {if he had lived today. He had a beautiful voice and sang for us many popular songs.} He was a natural vagabond, and his business fitted his character. I doubt if he ever paid for a night's lodging or a meal. He was welcome everywhere.

I did not lack for friends of my own age. Our nearest neighbor had a son, Herbert Northrup, a few months older than I, and from babyhood we were {the closest of} friends. He was quiet, blue-eyed, and tow-headed, and I was talkative and gray-eyed and with hair as black as an Indian's. We seldom quarrelled and our hours spent together were {of the happiest. We were always teasing our mothers to allow us to visit each other.} We both learned to read when very young, because each of us was an only child, and had many hours of loneliness; learning to read was the one way of amusing ourselves, so we each harassed our mothers to tell us the names of the letters. I learned many of mine from the inscriptions on our kitchen stove.

{One of our neighbors, Mrs. Beverly, a stout, pink-cheeked elderly lady whom we both loved, who always wore lace folded inside her surplice waist fastened with a great cameo pin, and who wore a lace cap on her white hair, presented us with *First Readers*. I do not know how old we were then, but I had my daguerreotype taken on the day that I was four years old, with my *Second Reader*, bought that very day, in my hand; undoubtedly Herbert had the same book,} for we always insisted on being together in our readers and other studies as well. If one of us borrowed a book, each always asked the privilege of lending it to the other. His father was a victim of tuberculosis and there were times when Herbert spent weeks with us, when Mr. Northrup was very ill; we rejoiced at the privilege and did not realize the tragic reason for it.

No book gave Herbert or myself complete satisfaction until it was shared with the other. We would sit together by the hour and each reading busily. Our parents remonstrated with us, telling us to play or visit; we listened to them tolerantly, knowing that they could never understand how we were happiest together when reading. This way of entertaining each other lasted until we were grown. {One winter, a sympathetic teacher let us sit together in school, a blissful arrangement after we were sure the other pupils would not laugh at us—for in our school the boys sat on one side of the room and the girls on the other. Unwise remarks about what seemed to be our inevitable mutual relation fell off, leaving us untouched.} No girl could have been more fortunate than I in intimate boy companionship. Herbert was a thoughtful, {keenly} intelligent, refined, {pure-minded} lad who liked me as much as if I had been a boy and I liked him as much as if he had been a girl.

I was to continue fortunate in the respect; for, later, after Herbert's family had moved away, my cousin Marian Herrick, her husband and her four boys came to be our near neighbors. Of these boys two were near my own age and two younger. They were bright, happy, sweet, modest boys and {not in all the years of my association with them} did I hear an improper word from one of them or witness an act that could have been criticized by our parents. Blessed is the girl who learns early in life that men are good.

{I had one dear girl friend, Alice. Her mother, who had her to support, worked for us several years and my parents invited her to bring the child with her as a companion for me. Alice was a dear little girl whom I loved devotedly and with whom I never quarrelled. We liked the same plays and were naturally congenial. We were treated impartially by my parents and relatives. My kind uncle, Lucius Botsford, who always brought me candy or other gifts when he visited us, gave the same to Alice; in one case I remember it was cloth for dresses and we were enchanted to have them just alike.}

{I had many pleasures in life, and these were the more appreciated because they did not occur too often.} My greatest {happiness} was when I was allowed to visit the home of my Uncle Harvey Little, about a mile from our own home. My Aunt Sarah had taken me and cared for me when I was a year and a half old, while my mother was ill {with fever}; I loved her {passionately} and always called her "Ma Sarah." She was {an extremely} attractive and intelligent woman; she had been a teacher and was cultured and stimulating. Uncle Harvey was a big, handsome man, who had a fascinating way with children. My two cousins, Kate and Lidie, were popular young women {socially}; both were beautiful {physically—Kate petite, pale, blue-eyed, black-haired; Lidie large, blue-eyed and blonde.} I {fairly} worshipped them both. They permitted me to look at their ribbons, laces, and jewelry to my heart's content. Their beaux made much of me, {evidently} to win approval from the girls. Both had excellent taste in dress and were in my sight a whole art gallery of beauty {and uplift}.

The house was a long story-and-a-half structure {that had been added to at various times. At the kitchen-end}, upstairs, was one room which was a repository of all the papers and magazines, treasured for years. Curled up in the low window I reveled in this literature {by the hour. Above the parlor-end of the house were my cousins' bedrooms}, in one of which was {their Aunt Jane's} dulcimer, a stringed instrument to be tapped with padded hammers, {held in either hand}. It tinkled under my efforts, and I was enraptured with my own music. The sitting room had a fireplace and I still remember my {intense} enjoyment when I was allowed to stay all night and sit with {Rover}, the dog, before the roaring fire, my feet proudly encased in my Aunt's much too large slippers, while my Aunt and Uncle read by the table and Grandma Little knitted in her chair by the hearth corner.

One summer during the Civil War my cousin Lidie Little taught our school. {She brought} beauty and happiness to us all. She covered the marred walls of the school room with boughs from the nearby woods. The {red,} rusty box-stove she covered with flowers and ferns. She was an artist and had painted many pictures; on the last day of school she gave each of us a card, with her name and a flower upon it, {which we treasured for years. The naughtiest boy in school} wept {copiously, as did} all of us, when we bade her good-bye, for it was tragedy to us that she would teach us never again.

The Civil War made a deep impression on me. I had many cousins who enlisted and who came to visit us during their furloughs, dressed in blue with buttons that were gold to my eyes. I had mastered the *Fifth Reader* when I was eight years old and was able to read the newspaper accounts of battles and the lists of wounded and dead. I scraped linen with a knife to make lint with which to dress wounds, and helped knit stockings and wristlets for the soldiers. I remember the pall that fell over us when Lincoln was killed.

{Company was always a pleasure to me, no matter who came, and we had visitors often; going visiting with my parents was also an interesting and often a happy experience, especially when hostesses were thoughtful enough to offer me cookies, to keep me from what seemed imminent starvation before the rather late dinner was served.}

I was early taught to work. I learned to sew before I was four years old and to knit when I was six. I had to knit my own woolen stockings after I was seven. My stint was to knit ten times around the stocking each day and it seemed an interminable task. I pieced a bed-quilt before I was ten and have it now, each block a memento of a garment of my own or of some friend.

Mother had good taste and I always had one "best dress" {that was pretty and becoming}. Mother was also abreast of the times and adopted the bloomer costume for everyday wear for herself and for me. The full skirt stopped at the knee, but the legs below were encased in wide trousers of the same material that reached almost to the top of the shoe. For summer I wore a Shaker bonnet, a straw sunbonnet trimmed with material like my dress, usually pink calico. Other women and children of our community dressed thus for "everyday", but not for "best" nor for public appearance. I remember meeting a smart equipage filled with city people {(or so I guessed)} when I was coming home from school one day. A lady looked at me through her lorgnette and exclaimed, "What an extraordinary costume!" and I thought, "What an extraordinary lady!".

Going to school in winter was strenuous work. {There was snow always and} the fenced roads were drifted full, {so that traffic was through the fields}. Often the neighbors and my father would break open the roads with ox teams before we could get to school or get home. One blizzardy day our heroic schoolmaster {froze both hands} holding his shawl in front of us younger children while he walked backwards until our house was reached. I always wore copper-toed boots in the winter, and as I remember, the tops were usually filled with snow {by the time I reached school or home and had to be taken off and emptied}.

Many duties fell to my share in our busy farm life. The summer I was nine years old I washed the breakfast dishes and the milk pails and swept the dining room and kitchen before I went to school. At night I washed the supper dishes and the milk pails (how I hated washing the two large carrying-pails!) and went to the garden and dug the potatoes for the next day's meal. I also had the chickens to feed and a canary to care for. The hired girl was sick and away that summer, {I remember,} I remember also that I was struggling, quite successfully, with compound fractions {in my arithmetic} that term; {but I am sure} I never rebelled, even if the days were hard.

One of the {privileges and} joys was going barefoot from early spring until late autumn. {It was a precious privilege.} I was wont to play I was a princess occasionally, for I was very imaginative. Mother told me that if I were a princess I would have to wear shoes and stocking all summer, and never again did I play that game. "Poor princesses", I called them, and pitied them sincerely.

The great events of the year were agricultural fairs and circuses; the latter not always an annual event. How I gloried in the gorgeous spangles of the lady riders in the circus! Seeing {them} display was a great stimulus to my imagination {and a means of real culture, I am sure}. Later, when the family had gone to the village, I would array myself as best I could, and, standing on the back of our pet brood mare, pastured in the orchard, I would do my best to imitate the circus ladies; but my inconsiderate steed usually scraped me off with the help of the low-branched trees.

The "ladies' pavilion" at the agricultural fairs was to me a glorious place: pictures painted by the exhibitors; patchwork quilts; embroidered linen; wax flowers; framed wreaths of {flowers made from seeds}, or perhaps a family hair-wreath (locks of hair wired into flower shapes); elaborate beaded broadcloth skirts made for themselves by squaws, who also exhibited beaded cushions and mats. {There was also a flower show that seemed heavenly.} Always in the afternoon there was a game of lacrosse by the young Indians of our Gowanda reservation of Senecas—splendid athletes they were, too. Then, {of course}, there was the meeting of many friends, which meant much to my parents—and to me too, who loved everybody.

Our fairs and circuses were always in Gowanda, {as that was} a much larger village than Otto. We were half-way between the two, but the ride to Gowanda was far more interesting, because we had to cross "The Breakers at Forty," which means that we had to go down one side of a gorge about 200 feet deep, cross the South Branch of the Cattaraugus Creek, and climb up the other side of the Gorge, an exciting {experiment. Why gorges were always called "The Breakers" is still a mystery;} they were favorite places for picnics and excursions and afforded impressive and picturesque scenery.

{I usually attended Sunday School in the old North Otto Methodist Episcopal church. I had a sweet teacher, a sister of my father's first wife, whom I called Aunt, and undoubtedly she was the lodestone that drew me there. Also I loved to commit verses of the Bible to memory. However I was a heterodox youngster; for, when my teacher explained how Christ suffered for my sins, I wept and said I would not have it so, and that my mother always spanked me for my sins and this settled the score. From that time to this, the doctrine of sin washed away by Christ's blood has seemed to me unfair and unjust and also quite impossible. Yet no word in my home had been said about this; my revolt was entirely my own. I asked my mother about it, and she, in her dear Quaker way, told me that Christ was our Elder Brother, who came to teach us to do right; and that, if we had done wrong and truly repented, we could start again on the right path.

Always in Sunday School I was asking puzzling questions, which were answered by some quotation from the Bible, instead of reasonably; and I finally came to regard the Bible as a refuge for ignorance and a stifler of reason, a prejudice that remained a secret in my mind until after I too reached the age of reason and came to realize its majesty and beauty.}

Every spring and fall we were visited by Seneca Indians, since we were on the road that led from Gowanda to the Salamanca reservation. {As I remember them}, the men were tall, gaunt with deeply lined faces; the hooked nose and the high cheekbones and piercing eyes made them impressive; they were taciturn and dignified. The squaws {were} usually fat and {always} wore broadcloth skirts embroidered with beads. They always had baskets and bead work, and bartering these wares for food. All our baskets, from the bushel size for grain and potatoes to the dainty pink and green or blue dinner basket for me, we acquired {thus}. Father and Mother were always kind to the Indians; {I remember that} when a terrible sleet storm overtook a company of them one night, they were brought into our kitchen and camped there for the night. I remember well also the thorough cleaning mother gave the room after they left. In the spring, when the cows freshened, the calves were killed when three days old. The Indians regarded this veal as a great treat and, {of course}, it was given them free of cost. The story of the Indians on our reservations is a sad one. They owned the best land, but did little in the way of cultivating it. Whisky, sold by unprincipled saloon-keepers in the villages, wrought havoc, especially with the men, {who now, like the squaws, are fat}.

When I was ten we moved to the house opposite the school, and, for the first time, I had a room of my own. This seemed a luxury, although it was very plain, its white-curtained windows giving a view of the orchard.

This year, for the first time, I was a naughty {girl} in school. Our teacher was a sentimental person who had made an unsuccessful marriage, and {she was quite} unfitted for teaching. Her discipline was capricious, {to say the least.} Once she decided to whip me, and seized a long apple-tree switch which {was her weapon of battle}. I ran out of the schoolhouse into a cornfield. She came after me; I kept near enough to her to know where she was and far enough away so she did not know where I was. After a half-hour, while all the pupils were holding revel in the school-house, she gave up. I went home quietly, returned in the afternoon, took my seat as if nothing unusual had happened, and she too {acted as if nothing had happened.}

{I graduated in English Grammar under her tutelage. We had Brown's old Grammar and} I demanded reasons for rules and explanations, so that I could understand. She was no expert {in this line}, and being annoyed, finally said: "Anna does not seem to get along well as the rest of the class; hereafter I will hear her recite by herself." {Later in the day} I craftily asked her "will you hear me recite all I can learn?" She said, "Of course." I had a remarkable ability to commit words to memory, whether they meant anything to me or not. I studied grammar exclusively until the next afternoon, and asked her to hear my lesson {first after recess}. I repeated the grammar rules, through the remainder of the book. She tried once or twice to stop me, but I said, "You promised to hear all I could learn." I finished grammar and cordially hated the study until I came to an appreciation of it after I studied Latin.

It had been a tradition in our school that one afternoon each summer we should move from the schoolhouse to the woods and recite our lessons there, always {a perfectly} orderly performance. {This summer,} during afternoon recess I climbed a tree, {which was} one of my favorite diversions. I was coming down peacefully when the teacher exclaimed sharply: "Anna, come down out of that tree immediately, recess is over." At which I stayed my downward course and announced that I would recite my lessons from there, and I did. A few years later when I was a teacher in that same school, and we were having school in the woods, one of the older girls said, "What would you do if one of us climbed a tree as you did when Susan Lee taught?", at which an older boy said, "We'd better not try it; Anna would climb right up after us."

It was surely a period of badness for me. I remember that a schoolmate, a sweet, refined girl, and I began swearing when we were alone together. We used every oath we had ever heard and swore at everything {and anything}. One day we saw an apple-tree tent-caterpillar on the fence and we called it every wicked name in our vocabulary, at which it lifted up the front part of its body ad swung back and forth; we were awestruck and concluded we had best stop swearing, {which} we did. The disturbed insect had made this motion to frighten away parasites, but when a mere worm turned on us we thought it was time to reform. What our mothers would have thought of our performance, if they had known, was one element in our enjoyment of our wickedness.

The next year my father sent me to Cattaraugus village, {to school}, where I could see Herbert Northrup every day, for he and his mother lived there; and where I could visit my uncle, Lucius Botsford, and Aunt Mary; often, {Aunt Mary} always gave me something very good to eat.

The summer that I was thirteen father bought land near the village of Otto and built upon it a barn. The next summer we moved into the barn while the house was being built, as we were obliged to give room and board to the carpenters. The barn had never been used, {as such,} and made a very commodious residence. The stalls were made into bedrooms and the carpenters slept in the hay loft; never before had any of us had so much fresh air for sleeping, and all agreed that never before had they slept so well.

It was a rapturous summer for me, for there were as many new experiences, and new friends. {Never was there a more thrilling experience than} watching our new house grow. It was a Gothic cottage with six gables and a dormer window. {The builder was a man of ideas and} the house was painted cream yellow, the trimmings white and the blinds pale pink. Although I have since then roamed 'mid pleasures and palaces, I still think it was a beautiful house; the scroll work in the sharp gables and the spires fitted the style of architecture. The house was set on a side hill above the road, with the orchard at one side and behind it, and it made a pretty picture. The view from the piazza was eastward across a wide valley, with a stream winding in and out the "kneeling hills." It was from this piazza that I learned the exquisite coloring of the eastern skies at sunset.

The house was pleasant inside, with its large white {painted} kitchen and pantry, the dining room opening on the piazza was only used as such when the company was too large for the kitchen {fall-}leaf table. The parlor, with its dignified walnut and green rep. furniture and marble-top tables, seemed {quite} grand, as did the parlor bedroom, with its big walnut {bed and} furniture; the walls {of both} were papered with gray and green paper that looked like velvet. However, the special charm of the house for me was my study, a chamber with a dormer window overlooking the orchard. {This was not a bedroom,} it had a red carpet and lace window-curtains which seemed to me the {very} acme of elegance. A comfortable couch where I could lie down and read, a walnut bookcase and writing-stand, and chairs and rocker to match, {were its furnishings}. Never have I had such blissful hours as {those I spent in that,} my very own room.

There was a "select school" in Otto, {conducted by Miss Maria Calver and her younger sisters, Jennie and Mary.} I attended this school for the first year after we moved into our new home. {The Calvers} were superior women, and were cultured and interesting; the two {younger} were my life-long friends, as they married and lived near us. {It was} in this school that I saw pupils taking lessons in oil painting; I longed to be one of them, but I was consoled by taking a few drawing lessons. I met here Etta Holbrook {and Mary Hunt} and formed lasting friendships {with them.}

Etta Holbrook was the niece of Mrs. Constant Allen and was living with her {that year}. Mr. Allen was one of our wealthy men in Otto. He was handsome and dignified and a lover of good literature. Mrs. Allen {was a woman of great force of character. She was dark and her black eyes were keen and expressive. She} had been a teacher in {her own state of} Vermont, and had chosen to come to Otto to teach, where she met Mr. Allen, then a widower, and married him. Their home was a rambling {story-and-a-half} structure set in beautiful grounds at the edge of the village. {It was} to me a symbol of all luxury, elegance, and culture. The mahogany furniture of the parlor and library, the book-cases filled with books, the handsome silver table-service, the spacious sitting room with comfortable chairs and piano, impressed me profoundly. The many oil paintings and engravings on the walls filled me with awed delight. {More over,} the master and the mistress of this home were {cultured people}. They read aloud to each other and {often} I was permitted to listen when I was their guest. Poetry, essays, political speeches, magazine articles, were read so well that it was a {privilege to listen}.

{Mr. Allen's children by his first marriage were married and away, and there were no children of the second marriage. Mrs. Allen supplied this want by inviting her nieces and nephews from Vermont to stay with them. Also Mr. Allen's nieces were often there, so} there were always young people in the house, which was an added attraction. {Among these was Etta Holbrook, who has been a beloved and helpful friend to me these many years. There was a boy, her brother Martin, who was a thinker and a lad of rare promise when I knew him best. I remember that when he was about fourteen years old he asked me once what I thought about death and life hereafter; of course I told him I didn't know, at which he said: "I think God owes us something, even if it is nothing but an explanation."}

As my home was a mile away from the village, I was welcomed at the Allen house during stormy nights, {for all the years of my school-going}. Father liked to have me there, for he knew Mrs. Allen would not permit me to go on the streets in the evening. {Also, one of the most inspiring teachers of my girlhood, Jennie Marsh, lived with the Allens, for it was a hospitable house, and her companionship was stimulating.} As I look back on my early life I can see that Mrs. Ann French Allen was the one {above all others} who aroused my ambition for a higher education, and implanted in me a desire to make my work in the world count to the utmost of my ability.

{I remember that} one morning when I called upon Mrs. Allen she had a newspaper in her hand and said: "Anna, here is your chance for a University education. Ann Arbor has opened its doors to women. Your Aunt Charlotte Willits lives near Ann Arbor and you can live with her." This seed, once planted, sprouted and grew. Later I prepared to enter Ann Arbor, when Cornell gave me a chance nearer home for a University course.

There were two churches in Otto, {Congregationalist and Methodist,} and the membership of the two included the best citizens in town. Nevertheless there was often hot rivalry between them, and this, I remember, was echoed by the children. "You are a damned Methodist," or "You are a damned Congregationalist," I heard on the school grounds, {and these epithets often resulted in a general battle}. My father was afraid that I would be influenced to join a church before I had reached the age of reason; so he insisted that if I attended the Sunday School of one church I must also attend the Sunday School of the other, and alternate my attendance at church services also. This had the desired effect, and kept the two balanced as far as my interest {was concerned. I remember that} when a most lovable man {came as pastor to the Congregationalist Church} he called on father and asked why he was not a church member. "I live in peace with *all* my neighbors." answered Father, with a smile, then they both laughed and were good friends {ever after}.

When I was fourteen, the teacher in the primary room of our village school was ill, and had to leave six weeks before the term ended. I was asked to take her place. I {secured} a third-class certificate without examination and entered a noble profession joyfully. It was hard work, but {it was} highly entertaining. I received three dollars a week and "boarded myself". At the end I had $18 and told my father I wanted to spend it for books. He proposed that we have a great {day} and go to Fredonia, N. Y., where was the nearest book-shop, {and make the purchase}. I have most of the books still; and this is the list, showing Mrs. Allen's influence: the complete works, in one volume each, sheep-bound, of Shakespeare, Moore, Burns, Byron, Scott; "diamond editions" of Tennyson and Longfellow; a half-dozen paper-covered novels by Dickens and Scott; and the owner of the shop gave me, *Faith Gartney's Girlhood* and *Hitherto*, both by Mrs. A. D. T. Whitney. The riches of Golconda were as nothing in my mind compared with my own when all these books were on the shelves in my study; and eighteen dollars {was the investment}. I especially reveled in the poetry. I bought the volume of Byron because, when Mrs. Allen found me reading *Don Juan* in her {volume}, she took it away from me. I'll never forget how I waded through that poem in my own book, trying to find out what was wrong with it, {but failed}. I thought it was the stupidest poem {ever written. Don Juan's philanderings were too far beyond my thought and horizon to seem more than a hopeless muddle.}

In 1871 there was no high school in Cattaraugus County. However, there were two seminaries under the direction of the Methodist Church. The nearest was "Chamberlain Institute and Female College" at Randolph, about eighteen miles from Otto.

In September, father {took} me and my precious trunk and a bundle of bedding in the wagon and drove to Randolph. The Institute was situated on a hill between two villages and consisted of a brick {dormitory}, one wing for the boys and the other for the girls, and a wooden building {given over to} classrooms. The offices and dining room were in the main part of the brick building, also rooms for the literary societies. The table in the dining room accommodated fifteen or twenty {each}, boys on one side, girls on the other, and a professor to preside at each {to keep order}.

The teachers were superior in character and attainment. The principal, James T. Edwards, was an able man of long experience {in teaching} and was especially brilliant in the physical sciences. His wife was the preceptress, a fine-looking woman, dignified and a successful teacher of French and painting. Darius Baker, who taught Latin and Greek, was afterwards {for many years} a judge in Newport, Rhode Island. Isaac Clements, who taught mathematics, was {in later years the head} the principal of Cazenovia Seminary.[4] These {three} men were graduates of Wesleyan University. They were men of high ideals and had great influence upon us all. The teachers of music and penmanship were also fine people.

For the first week life was glamorous. New teachers, new friends, new studies, new environment, all seemed wonderful to me. There were brilliant young instructors, and also brilliant pupils, as later life proved. {Will Blake and Frank Thorpe both made records as teachers in secondary schools in New York City, and there were others who have attained honors. My own very close friend was Sarah Burlingame, a beautiful girl who later became Mrs. Prentice Webster of Lowell, Massachusetts.}

{My special boy friend was David Jack, who, after a brilliant record in Wesleyan University, became an eminent lawyer in Bradford, Pa. David and I were the only pupils in college preparatory course in our class and thus we were thrown together. As he was of about my age, he was naturally attracted by the younger girls; and the authorities, recognizing that we were merely good friends, gave us more liberties than were usually accorded to a boy and girl. We studied together often. Dave had a better mind than I and had better grades than I in Latin and Mathematics; but he hated English and

---

4. Specifically noted in 1953 edition (p. 71), as "Cazenovia Seminary, in Madison County, New York."

I overtopped him there to the extent that I was made salutatorian when we graduated, which I considered unjust. We remained firm friends as long as he lived. He married one of my mother's cousins, a beautiful girl, and their life together was most happy.}

The eldest daughter of our principal, Grace Edwards, was a child of ten, and one of her dearest friends was a little girl whose family lived in Randolph, her name was Martha Van Rensselaer and I saw her often, never dreaming how closely she would be associated with me {in later life}.[5]

We had many activities at Chamberlain Institute and I was in them all. A literary society {met every week}, where we debated, orated, and declaimed; we also "published" a paper. Each winter there was a competitive oratorical contest. We {were given our topics and} could have no help in writing orations, but had training in declaiming {them. The judges were people selected from the town, Judge Henderson being one.} In the first competition it seems that a majority of the judges decided I should have the second prize; {but Judge Henderson thought otherwise and said I should not have the second prize}—if I was not given the first prize, I could not have any and he would give me {one. What happened was that} from him I received a {beautiful} set of Scott's novels {complete}, a much handsomer prize than either of the other two. I {was overcome and wanted} to weep. These books have been a joy to me {all my life}. The next winter I was given first prize, a set of Elizabeth Barrett Browning's poems.

{There was} one phase of life in Chamberlain Institute that I found very unpleasant—the pressure put upon me, mostly by my schoolmates to "experience religion." They felt that my lack of faith was sending me {on the broad path} to perdition. At first I did not attend weekly prayer-meetings, then I was accused of {fear lest I be} "converted", so I went regularly and sat there like a wooden image, unimpressed. Meanwhile I developed a sharp tongue against these onslaughts on my spiritual life and inside {I} was ugly and rebellious. One night, after prayer-meeting, {Professor} Darius Baker called me into his office and gave me a "straight talk." He {said that I should} not go to prayer meeting; that it was a damage to my character, {as it was} making me cynical, {and cynicism narrowed and contorted character.} I {meekly} obeyed, and the bitterness of the battle remained with me. Just before I graduated

5. Footnote from the 1953 edition (p. 71): "Minutes of the Cornell University trustees record that Anna Botsford Comstock, the first woman professor at Cornell, was appointed Nov. 8, 1898. Martha Van Rensselaer came to Cornell as an assistant in 1900 and was appointed a professor, as was Flora Rose, after the Cornell University faculty approved the appointment of women as Professors of Home Economics, Oct. 18, 1911.—R.G.S."

Dr. Edwards took me aside and labored with me, and finally said with tears in his eyes, "I believe that sometime we shall believe alike." I answered, "I cannot believe it, for so many of the attributes of your God, such as jealousy, revenge, and sending to eternal torment poor mortals, are the attributes of a devil," {and that ended it}.

{However,} it was not until I went to Cornell, where no one {cared a flip about} my beliefs {and it was taken for granted that I could look after my own soul,} that I became tolerant. I had met intolerance with intolerance. Cornell taught me again the lesson taught me by my parents, to respect the spiritual experiences and religious beliefs of others. I have never had an argument with any one about religion since; and I have counted among my intimate friends people of every creed, {from Catholic to Buddhist}, and people of no creed at all. I {quite} agreed with my Shinto friend, S. Hori, {when he} said: "No man has any more right to talk to me intimately about my religion than he has to talk to me about my wife." That early experience {has always} set me firmly against propaganda {when I could "spot it" as such}.

I graduated from Chamberlain Institute in June, 1873. My Latin salutatory I declaimed {from the stage}, and to the {disgust} of my many friends, who had been in the habit of coming to our public exercises to listen to what I had to say. I certainly had gained much from my stay at Chamberlain Institute. I had learned to {use my mind, and made many contacts with} cultured and superior people, and had been very happy in my friendships. {Of course} I had some "love affairs"; but they {were harmless and} did not do more than to exercise my emotions healthfully. I had my eyes fixed upon a University education and could not let anything happen that would interfere with that goal. {My} ambition was my insurance against sentimental {infections. As a matter of fact I was never popular with young men. I was too independent for one thing, and I did not appeal to the masculine taste. On the other hand,} I always had good friends among the boys of my acquaintance, friends on whom I could rely and who builded strong my faith in manhood.

The next year I taught school in Otto, and I enjoyed the experience. The summer of 1874 my parents and I spent with relatives in "The West." {We first visited my father's sister, Charlotte Willits, who with her daughter Helen and her son Eugene lived in Delhi, Michigan. They were of the best in every respect. We also visited at Monroe, Michigan, an older son, Edwin Willits, who later represented his district in Congress. Thence we went to Chicago and to West Chicago to visit mother's sister Betsy and her family, almost all of them married and in homes of their own. Among them was

Harlan Sanders, the portrait painter, and Calvin Sanders, whose daughter Bertha, then a child, was later a water-color artist and exhibited her pictures in a Paris salon.}

{From there we went to Aurora to visit the family of Alvin King, beloved by both my parents; thence to Elgin to visit Miss Addie Wing, an elder daughter of Charlotte Willits; and there we met for the first time her daughter Kate, now Mrs. Kate Sprowls of Los Angeles. It was a thrilling summer, meeting all these relatives, only a few of whom had I ever seen, and all of whom interested me.}

We tarried so long in the West that I did not enter college that fall. Instead I took lessons in German with the principal of our village school, {Mr. John Burns, a fine man who later made a notable record as a lawyer}.[6]

I first thought of Cornell when, during my last term at Chamberlain Institute, one of our graduates who had entered Cornell talked to me about it. He said: "It is a great place for an education; but if *you* go there you won't have such a gay time as you have had here, for the boys there won't pay any attention to the college girls." I thought seriously and finally concluded: "Cornell must be a good place for a girl to get an education—it has all the advantages of a university and a convent combined."

I started for Cornell in November, 1874, entering at the opening of the second term. I stopped at Elmira on my way, and John Hillebrand, Cousin Fidelia's husband, came with me from there to see me settled. It was discouraging business, but we finally found a room, with a Mr. and Mrs. Harvey, in a house on East Seneca Street {just below Spring Street}, and a place to board {with a Mr. and Mrs. Halsey in a house on the opposite side of} the street.

{There were then a few scattering houses on East Seneca Street above Spring, and a few on Eddy Street: but there were no paved side-walks anywhere. Now and then there was gravel on a sidepath.} I climbed up to the University as best I could, thankful that I was a country girl and accustomed to bad roads. Cascadilla Place was a forbidding{-looking} structure, {but} it housed many professors and their families and {many} students. The bridge across Cascadilla Creek had a low wooden coping; the {beautiful bridge of the present day was built and} given to the University many years later by William Sage. Where the old Armory {now} stands was the small wooden {railway}

6. In the 1953 publication, here ends Chapter 4, and Chapter 5 begins from this point forward. This next section served as an article in *A Half-Century at Cornell 1880–1930: A Retrospect of The Cornell Daily Sun, 1930* (pp. 25–26, 72) entitled "Pioneers Among Women by Anna Botsford Comstock." —KSt.

station {of the Elmira, Cortland and Northern R. R.}. It was a terminal station, {as at that time the road was finished no farther.} The railway had been admitted to the campus to bring material for the University; but the station was no ornament. {There was a little ravine north[7]} of it which was crossed by a wooden bridge. There were two houses on Central Avenue, one of them Professor [Thomas F.] Crane's and the other belonging to the Commandant. Sage College and Sage Chapel were in process of building. Morrill Hall, then called South University, and White Hall, then called North University, had classrooms in their central portion but at the ends were dormitories for {boys} and at the top of each was a large lecture room, {Room K and Room T}. Geology, zoology, and physiology were taught in McGraw Hall, {though} the central portion of its first floor was {given to the library}. Of Sibley College only what is now the west section was completed. The engineering department had the first and second floors, and botany the upper floor.

A large wooden building [The Laboratory] occupying a place west of that given to Goldwin Smith Hall held the departments of Chemistry, physics, and veterinary science. On East Avenue, President White's house and north of it the houses of Professor Willard Fiske and Dr. [James] Law were completed. The farm-house, with its orchards and barns, occupied {nearly the place} of East Sibley and Lincoln Halls. {There were} a few old oaks and pines on the campus, but the elms were all just planted and protected by their boxes. {However} it was not a bleak place, because {from almost any point there was a} glorious view of Cayuga Lake and the valley {, lost now behind the trees}.

I found I must take several examinations in order to enter, and {this} was discouraging. I had not had enough German to enter the class; but I saw a Masonic pin on the vest of the professor in charge. {My} father, thinking I was to be plunged into a strange and dangerous world, had given me his Masonic pin and a letter from his lodge asking all good Masons to be kind to me. Armed with these, I called upon Professor Bela P. MacKoon in his house; he {was a man who} struck terror to the hearts of his students, but he was an excellent teacher. I presented my credentials and no one could have been kinder to me than he; he made me come to him for the needful lessons and would take no pay. Before I joined his fear-stricken class I was convinced that, if his pupils knew how really kind he was, they would not mind so much the lash of his sarcasm.

At my boarding place were {six or seven} Brazilian students. They were young and had had only a few months' study of the English language; they

7. In the 1953 edition, "South of it was a ravine . . ." (p. 74) —KSt.

found their university work hard and discouraging, and were homesick. {Although} they were {so} young, they wore beards or moustaches or, both, which made them seem much older {than they were}. I found them serious, quiet, polite young men. Luckily I was not the only {one of my sex} at the table, for {Mrs. Halsey} always presided and one of her daughters usually sat with us.

One day, when I had been obliged to take two unexpected entrance examinations, I was low in my mind and looked longingly into the depths of the Cascadilla gorge as I crossed the bridge. {As I seated myself at the dinner table} a letter from my mother was at my plate, into which I gave a {surreptitious} glance. She had sensed my homesickness and was {sweetly} sympathetic. It was too much for me; I felt the tears coming, and fled to the other room, ashamed of my lack of self-control, but I recovered soon and came back to the table. Lo and behold, all the Brazilian youths were weeping, their tears rolling over their beards into the soup; they were just homesick lads, although they looked like men! I had never seen men weep, and I began to laugh {hysterically; then} they laughed too, and we ate our dinner in sympathetic sadness and cheer.

My room {at Mrs. Harvey's} looked out over town and valley; it was frankly a bedroom, and two students, William Berry and Spencer Coon, had their room off the same hall. {However,} I was not disturbed by this, since I expected no social {intercourse} with gentlemen. Imagine my dismay {a few days later}, when answering a knock at the door, I discovered {there} a tall and dignified {young} man who evidently expected to be invited in. I stood guard firmly, while he explained that he had called to invite me to join the Christian Association. I thanked him and he retreated. {Soon} my neighbors called on me, and since they knew it was my bedroom, I managed {in some way} to express my dismay at having no other place to receive callers, but they were cheerful and seemed to think it was all right.

That night I asked {Mrs. Harvey} if I might receive callers in her parlor and she refused. {Later} she suggested that I take another small room for my bedroom, saying she would help me make my room into a study, where I might receive callers without embarrassment. When we {had finished}, it was an attractive room and greatly needed, for I had many callers, some women students came, but more men, naturally enough, as there were but few girls in Cornell {at that time}. It seemed that my {boy} friend of Chamberlain Institute had a mistaken {idea about the social} ostracism of girls at Cornell.

There was a ball in Library Hall at Thanksgiving. Mr. E. F. Jordao, a dignified and handsome Brazilian who sat at table with me, invited me to go.

I consented, {of course,} as that seemed the only courteous thing to do, and I sent home for my evening dresses {(two was all I had). I had not brought them along}, thinking I should not need them. {However, this and other invitations to parties in the homes of Ithacans worried me lest I was not doing the correct thing socially.} All was strange to me, and both my landladies were newcomers to Ithaca. I took my life in my hands and called on Vice-President William Channing Russel, who looked so fierce and was really so gentle. I told him of my perplexities. He {said I should not} go anywhere with Brazilian students, as they were foreigners with very different customs from ours. I told him I had promised to go this time, but I would not go again, at which he remarked that "advice to young people always made them more determined to go their own way." However, we had on the whole an amicable conference, which was the beginning of a friendship {that lasted as long as he lived}. I went to the ball with Mr. Jordao, and no Puritan youth could have treated me with more courtesy and respect. I enjoyed it all greatly. The first people of Ithaca were in attendance and it seemed to me a brilliant affair. Professor Russel was certainly wrong about the Brazilian student I knew. They were gentlemen all{, judged from our standpoint, so far as I was able to discover. Later one of them, Mr. de Mello-Souza, married a sister of Professor Charles Crandall}.

As a result of my appeal to Professor Russel, his wife, a {very} superior woman, called on me and I was invited there for dinner, {and felt honored}. Ruth Putnam, a classmate of mine, was living with them, and she too called on me, which was pleasant. She {also has been} a lifelong friend.

In those days there was little afternoon work in the University, except in engineering.

{At least} I had none, although I studied both botany and zoology and had laboratory periods in both. The zoology lecture room, {an Amphitheatre,} was in McGraw Hall {on the second floor. The professor stood with his back to the door that opens into the museum. His laboratory was back of the raised seats and under them. We had to climb two flights of stairs to reach} the botanical laboratory in Sibley college. {I shall never forget how happy were} Professor Prentiss and Instructor W. R. Dudley when in the next year they were moved to Sage College, {where their lecture room adjoined what seemed then luxurious laboratories}.

President White had furnished a room on the first floor of White Hall for the literary societies. The pictures on the walls and the bronze statuettes {which were also his gift were beautiful and impressive}.

The days were busy and happy. We climbed up to the University through snow and slush and sometimes on ice. {I made the sage} observation that the native Ithacan was never self-conscious when he fell on the {icy walk}; he got up {as well as he could}, and never looked {to see if someone had observed him}. Not so did the recent comers take their tumbles; {before they made effort to arise} they looked around furtively to see who might have witnessed their humiliation. There was a steep place by Cascadilla up which, one icy morning, a South American student was carefully climbing and which I was about to attempt. Just as he reached the top he slipped and came back down on all fours, landing at my feet. I was glad I did not understand the language he was using.

When spring came there were walks in the woods {after flowers} for the botany, and there were boat rides on the lake, and {many} scrambles through the gorges. I had two {very kind} friends in the young men in my house, Will Berry and Spencer Coon, both of the class of '76, excellent students, with high ideals and deeply interested in their {university} work; they were {both} good companions and {very} thoughtful for my enjoyment. The lake was our favorite play-place. {It was very different then.} Two great side-wheel steamers made connections between the New York Central Railroad and Ithaca. (I still maintain that a side-wheeler is the most beautiful and swan-like craft in the world.) As we paddled out through the inlet we passed many barges, some of them with picturesque families aboard, their multi-colored wash flapping in the breeze. There were small sail boats in plenty and no cottages along the shores to take away the wildness that was their charm. There was an interclass regatta that was thrilling. The seniors spilled, the juniors stopped to rescue them, the sophomores were impeded by the mishap, but the freshmen rowed manfully on and won the race.

That summer was, {to say the least}, emotional. Will Berry and I had arrived at a stage in our relations that made a consultation with our parents desirable. On our way home I stopped at Forestville and met his father and mother and two sisters—excellent and interesting people. A little later Will came to Otto and visited my parents and our engagement was approved by both families. {Alas! It was one of those} affairs that in less than a year fell by its own weight. It was too emotional to meet the realities of life. I went with him to his senior ball in 1876 just to prove that there was nothing left of our tempestuous relations, and that night we bade each other a calm good-bye. I saw him only once afterward—when he called on us after I was married. He had a brilliant career as a newspaper man, working for several years on the New York Sun, then the Mecca of newspaper men. But he was too high-strung for the demands upon him. {His brain snapped and an asylum shrouded his last years, a sad ending for a beginning so promising.}

I returned to Cornell in the fall of 1875, rejoicing that Sage College was finished. It was a {beautiful} home {for us}, and highly appreciated by those of us who had experienced the difficulties of living in town. There were {two or three} small reception rooms {besides} the large dining room, all well furnished. My room was on the second floor on the north side and very pleasant. My roommate was Minerva Palmer '77, a beautiful Quakeress, and our companionship proved ideal. There were only thirty {of us} in the big dormitory, so only the first and second floors were in use. {With a front room or two} on the third floor. {Mr. and Mrs. Kinney, people of experience from Oberlin, had charge of the building and the refectory.} As thirty was a number too small {to run} a kitchen and dining room {for them} with profit, it was deemed expedient to give men students the privilege {of table board}. The dormitories in White and Morrill Halls were full of students, some of whom had formed an eating club in a tenant house, just behind the President's, called "The Struggle"—"for existence" {being dropped as too long for daily use.} I think David Starr Jordan[8] gave the club its name. Later the Kappa Alpha and Psi Upsilon fraternities built their chapter houses on the campus, and these groups had tables in the Sage dining room.

Although we were few, college spirit was with us. Ruth Putnam came to my room one evening asserting indignantly that the freshmen were holding a meeting {in a room of one of the class} and she averred something should be done about it. Something was done immediately; water from a pitcher was dashed over the transom to dampen freshman ardor. But it did not work that way. They {indignantly} made a sortie upon us, and as they outnumbered us, there was a {desperate} struggle on the stairs and a rumpus in the halls which shocked everybody not in the squabble. {Especially did it shock Mr. and Mrs. Kinney, who had been accustomed to deal with milder spirits in Oberlin.}

The fracas resulted in the organization of a student government association in Sage College. {Julia Thomas (later Mrs. Irvine, President of Wellesley) was elected President and} a committee appointed to make rules for our guidance. These rules, finally unanimously adopted, {were not so many, but otherwise} were not unlike the rules of the self-government association of today, with the exception of the one restriction that the women students should not bow to their men student friends on the campus. We were so few that it was embarrassing to {recognize or} be recognized in the crowds passing to and

8. Inserted in the 1953 edition (p. 79), ". . . David Starr Jordan (later President of Indiana and of Stanford Universities) . . ." —KSt.

from classes. As soon as we explained to our friends the reason for ignoring them, they not only accepted the dictum, but confessed relief.

President White and Mr. Sage both thought we should have a chaperone in charge of Sage College, but we {resented this and} would not have it. We came to Cornell for education and had been reared to care for ourselves; chaperoning we considered insulting to our integrity. However, I must confess that some of our rules were made to govern any girl who {overstepped} our ideas of propriety. We had a happy social life in Sage that first year. The gymnasium {was where the kitchen now is}, and was reached from the front hall via a covered porch. We had dances there every Friday night; sometimes there were girls only, but more often our men friends were invited. {I remember that} one evening the entire Kappa Alpha Fraternity came and we had a pleasant evening, a social affair probably not recorded in the annals of that {organization. I remember that} one of the members, {Mr. Ballard}, made each girl with whom he danced promise to bow to him when she met him on the campus. {I am sure that} we all promised, but I doubt {if any one fulfilled her promise; I know} I did not, although he was a nice lad. But lads, however nice, could not break our rules.

We had musicals; Professor Estevan Fuertes,[9] {being a leader in giving these.} He played the flute exceedingly well and he brought with him players of the piano and violin. We also had readings by Professor [Hiram] Corson. He read Shakespeare to us and also read from modern American writers, {Bret Harte, and George Cable, and others. We appreciated this greatly, for} I had never heard anywhere such perfect rendition of the spirit of the printed word {as Professor Corson gave.} Since he read {to us without compensation}, we thought we should do something to show our {appreciation}, so we bought a reading chair for his study, and planned to give it as a surprise. To make sure of his presence at the function, we took his son Eugene, then a sophomore, into our confidence. He met our committee on the morning of the day {when the gift was to be bestowed in the evening and declared:} "Pa is {awful} cross this morning, but I think he will be {here on time}." A {worshipful maiden lady} on our committee was shocked at this statement, but the others of us were delighted; it made our professor seem more like other men, {for if ever a mortal looked the superman}, he did—tall,

---

9. Inserted in the 1953 edition (p. 80): "The father of Louis Agassiz Fuertes, Cornell's famous bird artist, whose paintings illustrate the two volumes of *Birds of New York*, published by New York State; and part of the three volumes of *Birds of Massachusetts*. Many of the original paintings for *Birds of New York* are in the New York State Education Building in Albany, New York. —R.G.S."

spare, with flowing beard and hair rather long, his gaunt face illumined with eloquent {eyes that at times were piercing}.

There were interesting personalities among us at Sage College that first year. I remember {most distinctly the following}:

Julia Thomas {(Mrs. [Charles J.] Irvine)}, tall, {spare, and always} dressed in a {rather} masculine fashion, her skirt reaching to her shoe-tops while most of us wore ours barely clearing the ground. Her hair {was cut} short; {this and} a sailor hat and a cape coat, added to the masculinity of her appearance. She had a strong face and very keen eyes. She was {very busy} studying for her A. M.[10] and did not encourage acquaintance; {however, she had great} charm of manner and every word {from her lips was} interesting. She {was, some years} later, President of Wellesley College.

Martha Carey Thomas was in appearance an ideal of purely intellectual young womanhood. Her broad forehead, {her} clear cut features, {her} hair drawn smoothly back to a Grecian knot, {all} gave the impression of scholarliness. She was dignified and cold to all but a few. She had come to Cornell to study {and she did} not waste her time on social {intercourse}, nor did she think we were worth while {anyway}. A great work in founding Bryn Mawr College lay in her future.

{I found}, in my limited acquaintance with these two Misses Thomas, who were to be presidents of colleges, this difference at that period of their development. Martha Carey Thomas {did not care a flip for humanity}, while Julia Thomas had {a heart} for her fellow mortals. {Many} years later I met Martha Carey Thomas and {found her greatly changed in this respect. She had grown} kinder and more gracious {and was ready to give help where it was needed. I was charmed by her attitude.}

The most beautiful girl in Sage was Margaret Hicks. {Tall, slender, graceful and dignified, her face as delicate and exquisite as a cameo, she was a delight to the eye. She was studying architecture and married, later, Arthur Volkmann, one of her fellow students in that course.}

Harriet May Mills, a pretty girl with a round face, red cheeks, large dark eyes, and dark, wavy hair, was Miss Hicks' room-mate. {Perhaps she was the last one we would have thought of as} a future leader on the fighting front of woman suffrage. {Another beautiful girl was Anna Louise Head. She had a peachy complexion and pleasing manners. None of us wondered that she won the heart of one of the most brilliant men that ever graduated from Cornell, Dr. N. Archer Randolph.}

---

10. Master's degree.

Ruth Putnam was always an influential {person in her environment}. She was short, stout and had {beautiful} red {crinkly} hair. We all knew that she was well aware of her superior social position as member of the illustrious {Putnam family}, yet she was never a snob. Her historical works have brought great honor to the class of 1878. She also did excellent work as {an Alumni} Trustee.

Susanna Phelps (later Mrs. S. H. Gage) was one of the most charming of us all. {She was} short in stature, with {a most} attractive face and beautiful eyes and, in addition, winning manners, keen wit, and a joyousness in life that was infectious.

{There were also two inseparable friends, Lisette Jones, black-eyed, handsome, and vivacious, and Jenny Beatty, (later Mrs. A. J. Loos), whose sweet and gentle ways made her loved by all who knew her.}

{Outside of Sage}, in Cascadilla, lived the most striking young woman in the University, Harriet Tilden (Later Mrs. William Vaughn Moody). She was fine-looking, with a superb carriage and a winning dignity. {She was wealthy and} her clothes were always elegant and in perfect taste. We in Sage saw little of her {or her room-mate, Miss Ida Bruce,} but we all regarded her as a {most attractive and} splendid personality. We were wont to weave romances about her; and sundry gossip of her engagement to one of our most brilliant young professors thrilled us. {I am sure that} none of us would have been surprised {to know that} she would marry a poet and do effective work for her Alma Mater when she was elected trustee.

{On the whole, we were happy together in Sage College that year 1875–6.} One great privilege we had in the frequent visits of President White. He gave us talks on various subjects, from our proper behavior to the art of the Renaissance. More than that, he invited us to his home, where we met {the exquisitely} beautiful Mrs. White, whose {simple} graciousness charmed us all. There we gazed at treasures in {beautiful} books and pictures which President White himself {showed and} explained to us. {I shall never forget the feeling of exaltation I experienced because of that inspiring evening.}

I was taking President White's course in the history of the Reformation this year. {I was never so swept off my feet by any other course I had ever taken.} He revealed to us history in all its relations to literature, religion, thought, art, architecture, and music, as well as to nations, wars, and {people. I was} so eager a student that I read thirty volumes in connection with this course in one term. I read avidly in the library every afternoon and Mr. White {loaned} me some books from his own library as well. {I still have the syllabus of these lectures with my notes in class. It is to me a treasured volume.} It seems to me a pity that we have so crowded our curricula in these days, that a student would find impossible {such a glorious course of reading as I found time for that year.} My mind and my vision expanded in leaps {and bounds through this experience.}

{Another privilege} we appreciated was Sage Chapel, with its sermons by eminent divines {of all} denominations. {I shall never forget} when Henry Ward Beecher came, how the chapel was crowded {to the limit}, and the windows also were filled with eager {heads, to which, presumably, suspended bodies were attached.}

Hjalmar Hjorth Boyesen, already an author, {was a social factor with us that year.} Young, enthusiastic, he was an interesting figure in the Sage drawing-rooms in the early evenings, when we were wont to gather there. My first meeting with him {the year before} was an embarrassing moment for me. I was struggling against a strong wind between Morrill Hall and McGraw and lost my hat, which went {gaily} tumbling over and over in full view of oncoming students. Professor Boyesen chased it, rescued it, and presented it to me with a profound bow, removing his {high} silk hat with a flourish, {meanwhile}, to the obvious joy of our passing audience.

{This year} I was in his course in the history of German Literature, the first part of which was given to folk-lore. He was an interesting lecturer, but restless; often he would begin a topic on the platform in front of us and finish it at the window {gazing on the scenery} with his back toward us. {He was} in appearance a typical Scandinavian; yellow curling hair and beard, milk-white complexion, rosy cheeks, and {very} blue eyes. It happened {quite miraculously} that our neighbor of ours, when I was a child on the farm, had loaned me a fat book of fairy tales, both English and German. I read and re-read this precious volume {with an avidity possible only to a country child whose books are few. Thus} I was familiar with many of the folk-tales given in this course, and Professor Boyesen once said to me:

> "Miss Botsford, I have not found among my students any other so familiar with German folk-lore as you. I think you must have given much time to it."
>
> "Yes, I have given many happy hours to it," I answered, without further explanation.

Professor Boyesen was educated in Europe and was not accustomed to our {familiar} ways. He {joined the Psi Upsilon Fraternity and} ate at Sage dining room {with that group}. After a provocative incident, he {confided} to Professor Lazenby one day: "Cornell students have no more idea of caste than a cow," which delighted us {greatly}.

The first year in Sage was notable for many things. There were among us several older women, teachers who had waited for the doors of a university to open and to give them opportunities for advanced studies {as a help in their profession; there were} serious-minded girls who studied hard, some of them typical grinds; and there was a sprinkling of those who were gay and socially-minded. Some of them came from luxurious homes, some from families of {high} culture, and some, like myself, from village or farm, where in that day cultural influences were more or less accidental. Some were good to look upon and some were not. When, in recent times, I have heard complaints about the younger generation, I have thought of a slim girl of the class of '79 who succeeded in keeping engaged to two Cornellians who were roommates for an entire year before discovery revealed her double devotion—a feat that Cornell {flappers} of today could scarcely equal.

Among the pleasantest of our social events were the Delta Upsilon "Quarterlies", {dances given once a term in the society's rooms in a village block. Delta Upsilon, not being a secret fraternity, had the advantage of being at liberty to use its chapter rooms for social purposes.} These dances were informal and delightful. {I remember well} one which was a mask costume party. {Recently} I chanced to find my costume in a trunk of bygones. I personified "Night"; over a black silk gown that trailed I wore a long drapery of black tarlatan set with silver stars. My long black hair was loose, the tarlatan veil was fastened on my forehead with a silver ornament, and my black domino was edged with stars. Of course I made the costume myself. I was a sombre figure, {in the gay throng}, but I am sure no one else had a gayer evening than I.

All fraternities had their chapter rooms in {the city} blocks in the early days. The first fraternity house was built by Alpha Delta Phi in Buffalo Street, {just above Spring Street}. Kappa Alpha was the first to build on the campus and Psi Upsilon followed soon after. President White was in favor of allowing the fraternities to build on University land, as he thought it best for the students to be {away from the town and} near their work.

When Commencement came, the visiting trustees were lodged in Sage and we met them socially. Among them was Erastus Brooks, {a man of advanced years and of great personal charm}. I had the privilege of a long talk with him about the education of women, and he said to me impressively: "There will come a time when every room in Sage College will be taken, for young women will seek the advantages of Cornell. I shall not live to see this, and perhaps you may not, but the time is surely coming." I have lived to see two great dormitories besides Sage filled and overflowing. However many other halls may be built, Sage College will always be {most} important, not only because it was the first, but because this magnificent gift of Henry Sage secured the rights and privileges of Cornell University for women students forever. {It was} the bargain Mr. Sage made with the University Trustees and the State of New York. There have since been several times when we were profoundly grateful for his foresight in this matter.

At this point in my college story it is high time that I "{page} John Henry Comstock". He had called upon me in February {while I was at Mrs. Harvey's}. He tells me with vivid memory how he dreaded to make this call, and had postponed it as long as possible, but {that he} came away feeling it was time not wasted; he confided to his roommate, {Charles B. Mandeville}, that it was not half as bad as he had feared. I remember that he kindly offered to do anything he could for me and that I liked him; and my landlady, who took a motherly interest in my callers, told me he was highly esteemed. Probably, if we had {dreamed} what Fate {had up her sleeve} for us, he would not have come, and I would have bolted my door against him if he had {come}, since we both at that time were dreaming of futures with other persons.

I was in Mr. Comstock's class in the winter of 1875 and I liked his clear way of presenting what seemed to me, a very complicated subject. I must have studied well, for I still have my term paper, marked 95 by Instructor Comstock's blue pencil. A letter to my mother {states}: "Mr. Comstock called and stayed about two hours the other evening; he is very nice." In a previous letter I had written: "Mr. Comstock (the gentleman of whom Jennie Bartlett wrote me) took me through his laboratory after the lecture the other day; he is our lecturer in zoology now. Such thousands of insects I never saw before! Then we climbed up and saw his chum, Mr. George Berry, ring the chimes, which was very interesting. Mr. Comstock is one of the kindest of men. He is a young fellow, still in his twenties, and he has lectured in the University for two years past. Report says he is engaged to Docie Willett, but don't mention it!" Our relations were amicable and casual during the remainder of that year. During the Spring term he was very busy preparing lectures for a summer school in Peoria, Illinois, and I saw little of him.

It was in the autumn of 1875 that my real acquaintance with Henry Comstock began, {the first year in Sage}, when men came there for their meals. We were allowed to invite {any of} our friends to sit with us at {the} table. I asked for Mr. Comstock and Dan Flannery '76, who was one of my preparatory school friends; both were rooming in Morrill Hall. {Mr. Lazenby and one or two other men sat at our table also.} I was told afterwards by {Mr. Kinney}, the manager of Sage, that Mr. Comstock asked if he could sit next to me, since I was the only girl in Sage with whom he felt acquainted.

Susanna Phelps {(Mrs. Gage) and Rose Eddy, her room-mate, were the others} at our end of the table.

We had very happy times at meals. We were so gay and laughed so much that we were looked at askance by some representatives of dignity and decorum; but {at that time America was a free country and we were Americans, so} we laughed as we chose. Susanna had a laugh of such silvery sweetness that it ought to have redeemed us. {I find the following} in a letter to my mother: "Did I tell you that Mr. Comstock sits next to me at table at his own request? He is very pleasant and the very essence of kindness. This afternoon he invited me to go and gather moss and autumn leaves in the gorge. We had a charming time." After this, {I note}, he often invited me to walk; once I write: "We walked three hours, such a grand walk. Mr. Comstock and I thoroughly understand each other and that is why we are so thoroughly friends." But we apparently did more than walk, for I state in a letter of Nov. 28, 1875: "On Thanksgiving Day Mr. Comstock took me for a drive to Enfield Falls, {a place of resort} about six miles from here. It was a beautiful day and the scenery magnificent. We had dinner at a charming, old-fashioned tavern. We returned about 4 o'clock." I {later} reassure my mother by saying: "Mr. Comstock is noted for being a young man who is a sort of a general friend to young women of his acquaintance, but never wastes any sentiment upon them."

In March, 1876, there came a break in Mr. Comstock's work {from a very sad cause}. One reason for the good friendship {and reciprocal understanding} between him and myself, {was because} I knew of his relations to Jennie Bartlett, '77. She {was, in a way, a member of my family and, although I had seldom seen her, I knew her as} a beautiful girl in both face and character, and it was she who gave me a letter of introduction to Mr. Comstock. The two were not betrothed, but were very dear friends; and I knew that he looked forward {to the time when he should win her}. It was discovered in this winter of 1876 that she was a victim of tuberculosis, and her mother took her to Florida. Mr. Comstock, with his usual directness, went to Dr. Wilder {with the matter} and obtained leave of absence from the University. He sailed March 18th {on the S. S. "Champion"} for Charleston on his way to Florida. {For some reason} there were many clergymen on board {this boat, and} although Mr. Comstock was still a member of the Methodist Church, he {evidently then, as ever afterward, greatly} disliked theological discussion. A letter from him declares: "I hope I shall never {hear of my going} to sea again with several clergymen. It is hard luck; one of them talked me nearly to death." It was a very rough voyage and he confesses that many times he wished himself aboard a schooner, or some other craft that would "keep its keel under it." He sailed up {the} St. John's River on March 24th {on the steamer "Davis Clarke."} Florida in 1876 {was vastly different from Florida of today.} Its development had hardly begun {and he found it a "terribly uncivilized country, no railroads, no telegraph lines, no nothing."}

It was at Fort Reed, {at Dr. Foster's} sanitarium, that Miss Bartlett and her mother found an abiding place; Mr. Comstock found a boarding place not far away, where he was of even more interest to an army of cockroaches than they were to him, for they ate the binding off his books and the mucilage off his stamps. {However}, he was now able to do {all that lay in his power} to make happier the life of the girl whom he loved. {She told me afterwards how kind he was to others besides herself, and how soon he gained the favor of the sanitarium household.}

He had many hours in which to explore the country and give free hand to his activities as a naturalist. He writes: "This is the richest entomological field in which I have ever worked. I have studied my specimens only a little as yet, but I think I am finding many things new to science. I am making notes, and if health, etc., permits, I shall probably have material enough for a thesis. I have begun systematic work on the Orthoptera [an order of insects containing grasshoppers, crickets, cockroaches, et al.], especially the Acrididae [a family of grasshoppers]; and already made some important observations on geographic distribution and mimicry; my list of probable new species is astounding to me. Leland Howard collected grasshoppers in Ithaca last year and obtained, I think, about 22 species. I collected in a single day {last week} fifteen species." {He had some quite exciting experiences on his collecting trips. Once he saw something moving between two logs in his path; he thought it was a rabbit at first, then discovered it was a section of a snake; he jumped back, unscrewed his net handle, his only weapon, but the reptile passed on peacefully.} In addition to his care of the invalid and his interest as a collector, he had time to be a useful citizen of Fort Reed, for he writes to Lazenby: "I am tired today because I worked yesterday fighting wild fire until I was forced to lie down on the ground. It came near destroying the village."

The Florida experience ended sadly. Miss Bartlett did not {gain and she definitely} decided that marriage was out of the question for her, although {at that time} she did not anticipate a near approach of death. Her decision was a hard blow to Mr. Comstock; and probably no one better than I knew how hard. He came home early in May {on the schooner "Flora Woodhouse"}. Luckily for him he had {a beloved} work which was calling him to action, and he wrote from Fort Reed: "I shall come home soon. If I stay much longer it will break upon my summer work at Ithaca, and, as I was away last summer, it will not do. The work I shall do there is breeding insects and it is necessary to begin with the season to have the work amount to much."

{I remember how} we all welcomed him back to Ithaca. Since {no one but Dr. Wilder, Mr. Gage, Mr. Lazenby and myself} had known of the real reason for his Florida trip, and as Mr. Comstock and I took frequent walks together that spring, we heard rumors as to our future relationship which amused us {greatly} because they were {so false}.

Anna Botsford Comstock, n.d.

CHAPTER V

A University Professorship and Marriage, 1876–1879

Chapter V in the Comstock manuscript relates the courtship and early days of marriage of Anna Botsford and John Henry Comstock. This chapter shows Mrs. Comstock's use of "thee" rather than "you" and the formal "Mr. Comstock," whereas in the 1953 edition a more informal tone had been used instead. In the early chapters of her manuscript, Mrs. Comstock addresses her husband with names or terms appropriate to his age. From this point forward, once he procured the milestone of his assistant professorship designation from Cornell in 1876, Mrs. Comstock refers to her husband as "Mr. Comstock" almost exclusively. Mrs. Comstock did not refer to husband as "Professor Comstock," and only as "Harry" in familial settings. The 1953 edition may lead one to believe otherwise. A second interesting point about this manuscript chapter is that it ends abruptly. No continuation of Mrs. Comstock's final thought carries over into the next chapter. The page(s) may have been removed, lost, or destroyed.

The summer of 1876 was a busy one for the Instructor {in Entomology at Cornell}. He sprained his ankle {the last} of June, just when he wished to be observing the habits of *Corydalus*, and he complained because that insect had no notion of taking a vacation to accommodate a lame entomologist. He gave his forenoons to dissecting and writing and his afternoons to his collection and catalogue. He also had some relaxation. He wrote exultantly of the {boat} races [at Saratoga] that "Cornell won all the races." His friends

{Scofield and Lazenby} spent {many} evenings {in his room, the three playing} draw poker with matches for chips; {it is needless to add that} they never played for money, a commodity much scarcer than matches. {He also took long drives with the Jayne family, and} he continued to read French novels in the original. {It was about this time that} he read *The Count of Monte Cristo* in six small {paper-covered} volumes. His devotion to this {work} lasted for years, and many times, when he was tired and needed complete change of thought, he would carry one of these volumes {around} in his pocket to read at every opportunity.

He was at this time working on his thesis for the M. S. degree, the subject of which was the internal anatomy of *Corydalus cornutus*. {Miss Gabrielle Clements (who earned the B. S. degree at Cornell in 1880) was making drawings for it.} He writes {an enthusiastic letter regarding his investigations} of this interesting insect, which abounds in the streams about Ithaca:

> "I have done a glorious week's work. I spent Monday and Tuesday on drawings and then it occurred to me that, as the water was very low, it would be a good time to collect in Fall Creek. When I started into the field I was blue and half sick. {I had been applying myself too closely to my laboratory, which accounts for it physically; and} I had just discovered that all my specimens of *Corydalus* were useless for the study of the muscular system {which is a part I had begun to study. This accounting for my blueness mentally.} It is the larva that I am at work upon; my specimens were collected late in the season, just at the time they were about to change to pupae; {in fact} their internal organs had already undergone a change which rendered the specimens unfit for anatomical study. This was staggering. What should I do? Stop work on *Corydalus* until next spring, when the new brood will be large enough to dissect? No, I will not stop work altogether. I will look for little larvae; as the eggs were probably laid in June and July, they must have hatched ere this. The young larva has never been described and it will be worth my while to do it.
>
> "When I reached the creek, I found the water very low and within fifteen minutes I had found several larvae about a half-inch in length. This was glorious. I pulled off my shoes and stockings, rolled my trousers above my knees, took off my coat, rolled up my shirt sleeves and went to work. A few minutes later, on turning over a large stone, I saw a large object crawling on the bottom of the stream; it looked familiar, could it be? No, impossible! The reflection of the light upon the water was such that I could not see the specimen clearly. Involuntarily I seized it, but as it squirmed in my hand I dropped it with a shudder like a frightened girl; fortunately, I dropped it into my pail,

and there it was beyond a doubt a magnificent, apparently full-grown larva of *Corydalus*. What a strange thing! This fellow had evidently forgotten to undergo its metamorphoses in June and was loafing around two months behind time. Presently I found another loafer, and then another, and then several little loafers about half grown; and then I began to be conscious of the dawning of an idea, i.e., *Corydalus cornutus* does not become full-grown in one year, as is generally supposed. The little fellows about a half-inch long were hatched from eggs laid this year; the half-grown fellows are one year old, and the large specimens are two years old and would have become full-grown next year. Thus, it requires three years for this insect to reach the adult stage. This is an interesting point, but the thought which made me happy was that I need not now stop work for want of specimens.

"I found but few specimens until yesterday, when I learned another thing which is very valuable to me. I had turned over every stone on several acres of creek bottom and found perhaps a dozen specimens. I then learned that this larva, as a rule, lives under stones in that part of the stream where the water is swiftest, sometimes where the water is so swift that a man can hardly stand against it, although it be only knee-deep. I turned over stones in such places and saw the larvae; but the water would sweep them away ere I could seize them. Another idea dawned, I will take a dip net, and, holding it in the current with one hand, at the same time turning over stones in front of it with my other hand, I will catch some of these fellows. I did so and caught as many as seven at a time. Yesterday and to-day I caught about 80 specimens, enough to keep me dissecting a year or two. Need I add that I forgot my blues and indisposition? {Then he added,} "I should like to spend ten years on my thesis and employ an artist the whole time. I feel that I could do something that would advance science and be an honor to my Alma Mater."

That summer Mr. Comstock published a syllabus of his lectures, {which} was the first step toward the textbook that then he hardly dared dream of writing. He {says}: "I sent you a copy of my syllabus last week. I did it with hesitation, for the book amounts to little when not supplemented by lectures. It is only an outline of the lectures with references to authors; and, {too}, it was written under very trying circumstances. I hope to write a better one ere many years. {I already look on this as a boyish effort.}"

He had more students in his laboratory in September than he had expected. Leland Howard was specializing in Entomology as a senior. Little did he or his teacher dream of the momentous import of {this fact. Just at this time extra work loomed up before the young instructor}. Dr. Wilder undertook to give a course of lectures at Michigan University and also at Bowdoin College. This {entailed} his absence from Cornell all winter, and Mr. Comstock was to give the course on vertebrate zoology in the winter term. {He had fifteen new lectures to work on for which} Dr. Wilder would pay him $150.00. {Dr. Wilder advised him not to work on the lectures but to keep on his thesis. However, this was not the nature of the man. All his life, if he had lectures to give, he worked on them and let other activities lapse.}

It was during September that Mr. Simon H. Gage was called home by an epidemic of diphtheria in his family. His brother and the latter's five children died of {this dread} disease; {later,} Mr. Gage contracted it, and {Mr. Comstock} telegraphed him he {would come and} take care of him if necessary. Fortunately, his was a light case {and this was unnecessary}, but the incident shows the devotion of {Mr. Comstock} to {this friend at the beginning of} a friendship that was to bring happiness to both for half a century.

Mr. Comstock's thorough manner of working is indicated {by the way he began compiling a slip} catalogue of references to all {possible literature} on insect anatomy to aid him in writing his thesis. It was during this autumn that he was first invited to speak before the Western New York Horticultural Society, and it was suggested that he become entomologist {to} this organization. He feared he did not have the time to do justice to the position but felt that he owed it to the University to accept it. The following January {Mr. Comstock} read his first paper before {this} society and was gratified by {the manner in which it was received. He continued to read papers before this} important group of practical men for many years {after}.

In October of this year he made a visit to the Centennial Exposition in Philadelphia, {one of the attractions of this trip was the opportunity for} looking up references in the library of the Academy of Sciences {and the other was the meeting of Professor Leidy and hearing him lecture.} He {writes}:

> "I did not expect to find much in the entomological collections at the Exhibition; but I was decidedly surprised to learn that the American Entomological Society had no biological collection. It shows what I knew before, that the members of the society, among whom are the leading entomologists of this country, have studied species as adults only. I hope that before the next Centennial, entomologists will learn that it is as important to know what insects do, as it is to know their names. I expected to learn much about the arrangement of museums, but as yet I have obtained hardly a single idea that is new and practical. The exhibitors have aimed to produce an artistic effect rather than to give instruction. On the other hand, the library of the Academy is as

good as I expected to find it; and of course, I had no idea of the magnitude of the Centennial Exposition."

{One of his special pleasures during this trip was the companionship of his dear friend and classmate, Bennie W. Law.}

{". . . the new species of some one order. C. V. Riley is really the only economic entomologist that I know of in this country, and he is already doing very well. I had a talk with Professor Russell a few days ago. He seemed to feel very sad at the thought of my leaving. His 'I don't want you to go' did me much good, for it is nice to know that one's work is appreciated by some one. Dr. Wilder does not think I will leave. He expects the trustees to do something as soon as they discover that I am likely to go. And if I should go, he thinks they would call me back in a short time."[1]}

In December 1876, the trustees {made Mr. Comstock} Assistant-Professor of Entomology at a salary of $1000.00. Professor Russell was so delighted with this promotion that, after an evening session of the trustees in town, he walked up the hill to Mr. Comstock's room in White Hall and awakened him to tell him the good news; he carried a similar message to W. R. Dudley.[2]

{It was soon after he was made Assistant Professor that} he spent the {holiday} vacation at my home. His picturesque arrival I shall never forget. It was very cold weather, and his train was late, so that the regular stage, connecting our home town with the nearest railroad station did not bring him. A little later he appeared in a livery {open} sleigh. It was the fashion for a man to wear a silk handkerchief folded cornerwise as a scarf to protect the throat. This was a zero day and with {Mr. Comstock's} usual directness {he} tied this handkerchief over his ears, the free corners flying in the blasts and the whole topped by his hat. {However,} my parents like practical young men and he made a most favorable impression upon them. That was the beginning of a

---

1. John Comstock to Anna Botsford, no date. She included the quote in the manuscript, but the section was rewritten in the 1953 edition (pp. 92–93) as follows:

"Mr. Comstock had now been serving as an instructor for three years with little prospect of advancement in salary. The University's financial means were restricted, and he feared that at Cornell he might have to continue to be an instructor for many years. There were tempting positions open for teachers elsewhere. But he felt that in the United States, the importance of economic entomology was gaining recognition and that ultimately, he might attain a better position in that field than in teaching other subjects. He talked the matter over with Vice-President Russel, whose "I don't want you to go" did him much good and settled him down again to his work. He did not wait long for advancement." —KSt.

2. In the 1953 edition (p. 93): ". . . Instructor William R. Dudley, later Professor of Botany at Stanford." —Ed.

near and dear relationship between him and them, {that was to last and} be a happiness to them {as long as they should live. They} looked with favor upon the friendship between their daughter and this energetic, enthusiastic, industrious young professor. They apparently saw which way the wind was blowing and welcomed the probable result. It was {here} at Otto at this time that {Mr.} Comstock gained the family name of "Harry," which {has} clung to him all his life.

I remember clearly {his} personal {peculiarities} in those days. He was very active and moved with a rapidity that gave the observer a breathless sensation. {A cousin asked me sotto voce after observing him cross the room, "Anna, does he ever strike fire?" He was much unconsciously restless, even when he sat reading he moved constantly, and as I was to discover later, much to the detriment of his trousers.[3]}

He was absolutely fatal to the tidies with which the housewives of that day were wont to decorate {the backs of} easy chairs; he usually {rose triumphantly with} a tidy on his own back. {I also remember in those days that his activity was very expensive in the matter of shoe leather.} He always stood straight; his face was deeply lined, and if he became bored the lines went deeper, giving him a remarkable old look.

We had a happy visit, but there was no engagement to announce until several months later. We were becoming very well acquainted and the companionship on which our marriage was based was steadily becoming {closer and} more important to us both.

After {his} return to Ithaca he was quite excited {for a little time over} the prospect of joining a party of sixty students to make a trip around the world, in which he was to go as zoologist, but this did not materialize. He now definitely planned to work in economic entomology at Cornell and had an ambition, {when Dr. Fitch's position should be made empty by his retirement, to fill it himself and} become State Entomologist of New York. This dream, {as a matter of fact, he} never {was to have} fulfilled, {but it prevented him from accepting the position on the world-expedition}.

That winter {he} gave a course of lectures in Vertebrate Zoology to a large class and was most successful. {The class cheered him lustily at the end of the first lecture and continued to be appreciative and cooperative the entire term. His classmates, Lazenby and Dudley, attended the lectures, and also Mr. F. W. Simonds, the geologist.} His small laboratory was full of students, and he says of them: "I wonder what these men would do if they

3. This recollection was reworked in the 1953 edition (p. 94): "My father, who loved to tease me, asked sotto voce, 'Anna, does he ever sit down and sit still?'"

had to determine these species of insects alone as I did; still I suppose if I had had a teacher I should have bored him to death in the same way that these fellows do me, they are so fearfully careless." This was the feeling of the young teacher; later he learned, {as few men} do, the patience needed to start a beginner on the pathway to science.

It was in January of 1877 that {he} sent me India ink in the stick with direction as how to use it, pens, a drafting board, and a T-square, so that I could try my hand at {scientific} drawing. I still have those first attempts at drawing insects, and now, instead of scorning them, I think they are rather good.

In the Spring of 1877 {Mr.} Comstock made an application for a building lot on {campus. It was the one} he had always longed for, on the knoll at the {extreme} north edge of the campus. {The place} now is occupied by the Baker {Chemical Laboratory}. He was gratified to be able to make a lease of a large lot, 150 feet {front} and 300 feet deep, that commanded a view of the {lake}. He began to plan a home for some future time and did not seem to be in doubt as to who would share it with him.

{About this time, he first made himself felt in the faculty. There was a rule that hazing should be punished by expulsion. In White Hall one evening a group of students, including some freshmen as well as graduates, planned to visit two freshmen in the same building and have some fun. The freshmen met them with pokers by way of battle axes, and the visitors, like Riley's visiting baseball team, realizing that "they were not as welcome as they aimed to be," retired at once, as they had no thought of hazing or of any physical coercion. Mr. Comstock knew of the affair and was surprised to find that the freshmen had reported it to the faculty in such a fashion that the authorities called up sixteen men with the idea of expelling them all. He worked hard to give the sixteen fair representation and, after two long sessions, four were cleared and the others put on probation. This was a decided victory for the young professor and he remarked: "It seems as though many of the professors have forgotten their boyhood and cannot understand how young men feel and think."}

In February 1877, {Mr.} Comstock began copying his business letters in the old-fashioned screw-press letter books. The many letters to entomologists all over the country copied in this book show his activity in building up the collection of insects for {the} University. He asks Dr. Scudder[4] to send

4. In the 1953 edition footnote (p. 95): "Former Harvard University Librarian. He worked with Orthoptera and with fossil insects and wrote the *Butterflies of New England. How to Know Butterflies*, by the Comstocks, is dedicated to Samuel Hubbard Scudder. —G.W.H."

him types of the families and genera of common Orthoptera, and to keep in return, any insects that {he} collected in Florida; he issues a circular to the members of the Western New York Horticultural Society about the apple-leaf-folder, {which was} a new pest. Of course, all the letters were written by hand and also the circular, which was {mimeographed}.

In the spring term he gave a course of lectures on entomology; only three students were required to take it, but he had more than fifty attending the course, among them Mr. [Simon H.] Gage and Susanna Phelps. {He} had to turn many students away from the laboratory for lack of room.

After his term's work was completed, he gave a course of lectures at Vassar College. {Professor Orton, in charge of zoology at that institution, was away on a leave of absence, and Mr. Comstock was very glad to give the lectures from every point of view.} He wrote that he sometimes felt a little odd when he {was alone with} one other man in a dining room with 357 girls. {He soon made friends with Professor Priscilla Braislin, a gifted and beautiful woman who had charge of the mathematics at Vassar for many years. This friendship with Professor Braislin continued as a source of great happiness to to us both. He also became acquainted with Maria Mitchell, the Professor of Astronomy, and had a great admiration for her.}

All of this work proved to be more than he could stand, and later in the summer he had a hemorrhage of the lungs. He came to my home at once, and, after consultation {with several people of experience,} he went to Buffalo and placed himself under the care of {Dr. Foster}. This eminent physician found that his patient was breathing with the upper part of his lungs only and had thus strained them to the bleeding point. The treatment consisted chiefly in teaching him to breathe {abdominally}; after this was once {thoroughly} accomplished there was never afterwards any trouble with the lungs. {It was a very anxious time for us and we were greatly relieved that Dr. Foster's diagnosis and treatment proved so efficacious.}

{Mr. Comstock had tied a hammock for me, an accomplishment he learned at Vassar, and this was hung in my sanctum; in it he rested and recuperated and practiced his breathing exercises during the remainder of the summer. Meanwhile I was taking up the study of entomology along many lines and was making pen drawings of insects for my lover's approval. I was also painting pictures in oil, or copying those that I liked, with the idea of ornamenting our future home.}

As {Mr. Comstock} did not have to lecture during the fall term, he was able to bring some of his work to Otto and so remain with us until his recovery was complete. I remember that during the Christmas vacation I painted while he read aloud from Lewes' *History of Philosophy* and Draper's *Intellectual Development of Europe*. We were surely serious-minded young {folks}.

{Early in the Spring of 1878 Mr. Comstock was again working on our lot on the campus. He staked out the garden in April;} he had also let the contract for the {house, and the cellar walls of this wonderful structure were laid early in the spring. He was quite busy in the University also, for he had forty students in his lecture course and eighteen in the laboratory. During this spring a great event for him occurred;} he went to Rochester and bought for his laboratory three microscopes, stands, and seven objectives, and a triplet pocket lens. {The riches of the Indies were as nothing to these treasures in his opinion; he rejoiced that Bausch and Lomb had granted him 20% discount for cash. He was sure that with this equipment the work in the laboratory would be lightened by half.}

He writes {of the house}: "I cannot tell you how strongly I am becoming attached to our little home. {And if the partially built house is so dear to me what will the final home be?} I am more than glad to tell {thee} that the critics, so hard to please, pronounce Fall Creek Cottage an 'architectural success'; {many have told me that they thought it the prettiest house on the campus.} Leal Howard {came to me to-day and said: "Professor, I think your house is just as pretty as it can be!} It is pretty from {any direction."}

On the first of July 1878, {Mr.} Comstock was invited to {be one of the entomologists to} go into the South and investigate {the life habits of} the cotton-worm {[Alabama argillacea]}, with the {idea} of halting its ravages. It seemed an excellent opportunity for him to do field work {that was at the same time} research. Moreover, the salary of $100.00 a month and expenses was most acceptable, for the house must be paid for. C. V. Riley had been {in the position of} Entomologist {to} the U. S. Department of Agriculture only a short time, but the appropriations had already been made for the work. {It was finally decided that} the cotton belt be divided into {three} sections, Riley to have the eastern, A. R. Grote the middle, and Comstock {the most} southern section.

Mr. Comstock started from Washington on July 19th for Dalton [Georgia], and he was amazed at the damage done by the pest which he came to study. He {writes}: "It appears by myriads and often completely destroys the crops in some localities, ruining many people. The planters with whom I have conversed talk in a hopeless sort of way. They think when the worms appear nothing, but an intervention of providence can save the crop."

He settled for the summer in Selma, Alabama, as this was one of the chief regions for cotton growing, {and} the insects had made great havoc there. He sent me {the following} description {of the Canebrake Region}: "The Canebrake is a tract of land extending from the Junction just west of Selma to Demopolis and is about twenty miles in width. This is the field of my observation. This region is called Canebrake because in early days it was an almost impenetrable jungle of cane. It is now cleared and is the richest part of Alabama, both in point of fertility of soil and in wealth of inhabitants. {The region is not low or marshy, as we would naturally picture in our minds when we hear its name; quite the contrary, it is a high and dry tract of country, being in fact the watershed between the Alabama and Tombigbee Rivers. At this season hardly a bit of water is to be seen. The streams are all dry except the rivers. The soil is very shallow and rests upon a soft limestone rock."}

{Mr. Comstock} enjoyed {very much} his association with many of the men whom he met during this work. It was his first experience with the South and southern people, and he found that he was obliged to modify many of the ideas gained through his strong abolitionist and republican affiliations during the Civil War. {I quote from one of his letters}:

> "Captain R. M. Nelson invited me to go with him to his plantation. He is a very fine man and the days which I spent with him were very profitable to me. {We learned much respecting insects; but it is not of that that I wish to write.} We occupy the same bed; and one night we lay awake till two o'clock talking. I wish {thee} could see and talk with some of these men. The men of the South are noble men, or I have been very fortunate and met only the best. I wish our people of the North could see them nearer and not be obliged to depend on the reports of politicians who are more anxious to further their own ends than to tell the truth. As Captain Nelson said: 'I wish the people of the North and of the South could be brought together like the right and left pages of a book when we close it'. If that could be, the suspicions and jealousies now rife would disappear. {I have seen very much of which I must not take the time to write; I was here at the election last Monday and visited several of the voting places. I never saw a more quiet election.}"

{In a later letter he writes}, "I believe I have not told you of my return from Huntsville. It was a very pleasant one. Governor Chapman made me acquainted with General L. P. Walker, who was the Confederate Secretary of War. General Walker was going to Blount Springs that day and we were together from early morning until the middle of the afternoon. After General Walker left me Senator Morgan, who was returning to Selma, took his place. This gave me excellent company all day. I have become very well acquainted with Senator Morgan. I first called on him in an unofficial way, afterwards socially. Then he took dinner with me at a hotel. He has done much to make my stay here pleasant."

{Mr. Comstock's industry surprised the people of Alabama; but he was really very careful. He did not go out in the middle of the day and he kept out of the night air. He also took a dose of quinine every morning, carried a sun umbrella, and went into the field on horseback when possible. "If you can devise a means of ridding us of the cotton worm, you will be the greatest benefactor that the country has known."}

The date of our wedding had been set at about the middle of August and I {very much} disliked a postponed wedding, largely out of superstition. So at first, to please me, he planned to come north to be married and go back to his work. But I could see that he thought this was not wise, and I soon agreed with him. By the middle of August yellow fever broke out in Mississippi. Selma was quarantined, and trains went only to Demopolis. Day after day the yellow fever was closing in a ring about the region where my lover was working and, {it must be confessed, that} I and my family were not {very} happy during these last weeks of August. I found it rather upsetting to get love letters that had been fumigated for yellow fever.

{However,} on September 4th Mr. Comstock was called to meet C. V. Riley[5] in Nashville and he felt that he had finished his work, as he had watched the cotton-worms disappear. At Nashville he and Riley wrote a quarterly report of the work and then Mr. Comstock went to Atlanta. It was while he was with Riley in Nashville that he made the arrangement, so fraught with later results, for Leland Howard to come to Washington as Riley's assistant.

{From Atlanta Mr. Comstock went to Albany, Georgia, with Professor Willett, whom he found very pleasant and most congenial. Later he went to Macon and was the guest of the Willetts, an experience which he has treasured in his memory. Once in riding with Professor Willett in Southern Georgia the train stopped at a little station and the Professor said: "This is Andersonville and right there in that valley was the prison".}

{He} started North on September 24th and reached Otto October 1st, a leave of absence from the University having been granted him. {It is needless to expatiate upon the gladness we experienced when finally, we saw him again.} While in Georgia he had been the victim {of ague [malaria]} and he still suffered chills every other day, so we chose a 'well' day for the wedding. To our dismay two days before the event he changed his chill and was due to have one at the exact hour of the wedding {on the 7th}. I pictured my horror

5. Included in 1953 edition (p. 98): ". . . C. V. Riley, Chief Entomologist in the United States Department of Agriculture . . ."

should his assent to the minister's questions be made with chattering teeth; but the excitement of the event scared off the chills and he did not suffer from this disagreeable disease more that autumn.

The seventh of October 1878, dawned bright and beautiful. We can vouch for it because long before dawn we were up and at sunrise were on our way to East Otto, a distance of seven or eight miles, to attend the wedding of my brother playmate, Herbert Northrup, {to Miss Addie Beach. True to precedent,} Herbert and I, who had always done everything together in our childhood, were now to be married on the same day. It would be a small {matter now to cover that seven miles in an} auto, but it was quite a different matter {to do so} with father's pursy span of mares {(father's ideal of a good horse was one that was so fat that its ambition and tendency to shy were dulled). However}, it was a beautiful drive among the Otto hills, gorgeous in autumn coloring. We reached {our destination} with time to spare before the {very lovely home wedding at the} Beach homestead {took place}; and then we drove back for our own afternoon ceremony.

Our house was decorated with evergreens and autumn leaves; the arch under which we stood was made of hemlock twigs and hazel blossoms. {The latter flowers} we both loved because of our enjoyment of Whittier's poem about them. The guests were near relatives and a few intimate friends, and {of course} the wedding party of the morning. The Principal of Chamberlain Institute, where I prepared for college, Professor James T. Edwards, performed the ceremony, which seemed to us very impressive and solemn. {Directly} after {this} a wedding supper {was served, and} the two pairs started off together on a double wedding-journey. There was no need to wait for change of costumes because we were married in our traveling clothes. I shall never forget my father's little speech to his new son: "You are our son and belong to us, as Anna does", {which} proved a true prophecy; for, {as long as my parents lived, he was a true and} devoted son to them, and they regarded him {ever as such}.

The journey with the Northrups lasted only as far as Buffalo for they went off for a month's travel. {Far otherwise was it with us. Mr. Comstock was due to get back} to his teaching {as soon as possible, as he was already late;} so we went to Rochester {and spent two days with my college chum, Minerva Palmer, while we selected} furniture for our little home, {to the extent of} a hundred and fifty dollars {worth, which amount bought} a great many furnishings {in those days. It was a memorable visit in several ways. Mrs. Phoebe Palmer, Minerva's mother, was one of the most remarkable women I have ever known, a Quakeress, perfectly poised, with wide experience, broad sympathies and a charming personality, whose every word seemed to have special weight. The advice she gave us both, and especially me personally, proved a lifelong treasure of wisdom and guidance.}

The evening we returned to Ithaca we were met at the train by a group of dear friends, {Messrs.} Gage, Mandeville, Dudley, Lazenby, Howard, and {Misses} Lena Hill and Susanna Phelps.[6] They escorted us to supper at a restaurant and to the {finished} home which neither of us had seen. Mr. Mandeville had had the carpets put down, but there were no chairs, so we sat on the floor in the parlor and visited, all talking at once, and {later}, "Mandy" sang two {very sweet} songs to us in his {heavenly}, high tenor voice. The party then {exhorted} us to the home of Professor Roberts,[7] which was the old [Ezra] Cornell farmhouse, standing where the {east end of} Sibley now stand; {its orchards and barns covered the ground now occupied by Lincoln Hall}. Professor and Mrs. Roberts were very kind to us; {they entertained us delightfully in their home during the time that we were settling our house. This was their wedding present to us}, and nothing could have been of greater help, since theirs was the only house near {at hand. Moreover, then} began the friendship that lasted strong and loyal {for a lifetime}.

We were {very} proud of our little {new} home, Fall Creek Cottage. It stood where the north-east[8] corner of the Baker {Chemistry building} stands, and it commanded a wide outlook over the campus and the Lake, {for in those days the trees were young and did not shut off the view as they do at present. It is true that} the old farm barns, {by no means beautiful,} were directly below and in front of us, and a winding road through a cornfield was the only approach to our dwelling from what {is now} the corner of East and Reservoir Avenues. {Our house was so placed that the lot which went with it was almost an estate; we found it rather too large when it came to keeping the lawn in order.} The house was pretty and compact and the special pride of its designer, Professor [Charles] Babcock, {who was at that time} head of the Department of Architecture {at Cornell}. On the first floor there was one large room on the west side, a cheerful living room with {the open} fireplace {at its middle}; a hall and stairway divided this from the dining room at the southeast corner of the house and the kitchen and pantries at the north. On the second floor the rooms were {the same}, a large west room, used later as a study, and two bedrooms, {while} on the third floor there was

6. Expanded in the 1953 edition (p. 99): ". . . Simon Gage, "Mandy" Mandeville, W. R. Dudley, W. R. Lazenby, Leland Howard, Lena Hill, and Susanna Phelps."

7. Noted in the 1953 edition (p. 99): "Professor Isaac P. Roberts, Professor of Agriculture and later, Director of the Cornell University College of Agriculture and Agricultural Experiment Station.—G.W.H. and R.G.S."

8. Corrected in the 1953 edition (p. 100): ". . . the northwest . . ."

a large square tower-room with closet, a hall and an attic. {If we had had a palace we could not have been prouder, and surely not half as comfortable.}

We were so happy and interest {in it all that everyday was like a part of a continued story,} our cares and our perplexities {simply added to the interest. One of the amusing incidents of our early housekeeping occurred} shortly after we were settled; {we had invited Mr. Mandeville and some} others to dinner and had laid our first fire in the {parlor} fireplace. When we saw the guests coming {Mr. Comstock} lighted the fire and the smoke poured out into the room. We had to throw water on the blazing wood and open all the windows, which gave the approaching guests the impression that the house was on fire. This was a terrible blow to us, for {Mr. Comstock} had directed the architect to "build two fireplaces and as much of a house around them as a certain sum would permit." The one in the dining room we had found perfect from the first, {but to have the one in the parlor smoke was a crushing blow.}

The next morning {beheld a memorable sight.} I heard a queer noise on the roof and stepped out to see what it meant; there stood {Mr. Comstock} on the peak of the roof with a window weight attached to the end of a cord and was "chugging" it up and down in the recalcitrant flue. He had donned his oldest coat, which happened to be a Prince Albert, and an old hat whose brim was blown back by a gale of wind that was flapping the tails of his coat {in a wild and unseemly manner. It was a sight for a cartoonist. However, appearances were nothing to him!} He was loosening two {scuttles full} of mortar which the masons had carelessly dropped {and so closed} the flue; ever afterwards the living room fireplace was {to us as perfect} as we had anticipated.

Fireplaces had gone out of fashion fifty years before, with the advent of stoves. Now, with houses warmed by furnaces, their aesthetic value began to be appreciated, but as yet there were no dealers in andirons within our ken. {Mindful of this, Mr. Comstock had} haunted junk shops and had picked up one {beautiful} old pair of brass andirons in Syracuse, another pair in New York, and a shovel and tongs in Washington. It was several years {later} that these articles were again manufactured for the market.

On Thanksgiving Day, we invited in the friends who had welcomed us, to eat with us our first turkey. Mr. Comstock's direct methods came again into play; he had never carved a turkey, so he spent a part of the morning in the Museum studying the skeleton of this delectable bird; and when he carved the turkey for dinner he did it with so much assurance {and aplomb} that no one even smiled. He had his cares that morning as well as I, {for, directly} after breakfast, we {made the perturbing} discovery that we had no platter big enough to hold our turkey, and {Mr. Comstock} walked {to town and back to secure} an ample dish.

I had a conviction that, in order to know how to manage a house, I {should} do all the work myself. This was both good philosophy and economy. I knew how to perform all the {several} household tasks, but had never mobilized them into day's work, and I found this more of a problem than it had seemed, {however, I did it, I am glad to say}. I did all of the washing even, and {a pair of} strong young arms and hands that soon became skilled ironed successfully {Mr. Comstock's linen} shirts, collars and cuffs, a feat which I now regard with {awe}.

An incident which taught me {facts} about pies and also about my husband occurred during those early weeks of housekeeping. I had {never} mastered the art of making just enough pastry for one pie and the day I made cranberry pies, which had no upper crust, I had so much dough on hand that I had made three {pies. Now} since there were only two of us for dinner, it seemed that I had enough dessert on hand to last nine days; however, {on the third day} my new husband mutinied and declared he would eat no more pie. I maintained that we would {just} have to use it because we could not waste {as much as that,} at which he took the offending pies and threw them into the garbage, {an act which I remember both} shocked and scandalized my frugal self. {I find that I wrote my mother soon after this: "I get along with the cooking; I have not had bad luck with anything yet, except with some turnips that were so very strong of turnip that Harry feared the finished product might prove intoxicating."}

{Another incident of these first weeks taught me a lesson that has been of great help in solving my servant problems. I had been invited to an afternoon tea at the home of Mrs. Prentiss. The Prentisses had been married that summer also and built a beautiful home on the campus. I had worked hard all the morning and thought I had my house in order when I went out. Mrs. Prentiss, a woman older than myself and of much experience was an exquisite housekeeper; she had furnished her home most tastefully and with the aid of two maids, kept it in beautiful order. I admired vastly the daintiness of the appointments in her home; when I came back to our house and opened the front door, I discovered that I had forgotten to dust the stairs before I went, and the sight of them was too much for me. I sat down on the lower step and wept from sheer discouragement. I took the lesson to heart that a housekeeper may try her best and yet fail to do everything just as it should be done, and during the rest of my life my maids were dealt with considerately in consequence. In fact, that year of housekeeping taught me how to deal with the human hazard in housework and to it I largely owe the fact that people who have worked for me have always cheerfully done their best.}

Although our house was so isolated from town, a grocer's wagon came twice a day, a meat wagon once, and the milk wagon morning and night {so we did not experience any great inconvenience from our isolation. Of course} we were very economical and had our first ambition, the paying off the mortgage on our little home. {The following incident shows how very careful we were in our expenditures.} Professor Russel came to call and rapped on our front door with his {devoted} knuckles {until he got a response. As} we opened the door, he said: "My dear children, you must buy a door bell, it is an absolute necessity." {Of course} we obeyed but we felt rueful over the $3.50 that {this door} bell cost us {even though it had a clarion ring that might wake the dead as even our distant neighbors.} It was a good bell and it lasted as long as the house stood.

At this period Cornell University was a small institution and the faculty families were very {friendly}. Every one called on us and we returned the calls promptly. {I note} in a letter to my mother that I said: "President White stayed about two hours the first time he called and made us most extraordinarily happy." Dr. and Mrs. Caldwell[9] gave us a reception at their home; and Mrs. Howard, mother of L. O. Howard, {afterward Mrs. George Harris}, gave a reception to the Delta Upsilon fraternity in our honor, especially to introduce me to my husband's and her son's fraternity brothers.

We had much company in our home. This was the first time {Mr. Comstock} had ever had a home of his own and he {writes} to my mother: "I never before appreciated how much happiness one may have in entertaining one's friends in one's own home." {Two experiences} during the first month in our home are memorable; {one was} the establishing of Mr. Simon H. Gage in our tower room, November 11, 1878. It had been one of {Mr. Comstock's} dreams to have Mr. Gage have a room in our house {and now the dream came true. The other happy incident was a visit from Mr. and Mrs. Bennie W. Law who had just been married and were on their way to Cuba. It seemed prophetic that these friends, who have been lifelong, should come to our house so soon.}

Despite housework and visitors, we found time for intellectual pursuits. We attended President White's lectures at {twelve o'clock} every day. I doubt if either of us ever found lectures so stimulating and interesting as those

9. Noted in the 1953 edition (p. 102): "George Chapman Caldwell, for whom Caldwell Hall is named, was Professor of Agricultural Chemistry at Cornell from 1867 until his retirement in 1902.—G.W.H. and R.G.S."

which he gave on The Reformation. Moreover, we had writing of our own to do. Mr. Comstock was obliged to write his report of his [cotton-worm] investigations in the South and send it in as soon as possible. I gave him every spare moment of my time, sometimes copying his manuscripts and sometimes writing at his dictation. Mr. Gage also helped, and it was finished by middle of November. I shall never forget how Mr. Comstock toiled on this, for it was {really} his first {scientific} writing of any considerable importance. {From the first} he wrote laboriously {and all his life it has been the same}. His method was to think carefully and place his facts logically in his mind and then to find words to express his thought. There {is} no doubt that his lucid, terse style {of scientific writing} which has won him so much praise is the {direct} result of his difficulties {in expressing himself with the pen}.

The University had the trimester system {until late in the nineties}, the second term began January 15, 1879. Mr. Comstock had three students in his laboratory of whom he was especially proud, L. O. Howard, William Trelease, and Henry[10] Curtiss. In those days laboratory work was {rather an annex} to lectures than the integral part of a course {as now given}. While, {of course}, Mr. Comstock's work as lecturer and teacher was quite apart from my duties, we worked together then as later. He used to help me wash the dishes and I used to go to the laboratory and help him in all ways possible. I {very much} enjoyed putting the laboratory in order. I wrote his business letters at his dictation, and {I began making} diagrams to illustrate his lectures in invertebrate zoology. {I remember I used} holland curtain cloth and oil paints. I also made stencil outlines for his lectures. Thus we worked hard during the days; evenings we had company or went to receptions or lectures at a rate that seems, {at this date,} veritable social intoxication.

I think our house was, {from the first,} a hospitable place. I remember that first year we had a visit from Professor and Mrs. Straight of Oswego Normal, parents of Willard Straight, {very superior people[11]}. We also entertained President and Mrs. White, Dr. and Mrs. Caldwell, Dr. and Mrs. Wilder, Mrs. Howard, and our {dear} friends Mr. and Mrs. Henry Lord. I find a note of my household activities that I gave my mother: "My week is systematized as follows: Monday forenoon, do the washing, afternoon, laboratory,—Tuesday {all day}, laboratory,—Wednesday forenoon, iron,—afternoon odds and ends of housework,—Thursday, cook and bake {whatever needed}, afterwards laboratory,—Friday {all day} laboratory,—Saturday sweep and dust the house from top to bottom and mop the kitchen." I also told of days that

10. In the 1953 edition (p. 103): ". . . Cooper Curtice."

11. Added in the 1953 edition (p. 103): ". . . for whom Cornell's student union building is named."

went wrong: "Monday was certainly blue, the clock stopped, the telephone line was broken, the grate in the furnace melted down and not another grate like it this side of Boston! The buckwheat cakes for breakfast were overburdened with soda, the bread was dry, and the coffee like dishwater. In fact, everything was so ridiculously desperate that we laughed until we cried." It is an interesting fact that we had a telephone on the campus before {it} was in general use. Professor Anthony built the line because he wished to experiment with it in his course of physics.[12]

The entomological department of Cornell, {however small}, started {in its career} to interest and instruct the farmers. There was a large Grange meeting held at Ithaca in {the fall of} 1878 and we {took} the members in relays of eight to ten {at a time and showed them} what seemed to them—and to us—the wonderful collection of insects, which consisted of a few boxes. Mr. Comstock had a letter-head printed which gave practical suggestions as to the best way to send insects for identification. This proved very useful and many insects were received from all parts of the state.

{Mr.} Gage gave his first lectures {this year and} we attended them. I began to study the microscope with him that winter. He {was} a part of our family life. His future wife, Susanna Phelps, {and Lena Hill} were with us much. Mr. Comstock {then} had eighty {pupils} in his lecture class in invertebrate zoology and I was deeply gratified to see the attention and devotion they gave him. It was {always the case with} him that the {harder} his subject, the plainer he made it to his class. We began that first year an enterprise that we carried out as consistently as possible for forty years, the entertaining of {Mr.} Comstock's students in our home. We invited his laboratory class of nine to tea; I, {of course}, was the cook and the menu was scalloped oysters, chocolate cake, lemon layer cake, pickles, jelly, sliced oranges, tea and coffee. {This Spring} another edition of Mr. Comstock's Syllabus of lectures was published, {and they cost the} students five cents {apiece}.

Early in the Spring of 1879 we had a rare treat in a visit from Professor Braislin of Vassar College, who spent her vacation with us. She was a charming woman and we enjoyed {every moment of} her stay; we shared her with as many of our friends {as we could}. One event of her visit was notable. Gilmore's Band gave a concert in town and Professor Anthony connected our telephone with [two miles from] the music hall and gave us two receivers. Mr. Comstock invited Professor Braislin to attend the concert with him

12. Footnote handwritten in the manuscript (p. 5–28) by Herrick, but not included in the book: "William A. Anthony was Professor of Physics."

and Mr. Gage invited me, and we all sat in our front hall and listened to the concert, which seemed almost a miracle to us.

With the trimester system we had fairly long vacations at Christmas and Easter, which we spent at Otto with {my people}; we returned to Ithaca laden with as many farm products as we could carry and {which materially} lessened our living expenses. That year Mr. Comstock had his salary of a thousand dollars, and {of course} we had extra expenses in beginning housekeeping, but we saved more than four hundred dollars to pay on the debt we owed on our home. This illustrates the difference in living expenses between {then} and fifty years later.

{I have often thought in later years of the Cornell Faculty as I knew it as a bride,—a bride who had also been a student and who knew the professors in the classrooms whom—[13]}

---

13. Here abruptly ends Chapter V of the manuscript. There is no continuation of this thought into the next chapter. The page(s) may have been removed. In the 1953 edition of the book, this point ends Chapter 6. —KSt.

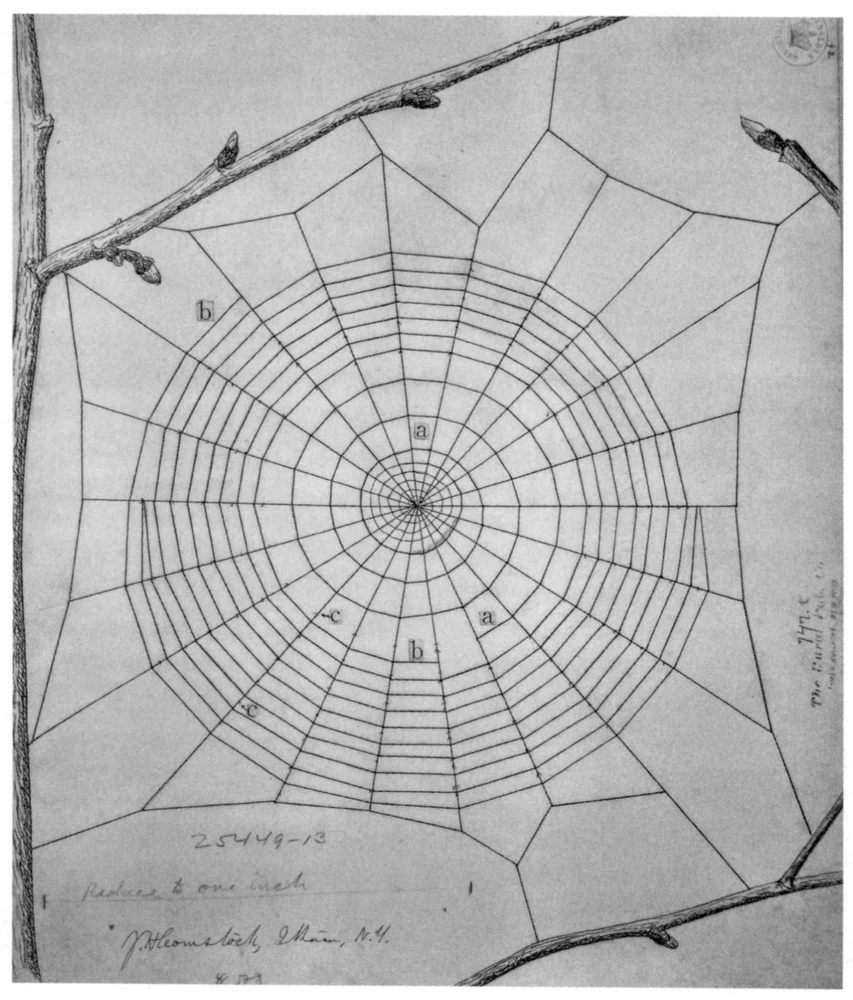

Drawing of spider web by Anna Comstock, n.d.

Chapter VI

Entomologist to U. S. Department of Agriculture

(Life in Washington as United States Entomologist, 1879–1881)

In Mrs. Comstock's manuscript, Chapter VI and Chapter XVII are the next-to-longest chapters (at fifty-five pages each) after her autobiographical Chapter IV (sixty-six pages). Researchers and readers benefit from these additional pages because we learn more about Mrs. Comstock's personality and interests, which are revealed in her descriptions of their life in Washington, of the entomologists who worked with the Comstocks there, and of their social connections. Many paragraphs of this information were not included in the 1953 edition and are now returned to this chapter. As with the previous manuscript chapters, the paragraph, format, and most punctuation are Mrs. Comstock's.

Early in April 1879, news came from L. O. Howard that Dr. C. V. Riley had had a disagreement with General [William G.] Le Duc, the U. S. Commissioner of Agriculture, and was about to resign [as United States Entomologist]; Mr. Howard suggested that Mr. Comstock try for the place. It seemed a great opportunity for a young man and when General Le Duc came to Elmira to address a Grange meeting {Mr. Comstock} went over to see him and {make} a formal application for the {place}. He pointed out he had worked on the cotton-worm all the preceding summer and would be able to finish the report which must be forthcoming from the Department of Agriculture this year. {However, days went by and} we heard nothing until the last of April, when a bomb struck Fall Creek Cottage in the form of a telegram from General Le Duc asking Mr. Comstock to come on to Washington on important business. Telegrams came from {C. V.} Riley and {L. O.} Howard saying that Riley had resigned. {However,} money had been granted the Department to carry on the cotton-worm investigation and this must be finished. Howard wished Mr. Comstock to come because he wished to work with his former instructor, and General Le Duc wanted him because he must have a man who could finish the cotton-worm report in a way that would bring honor to the {Department}.

Mr. Comstock {secured a temporary} leave of absence and went to Washing April 29th, 1879. {Naturally he was greatly} excited over the prospect of a change of work. He found everything ready for him on his arrival; the position was tendered to him fifteen minutes after he had called on the Commissioner and he took the oath of office May 1st. {The following is an excerpt of his letter} to me: "My talk with Commissioner Le Duc was very satisfactory. I said to him everything I wished to say and it all met with his approval. When I told him of my desire to keep clear of politics, and simply devote myself to scientific work, he assured me that the latter was all that he would expect me to do; that politics belonged to the head of the department and added feelingly, 'the head of a department of the government needs a skin as tough as that of a rhinoceros.'"

Thus Mr. Comstock entered upon his duties as Entomologist to the Department of Agriculture and into a very cordial association with Commissioner Le Duc, {who always did his best to help him in every way}. The Commissioner was a true friend and a very considerate superior officer. {In the same letter I also find the following}: "Leal [Howard] is almost too happy to contain himself; {in fact} we both were fairly wild last night, I never knew that two men could talk as fast as we did."

Now that {he} had {definitely} been appointed Entomologist {of the U. S. Department of Agriculture, Mr. Comstock} asked for a two-year leave of absence from {the University}. This was granted on the condition that he return for a fortnight in May to complete his course of lectures. {The question as to who would take his place at Cornell was a troublesome one. Mr. Comstock was anxious to have William Trelease take the work, but} Dr. Wilder {thought it better to try to get} William Barnard.[1] {Very soon Mr. Comstock needed Trelease for field work on the cotton-worm investigation, so Henry Curtiss[2] took charge of the lab and Barnard was appointed for the two years following.}

---

1. Footnote in the 1953 edition (p. 107–8): "Afterwards assistant entomologist, for five years, in the United States Bureau of Entomology in Washington. In 1886 he went to Drake University as Professor of Biology. His untimely death the next year, 1887, brought to a close the promising career of a real scientist. —G.W.H."

2. Corrected to Cooper Curtis in the manuscript, however, the name does not appear in the 1953 edition. —KSt.

It did seem almost cruel to have our small home disrupted just as we had begun to appreciate what a home meant. At first it had seemed like a wonderful plaything, but now it was a real abiding place. I invited Susanna Phelps to stay with me during Mr. Comstock's absence {and Lena Hill also spent part of the time with us. I remember one perfect day when I was invited to go with her and Mr. [Frank H.] Severance boating on the lake. Though the two were married later, their romance at that time had not reached the state for expression and a chaperone was more of a help than a hindrance to happiness. The day was perfect; a soft spring haze covered the hills, and the lake was so mirror-like that two wild ducks swimming across made a 'W' that reached half way of its width. The next week a poem by Severance appeared in *The Cornell Era*; beginning:}

{"So fair a day ne'er dawned before
To make all other days seem drear."}

Mr. Comstock was very busy in Washington. The work immediately before him was to finish the investigation of the cotton-worm and write a report of it. The staff at that time consisted of {Comstock,} Chief Entomologist; L. O. Howard, Assistant Entomologist; and Theodore Pergande for special work in the care and rearing of insects. The letter had been brought to Washington by Riley. Mr. Comstock liked {him very much}, considered his work most valuable, and asked him to remain. {Mr. Comstock} desired to go south at once to see {for himself} the conditions relative to the cotton-worm, but he was obliged to modify his plans. He had been told that there was about {one thousand one hundred} dollars {of an unexpected fund} at his disposal, but {Riley had left a good many} unpaid bills that had to be met, consequently but one field assistant could be appointed. {He} chose William Trelease, who came to Washington May 7th, and was at once commissioned and sent to Selma, Alabama, to continue the investigation.

{It is interesting}, in contrast {with present conditions, to note} the salaries {of the men} in the Division of Entomology: {Mr.} Comstock, {Entomologist}, $2000.00; {L. O.} Howard, {Chief Assistant}, $1200.00; {T.} Pergande, {Assistant}, $750.00 which Mr. Comstock soon raised to $1000.00. George Marx, the artist, received $5.00 a day, and the copyist $2.00. All the letters were written by hand. Although the staff was small, Mr. Comstock was full of joy at the prospect of so much assistance and wrote: "It is just glorious, the facilities for work here. Just think! The appropriation for my division for next year is $5,000.00 and this does not include my salary. The entomological books come out of another fund and the insect cases from the furniture fund. I feel sure that I shall be able to write a very valuable report next winter. One of the good things so far, is the discovery of the eggs of the peach-tree borer. Leal [L. O. Howard] is a great help to me. {I don't know what I should do without him. And Pergande is a jewel.} I do not know how long it will last, but the Commissioner is interested in our work. Before going to him about anything I make up my mind fully concerning it and then ask his advice and he always seems to agree with me."

About this time, I received a scolding from my husband which set me aright for the rest of my life. I had innocently enough used one of his stamped departmental envelopes in writing him {personally}. I {naturally thought} that he was the U. S. Entomologist had had all the rights there were; but I was enlightened in his next letter, which {declared}, "You must not use official stamps on private letters; the penalty for it, in case of detection, is three hundred dollars each offence, which would buy ten thousand ordinary stamps; and that leaves the question of right and wrong out entirely". {This shows Mr. Comstock's attitude, and} no one could have been more careful than {he}, during his connection with the Government, never to infringe upon the spirit or letter of the law in using franking privileges or official postage.

He returned to Ithaca the last of May to put his affairs in order, rent the house, store some of our goods, and {above all} to finish the lectures, and then he was laid low with the mumps. {He was really ill and Professor} Gage and I took care of him. I recalled that one of the standard remedies, or rather alleviations, for fever in my own home had been that of bathing the patient in cool water, but {Mr. Comstock, all his life,} was very sensitive to the cold. Brother Gage and I administering the bath and I was trying to cool his hot spine when he groaned between his gritted teeth: "I'll be damned if I believe in this kind of treatment."

I had worked very hard that spring and had had plenty of worry over various problems of leaving Ithaca. With a sick husband added, the situation proved too much for me. I learned then {a very important fact about myself},—that I was by both nature and temperament unfitted to care for the sick. I was very sympathetic and was always so worried myself that I worried the patient. When I could not do anything else, I stood around gazing at the sick one until we were both perturbed and unhappy. I {was physically awkward in doing the necessary things in the sick room; and} I learned early {in my career} that when a member of my family fell ill, it was best to send for an experienced nurse.

I went to Otto for recuperation and rest, after {Mr. Comstock's} recovery. He remained to finish the lectures and {then}, securing the help of a packer, emptied our little home, rented it for $250.00 a year and sent our household goods to Washington. I had a letter from Mr. Gage telling how enthusiastically Mr. Comstock's classes greeted him on his return, and how they cheered at the end of the last lecture.

When {Mr. Comstock} started for Washington I joined him at Elmira, New York. {Our journey was made pleasant by the company of Rutherford Hayes, Jr., who was a student at Cornell at that time. We found him both witty and interesting; later he called on us at the Department several times, and we still have a pleasant memory of him.}

{We arrived in Washington June 13th and Mr. Howard met us at the station; he had secured temporary rooms for us over a restaurant in which we could take our meals. Howard was usually with us but at the end of two weeks, when I pulled a cockroach out of my soup, I mutinied. The two men laughed at me, but I said to them, "Look in your soup." They did, and each found a cockroach well cooked and mingled with sweet herbs. We changed restaurants the next day.}

{One of our earliest experiences in Washington occurred} the first day of our stay there. Dr. [Thomas] Taylor and his daughter invited us to join them with a party of friends, among them several Congressmen, {on} an evening trip on the boat down the Potomac. Dr. Taylor had charge of the Division of Microscopy in the Department of Agriculture. When anything {came to the Department} too small to be observed with the unaided eye, it was handed over to him for examination through the compound microscope. The specialist {now} would smile at such an arrangement. Dr. Taylor specialized in mycology more than entomology and all specimens of insects were studied in our offices.

The trip down the Potomac was an eye-opener to me. The Taylors {were very nice to us and} introduced us to five Congressmen {and some other people}. My provincial soul was scandalized by the conduct of four of the Congressmen. I made the following note: "They were fooling and flirting with some girls in an outrageous manner; I was actually ashamed to be seen looking at them. I was relieved to find that none of them were Democrats". {Luckily, we also made the acquaintance of Dr. and Mrs. [Ferdinand V.] Hayden. Dr. Hayden was at the head of one of the first of the United States Geological Surveys, and we found the two very charming companions.} Two years after this experience, when Mr. Comstock was trying to put the Entomological Division on a broader basis, he found Congress cool to his plans. Dr. Taylor then said: "Well, I gave you a chance to know some influential Congressmen when you first came here, and you made no use of the opportunity, so what can you expect?"

We began, {almost at once}, hunting for a house. {We} were fortunate in finding an apartment on F Street between Eleventh and Twelfth, N. W. The house had been originally a dwelling for people of means and was built with special reference to the Washington climate, with thick walls, large rooms, and high ceilings. We had two large rooms on the second floor with folding doors between, a large hall bedroom, a roomy bathroom, and a balcony porch; we {secured the suite for the modest sum of} $20.00 per month. The rooms were so large that they engulfed all of the furniture which had been so ample for Fall Creek Cottage; but after we were settled the apartment seemed homelike and pleasant and we felt fortunate to find such quarters, near {several} restaurants and only a fifteen-minute walk from the office.

The servant who cared for us was {a never ending} source of interest to me, for I had never, hitherto, come in contact with colored people. Nancy {was a character; she was rather} large, {very} homely, and always wore a colored handkerchief-turban around her head, and was {always} clad in two skirts, the lower one of which trailed on the floor. With this amazing arrangement of skirts, she wore any kind of a waist, nearly always out at the elbows and usually gaping in various places.

In appearance she was a towering ragamuffin. {However,} she had beautiful manners and a sweet voice. Not if I had belonged to the aristocracy could I have had my visitors ushered in with greater courtesy and dignity, {than that evinced by Nancy}. She lived in the back kitchen on the first floor which, {without exception,} was the most hopelessly disordered and dirty room I had ever seen; and yet, {on occasion}, she would cook a meal there which she would bring up on a server, arranged daintily on spotless linen,—a meal fit for the gods. I often ate these repasts, knowing {perfectly well}, that if I had seen them cooked, I would not have touched a morsel.

Nancy had been a slave in a Virginian family and was very proud of the standing of her white folks, looking with {lofty} disdain on other colored people less favored. I said to her once, "Nancy, isn't it true that you have to work much harder and have more cares now than when you were a slave?" Her answer was, "Yes, honey, I has to work a heap harder and I has more 'sponsibilities, but I'se a heap easier in my mind." The only recreation Nancy ever had came through her membership in a burial society. She paid a small amount each month, which ensured her a decent burial when she died, and also gave her a ride in a hack to the funeral of every member of the society {who died before she did; this meant a ride quite often. She was honest, industrious and faithful, and in her own way efficient.}

As soon as we were settled, I went every day to the office to help my husband with the many details of {the Department}. I had no housework to do and rejoiced that I was able to be of some use where I was needed. As a result of this, we experienced a great surprise. {The last} of June, Commissioner Le Duc came into the office, where I was busy, and asked me if I {liked to work for my husband. When assured that I did}, he asked me if

I would object to pay for my services. I answered that I had never thought of such a thing, {as} I knew that there was a rule against two of the same family being employed in one governmental office. He answered: "Rule or no rule, you shall be paid for your services. If they do not wish me to pay you, then they must give a better salary to Mr. Comstock." He appointed me then and there as a clerk at a salary of $900.00 and made me {a} very happy {woman}.

Commissioner Le Duc was anxious to help the impoverished South and he was about to make an attempt to introduce silk culture there. I was to help in this enterprise. However, nothing could be done with silk worms before the coming spring, so I began as a general helper. When Howard had to attend to other work, I wrote letters. I also wrote entomological notes and answered queries for the agricultural papers. Mr. Comstock read and verified what I wrote, as his name was, {naturally,} signed to such articles.

The entomological division was housed in two rooms on the second floor of the old building of the Department of Agriculture. The center of this floor was {given over to} the museum. Mr. Comstock's office was a long, narrow room, with the word "Entomologist" emblazoned above the door. As people came through the museum, we could hear their conversation through our open transom and, at least a dozen times a day, some one would look up and spell out the word and say, "Oh! Bugologist," and then laugh at his own {exceeding} wit. This amused us at first but, after we had heard it scores of times, it palled upon us, and when one day some man looked up and said "Entomology, syntax, and prosody," we were all so delighted that we cheered, much to his mystification.

Mr. Comstock had been the devoted friend of L. O. Howard for years, and naturally we were more intimately associated with him than with the others. Especially {intimate was} the discussion between the two men as to the policy of the Division. During our two years in Washington, Mr. Howard was our greatest and happiest social resource. He and his Cornell chum, J. McKay Borden,[3] played whist with us evenings or went with us to the theater or on excursions. One experience, often repeated, has been an especially zestful memory. We were all {beginning life and} saving money as fast as possible. {We} soon discovered the sure way to save was to take the amount that we thought we ought to put by from the pay check and put it in the bank, reserving only what we deemed necessary for our expenses for a month. Too often some good play would come to one of the theaters during the last week of the month, when we were all reduced financially to

3. In the 1953 edition (p. 112): changed to "J. McK. Borden." —KSt.

the price of our meal tickets. Under such distressing circumstances Howard always came to the rescue; he had a watch which he had inherited and which he did not use; he would take the watch to a pawn shop and get a six-dollar loan upon it and we would all go to the play, enjoying it all the more because of the way that we had achieved the wherewithal; {and then,} on the first of the month we paid up, the watch was redeemed and laid aside for the next emergency. Those who have had the pleasure of knowing Mr. Howard {socially during the later years of his life, I think, can well} understand how much his society meant to us in those days. He {has been} one of the most interesting men in Washington, which is saying much, and he had, {moreover,} the power of winning admiration and affection, to a remarkable degree. His wit has been the much prized alleviation of after-dinner speeches for three-score years.

Theodore Pergande was a small, delicate-featured, bearded German with a {very} gentle manner and {very} lovable character. He was about thirty-nine years old and had come to America before the Civil War. A rich man in the town where he was born in Germany wanted him to become a Catholic, marry his daughter, and go into business with him. Pergande told me that he would have liked the partnership with the man but he could not stand for either the church or the daughter, so he came to America, served in the Northern army during the entire period of the war, after which he married a pleasant, thrifty little German woman who took good care of her husband and their {little} daughter, {an only child}. He was {an indefatigable} worker, faithful both to his task and his fellow workers; he wrote an exquisitely fine hand as legible as print, and his notes on the insects he studied were of the greatest value because of their accuracy and careful description. He was ambitious to write in perfect English, so he began studying Shakespeare. Mr. Comstock and {Mr.} Howard had many a secret chuckle over notes on some minute insect, written in true Shakespearean diction.

{His [Pergande's] carefulness of observation was well exemplified in a conversation he had with Doctor A. S. Packard[4] who visited our offices one day.} Pergande {had found} the male of a scale insect which had never before been {discovered}. Dr. Packard said, "You are fortunate to have so many of these rare insects." Pergande answered with a smile but very

4. Inserted footnote in the 1953 edition (p. 113): "Dr. Packard's *Guide to the Study of Insects* (1869), is among the earliest books devoted entirely to insects; while his *Text-book of Entomology* (1895) is a mine of information on the insect world. —G.W.H."

earnestly, "Fortunate? No, not fortunate! we hoont for them." Pergande was not fitted {by mind or education} for independent scientific work, but his knowledge of insects was great and, as an observer in a scientific laboratory, he was invaluable. He could mount most minute insects to perfection; his slender hands could manipulate with exquisite precision the wings of the smallest Tineid [moth]. He loved his work and loved to discover new things. When my mother once wished him a long life he answered: "Jes, jes, I hope so too, dare are so many tings to find out and I hope I live to fine dem."

Dr. George Marx was a striking character. He, too, was German, {but of a very different sort from Pergande}; he was tall, blonde, handsome, and carried himself with great dignity. He had studied medicine, but he liked scientific work better, {and he had been appointed by C. V. Riley as artist for the scientific divisions of the Department}. He was an excellent and painstaking artist. His pictures were not only accurate, but he had the feeling of an artist and he made them beautiful when it was possible. His wife was a typical German frau of the upper class, devoted to her home and her husband and to music. Dr. Marx {himself was a specialist and} an authority on spiders. He was {extremely} witty and often entertained us when there was a lull in the work. The systematists had wrought chaos in the genera of spiders; there was a tangle of synonyms hard to unravel, and in recounting his perplexities {he} said one day: "I shall tell you about it. The man who studies spiders stays out with his friends an evening, drinking much beer, comes home late, wakes up next morning with katzenjammer; his breakfast is late, his coffee muddy, his eggs bad, his wife is cross, and he says, 'God damn' and goes up stairs and erects a new genus."

{Once} one of us remarked, "the spirit is willing, but the flesh is weak". He repeated it in German and then translated it back into English, "The ghost is willing, but the meat is weak"—a saying which we remembered long and which relieved many a trying situation.

With this congenial staff the work went {on most} satisfactorily. {There was a vast amount to do, for} Mr. Comstock was obligated to get out the report on the cotton-worm {which Riley had begun}. He had the report which he himself had made while in the cotton fields the previous summer, {as a nucleus} and he built his report around that.

We wrote all of our correspondence in long hand, but the task of writing the letters was, after all, only a minor part of the work. Often before a reply could be made to a letter, much time had to be spent in determining the identity of the insect in question and then in searching the literature for facts concerning its habits, life history, and control.

I early learned a lesson in proprieties of {red tape}. When the mail was ready I would take it down stairs to the mail box. After some weeks of this, Commissioner Le Duc called me into his office one day and asked, "Why don't you send your mail down by your porter?" I replied, "It is more trouble to find {Henry} than it is to take it down myself." "I know it is," he said, "but the porter is here to do those things and you must let him do them."

Mr. Comstock sent out a letter to twenty-five leading agricultural journals, offering to answer, to the best of his knowledge, queries about insects and their control. He received many appreciative answers and, henceforth, writing replies to these queries was a part of our regular work. This was really a wise move, for many of the journals had been inimical to the Department; the *Prairie Farmer* had been a bitter critic of General Le Duc and the editor wrote a very warm letter of commendation to Mr. Comstock for his offer.[5]

Mr. Comstock adopted a broad, wise policy regarding the work and development of the Entomological Division. He decided to keep the work practical and widely useful, and to build up a collection of insects. He {planned to give over} all of the systematic work {of} the collections to specialists and to pay them for their {time and} labor. {He thus hoped to bring} into close relations with the Division of Entomology the most eminent entomologists of the United States.

During the last week of August 1879, there was a meeting of the A. A. A. S.[6] at Saratoga [New York] and, although he could ill afford the time, {he went to this meeting}. He thought it was important to meet the entomologists who might be there; he had written a paper for the occasion on the Coccid-eating moth *Laetilia coccidivora*. The results were even better than {he} expected. He met there for the first time Professor Charles H. Fernald[7] and began the friendship that lasted {as long as Mr. Fernald lived}. He {also met} Dr. Samuel H. Scudder again, and {had a talk with him} about his aims for the Division. Dr. J. A. Lintner, President of the Entomological Club, asked Mr. Comstock to give the Club an account of what he was doing in Washington and of his plans for the future. After he had finished his discussion, Dr. Scudder arose and said that now at Washington there was a nucleus of

---

5. The preceding three paragraphs are in a different order in the 1953 edition of the book. This rearrangement is particularly noteworthy for this is the first major example in the editing that disrupts Mrs. Comstock's flow of thought and diminishes her voice. —KSt.

6. American Association for the Advancement of Science.

7. Footnote in the 1953 edition (p. 115): "Head of the Department of Entomology, Massachusetts State University, and author of numerous papers on the Microlepidoptera (small Moths). —G.W.H."

what ultimately might be a national museum of entomology and, since there was a man in charge of it who was in earnest and who held broad ideas about the development of the work, {felt} entomologists everywhere should give him support and aid. After the meeting Dr. William Saunders, editor of the *Canadian Entomologist*, spoke most encouragingly to Mr. Comstock, as did several others. {A special joy at the Saratoga meeting was a reunion with Prof. S. H. Gage who also read a paper there. The two men took an evening walk of nine miles together to talk over all they had in mind. On his way home Mr. Comstock visited Professor Braislin in her home in Burlington, New Jersey.}

{The first of} October 1879, Mr. Comstock introduced a great innovation in the office: he bought a {Remington} typewriter. There was one of these machines in the Commissioner's office and ours was the second in the Department of Agriculture. {Of course} we had no typist, but Howard and I learned to use it. Probably an expert typist today would smile could she have seen our achievements of which we were so proud. Another purchase for the division was a microscope costing $200.00. {In addition, Commissioner Le Duc, of his own accord, ordered for us} 500 insect boxes at an expense of $1,500.00.

{Meanwhile} all of our efforts were directed toward finishing the Cotton Report, but Mr. Comstock's time was so much interrupted by visitors that he had a very difficult time writing. I worked every spare moment, editing the answers to the questionnaire which had been sent to the cotton growers the year before. These answers were supposed to be of use in giving information that would help to oust the cotton-worm, and it was understood that they were to be a part of the report. Thus they had to be prepared for printing, although both Mr. Comstock and {Mr.} Howard were of the opinion that they were not worth publishing. I {also} had another very interesting piece of work {which consisted of} examining all of the moth-traps {on file} at the patent office to see, if, {by chance}, any of them could be used in trapping the cotton-worm moth. Of all the absurd plans for capturing insects some of these patents were the cap-sheaf. {One presupposed} that you would catch the insect {in the fingers} and put it in the trap.

The labor on the Cotton-Worm Report was pushed steadily. In those days all manuscripts had to be copied by hand before being sent to the printer; {in November} four copyists were detailed for this work at a cost of $500.00. One day we had a scare: General Le Duc came to the office and very pleasantly announced that he had come to talk about cutting down expenses, as {there were} only $570.00 left of the appropriation,—not enough to pay Howard for the rest of the year, to say nothing of Pergande and {myself}. Mr. Comstock was dumbfounded for he had supposed that there was a balance of $2,000.00. The next day we went over the accounts with the disbursing clerk and found to our great relief, that $1,000 had been lost in adding {up the} column.

Our official and private life was very happy, except for the growing differences between C. V. Riley and Mr. Comstock the reasons for which were as follows: in 1877 an Entomological Commission had been formed for the study of the Rocky Mountain locust. {C. V.} Riley was at the head of the commission and associated with him were Dr. Cyrus Thomas of Illinois and Dr. A. S. Packard of Rhode Island. {The} Commission {was given an} appropriation by Congress {and was} placed under the Geological Survey of the Department of the Interior. {A year later C. V.} Riley was made U. S. Entomologist and {a beginning was made on} the investigation of the cotton-worm. The appropriation for this was made to the Department of Agriculture and not to the Entomological Commission: all of the work done by Mr. Comstock and others in the cotton fields of the South {was paid for from} this appropriation, and the Commissioner of Agriculture was in honor bound to get out a report to justify the expenditure {of money}. The quarrel between Le Duc and Riley was a personal one, and when the latter resigned {his position} he claimed that all of the data on the cotton-worm and all of the specimens of insects sent in during his official connection with the Department of Agriculture belonged to the Entomological Commission,[8] and therefore he took them with him when he left. If Mr. Comstock had not had a copy of his own report he would have been without any data {whatever,} except the useless answers to the questionnaires, {with which to make the report for the Commissioner.}

Mr. Comstock and Dr. Riley had been good friends and {the former} anticipated no trouble {whatever} when he went to Washington. He {had many talks} with Riley {and actually} pleaded with him to return the notes on the work {already done, together with} the specimens collected while he was in the Department of Agriculture, but to no avail. Finally, the men went apart. General Le Duc, through the Attorney General, forced a return of some of the specimens and some of the manuscripts. The insects had been put in Dr. Riley's private collection. Mr. Comstock saw the dangers inherent in such a practice and {made a rule} that no one connected with the Division of Entomology should have a private collection of insects.

8. In the 1953 edition (p. 117): ". . . Entomological Commission of the Department of the Interior . . ." —correction made by R.G.S. (p. 6–18 in the manuscript). —KSt.

The break with Dr. Riley hurt Mr. Comstock deeply, {later}, after we returned to Ithaca, Riley made us a visit, during which he and I kept up {a most} amiable conversation but Mr. Comstock remained rather silent. The quarrel had been distressing to me. I would rather give up anything than have trouble about it,—one reason why I could never be an efficient executive.

We had an interesting summer even though it was hot. Mr. W. A. Henry, then a student at Cornell, had become through Mr. Comstock's recommendation an assistant to Riley in the work for the Entomological Commission. Mr. Henry, at that time, revealed the remarkable ability power which afterwards enabled him to do such remarkable work while Professor of Agriculture at Wisconsin University. He had never been South before and the colored people were a never-ending source of interest to him; and as I too, was interested in them he often took me to entertainments given by the negroes. We were always careful to act serious and respectful for we were genuinely interested. Sometimes, however, we were unable to refrain from smiling inside at their anthropomorphic remarks on religious subjects and their jumbled metaphors when excited.}

{In July W. R. Lazenby visited us. He had been commissioned by General Le Duc to gather statistics in agricultural colleges. While he was with us, one Sunday, we made our first excursion on the canal that stretched along the banks of the Potomac. The scenery was beautiful and restful; the still waters reflected the huge sycamores, their branches intertwined with the vines of the grapes and the trumpet creeper. Now and then we gained a glimpse of the Potomac dotted with many green islets. The union aqueduct bridge was a wonder to us then. It's single stone arch of stone, 224 feet from pier to pier, made it seem to us the most wonderful bride in the world. I remember I saw three snowy herons that day.}

{Sundays were our only days for rest and change. We often went over to Alexandria and attended services in Washington's church, afterwards wandering about the churchyard deciphering the quaint inscriptions on the headstones. There was one to Dinah Crowe, but the stone cutter not having calculated his space well had been obliged to engrave her name "Dinah Crow". There was another interesting old cemetery in Alexandria. Its walks were bordered with box and, I do not think I have ever got a whiff of boxwood since then that it has not recalled that old burial place. However much we wandered about in it, we always ended by visiting the grave of the "unknown woman", the tragic mystery of whose death is detailed on the tabular gravestone. Often, we crossed the Potomac on a ferry from Alexandria, and wandered about in the woods gathering ferns, or, perhaps, practicing with a revolver at a mark set up against driftwood along the shore. We always found wood-ticks on us in the evenings after these shore wanderings.}

We had many visitors at the office—some who knew us, and others who had something to say or ask. Among others came Dr. Mary Walker. Mr. Comstock had roomed with her nephew {in college} and had met her in Ithaca. I had never seen her before and I was {greatly} interested in her appearance, and {especially in her} personality. It was surely the irony of fate that she, of all women, should elect to wear trousers and fight for the privilege; she was in {face, voice, stature and in} every {other} way essentially feminine; {her round face was much wrinkled, her short hair was streaked with gray; her suit consisted of} trousers, coat and vest, and she wore a man's derby hat. {She was perhaps fifty years old but} her voice was that of an old woman. Despite her man's garb she walked mincingly, like an old-fashioned lady going to church; {however,} she swung her cane jauntily. {Although she was peculiar}, she was a brave {little} woman who had earned her right to dress as she pleased through her work as a doctor in the hospitals and on the battle fields in the Civil War. She had borne imprisonment, repeated arrests, and endless jeers, but she had stuck to her principles that a man's costume was {much} better fitted for active work than a woman's. How she {must} rejoice if she {can look down from her heaven, which I am sure she is enjoying, and see our girls of today in knickers going about the streets with calm assurance. Certainly, the sight would make her heaven happier.}

Commissioner Le Duc was {a character. He was a man} of indomitable will and combativeness, imperious, and impatient at obstacles, not very tactful, but loyal and devoted to the people he trusted, or to a cause he had undertaken. He was a big, handsome man with abundant gray hair, gray pointed beard {and rather portly but active. General Tecumseh Sherman once said to a friend of ours, "O, I used to know him when he was Bill Duke, years ago when I was a red-headed, barefoot boy, and Bill was a shock-headed barefoot boy. He and Garfield and Blaine and I all used to go to the District School together in Ohio. Bill Duke was a little thick-headed in those days but he had a good heart."} He was nearing the age of seventy-five when we knew him. He {had fought in the Civil War and} was made Brevet Brigadier General of the U. S. V.[9] {He fought by the side of Thomas at Lookout Mountain and was wholeheartedly devoted to his superior officer. He used to tell me of General Thomas, his voice thrilling with emotion. He} was {rather} overbearing at times, with {newspaper} reporters, which {was the

9. United States Volunteers.

underlying cause of} bitter attacks on him in certain {journals}. After one of these attacks some reporters came up to the Department to get his reaction. He pointed to a span of mules {that happened to be} standing {on the roadway} and said; "Gentlemen, I am too wise to start a kicking match with those mules,—I have nothing to say." We were associated closely with him for two years and had an excellent opportunity to judge him. We found he had always fore-most in his mind {and efforts}, the welfare of farmers and the advancement of agriculture. {After he retired, he went back to his native town of Hastings, Minnesota, and, in his later years, became deeply interested in life after death. After he was ninety he wrote a remarkable pamphlet entitled: "If a man die; shall he live again? Job XVI-14. When, where, how?" I had several letters from him concerning this publication and he seemed mentally as vigorous as ever.}

{By the middle of November, the Report was nearly completed, and I went to Otto for a rest, when the Report was sent to the printer Mr. Comstock followed me. It was wonderful vacation. There was so much to talk about with the parents; and the Cattaraugus hills were beautiful in their rich autumn coloring. On our way back, we stopped at Ithaca and had a delightful visit with various friends, especially with the Roberts, Mr. Howard, and with Professor Russel, who seemed to feel our absence more than did the others. Mr. Gage returned to Washington with us, and soon after we arrived Professor [C. H.] Fernald was our guest also. The two men visited interesting places in Washington while we were at the office, and, during the evenings we went to the theater or called on friends. Although we were not housekeeping, we had much company. My college chum, Minerva Palmer, at that time studying medicine in Philadelphia, spent several days with us. One of our interesting excursions was through Alexandria. At Washington's church we made friends with the old sexton, who voluntarily acted as our guide about the city. He took us to Washington's lodge room, showed us his chair, the charter granted to the lodge when Washington was Master, the silver trowel with which Washington officially laid the corner stone of the Capitol, and a handsome silk Masonic apron embroidered for and presented to Washington by Madame Lafayette. My father was a very devoted Mason and I had been reared to hold this order in great respect. Therefore, that visit to Washington's Lodge made the Father of his Country seem more real and human to me than he had ever seemed before. We also had visits from Dr. Edward L. Nichols, then a fellow at Johns Hopkins. Through Dr. and Mrs. Caldwell of Ithaca, we had the acquaintance of Professor and Mrs. Doolittle. Professor Doolittle was a mathematician of very great eminence and was employed in the Coast Survey; he was quite absent-minded, so much so that I thought he was deaf since I had to shout to get his attention. One day when he and his wife were calling, I said to Mr. Comstock, in my ordinary tones, "Speak louder, he is deaf"; his face showed no signs of having heard, but Mrs. Doolittle, who was a happy, wholesome and understanding woman, began to laugh and said cheerfully, "He is no more deaf than you are."}

{We were seeing much of my cousin, Congressman Edwin Willits and his family; the latter consisted of his wife, and his daughter, later the wife of Judge Bordwell of Los Angeles. Helen Willits, a younger sister of the Congressman, was also with them that winter. Cousin Edwin was a graduate of Ann Arbor, and a classmate of Professor Moses Coit Tyler. Mrs. Willits was a teacher and she never gave up her studies completely, as do so many women after marriage. I remember all that winter that she and Edwin were reading French literature together in the original. Their only son, George Willits, had graduated from Ann Arbor in 1878 and was then a brilliant young lawyer in Chicago. While my cousin Edwin was old enough to be my father, cousin Helen was only a few years my senior. It seemed very good to us to have relatives in Washington and we were often together.}

{The first official entomologist of the Department of Agriculture was Townend Glover, who had retired some years previously. He was a most eccentric man, interested in all forms of plant and animal life. He had remained a bachelor and his room became a jumbled museum of a heterogeneous collection of living and dead animals and plants and a miscellaneous assemblage of curios and pictures. We called on him in Washington and the following letter to my parents gives a faint impression of his room and its contents:}

> {"We went to call on Townend Glover, the former entomologist of this department. He is an old man (a bachelor) and completely broken down in health and mind; he has an adopted daughter of whom he thinks a great deal, and who is to be married soon, and with whom Mr. Glover will live. She was not at home. I wish that I felt equal to describing his home to you, but it was so strange I cannot do it justice. There were several cases filled with books. The walls were covered with pictures, many of them of animals. There were two or three glass aquaria with fishes in them and two ingeniously contrived little fountains playing all the time; one was made of red glass and around the tube that threw a jet of water was the figure of a coiled snake. There were three large cases filled with stuffed humming birds that had been killed in South America; they were exquisitely tinted with every color of the rainbow. On top of the book cases were stuffed birds. Some from South America were very brilliant in color. On one case was a huge owl

holding a book in its claw and wearing a pair of spectacles. There were a dozen cages of live canary birds which he had trained to sing, and several cases of brilliantly colored insects fastened to artificial plants and looking very alive. The windows were full of plants. On one side of the room, among the pictures, was a stuffed bear's head; on another a wild cat's; on the other a dog's head carrying in its mouth a powder-horn and over the door was a huge pair of antlers. For rugs on the floor there were a lion's, a leopard's, and a wolf's skin. His own paintings fill ever so many books; I never saw more exquisite pictures of flowers and insects than he had painted. He has painted some very pretty landscapes in oil too. He had an Indian scalping knife and belt with a scalp attached, although he said very quaintly, "I did not take it myself". He was born in Brazil (of English parents); but as his parents died when he was young, a German family adopted him, and he lived almost all his life in the United States. He has travelled over North and South America and Europe and part of Africa, but he is so broken now that he cannot tell much of what he has seen or done. He treated us in old English fashion giving us fruit (apples, pears, peaches), cake, and wine. I have not told you half of what we saw in that chamber of wonders."}

Early in January Mr. Comstock began a problem of research which he and Mr. Howard had been considering for some time, an investigation of the scale-bugs and other insects affecting citrus fruits.[10] This was especially important in view of the growing citrus industry in California and in Florida. Mr. Comstock wished, {personally,} to plan and supervise the work. General Le Duc was {most} encouraging and gave him letters of introduction to the Senators and Congressmen from Florida. When {Mr. Comstock} went to the Capitol with these letters, Cousin Edwin Willits,[11] introduced him to the men. They received him most cordially and gave him {many} letters to prominent orange-growers and, armed with these, {he} started for Florida. While I should have liked above all things to go with him, I felt that my work and my presence in the office were essential, and this made me content to remain {behind}.

Mr. Comstock started on this journey with as much of the spirit of the explorer as did Columbus when he set sail for the unknown lands of the West.

10. Preceding this sentence, R.G.S. wrote in the manuscript (p. 6–26): "The Report went to the printer late in 1879," which appeared in the 1953 edition (p. 118). —KSt.

11. In the 1953 edition (p. 119) edited to, ". . . my cousin Congressman Edwin Willits . . ."

In a letter written on the train on his way South, {he} exclaimed: "O, the Coccidae! I want to get off the train and examine every tree I see for specimens." He stopped for a day at Macon, Georgia, {and renewed his acquaintance with Professor and Mrs. J. E. Willett, whose guest he was. He and Professor Willett} spent a morning in the field collecting. Among the insects which he sent back as a result of this morning's work was a leaf miner in the needles of the southern pine. From Macon he went to Brunswick, Georgia, and took {the steamer "Florence"} to Fernandina, Florida. It was a small steamer that traversed St. Andrews Sound, upon the waters of which he saw thousands of wild fowl, especially ducks. From Fernandina to Jacksonville may be about thirty miles as the crow flies, but the train was from 11 A.M. to 5 P.M. traversing this distance, "through pine woods all the way, any one mile of the route appearing like any other, the country {perfectly level}, as level as the sea when calm. The long-leaf pine with its magnificent slender leaves, the saw palmetto and wiregrass, were all we saw of vegetation except when we passed hammocks; in these were many shrubs bearing red and black berries."

At Jacksonville he called {at once} on Dr. C. J. Kenworthy, {whom he found "an elderly gentleman, tall and pleasant and whose residence is very fine." Dr. Kenworthy was} an influential man and obtained passes for Mr. Comstock over every railroad and on nearly every line of boats {in the state which was a great help.} Mr. W. H. Ashmead, {then a young man of twenty, just married, was very nice to} Mr. Comstock and gave a dinner in his honor to which all of the local men of science were invited. Mr. Ashmead was the proprietor of a bookstore in Jacksonville, but he was an entomologist by avocation {and had} made collections of Florida insects. Later, he became connected with the Department of Entomology in Washington.

There were few railroads in Florida {at that time and}, in order to reach the various plantations, {Mr. Comstock} had to travel by boat, {with} horse and buggy, and on foot. He {succeeded, however, in} visiting several large orange groves in which he collected many scale insects and sent then on to Washington for further study. At Mandarin {he visited the Crane plantation where} he met Mrs. Harriet Beecher Stowe {and her husband, who were guests of Mr. Crane. He was greatly} impressed with {Mrs. Stowe's} strong personality.

At Alexander's Landing on Lake Beresford he found a large waxy-scale insect which he called the barnacle scale.[12] Here he also discovered the caterpillar[13] which bores a tunnel down the leaf stem of the water-lily and lives in the burrow several inches below the surface of the water. The following

12. In the 1953 edition (p. 120): "*Ceroplastes cirripediformis*. —G.W.H."
13. Ibid.: "*Bellura melanopyga*. —G.W.H."

letter in which he describes his trip in quest of the sweet-potato beetle[14] gives an excellent idea of the difficulties of travel with which he had to contend:

> "I learned at Manatee that the sweet-potato beetles came from across the river a short distance and if I were to cross over to Palmetto I could get a horse and drive out to Daniel Gillett's place where the beetles were to be found. I went across the river and tried to hire a horse but one was not to be had. Mr. G., I was told, lived eight or nine miles away, and, although it was then 3 P.M. and I was {quite} tired, having been running about in the cane all day, I determined that I would not leave that section without learning something about those beetles, so I started across the prairie on foot. Just before nightfall I reached a house where I inquired the way and was told that the place was only a mile further on,—that I was to go through a piece of woods and there I would find a trail which led to Mr. G's. I found the trail and followed it for a distance, but it soon forked. I took the larger branch. I did this several times, each time the trail becoming fainter. At last I found myself in the open prairie where no path was to be seen by the dim light remaining. Night soon came on. I could not see the stars and so had no idea in which direction I was going. {I wandered about with but little idea of the direction as} I had lost my bearings while following the winding of the trail across the prairie. At last I struck a road which I felt sure was one {I was in search of, the one} leading to Mr. G's place. I followed the road, came to {a piece of} woods, crossed a creek; {the creek was} about the same size as the one which I had crossed in the woods through which I passed just after receiving my directions. This made me think it was the same one and that I was returning in the direction of Palmetto. Not being sure, I followed the road a mile or two, then finding no residence I retraced my steps to where I first struck the road and went on much further. Finally, I decided to camp and was looking for a place at which to do so when I saw a light. This gave me new strength. I hurried on {a distance of} a mile and found some trees on fire in the woods. {Then} I was discouraged and began to make preparation for a camp. Before doing so I shouted long and loud and had no answer. Before I had my camp arranged I heard a dog bark. Then I felt sure I was near some residence or camp. By going in the direction of the dog I reached the house of a son of Mr. G. He put me on the right road.

14. Ibid.: "*Cylas formicarius*. —G.W.H."

"Finally, late at night I reached my destination foot-sore and tired, only to learn that Mr. G. had dug all the potatoes the week previous. My bed seemed good that night. In the morning I found that no horse could be had for the return trip. In the meantime, I had been thinking over the proposed trip to Tampa, Fort Mead and Ocala and concluded that with the delays incident to travel in that country it would take me till the middle of March to make it. The "Lizzie Henderson" was expected back on her return trip from Tampa at noon. I thought that perhaps if I could get back to Manatee in time I would take passage on board her. I was fortunate in obtaining the company of a lad who was going to Manatee; and, as soon as we had breakfast of the grits and bacon, we started. I found my companion was a good pedestrian. We walked to Palmetto, nine miles, in two hours and a half. There, after talking for a half-hour to a fellow, we induced him to rent his boat to us to cross the river. When we reached Manatee, the steamer had not come and there was no doubt as to the best plan for me to follow. I was so foot-sore and weary that I could hardly step. It was of no use to stay in the field as I could not go about the groves in that condition in a country where there were no men to be hired. I took the steamer when she came. I reached Cedar Keys yesterday (Sunday) and left there at five o'clock this morning. I have now to see the Orange lake region {and to meet Hubbard} and then I shall come home."

On the morning of February 4, he left Titusville on the sailboat "Mist" bound down the Indian River for Rockledge, where he {visited Mr. H. S. Williams and} examined the orange trees in that region for scale insects. The trees in that section proved as a rule free from insects but he did find the cotton strainer {[*Dysdercus suturellus*]} at work. From there he went across country in a wagon drawn by mules to Lake Poinsett, where he boarded the steamer "Fox" on the return trip to Sanford. He was having trouble with his specimens: "As they were collected in the rain I did not dare to do them up ready to send by mail for they would certainly mold before reaching Washington, so I have been obliged to spread the leaves out to dry and watch lest the larvae escape. I have several boxes which I have got to restock with food at Sanford before sending."

While my husband was going through these experiences I was having rather {pleasanter} diversions in Washington. I went with {the Willits family} to a reception at the White House, {a very} important event to me. Mrs. Hayes received us graciously; she was a woman of vivid personality. Her rich, dark coloring, her dark hair combed smooth and low over the ears, her dignity {of manner} and yet {her attitude of} true friendliness, made her seem to me the ideal of what our President's wife should be. She had hurt her popularity in Washington in the diplomatic society, by her refusal to have alcoholic beverages served at the White House table. It certainly required courage to take this step {and she was quite equal to the situation}. Her stand on prohibition {undoubtedly} won her many friends {in the United States}.

Thanks for my cousin Edwin I was {enabled} to hear {[Charles Stewart]} Parnell describe vividly the sufferings of the people of Ireland under the Land-tenure laws, in a speech before the House of Representatives. {In personal appearance}, Parnell was {very} attractive. His face {was} pale and refined and in his bearing, he was an aristocrat; he was about as much like my conception of an Irishman as a lily is like a peony. He spoke without {enthusiasm} or oratorical embellishment, but his terse sentences were {to the point and very} effective.

Meanwhile in Washington we were co-operating with Mr. Comstock in every way possible. Almost every day specimens arrived from Florida to be taken care of and studied. {In fact,} the many living specimens that he sent kept us busy, for he was keen to get every insect that had any relation to citrus fruits or other Florida crops. I had apparently acquired enough skill with the typewriter so that Howard dictated letters to me. I also worked {at all possible moments} in transferring the old insect collections into the new boxes.

I found life too full for loneliness. I went with the Willets to see Lotta Crabtree in her characteristic gamin plays, a genuine pleasure. I also saw Fanny Davenport as Lady Cecil and I heard Mrs. Scott Siddons read; all these opportunities meant much to me. {We also had some diversions in the office. One day some Scotchmen of the Parnell party visited our museum. The lady in charge of the exhibits was a very prim spinster and I saw her casting horrified glances at the bare brown knees of the Scots. Afterwards I asked her if she was not shocked at the spectacle, at which she replied with a sniff: "Ah, yes, yes. I heard some of them say the Scotchmen had legs, but I didn't see them; I never see things that are not proper for me to see."}

One day I received a pleasant call from {Mr. W. G. Gibson}, who had been with Mr. Comstock for several days in Florida, and he said {to me}: "Mr. Comstock is the most economical man I ever saw travelling at government expense." {This was quite true always}; he was as careful of the money of the government as if it had been his own.

The last of February {Mr. Comstock} returned to Washington very much pleased with the work he had accomplished in Florida and the interest he had aroused among the orange growers. Soon after his return, {a happy event occurred}. My parents came to spend a week with us. It was a great joy to show them the Washington they had read about, and the Mount Vernon they had revered. It was {a means of} education to us to go with my father to the

Houses of Congress. He was an old-fashioned farmer with New England traditions, who read and thought about what he read; consequently every man of prominence in {the House of Representatives or in the Senate}, was known to him through his support or his rejection of measures for the country's good or harm, {and my} father was never in doubt as to whether measures were harmful or useful. During his visit he was able to hear many men speak whom he had long known through their political careers; and it was undoubtedly the greatest experience of his life to see their faces and hear their voices. Cousin Edwin was amazed at father's knowledge of the public records of so many of his colleagues. Mother was more interested in the beauty of the Capitol, the statuary, the pictures, and the {beautiful} parks. The visit meant more to them both than we of the present day can imagine.

On March 10th the silkworm eggs {arrived} from China with {a large number} of them already hatched, probably because they were kept too warm in transit, and General Le Duc was deeply disappointed. Mr. Comstock had been called to Long Island for consultation concerning the ravages of some insect pests, so Pergande, a woman clerk and I, working in almost freezing temperatures, cut the cards, packed, wrapped and franked one hundred-and-fifty boxes of silkworm eggs in one day. {I remember} my fingers insisted on tying knots all night in my dreams. By doing this work so promptly we were able to send to each person 4000 unhatched eggs.

On May 18, 1880, a copy of the *Report on Cotton Insects* was on the desk of every Congressman, although it was not officially published until a few days later. On the strength of the report Representative Aiken of Georgia made a speech in favor {for} a larger appropriation for the Department of Agriculture and raised the salaries of the heads of the divisions {from $1900 to $2000}. The publication of this volume was a great occasion for us. There were 343 pages of the *Report* proper, ten pages of which were given to a very valuable bibliography, and 170 pages of appendix and the answers to circulars. We were very much pleased over the colored plate frontispiece representing a cotton branch with blossoms and the cotton-worm in all its stages, an excellent and artistic picture, painted by [George] Marx and lithographed. There was also a lithographic plate of the nectar glands by [William] Trelease that was most satisfactory. The report was well received, and Mr. Comstock had many letters of congratulation and of appreciation from scientists. Dr. Hagen's[15] letter was most characteristic: "It is a very good and very sensible

15. Included in the 1953 copy (p. 124): "Dr. H. A. Hagan, with whom he had studied in Cambridge, Massachusetts . . ."

work; and what I like more is that you stand on your own legs." Following these words of approval was a rebuke to Mr. Comstock for wasting the government money by printing the appendix. Mr. Comstock replied that he agreed with him entirely, {but that} this appendix {matter} was all that Riley had left of the work done the year before and he was obliged to print it.

The most gratifying of all the commendations of this report came from Charles Darwin, who thanked Mr. Comstock for the volume and said that he found in it many interesting things bearing upon the theory of {natural selection}.

The agricultural editor of the *New York World*, Dr. L. C. Benedict, wrote: "Your {Report on Cotton Insects} has not only been largely copied from but heartily commended to the large class for whose benefit it was prepared, {in *The World*}, which is evidence of what we think of the work. I cannot refrain, however, from adding, that I consider it a most valuable book, which ought to be in the hands of every cotton planter."

In July 1880, we started on a memorable journey to the Pacific Coast. Congress had granted an appropriation of $5,000 to the Entomological Division and Mr. Comstock felt that he could not do a more valuable work than to finish the investigation of the scale insects infesting citrus fruit trees. It was arranged that I should take charge of the laboratory while Mr. Comstock did the field work in California. In Chicago and Omaha Mr. Comstock succeeded in getting free transportation for us to Salt Lake City, which materially lessened the expense for us personally as well as for the Government. Between Chicago and Omaha, we had our first experience in a dining car, a luxury that had not yet reached the eastern railroads. It seemed quite wonderful to us to sit at table and eat while we were viewing from the windows the crop-covered, rolling lands of Iowa. Those who use the dining cars of today little realize how great this luxury seemed to us.

All one day we followed the Platte River, the bottom lands of which are about thirty miles wide, bordered by bluffs. We were able to observe, along the north shore of the river, the old immigrant trail over which so many passed when seeking their Eldorado. We were awed by the tragic fate of scores of these pioneers, for here and there could be seen the board markers of the graves of those who had died along the way. We suddenly awoke to the sad realization that we were passing near the unknown grave of Mr. Comstock's father, who had died somewhere along this trail thirty years before.

The ride from Ogden to Salt Lake City was a revelation to us. The Oquirrh Mountains beyond the lake {and} the beautiful green of the fertile valley between us and the lake, and the lake itself, by the light of the sunset all made a picture we could never forget.

The Mormons had always been to us a strange, almost a mythical people. We gained a new respect for them when we realized that the beautiful valley we were gazing upon had been a desert of sage brush, before these people {had come, and} brought water for irrigation from the mountains, changing the desert to a garden. The more we saw of the Mormons and their work, the more we admired their pluck and their industry. We found {the city itself} very attractive. I think the thing that impressed us most was the open irrigation. Dashing along each street at the side was a stream of {pure} water brought from the melting snows of the mountains.

Mr. Comstock met the most prominent fruit growers of Salt Lake and found them not only intelligent but eager for assistance in fighting their various insect enemies.

There had been a personal interest from the first in this journey of ours. {Mr. Comstock} had not seen his mother since he was a boy of thirteen and had never seen his step-father nor his little sister.[16] {Thus} it was with {great} eagerness that we took a side-trip from Sacramento to visit our family. We went first to Marysville, {which was then} a lively town of five thousand inhabitants. {It was a city of} pretty houses embowered with flowers and trees. From Marysville we took a train to Oroville and {then} a stage for 22 miles to Forbestown. We were vastly interested in this region, which we had come to know through reading the works of Bret Harte.

We found our people in their mountain home, the view from which was superb, but we were so happy to see them {all} that we could give scant time to gazing at {the magnificent} scenery. {Mr. Comstock} found that his mother had failed much in health but her splendid spirit remained. She made light of the trials of life and made the most of its joys. Margaret was {a pretty}, attractive child of nine with long golden curls and {with} eyes as blue as the skies. We found our stepfather a very interesting man; his many years of pioneer experience in California had yielded him a wealth of wisdom and knowledge. His keen wit and his ability to tell a story well made him a delightful companion. He was the owner of placer mines, some of them fairly good, and some worked out. {I remember} while there that he "panned out" some gold for me that {later} I had made into jewelry. He had formerly owned two hotels in the mountains and it was a joy to hear him tell of his experiences as host to the various actors and minstrel troupes that had come up to entertain the miners, in the golden days.

---

16. Included in the 1953 edition (p. 126): "(Margaret Dowell, born February 1, 1870)."

{Mother} and sister Margaret went with us to San Francisco and thence to Santa Rosa to visit Mr. and Mrs. Nelson Carr, who had a delightful home on a ranch about seven miles from Santa Rosa. Mrs. Carr was Mother Dowell's sister and our Aunt Hannah.

Uncle Nelson Carr was prominent among the agriculturists of the region, and almost immediately took Harry with him to San Francisco to attend a meeting of the State Horticultural Society, where Mr. Comstock met Mr. Wickson of the *Pacific Rural Press* and Professor [Eugene W.] Hilgard of the University of California, both leaders in agricultural matters in the State, {and he also met other prominent agriculturists.}

{Later, when we started south, we visited the University of California, and Professor Hilgard. I shall never forget} my first impression of the California climate, as exemplified in San Francisco and Oakland. Palms had the effrontery to grow in the parks and around the grounds of private estates, and there were quantities of calla lilies in front yards and gardens; and yet, for twenty of the twenty-four hours of the day, I was shivering with the cold. {However,} we were {quite} warm enough on our journey down through the San Joaquin valley. Harvesting was going on in the grain fields that stretched out quiveringly under the heat of an almost tropical sun.

{Our journey was marked by a painful experience.} The day before we started for Santa Rosa, we had climbed to the crest of a hill {on Uncle Sam's ranch to obtain} a view of the ocean; we evidently helped ourselves up by grasping the shrubs along the steep pathway and these shrubs were poison oak. {Had we seen poison ivy on our climb we would have shunned it, but the poison oak was a new plant to us; and}, as {Mr. Comstock} was {very} susceptible to its poison, the result was disastrous. He suffered terribly and by the time we reached Los Angeles his hands and face were swollen until he looked as if he had been a loser in a prize-fight. He was {highly} embarrassed on our arrival at Los Angeles by finding awaiting him there a number of important men and the mayor of the city invited him to a banquet that night, which of course he had to {refuse}.

{We stopped at the Cosmopolitan Hotel on Main Street near the Plaza but soon found an excellent boarding house on a hill accessible from a horse-car line. We were able to rent two rooms, one with excellent light which we used as a laboratory. From our windows we looked on the one side over the scattered homes of the city and on the other, across the desert to the mountains. One day I saw what I thought was a thunder-storm sweeping toward us from the desert. I was unable to understand the panic of our hostess and her daughters as they flew to shut the windows and doors, until I realized that it was a sand storm; and then gained a lesson on the power of sand to sift through crevices.}

{We were now living for the first time in our lives in an irrigated region and it was hard for us to realize that every green thing in sight owed its verdancy to the water of Los Angeles River. The population of the town at that time was about twelve thousand and was largely Mexican. Spanish was the language of the streets. However, there were many German and French people and a large number of Chinese.}

Mr. Comstock was very cordially received by the fruit growers, and Mr. [S. W.] Niles, {one of his} Cornell classmates, {was especially kind and} drove with {Mr. Comstock} to visit many orchards. {One day we drove to Pasadena. We had rather a long ride through the desert that then lay between that village and Los Angeles. But even then, Pasadena was a beautiful town of orange groves. We visited here most happily, Professor Ezra Carr and his very remarkable wife. He was superintendent of the school of the State at that time, and she was a potent influence in the educational as well as the social life of the western world. At that time, we could have bought half of Pasadena for a hundred dollars an acre with water rights, and we were tempted to invest.}

{Mr. Comstock went with Mr. Niles to Santa Barbara and met the leading horticulturists there. I could seldom get away from work, but I remember once that I went with Mr. Comstock to visit the ranch of a Mr. Rose who had 500 acres of orange trees and twice as much in a vineyard. He paid the government that year $30,000 in taxes on the wine which he made. We also visited that day the Chapman orchard and the ruin of the mission of San Gabriel.}

{However, the most valuable place for Mr. Comstock's work was the Wolfkill orchard which covered many acres including the site of the present Union Railroad station. This was the oldest orchard in the State and consisted of large, stately trees thirty feet or more in height, which were kept vigorous by the best methods of culture. Mr. Wolfkill was a Spanish gentleman and was very courteous and kind to both Mr. Comstock and myself. His superintendent at that time was a young Scot by the name of Alexander Craw whom Mr. Comstock found most intelligent and helpful, and who in later years did much for the economic entomology of California.}

I was kept busy caring for the insects which {Mr. Comstock} brought in, making notes on their habits, and drawings of those that could not be well preserved. I remember how excited we were when we found the males of several of the coccid species, and I made careful drawings of each. These drawings helped us to {come to} the conclusion that these ephemeral individuals were of little use in determining species.

One of our fellow boarders was Mrs. Caroline M. Severance, a most interesting woman, and a potent force later in developing educational facilities in Los Angeles. Kate Douglas Wiggin pays her enthusiastic tribute in "My Garden of Memory".

We left Los Angeles about September 30th. At our last luncheon, our landlady, anxious to show us what California could do, had seventeen varieties of ripe fruit on the table.

We visited San Jose, and Mr. Comstock, working in the orchards there, found a scale insect that was doing much damage and which he named appropriately the "pernicious scale", *Aspidiotus perniciosus*. By some twist of fate, the insect soon became known as the San Jose scale, much to the disapproval of the inhabitants of that beautiful city. Dr. C. L. Marlatt has since traced the scale to its original home in China.

We went again to Santa Rosa and, on our return, the whole [Dowell] family came with us to San Francisco. {Mother} and sister Margaret went with us as far as Sacramento where we bade them {a sad} farewell. That night we stopped at Truckee and visited Lake Tahoe.

We stopped at Yank's, a well-known hospice on the shores of Lake Tahoe. For a day we gave ourselves up to the admiration of the beauty of this sheet of water, hardly realizing that it lay with its unfathomed depths and mighty mountain wall six thousand feet above the level of the sea.

We spent the sunset hour amid the glories of Emerald Bay gazing {with longing eyes} up the snow-clad sides of Mount Tallac, whose rugged brow hung five thousand feet above us. The desire seized us to mount those heights and view the beauty of Tahoe from the summit. {We casually mentioned our desire in the evening in the presence of} Yank, our ubiquitous host, {who} assured us that he could furnish conveyance the next day for the excursion. {With expressions of premature gratitude, we accepted his offer.}

We arose early the next morning and with our fellow excursionists, {Mr. and Mrs. H.}, started out in an old stage coach drawn by two rawboned balky horses with three Indian ponies trailing behind. At Soda Springs we left the coach and mounted the ponies for the final ascent, while {Mr. H.} remained behind to fish. It was a stiff, {steep} climb but the view from the summit was magnificent. We had not realized the steepness of the trail until we began the descent. The ponies were cautious and sure-footed, but it seemed, at times, as though we must pitch over their heads into the depths below. When we finally reached the level area about the Springs we found {Mr. H.} with a fine string of trout. Our strenuous exercise and meager lunch had given us {a} ravenous appetite. We, {therefore}, decided to build a fire and make a supper of the roasted fish. My memory still recalls it as one of the most delicious meals I ever had. By the time the supper was over it was dark, and we were {frightened} at the thought of returning in the coach over the awful eight miles of road along which we had painfully toiled in the morning. Our doubts were soon {and irrevocably} settled by the horses who balked beyond {any of} our powers of persuasion, {while} one of them kicked a whiffletree into slivers. We {made up our minds} to camp over night and soon had a great fire roaring. With the coach cushions for pillows and the men's coats for covers we passed the night as best we could. With the return of the blessed daylight, we finally reached Yank's Inn a tired, hungry lot of people and horses but with an experience not easily forgotten.

{We came} from Chicago {by the Baltimore and Ohio Railroad} through mountains that were covered with {the most} brilliant autumn tints {and which gave us great delight. We thought that} our visit to California had given us a new insight into the beauty and grandeur of nature, {hitherto unknown to us}, and yet the experience had unsealed our eyes to the beauty of the East.

After our return to Washington we changed our mode of living. We rented two additional rooms on the back hall of our apartment, using one for a dining room and the other for a kitchen. Cousin Helen Willits came to us to take care of our light housekeeping. She longed for another winter in Washington and we were more than glad to have her with us.

The coming Presidential election seemed likely to be an important event to us. Commissioner Le Duc was a personal friend of [James A.] Garfield and if the latter were elected we had ground to hope that much could be done for Mr. Comstock's work. A letter to me from my cousin Stacey Cochrane, who once tried working on the Erie Canal and later, {for years,} was an editor in South Dakota, summed up the situation in a manner that pleased us. He said: "It is a great thing for the American boy to know that, although he may be poor and friendless, he can go on the canal, then go to school and get an education, and by and by the people will call him a thief and a liar and elect him President. Then he can have half of the people find fault with everything he does and the other half to admire everything he does no matter whether they know anything of the results or not. Then after a while he can die and have a grand funeral and after a while a monument will be raised to him and sporting men will name their fast horses and fighting dogs after him. My motto is 'Go on the canal, young {man}!'".

Garfield was elected [President of the United States] but some how we did not feel confident that all would be well with us. Mr. Comstock was able to get Professor Charles [H.] Fernald to come for the winter and work on the micro-Lepidoptera for the annual report. Mrs. Fernald was also an entomologist {of standing} and, she offered to work on the Tineids of the collection free of charge, a kindness {which was} greatly appreciated, for the collection at the Department of Agriculture was in a {very} sad way. The Fernalds brought with them their son Henry, a boy of fourteen, who was even then an {excellent} entomologist.

Mr. Comstock began in earnest on a more scientific and detailed report on scale insects for which I gave three days of every week to the making of drawings from the microscope. With an eye-piece micrometer marked with rectangular spaces I studied and portrayed the pygidiums of the female coccids. I was thus enabled to differentiate the fringes with their lobes and spines, characters upon which Mr. Comstock later based the specific difference of these insects. I worked out the anatomy of the individual coccid as it appeared under the microscope, and then my task was done. {He took} the collected drawings, classified them and combined their characters with others, and thus built the foundation for the classification of the {Coccidae} of America.

There was but one book that gave us definite help in the studying the *Coccidae*; it was written in French by the eminent {Frenchman}, Monsieur Signoret. We had paid $20.00 for the volume and considered it money well spent. After I had made many drawings Mr. Comstock sent specimens to Signoret for determination and also one of my drawings of a male coccid. {In his letter} in reply he said: "The drawing of the male is magnificent. It was made by the hand of a master. I wish I could make as good a one. Without impertinence may I ask if the artist is your wife or sister?" I think this commendation did much to start me on my career as a Natural History artist. M. Signoret was {very} curious as to the means used to print our letters. The typewriter had not yet appeared in France.

Early in January 1881, Washington experienced a temperature {often} below zero accompanied by a very heavy snow storm. This caused so much suffering among the poor that a mass-meeting was held to raise money for their relief. {However,} there was an amusing side to the experience, for everyone wished to go sleighing, since the opportunity was so unusual. The contrivances invented to enjoy this sport were laughable. Iron runners were put on the axles of carriages and wagons giving them a long-legged spidery aspect; dry goods boxes were set on runners and we saw one horse hitched to a stout rocking chair. Pennsylvania Avenue was gay despite the cold. The reckoning came when the snow thawed, {a month later}. I remember a river flowing between Pennsylvania Avenue and the

Department of Agriculture. We took a street car to the office and had to stand on the seats to escape the two feet of water on the floor.

About this time, we had a visit from Dr. A. S. Packard and Dr. [Cyrus] Thomas. A law had been passed placing the Entomological Commission under the Department of Agriculture and these gentlemen came to see Commissioner Le Duc concerning it. That ruthless soldier said to them: "All right, gentlemen, if there is work to do and you can do it better than anyone else, you may do it; but if you work under this Department you will do it a damn sight cheaper than you ever have done. You won't get any more salary than Comstock does." The Commissioner brought the men to our office and {I remember that he} said to Mr. Comstock, "Show them the drawings that your wife made and read them that Frenchman's letter" which was rather embarrassing.

We were having very pleasant times socially; so many of our friends came to see us. {I remember one evening we had} David Starr Jordan and Frank Carpenter, a Cornellian who went to Brazil with [Charles Frederick] Hartt, and who had just won a thousand-dollar prize for a poem on a subject connecting the two Americas with a railroad. {Mr. Howard was with us on that occasion and we had a happy evening.}

Many other friends came to see us—Dr. [James] Law of the Veterinary College at Cornell; Mr. George Harris, the Librarian at Cornell; {and later our friend,} Susanna Phelps came {for two weeks, to our great joy. Still later came my childhood friend, Etta Holbrook.}

That winter we heard John McCulloch in his entire repertoire and I have yet to see as perfect a *Richelieu* as was his, although he probably ennobled the part. We also saw Mary Anderson, young and very beautiful, in *Ingomar*. And {it was our privilege to hear} Sarah Bernhardt, which was a revelation to us of artistic interpretation. It was a sad little play and she made an indelible impression upon us. {She had a fine} audience also; I remember seeing there [George] Bancroft {the historian}, John Hay, and Frances Hodgson Burnett.

{One very unhappy circumstance occurred early} in March. Our dear friend William Channing Russel was asked to resign {his position as} Vice-President of Cornell University and also his professorship of history with no reason given. This was a {great} shock. We could have understood why he might be called upon to resign the Vice-Presidency for that office had brought him in unfortunate contact with students; it had in fact made him do the disagreeable work of the President without the other compensations. {However}, as a teacher of history he had always been {most} successful {and no one could give a reason for his forced resignation of that post.}

This summary dismissal of a scholar[17] and a man whom we revered was a blow to us. Mr. Comstock called a meeting of the Cornellians in Washington and the following petition was transmitted by them to the Trustees:

{Washington, D.C.
To the
Executive Committee of the
Board of Trustees,
Of Cornell University}

"We the undersigned alumni and former students of Cornell University now residing in Washington have learned with great surprise and the deepest regret that you have requested the resignation of Vice-President W. C. Russel from his executive and professional positions.

"Believing as we do, that no officer of the University has labored more faithfully for the welfare of the institution than he has done, and that his labors have been eminently successful, we can see no reason why this step has been taken. And we respectfully but earnestly request that the matter be reconsidered, and that Professor Russel's resignation be not accepted.

"We are loath to believe that the time has come when our beloved Alma mater seems to reward one of its most faithful and efficient officers with degradation and disgrace; and the belief that your honorable body has been deceived by some malicious persons; and the hope that you may be induced to reconsider the action you have taken and render justice to one who is now greatly wronged, enables us to make this request quietly and respectfully."

This petition was never {granted any} reply. Moreover, this manner of dismissing a professor was {continued}, in an even more {brutal} manner, in the case of {Professor [Charles C.] Shackford}, who received the first news of his resignation {of the chair of rhetoric and general literature in 1885} through an item in the {daily} paper.

The appropriations for the {Entomological work} passed {the Houses of} Congress, giving the Division of Entomology $16, 200. Although, after the inauguration of Garfield, the prospect that General Le Duc would be

17. Inserted as footnote in the 1953 edition (p. 132): "Of the Russel case, see Walter P. Rogers, *Andrew D. White and the Modern University* (Ithaca: Cornell University Press, 1942), pp. 150–154. —G.W.H."

retained was not {very} bright, {yet there was nothing for} Mr. Comstock to do but to go ahead and plan the work, {as he wished to have it carried out}. He {made a trip to} Baltimore, Philadelphia, New York, and Boston to engage entomologists of standing to assist in carrying on the work of the Division. He put his plan for a practical Division of Entomology before the entomologists of the country with {most} flattering results.

The fight in the Senate between President Garfield and Roscoe Conkling of New York so occupied the President that he had no time to consider the Department of Agriculture for many weeks. However, on May 19th, General Le Duc was removed, and George B. Loring of Massachusetts was made Commissioner {of Agriculture}. We had heard that C. V. Riley had been {working hard to have} Loring appointed, but we knew {also} that he had worked {equally} hard to have Orange Judd appointed {to the same position}. The farmers, especially the Grangers, were very indignant over Loring's appointment, {as their candidate received no attention}.

{Very} soon Mr. Comstock had an interview with Loring which seemed favorable. Mr. Comstock certainly had strong backing. Both of the New York State Senators and {also Senators Frye and Blair, as well as the} Senators from Michigan, did their best to have Mr. Comstock retained. {However,} it was from the scientific men of the country that the strongest influence came. The following letter from Dr. Samuel H. Scudder {of Cambridge} reveals the attitude of the prominent entomologists:

"Washington D. C.[18]

My dear Mr. Uhler:

"You do not need to enlarge at all upon the labors of Mr. Comstock, to enlist my sympathy for him. I know for myself that no person has yet filled the post he occupies in half so faithful or efficient a manner. I have commended his work on every occasion, for it seems to me admirable in every way, thorough, honest, fearless, well judged; while his industry is beyond all praise. He is making his special department thoroughly respected for the first time in its history; and I, for one, will defend his moral right to the place (by virtue of the dignity he has given it) against all comers, be they my dearest friends or the most distinguished scientific men in the country. Command my services in this direction in anything I can do, and I will thank you for the

18. In the 1953 edition (p. 133): changed to "Cambridge, Mass."

chance. You are at liberty indeed, to use this letter in any way, in which you think it may serve him.

Very cordially yours,

Samuel H. Scudder"

{With} all this excitement we had to work steadily on the Annual Report which must be handed in by June 15th. After this had been accomplished, I went to Otto for a little vacation: {I went} knowing that the axe might fall July 1st, but I hoped for the best.

One happy, care-free afternoon I had before I went, when Mr. G. K. Gilbert took me to visit [W. H.] Holmes, the artist for the Geological Survey. Mr. Holmes's sketches of the western desert were {very fine and gave me great joy}. Mr. Gilbert thought that Mr. Holmes might help me to find a teacher who could give me instruction in drawing, especially for my work with pen and ink. Mr. Holmes said he knew of no one, so I had to keep on {and do} the best I could {by myself. However,} my drawings for the Report made a good showing and Loring deigned to praise them. I had much to encourage me. Howard told {Mr. Comstock}, concerning my drawings of chalcids, "It was the rarest thing that she made a mistake or overlooked anything: and she found lots of things that I didn't see in my descriptions."

Mr. Comstock had a personal interview with President Garfield who said that he had talked with Loring and that he thought {the latter} did not intend to make any changes in the heads of Divisions. In closing he said: "If you have any trouble I will take your letters of recommendation under consideration myself." This was most encouraging.

Letters from Entomologists all over the country came pouring in. The *Nation* had an editorial most complimentary to Mr. Comstock. The Boston Natural History Society sent in requests for his retention.

{Dr. [P. R.] Uhler,} librarian of the Peabody Library in Baltimore, came over to Washington to interview Loring. {Out of a clear sky} the Secretary of the Pennsylvania Agricultural Society came to see Mr. Comstock and told him that the four largest Agricultural societies of Pennsylvania were backing him. Mr. Scudder sent Loring a petition signed by thirty-six entomologists asking for the retention of Mr. Comstock. Professors Cooke and Beal of the Michigan Agricultural College and the Michigan State Agricultural Society wrote letters of similar purport.

Then came the tragedy—the shooting of Garfield and {for days and weeks} all was in suspense while he made his fight for life. This tragedy had direct results for us, for had President Garfield lived, we had every reason to think he might have insisted on retaining Mr. Comstock. Although Loring had previously promised Riley the position, yet with all the pressure from the scientific men from the country and some personal politicians, {he} dared not throw Mr. Comstock out, so he {compromised}. He presented a plan for having both Riley and Comstock {as workers} in the Division. As a matter of fact, he {said in so many words}, that he did not "care a tinker's damn about {Mr.} Comstock's work or plans." He simply took this way to satisfy those who had declared against Mr. Comstock's removal. {Of course} Loring's plan was quite impossible. It would have been difficult to have two entomologists managing the work of the Division {had they been entirely harmonious, and Mr. Comstock} refused {positively} to consider this proposition.

{Mr. Comstock proposed to} Commissioner Loring that he be granted a salary of fifteen hundred with five hundred dollars ($500) for illustrations and on thousand dollars ($1000) for an assistant in order that he might carry out the following work in Ithaca:

{First;} to complete the monograph on scale insects,
{Second; to} prepare for publication accounts of the insects bred and studied in the Division under {Mr. Comstock's} direction,
{Third;} investigate any entomological subjects which the Commissioner might refer to him.

The Commissioner acceded to this {proposition} and established an entomological station at Cornell, a valuable enterprise in which he took not the slightest interest, and which he allowed to lapse for lack of support {after one year}.

After the first wrench that caused us to throw aside our ambitious plans for {the} work in Washington, we found that we were entranced with the prospect of carrying on the work at Ithaca and {living in} our attractive little home. The only drawback to our entire happiness was the dismissal of Professor Russel and the feeling that the Cornell trustees had the power to dismiss a professor at any time and give no explanation. This was a cloud that darkened Cornell skies {for many years thereafter}.

Mr. Comstock handed in his resignation to Commissioner Loring on July 5th, to take effect on August 1st. Before {Mr. Comstock} left Washington, after many interviews with Loring, {he} wrote me, "So thoroughly have I lost confidence in Loring that were he and Riley to have a row to-morrow, and he were to invite me to come back I should hesitate to accept." Extracts {from the letters of Mr. Comstock} which he wrote me show well his way of taking reverses {of his plans}:[19]

> {"... following a phantom, although at times the road has been rough it has more often been a pleasant one; and while the principle object of my pursuit has banished, I find that the prizes which I have picked up by the way are far greater in value than I had any reason to hope to obtain.}
>
> "I feel my personal disappointment but little. I look upon my case as simply an exponent of a system, the existence of which should make the heart of every lover of our glorious country ache with shame. And too, I feel very sad to believe that entomology cannot have in the near future what we believed was in store for it.
>
> "Still everything is not lost; my administration and the struggle which accompanied its close will have an effect on entomology. The attention of every American entomologist has been called in a most forcible way to the existing state of affairs, and to what might be, and the end is not in sight.
>
> "And how much we have grown in the past two years! We will take up the work at Ithaca with much more confidence than we laid it down. We will have a happy home. We will give my students the best facilities for obtaining an entomological training that can be found in the world. And we will do some original scientific work.
>
> "I am now planning my Ithaca work as enthusiastically as I have planned anything. Just now I am at work on a plan by which the students, after the first term, shall do original scientific work. In that way I shall have a large corps of assistants and they will get the best training."

19. Page(s) are missing at this point. Page 6–55 of the manuscript is heavily crossed out with pencil and blue china marker, with "End of Chapter 6" written and circled at the bottom of the page. —KSt.

Insectary on Cornell University campus, n.d. (circa 1900).

Inside of the Insectary with Professor Comstock.

CHAPTER VII

Return to Cornell

This material makes up Chapter 8 in the 1953 edition of the book, and the focus was placed on Mr. Comstock's return to Entomology at Cornell University. In this manuscript chapter, Mrs. Comstock places the emphasis on organizing their lives upon their return to Ithaca. Also, in a section previously omitted, Mrs. Comstock credits her husband with inspiring her to pursue nature study work. The paragraphing and punctuation style are Mrs. Comstock's.

Early in August [1881] we returned to Ithaca and began the work of settling the laboratory and home. {The cleaning and the} paper-hanging {of the latter} added to the confusion {of it all}. It had been decided that Cousin Helen Willits should come with us to Ithaca and pursue her studies in the university. She was to have charge of the house in order that I might have time to finish my drawings for {the Coccid Report}. In addition to all his other work, {Mr. Comstock} enthusiastically began planting a strawberry bed and setting out raspberry and currant bushes, all {of which he did} with his own hands, at odd moments. He {also} bought a carpenter's bench and tools, which he installed in the cellar; {and was very proud of} this acquisition {which, in fact}, helped us out in many an hour of need. {Indeed}, that fall he made a herbarium for Helen which stands staunch and strong in our cellar today. I wrote my mother: "The only drawback to Harry's happiness while at his carpenter work is lack of company. He usually, on some pretext or other, inveigles either Helen or myself to go down there with him. I think if he could have his carpenter bench in the parlor he would be entirely happy."

We {secured} a maid fresh from the bogs of Ireland, ruddy as to cheeks and blue as to eyes and with the single accomplishment of being able to wash windows. With Helen's patient training Katie developed into a capable, efficient {servant}, loyal and willing. {It was during this} summer that Katie pale with fright rushed into the parlor where I was receiving callers, and cried, "Ooch! Koom in the kitchen, the divil is on the doorpost". I hurried to find a large adult {*Corydalus cornutus*[1]} on the door casing, snapping his great curved jaws angrily. I {really} did not wonder at Katie's characterization of the creature.

In September, President Garfield {succumbed, after his long and brave fight for life}. On September 28th, President White pronounced an eloquent memorial address {on Garfield} in our University chapel, {which was beautifully} decorated with flowers for the occasion. Soon another sad event occurred, the death of Jennie McGraw Fiske [donor of the Cornell chimes]. She and Professor Fiske had come from Europe, expecting to take possession of the beautiful home that was then nearly completed,—the notable Fiske-McGraw mansion—on the site of the present Chi Psi Lodge. She never saw {the beautiful home} but her funeral was held there.

{It is now rather hard to realize the difficulties we were experiencing then in the mere matter of daily living. We had, at that time, no mail delivery and we were obliged to go to town on foot or in an omnibus to get the mail at the post office.}

We entered wholeheartedly into the University life. We were all {very} glad to have Professor Moses Coit Tyler added to our faculty and we attended the first course of lectures {which he gave}. We went regularly to the University Chapel and rejoiced in the privilege of hearing the great preachers who came to Cornell, Phillip Brooks, Lyman Abbott and others.

{In October we attended the wedding of DeForest Van Vleet at Dryden. We drove over with Professor Gage, and it was an all-day event to drive twelve miles, attend a wedding and return. The big old house of the bride's family seemed to us grand; and the wedding with the flowers and bridesmaids very elaborate. The experience of watching the ceremony gave Professor Gage a chill, for he realized that he was soon to be a participant in a similar function.}

{That fall} the eminent English [historian, Edward A.] Freeman, gave a course of lectures at Cornell which we attended. Unforgettable was his

---

1. Footnote in the 1953 edition (p. 138): "An aquatic insect with a wing-expanse of four to five inches; the male has long curved mandibles.—G.W.H."

appearance and method of lecturing. He was {quite} stout and had an immense beard which gave him a patriarchal appearance. He was a victim of gout and with one foot encased in an immense slipper and elevated on a foot-rest in front of him, delivered his lectures, sitting. He read his lectures from a manuscript with the inflection of a country schoolboy who lets his voice slide down at every period.

President White, who had been American Minister to Germany {during the years} from 1879 to 1881, returned this fall, and we were happy to have him back. He and Mrs. White were {very} neighborly and often called upon us. On one occasion, I was {greatly} interested to hear Mr. White's private opinion of President Garfield. He said that Garfield had been a strong man but no upholder of the Civil Service; he related to us some very shocking stories of the manner in which able and efficient consuls {were turned out of office and their places filled} by inexperienced politicians. He maintained that, although people had the idea that Garfield was a reformer, he had begun his administration as badly as any President in history; and that he believed that there had been less hope of Garfield {in this respect than there was of} Arthur.

As Mr. Gage was to be married soon, he did not again take a room in our house; but he came to us for his meals and, as ever, added greatly to the family cheer. {I remember that year he} was working with Dr. [Burt G.] Wilder on the "Cat Book", {which was} a laboratory manual for the dissection of the cat. Dr. Wilder had introduced a new nomenclature in describing the relations of anatomical parts to each other and in a measure, this appealed to Mr. Comstock. The discussions between Gage and Comstock were characteristic. They would argue excitedly and pound the table for emphasis, until my gentle cousin Helen was frightened, fearing that they might quarrel. {However, each} discussion ended suddenly by the complete yielding of one or the other, with "Well, I think you are right, Brother Gage", or "I think you are right, Brother Comstock".

That fall my father and mother came to visit us for the first time in our Ithaca home. They found much to interest them. Father was especially interested in the University farm and the stock; it was during this visit that he {made arrangements for the purchase of} two {well-bred} Holstein cows which {later} added {much} to the value of his own herd.

{Father quite disapproved of Katie's waiting on the table instead of sitting at the table with the family. However, he did not say much, but one day at dinner murmured musingly; "If I were a big, blue-eyed, red-cheeked young woman, I should hate to come and go at the tinkle of a little bell."}

A {quite} momentous event occurred just before the opening of the University in the fall of 1881. The entomological laboratory in the tower of McGraw Hall, had become so crowded that it could not longer accommodate the students, and Mr. Comstock was given a new laboratory on the second floor, north end of White. Adjoining this laboratory was a small office. {Mr. Henry Turner had been appointed as} an assistant so that Mr. Comstock could find time {to carry on his work} for the government. The new laboratory seemed {actually} palatial, and yet, as the years {wore on, more and} more room was needed until the whole north section of this second floor was given over to entomology.

In November of 1881 the University raised the salaries of the assistant professors from $1000 to $1200 and {that fall} we paid $200 on the mortgage of the house, thus reducing it to $900. {It was} about this time that Mr. Comstock began seriously to write a textbook for use in his classes. {He began this} although he still had much to do on the Coccid Report. He took a lamp to the laboratory and worked there nights. A telephone had been put in the laboratory, so I could reach him if necessary, and this seemed a great luxury.

{An event of importance to us all was the wedding of Professor Gage to Miss [Susanna] Phelps. After the Van Vleet ceremony,} Professor Gage had shown signs of nervousness when his approaching marriage was discussed. He feared that the Episcopal ceremony {by which he was to be married} would be a long trying rite. He confided his fears to {Comstock}, who hunted up the Prayer Book and with great gravity began to read to him the visitation of the sick, doing a little judicious skipping {here and there}. Gage's face grew more and more serious until he finally began to suspect something wrong, and took the book to see for himself, at which Mr. Comstock and I laughed until we wept.

We went to Morrisville for the wedding, which took place in the Phelps home, the house which now contains the village library, a gift from Mrs. Gage to her native town. It was a very beautiful wedding, and the dear twain made one, were soon in Ithaca, where the four of us, now joined in double bonds, began anew an intimate friendship, which lasted without interruption for more than thirty years {until Mrs. Gage's death}.

{During this year we had two notable non-resident lecturers from Ann Arbor. The first was Charles Kendall Adams, who lectured on English history; and the other was Henry Carter Adams, who gave a course on the tariff, especially of England and America. We attended both of these courses of lectures; and became quite well acquainted with both of these men, never dreaming at that time that one of them would be President of Cornell and our nearest neighbor for years.}

{Another pleasure that came to us this winter was the return to the University of John Casper Branner, who was a classmate of Mr. Comstock but who had gone to Brazil with Charles Fred Hartt before he received his degree.

Now, after seven years of geological work in Brazil, he returned to Cornell to finish his studies and to receive the degree. He was born on a plantation in the South before the Civil War and was drafted into the Confederate army before he was sixteen. He was a man of supreme social charm, being extremely witty and very adaptable. He and Professor W. R. Dudley often came to our home that year, adding greatly to our enjoyment. Many years later we renewed our intimacy with Dr. Branner, when he was a professor of Geology at Stanford University, and later Chancellor of the same institution.}

{Our mode of entertainment during this period at Cornell is illustrated by the supper to which we were daring enough to invite President and Mrs. White, Professor and Mrs. Moses Coit Tyler, and Professor and Mrs. G. C. Caldwell. The table cloth was a "turkey red" damask, solid in color and quite elegant, costing as much as the best damask. The dishes were white china decorated with flowers, hand-painted, and to me seemed very beautiful and unusual. They looked particularly fetching on the vivid red table-cloth. My husband had just made me a present of certain silver dishes that added much to the beauty of the table. These consisted of a butter dish, with a hinged cover and a place under the glass bottom for chopped ice; also, a silver, vase-shaped holder and twin pickle-caster. These articles and their use would scarcely be recognizable today, but they seemed very important to me then. For food, we had pressed chicken, canned salmon (a luxury that had just appeared on the market), hot biscuit, cheese, pickles, and canned peaches for the first course. The dessert was floating island, chocolate cake, and fruit; tea, coffee, and milk were the beverages. I wrote my mother that I rather dreaded entertaining the Whites, who were accustomed to so much elegance in their home, but I was very sure I could entertain as well according to our means as the Whites did according to theirs. It certainly turned out all right for, like all thoroughbred people, our guests were simple, sincere, and sympathetic and would never dream of criticizing.}

{Mrs. Caldwell's "Kaffee Klatches" formed an important part of the social life of the wives of the faculty. We were invited to her pleasant home on Central Avenue from 3 to 5 in the afternoon; we brought embroidery or knitting and chatted busily while we worked. Excellent coffee and cake constituted the simple but satisfactory refreshments and gave the name to the function. Our hostess was a wise and benign woman but could say things on occasion that were pungent and pertinent. So, while we younger women basked in her benignity, we were very careful not to incur her criticism. She was a very potent influence in my development as a social factor at Cornell; I was wont to consult her on all perplexing questions and had perfect confidence in her judgment. Through the years our friendship waxed stronger and sweeter.

I have never ceased to miss her during the many years since her death. I have been grateful that she left a daughter, Mrs. Grace Chamberlain, much like her, who has been very dear to me in my later life.}

{In March (1882) Mr. Comstock made an address before a Teachers' Institute held in Ithaca. I listened attentively to his plea that teachers should interest the children in their natural environment. In all probability, listening to that address awakened in me the interest which later developed into my chief work in life.}

{One of the} important improvements in the entomological laboratory that spring was a new cabinet of white ash which Mr. Comstock had had built for the insect collection. It was about 17 feet long and 9 feet high and deep enough to hold insect boxes 2 feet square; it had 8 sections for holding the boxes, each of which could be pulled out like the drawer {of a bureau}. Mr. Comstock had put much thought on the best means of building up a collection of insects. One of the problems was that of adding acquired specimens to the collection, which meant the repinning of a whole box of insects in order to insert the additions in the right places. To meet this problem; he devised a system on the plan of the card catalogue; i.e., blocks of cork, later of wood, in multiples to fit the box. This system allowed new entries {without the repinning of specimens}, by {simply} shifting the blocks. It also gave opportunity for making the boxes tighter and more nearly pest-proof, for both the bottom and top of each box could now be made of a single pane of glass. Another problem connected with the collection was to find a way of preventing the loss of alcohol from straight vials containing specimens when laid flat on the blocks. The difficulty was eventually met by devising a quadrangular vial with the neck bent sharply upward. The form of bottle became known in the laboratory as the bent-neck vial. Mr. Comstock possessed considerable mechanical skill and when he gave his thought to this type of problem the result was usually effective and practical.

Mr. Comstock's influence as a teacher was steadily growing. The outline of study of a grasshopper which he had written for his own use in his laboratory, as an introduction to insect anatomy, was adopted that spring for use in the entomological laboratories of the Universities of Iowa and Wisconsin.

The number of students at Cornell was very small that year (1881–1882). Mr. Comstock had only twenty in his lectures and ten in his laboratory that spring, the smallest class he ever had {in his entire career as a teacher}. His lecture class increased to thirty before the term was far advanced.

{During the spring Mr. Comstock and cousin Helen continued their botanical collecting. I went with them on their excursions and for the first time undertook to sketch in water colors.}

On the 28th of June we finished the report on injurious insects for the Department of Agriculture[2] and sent it to Washington, knowing {quite well} that this would be the end of Mr. Comstock's connection with the Department despite Commissioner Loring's promises of future work. {Mr. Comstock} had utilized every possible moment in writing it, and I had worked every day on the drawings. While the Report discussed some insects of economic importance aside from the scale insects, {the main part, over} 100 pages, was devoted to the *Coccidae*. We were {very} proud of this Report at the time; and we would have been even more so, had we known that it would become the basis of all future work on this important family. The part of the report devoted to the parasites was written by L. O. Howard and included many of my drawings of the chalcids.

After Commencement we went to Otto and remained there until August when we, {accompanied by cousin Helen, and my girlhood friend, Etta Holbrook of Otto,} went to the meeting of the A. A. A. S. at Montreal. We stopped at Oswego on our way, where we visited all branches of the Turner family. I was especially interested in our visit to Captain Turner; he was Mr. Comstock's "Pa Lewis" whom I had never seen. He was a large fine-looking man with white hair and ruddy face; he talked in tones of thunder. He had once been very profane but {now, for a long time, had been a} "professor of religion"; and {Mr. Comstock} said that his way of saying "God bless him" was very reminiscent of his former "God damn him." {He} was so excited and happy over our arrival that, at dinner, he forgot to say grace until after he had begun to eat; then suddenly he raised his hand and thundered: "Hold up; and we will ask the blessing of God!" I wanted to laugh, but when I saw my husband drop his fork and bow his head as calmly as if this was the usual method of procedure, I suppressed my smile.

I enjoyed Pa Lewis greatly and have always been glad that we made this visit, for {we} never saw him again. We took a long drive while at Oswego, visiting all the schools where {Mr. Comstock} had been a pupil, and the schoolhouse where he had taught. We also called on many of his {old} friends.

---

2. Footnote inserted in the 1953 edition (p. 141–42): "*Report of the Entomologist of the United States Department of Agriculture for the Year 1880*, by John Henry Comstock, 1881. This report contains the notable work on the Coccidae by which Professor Comstock established for the first time a simple, accurate basis for the classification of the species of scale insects in the important family *Diaspidinae*. The work was based on the characters of the pygidia (posterior segments of the body) drawn by Mrs. Comstock from the actual specimens and illustrated in the report by many fine plates. The article by Dr. Howard on the parasites of the Coccidae established his reputation at this early time as an authority in the field of insect parasitism. —G.W.H."

A.A.A.S.[3] was in its youth and the novelty of holding the meeting in Canada was a special inducement to attend. Montreal was most hospitiable [sic] to its scientific guests and the meetings were {very} successful and enjoyable. Mr. Comstock read a paper before the Agricultural section and C. V. Riley, who was present, attacked him quite rudely. {Mr. Comstock} kept his temper and answered in a few quiet words that made controversy impossible. Later, several of the entomologists congratulated him on his manner of dealing with the matter.

On our return, we visited Quebec, {and from there turned south to see} the White Mountains and {to visit} Boston {with} its many historic buildings and monuments. From Boston we journeyed to Orono, Maine, to visit Professor and Mrs. [C. H.] Fernald. The State University [of Maine], {at that time}, had four dignified buildings on an attractive campus and a faculty of about twelve professors and instructors. {We had a charming visit with the Fernalds and}, on our return to Boston, went out to Cambridge to visit Dr. and Mrs. [H. A.] Hagen.

{The Hagens were very kind to us and took us for} an extended drive around Cambridge and Brookline. Dr. Hagen always seemed to consider Mr. Comstock as his chief disciple in America. {It was during this visit that Mrs. Hagen told me of the following incident} when we were discussing the difficult servant problem in America: A nobleman from Europe was visiting them {(I think it was Baron Osten-Sacken)}. Mrs. Hagen had no regular servant but was able to get a woman to come in to cook the meals and wait upon the table while she, {herself}, attended to the other housework. At the Baron's departure, he said to his hostess: "I have tried in vain to see the maid who has kept my room in such good order, but I have been unable to find her. I have left something for her on my bureau." Mrs. Hagen said, laughing, "I thanked him, and I think I enjoyed spending that $2.50 more than any other money I have ever spent."

{Two or three} momentous decisions were made this autumn. I determined to go back into the University and take the course in science which my husband had taken, and get my degree. Mr. Comstock thought I should have more training and knowledge in the sciences allied to entomology; and {he thought} I would be better satisfied to have a degree. I was allowed the same privilege of free tuition that, {in those days}, was granted to children of the professors. Thus, I could register for a minimum number of hours, which would allow me time for my other work. We also had come to the

3. In the 1953 edition (p. 143): "The American Association for the Advancement of Science . . ."

conclusion that I must learn wood engraving to illustrate the *Manual for the Study of Insects*[4] that Mr. Comstock was to write as soon as possible. I saw an advertisement of wood-engraving tools with a booklet of directions and promptly sent for them; and with my usual daring in untried paths I went at it. {Of my success with this equipment I will speak later.}

That autumn the trustees raised the salaries of the professors $250. We were delighted that Professor Gage's salary was increased from $1000 to $1500.

President White went with Dr. Wilder and Mr. Comstock to Ward's [Natural Science] establishment in Rochester. The President became enthusiastic over the beautiful models of invertebrates, made in glass, by the Blaschkes of Austria. He saw new possibilities of the department of invertebrate zoology at Cornell, and as a result, the appropriation for running the laboratory was raised from {its customary} fifty dollars per year to six hundred and seventy-five and Mr. Comstock was given, in addition $1200 with which to buy a set of glass models to illustrate his lectures, and $300 to buy museum specimens of invertebrates. {Mr. Comstock was highly} delighted and encouraged. He engaged a student assistant, {Mr. F. M. Chappell, at fifteen cents an hour and} thus was able to get rid of much drudgery. {He} also kept {Mr. Chappell} busy at odd moments in pinning and mounting specimens, thus adding many new boxes of insects to the collection. All this constituted one of those unexpected leaps forward after a long period of waiting {and discouragement} that have characterized the growth of the Department of Entomology. {It was} during this period that running water was brought into the laboratory and Mr. Comstock {was able to} establish a series of glass jar aquaria which enabled him to show his students aquatic insects in their natural element.

President White went with Mr. Comstock to Rochester to select and buy the glass models. As they did not spend all of the appropriation for the models, a part of the money was used for the purchase of other needed specimens.

On the way back from Rochester, President White sat with {Mr. Comstock and told him to go ahead and correspond} with leading entomologists {and find} what collections were for sale and he would get the money as fast as possible. {Mr. Comstock} was greatly encouraged and confided to me that he expected to build up the third best collection in America. The Cambridge and Philadelphia museums, {having had hundreds of thousands

4. In the 1953 edition (p. 144): [title] changed to *An Introduction to Entomology*.

of dollars and many years ahead of him}, he could hardly expect to overtake. His idea, consistently carried out, was to limit his collections to North American insects.

A considerable part of the *Report on Scale Insects* which Mr. Comstock had prepared for the United States Department of Agriculture was left out of the annual report by Commissioner Loring. {The alleged} reason given was lack of space. The Cornell Experiment Station, {recently inaugurated}, proposed to publish this as a *Bulletin*. As some of the illustrations were outline figures on wood I was asked to engrave them and was given $50.00 for the work.

I had been practicing with my tools, {which were very} shallow and which later my teacher, Mr. Davis, characterized as "very curious." But I managed to engrave those complicated outlines and did a fairly good job, meanwhile getting "loads of experience." I remember I lamed the muscles of my arm in the process, something that would have seemed ludicrous to a skilled engraver.

{This year} I took an added responsibility and on November 4, 1882, I joined the Kappa Alpha Theta sorority. This was the first sorority established at Cornell; and many of us would have preferred that none should ever come to our University. However, this one was established, and others were sure to follow. I was too democratic and catholic in my tastes to be in sympathy with any organization that was exclusive, and I had little use for secret societies of any kind. I consulted President White on the subject and he advised me strongly to join this first sorority, because, he said, I might have a wise influence within it, and also upon the policy of the relations of the sororities to each other when others should be established. Membership in the sorority has brought me many {sweet and} happy friendships and enriched my life by the close companionship of many noble women {whom I would scarcely have known otherwise}. Through it I have been closely and constantly associated with a group of women students during the {forty years past}. It has brought me a great deal of extra work and care and caused me much mental anguish at times. It has been also, in some measure, a barrier between other students and myself, {which has been to me} a source of much regret. I have seen both boys and girls develop splendidly under the spur and responsibilities of fraternity life—and also, I have seen others ruined through it. I believe it would be better for colleges and universities if the social life were to center in clubs which had their inception in some special interest or activity, rather than in {Greek-letter} fraternities, where the membership is restricted to personal choice or caprice, and which are, at their best, a menace to the democracy of an American institution of learning. With all due modesty I think I may say that I have exerted an influence that has been felt in three directions; {the keeping of the relations} between the sororities friendly; the widening of the sympathies and interests among my sorority sisters, and the impressing upon the members of my chapter a sense of their responsibilities to their sisters and to the University.

I was never a good nurse, but I was a good doctor. Mr. Comstock came home from a meeting of the Western New York Horticultural Society in Rochester with a terrifying cold. I {promptly} gave him a "hemlock sweat," a remedy employed by my New England ancestors. It broke up his cold, but he was weak {as a rag} for days after. Later, he had lumbago and the doctor told me to paint his back with iodine. His back was so white and smooth that, as I dipped my brush in the colorful liquid, my artistic instincts were aroused, and I painted a lake, with a forest on the far side reflected in the still waters. I did not dare tell the patient what I had done, but {our dear Dr. Winslow took great joy} in telling him of the beautiful outcome of his lumbago.

This year Dr. [E. L.] Sturtevant, head of the State Experiment Station at Geneva, offered Mr. Comstock one hundred dollars a year and his travelling expenses to do {the active} entomological work for the station. {At this time} Dr. Samuel H. Scudder planned the starting of a scientific periodical and asked {Mr. Comstock} to become a regular contributor, which meant a further addition to his {salary}.

While Mr. Comstock never called the roll in his classes he kept in touch with his {pupils} through weekly quizzes, and this term he looked over fifty of these examination papers every week. Three of the faculty wives attended his classes and he felt {very} much complimented. The glass models added {much} to the interest of his work.

The first term, when {Mr. Comstock's} work was entirely on entomology, we entertained the {entire} class one evening at our home. We also did {much} other entertaining of the {girls} of my sorority, and the boys of Mr. Comstock's fraternity.

It seemed best for us that I finish my University course as soon as possible, so we {concluded to} give up housekeeping and take our meals at Sage College. This brought us into rather close association with many of the women students and resulted in much more gaiety on our part than we had anticipated.

I registered for the largest possible number of hours and Mr. Comstock took the course in physics with me; if any of the instructors in that department {at that time} had been as good as he in explaining to me the mysteries of that science the class would have had an easier time. Several of the {girls} in the class used to come to the house to get the benefit of Mr. Comstock's explanations. He could always make the most abstruse subject clear, a faculty contributing greatly to his power as a teacher.

After commencement I went to Otto, but Mr. Comstock remained at home because he had much to do for the department at Cornell; he was also writing the article on Hymenoptera[5] for the *Standard Natural History*. He lived at home and took his meals at {Mrs. Crittenden's}, a popular boarding house on Eddy Street. Professor [W. R.] Dudley[6] also ate there, and the two had some delightful excursions together collecting. {Mr. John M. Stedman}, then an undergraduate, was working for the department and Mr. Comstock was teaching him to collect and care for the living insects in the breeding-cages in the laboratory. {He} wrote me: "I tried today for the twentieth time to impress upon him that I want all data respecting insects saved. I like him very much, but his is a very, very young boy and I have to watch every step of his work." {He} describes his day's work: "I work on the *Hymenoptera* article all of the mornings. Afternoons I have to go over the notes and the breeding cages and attend to my correspondence. I have found a caterpillar in the seed of the currants that seems very important. It causes the fruit to shrivel and is quite common here."

This was the first year of a very important change in the Entomological Department at Cornell. Mr. Comstock was to remain in Ithaca and work during the summer and have three-months' vacation in winter. He proposed this, {as it seemed} to him the only way in which he could develop his collections and data concerning injurious insects. He had no thought then of establishing the summer school in Entomology, that came many years later.

Unfortunately for his plans {this summer} I fell ill of fever at Otto and he came on at once. There was no nurse to be had in that country village, and as my mother was not well, {Mr. Comstock} nursed me through nine weeks of low fever. He was an excellent nurse and was a great comfort to me, because of the telepathy that had always existed between us, and which now reached an amazing perfection. All I had to do was to wish for something and he immediately responded, which relieved me of the effort to speak. It was a discouraging summer, but the last of September I was well enough to

---

5. Footnote from the 1953 edition (p. 147): "Hymenoptera, an order of insects with four clear, membranous wings, familiar examples of which are the bees, wasps, and ants. —G.W.H."

6. Ibid.: "Dudley was a Cornell graduate who, with David Starr Jordan, explored the flora of the Cayuga Lake region. A leader in the conservation of plants in New York and in California, Dudley led in the conservation movement for the preservation of the giant redwoods, *Sequoia gigantae* and *Sequoia semper virens*, and of other trees shrubs, and flowers, while a Professor of Botany at Stanford University. —R.G.S."

return with him to Ithaca, a shadow of my former self. The parlor of our little house was filled with flowers, from friends, when we arrived.

Mr. Comstock had finished the first part of the *Hymenoptera* before he left Ithaca. He worked on the second part at odd moments while he was nursing me. I remember well he worked out the history of the little carpenter bee, *Eumenes fraternus*, by bringing in the stems of the sumac and raspberry and entertaining me with the story as fast as he was able to decipher it. This is why in my {volume}, the *Ways of the Six-Footed* I entitled this "The Story We Love Best".

{Mr. Comstock}, that fall, joined a Republican revolt against Blaine and brought all his influence to bear in favor of [Grover] Cleveland, {and Hendricks}. From one of the political meetings which he attended {during the evening}, he did not get home until 1 a.m. He was in bed with a sick headache the next day. I cheered him up by telling him that nowadays men did not often have a chance to suffer for their country.

As my strength returned my hair fell out—my hair had been my chief claim to beauty for it was {very} thick and {very} black. But I had to have it cut off and, as usual, I spent no time mourning over what could not be helped. Bobbed hair was unheard of in those days, so I had to become resigned to appearing different from other women. I wore my hair short for about two or three years because I found it {very} convenient and time-saving. Then {Mr. Comstock} announced {to me} one day: "My dear, one member of our family must have long hair; shall it be you or I?" I took the hint and let my hair grow again.

In those days students at Cornell had to write theses for the degrees of B.A. and B.S. I wrote mine with Professor Gage, on "The fine anatomy of the interior of [the larva] of *Corydalus cornutus*." The work was most interesting; I imbedded tissues and cut sections and wondered at the beautiful structure of this horrible-looking creature's insides. I told Professor Gage that a Dobson [a larva of Corydalus] was like a stained-glass window; it could only be appreciated when looked at from the inside.

This spring, Mr. Comstock and I attended a course of lectures on Public Institutions by Franklin B. Sanborn, the biographer of Thoreau. His lectures were interesting although wandering and sketchy. The great value of the course lay in our Saturday trips to visit {such} institutions as we could {conveniently} reach,—Willard {Insane Asylum}, Auburn Prison, Elmira Reformatory, our own County House and jails. After these visits he [Mr. Sanborn] would give us the latest ideas as to how each should be conducted; and I believe that we all regarded the course as {most} valuable in training for citizenship. Professor Sanborn {was} a charming man socially {and} was frequently a guest in our home. He was a {true} transcendentalist {and}, as an example of his methods of thought {the following} incident is pertinent: There had been a scandal in the University through the theft of examination papers from the printing office. Professor Sanborn planned to avoid any such danger, so he had his examination papers printed in Boston. His class was large and, for examinations, was divided into two sessions, forenoon and afternoon. To the astonishment of the morning section, the examination papers contained the questions for both sections. Needless to say, the afternoon section was well prepared.

In June [1885], I received my degree, taking my diploma from the hands of President White, the last class that was so honored. {At this commencement} Mr. Comstock asked that his salary be raised, stating that the Doctor's Bill {of the summer before}, of several hundred dollars, was not yet wholly paid. His request was not granted but it brought us a beautiful experience. Professor Henry S. Williams came to {Mr. Comstock} and handed him some bonds and told him he could have the use of them as long as he needed. All our lives we have been grateful to this noble, kindly man {for this help}. Later it was through his influence that his brother, George R. Williams, {then} a trustee, {came and} looked over the Entomological Department and talked with Mr. Comstock about his plans for its development, a visit that resulted in an advance of {Mr. Comstock's} salary.

In the summer of 1885 Mr. Comstock {had} his first real summer term in entomology. He had sixteen students, several of them graduates, and he found his class most satisfactory. It was the beginning of a policy that, {later}, made his work so {very} successful. It offered an opportunity for a graduate student to do a trimester's work in the summer, and many came {to study}. His plan was to give two mornings each week to collecting and studying in the field and {spending} the rest of the time in working up the material {thus} collected. As there were no other classes, these students gave all of their time to entomology. The varied environment of Ithaca {afforded} a wide range of forms and the summer season was the best {period} for the study of insect life.

{This summer our very pleasant acquaintance with Mr. Grove Karl Gilbert of the U. S. Geological Survey was renewed. He was interested in the geology of the region of the Finger Lakes and came to do some field work. One of us went with him on his days of exploring and it was a delight to do so, for, aside from his being a very interesting companion, his ability to read the history of a landscape seemed to us like magic.}

I had sent some of my scientific drawings to the New Orleans Exposition, which took place that year, and received first honorable mention. I still have {somewhere} the blue ribbon of {the} award signed by Julia Ward Howe and Isabel Greeley, {and a diploma}. This recognition encouraged me so that I took up my engraving with new vigor.

Charles Kendall Adams was inaugurated in November [1885], as President of Cornell University, and occupied the residence next to ours on the campus, {living there during his entire incumbency}. As a result, our end of the campus was {re-}landscaped and became a more important section. President Adams' household consisted of his wife, a fine dignified woman, who sacrificed much of her time and strength in caring for her invalid niece, {a very bright and} interesting young woman and a great sufferer. President Adams' mother was also with them, the highest type of New England womanhood {of her generation}. "Grandma Adams" we called her, and we loved her devotedly. She was seventy-eight years old, keen, intelligent, and simple in her ways of living.

In the fall of 1885, {Mr. Comstock} had trouble with his eyes and had {to put on} glasses. There were several cases of typhoid fever this autumn and the burden of seeing that they were properly cared fell on him because he was president of the "Student Guild," an organization to which students contributed small sums each year to cover expenses in case of sickness. There was no hospital {of any sort} in Ithaca {at that time, nor for} many years after.

{We} were very disappointed at having no children of our own and thought seriously of adopting a child. Had an attractive child for adoption appeared within our range of vision, we should certainly have taken it.

{We both} worked very hard and our only hours of rest came when we took long drives with our pony over the picturesque hill roads about Ithaca. These drives were usually taken on Saturdays. Sundays we {regularly} attended chapel twice; our reward that autumn lay in {having} Lyman Abbott, Edward Everett Hale, H. R. Haweis, {the famous English professor}, and Washington Gladden. {The year of} 1886 I did {much} social work for the Cornell Christian Association, despite my too liberal views. {I think it was Charles Thurber} who explained it by saying, "Mrs. Comstock may not be much of a Christian but she is great as an association—."

Mr. Comstock had definitely asked to have his salary raised. He had a long talk with President Adams about his ideals for his department {and the President} seemed interested but said he considered entomology as a part of zoology and thought it could be cared for by an instructor {in that subject}. This {was only one} instance illustrative of President Adams' lack of vision and of real interest in the scientific work of {the} University. {His horizon was bounded by Ann Arbor experiences and prejudices.} He was so different from President White in relation to science at Cornell that {everyone} felt discouraged, and our {wonderful} Professor [William A.] Anthony, head of the Physics Department, resigned. President Adams was a good man and an able {one}, but he had little imagination. However, he learned by experience and his troublous seven years as President of Cornell produced a crop of wisdom in him which the University of Wisconsin harvested later.

Mrs. [Simon] Gage had {been} interested in wood engraving {and, as she was} always practical, she had sought instruction in this art. She was receiving correspondence lessons from Mr. John P. Davis, teacher of wood engraving at Cooper {Institute} in New York. I read his letters and concluded that I would like to study with him. Accordingly, I made arrangements to go to New York soon after Thanksgiving.

In New York, Professor [W.C.] Russel met me at the train and took me to a boarding house in Washington Square where he and his daughters lived. This was convenient for my work at Cooper Union and gave me a delightful society at table. {I remember Lawrence Abbott was at our table.} The experience at Cooper Union was a wonderful one {for me}. Mr. Davis was a {remarkable man and so} lovable {as he was remarkable}. He was a gifted teacher and a true artist.

The room devoted to our engraving class {in Cooper Union} was long and high and {more or less} dingy, {like most work rooms in New York City}. It was well lighted by {plenty of} windows on one side; by an arrangement of sash shade the light came in above our heads and fell upon our work. The opposite wall was hung with well-selected specimens of wood engravings. We sat at one long table, under the windows and facing them; each of us {had before her} a block of boxwood {upon which she was} working, placed upon a leather cushion, filled with sand to insure solidity; each had her tools {at her right hand} and the study from which she was engraving placed against the wall in front of her; most of us worked with an engraver's lens, held high above the block by a standard; but some used spectacles that magnified.

In 1885 there were {perhaps} a dozen of us in the engraving class; and we came from the four corners of the United States. {I remember vividly the two charming girls from Maine who sat at my right. They were "dead" in earnest, and worked early and late to master their art. They were rather envied by some of the rest of us, because they had cosy rooms in the working-woman's apartment house, which was inaugurated and supervised by that gracious philanthropist, Grace Dodge. This house was fitted up with special rooms for cooking, so that those who wished could get their own meals.}

Our red-letter days were the three mornings of the week when {our teacher,} Mr. {John P.} Davis, {came to us}. It is a little difficult now after {these} many years to {describe just what he was to us, or how we adored} him. When we heard his step outside the door and saw {his face as he} came in with a breezy good morning and {an infectious} genial laugh, we {at once experienced an} elation {and our perplexities vanished in the sunshine of his presence.} He {told us plain truths} about our {inefficiency and lack of skill but told them so sweetly} and {so} tactfully that we felt honored rather than disgraced.

His criticism was {of the} constructive kind; {the criticism that resulted in creation rather than mere destruction}. He {took} us in turn, sat at the side of each, took the tool from the unskilled hand and cut {with it} wondrous lines upon the block. {He talked with us and} his conversation was {ever} sincere and earnest yet graced with flashes of {keen} humor. It was almost as much of an education to us as were his lessons upon the blocks.

He was wont to tell us that we must see, and feel, and live, before we could expect much of ourselves as artists. {One day} one of the pupils asked him in despair, after he had given her a lesson upon her block, "Oh, Mr. Davis! How shall I ever learn to cut a line so full of feeling as this?" He looked at her with a {doubtful}, puzzled expression {for a moment}, then his face lighted up as he {exclaimed}, "Read, Browning, my dear child, read Browning."

We knew that {he} had a studio in a mysterious Somewhere; and {at this studio met at stated intervals the} Society of American Wood Engravers, a coterie of masters whom we mentioned with bated breath. {Some of our number} had met a few of these demi-gods, Kingsley, King, and French, {and we looked upon these favored girls with an awe only equaled by that vouchsafed to the girl who had, in some mysterious manner, come into possession of one of Juengling's tools.}

Two years later, {through the grace of the master}, I was allowed to work for a time in this studio, this Elysian Field where our Olympians met {and disported themselves}.

The memory of the happy days {spent in that room of enchantment} remained throughout my life as an inspiration. My bungling hand forgot to blunder when the master stopped his own work to read us pages from *Saul* and *Paracelsus*, {or} to teach us art from Andrea del Sarto and Fra Lippo Lippi, or to sing to us {in sweet sympathetic voice}, passages from *The Creation* or *The Messiah*. With music in our ears, the spirit of Browning in our souls, and the Grace of God as exemplified in our teacher, in our hearts, small excuse had we {that} we did not also become masters.

That winter I spent about six weeks under Mr. Davis' instruction and then came home to practice what I had learned. I had always taken insects as the subjects of my lessons so that if the results were good, the engravings could be used in {the} textbook. In addition to my work on the engravings for the book, I did some line engraving for one of the professors in engineering.

The Spring of 1886, Mr. Comstock had more than thirty students in his courses in entomology. He was so busy teaching all day that he tried to write on the textbook in the evenings. He began to use the typewriter, thinking that it would not tire him so much as writing by hand; but, {as I recall}, the experiment did not last many months. In the spring he began a new phase of entomological instruction, {namely, that of} apiculture. He obtained three colonies of bees which he divided into five, and we were all {very much} interested in seeing them established in the area east of our {lot}.

{It was in the spring of} 1886 {that} the honorary society of Sigma Xi was formed at Cornell. There had been a feeling for some time that a society for the recognition of students in Science should be established, comparable to Phi Beta Kappa for students in Arts. The engineers were especially keen for such an organization. {Professor Orndorf and} one of the instructors {Mr.} Frank Van Vleck, were the prime mover{s} in the enterprise. Mr. Comstock represented zoology, as Dr. Wilder was opposed to any kind of Greek-letter society. Professor Henry S. Williams, who represented geology, was {of great} influence in forming the policies of the organization. At first it was thought that Sigma Xi might be limited to Cornell University. {But other} institutions were interested and chapters {now exist in all of} the leading universities in the United States. In December 1888, Mrs. S. H. Gage, {Hattie Grotecloss (Mrs. Charles David Marx), Mary Julia Snow, Professor of Botany of Smith College,} and I were elected the first women accorded this honor.

{In June} Mr. Comstock finished his term's work and went with {Mr. Van Vleet} to the Adirondack's for fishing. {This was done as a "life save" to give} him a rest {and change} before his summer teaching {began}. He became {enthusiastic and} expert in trout fishing and {derived both} pleasure and recreation {from it}.

{As} our friend, Charles H. Thurber graduated {that} June, I entertained his {father and mother} and his aunt and uncle, {Mr. and Mrs. William Aber}, during Commencement week. {Later}, Mr. Thurber was made private secretary to President Adams, and had a room with us during this summer. {Our chief memory of him that summer was his frequent need of "first-aid".} He learned to ride a high wheel, the only kind of a bicycle known then. {Rarely} a day passed for the first few weeks that he did not come home for bandages {and court-plaster}; but he was no quitter and rode on to final success. The next year {Mr. Thurber} was made Registrar and did a heroic work in starting the present card system, {with} dear old Dr. [William Dexter] Wilson's rather sketchy {statistics}.

The summer term of entomology kept {Mr. Comstock} very busy, but the wisdom of his judgement regarding the advantages of the summer season for the study of insect life became more {and more} apparent. The following {announcement} was the first formal {statement} concerning the summer course in entomology.

"Cornell University
Department of Entomology and General
Invertebrate Zoology

Summer Course of 1886

The summer course in Entomology and General Invertebrate Zoology of Cornell University, will begin Monday, June 21st, and continue ten weeks. The course will be given at the University and will comprise lectures, laboratory practice and field work.

The laboratory and field work will be arranged with reference to the needs and attainments of each student. After completing an elementary course in either general zoology or entomology the student may select some subject in systematic zoology, economic entomology, or insect anatomy for special investigation. It is planned to have the work of each student, as far as possible, an original investigation. The chief object of the course is to give training in methods of natural history work.

Members of this class will have free use of the library and all other privileges of students of the University. Tuition will be free to college graduates, and to undergraduates taking regular courses in this University; for all other persons the fee for the term will be $25.

Those desiring to join the class should make application before June 10th. Address:

Professor J. H. Comstock, Ithaca, N. Y."

{Mr. Comstock} attended the meeting of the A.A.A.S. at Buffalo in August, and we went to Otto for our vacation. Mr. G. K. Gilbert, who had attended the meeting, went with us. He {greatly} enjoyed our beautiful Cattaraugus hills, and my mother and father enjoyed {him}. During this vacation, {Mr. Comstock} and {my} father had glorious days hunting bee-trees, a diversion that took them over hill and dale, {now} beautiful in early autumn coloring, {and yet not sufficiently strenuous to be fatiguing}.

Cornell opened this fall with 300 freshmen, a {very} large class for any university at that time. This made about 750 students at Cornell, {all told, and we all felt encouraged. There was a change of courses and} Mr. Comstock had only 35 attending his lectures, but his laboratory was crowded {to its utmost limits}.

In October we rejoiced with Professor and Mrs. Gage in the birth of their son, Henry Phelps Gage. President and Mrs. White returned from Europe this autumn and we were all very happy to see them. George Burr[7] had been searching libraries in Europe for Mr. White and had discovered a valuable manuscript lost for 300 years. {We were} all {very} proud of his success. In November I went {back} to Cooper Union for further {work with} Mr. Davis with special reference to the engraving of insects.

Mr. Comstock had been so discouraged after his talk with President Adams about the future of his department that he concluded he had made a mistake in his profession and sent for catalogues of medical colleges. I felt that with my two resources as natural history artist and engraver, I could probably keep ourselves going while {Mr. Comstock} was studying. After reaching this conclusion we were surprised and delighted to learn that the trustees, {through the influence, presumably, of George R. Williams and Judge [Douglas] Boardman,} had raised Mr. Comstock's salary to $2500.

From New York, where I was studying, we went to Otto for Christmas and with the new year, 1887, returned to Ithaca full of enthusiasm for our work on the [entomology] textbook. {Mr. Comstock made it a rule to work nights at the laboratory, although after teaching all day he was too tired in the evening to do his best.} He also began experimenting with photographing my drawings and printing them on the box-wood block. {This assistance to engravers} was just coming into vogue {and it was of great use}, since the engraver had {the original drawing to look at while engraving. Mr. Comstock} soon became expert in this. He made a black box three feet long, just long enough to admit the printing frame at one end; by pointing the other end toward the sun he was able to get the direct rays and thus make a sharp print. {Mr. Comstock} was {quite} firm in refusing invitations for evenings. {I remember} he made an exception when my sorority, {K. A. O.[8]}, gave a faculty reception at Sage College, the first time a sorority had dared so much.

7. Footnote from the 1953 edition (p. 156): "George Lincoln Burr had been a student of history under President White and was one of the Comstocks' best friends. Burr stayed at Cornell and became Goldwin Smith Professor of History. —R.G.S."

8. Kappa Alpha Theta.

The girls made the cake at my house, while Mrs. [Estevan] Fuertes allowed Beth Boynton (Mrs. Frederick Coville), the use of her kitchen {in which} that capable young lady cooked a wash-boiler full of fowls and made a delectable chicken salad.

In February, a Farmers' Institute was held at Cornell. Mr. Comstock and I wrote letters and addressed circulars or invitations to help Professor [Isaac P.] Roberts [Director of the College of Agriculture]. The Institute was a great success. The chief speaker was my cousin, [former Congressman] Edwin Willits, {whose} address was so {excellent} that Professor Roberts had it printed at his own expense for {the future use of} his students. In 1885 Cousin Edwin was made President of the Michigan Agricultural College at Lansing, {a position} which he filled {most} successfully for four years when he resigned to become Assistant Secretary of Agriculture {under "Jerry" Rusk}.

Mr. Comstock made addresses at other [Farmers'] Institutes that winter. One was held at Oswego, which enabled him to visit Captain Turner again. {He} was also asked to edit the entomological section of the *American Naturalist* this year, a position which he filled for three years. This spring term of 1887 there were twenty attending the lectures in Entomology. The laboratory was full and there were seven taking apiculture. One of the experiences of this class was the cutting of the "bee-tree" and the transfer of the bees to a hive. Professor Goldwin Smith was visiting President White and both of them came over, put on veils, and inspected the tree and the hives. Mr. White came over afterwards and, protected by a veil, examined the {hives} with Mr. Comstock.

The social event of that spring was a reception given by Mrs. Ezra Cornell aided by her daughters, Mrs. [J. B.] Blair, and Miss Mary Cornell. {It was given} to celebrate her 76th birthday. Mrs. Cornell was a woman of great dignity and {it was a privilege} we all prized, this opportunity of meeting her.

Just before Commencement (1887) our whole community was {shocked and} grieved by the sudden death of Mrs. [Andrew D.] White. We had been present at a party at {President} White's only a few days before and Mrs. White had seemed as well {and as charming as ever. We could not realize that we would see her no more.} We were afraid that her loss would have an injurious effect upon Mr. White's health, {as he} was never robust. {The entire University community was plunged into sorrow.} Mrs. White was gentle, thoughtful, and considerate of others. These characteristics, added to her delicate beauty and gracious manner, had endeared her to everyone. I spent the day after her death at the house of mourning, giving what help I might. To add to the sorrow of this Commencement, {Miss Ida F.

Pearson}, one of our fairest young women students, {lost her footing and} fell into Cascadilla gorge and was killed.

In June {Mr. Comstock} took another vacation trout-fishing, {at Jock's Lake, near the Fulton Chain} in the Adirondacks. Charles Wing, later {and for many years} professor of Civil Engineering at Stanford University, was one of the party; and through this experience of camping and fishing together began a friendship {that still stands firm and true. Mr. Comstock returned,} brown and vigorous, and with a {great} basketful of trout which we shared with President White, the Adams' family, and other neighbors.

In August both Mr. [Grove Karl] Gilbert and John P. Davis came for a visit; the former for two or three days and the latter for two weeks. {I remember an incident that occurred} after luncheon the day of their arrival. We were on the piazza and some laborers were digging a ditch on the {grounds} below the house. Our bees did not like this intrusion and attacked the men, who protected themselves by throwing loose soil at them. Mr. Davis took Mr. Gilbert to view the fray and cried, "Geology versus Entomology! Which do you bet on?"

Mr. Davis gave me lessons during the mornings in engraving and in the afternoons, we went sketching. We were sketching on the shores of Beebe Lake on afternoon when he suddenly dropped his brushes, stood up under a great hemlock and sang, from Handel's Creation, "The Brook". {The setting, his excellent voice and his rendition of the song made it an experience for memory's treasure house.}

{Professor} George L. Burr was with us much this summer; he used to come to supper early enough to play tennis on our lawn court. Mary Roberts, the daughter of Professor [Isaac P.] Roberts, {was also a frequent visitor}, and Gertrude Van Dusen, then a cataloguer in the Library, {was with us often and} stayed with me while {Mr. Comstock} went to New York in August to attend the A.A.A.S.

{Mr. Comstock} had worked hard preparing a paper for this meeting while he was teaching, but he felt repaid through the interest and appreciation accorded it. C. V. Riley was at the meeting {and} in a {very} conciliatory mood; Mr. Comstock met him {in a similar attitude} and the hatchet was buried {once and for all}.

As soon as the term closed, the last of August, Mr. Comstock and Mr. [John] Stedman and I went to Maine to collect material for the course on invertebrates, which {Mr. Comstock} always gave preceding the course in entomology. We settled at Linekin on Booth Bay, {living at the home of Captain Blatchford}.

{Mr. Comstock and Mr. Stedman took possession of} a fish-house on the beach and turned it into a laboratory. {Here they kept their can of} alcohol for preserving specimens, {an object of} fascination for idlers of the village, {who stoutly maintained} they smelled it a mile away. Mr. Comstock was afraid that the temptation in this prohibition state might be too strong, so he hastened to put {various} animals to pickle in it. We had the use of {Captain Blatchford's} sail boats and row boats for our collecting. The sea fauna is {very} rich {along that coast and the} most interesting of any that we ever found {so far as the} quantity and variety of forms {are concerned}.

On our way back to Ithaca we made a visit at Wellesley College {to see Mary Roberts, who is teaching there. While there} we had the great pleasure of dining with Alice Freeman Palmer, who was President {of the college}.

When the term opened [in the autumn of 1887], Mark Slingerland entered as a freshman {with another boy from Cattaraugus County, Albert Bird.} Mark had been one of my pupils when I taught school in Otto and I had found him an exceedingly bright boy. I had encouraged him to come to college {when I heard that he had aspirations for a higher education}, and I had promised to find him some work {so he could} pay a part of his expenses. He {had studied geometry for entrance by himself and} passed the Cornell examination with a high grade. Clara Kerr, the daughter of a cousin of my mother, entered with the same class. She was with us much during her college course and was always a joy to us.

In October, our {dear} friend Gertrude Van Dusen, sailed for Europe for a two-years stay. Another event of this autumn was a visit from David Starr Jordan, then President of Indiana University and alumni trustee of Cornell. Also, Professor and Mrs. Benjamin Ide Wheeler came to live in the second house from ours.[9]

Mr. Comstock had taken a great interest in organizing the Experiment Station at Cornell. Mr. Austin Wadsworth was at that time President of the New York State Agricultural Society and was {ex officio} a trustee of Cornell. He was interested in our experiment station and came to Ithaca to look into the matter. President Adams invited Mr. Comstock to dine with him. A short time after this {Mr. Comstock} spoke at a Farmers' Institute at Albion, N. Y. and I went with him. There I met Mr. Wadsworth {for the first time}. I had {been interested in} reading about the Genesee Valley fox hunts and knew that Mr. Wadsworth was the owner of {the famous} fox hounds, {a fact which, for some occult reason}, had prejudiced me against him, and I was {quite} unprepared to find him such a {truly delightful} man. I felt

9. Footnote from the 1953 edition (p. 160): "Later, Dr. Jordan became President of Stanford University and Dr. Wheeler, President of the University of California. —R.G.S."

acquainted with him at once, and when he came to Ithaca later to stay several days to perfect the organization of the Experiment Station, we invited him to stay with us,—an invitation we should hardly have given had we known of the luxury in which he lived at home. He was a {charming} guest and entered into our simple life as naturally as if born to it. He was interested in my engravings.

{Although Mr. Comstock consistently tried to keep his evenings free for work, he sometimes made exception. We took our charming young cousin, Clara Kerr, to the Military hop, and the Junior Ball from which we returned at 4 A.M. Mr. Comstock felt the need of more exercise so he and H. E. Summers, then a graduate in entomology, were wont to box in the laboratory after the students had departed at five o'clock. It was the most intriguing event I ever witnessed; and I witnessed it as often as possible from the safe vantage of the top of the laboratory table. Summers was very tall and lank with very long arms and very agile. Mr. Comstock was a pigmy beside him but quick and active. His only chance of hitting Summers was to dodge under his hands and come up within the circle of his arms and hit him a rapid clip before the same long arms could retire far enough to retaliate. I used to be so weak from laughter after seeing one of these bouts that I had to be helped off the table.}

In March we both spoke before a Farmers Institute at Hornellsville. The happy side of the farm life had always appealed to me, and the conductor of the Institute, {Mr. Woodward of Batavia} asked me to give a cheerful message to the assembled women.

In March, the manuscript for half of the textbook, *An Introduction to Entomology*, was sent to the printer. Mr. Comstock was determined that my engravings should have the best possible printing. Therefore, he chose the DeVinne Press of New York, famous for {the way it printed} the engravings in magazines. The cost was greater than with other printers, {but Mr. Comstock was quite determined to have the best}. He had forty students in entomology this spring term and the laboratory was crowded, but he hoped to have the textbook before the end of the term. Vain hope!

The Hatch Bill establishing experiment stations at the Land-Grant Colleges passed Congress and was signed by the President [in 1887]. Professor [I. P.] Roberts was made Director of the Cornell Experiment Station which pleased us {much. There had been} delay in getting the bill through so that the funds were not made available until the last of April. Since this was too late for starting experiments {it was determined} to use the money for equipment. Mr. Comstock reaped the benefit of his dreams for his Department and asked for an Insectary,—a greenhouse where he could grow the plants on which insects feed and study the life histories and habits of the injurious species. Because he had his plan ready, he {was awarded} a goodly share of the funds, and by May {14th} the ground was staked off for the building just behind our home. The contract, providing for a two-story cottage with a glass house sixty feel long attached to it was let for $2500. The two rooms on the first floor, one on each side of the entrance hall, were to be used as offices; one room upstairs was for storage and the other for a student janitor. There were two divisions to the conservatory, one {which could} be used as a hot house and one which could be kept cold. There was a dark room for photography, and running water for aquaria; outside, there were several pits bricked up, for holding root cages with glass sides in which plants could be grown and which could be lifted out to observe the habits of insects infesting the roots. This was the first building of its kind in the world, and Mr. Comstock coined for it the name, "Insectary"; later he was asked to define the word for the *Century Dictionary*. Mr. Comstock was also given $400, for a microscope and money for two student assistants; I {informed} my mother: "Harry is the happiest entomologist in all America." As the appropriation had to be spent by Just 1st, the work on {the building} was hastened and {Mr. Comstock} watched every phase of its erection {with deep interest. However,} in June he tore himself away for a fishing trip in the Adirondacks {with Mr. Van Vleet.}

{George Tansey, a member of Delta Upsilon, with whom we had become acquainted early in his course, and who had been a frequent visitor at the house, graduated in June 1888. He was a remarkable young man, both in personality and in achievement. We had found him delightful socially and it was with genuine sorrow that we bade him good-bye. He cheerfully maintained that it was not "good-bye" and that we should keep alive the friendship so firmly established. I said, "I have heard such statements before, but when a young man gets out in the world of business we lose touch with him very soon." "You will find it is different with me," he answered, and so it proved. For the thirty-eight years since that June until his death we kept in closest touch. For many years after he went back to St. Louis to study and practice law, we received every week some token of his thoughtful friendship,—a book, a paper, a letter, a poem cut from some periodical,—always something interesting.}

{In the summer term [of 1888], this year, Mr. Comstock admitted several students who had failed in their work during the year and wished to "make up." He did this at President Adams' special request. They were a poor lot, and, although Mr. Comstock gave them personal attention and tried to help them, his efforts were futile. So, at the middle of the term he called them into his office and told them that even if they should do good work for the remainder of the term, their record was so low that they could not pass. Naturally they were disgusted. One of them went back in the laboratory and gave to one of the regular students his collection of insects. "Don't you want them yourself?" he asked, "No, if I ever see another bug I am going to kick it" said he. A row of headstones appeared in *The Cornellian* inscribed with "Entomology, Summer Term," and from that time on Mr. Comstock was never troubled with this kind of students.}

We moved into the insectary the first week in July [1888], as it was practically completed. {The Insectary} was {a matter} of great interest in our neighborhood. Mr. White was enthusiastic about it, but some looked {at it askance. I remember that} Professor Moses Coit Tyler, after looking through the building, said he hoped we would keep the windows closed and all of the bugs {corralled} inside. Mr. Comstock assured him that of all the insects that we {should} rear there, {there would not be one among them that would not rather die than try to} take a bite out of a professor; for of all creatures, insects were the most "notional" about their food. I found a north window in the Insectary office which gave me a {very} good light for my engravings and {it gave me a charming outlook into the woods with} a glimpse of the lake.

My father had rented his farm (the one on which I was born) for twenty years, and it had steadily deteriorated. He and mother concluded to return to it for one year and try to bring it back. Father was seventy years old and {very} well and strong. Mother was sixty-five and far from well, but she was so interested in {the change and} the experiment that she improved in health during the summer. It was a valuable experiment for it helped bring up the farm and it taught my ambitious parents that they were not so strong as they thought they were when it came to farm work.

{Mr. Comstock} and I enjoyed our vacation that {year very much}. We slept {at our cousin's, the McCutcheons, who lived} in the little homestead where it was the delight of my childhood to visit. We spent our days on the farm, and I renewed my acquaintance with the trees of the virgin forest still standing near the house, and with the birds, {for it was the haunt of} the hermit, the wood, and the Wilson thrushes, the teacher-bird, and many others. The view from the farm was magnificent,—rolling hills with their farmsteads and along the western horizon, blue Lake Erie, thirty miles away.

Cornell had an entering class of four hundred that fall [1888] and we were all greatly encouraged. {This year} George Burr came to live with us; he had not been well and needed the regularity of home life. We could not give him a room in the house, but he chose to room with the {boy} in the new Insectary {as he did not enjoy rooming alone.}

It was during the autumn that we went to Geneseo to attend a Farmers' Institute and were Mr. Wadsworth's guests at the beautiful old "Homestead," a great house filled with treasures collected by three generations {of cultured people} who had travelled far and wide {but who loved this country and their home. The atmosphere of the place appealed to the imagination, as well as to the spirit.} For thirty years we visited Homestead, at least once a year.

{On November 1st, the first part of the textbook, *An Introduction to Entomology*, was published. When finally, the book appeared, we both experienced the slump common to authors and artists at such times. We felt discouraged and thought the volume—}

The first part of the textbook *An Introduction to Entomology*[10] was published on November 1 [1888]. When the book appeared we, both felt the depression common to authors and artists at such times. We were almost discouraged, for the book did not seem to amount to much after all our labor. But when letters began to come from entomologists expressing their appreciation of it we felt more cheerful. {Mr. Comstock sold} fifteen copies in the first week and that seemed to augur well for the future.

---

10. Footnote from the 1953 edition (p. 162–63): "*An Introduction to Entomology*, by John Henry Comstock, with many original illustrations drawn and engraved by Anna Botsford Comstock, 1888. This book of 234 pages, bound in paper, treated of only eight of the twenty-five orders of insects that Professor Comstock described in his much later and more elaborate *An Introduction to Entomology* (1925). There was no second edition of the paper-covered book. Instead of completing it with a discussion of the remaining orders of insects, the Comstocks planned and in 1895 published an entirely new book, *A Manual for the Study of Insects*. —G.W.H."

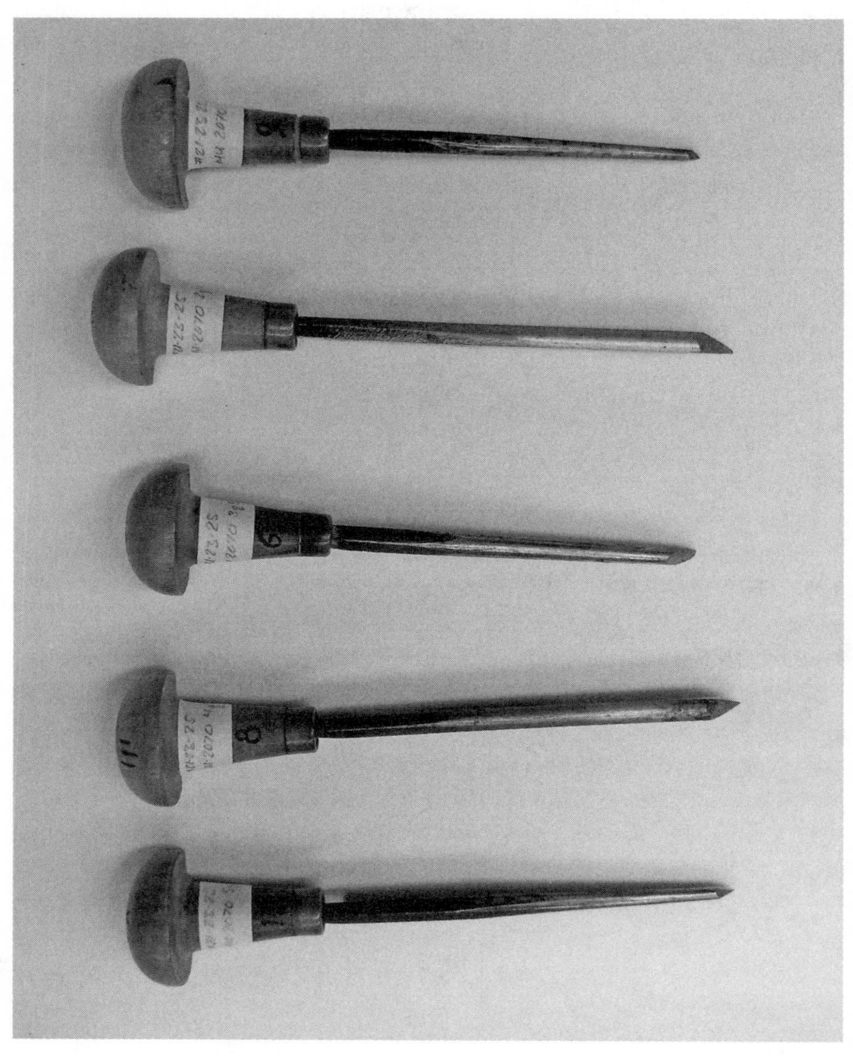

Anna Comstock’s wood-carving tools.

CHAPTER VIII

The Year 1888–1889; With a Winter in Germany

In Mrs. Comstock's manuscript, this chapter is slightly longer than twenty-seven pages, and a significant portion was culled for the 1953 edition of *The Comstocks of Cornell*. In that edition, this manuscript chapter is equivalent to Chapter 9 and is just over nine pages in length. A substantial portion of the Comstocks' trip abroad to Germany was removed from the book. In this current volume, the paragraphing and punctuation styles are Mrs. Comstock's.

For a long time, Mr. Comstock had struggled with the German language, in which so many treatises on zoology were written. He had {finally} concluded that a winter in Germany was necessary before he finished Part II of the textbook {[*An Introduction to Entomology*]}. We sailed on the {S. S. Waesland of the Red Star Line}, December 15, 1888.

{We left the house in care of Jennie Fleming who had a friend with her for the winter. Jennie was greatly beloved by us all; she had mastered her secretarial work so that she had been of great assistance to Mr. Comstock in preparing the manuscript for the press. Now we left her in charge of the sale of the book. Mark Slingerland, who was then a student assistant in the Insectary, was to help her and we were sure all would be well.}

We had a very pleasant voyage, {although some days of it were} rather cold because the Captain would not allow the ship to be heated for he had a cargo of cotton and was afraid of fire. There were only seven first-class passengers; {one of these was Mr. George Emerson, now for many years a lawyer in New York City. He was born and educated abroad but was a citizen of the United States and intended to study law after he visited his family in Munich. We came to like him very much and probably influenced him to study law in later years at Cornell.} We landed at Antwerp December 28th. We were greatly interested in the two-wheeled carts loaded with milk and produce, and {admired} the hard-working dogs which drew them. {We had an absurd experience through our inability to understand the French language. We wished to go to the opera the night after we arrived and asked our concierge how much we should pay for ordinary seats, and he said fifty cents. We found the place and tried to buy the ticket but were told the cheapest was $1.00. Mr. Comstock remained firm and by pantomime declared we must have two seats at 50-cents each. The two men gesticulated and talked like mad, but we stood there obdurate. Finally, one of them who went to consult some one, returned, and gave us our tickets. We were conducted up and up and up long winding stairs until we finally found ourselves in a dusty, spider-webby box. We had gone to the box-office and demanded tickets for 50-cents and here we were at the top of the theater with eight tiers of boxes directly below us. We were so far above the stage that the singers looked like puppets striding about, and to crown our embarrassment, we saw several of the Waesland's passengers in seats far below us, looking at us through their opera glasses.}

From Antwerp we went to Aix-la-Chapelle and visited Charlemagne's cathedral, thence to Cologne and paid awed tribute to the beauty of its cathedral. There we took a "Gepek" boat up the Rhine from St. Goar to Mainz. Although it was winter, the fields were green and the Rhine, with its high terraced banks and ancient castles, seemed to us a page from a fairy tale. From Mainz we went to Karlsruhe where our friend, Gertrude Van Dusen, was {established with two of our Cornell girl friends, Mary and Helen Corser.} We found accommodations {in their pension} and Mr. Comstock began German lessons with the daughter of our hostess, {Agnes Richard. Mr. Comstock's} early attempts {with German} were {often} amusing. He was trying to tell his teacher {something} about bees in German, and she began to laugh but would not explain why. {Later, she told Gertrude that he insisted} on calling bees "beine" instead of "bienen" and had given her a lecture on the habits of social and solitary *legs*.

In Karlsruhe we went to the theater and opera often. {There we saw "Carmen," for the first time, magnificently sung and acted. There, for the first time, we came in contact with} the privileged military of Germany. The front rows {at theater and concert} were reserved for the officers. Between acts they were wont to stand, face the audience, and inspect it {leisurely} through their opera glasses.

Gertrude Van Dusen went with us for the winter in Leipsic. We stopped at Heidelberg, as Mr. Comstock wished to pay his respects to Baron Osten-Sacken, a noted entomologist. We went on to Frankfort and thence to Eisenach, the home of Luther. We had both attended President White's lectures on the Reformation and every event in Luther's life was fresh in our minds. Our visit to the Castle Wartburg, where in seclusion for safety he translated the Bible, was full of interest to us. {It caps a hill 600 feet above the city and had been partially restored. The strange} old pictures, the majestic arched ceilings, the galleries, the dungeons, and the armor worn by the Crusaders {made us feel that we} were visiting the middle ages. Luther's desk and the spot on the wall where he threw his ink-bottle at the Devil made us feel that he had but recently departed. Some one told us that the ink spot was renewed as often as it became faded, but that took {nothing from its reality} to us.

In Leipsic we took rooms with an old peasant woman who had cooked for the nobility. We had a {very} pleasant sitting room in which our landlady served us bountiful meals. {In addition}, we had two bed rooms furnished with plethoric beds and short feather "decken" which we never learned to use with {any degree of} comfort. Mr. Comstock {at once} arranged for his University work under [Rudolph] Leuckart, the {celebrated} zoologist. The officials were {very} kind and the professors said things to him in German about his book which he guessed by the expression on their faces, were complimentary. In Leuckart's laboratory {he} met Professor Harry [Henry Sherring] Pratt, a graduate of Ann Arbor and who, for many years {now, has had the chair of} Zoology at Haverford. {Mr. Pratt was very kind to us and we enjoyed his society very much.}

There were about 4000 students in the University [of Leipsic] and apparently their ages were about those of the Cornell students. {However,} they looked very different from our students, {for most of them belonged to some college society,—Chor—, and each Chor had its own} special cap decorated with bright colors. {Many of the students had} faces {badly} scarred from cuts received in duels. {At the time, dueling was forbidden in Leipsic, but the students were in the habit of going to Halle for this diversion. They fought with two-edged swords and with body, eyes, and arms protected so that only the face was exposed.} Women were not admitted to the University {at that time}, but Professor Leuckart permitted Miss Van Dusen and myself to attend one of his lectures, asking only that we come early and depart late—before and after the regular students. Professor Leuckart came in like a shot after the class was assembled and talked like a Gatling gun, so rapidly did he eject his explosive words.

{We were greatly interest in the student life at the University. At that time the civil authorities had no control over the students. If a student was disorderly, or even if he committed murder, a policeman could only take his name and report him to the University authorities. If the offence was criminal, the University handed him back to the Courts, but if venial, the student was sent to the University prison where he was locked in a cell for a certain time. If the offender belonged to a Chor he hung his cap out of his cell window to tell his brothers of his plight, and they would hasten to visit him, bring him beer and food, and help him while away the time. The day we visited the prison the jailor was away, but his cheerful daughter, a girl in her teens, took the keys and showed us around. She took much pride in displaying two or three prisoners who pretended to be asleep.}

{We heard so much of the students excursions to Halle that we visited this city ourselves and were interested in its ruined castle and great medical school, a part of its venerable university. But we were most interested in the ancient people of Halle, the Halloran, of which there were then about 100 left. They were not originally Germans and had not intermarried with them. The men were stalwart and handsome and very much finer looking than the shorter Saxons, who seemed to us almost pygmies. The Halloran men wore handsome costumes much like that of George Washington—a three-sided hat, short pants, with buckles at the knees and on the low shoes. Each year, from time immemorial, they had been allowed to send a delegation of three men to the Emperor (or formerly the King) with presents of salt and sausage of their own manufacture.}

{We went to the theater or to the opera almost every night. We secured excellent seats for 35- or 40-cents and were delighted with the general excellence of the acting of the stock company. We saw Schiller's *William Tell* on Children's Night when there were at least 500 small boys in the audience. They became greatly excited when Tell shot the apple from his son's head. The plays for the children were delightful and we often went to see the fairy stories played. We also went to see the "Puppenfee", ("Fairy Doll"), played by the children themselves under the direction of the theater. The performance began at 6 o'clock and was over before 9. The ballets by the children were the prettiest I ever saw anywhere.}

{We attended the *probe concerts* every Wednesday. These were the final rehearsals for the subscription concerts and came at nine o'clock in the morning. The orchestra was led by Nikisch who one year later came to America to lead the Boston Symphony. After we had experienced nearly three hours of rapture in the hall, it was always a shock to come out and find the students of the Chor of blue caps, who always attended these rehearsals, ranged in rows in the open area in front of the Opera house, making observation on all of us as we descended the long flight of steps facing them. They looked us over and made amusing remarks about us while we were helpless to retaliate.}

{We attended a concert by Frau Emma Schumann. She was then about 70 years old. She had a fine, strong face; her white hair was combed down plainly and partially covered with a black lace cap with long lace tabs at the sides. She wore a black silk dress, Quaker-like in its plainness; her hands, wrinkled and old, gave no inkling of their wonderful strength or magical power. The house was packed, and the air was saturated with admiration and enthusiasm for the great pianist. She played her husband's compositions only; after each of which, the audience cheered and cheered, and called her back repeatedly; at the last the people mounted on the seats and waved their handkerchiefs, while many were weeping. It was a thrilling experience.}

{Every Friday noon we went to hear the Motet Choir, established by the elder Bach, and which went from church to church on Sundays, but on Friday noons, always sang in a church near the University. It was a boy choir of about seventy and I believe the music was the most heavenly that I have ever heard produced by human voices. Students hurrying from their classes filed into the transept where they stood facing the choir and the audience in rapt attention to the singing. Certain ones always came with their "soul pals" and during particularly beautiful passages they would turn their eyes upon each other languishingly. This sentimentality between boys, shown so regardless of spectators, was a new and interesting phase of masculinity to Miss Van Dusen and myself.}

{In a letter March 6, 1889, to the home folk, I give the following description of our brief glimpse of the King and Queen of Saxony while they were on one of their visits in Leipsic:}

> {"Although Germany is now an Empire ruled by an Emperor from Prussia, each of the German states has its own ruler, a king or a duke, who are the descendants of its own line of rulers and who still have the government of the state within certain limits. These kings maintain their own courts in their own countries, just as much as they did before the days of the Empire. The King of Saxony, for example, is much beloved by his people, and is a very good man. Saxony is not half the size of New York State, but it is a very important part of Germany because it is enormously wealthy. The rich people there are much richer than our rich people at home, if you except our millionaires. Saxony has over 3, 000,000 inhabitants and, before the Empire began, the taxes were light. But now the standing army costs a great deal. King Albert of Saxony has his court at Dresden, but he also has a palace here in Leipsic and comes up here every year for visits, over which the people make a great ado. He came up a week ago Monday and all the time he was here the green and white striped Saxon flags were flying from every important house in the city.}

{"We heard that the King and Queen were going to visit an Industrial School for servant girls near us so we kept watch for them. Friday morning, we saw the school building and an immense photograph establishment next to it, draped in flags, and a crowd waiting about the door. We got hastily into our wraps and rushed down the stairs to join the loyal crowd of servant girls, baggage men, market women, and chimney sweeps who were waiting to catch a glimpse of royalty. We were just in time. The royal party was going from the school to have their photographs taken in the gallery. First came some policemen who made the crowd stand back. Then came a magnificent officer with lovely gold braid looped on his shoulders and uniform. I called him immediately "The Beautiful." Then came some people who were accompanying the royal party and then the—Oh Bliss! The King and Queen, arm in arm. We stood on our republican tip toes and gazed with all our democratic eyes to see how Royalty looked. The King was a fine looking old gentleman with white burnsides (whiskers) and was dressed in uniform with a helmet on his head. He looked venerable and soldierly. The Queen was a pink-cheeked, rather stout woman, and was dressed very plainly; she wore a dark green dress, a plush dolman, and a bonnet with a lace face veil. She looked sweet-tempered and benignant. A feeble cheer went up from the rabble, which we were too engrossed to join; but we were quite scandalized over its feebleness and wished for a lively American crowd to teach them how to yell, when great people were passing by. After the monarchs disappeared in the atelier we went around and gazed at the carriage and turnouts. The carriages were coupes with modest little crowns painted on their panels. The horses were dark chestnut, very handsome in gold-plated harness with two rows of gold bells extending on each from the lower part of the collar back to the hook for the check rein. Oh!, but the footman and coachman. There was royalty for you! They were dressed in pale fawn-color coats reaching to their feet and trimmed with black and silver braid. Each wore a black "stovepipe" hat ornamented with a wide band of silver. The coachmen had on wide, black fur collars but the footmen had none. Pretty soon the policeman acted uneasy and scolded the children for pushing up so close. "The Beautiful" came out of the doorway of the atelier and gave orders to the policemen, the coachmen, and the footmen. Then he signaled a man to bring him a horse that had been standing there blanketed and saddled, and he put his beautiful foot into the beautiful stirrup, gave a jump and up he went, landing just right. He then pranced around on his horse until the Queen with one of her ladies came out and entered a carriage. The guests climbed into another—and then the King with his gentlemen got into a third. (The King's footman had a most remarkable hat with the sides rolled up and many green feathers on top of it.) Then came a "no count" carriage, which took the soldiers and policemen who accompanied the train. "The Beautiful" galloped on ahead and cleared the way. The bells jingled; the coachmen put on style, the footmen looked and acted as if they were each and every one kings, and off they went.}

{"We came back, highly delighted and edified. We were glad that our first King and Queen were such very respectable looking people; and we felt that we had done our duty to ourselves and the monarchy. Yes, we came back with our minds improved too, because we had found out that the grandeur of royalty consisted of the style and show which the servants put on. Royalty itself was just a nice lovely old couple, good enough to be anybody's 'Pa' and 'Ma'."}

{The German newspapers irritated us by ignoring American news unless it was a murder or some scandal which could be used slurringly. The policy of the German government was to make its people forget that there was such a place as America, to which they might emigrate; and in case it was remembered it must be considered a most undesirable country.}

{The rites at the railroad station interested us. The officials were so attentive that a mistake was practically impossible. The classes of cars irked us, as did also the waiting rooms for 1st, 2nd, 3d, and 4th class passengers in every station. When a train was ready to start the conductor, in blue cap, blew a little whistle. The station master, in a red cap, rang a bell, the engine tooted, and the train moved.}

{We experienced the preliminaries for leaving a city when Miss Van Dusen left us for a few days. She was ready to start, bag and baggage, packed in a hack, but the hackman refused to budge until she showed him her police permit, to live in the city of Leipsic, which was stowed away somewhere in her bags. It was a hectic ten minutes before we unearthed it, for it was almost train-time. We all felt we should like to get back to a country where even the most doubtful character might at least leave a city, without being obliged to satisfy the hackman as to his antecedents and mode of life.}

We left Leipsic in March and spent a week in Dresden {enjoying greatly the art galleries; we were filled with wonder as we visited the palace and beheld the crown jewels. Thence we} went to Berlin for a week. When we entered the art gallery in that city, the first thing that met our astonished eyes was a group of my own engravings of moths and butterflies in a case near the entrance. An exhibit made by the Society of American Engravers had been borrowed by the Berlin Art Gallery. {Naturally, I was very much delighted.}

Emperor William {was a young man and had only begun to exert his power as a ruler. We often saw him} out driving. We recognized him by the long white plumes on the hat of the footman who always sat in front on the high seat with the driver. As he passed, men on the street lifted their hats and he gave a military salute. One morning, rather early, we were walking "Unter den Linden" and the Emperor passed. Mr. Comstock lifted his hat; I waved my handkerchief, and the Kaiser Wilhelm saluted; when we discovered we were the only pedestrians in sight we "soaked up" all the glory. I asked President White after our return what he thought of the young Emperor and he answered: "He will either make or break the German Empire; only the future can reveal which." {The broken Empire is now the answer to that question.}

{We returned on the Red Star Line, S. S. 'Westernland', an excellent ship, with Captain Jamison in charge, a most admirable man in all ways.}

{Our reactions concerning} Germany {and its people} may be briefly stated: It is a great country, but the government is too paternal. The magnification of the military is exasperating to an American; often I had been obliged to step off a narrow sidewalk to let a haughty officer pass, and it 'went against my American grain.' We liked the subsidized theater and we adored the German music. We found the Germans themselves a kindly, childlike folk, with much charm. We thought the German women were much too servile to their lords and masters. {I remember how} our hostess reproved me because she {was actually shocked when} Mr. Comstock brought home the bundles after we had been shopping: "[You] should have carried the packages and not the Herr Professor." {The German women were wonderful housewives and seemed to knit interminable; we knew several who knit all the underwear for their families. Music was the only intellectual resource that they had in evidence. Many of them were good pianists and at concerts always a large number of women were following the scores.}

We were very happy {to be at} home again. {We loved our home, Cornell, Ithaca, and America more than ever before.} The sale of {the book[1]} was quite satisfactory and now we must finish it.

---

1. Included in the 1953 edition (p. 166): ". . . the first part of Mr. Comstock's *An Introduction to Entomology . . .*" —KSt.

{We found Mrs. Adams, wife of the President, quite ill and she died in June. She was a fine woman and a kind neighbor, and we grieved over her going.}

The summer term of 1889 in entomology was well attended and {Mr. Comstock}, as usual, enjoyed the summer teaching {very much}. He {felt that leading his pupils to see the} insects living in their natural environment {was most important}. He had now two students, Mr. [John Moore] Stedman in the laboratory and Mark Slingerland in the Insectary. {The latter} had come to college with no definite idea as to his future work. {He took the} lectures in invertebrate zoology given by Mr. Comstock and there learned {for the first time} that caterpillars changed to moths and butterflies; {this seemed so wonderful to him that he could scarcely sleep at night for thinking of it. I had known him from childhood, and as he had to earn his way, Mr. Comstock} had given him work in the Insectary, and soon discovered that {his} interest in entomology {was so great that he} would make a good assistant. {The story of his future growth to eminence none of us could have foretold then, and he least of all.}

{The summer was lost to me. I had had a recurrence of fever every summer since the long siege in 1884. This year it was more persistent and in August Mr. Comstock took me to the Sanitarium at Dansville, New York. Jennie Fleming came with me, as I was not ill enough for a trained nurse but too ill to be left alone. Jennie was a jewel there as in our home. She read aloud to me, but above all she entertained me with her talk. She went to the dining room for meals and her sense of humor and dramatic instincts were so keen that she always came back with an interesting story of some sort.}

{After the [summer] term closed Mr. Comstock came to Dansville for two weeks and while there had an attack of acute indigestion which made him, too, an invalid for several days. In October I was well enough to go to Otto for a time and did not return to Ithaca and work until November.}

This autumn (1889) Mr. Comstock began to write some entomological articles for the *New York Ledger*, {which had come under new management}. The price offered was generous, but that alone would not have made {Mr. Comstock} undertake this writing. He felt that the future of economic entomology lay in arousing and educating public opinion {to its importance}, and he believed that these articles in the *New York Ledger* would reach {a class} untouched by other more serious periodicals. {I remember the interest of his friends and} colleagues when they heard he was writing for the *New York Ledger*, "What are you writing?" they demanded. "My Story is called *The Barber's Washerwoman*, or *The Bloody Stocking*," {was his instant reply}.

I was tempted to illustrate his articles, but he thought {otherwise}. He wrote me at Otto: "There is no necessity for earning money; it is much more important that the book should be finished.[2] I do not intend to do any more outside work for remuneration after I get these articles done, till the book is finished. And if you feel as I do about it, you will not do an hour's work on anything else until the book is done. I think it will be well to make figures for my bulletins provided they will be of use later in the book, but not otherwise; and I hope you will not think of making a single figure for anything else. Our lives would be a good deal of a failure if one of us should break down before the book is done. It is to be *our book*; not a book projected by us and finished by some one else."

{This shows well his singleness of purpose in writing this text for students. We had been amazed at the number of copies which had been sold of the first half, and were, of course, encouraged.}

{I did not return to Ithaca until October as the doctors thought I should rest at Otto for a time.} As soon as I returned I began work on my engraving. {The Insectary was an ideal place to work and so near the house that I found it most convenient, although later I moved back to a studio connected with the laboratory.}

{Miss} Van Dusen came back [from Germany] to her work in the library and {it was a great pleasure to have her} with us often. {A niece was staying with Grandma Adams and we saw much of both of them.} The Gages moved into their new house on South Avenue, and were therefore permanent neighbors, to our great satisfaction. Thanksgiving we went with Professor [George L.] Burr to his home in Newark Valley. He had become an established member of our family {and lived with Mr. Comstock while I was at Dansville}. His father [Dr. William J. Burr] was the typical village doctor {of last century}, skillful and with a wide knowledge of the world in politics and science; a man on whom a large community depended for sympathy and advice and his professional service {in sickness}. His {dear little mother} was a {sweet} sensitive woman, very efficient in her home and community. Their home was a large, old-fashioned house full of {real} comfort and replete with good housekeeping. We had oysters, turkey, chicken pie, pumpkin and mince pies, and tapioca cream—{just the} bountiful Thanksgiving dinner {of an old-fashioned home.}

Mr. Comstock worked steadily on the book during the evenings. This made our social life {very} one-sided. I recall that Jack [John Wilson] Battin,[3]

---

2. Footnote at the bottom of the manuscript (p. 8–15): "*An Introduction to Entomology*, the second part.—G.W.H."

3. Footnote by editor Herrick in the manuscript (p. 8–16), and then heavily crossed out: "John Wilson Battin, '84–'86, '88–'90 Ph.D."

a young Quaker belonging to Delta Upsilon, invited me to attend the Military Ball in the armory and {Mr. Comstock} insisted that I go. My escort came for me in full dress, silk hat, white satin waistcoat and white kid gloves while I wore a crimson velvet evening dress with long train and carried the great bouquet of roses {he had sent}. We wondered what our Quaker grandfathers would {have thought} if they could have seen us and agreed that they would have turned over in their graves.

{George Emerson, in the Law School at Cornell, with his youngest brother, Edwin Emerson, Jr., in the College of Arts and Sciences, were frequent guests of our household. They were two very different types of men. George was of the stable, dependable, responsible kind while Edwin, almost a genius, of most interesting personality, was brilliant but erratic. He was a lovable boy, and even I who knew him so well could not have prophesied his pyrotechnic career. He became a newspaper man, a Rough Rider with Roosevelt in Cuba in the war with Spain, was arrested as a spy in Porto Rico [*sic*] and only saved by his assertion that he was German and could not speak or understand English; a revolutionist in Mexico; a newspaper correspondent in the Japanese-Russian war, where the Japanese held him prisoner and made him break wild horses for the army; and during the last war a subject for international bickerings in Germany and a terrible thorn in the side of Mr. Gerard, our Ambassador to Germany before we entered the war.}

{We} spent the Christmas holidays at Geneseo with Austin Wadsworth. {There were other interesting guests there as usual. I believe this was when we first met Miss Anne Miller of Geneva, an old friend of Mr. Wadsworth. She was in poor health then. Our friendship which ripened in later years, was then begun}. The winter of 1889–90 was spent largely at Otto. Mr. Comstock brought his writing there and I, my engraving. We returned to Ithaca for the Spring term. This Spring the Faculty held 'socials' every Saturday night in Barnes Hall, the new Christian Association building, which had been given by Mr. A. S. Barnes, {the} publisher. {We had come to the conclusion that} the University was growing so fast that we needed some regular informal social function to keep us acquainted {and hold us together}. Mrs. Gage and I {also} gave a {joint} reception to the young women in the graduating class and the Cornell graduates who had married {into} the Faculty. {Thirty of them came and we felt that it was a large affair concerned only with Cornell women.} There was also a Sigma Xi reception which was of importance to us as Mr. Comstock was president {that year}.

{In July we all were rather shocked to read in the papers that President Adams was married to Mrs. A. S. Barnes, the widow of the man who had given us Barnes Hall. A scant year seemed a short time to bury one wife and achieve another. But we were too loyal to him and to Grandma Adams to say what we felt.}

{It was later in that summer that President White spent an intimate evening with us and told us of his approaching marriage to Helen Magill, daughter of the president of Swarthmore College.}

I did some drawing and engraving for Professor Bailey for the *Experiment Station Bulletin*. I was also working hard on moths and butterflies for {Mr. Comstock's} book. I sent some proofs on to Mr. Davis for his criticism and was made very happy when he wrote me:

> "I can hardly believe you trembled when you enclosed me the proofs of your admirable work. To me they are a cause for wonderment and admiration. I notice an earnest study of Marsh (a great engraver) in their technique; and then you have the knowledge of your subject, and Harry keeps you right as to structure. These little insects seem to possess a superlative accuracy such as no mere engraver could give. Proud as I am to own you as my pupil I can but feel that in this department of our art you could be my teacher."

This year [1889–90] Mr. Comstock inaugurated a new plan of work. He found that after a day in teaching, he was too tired at night to do efficient writing on his textbook. Since his laboratory was filled with student's from 8 A.M. to 5 P.M., he had no time to write during the day. He therefore formed the habit of rising at 4 A.M. Preparations were made for him the night before so that all he had to do was to warm the café au lait and cook an egg. This took but a few minutes and he had three hours free to work when his mind was fresh and when there were no students around to interfere. {Of course} this mode of life meant going to bed early, and there is where most men would have failed, but not {Mr. Comstock}. The laws he made for himself were as those of the Medes and Persians. He retired at eight o'clock {punctually}, making {very} few exceptions. {If we chanced to have} a parlor full of callers {or guests}, he explained the situation if he felt well acquainted with company, otherwise he quietly stole away and {trusted to my tact} to explain. It was a heroic mode of life, but it accomplished {the} purpose. The manuscript for the textbook grew {most} encouragingly and the pace once set was easy to follow. But the old adage applied—"if a man gets the reputation of arising early he can be abed all day." As soon as the textbook was finished Mr. Comstock changed to the ordinary schedule of living, but for years {and years} people believed he still arose at 4 A.M. {It was his way of solving the problem for a professor of science who had to teach in a laboratory all day and who wished to be an investigator and writer as well. All these years} he had only one student assistant in the laboratory. It was in 1890 that his first full-time assistant was appointed. That year, Mark Slingerland was made assistant {in the Cornell Experiment Station} at a salary of $500 for the first year and $750 the next. It was also this year that Mr. Comstock's salary was raised to $3,000.

Slingerland did not help teach. Students were still the rule as laboratory helpers. After [John M.] Stedman graduated, Alexander McGillivray took his place. {He was deeply interested as a boy in insects and had collected, classified and studied them. He wanted only one thing at Cornell and that was to study entomology as a special student. It was through Mr. Comstock's influence that he finally completed his course and graduated from Cornell. He was a boy of beautiful character with gentle and winning ways, but he had a Scotch back-bone and was an excellent teacher—most exacting as to the student's attainments. No student could pass through his hands and not know the subjects taught in that laboratory. Later, he was for many years a professor in the Entomological Department at Cornell and was finally} called to the head of the Department of Entomology at the University of Illinois.

{The summer of 1890 was a busy one. The class for the summer term was of goodly size and we were both working hard on the textbook. In August, our friends, Mary Roberts and Albert Smith, were married and as professor and Mrs. Roberts were away, they were guests at our house until they moved into their own. Professor and Mrs. David Marx left Cornell for Wisconsin University that summer, much to the regret of us all.}

Among those who frequented our house was a young Russian, Alexis Babine. He had been in the University of Moscow but had become tired of the restrictions in Russia and having found in the library {of Moscow one of the} early catalogues of Cornell University which promised students manual employment for pay {while they studied}, he learned the carpenter's trade and came to Cornell. He arrived {twelve years after the catalogue was published} and found the plan of combining manual and mental labor had been abandoned {as a University enterprise. However, Eugene Schuyler had given Cornell a library of Russian books, but no one here could read Russian. Dr. A. D. White, who chanced to meet Mr. Babine, gave} him work in the University Library, cataloguing the Schuyler collections. {We found Mr. Babine very interesting and a man of high ideals and absolute integrity.} He was afterwards Librarian at Indiana University and then at Stanford University and later connected with the Library of Congress. He was caught in Russia during the last war and made his escape from the Soviets through the influences of the American Relief, for which he was interpreter. He came back to Ithaca and again found a position in the {Cornell} Library. He had written a history of the United States in Russian, having begun it at Cornell under Professor Moses Coit Tyler. This history was {accepted and} published under the Czar and has been republished by the Soviets, probably because it discusses the problems of democracy exemplified in the United States. Under the Czar's regime Mr. Babine received royalties on the book, but not under the Soviets.

{Mr.} C. V. Riley came this fall to look over the Insectary and to see Mr. Comstock's new methods for caring for insects {while studying their habits and also to examine the block system and the cases for the collections}. We invited him to tea and had a very pleasant visit. {Riley was certainly a forgiving person, to be so amiable after all the hard things Mr. Comstock had said to him}—just before he left he {was with me alone and} said, "Mrs. Comstock, it was better for Comstock that he came back here when he did for this is one of the best entomological positions in the country and a much happier one than the Washington position." I answered, "Yes, it was the best thing that ever happened to him {when he was forced out of Washington}."

Mrs. Adeline Prentiss started a day nursery in town but made it really a kindergarten. In those days Ithaca had a slum in the region of the [Cayuga] Inlet {and there was} poverty and misery {there as well as} vice. Mrs. Prentiss had each child provided with a little table, tablecloth, dishes, dish cloths, and {wiping} towels and with these the children were taught the proper way of setting table and washing dishes. Each had a bed about 2 feet long furnished with sheets, pillows, slips, and blankets and were taught how to make {beds} properly. Each child had a little washtub and board and was taught how to wash clothes. The enterprise was supported by private subscriptions and many of us in the Faculty were contributors for years.

In November I went to New York again for more lessons in Mr. Davis' studio. {Mr. Comstock} came to New York while I was there. He was called there as an expert witness in a lawsuit. A cargo of wheat had been injured by the weevil, and the owner sued the ship owners for damages, maintaining that the damage had been done while the cargo was enroute from Chicago to Buffalo. {I was very glad he had come, and we had delightful times together. It was helpful for me to be near Mr. Comstock when I was engraving insects for I often needed his advice and criticism.}

{Alas! Clouds were coming in the Adams' skies that threatened to shut out all the sunshine. Mrs. Adams, charming personally, brilliant mentally and with many other good qualities, was evincing a jealous disposition. She was especially jealous of dear, good, staunch Grandma Adams, and was making her very unhappy. She was also doing queer things, like calling up Mr. Henry Sage in the middle of the night to confide her troubles to him, of all men.

I felt that she was slightly demented, and I did all in my power to smooth things over and keep her calm. She suddenly made up her mind to go to New York and entreated me to go along. I could ill spare the time, but I went. The only comfort I got out of it was that Mr. Davis took me to the Grand Opera to hear Siegfried, and at his studio I met Emily Sartain, daughter of the eminent steel engraver.}

Soon afterward I returned, President White came over to talk to Mr. Comstock about David Starr Jordan's success as President of Indiana University. Senator and Mrs. [Leland] Stanford were his guests and had come to ask his advice in selecting a president for Stanford University. I think they hoped he would take the position himself {but he could not} consider it. I told him all I knew of Jordan and later he sent for me to come to his house and talk to the Stanfords, which I was very glad to do. Senator Stanford was a large man, florid, and with white beard and hair. He was keen and reticent. Mrs. Stanford was large, dark-complexioned, dark-eyed, and very dignified. I told them something of Jordan's breadth of vision as an educator and of his high standing as a scientist. They asked me about Mrs. Jordan and I {gave tribute} to her high ideals, excellent scholarship, and integrity. From Ithaca {they} went directly to Bloomington, Indiana, and invited Jordan to be the President of {this precious} university which they were founding as a memorial to their {dear young son, who had died before reaching manhood}. President White said to me afterwards, "You carried a high hand with Senator and Mrs. Stanford and you nominated Jordan for their president"—but this was his way of being pleasant.

In February [1891] Mr. Comstock was feeling very tired and miserable and finally {concluded to accept the invitation of Mr. and Mrs. Bennie [Benedict] Law and} go to Cuba for a rest and change. The long hours of hard work had resulted in an unhappy nervous condition and a rest was imperative. It was quite as imperative that I stay home and work, although I longed to go with him. {As a matter of fact}, I was {horribly} upset by {Mr. Comstock's} breakdown and worried over the outcome. None of my friends realized this, except my neighbor, Mrs. Benjamin Ide Wheeler, whose understanding and sympathy {that winter} filled my heart with love for her {which has never been dimmed or diminished.}

{A note} this winter from Dr. A. J. Lintner, {who was} New York State Entomologist, is among my treasured memories. We had {met} Dr. Lintner at the Farmers' Institutes and had come to know him. He was a man of great {dignity and very} reserved. When he heard of Mr. Comstock's ill-health he wrote to me a very sympathetic letter, full of solicitude for {Mr. Comstock's} health, and kind words of praise for the proof of a moth I had engraved and sent him.

{Mr. Comstock} came home April 7th much improved in health but still far from strong. Our good Dr. Winslow believed he did not get enough nourishment from his food and advised a cup of hot milk between meals. All that spring, one of my chief cares was to see that he had this {nourishment. He} told me, with an injured air, one day that what he needed most was sympathy but that I gave him {only} hot milk. This remark afforded {me good} evidence that I had kept my worry about him from his knowledge. I would not have dared to tell him how discouraged I was about his health. My mother visited me soon after {Mr. Comstock} returned and I found her in an even worse condition than my husband. I went to Otto for a few days rest when {Mother} went home. After I came back, we began to take our meals at the old Cornell farmhouse which had been moved to the corner of East Avenue and Forest Home Road {near the south end of Triphammer bridge and transformed} into a boarding house.

In May, President Jordan and two of his Stanford professors, [Joseph] Swain and [Oliver P.] Jenkins, visited us. Dr. Jordan asked Mr. Comstock to take the chair of entomology at Stanford at a salary of $4,000. But {Mr. Comstock} had built up one entomological department and he did not feel equal to establishing another. Finally, it was arranged that Mr. Comstock should go to Stanford for three successive winters and give the lectures with an instructor engaged to care for the laboratory the entire year. It pleased me {very much} when Dr. Jordan told me that Mrs. Stanford had asked that I come to Stanford.

In June, Gertrude Van Dusen and I accompanied {Mr. Comstock} on his fishing trip to the Adirondacks. We went by rail to Prospect, where we were met by team and taken 20 miles to Wilmurt. From there {"Ev" Evans}, a big Welshman {and a fine} driver, took us on a buckboard, drawn by great Percherons, for fifteen miles over rocks and stumps to Jock's Lake where there was a well-kept hotel, Forest Lodge, the headquarters of the Adirondack League Club. From here it was easy for {Mr. Comstock} to reach West Canada Creek, which was his favorite fishing ground. {Jock's Lake was one of the most beautiful in all the Adirondacks. Its high wooded shores gave one the feeling that it was the heart of the wilderness.} The last week of our stay, G. K. Gilbert joined us, and we all felt that it was an ideal vacation.

That summer there were 27 students in Entomology. They crowded the laboratories {for each student worked all day, studying insects and classifying them} except for the field days twice a week for collecting. Many were advanced students {which complicated the work} and made it more difficult for Mr. Comstock. {However}, the hot milk treatment had helped him {very much} and he stood the summer better than I had expected.

We had been {taking our meals at a} boarding house {during the summer, but I felt Mr. Comstock} was not getting the proper food, so although I could get no maid for a time, I threw engraving to the winds and became cook as well as housekeeper at Fall Creek Cottage. {At the end of the summer Bessie Markham came to help me with the house work. She was a most interesting and attractive girl and was working to help her sister Mary through Cornell. There were always interesting things going on in our house while Bessie lived with us. Her dramatic instinct and imagination and cleverness in telling a story cast a ruddy halo around daily life and gave us all the feeling that indeed our little world was a stage and we were all interested players. Later, Nettie Bovier came to help in the house work. She was a fine girl of strong character, unshakable loyalty and strict in integrity. She and Bessie worked well together, and my household ran on "ball bearings". These two have been our lifelong friends.}

In September Mr. Comstock and I spoke before a Farmers' Institute at Fredonia. {I do not remember Mr. Comstock's topic, but} mine was "Some Uses and Abuses of Education", and I wonder now what I found to say on that subject. From Fredonia we went to Otto for a little rest until college opened.

Our new library at Cornell was dedicated this fall [1891]. We were all so proud of it {although Gertrude criticized the Campanile, saying it looked like a freshly sharpened lead pencil. But} it seemed such a large building we could hardly imagine it full of books. We did not dream that we should live to see it overcrowded and {quite} inadequate.

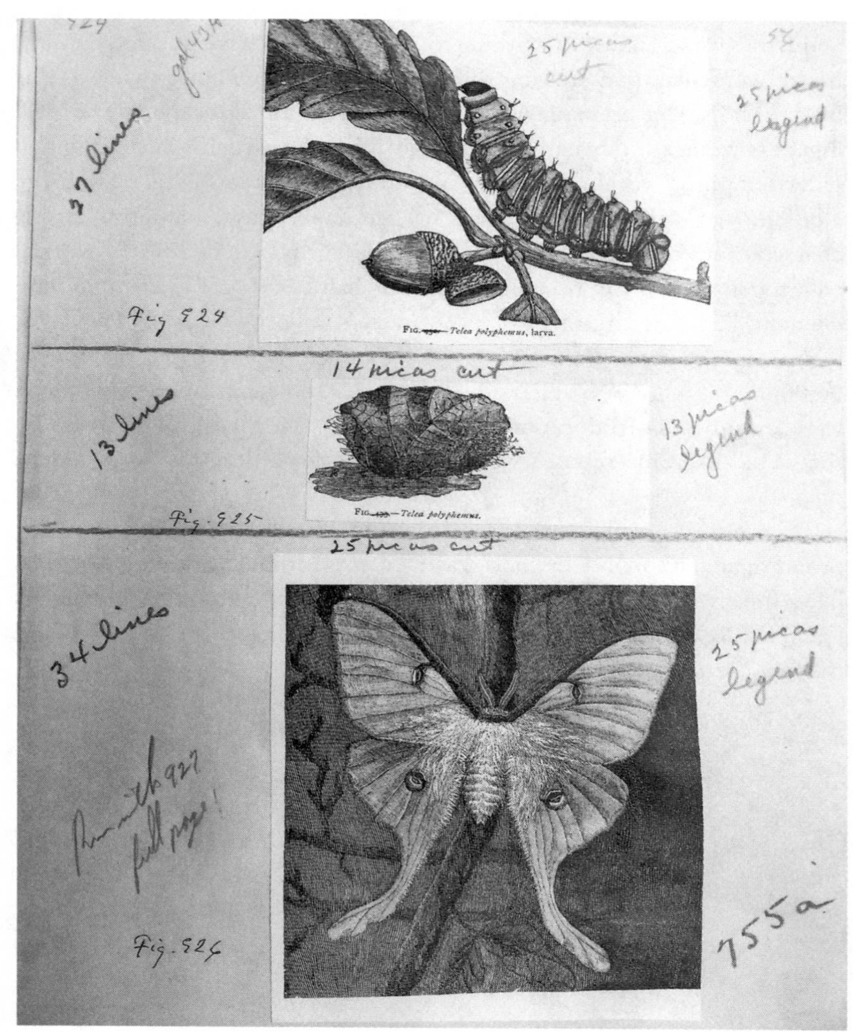

Publisher's proof of a page from *The Manual for the Study of Insects.*

Chapter IX

California and Stanford University

As with the previous manuscript chapter, this chapter has large sections that were not included in its equivalent Chapter 10 in the 1953 edition. The middle section of this manuscript chapter became an amalgamation of the manuscript chapter with pieces from four to five manuscript pages, reassembled to one page, for the original 1953 book. The alterations, which made sense in the mind of the Glenn Herrick et al., diminished Mrs. Comstock's voice. Here these omissions are returned, and the paragraph and punctuation style are Mrs. Comstock's.

We left Ithaca for Stanford University on December 23rd, 1891. Our cousin, Clara Kerr, having finished her course at Cornell, {concluded} to take a graduate course at Stanford and be with us during the winter. {We decided on the Northern Pacific route and although it was} midwinter we found the journey overland most interesting. When we crossed the timber lands of Wisconsin with their infrequent settlements we felt that the United States was indeed a new, virgin country. The snow-covered plains of North Dakota, dotted here and there with forlorn little farm houses, seemed to us desolate; and we pitied the horses and cattle pawing in the snow to find mouthfuls of frozen grass.

The Mountains of Montana and Idaho won our {enthusiastic} admiration; they were so glistening white in their snow-caps and so blue in their shadows. We learned to pronounce Helena properly. We had always called it He-le-na but now we found it was *Hel*-e-na and from the stories we heard about it from a man who lived in Butte, it seemed quite fitting to put the emphasis on *Hel* in pronouncing it. However, the man from Helena gave us quite as lurid a picture of Butte. {It was the} first {time we had come in contact with the vigorous loyalty of the denizens of far western cities who considered it pretty nearly a personal insult to hear a neighboring rival town praised.} We admired Tacoma with {its wide streets paved with planks and} beautiful Puget Sound stretching {his} feet. We were surprised to find it took eight hours to go from {Tacoma} to Portland, and {we} felt cheated because the mountain {peaks and} ranges were hidden in clouds. As we came south through California, we saw {much} evidence of placer mining, and in the Siskiyous we were stopped by six feet of snow. Eight {important little} wood engines {with their inverted bell-shaped smoke-stacks, puffed and grunted and shoveled and at last opened up the track. At six o'clock} we were moving through walls of shoveled snow ten feet high, {and at eight} we were looking out on palm trees and the air was as balmy as in May. When we arrived at Palo Alto we found it {had no depot}, simply a platform; a bus drawn by {western} ponies, took us through the Sphinx-guarded portals of the Stanford grounds and down the broad avenue, lined on each side with baby palms, and then the beautiful Quadrangle met our eager gaze.

{It was beautiful then, though it was only a section of the finished structure.} The pale yellow of the building stones with the red-tiled roofs were beautiful against the green hills and the mountains beyond. {The quadrangle with its arcades seemed like castles in Spain. From the first, there was a glamour of enchantment over it all,—the big circles filled with tropical plants, then very young; the glimpses of mountains through the arches and the arcades, the broad stretches of green near by, the gnarled oaks that dotted the distant fields, all made a noble and unique picture.}

Our destination was Encina Hall, {the boy's dormitory}, a handsome stone building a little distance from the "quad". {Encina was new and} "spick and span"; its handsome entrance, wide halls, and dignified dining-room {were impressive}.

I {had the unique experience of being} the only {female} in the {entire} establishment; even the servants were Japanese men. I was permitted to go to the dining-room for a late breakfast, but my other meals were served in my room by a Japanese servant, who bowed low as he entered and {continued} bowing, {until he had put my tray upon the table. Then, with many low bows, he backed out of the room as if I were royalty indeed.}

The manager of Encina {was a Mr. Adderson, a large man with much dignity and, to me, rather overwhelming presence, (the boys were not thus impressed). He} had been majordomo to Queen Liliuokalani in Honolulu, and he had manners equal to the position. {Mr. Adderson, arrayed in a dress suit, frequently knocked at my door, and entering with a courtly bow, would ask if everything was to my liking; I always assured him that it was.}

{Mr. Adderson believed in making rules that must be obeyed, and one rule was that, after a certain time in the morning, no one was admitted to the dining-room, and he stood guard to see that there was no infringement. He was quite as strict with the professors who were living in Encina as with students and they often had considerable difficulty in achieving breakfast.}

{Among the professors were Melville Anderson, one of Mr. Comstock's classmates who was at the head of the English Department at Stanford. One morning while I was at breakfast, Professor Anderson came in late, getting in while Mr. Adderson's attention was directed against some students who were doing something of which he disapproved. I asked in awed whisper: "How dared you?"

"What would he have done to me if he had caught me?"

"He would have roared at you." Then said Professor Anderson in his deepest bass voice and most impressively,

"I would have roared back at him."}

{The picture of the two big men standing, roaring at each other like infuriated bulls was beguiling.}

Our {large} sitting room had windows on the side through which we {gained} a view of a wide plain, very green from recent rains and {bordered by pines and eucalyptus trees. Beyond the plain rose the blue}-purple mountains, and through the windows {filtered sweetly} the songs of the meadow larks. Mrs. Stanford had sent {over a handsome pair of} large vases, which filled with flowers, {made the room very pretty}. One morning they were filled with narcissi, and because of the heavy fragrance I had set the vase on the window-ledge at night. The next morning, {vases and narcissi had disappeared}, although the window-sill was at least fifteen feet from the ground. Near the close of the term {the vases suddenly} reappeared on the window-ledge, with a note thanking me for the loan {of the vases} and assuring me that certain young ladies of Roble Hall (the girls' dormitory) had enjoyed the flowers {very much}. Our loss was not so important as that of {Ex-president [Benjamin]} Harrison, who {innocently} put on the window-ledge some bottles of {fine old} wine that Senator Stanford had sent him. {Ex-president Harrison} did not get even the bottles back, {and I doubt that he enjoyed this superlative bit of student impudence}.

The unmarried professors, and those who had not yet brought their families with them, lived in Encina. {Dr. John Stillman, Douglas Campbell,} Edwin Woodruff,[1] {Melville Anderson}, and Martin Sampson[2] were there, {and both altogether satisfied with} the rather limited variety of food provided in Encina. To relieve the monotony, I began making after-dinner coffee in our room and inviting those who wished to come and partake. {Often, we read a story afterwards to those who had the leisure to remain.}

The President's house was Escondite Cottage {in which Dr. Jordan took great interest}. He related mysterious stories of the Frenchman who built it after the plan of Le Petit Trianon, and who later absconded because of some financial irregularities, {the incident which suggested the name for the cottage. We spent man happy hours within the tapestried walls of Escondite with President and Mrs. Jordan. As a guard to} the gates of Escondite, President Jordan kept a chained monkey {who had an anti-feminine complex}. It was {most} exciting to pass through just beyond the reach of his chain while he was making {every} savage efforts to get me. He was quite amiable with men, but he hated women.

The Quad housed all the lecture rooms, laboratories and library and {I believe, that year,} the engineering {laboratories and workshops. The row of} Professors' houses were the only buildings near the Quadrangle and only a few of them were finished.

Electric lights at the dormitories and in the professors' houses also, {had regular habits, one of which was} going out promptly at 10:30, {no matter what was doing socially. Many were the dances and other social functions} we attended, {that were left in darkness at 10:30} and finished by the dim light of candles.

{One day I put a card} on the dormitory bulletin board stating that {I} would be at home Thursday evenings to the students of Encina who wished to call. Many of them came {from time to time, Lyman Brown, Cyrus Miller, Shirley Baker, Charley Field, and others. There were an interesting group of young men facing life joyously and competently. I never think of them without saying "Heaven bless them." Stanford University students were from the first musical and had a feeling for poetry. The Encina} boys improvised some charming concerts. I do not recall ever passing through the Quadrangle of a moonlight night that I did not hear, {somewhere} along the arcades, singing, accompanied by guitar or mandolin.

The professors called to Stanford from the Eastern colleges {soon} found that {they had a} different {variety of} students {to deal with from those to

1. From the 1953 edition (p. 175): ". . . who later became Dean of the Law School at Cornell . . ."
2. From the 1953 edition (p. 175): ". . . who became head of the English Department at Cornell."

which} they were accustomed. The outstanding difference was entire lack of respect or reverence for a professor as such. This was a disturbing {factor} to the uninitiated, and the success {or failure} of the professor depended upon the manner with which he met this attitude. Luckily, President Jordan, {to a large extent, called young men to the faculty at Stanford}. Perhaps {it was easier for them to measure the situation and, too, they} did not have so much dignity to hurt. Edward Holden, then at the head of the Lick Observatory, once said to me, "Oh, the youth of Jordan's faculty would make the gods pale with envy."

Mr. Comstock had {very} enthusiastic {and fine} students in all his classes. {His simple way of teaching}, not men or women or students, but just other human beings, {forefended trouble of any sort and won the whole-hearted} attention of his classes.

{As an offset to the lack of reverence the students evinced} for the untried professor, {was the chivalrous} devotion they gave to one who had gained their confidence. {In those days, each freshman selected a major professor with whom to specialize and with whom to take counsel regarding the studies to be pursued. Thus, the student body was divided into camps, so to speak, for each student was sure his or her own special major professor was the best in the university, or in the world, for that matter.}

I gave a lecture on wood engraving, as I had my work with me and plenty of illustrative material. It was my first University lecture and I was gratified at the interest in the art which I aroused. {In 1925 when we met Professor [Frederick G.] Krauss at the University of Hawaii, he told me that through all these years he had remembered the lecture and had always been interested in wood engraving.}

{Mr. Comstock took to riding a bicycle that winter for exercise. The high bicycle, which came so near ending the career of Bert Thurber in 1887, had finally given place to a lower machine easier to manage, but at that time, in 1892, there were not many in use either east or west. I, too, learned to ride a bicycle in the big comfortable Quad where there were soft flower-beds into which to tip over.}

Mr. Comstock addressed the fruit-growers of San Jose {and in this beautiful town we found old friends, the Washburns. Mrs. Washburn was sister of our dear friend Mrs. Henry Lord, and we had known her and her daughter Lucy and her son Arthur in Ithaca.} It was here that we experienced one of President Jordan's characteristic jokes. Dr. Jordan said to us: "The Leibs at San Jose expect you to visit them when Mr. Comstock goes to meet the fruit-growers." {I think Judge Leib was a trustee of Stanford then, but it may have been later.} Accordingly, we appeared on the Leibs' threshold and were made welcome but discovered afterward that they had not expected us nor had they sent us an invitation. We were {greatly} mortified and would have left at once, but they were good sports and insisted on our remaining. {We found Judge and Mrs. Leib delightful and the children charming.} On our return we reproached Dr. Jordan for doing such an outrageous thing, and he answered calmly, "You are all such nice people I thought you ought to know each other."

{We found opportunity} over the week-ends to visit {near-by} points of interest. We "did" San Francisco in a way that no tourist {will ever do it again. We visited Chinatown at midnight with a guide}, after going to the Chinese theater. We saw the gorgeous Joss-house, {their} restaurants where {pretty, Chinese} girl-slaves, {in gorgeous dress}, waited on the guests, and then we threaded our way, {stumbling up and down unexpected steps}, through opium dens. {The passages were so narrow our elbows touched the walls and so low our heads bumped. The small rooms were like fetid nests, bunk above bunk, wherein lay dazed men, some of them still smoking opium, others in the realms of the opium smoker's paradise, their dull eyes seeing naught of this world realities.}

{San Francisco was a shameless city in those days. Brothels, opium dens, and gambling houses had their place in the midst of the business section of the city. I remember how shocked I was then, while going from Stanford with my young cousin Clara Kerr and a young Professor, from a shopping street to Market, the main street in the city. We took a short cross street and found it lined with brothels, the denizens of which shouted at us as we passed. The chief business block of the city was infested with prostitutes who vaunted their trade under the camouflage of "masseuse."}

We had the pleasure of being entertained at luncheon by Adolphe Sutro at his home on Sutro Heights. {He was a handsome} dignified gentleman, {cultured}, genial and entertaining. {I remember} at the end of a course at luncheon he took a bit of bread, and {very cleverly} molded it into two little animals, which he presented to me as original works of art. He {drove} us over Sutro Height, {and showed us the} great possibilities of them as a park; and showed us the public baths, which he had given to the city. {He was a man of benevolence and broad vision and the city he loved will be eternally indebted to him.} He was a striking figure on the street, tall and handsome, and {always} wearing a brimmed light-gray hat {and top coat to match}.

{We left Stanford at the end of the semester and as soon as we reached Ithaca, Mr. Comstock took measures to have Mark Slingerland's salary raised to $1200. He showed promise of being a very valuable man in Economic Entomology and Mr. Comstock wished to keep him.}

{This spring [1892] we found the University restless and in more or less of a turmoil. President [Charles Kendall] Adams had not been wholly successful in his policies and had clashed with the trustees. His lack of appreciation of the sciences had made him unpopular with the science professors. However, the idiosyncrasies of his second wife probably brought on the crisis, and he resigned as President of Cornell in May (1892) and} Jacob Gould Schurman {was elected to the position. Dr. Schurman had filled the chair established by Henry Sage in Moral Philosophy and it was Mr. Sage who elected him. There were many who desired} Benjamin Ide Wheeler {instead, and for some time we were uncertain which would be elected}. Both have had long and successful careers as University Presidents. Both were eminent scholars before they were made executives and neither did much as a scholar afterwards. It remained for the early years of the 20th century {to hammer home the lesson that a} University President must be primarily an executive and that his presidential duties inevitably crowded out and starved his research work and his writing of books as well as his teaching.

{We were genuinely sorry for the trouble which had come to President Adams, especially to his mother, who was deeply grieved and hurt over her son's forced resignation. It was a pity that she did not live long enough to witness his success as President of Wisconsin University. His experience at Cornell had proved to be the making of him as presidential timber; and perhaps his brilliant, erratic wife had learned a lesson also.}

{Soon after our return we were guests at a dinner at President Schurman's at which was present also, Dr. [Charles A.] Briggs, the minister who had been tried for heresy. He was a quiet, gentle-mannered man and, as I recall, his sermon in the Chapel seemed very orthodox.}

In the autumn of 1892, my cousin, Glenn W. Herrick came to live with us during his college course and was a joy to all. He roomed in the Insectary with Professor Burr and cared for the greenhouses, and the furnace. I had named him when he was born so I felt, after his mother's death, as if he in a measure belonged to me, and I was {very} anxious that he should have a University education and {very} happy to have him a member of our household. His subsequent development into a scientist of note and a superb teacher has given us heartfelt joy and pride.

Mr. Davis had urged me to engrave a block for the Chicago Exposition and I had promised although I had begrudged the time. The subject was night moths, and as there were several I called it "A Moonlight Sonata."

In May (1893) I had the pleasure of taking my mother and father to Chicago to see the Exposition. It was a great occasion for them and for me. Of course, I hunted up the wood engraving exhibit and had the thrill of seeing my "Moonlight Sonata" and many of my moths and butterflies hung, with the work of the great masters. However, when it came to giving awards, the judges {threw me out} of the competition with the bank-note engravers, because of the specialization of my work. I thought this was fair enough. {While I was away I invited one of Mr. Comstock's students who had been a teacher at Northfield to stay at the house and be company for Mr. Comstock.

This began our friendship for Mary E. Hill which has brought us her loyal companionship during all the years since.}

At Commencement time (1893) we were so busy finishing the book that we took a cottage on the lake shore for two weeks to avoid the social distractions of the season.

{The summer school in entomology was not as large as usual owing to the Exposition, and we were both glad, for we were working at top speed to finish the book, the first part of which was in the printer's hands.}

The last of October Mr. Comstock was sent by the University to an Agricultural Congress at Chicago. Thus, he saw the Exposition and had a week away from teaching and labor on the book. {Vernon Kellogg was studying at Cornell this autumn and was staying with us. He had come to be regarded as a real member of our family. He was to go to Germany for study later in the year.}

The notable event of this year (1893) was the publication of the *Wilder Quarter Century Book*, a memorial to Dr. [Burt G.] Wilder for his twenty-five years of teaching at Cornell. Many of his old students contributed to it, but the burden of the publication fell on Mr. Gage and Mr. Comstock. It was a success in every way. Mr. Gage and {Mr. Comstock}, both, realized fully how much they owed to Dr. Wilder, especially in training and encouraging them as investigators. They were glad to make public acknowledgement of their gratitude.

The work on the book went slowly. There was so much teaching to do during the autumn that Mr. Comstock asked Dr. Jordan for a leave of absence for this winter with the recommendation that the instructor, Mr. W. G. Johnson, carry on the work. This gave him an opportunity to spend his three months of vacation writing. My Mother was in such poor health that I was called home, leaving Mr. Comstock and Glenn Herrick to board at Sage during my absence. {I took my engraving with me and my house helper, May Hart, but I did not bring her back, for she married a fine man of my native town and was a great blessing to him and to her step-children.}

Mr. Comstock's letters to me this winter were full of joy in his freedom from teaching, "It seemed so good to have practically only one thing to do." He spent two solid weeks working out the classification of the Geometridae,[3] the results of which are condensed to a page in the "Manual".[4]{Mr. Ephraim Felt, at first, and later Rufus Pettit, helped make the drawings of wings; both

---

3. Footnote from the 1953 edition (p. 178): "A family of moths, the larvae (caterpillars) of which are commonly known as "measuring worms." —G.W.H."

4. Ibid. (p. 178): "*A Manual for the Study of Insects*. —G.W.H."

were students at Cornell at that time.} Mr. Comstock put much enthusiasm in his work. He says: "The chapter on Lepidoptera,[5] I am sure, is going to be a delight to us. I believe in it more and more. I think it will put the study of the order on a firm basis at once and it is not going to be difficult." His prophesy has indeed come true, but lepidopterists in general were slow to adopt his classification. However, thanks to the "Manual" and the many students Mr. Comstock has trained, his classification is used everywhere now.

{The laboratory was furnished with two new cabinets, and Mr. McGillivray and Mr. Herrick worked all their spare time in arranging the collections of Lepidoptera in the cabinets, according to the new classification.}

{In January, (1893)[6] the new dairy building was dedicated. Thirty members of the Legislature came to the ceremonies and the banquet and promised state support for Agriculture at Cornell. Despite President White's influence, the Department of Agriculture was more, or less looked down upon by students and only a few chose it. When the appropriation was made for the Dairy Building, Professor Roberts insisted on giving it a site on the campus. It was a gem architecturally, Professor [Charles Francis Osborne] having been most successful in planning it. It was so beautiful that Benjamin Ide Wheeler called it "The Temple of Bos." It is now the north section of Goldwin Smith Hall.}

{On January 31st the faculty and trustees gave a surprise party to Mr. Henry Sage on his 80th birthday. Mr. Comstock wrote of it, "It was the most impressive ceremony I ever took part in. Mr. Sage's response was magnificent. Among the congratulatory letters was one from President Cleveland."}

{Although Mr. Comstock and Glenn Herrick were alone in the house they managed to have some social life nearly every evening before time for work and study. A fire was built in the living room and George Burr came and read aloud for a time. Mr. Comstock sat next to Professor Kate Edwards of Wellesley at Sage dining hall, where Mary Rogers became one of his new acquaintances. He often spent an hour with Gertrude Van Dusen and went with her to hear Alexander Salvini; it being the first time Mr. Comstock had seen a play in our new Lyceum which everyone thought so beautiful. There were also dinners with the Barrs[7] and other neighbors.}

5. Ibid. (p. 178): "An order of insects having their wings clothed with minute delicate scales. The order embraces the moths, butterflies, and skippers. —G.W.H"

6. Corrected to "1894" in the Comstock manuscript, however, this section was not included in the 1953 edition. —KSt.

7. Professor and Mrs. John Barr.

{There was always one peculiarity of my husband,—he regarded social functions coldly and regarded himself as unsocial, but he always managed to be present at interesting gatherings and always gathered new friends wherever he went.}

{Mr. Comstock} joined me in Otto in the spring vacation. As usual, when we returned to Ithaca, we found plenty of work to do. Mr. Comstock had to begin teaching immediately. He began again his early rising at 4 A.M. and working on the book. Part I of "The Introduction",[8,9] {which had already been published,} had been in use in his laboratory long enough now for him to realize more clearly what kind of a book was needed at that time in entomology. He, therefore, concluded to modify and simplify the book, in reality to write a new book, allowing Part I to stand by itself for the time being. This change did not affect my work, for the plan of illustration remained the same.

Wednesday afternoon my studio was open to visitors, and usually a goodly number came. I believe that many people, through a study of wood engravings by the masters which were there on exhibition, learned to appreciate pictures in black and white and to realize that the nuances of tone at the command of the wood engravers, could perfectly interpret color.

After the introduction of photographing on the block, the engraver had the opportunity to study the color of his original. Immediate success followed. Philip Gilbert Hamerton, in his *Graphic Arts*, says:

> "Tone, in wood cutting, depends upon the management of greys, and I cannot but heartily admire the almost unlimited ingenuity with which the Americans vary, not only the tone, but the very quality of these intermediates, getting not one gamut only but several, with the faculty of going from one to another on occasion, as if changing the stops of an organ. Some of their greys are pure and clear, others cloudy; others, like 'veils of thinnest lawn'; others, again, are semi-transparent, like a very light wash of body-color, and whatever may be their quality it is always surprising how steadily a delicate tone is maintained in them. As for texture, these engravers seem to be able to imitate anything that is set before them."

This study of color and texture on the part of our engravers had the inevitable result of changing them from engravers to artists. A group of them, led

---

8. From the 1953 edition (p. 178): ". . . *An Introduction to Entomology* published in 1888 . . ."

9. A crossed-out note in the Comstock manuscript was written by Herrick about this particular book: "Nothing more was ever done with this Part I." —KSt.

by Elbridge Kingsley, began engraving their own creations with remarkable results. Of the original engravings, my collection embraces the following: "New England Slums" and the "White Mountains" by Kingsley; an exquisite autumn hillside by my teacher John P. Davis; a superb picture of "The Pirate's Cave" by Victor Bernstrom; "Evening on the Wissahickon" by A.M. Lindsey; and his "Daughter Clara" by Frank French; the finest portrait of Lincoln, extant, engraved by Gustave Kruell from the death mask; an exquisite study of birches by Edith Cooper; "Winter Sunshine" by William B. Classon; a "Scene in France" by W. M. Aikman; and my own "Moonlight Sonata" and "Two Incarnations."

I was the third woman to be elected to the society of American Wood Engravers. My work from the first was original. I worked always with the insect before me. Undoubtedly, I would have made sorry business of interpreting the work of another. It was because my work was all original that I was elected to this body of {splendid} craftsmen and artists, an honor I have always greatly valued. The group of engravers, who became their own artists, was called "The Original Wood Engravers" and had for their sign, a woodpecker working on the side of a tree, {a conceit of Mr. Davis', I am sure}. My collection of wood engravings consists of proofs on Japanese paper signed by the engravers and given to me by them. There are about 300 proofs in the collections, which would be quite impossible to duplicate now. I took great pleasure in willing the whole collection to Cornell University.[10]

The summer school in entomology was especially successful this year. Students from other colleges, many of them graduates, had come to realize the character of the work in entomology at Cornell. The class of students in the summer school was, therefore, of a high order, a quality that contributed greatly to the satisfaction of all of us.

We gave our usual evening reception to the students this summer and as there were about thirty of them we had to put lanterns and rugs on the piazza to accommodate them. Mr. Comstock did his writing on the book in the early mornings and I worked on the engravings from 8 A.M. to 6 P.M. After supper we often went for bicycle rides for recreation and exercise.

In August Mr. Gilbert visited us and went with Mr. Comstock to the American Association for the Advancement of Science held in Rochester, where

---

10. Footnote from the 1953 edition (p. 182): "In addition to the two collections described above, Mrs. Comstock's gift to Cornell included the originals, or copies, of the hundreds of engravings she designed and executed to illustrate the books written by her husband and by herself. Both artists and scientists praise and value this group of engravings by Anna Botsford Comstock, because of their combination of scientific accuracy and of artistic values. All of these collections are now (1952) in the Treasure Room of the Cornell University Library. —R.G.S."

the latter gave a paper on "The Descent of the Lepidoptera; an application of the theory of natural selection to taxonomy."[11] Behind this address there was a long story. When Mr. Comstock wrote the Hymenoptera[12] for the *Standard Natural History* in 1884 he tried to classify the order by the wing venation and found it impracticable; but this subject continued to interest him and in 1887 he wrote for the *American Naturalist*; a review of a paper by Redtenbacker on "The homologies of the wing veins of insects." When he began to work on the Lepidoptera for the textbook, he found that chaos reigned in the classification of that interesting order. I remember how faithfully he worked week after week and month after month, before he began to see light. I was never so impressed with my husband's patience and dogged perseverance in search after truth, as while he was feeling his way in the dark in trying to find a logical and clear classification of the moths and butterflies by the record of their wing veins. He had blueprints, enlarged, of the wings of many species pinned upon the walls of his office at the laboratory. Finally, he found the thread to the labyrinth in the division of the order into *Jugatae* and *Frenatae*, based on the methods of holding the fore and hind wings together during flight. He was led to this by the study of Hepialus;[13] he decided that this was a primitive type which had retained the veins in the hind and fore wings in the same number and that the fewer veins in the hind wings of other forms, meant reduction and therefore evolution to a more specialized type.

{After he decided upon this, chaos was reduced to order, and the paper given at Rochester embodied his conclusions. I remember that those entomologists who listened to his address were too dazed by the overturn of the classification of the Lepidoptera to approve it.}

As the summer neared its end and we saw that we could not get the textbook finished this year, and as the need of money was always with us, Mr. Comstock wrote the article on "Insects" for Johnson's Encyclopedia; for which he received $150.00, while I made drawings for the Texas Experiment Station and received $50.00.[14]

I addressed several Farmers' Institutes this autumn in the Hudson Valley. Mr. Comstock was too busy to go but I enjoyed working with Mr. George Powell for I believed in his plan for helping the farmers. I was at the Millbrook

11. Footnote from the Comstock manuscript (p. 9–18) not included in the book: "A. D. Imms, a noted English entomologist, considers this work on wing venation to be 'one of the greatest advances ever made in the study of insects.' —G.W.H."

12. Footnote from 1953 edition (p. 179): "An order of insects with four clear, membranous wings, comprising bees, wasps, ants, and related forms. —G. H. W."

13. Footnote from 1953 edition (p. 180): "A genus of primitive, more generalized moths. —G.W.H."

14. In the 1953 edition, recorded as "$150.

Institute when the news came of Cleveland's election. Professor Benjamin Ide Wheeler, had taken the stump for Cleveland, although he was a Republican, and he was invited to be present at a dinner given to Cleveland in New York after the election. {At this function he} talked with a man who had been present at the interview between Cleveland and the Tammany leaders, and when Cleveland was asked to give pledges to repay Tammany for its support, he thought a moment and said: "I shall do what I can conscientiously for those who have worked hard for the party's success, but as to giving any promise or pledges I'll be damned if I will." {Richard Croker said, as they left the room, "Did you ever witness a scene like that?"}

Mr. Comstock had fifty students in Invertebrate Zoology this fall but not as many as usual in the laboratory and we both bent our energies to {completing the book}. I often worked nine hours a day on my engraving and {Mr. Comstock} put in three hours in the early morning and utilized every spare moment of the day.

{Mr. Davis came to give a lecture on wood engraving before the University and another lecture with an invited audience at Professor Gage's. He wished me to engrave a block for the Chicago Exposition and I promised but begrudged the time. The subject was night moths, and as there were several I called it "A Moonlight Sonata."

The last week in December 1893, we again journeyed overland. We were made happy by the warm welcome extended to us on every side at Stanford. There was a Faculty reception at President Jordan's soon after our arrival and I shall never forget that happy evening with our many friends. We found a place to live in a boarding house kept by Miss Dickinson. The food was much better than at Encina, but I missed our large, steam-heated rooms. The only means of warming our room was an oil stove, that somehow could not help giving off as much smell as heat. I never think of that room without shivering. Never in my whole life have I suffered so with the cold as during that winter.

Mr. Comstock was very happy in his work this winter, largely because Vernon Kellogg,[15] who had been studying with him at Cornell, came with him to Stanford. Kellogg was a graduate of Kansas and had registered for an advanced degree at Cornell. However, he could study only during periods when he could leave his work in Kansas and this winter of 1893 was one of those free periods.

---

15. Footnote from 1953 edition (p. 183): "On the recommendation of Professor J. H. Comstock, in 1894 V. L. Kellogg became head of Stanford University's Department of Entomology. He resigned in 1920 to become permanent secretary of the National Research Council. For many years Kellogg was associated with the Comstocks. —R.G.S."

We had come to regard him almost as a member of the family while he was at Cornell. His charming personality, his {delicious} sense of humor, his brilliance in conversation and his devotion to science made him an ideal companion. {He, too, rode a bicycle, so the two of them} went off together collecting often. I sometimes went with them when they did not go too far afield.

{I worked very steadily on my Exposition block and finished it.} I took with me to Stanford that year, a collection of proofs of engravings by members of the Society of American Wood Engravers. I showed them at Stanford and sold a goodly number. I also exhibited them at Sacramento at the invitation of the Women's Art Club of that city. This was for me a happy experience. The interest in the collection and in my lecture was most agreeable. The wife of the Governor gave a luncheon for me and showed me the Capitol and {the environs of} the city. When I left, the president of the society gave me a little box in which I found a beautiful gold brooch with a diamond in its center. When we passed through Sacramento on our way home, some charming ladies came to the train and brought me a tray of {exquisite} camellias to brighten our journey.

Quite different was my experience in San Francisco. I had shown some of the engravings at a meeting of the Women's Club of San Francisco and the members asked that I exhibit them to the students of the Academy of Art in that city, which I was glad to do. I stopped on my return from Sacramento and went up to the Academy to make arrangements. The man in charge told me it could not be done because there were no funds available for it. I told him that it was quite free and that I neither expected nor would accept any money for the exhibit; and I gave him the name of the prominent women who had asked me to display the engravings.

He looked at me doubtfully, spat copiously into a huge spittoon and called in another man as a witness to my assertion that this exhibit would cost the Institution nothing. {I was mad} by that time and determined to go ahead. I put up the exhibit alone, no one offering to help me; the [Grand] Mogul dropped in twice meanwhile, to tell me that there was no money for me in it. I smiled at him, thanked him and went on hanging the engravings, which was no small job. Then I sat down to await visitors. They soon came, at first a few, but the second day the room was full all day. That night the Grand Mogul came, apologized for his attitude, and excused it by saying people were always trying to beat the Academy. I said to him: "Well, now you know that there was someone who was glad to do something for the Academy without any compensation, and maybe there will be others." He thanked me and called the janitor to help take down the pictures. I departed triumphant.

{Mr. Comstock's mother and step-father moved that winter from Santa Rosa to Ocean View. Sister Margaret took some courses in English at Stanford and remained there the rest of the year.}

The experience that remains most clearly in my memory of that winter was the intimate acquaintance which I made with Irene Hardy; {she lived across the street with her adopted son, and took meals at our boarding house}. She was one of the most interesting persons that it had been my fortune to meet. She had been teacher of English in the Oakland High School {and a pupil of Edward Rowland Sill}. She had already made a reputation through her poems, when she was called to Stanford to instruct in English. She had exquisite literary tastes and her conversation was {always} of the sort that lifted thought to a {new and} higher plane. {I always came away} from a visit with her with a {conscious} spiritual glow and mental stimulation. "Anna Una," she always called me, and she wrote some sweet verses to me {later}. Her friendship {and companionship were to} enrich my life for many years {to come}.

In April, we returned to Ithaca, reluctantly leaving Stanford. We are both proud of Cornell, and glory in her achievements, but we loved Stanford with an intimate personal love that people rarely lavish upon institutions.

In the winter of 1894–5 the legislature appropriated $150, 000 to establish a veterinary college at Cornell [which opened in 1896]. This was a real triumph for our new President [Jacob G. Schurman, and for Dr. James Law,[16]] and we were all greatly pleased. As the winter passed the work on the textbook proceeded steadily. Mr. [Rufus] Pettit finished the drawings of the wings and Mr. [Alexander] McGillivray worked hard looking up names and authorities for nomenclature. Dr. A. C. White of the University Library, looked over the list of scientific names to correct the derivation and pronunciation of them. Great credit is due Dr. White for the care and time he spent in tracing the derivation of the more obscure names. The decision of Mr. Comstock to have the pronunciations given in each case made no end of work, but it has proved to be a most valuable asset of the book. {I find in} one of his letters the following: "This task we have in hand now is something over five hundred names to be divided into syllables, and the like of some of them neither the Latins nor the Greeks ever knew."

It was {quite} characteristic of Mr. Comstock's modesty that he should call his first textbook, which was really too advanced for college work in

16. Footnote from the 1953 edition (p. 185): "Dr. James Law, a member of Cornell's first faculty and first Dean of the New York State Veterinary College, had gained the respect of the New York State Legislature and of the New York State Agricultural Society, through his work with the farmers. —G.W.H."

those days, *An Introduction to the Study of Entomology*, a title which he has preserved in his last textbook published in 1924.[17] He planned to call the more elementary book *First Lessons in Entomology*. Later, when he saw how large the volume was to be, he concluded to call it, *A Manual for the Study of Insects*.

All this winter I was engraving steadily at Otto eight or nine hours a day. Getting proofs of the blocks was very exciting to us both. Finally, in March Mr. Comstock wrote me: "For the first time since I began work on this blessed book a job has proven less of a job than I expected it would. I reached work on the Tineids[18] Saturday night instead of Sunday as I expected to do. The work started off right from the word go. In fact, I got the Tineids on the run at once and I determined to keep them going as long as the mood lasted. It was done, and I think done well in forty hours and I had expected to devote a week to it."

Commenting on his classification of Lepidoptera he says: "As I look on the work I am not surprised that it has cost so much time. A greater shuffling of the families could hardly be possible. Still I have faith that my results will be accepted by the more scholarly entomologists. Of course, the amateurs will kick against the necessity of rearranging their collections."

Mr. Comstock's articles on "Evolution and Taxonomy", published in the *Wilder Quarter Century Book*, had made more of a ripple in the entomological pond than had his, "The Descent of the Lepidoptera" in the proceedings of the A. A. A. S.[19]

Mr. [H. G.] Dyar of Washington in the Canadian Entomologist said: "It is a valuable contribution to American Entomology and should be carefully read by all who wish to see a scientific classification take the place of a misty division in use in Lepidopterology." The entomological section of the Academy of Natural Sciences at Philadelphia gave a very interesting evening to the discussion of the wing vein classification of insects. Dr. Phillip Calvert [Professor of Entomology in the University of Pennsylvania] presented Mr. Comstock's paper. Dr. Howe said he considered the methods pointed out by Professor Comstock as the proper way to study. The question should always be asked of oneself when any new anatomical structure is found: "Why is it?"

Dr. Samuel Scudder probably did not understand or accept Mr. Comstock's views, but he wrote in a letter: "The man who confutes you will have to do a great deal of hard work."

---

17. In the 1953 edition (p. 186): "In 1925, . . ."

18. Footnote in the 1953 edition: "A group of very small moths, among which is the common clothes moth."

19. In the 1953 edition (p. 187): ". . . the *Proceedings of the American Association for the Advancement of Science*."

{The Weiner Entomologische Zeitung in noticing "Evolution and Taxonomy" says: "Nach eimer ansfuhrlichen Darstellund der Methods, nach welcer die Entwincklung (evolution) der Organe de Lebewesen—bei den Insecten besonders der Flugel—sur Aufstellung eines naturlichen Systems (Taxonomy) fuhrt, wird auf Grund dieser Methods ein neus Lepidoptern System auf gestellt. Es weicht in manchen Punkten Arbeit dem Lepidopterolgen ein besonderes Interesse, so wird sie doch die in derselben mit grossen Scharfrinne entwickelten aligemeiden phylogen-etischen Thatscacken und Schlusie fur jiden Systematiker eine wilmommen Lecture sein."[20]}

{Mr. Comstock was greatly pleased to receive an appropriation for $100.00 to purchase The Proceedings of the Entomological Society of London. That made $300.00 this year for books, which indicated the growth of the Department.}

{The last of March Mr. Comstock came to Otto for two weeks rest. One of the baffling hindrances in getting the book finished was the difficulty Mr. Comstock experienced in printing the blocks for me to engrave on account of the cloudy weather in Ithaca. Often a block was spoiled by delays and often the prints were poor, but as I always worked with the specimen before me this did not much matter. He writes: "I have had another time of it today to get the photograph for you. It was cloudy, and it took me two hours to make a print. I succeeded in getting an excellent one and after it was ready to send to you it turned black. I made some remarks to myself, being alone."}

{This spring term [1894] several excellent students registered for special advanced work. Mary Farrand Rogers, (Mrs. William T. Miller) determined to specialize in entomology. Elias J. Durand studied the specialization of insects for carrying pollen and Mark Slingerland went to Long Island to work on the cabbage maggot. The class this spring was the largest ever registered for the third term in entomology. Mr. Comstock writes: "I have had an awfully hard forenoon. The laboratory was full, and I worked thoroughly and carefully with each student. I worked with them every minute from breakfast until lunch."}

{As an instance of the general uses of our home I note that Mr. Comstock gave it over to my sorority for the initiation of a young lady of great charm, Miss Lillian Swift. In those days the sororities were obliged to have their

20. Translation by Benjamin Stevens, July 30, 2018: "The Viennese Entomology Journal, in noticing "Evolution and Taxonomy," wrote: After a detailed presentation of the methods according to which the development of the organs of living organisms (in the insects, especially the wings) leads to the establishment of a natural system, a new lepidopteran system is set up on the basis of these methods. While work on the lepidopteran gene is in some ways of particular interest, it will be a welcome lecture for any systematist in the same general phylogenetic action and conclusion developed in the large scale." —KSt.

initiations in private houses as Sage College would scarcely have afforded the privacy necessary to the rites of a secret society. Soon after I returned, and Mr. Comstock and Glenn Herrick had come home to board, they gave a reception to all the girls who had sat at their table at Sage and it was a gay occasion.}

{At Commencement, sixteen of the men who graduated in 1874 came back and they banqueted from 10 P. M. until 4 A.M. Mr. Comstock enjoyed the reunion very much.}

{The last of June Mr. Comstock went with L. O. Howard and C. H. Fernald to inspect work done for the extermination of the gypsy moth, which had begun its ravages in New England. He was not sanguine of success but said there was nothing else to do but fight the pest in every possible way.}

{The summer term in entomology brought many good students to Cornell this year; among them was Dr. Harry Pratt, who had been with us in Leipsic. There were many graduates and many experienced teachers. Mary E. Hill was in the class and lived with us that summer. She had been a teacher in Northfield after she graduated at Mt. Holyoke. We entertained the class one evening at the house very informally. It was a pleasure to associate with such people, quite aside from our common interest. Glenn Herrick had developed an attractive voice and was a great help at our reception.}

{As all of the boarding houses on the hill in Ithaca closed August 15th, three weeks before the closing of Mr. Comstock's summer term, some of his students were forced to leave or live a long way from the campus. This year we invited one of Mr. Comstock's favorite students, Miss Nannie Burke of North Carolina, to spend three weeks with us. She was a charming guest.}

{This summer, a group of us established the custom of having picnic suppers twice a week on the brink of Fall Creek Gorge on a point above the falls that gave us a view of the valley and lake. It was where the south end of the Stewart Avenue bridge is now anchored. It was a secluded spot, easily accessible and gave us a heavenly view. We name the place "Camp Camaraderie". There we would gather, each one knowing what his or her own contribution to the supper was to be.} {We built a camp fire, boiled our coffee, and after supper gathered around the fire, sang and read stories by candle-light, until the last sunset glow faded from the lake and sky. The regular members of this coterie were George Burr, Charles Hull, Mary Fowler, of the Library, who is known for her Petrarch Catalogues, and her sister Agnes, S. Henry Barraclough, now Sir Henry, of the University of Sidney, Australia, Mary Farrand Rogers, Glenn Herrick, Nannie Burke, Mary Nichols (now Cox), Julia Rogers, Florence Slater, Alexie Babine, William Miller and Alexander

Meiklejohn. The following song composed by Margaret Boynton, always ended our evening:}

{"Camp Camaraderie.
"On the lake there softly linger,
Gleams of sunset light,
Close the coming twilight hovers,
O'er our camp-fire bright.
Though to other lands we wander
Memory shall dwell
On the camp above Cayuga
Guarded by Cornell.
"In the gorge the rushing water
Croons a lullaby,
Distant chimes send us fair warning,
That the glad hours fly,
Gather closer, comrades, closer,
Friendship weaves a spell
In our camp above Cayuga,
Guarded by Cornell.
"Now the blaze is fading, dying
Still glows warm the heart,
Still we linger 'round the embers,
Loth are we to part.
Loth are we at last to murmur,
That sad word "farewell"
To our camp above Cayuga
Guarded by Cornell."}

{The work of the summer school interfered greatly with Mr. Comstock's writing while my household duties and social activities interfered with my engraving. We had a short vacation in Otto in September and then the fall term began.}

{Mr. Comstock organized his teaching time so as to give him as much freedom as possible. I too, found more time for engraving, and we actually saw the end of the task approaching.}

Stanford University was beginning to experience financial difficulties and in reply to Dr. Jordan's statement of conditions Mr. Comstock wrote: "I do not want to come to Stanford next winter unless it is best for the University, all things considered. As I am printing my textbook I shall be too cramped financially to make the trip this winter unless our expenses are paid. But if you can spare enough for our travelling and living expenses while there I shall be delighted to come. $750.00 will do this. I am unable to give any money to Stanford, but I shall be very glad to give my services for that term. Now, my dear friend, I want to do what you think is for the best interests of the University." Dr. Jordan answered immediately asking us to come. We left New York on December 28th, 1894, after having placed our book in the printer's hands.

{Vernon Kellogg had been appointed Associate Professor of Entomology at Stanford and our dear friend, Professor W. R. Dudley, had been made Professor of Botany, promotions which added to our happy anticipation for the winter. We found a room and board with Mrs. Morton, a very pleasant lady who was educating her children there. Professor Kellogg had his rooms near and ate with us. It was in his rooms and with his help that we made the index for the "Manual".}

{We were pretty sure that this would be our last winter at Stanford, for with Vernon Kellogg's appointment Mr. Comstock was not needed. He was very glad to have the department he started, carried on by one of the ablest of his students, and his dearly beloved friend as well. So we gave ourselves over to as many good times as possible. There were frequent and happy visits with our dear friends in Stanford University Faculty, especially with the Stillmans, the Marxes, the Branners and Elliotts. We also saw much of Professor Dudley.}

{We shall always remember a driving trip at a weekend with Kellogg and Dudley. On our drive over the mountain with Pescadero Beach as our objective, we stopped at a mountain inn where we found our bed reeking with dampness; we managed to sleep a little. The next night we were comfortable at the Beach and on Sunday we drove home by Spanish Town where there was a good hotel where we could stop for dinner; but when we arrived we found the hotel had burned. We were directed to the house of an Italian, as our only chance for dinner. It was an unpromising looking place, but we had to take our chances. The table had clean linen, but it was set in a shed near the kitchen. A very excellent soup was served by our hostess, then a baked fish, so delicious that we concluded to make our dinner of it, as it must be the *piece de resistance*. We were dumbfounded when roast turkey was served after this and we so full of fish. Then there was a salad, a delicious dessert and finally black coffee with cognac; red wine had been served with the meal. Professor Dudley, when he paid the bill, tried to express our appreciation, at which our host with a happy smile rejoined "You mak-a my heart gladda."}

{There were after fire after-effects from the damp bed. Both Mr. Comstock and I came down with the worst attack of la grippe that we had ever experienced. Kellogg escaped and came every day to cheer us. Well I remember our room at Mrs. Morton's. It was not very large, and as Mr. Morton had handsome old furniture our bed almost filled the room. We were glad of a wide bed for we both were very sick and needed room. As there was no chance to sit on a chair, Kellogg would perch on the footboard of our august bedstead and with his hat set rakishly askew (as there was no place to lay a hat down) he would tell us funny stories and a string of delightful nonsense that would make us laugh despite our misery.}

On our return to Ithaca, we found the "*Manual*" finished and we had all the happy excitement of reading letters about it and reviews, all of which were most satisfying to the author and engraver. However, our chief pleasure was the book itself; it was beautifully printed by the Trow Directory of New York and much pains had been taken in printing the engravings. It was a big, leisurely book, with ample spaces at the beginning and endings of chapters and with wide margins {to the pages}. The cover was pale gray, more beautiful than practical, with a silver spider web in one corner.

Mr. Comstock sent complimentary copies to teachers of entomology in the United States and within thirty days thirty institutions had adopted the *Manual* for a class text. This proved the wisdom of Mr. Comstock in publishing it himself. The publishers who had considered the matter concluded they could not afford to put the book on the market for less than $5.00 while we were able to sell it for $3.25. The publication of the Manual (1895) gave rise to the permanent establishment of the Comstock Publishing Company.[21] At the same time, Professor Gage wished to publish the fifth edition of his book on *The Microscope*. He wished to put it out in small editions and have it printed from the type so that he could rewrite it for each edition. Publishers did not look with favor on this scheme, so he and Mr. Comstock joined their projects under the name of the Comstock Publishing Company, and hired a student to fill the orders, pack and send the books. Neither member of the firm dreamed at that time that the Comstock Publishing Company would become a business house of considerable importance.

The *Manual for the Study of Insects* fulfilled all our dreams of its usefulness and more. It was the means of bringing knowledge of insects to the general

21. Footnote from the 1953 edition (p. 188): "The Comstock Publishing Company was tentatively established by J. H. Comstock and S. H. Gage in 1893 for the publication of the Wilder Quarter Century Book. A brief history of the Comstock Publishing Company, Inc. in the Comptroller's Report for 1934, pp. 197–198 (Cornell University Publication). —G.W.H."

public; it was placed in school libraries and public libraries, besides serving as a textbook in colleges and universities. At this writing, 1926, it is in its 17th edition; nearly 50,000 copies have been sold.

No sooner was the *Manual* fairly launched when we began work on *Insect Life*, a book of very different character, for the use of the teacher of children or the novice in reading facts from "Nature's Book." After a brief account of insect {physiology and methods} of the pond, the brook, the orchard, the forest, and the roadside. Then follows directions for making a collection and studying life-histories. I engraved may new illustrations, trying my hand for the first time in engraving landscapes. We had intended to publish this ourselves, but the Appletons heard of it and sent a very tactful and charming man, to get the book. Their offer to pay $1000 for my engravings decided us. We needed the money to help pay the cost of the *Manual*. *Insect Life* was published in 1897 and {now} after thirty years is still used by many teachers. The book was written at the very inception of the Nature Study movement at Cornell and was written with the needs of the teacher in mind. This year also, Mr. Comstock ad Mr. Kellogg wrote the *Elements of Insect Anatomy* for use in Entomological laboratories. This was {put out} by the Comstock Publishing Company.

Group photo of the Nature Study Department, 1899.

Chapter X

The Nature Study Movement at Cornell University; A Journey South to Study Spiders

Mrs. Comstock's manuscript Chapter X was divided to create both Chapter 11 and Chapter 12 of the 1953 edition. The editors of that edition omitted large sections of material that discussed Mrs. Comstock's early days in the nature study education movement. Comstock joined several key figures—Alice McCloskey, Julia Rogers, and Mary Rogers Miller—who were already involved in nature education initiatives at Cornell University with Liberty Hyde Bailey. Knowledge of McCloskey's, Rogers', and Miller's involvement was omitted from the 1953 publication as was an early publication effort by Mrs. Comstock, John Walton Spencer ("Uncle John"), and Martha Van Rensselaer to increase nature study education beyond New York State to the rest of the country. The paragraph and punctuation style are Mrs. Comstock's.

During the years 1891 to 1893 there was general agricultural depression in the East, and New York City found itself called upon, for the first time in history, to help people who flocked in from the rural districts in search of work. A conference was called by the philanthropists associated with the city charities to see what could be done about the matter. Mr. George T. Powell, who was director of Farmers' Institutes, was called in as an expert in a conference to consider the situation. Several at Cornell were invited to be present but I was the only one who was able to attend. At this conference (1895), a committee for the Promotion of Agriculture in New York State, was created with the following personnel: The Hon. Abraham S. Hewitt, Chairman, R. Fulton Cutting, Treasurer, and William H. Tolman, Secretary; William E. Dodge, Jacob Schiff, G. Howard Davidson, Howard Townsend, C. McNamee, Mrs. J. R. Lowell, Professor I. P. Roberts of Cornell, George T. Powell, and {myself}. Mr. Powell was retained as advisor. He maintained that poor farming was one of the reasons for agricultural depression, and that the only permanent remedy {would be} to interest the children of the rural districts in farming, and thus retain {the brains} on the farm instead of sending them to the city. He also declared that Nature Study was the means to use to interest the child in the farm.

The committee wished to {see for itself the} value of this idea of Nature Study, and Mr. R. Fulton Cutting gave the money {to initiate} Mr. Powell's {plan} in Westchester County, {where the results might be observed}. Mr. Powell undertook this task and asked me, with others, to help. The experiment was encouraging, and the committee was favorably impressed. Mr. Hewitt declared after the experiment in the Westchester schools, "This is too large a proposition for private responsibility; it must be carried on by the State." Accordingly, the committee arranged a conference with Senator Frederick Nixon, Chairman of the Ways and Means Committee of the New York legislature.

Mr. Nixon had always been deeply interested in the agriculture of the State, and in 1894 had established an extension course in horticulture from Cornell in his own county, Chautauqua. Mark Slingerland had conducted classes in entomology in this school. When Mr. Nixon, large, pink-cheeked and earnest, stood before us, and listened to the proposal for interesting children in the farm, he answered: "Gentlemen, I would rather have considered some plan for immediate help to the farmer, but if you believe this will help in the future, you shall have the financial support of the state. How do you plan to administer the money when appropriated?" Mr. Hewitt answered quickly and decidedly, "We have an efficient State College of Agriculture at Cornell, and the money should be given to it for this work." This decision was immediately ratified by the committee. As the outcome of these plans and decisions of the committee, and of Senator Nixon, the sum of $8,000 was given in 1896 by the State to the Cornell College of Agriculture for teaching Nature Study in the rural schools of the State.

{It was a great experience for me to attend these meetings and observe the reactions of these eminent men when this agricultural problem was put before them, a problem which was utterly foreign to their experience. They were keen to see the discouraging facts and open-minded in discussing remedies—open-minded, but by no means readily convinced that there was any panacea to be discovered. It was certainly a unique situation, this voluntary organization of men wise in their ways of city finances, ready and eager to give the benefit of their wisdom in helping the agriculture of their state.}

{The meeting of the committee were often held in Mr. Hewitt's study, a large room, very simple in its furnishings and very comfortable and homey in its atmosphere. Mr. Hewitt was a man of rich personality. His sincerity and good judgment were evidenced in his every word.}

{I was greatly impressed with Mr. R. Fulton Cutting, tall, aristocratic in every feature and gesture, and yet deeply concerned for the good of mankind. He of all the committee had the most imagination; he quietly met the expense of the experiment in the Westchester schools and was more deeply interested in the results than were the others.}

{Mr. Jacob H. Schiff was cordial and kindly, a person of power and ready to help. Mr. William E. Dodge, blond, dignified, and benign, was deeply in earnest and most eager for results. I shall always remember his beautiful hands, perfectly manicured,—so often inconsequent memories stay with us. Mrs. Josephine Lowell, was a woman of ability and charm; her interests lay in urban needs, although she was sympathetic with our efforts. It was a remarkable group and to its efforts to help the farmer we owe the Nature Study movement as carried on by Cornell, a movement that has affected the entire nation. I have always been grateful to the fates that, quite in their own mysterious way, made me a member of that committee for the promotion of Agriculture in New York State.}

To say that the Agricultural Faculty of Cornell was dismayed {when told the results}, is putting it lightly. Not one among them had even thought of the rural school curriculum since he left it as a boy. Professor Roberts, [Director of the College of Agriculture], suggested that, {first of all}, there should be a survey of the rural schools to find if any Nature Study was being taught. He {called upon} Mr. Powell, {Professor} J. G. Stone, Mr. John W. Spencer [a farmer] of Chautauqua, and {myself} to help in this work. We visited scores of public schools but found almost {no work of the sort} anywhere. As a result, Mr. Spencer {was called in to help} and leaflets for teachers were written by Professor L. H. Bailey, {Professor} George Cavanaugh, and {myself}. Later, Mr. Spencer started the Junior Naturalist Clubs, some years embracing 30,000 children in the schools of the State. Professor Roberts asked me to help by meeting the educators of the State and by presenting the idea at Teachers' Institutes. {The conductor of the Institutes, Mr. Isaac Stout, of the State Department of education at Albany, was very cordial and glad to have us work with him.}

{In history, it is an oft-repeated story that} the success of a movement for the betterment of the world has been dependent {on the genius of the man who first had it in charge}. It was therefore, fortunate for the Nature Study movement that in 1897, one year after the first appropriation was made for the work by the State, Professor Roberts placed the whole enterprise in the hands of Professor Liberty Hyde Bailey, at that time head of the Department of Horticulture in Cornell University. NO wiser step could have been taken. Professor Bailey is a great man from any standpoint, but perhaps his greatness is never more in evidence than in his genius for leadership. He had great vision concerning this Nature Study movement, and great faith, also. He was especially fitted for the work, for he had been born and had spent his childhood on a farm, and had, as gifts from birth, an innate love of nature {in all of its moods} and the poet's imagination {that gave him vision beyond his horizon}.

{. . . the idea at Teachers' Institutes. The conductor of the teachers' Institute, Mr. Isaac Stout, of the Department of Education, at Albany, was very cordial and glad to have us work with him. Thus, I began in a casual manner.[1]}

In the fall of 1894, {Mr. Comstock} bought of my father the farm on which I was born. He did this because the farm had rundown through poor tenants and the worry of it was too much for my father, in his old age. {Taking everything into consideration,} Mr. Comstock's career as farmer was one of the most remarkable achievements of his life. He knew little of farming and almost nothing of modern methods. But he went at the problem with his usual thoroughness. He sent for bulletins and purchased books and read them. He consulted Professor Roberts[2] {constantly,} and this friend and neighbor took as much interest in the affair as if Mr. Comstock had been his own son. When my father lived on the farm he kept forty cows, and young stock for replenishing, but now the farm was so depleted that the tenants could barely keep twenty cows. {Mr. Comstock} secured a neighbor, a young man, Edward Ryder, who was a cheese-maker and not a farmer, as foreman. Ryder, {however, was a young man of} intelligence and enterprise and cooperated enthusiastically in rehabilitating the farm. Mr. Comstock had to build a barn and a house and remodel {those that were there}. He built two silos which was considered foolhardy by the community. He planted forty acres to corn which was an unheard-of thing in that neighborhood. {The fields of corn in that region were small} when Mr. Comstock bought Hilltop farm; in ten years silos were built on all neighboring farms and the acreage of corn was trebled. Mr. Comstock was soon able to increase the herd to sixty cows in additions to the necessary teams and young stock.

The care of the farm added much to Mr. Comstock's activities, for he visited it {regularly} once a month; this meant leaving Ithaca, after the week of teaching, on Friday evening, spending that night in Buffalo, taking the train to Gowanda in the morning and then driving five miles over rough roads to

1. This paragraph begins with a sentence fragment that was crossed out in the Comstock manuscript. —KSt.

2. Added in the 1953 edition (p. 199): ". . . Director of the Cornell College of Agriculture . . ."

Hilltop farm, where he would work with the foreman on Saturday and Sunday mornings and return to Ithaca on the 11 p.m. train Sunday night. Nothing but his interest and enthusiasm could have sustained him through such effort.

The farm responded wonderfully to the new regime of a rotation of crops; miles of old fences were removed, and the fields made clear for cultivation. Modern machinery was bought and used. The herd was steadily improved and {thoroughbred} stock bought from time to time. The stables were kept clean and scales were introduced so that the milk of each cow could be weighed. The milkers wore white caps, trousers and coats while milking. People had told {Mr. Comstock} that he could never get help that would do this, but he found the help very interested in the records of the cows they milked, and entirely willing to wear the uniform.

{Mr. Comstock} kept the farm twenty years and it became one of the show places of the region. He lost two foremen meantime, as they bought farms of their own; and the third was on the farm when it was sold in 1916.

Mr. Comstock wrote Dr. David Starr Jordan in the winter of 1896–7, "Anybody can be a professor if he studies hard enough along one line, but it takes a man of wide knowledge of all the sciences to be a farmer."

{We spent the winter at Otto of course,—Miss Mary E. Hill was with us, a partial invalid at the time. The next year she taught natural sciences in the Burlingame School in Syracuse, so much had she recuperated. Mr. Comstock spent almost all his time on Hilltop planning the year's work with the foreman. He named all his thoroughbred cows after his special girl friends, so we had a Mary, Meg, Hilary, etc. in the herd.} After the text for the {*Insect Life*} was completed, Mr. Comstock did not undertake other writing for a time, since the farm took all his spare time and energy.

{The summer of 1897 I taught in the State Normal School at Chautauqua, and had for associates, Mary Rogers, one of Mr. Comstock's special students, also Mr. George T. Powell, who gave talks on agriculture and fruit-growing.}

{During my absence Mr. Comstock took his meals at Sage College and had with him at table George Burr and Margaret Schallenberger of Stanford University, who did much to relieve hi loneliness. He had also in the house with him, Seguya Hori, a Japanese, who was specializing in entomology and who was earning his way by helping around the house. He was of excellent character and lived with us during his entire college course and we all became genuinely attached to him.}

After the publication of the Manual, the entomological seminary adopted the name, "The Jugatae," and still carries on under this title. Mr. Comstock kept on with the wing-work at every possible spare moment and presented a paper on his further investigations before the Jugatae this summer. He had a large class and writes of one of his field excursions. "We had a glorious field day yesterday; it was a study of brook life in Fall Creek between Triphammer Falls and the swinging bridge. The class was very enthusiastic over it. I think every student got specimens of everything on the list that I made out before going." He continued to rise early, not later than 4 a.m. and to go to the laboratory to study and write.

On November 10, 1898 I received my appointment as Assistant Professor of Nature Study in Cornell University Extension. This was the first time a woman had been given the title of professor in Cornell University; and, although the title lapsed at the end of the period for which I was appointed, because of the objection of certain trustees to having women professors, yet the fact remains that President Schurman bestowed upon me this title. After the adverse decision of the Board of Trustees, I was appointed by President Schurman, Lecturer in Nature Study at the same salary, which I think was $1200.

This work of Nature Study propaganda had really engulfed my time by taking me hither and thither and upsetting my plans for drawing and engraving. So, it seemed best to let other things go and to take up the nature work in earnest. I was especially glad to do this {since Professor Roberts had put all this work} under the direction of L. H. Bailey, {than whom there was never a more helpful and inspiring man}.

{During the summer of 1899 and 1900 we had a Nature Study School at Ithaca.} We accepted only 100 pupils. Two days I gave them instruction in insect life, consisting of lectures, and field and laboratory work. Two days a week they were given plant study under Professor Bailey, and one day Professor Roberts gave them instruction in general agriculture. {The work was successful.} Glenn Herrick, who had taken postgraduate work at Cornell and Harvard and had been teaching two years in the State College of Mississippi, came {to help me}.

In February 1899, my father died of pneumonia. It was {a great shock to us and} a heart-breaking loss. He had been so much {to us both} that we did not know how to go on without him. We were grateful that we were with him and could give him every care. The funeral was on a blustering winter day with zero temperature, drifted roads and heavy skies; but just as we laid him away with the beautiful masonic rite of casting into the grave a twig of evergreen, the sun broke through the clouds and sent a comforting shaft of light over us and touched the snowy hills with a halo.

I did not return to Ithaca to work until late spring. {On June 8, 1899, we had a wedding at Fall Creek Cottage, Mary Rogers and William Miller. It was a pretty wedding with decorations of lemon lilies. William Miller assisted L. H. Bailey in writing *The Encyclopedia of Horticulture* and later, when Professor

Bailey was editor of *Country Life in America*, he worked on that journal and, later still, was editor of the *Garden Magazine*. Mary Rogers Miller assisted in writing the Nature Study leaflets for Cornell and also in the extension teaching. She was the author, later, of *The Brook Book*, a charming volume which she dedicated to Mr. Comstock.}

This year [1899][3] Mr. Comstock and J. G. Needham published a paper on "The Wings of Insects with Special Reference to the Taxonomic Value of the Characters Presented by Wings." Reprints of the article were sent to many entomologists abroad as well as in America.

The winter of 1899–1900 we went to California. Dr. Jordan wished Mr. Comstock to give some lectures on economic entomology to the Fruit Growers of California. {My mother went with us to visit near Los Angeles and spent some time with Mr. Comstock's mother and sister. Professor [Douglas H.] Campbell was travelling that winter and invited us to lie in his apartment, which made it delightful for us. Our housekeeper and cook was a Chinese called "Joe." He was a very interesting character, and did much that winter to initiate me into the mysteries of oriental thought and character. He had married a very pretty girl and he worshipped her. No matter how much work he had to do, he never asked her to help except in some trifling matter. We were to have a dinner party and at four o'clock I visited the kitchen and found Joe preparing dinner with one hand while holding the year-old baby with the other. I asked with some asperity, "Joe, where is your wife? If she cannot help get the dinner she can at least take care of the baby." Joe answered nonchalantly, "My wife, O she gone down to joss house to pray. She go every day at 4 o'clock. These women very superstitious." (The joss house was the middle section of their cabin in the back yard." On another occasion, Mr. Comstock, in opening a door, bowled over the baby and exclaimed; "You little heathen, did I hurt you?" Joe rebuked: "He no heathen Chinee; he native son California."}

{It was more like home that winter than any other at Stanford. We had family life and could entertain, and it was always a joy to live near Kellogg. We saw a great deal of our friends, especially Mr. and Mrs. Guido Marx. It was my first opportunity of visiting Gertrude in her home since her marriage. We returned to Ithaca in April as usual. Mr. Comstock had his regular teaching and of course the farm at Otto.}

3. Footnote inserted in 1953 edition (p. 193): "This year Mr. Comstock was given another assistant, William A. Riley, a graduate of DePauw University. After Mr. Riley had attained his Ph. D., he was made instructor and later Professor of Insect Parasitology. In 1918, Dr. Riley became chief of the Division of Entomology at the University of Minnesota. —G.W.H."

{During our stay} in California Mr. Comstock had trouble with a stoppage of the Eustachian tubes and was very miserable because of the roaring in his ears, and still more miserable with the prospect of deafness. As soon as his spring term's work was done he went to New York City under the care of Dr. Arthur B. Duel and went into the Manhattan Eye and Ear Hospital for an operation on his nose. After he had recovered from this Dr. Duel began to give electrical treatment to clear out the stoppage in the Eustachian tubes. All summer and during the autumn {he} went to New York {every week, or every other week}, for treatment by {this skillful physician} who {meanwhile} had become a personal friend.

The summer of 1900 we had another summer school in Nature Study {of 100 pupils} with the same plan of work as in the previous summer. {I had as assistant this year Franklin Sherman, who was for many years entomologist of North Carolina and later of South Carolina. For laboratory helper, I had Ross Marvin, who was working his way through the Department of Civil Engineering. He was a most efficient lad and had a very pleasing personality. While I have been writing this the news has come of his murder by an Esquimo [*sic*] while he was with Peary, during the successful expedition to the Pole,—a sad ending for a life so strong, ambitious and useful.}

The summer school was successful in every way but one, and that was,—our 100 pupils came from cities and the Cornell task was to reach the rural teachers. Therefore, this type of summer school was given up, and hence forward we did our teaching in the State Summer[4] Schools, which were attended by many rural teachers.

{This year Mr. Comstock had another assistant in his laboratory, William A. Riley, a graduate from Depauw University who had come to Cornell to study for his Ph. D. He was in poor health at first but steadily grew stronger and became a very able teacher and a great help to Mr. Comstock; after he had attained his Doctor's degree, he was made instructor and later Assistant Professor of Entomology.}

{This year, 1900, Mr. Comstock was given his first instructor, Alexander McGillivray, who had been a laboratory assistant while working for his Bachelor's and Master's degrees and now was given a regular appointment as instructor. When we went to Otto in the fall of 1900 we took with us as guests Charles H. Hull and William A. Riley. They were both interested in Mr. Comstock's experiment in farming, and it was a pleasure to show to them the beautiful Hilltop Farm and to have them in the Otto home.}

4. In the 1953 edition (p. 193): ". . . State *Normal* Schools . . ."

{Three years before, Mr. G. K. Gilbert, whom we always called "Charlemagne," had confided to us that he did not know what to do with his eldest son, Archibald, who did not seem interested in school or in anything else worth while. After talking matters over, he concluded to put him on our farm and let him support himself for a time at $8.00 a month. I found him a truly interesting lad; we had several long conferences during the year, and he confided to me that he thought it was silly not to prepare one's self for professional work and that he would like to be a civil engineer. His father had small faith in his son's ability to stick to work but I took him to Ithaca and became responsible for him. After completing his preparatory work, he entered Cornell and would have graduated in 1903 except that he became ill. He expected to come back to finish but was given work in the U. S. Reclamation Division where he made an excellent record. He did all the overseeing of the work on the Salmon River Dam and became a successful engineer.}

During the autumn of 1900 I {did much} lecturing at teacher's institutes about the [New York] state. Mr. Comstock was working {along different lines of investigation}, although his teaching required most of his time and strength. He wrote a leaflet on spiders for teachers published in our Nature Study series.[5] He had a {definite} plan that when he {should} revise *The Manual for the Study of Insects* he would take out the chapter on spiders[6] and publish it separately.

{We were very busy socially at Ithaca. The Schurmans entertained a great deal and we were often invited there. They were charming hosts, and there probably was never a more successful college president's wife than Mrs. Schurman. She was beautiful and sensible and enjoyed entertaining. She once said to me, "if I did not enjoy my own parties I do not see how other people could enjoy them."}

I lectured before the Teachers' College at Columbia this year and in many other places. The winter course in agriculture for {boys and girls} of the farm was established this winter {on a firm basis}, an important step forward. I gave a course on the Farm Library in which I tried to inculcate a love for books of Natural History and of United States history and for simple poetry. {I was also helping} Professor Filibert Roth, who was writing for our use a "First Book of Forestry," by reading the chapters as he wrote them. I also induced Professor George F. Atkinson, my neighbor and classmate, to

---

5. In the 1953 edition (p. 193): "... *Cornell Nature Study Leaflets*."

6. Footnote in the 1953 edition (p. 194): "This decision led to the publication of *The Spider Book* in 1912. —R.G.S."

write a book on botany for Nature Study. His "First Lessons in Plant Life" was the result; it is a charming book and {at the same time} scientific.

{Mr. Comstock was working on a paper on "The Skeleton of the Head of the Grasshopper" with one of his Japanese students, Mr. Koch.} He also had in his laboratory a student sent by Professor Aldrich of Idaho State College, Mr. Bayard Simpson, who later received an appointment in South Africa, did excellent work and, alas, died there. Simpson was a giant with a soft voice, gentle manners and shy disposition. I sought some subject for conversation when he called upon me and asked him what he had enjoyed most while in high school. I was nearly bowled over, {mentally}, when he bashfully murmured, "fighting."

As soon as the winter short course was finished I went to New York to Dr. Duel for an operation on my nose and tonsils. I was at the Manhattan Eye and Ear Hospital. It was a new experience to me. I was made ready two hours before being taken to the operating room and amused myself by reading Omar Khayyam. I was nervous and a little scared, but I found that passage, "This what you are today, what yesterday you were; tomorrow you shall not be less," reassuring. Omar must have lingered in my mind for when I came out from the effects of the ether and saw Dr. Duel bending over me with smears of blood on his white operating coat I murmured: "Hello, Angel of the Darker Drink." "A case of mistaken identity," answered the doctor, and I again relapsed into unconsciousness.

Professor Gage was working in the city at that time, and he came to see me every day, and many other friends came, among them Mr. Austin Wadsworth. After a week I went to the home of our friend, Mary Nichols Cox, [who had been awarded a Ph.D. at Cornell], who was living in New York at that time.

I returned home April 11, "revised and expurgated," and found my family glad to see me. I also found that my office had been moved to the second floor of the Insectary. I was glad of the change, for it was much more convenient to be near the house.

We were much interested in the new edition of "Insect Life" published this spring. Six colored plates of moths and butterflies had been added to it. With this addition the book remains as it was written in 1897 and the sales are still {considerable}.

This year (1901[7]), through Mr. John Spencer and myself, Miss Martha Van Rensselaer of Randolph, N. Y. was brought in to the Cornell Extension work with special reference to giving aid to the farm women. She had not lived on

7. 1953 edition (p. 195) indicates the year as 1900. —KSt.

a farm, but she had been Commissioner of schools in Cattaraugus County for two terms. She had been most efficient in her care of the rural schools and had had much experience in visiting farm homes. She was a young woman of broad sympathy and understanding and with great capacity for work. The story of how she developed the College of Home Economics from a very small beginning is a story by itself {as wonderful as true}.

In May our {dear} friend Mrs. Hiram Corson died. I spent days with the bereaved family {and was with Professor Corson often thereafter; he} had been the teacher and inspiration of both {Mr. Comstock} and myself when we were students and led us to the appreciation {and love of the best in} English literature. {He} was a man of wide culture, {an excellent mathematician}, and a thorough scholar. {He took an intelligent interest in the sciences and had a true sense of humor.} His career had begun as a reporter in Congress in the time of Webster, Jefferson Davis, Calhoun, Clay, Cass, Edward Everett {and others. Later, he accepted a position in} the Smithsonian Institution; and he came to Cornell in the early days of the University. His {striking and} impressive personality, his {remarkably} sonorous and pleasing voice, and his {perfect} interpretation of Shakespeare, Browning and {the other great dramatists and poets}, drew large audiences to his {public} readings.

After the death of his wife he spent much time with us {until his own death}. He was {an ardent} spiritualist and got {much} comfort from his belief.

I {should like} to pay tribute to the {personal} sympathy of President Schurman to those in sorrow. {I was at the home} when he came to see Professor Corson and his son, Dr. Eugene [Corson]. I shall never forget {his} touching expressions of sympathy which brought real comfort to the bereaved. {President Schurman} was a man who in his capacity as Professor or President walked alone; he had no intimate friends, but when sorrow {or loss by death} came to {any of us}, he was full of genuine {feeling and} sympathy {because of which} many learned to love him.

{Professor Vernon Kellogg spent a few weeks with us in early summer. He and Mr. Comstock worked together during the day and usually spend the evenings at the Town and Gown Club, of which Mr. Comstock was a charter member and to which he was much devoted since he had ceased his labors in the early morning.}

{Kellogg was not well, and Mr. Comstock went with him on a trip to Quebec via Lake Ontario and the St. Lawrence River. They made a pilgrimage to the Shrine of St. Anne of Beaupre' and, as biologists, were deeply interested to see a wooden leg among the crutches left there by healed cripples. Kellogg asked, "Is then a man, able, like a lobster, to grow a new leg to replace one amputated? 'Tis indeed a miracle."}

I went to Chautauqua again in July for the Nature Study teaching. {This time I had} as an assistant, William C. Thro, now Dr. Thro of the Cornell Medical School Faculty. Mr. Thro was one of Mr. Comstock's {excellent} students and he gave me {most} efficient aid that year, and for all the years thereafter that I taught in Chautauqua. We had large classes and the work was as satisfactory as possible {in the short time of} three weeks given to it. {Mr. John Spencer and Alice McCloskey were also there for the Junior Naturalist and gardening work. I saw Mr. Spencer give a practical lesson in gardening to kindergarten children and I marvelled at his success and his charm for the little folk.}

The summer term at Ithaca was as large as usual and Mr. Comstock had the happiness of having J. G. Needham, then professor of Biology at Lake Forest College, {to work with him}. Mr. Needham had taken his Ph. D. degree with Mr. Comstock in 1898.[8]

Mr. Comstock and [Vernon] Kellogg spent a week at Otto {and I joined them from Chautauqua. We visited Hilltop and had an enjoyable time} driving over the beautiful Cattaraugus hills. {The special reason} for Kellogg's stay with {Mr. Comstock} this year was the third revised edition of "Elements of Insect Anatomy," {which was then being put through} the press. Mr. Comstock {was working on the} revision of {the parts of} the head of the grasshopper which he had brought into line with his recent {investigations}.

During the stay at Otto, this September (1901), {Mr. Comstock} and I worked on "The Spider Book." We went collecting and he did some photographing. My mother came with us when we returned to Ithaca, for it was arranged that she should stay in her Otto home summers only, {with her cousin Mary King as companion}. I was very busy, for in addition to a University class of twenty in Nature Study, I gave a course of lectures to the teachers of Ithaca.

I was made happy {by being invited} by Professor Bailey to look after the poetry in "Country Life in America." We were all so eager to make this journal one of real {uplift physically and spiritually} to those who lived in the country. Professor Bailey had two things clearly in mind; one, to give practical help to farming and horticulture; and the other to lead people to appreciate the beautiful in nature and learn the many things of interest in the fields and woods. These ideals he held fast, and when he realized that the

8. Included in the 1953 edition (p. 196): ". . . with Mr. Comstock as Chairman of Needham's Graduate School Committee."

publishers had other ideals, he resigned his position as Editor. He said he had no interest in a periodical that should be called "City Life in the Country."

All the autumn, whenever there was an hour to be snatched, Mr. Comstock and I went out to study spiders,—he to make definite observations and I to enjoy the experience. I find the following note for October 21st . . . "Went spidering with Harry and saw spiderlings migrating, making a carpet of web over the grass." {One of my pleasures also was taking the Schurman children, Jack and Helen, for walks to observe things of interest. I am sure they taught me as much as I did them, their questions were so keen.}

{We had many students who were with us a great deal in the house. Margaret Schallenberger, who had come to Cornell to pursue special studies in psychology with Professor [Edward] Titchener and who afterwards did notable work in public education in California, was with us a great deal. We also saw much of Margaret Washburn, Benjamin Duggar and Arch Gilbert.}

In November I went to New York and Mr. Spencer met me there; we visited the schools of East Side and then the markets to see if perchance we might teach a little Nature Study in this great city through garden produce. My work in the Nature Study department at Cornell was varied. I helped wherever help was needed. It was in December of this year (1901) that I wrote "Trees at Leisure" for "Country Life in America," which, in my opinion, is as good a bit of writing as I ever did.[9,10]

In December I went to Grand Rapids, Michigan, to a State Teachers' Institute. Booker T. Washington was another speaker there and I enjoyed his address very much; I came to the conclusion that he had Irish blood in his veins, his humor was so delightfully Irish. I had great respect for him {anyway} for I {knew} from experience the force of his personality. When Mr. Comstock {was doing his writing during the hours of 4–7 a.m.}, he always had a short siesta after luncheon, and I stood guard vigilantly lest anyone should disturb him. {It was} during this sacred hour that I answered the door bell one day and found on the threshold a clever-looking young negro who wished to see {Mr.} Comstock. I invited him in but said he could not see {Mr. Comstock} at that hour. I am quite unable to remember how {he} did it. I am sure he was absolutely courteous and not oppressively insistent, but a little later I awakened Mr. Comstock and said: "There is a young negro

9. Footnote from the 1953 edition (p. 197): "This essay was republished in 1916 by the Comstock Publishing Company at Ithaca, N. Y. —G.W.H."

10. Article published in *Country Life in America*, February 1902, vol. 1, no. 4 (old series vol. 6—no. 8), pp. 105–9 (https://babel.hathitrust.org/cgi/pt?id=umn.31951000739012u;view=1up;seq=191). —KSt.

downstairs, Harry, and you will just have to see him now." Mr. Comstock arose meekly and went downstairs and became a permanent yearly subscriber to Tuskegee Institute.

{On New Year's Day, 1902, I went to Lockport to attend the wedding of Margaret Boynton to Phineas E. Windsor, now for many years Librarian at the University of Illinois. Mr. G. K. Gilbert was also there and came home with me. Mr. Comstock had hurt his leg and it was put in a cast, so he was unable to see Margaret married, a fact that did not worry him much for he always dreaded going to weddings. The dearer the people the less he liked to see them married; not that he objected to marriage as an institution, but the rites palled on him.}

{It was during this fall and winter that Phelps Gage and then his father were ill with typhoid fever, a great worry to Mr. Comstock and myself. My little neighbors, Jack and Barbara and Helen Schurman, were also ill, and for days I squeezed out enough time to read them a story.}

{In March, Mr. Comstock and I went to Washington to visit Mr. Gilbert, who lived with Dr. and Mrs. Hart Merriam. It was a privilege making the acquaintance of Dr. Merriam and his interesting wife and young daughters. Dr. Merriam we found genial and interested in many things. He had a fine collection of Indian baskets, several of the most valuable of which he had acquired by sitting for long hours in converse with trial chiefs and their wives. Dr. Merriam is so winsome that I am sure he could get anything from anybody by conversing with them.}

Mr. Comstock had been working on *The Spider Book* all of his spare time this winter [1901–1902]. {He had prepared a paper} with a Japanese student who could draw exquisitely, but couldn't do much else, on "The Skeleton of the Head of Insects." He had also written a paper on the "Wings of the Sesiidae," {and had written a leaflet on spiders for our Nature Study series}.

In April I went to New York and {stayed with Mrs. [Clara Kerr] Stidham while I} carried on an experiment in the Allen Street School in trying to introduce nature study from the markets, a thrilling experience, {written up later} by Carlyle Ellis for the *Cosmopolitan Magazine*.

{In May I entered into another literary enterprise. Martha Van Rensselaer believed that there was much in our leaflets for children that should be available to those outside of New York State and she had a scheme for doing it. Mr. Spencer was quite in sympathy with her in the matter, and between them, I too, became interested. To insure the business side of it we interested Mr. [A. W.] Stephens, who was at that time head of the Cornell Co-Operative Store, and we formed a company to publish a magazine called "Boys and Girls." The magazine had a career of seven years, although it was never a great financial success.}

{In the Spring term of 1902 Mr. Comstock had associated with him in the work on spiders, Cyrus R. Crosby, who was then a student and later Professor of Extension in the Entomological Department at Cornell. Mr. Crosby was an excellent student, especially in research, and Mr. Comstock found him an efficient and enthusiastic co-worker in studying spiders. Mr. Comstock wrote me thus in April 1902; "Mr. Crosby is proving very efficient help in the work on the Spider Book. He is taking hold in a splendid manner. He has a good command of the necessary language and is able to go ahead with the work with but few suggestions. We are at work now on the table of families."}

{I taught as usual at Chautauqua. Mr. William C. Thro was my assistant and Florence Margaret Cook, a teacher in Adirondack schools and destined to be a factor in our lives, was a member of the Chautauqua household. I had my mother with me for part of the time also. Another member of our household was Julia Rogers, sister to Mary Rogers Miller and later, the author of the "Tree Book" of the Doubleday Nature Series. Martha Van Rensselaer and her mother were with us also.}

{When I returned to Ithaca I found G. K. Gilbert was staying with Mr. Comstock and we celebrated, the two men, Margaret Schallenberger and I, by going to the circus. We moved to "The Hermitage" as soon as possible, at least I did. Mr. Comstock came whenever his teaching duties would let him, and Mr. Gilbert came when his geology explorations permitted. Mr. Thro came now and then but for the most part I was alone. The son of a nearby farmer, a boy of sixteen, used to come to stay nights at the cottage. I had to waken him at 4 o'clock in the morning and judging by the noise necessary to tear him from his dreams, a troop of wild Indians could have razed the place without his slumber being disturbed.}

{The last of August I went to Harrison, Ohio to teach in the week-long State Teachers' Institute. There, one of my co-workers was Wilbur Jackman, the father of Nature Study in America, and a man of high ideals and great accomplishment. I greatly prized this opportunity of knowing him. He believed that all elementary education should have as its foundation, Nature Study.}

{When I was teaching in institutes in the eastern part of New York, my mother joined me and we visited the home of her ancestors in Vermont. Her early ancestor was a Quaker and came to America soon after William Penn. Her great-great-grandfather had first belonged to the Friend's Meeting in the "Oblong" in Dutchess County but migrated with his nine sons to

Rutland, Vermont before the Revolutionary War. Her father had migrated from Danby to Collins, Eric Country in 1816. Because the members of her family were Quakers and would not fight they were persecuted by both Americans and British during the war. One of her great-uncles had cleared a piece of land in the wilderness and planted his crops. He knew that his life was threatened and each time after he came home from hunting he took his gun apart for fear he might be tempted to shoot a man if he were attacked. It was a superfluous precaution for he was shot from ambush as he stood in his own doorway. His wife, who must have been a remarkable woman, buried him with her own hands. She remained in the cabin until the crops were harvested and then with her four small children followed the trail through the wilderness to Rutland.}

During the fall and winter [1902–1903] I had collected some of my writings published in various periodicals and added some others to make a small volume. This was published by Ginn and Company in the spring [1903] under the title "Ways of the Six-footed."[11]

Mr. Comstock had worked on spiders during the preceding months and while we were at Otto I made several drawings for him. He felt keenly the need of more field work on these interesting creatures and soon after our return to Ithaca he started south to study them.

{During his absence, I had with me Julia Rogers and Margaret Cook who was studying at Cornell.} Soon after Mr. Comstock's departure (1903) the epidemic of typhoid broke out in Ithaca; it was a terrible experience; hundreds were ill, and the death toll was great. The public water supply had been contaminated; but the supply for the campus from another stream was pure, so we were safe. Mark Slingerland was very ill and we almost despaired of his life; {as a matter of fact}, he was never {a} well {man} afterward.

As a result of this plague {Mr.} Andrew Carnegie built {a filter} for the University and paid for the medical aid and hospital fees of all our working students who were ill. This act {has made Mr. Carnegie} dear to all Cornellians. During the epidemic I was able to repay an old debt. I {have already} told how Roswell Leavitt of the class of '72 nursed Mr. Comstock through an attack of typhoid. This year, Clyde Leavitt, son of Roswell, was taking graduate work at Cornell and lived in the most afflicted area of {the town}. I invited him to be my guest for the rest of the year. He came and escaped the plague.

11. Here ends Chapter 11 in the 1953 edition. The remainder of the Comstock manuscript Chapter X continues as Chapter 12 in the 1953 edition. —KSt.

Mr. Comstock started south in good spirits. {He spent a day or two with Mr. Gilbert at the Merriam's in Washington.} One of his characteristics is the way he drops out of hustling at high speed into a vacation mood. In a letter {written February 9, 1903, on the Southern Railroad} he says,

> "I learn this morning that we are four hours late and that it is an outrage, but I don't feel outraged. My only emotion evoked by the management of the Railroad is one of thankfulness that they hitched the dining car to a northbound train to meet us so that we had breakfast on time. The breakfast was good and so was the cigar and I don't care whether we get to New Orleans tomorrow or next day." . . . . "Here I am in New Orleans in a comfortable hotel. Immediately after breakfast, I started with a pocket full of bottles and have had a successful day collecting. It has been a perfectly clear summer day. I have seen a few flowers in the parks, a few flying insects, and one newly made orb-web. A good many jumping spiders are running about on the sunny sides of buildings; and, in their winter quarters, I have found representatives of several other families. I have collected continually for five hours, except when I stopped in a café in the old French Quarter for a dozen oysters and a glass of beer. But I have not been blind to the very interesting human world about me.
>
> "My way had led first to the levee where I could see this great river and the ships loading and unloading. Here on the sides of the warehouses I saw the remarkable Dictyna-like webs of *Filistata* and secured several specimens of the spiders, the first I had seen; and I found, too, what I think is *Oecobius*, which completes the series of families of curled-thread weavers that occur in the United States. This too I had never seen before.
>
> "Several hours were spent examining the sunny sides of buildings in the old French Quarter. I drifted along, at one time greatly helped by some bright-eyed kids. I gave no thought to direction and finally found myself beyond the city in an open field where there are many cows, each with a bell. Sunning themselves, on the warm side of a fence, there were several beautiful lizards much like the California swifts. From New Orleans I went to Lake City, Florida. As I was writing my name in the hotel register I felt something crawling on the back of my neck and concluded that a descendent of some of the many cockroaches that used to make free with me at Mrs. Wright's, 27 years ago, were welcoming me back. I calmly finished writing my name and put my pen in my pocket and then brushed off on to the

register a scorpion! I was delighted for I felt sure that this was an indication that I was to find arachnids in Florida.

{"I rather expected Professor Girrard to meet me at the station, but he was out of town and my message had been given to} Professor [H. H.] Hume who came to explain matters. Professor H., too, was to leave this morning on some Horticultural field work; but after we had visited awhile, he said that he would postpone his trip and would spend the day with me.

"You will remember that one of the most important things that I had hoped to find was the purse-web spider, the spider that I wrote to Glenn (Herrick) about. In our visit last night Professor {H.} told me of a curious spider that he knew. I recognized his account at once as of the purse-web and was delighted. I think it was this that made him change his plans. He took me today into a forest where there are hundreds of them. He took his camera and made splendid negatives of the nest, one of which I hope to use for a full page plate. He took me to lunch, not explaining, until after we were at his house, that he was alone. Mrs. {H.} had made plans to be away during his absence and she could not change when she learned that his plans were changed; but she left a fine "hurry up" lunch for us."

From Lake City Mr. Comstock went to Miami, Florida, where he was given a room in the subtropical laboratory of Dr. P. H. Rolfs. The following extracts from his letters give a clear account of his success in collecting and photographing spiders.

"I had a very comfortable journey last night. There was a rather stout German on the train whose face seemed familiar. I thought a long time before I could place him; and then concluded rightly that it was [E. A.] Schwartz, who you will remember was a slim man when we knew him in Washington 23 years ago. He is on his way to Cuba to study the cotton-boll weevil. I had a delightful visit with him, and a very profitable one, as he has collected in this place and could give me many suggestions."

". . .Well, I am settled for my laboratory work in just as nice a place as could be made in this climate. The subtropical laboratory is a beautiful cottage on the shore of the bay; and I have a room, about the size of your room in the Insectary, entirely to myself.

"I have rented a bicycle. It is about eight minutes ride from the hotel to the laboratory, over a splendid rock road. The roads here are even better than in the Santa Clara valley.

"There is a beautiful new butterfly very common here; it is about the size of the cabbage *Pieris*. This was so abundant in the Rolfs' orchard, that several hundred of them were on a single bush. Half as many butterflies as leaves; the most remarkable display of butterflies I ever saw! They are gentle creatures; one can easily pick them from the bushes, like the birds on the Pacific Islands. Several of them alighted on us and remained a long time. This strip of land between the Everglades and the ocean, about five miles wide here, is mostly like the northern part of the state, i.e. a pine barren. The pine trees are very scattered and have few branches; so that practically there is no shade; the ground is quite thickly covered by a palmetto. The number of species of plants and animals to be found in these barrens, is comparatively small and Schwarz told me that they are the same as are found in the northern part of the State.

"I found {Mr. Hendrickson} at the laboratory making some prints today and I knew then that it was proper for me to photograph on Sunday."

. . . . "I told you I had found *Nephila plumipes* Dr. Wilder's Nephila. I thought I had found two specimens, a young one and an adult. Now I think the supposed young one is some other species of Nephila. I have examined neither closely; but have left them on their webs out in the jungle. I have paid little attention to the smaller one, beyond noting that its web is of the characteristic form of *Nephila*; but with the old lady I have spent many hours; and I have spoiled a good many plates trying to photograph her web.

"This noon, when the maximum amount of light was leaking through the dense foliage I took an instantaneous plate, set the diaphragm wide open (a combination that would make a picture in the open in 1/100 of a second) and set the shutter at 2 1/2 seconds, then waited for a lull, for there are moments went the breeze does not stir the undergrowth. At the right moment I pressed the bulb and hastened back to the laboratory to develop the plate. Result, a magnificent negative. Not wishing to have all my eggs in one basket, I returned and took two more, both splendid negatives.

"I have developed such an affection for the old spider that I fear I shall be unable to put her in alcohol."

. . . . "The day has been a beautiful one, clear and with a comfortable temperature. It has been a very successful one in my work. The heavy rain of yesterday injured the webs so that the spiders were obliged to make fresh ones and I have devoted the entire day to photographing them. I secured some of the best photographs of webs I have ever made out-of-doors. There was less wind than usual so the difficulties were not so great. But I tell you my legs ache tonight. I made three trips into the jungle, each time with four plates; and between trips developed the plates."

. . . . "This morning I started out to get a photograph of the orbs web weaver, the most common one here. It is a difficult subject to get a background behind it. I examined a hundred webs and tried to get several. I would carefully cut away the interfering bushes and perhaps get the background placed, when some invisible thread supporting the web would be touched and the web spoiled. This happened several times but finally about noon I succeeded in getting a picture."

The epidemic of typhoid in Ithaca was a great worry to Mr. Comstock, especially after Mark Slingerland was stricken, and it required all my powers of persuasion to keep him from coming home. He could not have been of any use and it was a comfort to have him out of danger. He writes;

"While I was sick for the past two days I thought out a new method of photographing the hubs of webs enlarged. {Mr. Hendrickson (who by the way spent the entire day with me, it being Sunday) and} I made the apparatus for this new method and then tested it, and it worked.

It is used in connection with the vertical camera and the magnifying lens that I have. The first subject of our apparatus was a remarkable, two-tailed spider[12] with four large humps on its body which makes an orb web. It rests at the center, it's star-shaped body covering the hole in the hub. But the remarkable thing is that it decorates some of the radii, and frequently also some of the lines in the outer foundation with shining white patches of flocculent silk; these are very conspicuous. What are they for? They are evidently made of the same material as the stabilimentum of *Argiope*, but each patch is connected to a single line and waves free in the wind. Are they lures to attract insects to the web? I believe that is their function.

"After getting photographs of this, I mounted some specimens on glass of lantern slides. Then we took some view of the Station so as to show you what it is like when I return."

. . . . "I spoke in my note of this morning of doing the necessary things now before beginning to pack. I felt that getting pictures and specimens of the web of this angling spider was one of the necessary

---

12. Footnote from the 1953 edition (p. 204): "*Gasteracantha cancriformis*. See J. H. Comstock, *The Spider Book*, p. 513, for an account of this remarkable spider. —G.W.H."

things. Don't you think so? After lunch there was the making of some more photographs, the mounting of some more webs for more careful study after I came home, and the collecting of some remarkable spiders which I had not seen before and which as, yet I have only glanced at; and now I am dead tired.

After supper and a cigar, I feel O. K. and have enjoyed writing you this little note. You say it can't be too long."

. . . . "About snakes. That too is a saga. I don't take a step out of a public highway without thinking of them and haven't seen one! But damn the mosquitoes! There are sixteen about my head now. I don't think they are Anopheles for they are little black cusses that come right through the screens.

"One of them striking things one sees in Miami are the Seminole Indians that come out from the Everglades. They wear cotton shirts of various colors and gayly trimmed. One day when I was in at a photographer two of the men were having their picture taken. I asked the photographer to make a print for me and today I got it. I will try to send it tomorrow.

"I wanted to write you about these Indians and the Miami crows the first day I came, but other things crowded these two topics out.

"As to the crows, they are here in hundreds; they are the city scavengers. They keep just out of reach and that is all. They have a soft southern accent, as unlike the voice of the northern crow as is that of the southern negro from that of a northern white man. There is a tree under my window in which there are frequently 50 of these crows at once.

"I am very glad that you have taken Leavitt into the house; both for his sake and for yours. I know it will be a comfort to you to have him there.

"I shall make my plans to goto Austin. If anything happens to make you wish to stop me, you can reach me Monday p. m. or Tuesday a. m. at Lake City. After which I shall be out of reach till I get to Austin.

"As I closed up my work here and took stock of what I have accomplished I felt that the trip had been a great success. I have accomplished more in the three weeks that I have been here than I expected to do on the whole trip.

"It is now late in the evening. I have just returned from Professor Rolfs', five miles in the country, where I took supper and spent a part of the evening. Professor Rolfs returned last night from his trip to

> Jamaica; so I have had a chance to see him, and thank him for the aid that he has given me.
>
> "This has been a busy day. I shipped my freight this morning and spent the remainder of the forenoon packing my trunk."

Mr. Comstock left Miami March 8, 1903 and went to Lake City, where a letter from me informed him of Mark Slingerland's critical condition; he writes; "Since receiving your message I have been terribly broken up; but I have been forced to think and talk about other things. It came just as we were going out to lunch at the Humes. This afternoon I went into the field, but I could put no heart into my work. It was while there that I decided to start for home as soon as possible. This evening I was invited to supper with President and Mrs. T. H. Taliaferro. They are charming people from Baltimore."

A telegram from me met Mr. Comstock in New Orleans telling him the crisis had been passed and Mark would recover and advising him to go to Texas as he had planned—which he did. He was the guest of Professor and Mrs. William Morton Wheeler at Austin and his enjoyment of the stay with them has ever since been a happy memory. Certainly, they are two of the most delightful people that have graced University circles in America. Mr. Comstock writes:

> "I reached Austin (March 12, 1903) in time to take breakfast with the Wheelers and received a very cordial welcome.
>
> "This forenoon Professor Wheeler took me into the field where we found many things new to me. The collecting is excellent here, and the fauna is very different from that of Miami. Our collecting was done almost entirely by looking under stones. We found two kinds of tarantulas, several scorpions, and a considerable number of spiders new to me.
>
> "It has been a delightful day. Fortunately for me the Wheelers are not Sunday people. So Dr. W. and I have had two collecting trips, a long one this morning, and a shorter one this afternoon. Both of which were successful.
>
> "My stay at the Wheelers has been a delight and an exceedingly profitable one for the spider work. I had splendid weather the entire week till this morning, but left Austin in a pouring rain. I wish you knew Mrs. Wheeler—she is a charming woman.
>
> "I am riding through the land of the agricultural ant. It is an exceedingly abundant species here. One day Professor Wheeler pointed out the place where McCook camped when he made the observations for his book on these ants.

"During our walks, Wheeler has told me enough wonderful things about ants to make a large volume. He is making a very exhaustive study of the group.

"I had a whiff of Texas atmosphere this morning, on my way to the train. I was about 300 feet from a man when he shot and killed another man. I had heard the shots and saw the crowd gather about the fallen man. I then went on to the station. Before our train left Austin, I heard that the man that was shot lived only a few minutes."

. . . . "I had a fine day in New Orleans yesterday, spent the entire day collecting from the sides of old buildings and making notes. Came out here to Baton Rouge in the evening. This morning it has been raining hard and I have collected in old buildings. Have had an excellent morning's work.

"I am going to stay here till Thursday morning; which is a day longer than I had intended to stay. But Morgan wishes me to give a lecture Monday night."

"I had a delightful and very profitable time at Baton Rouge Sunday afternoon. [F. H.] Burnett, Professor of Horticulture, took H. A. Morgan and me down the river on a tug to a place where the levee was nearly destroyed, and 200 men were at work building a new one behind the old one. A turn in the direction of the current had caused the river to cut into the levee so that only a little shell, less than a foot in thickness at the top, kept this great river more than a half mile wide, from rushing over the country.

"I made a large collection here at Baton Rouge, yesterday. H. A. Morgan took a class of twelve men out with me and all collected spiders. We collected along the edge of the dike by some overflowed land where the water had driven the spiders to the shore of the lake.

"Among the spiders collected at B. R. was one which is a most remarkable instance of mimicry. It looks exactly like the dropping from a bird, and rests exposed on the surface of a branch or leaf."

From New Orleans Mr. Comstock went to Starkville, Mississippi to visit our cousin Glenn W. Herrick and his wife Nannie Burke, who was a former student at Cornell {and one of our household friends}. Glenn was professor of biology and entomology in the State College of Mississippi. It was too early in the season there to do much collecting of spiders. He says,

"I had a delightful and heart-satisfying visit with these cousins who seemed like children of our own.

"I can't complain as up to date I have not lost an hour account of rain, since I left Ithaca, and it has been a very rainy winter in all parts of the south.

"I do want, however, another half day of good weather here, as Glenn and I found nests of a turret-building spider yesterday and we want to go and dig the spiders out. We got one specimen and it is a different species from one that I found in Texas."[13]

---

13. The manuscript Chapter X ends suddenly at this point. The 1953 edition Chapter 12 concludes with the following paragraph: "Mr. Comstock also found there one of the most remarkable engineering spiders in his collection, *Ariadna bicolor*. He speaks of its 'nests of such marvelous engineering skill that I have never ceased to wonder at them.' (See J. H. Comstock, *The Spider Book*, pp. 300–301) —G.W.H." —KSt.

Butterfly engraving by Anna Comstock, 1891.

CHAPTER XI

"How to Know Butterflies" and the "Confessions to a Heathen Idol"

The reader may notice that as you progress through the Comstock manuscript, increasingly more sections had been left out of the 1953 edition. (Recall that you can determine this by the number of times the brackets occur around sections in this book.) By the end of the book, this process of culling has left out Mrs. Comstock's final chapters in their entirety from the 1953 edition. Mrs. Comstock's Chapter XI (in the 1953 edition this is Chapter 13) displays the beginning of this dramatic diminishment in earnest.

{Mr. Comstock} met me at Otto when he returned from the South, April 4th, 1903. After attending to the business of the farm we both returned to Ithaca. As I had much lecturing at the Teachers' Institutes before me, we continued to {take our meals at a boarding house}. Neither of us enjoyed this way of living, but we knew it was for the best and our usual way has ever been {to play} that we like whatever happens.

{President White returned from Germany this spring and it was a joy to have him back. He was given to early walks and often joined us on our way to breakfast.}

{The special happiness of this commencement was the coming of Professor and Mrs. Guido Marx and their children from Stanford,—it was Guido's 10th class reunion. As I had to depart for summer work soon, we established the Marx family in our house with Mr. Comstock retaining only his bedroom. He was delighted to have their company for the summer. The daughter Eleanor was seven and Guido three, and Sylvia 18 months, all charming children.}

The last week in June I taught in a summer school for teachers at the University of Virginia at Charlottesville. William Thro went with me to take care of the field trips and laboratory periods. It was a very interesting experience. The beautiful old college with its quaint buildings permeated with the memory and spirit of Thomas Jefferson together with the picturesque scenery around it gave us a new setting for our work. Soon after we arrived we made a pilgrimage to Monticello and our sojourn in Charlottesville gave us a {new and vital} interest in Thomas Jefferson and a respect for his educational ideals.

Mr. [Edward C.] Glass, a brother of Senator Carter Glass, and superintendent of schools in Lynchburg, {had the} school in charge. He seemed to me a rather remarkable man, especially in his broad vision in educational matters.

He said to me: "I have here in the colored High School the negro teachers who have come to get what I can give them. I have no money to pay for instruction for them and you are under no obligation to give them anything, but if you choose to lecture to them they and I will be very glad." Of course, I assented. Strange to say I found among the colored teachers better nature observers, by far, than I found among the white ones. I soon discovered a fact that has been a stumbling block in the way of negro education. The negroes look upon the white college men of their acquaintance as the truly educated. The white men of the South study Latin, Greek, and philosophy; therefore, the negro insist that only these studies educated anyone. A part of my work with them was to try to counteract their ideas in this {matter}. I talked over the matter with Professor Glass and he made the memorable answer: "They talk about the negro problem. There is none outside of proper education. If we educate them and widen their intelligence and their interests, the problem is solved."

{From Virginia we went to Chautauqua where the work was soon organized and successfully carried on. My mother came over from Otto to celebrate her 80th birthday, June 14th. From Chautauqua Mr. Thro and I went to Thousand Island Park to another State Teachers' Institute. Here we had a very large field class and we were both tired when we returned to Ithaca early in August.}

{Mr. Comstock had 33 in his summer term this year. He gave a course of lectures on spiders which was very popular. Many of his students took up the spider work, Miss Seeton of Cleveland among them. Mr. Alfred Hammar assisted in arranging the collection and in getting the specimens photographed; Mr. Comstock already had 560 negatives of spiders. Cornelius Betten began his work for his Ph. D. this summer and was the kind of student Mr. Comstock delighted in. My husband worked particularly hard this summer.

He writes, "I have many questions to answer which require looking up, and the lectures keep me on the jump. I have just delivered a lecture that I worked on every minute yesterday, and it was a good one if I do say it that hadn't oughter. In preparing the lecture I got a lot of material in shape for the Spider Book."}

{Mr. Comstock always insisted on good conscientious work on the part of his students, but he was always sympathetic with the human side as well. This is shown in the following quotation from a letter of July 12: "The first thing this morning was a case of discipline which had been on my mind several days. A young woman had copied another student's drawings and handed them in as her own. I was as gentle as I could be; but I told her she must begin at the beginning again and could not get credit for the work done. She has found the work very difficult owing, in part, to trouble with the eyes, and does not feel she can do it now so has withdrawn from the class. She leaves ostensibly on account of her eyes. I have taken great pains that no one should know the truth and she is very grateful and thanked me earnestly for my consideration. On top of this I had a call from Herbert Smith and his brave little wife. He is going to give up scientific work and devote himself to literature. He is writing short stories for the magazines. Poor people! They have had a hard, strange life."}

My problem in the Chautauqua classes was a difficult one. The teachers had no background of science, and it seemed best to get each one in the class interested in some phase of nature that she could follow by herself later. I found trees, ferns, birds, and butterflies adapted for this work.

All the butterfly books were too advanced for use in these courses and I had besought my husband to write one with me. The Appletons had asked for such a book and I needed it. Mr. Comstock, who objected to my summer teaching as too hard for me, wrote as follows: "I am devoutly thankful that the weather has been cool. That adds to the chance of your getting through the summer alive. The contract for {the} *Butterfly Book* came from the Appletons yesterday; but I shall not sign it until I see in what condition you are at the end of the summer's work."

I lived through the summer and we began working on the book soon after I returned. {We had a happy August with our beloved Marxes, and then went to Otto where I began in earnest the work on the butterflies.} Mr. Comstock was so occupied with constructing that he termed a "pig palace" on Hilltop that he had no time for writing during that vacation. We returned to Ithaca the last of September and had another happy week with the Marxes before they left us to go to Europe.

{We had become very much interested in Margaret Cook and the quite remarkable work she was doing in Adirondack rural school; and through our encouragement and help, she came to Cornell this autumn to pursue such studies as would aid her in her chosen work. I fitted up a room for her in Cascadilla Building and arranged for her to assist me so that she might earn enough for her current expenses. She was a remarkable girl, generous, temperamental, resourceful, and brilliant along certain lines. She remained an important factor in our lives as long as she lived.}

October 7, 1903 was our silver wedding day, but we did not mention the fact. We drove off in the country in the afternoon to celebrate by ourselves. We were {truly} surprised that evening by the Agricultural Faculty, the Wilders and the Gages, appearing at the Fall Creek Cottage, and presented us with a beautiful loving cup. Mark Slingerland had engineered the affair. Professor L. H. Bailey made the speech and it was full of feeling and affection. Miss Van Rensselaer smuggled in refreshments and we had a most pleasant evening {and to us most gratifying}, an experience that has ever warmed our hearts when we glance at the loving cup with its inscription written by Professor Bailey.

"We count the sum of gain and loss
To make things what they seem;
And find it all as pain and dross,
Save love and high esteem."

After my return to Ithaca from a course of lectures in November at the Phoebe Hearst Kindergarten School in Washington, D. C., we had so many interruptions that we were in despair of finishing *The Butterfly Book* and we held counsel; this resulted in our taking possession of a very small room on the floor above the entomological lecture room in White Hall. The room had a window and was heated. We called it "The cubby hole." When one of us retired to into it, only the other knew about it, and the one that knew never told. Thus, we were able to steal time for this book. Mr. Comstock had the help of Mr. [Alexander] McGillivray and so he was able to take an hour off now and then.

On November 13, 1903, I accepted the trusteeship of William Smith College, at that time a dream of a very remarkable man, Mr. William Smith of Geneva. {There were other trustees,—Mr. Chase and Mr. Henry Graves of Geneva. William Smith} was born in England and never went to school after he was seven years old. He came to Geneva as a youth and by thrift, hard work, and good management he had accumulated a property worth about a half million dollars. He {had never married and} had an exalted ideal of the place of woman in the world; he believed {she} should be educated and fitted in every way {to do her work of} motherhood. He wanted to found a college for women at Geneva. When I accepted the trusteeship {the problem was not solved} but Mr. Smith, then 87 years old, {made over} his property to the trustees to be used for this purpose. {We certainly had a problem before us. I owed my part in the affair to my friend Miss Anne Miller and her mother, Elizabeth Miller of Geneva.}

{Just before Thanksgiving Mr. Austin Wadsworth and his bride visited us. We invited President and Mrs. Schurman in to dine with them, also Edwin Woodruff and Ernest Huffcut. When we wanted a socially brilliant affair we always invited Woodruff and Huffcut, two of the most interesting men ever connected with Cornell. Huffcut was at that time Dean of the Law School and Woodruff a professor in it.}

{The prospects for the College of Agriculture were improving. It was this year that L. H. Bailey took the work of Director laid down by Professor I. P. Roberts, who had fought a long fight and retired, just as success was in sight. Professor and Mrs. Roberts joined their children in California and we lost two of the kindest and most helpful neighbors we had ever had. Professor Bailey somehow managed to get Governor Odell to visit Cornell in November. He was present at a meeting of the agricultural faculty and Professor Bailey, in a most able speech, placed the needs of our college before him. It was the beginning of a new growth for the College of Agriculture at Cornell.}

{Professor Bailey was not in good health and the weight of the office of Director was heavy upon him. His friends, especially Professor George N. Lauman, felt he must have a change and rest and settled on a trip to Bermuda for him, and then, looking around for some one to accompany him, asked Mr. Comstock and myself to go. We agreed. On December 23rd we finished the Ms. of "How to Know the Butterflies," and on Christmas night we took the train for New York. Our ship, the "Pretoria," was to sail at noon the next day. We came into the harbor of Bermuda on the morning of the 29th. The beautiful green shores dotted with white dwelling looked good to us. We stopped at the Princess Hotel in Hamilton. For three days we rejoiced in the subtropical landscape as we drove about over the island.}

{The voyage home was tempestuous. Professor Bailey was so ill that he fell in a dead faint. I was so ill that I could not imagine how I had ever walked or ever could walk again. Poor Mr. Comstock oscillated between Professor Bailey's state room and ours.}

{We found zero weather in Ithaca on our return. We had with us as a working student in the house this year, Alfred Hammar, a brilliant young Norwegian who had first migrated to South America. His interest in entomology had led Dr. Orville A. Derby, the state geologist of Brazil, and an old Cornellian, to advise him to come to Ithaca and carry on his studies. He was an aristocratic youth but the way he did his menial work made us respect him. He graduated with honor and was later in the employ of the U. S. Division of Entomology doing excellent work when through an accident he met an untimely death.}

This winter we bought a piece of land between the University's land and Forest Home called "The Pinnacle."[1] We knew that sooner or later the site of Fall Creek Cottage, our home, would be needed for a University building and we wished to find a place for a home near by. At that time a trolley line was projected from Ithaca to Freeville which would pass near our new possessions, and we began at once to make plans for a home.

{Although Mr. Comstock and I both worked so hard and gave so much of our spare time to friends, we were always wont to have was what we called "an orgy" by ourselves. I remember one very rainy summer night we packed up our supper and went to Camp Camaraderie and camped out under an umbrella.}

{This winter our colleague, Dr. George C. Caldwell, was obliged from failing health, to give up his University work, and our Mrs. Henry Lord passed away—two cherished friends, whom we missed greatly.}

Early in May, Governor Odell signed the bill giving Cornell money for {buildings for} The College of Agriculture. On May 12 the students paraded with floats and made a great show. One float showed the dairy girls and boys in white caps and aprons churning and making butter. Others represented other departments. One float, on which twenty nations were represented, showed the international character of the students of agriculture. There was a great banquet that night with Governor Odell present. There were many speeches. Mr. Comstock made a {very} excellent one. {He was always a good speaker at such occasions.}

This spring, our friend Albert W. Smith, was called to Cornell as Director of the College of Mechanical Engineering, a matter of much rejoicing to us. During the year and especially this spring we saw much of several Brazilian students. Mr. Comstock helped them all the ways he could and at Commencement they gave him a loving cup inscribed—*Ao nosso maestro, J. H. Comstock, como prova de estima e consideração A. Botellio, A. S. Coelho, L. Fagundes, C. Fagundes, J. Tibirica, W. Fagundes, 4 Maio 1906.*[2]

On May 21 [1904], our book "How to Know the Butterflies" was published, and we were delighted with the colored plates in it. We took a copy

1. Footnote inserted in the 1953 edition (p. 212): "This forested hill has been designated by the University as Comstock Knoll, a forest reserve, in the Cornell Plantations, dedicated to the conservation of natural resources and beauty. See Ralph A. Hosmer, *The Cornell Plantations: A History*, and the University Quarterly, *The Cornell Plantations*, edited by Professor Bristow Adams. —R.G.S."

2. "To our teacher, J. H. Comstock, as proof of esteem consideration A. Botellio, A. S. Coelho, L. Fagundes, C. Fagundes, J. Tibirica, W. Fagundes, May 4, 1906."

to President White {and to Mr. Lord} and to Professor Bailey and sent it to other friends. It was always great fun to give our friends our books {when they were published}.

The summer of 1904 I taught at Chautauqua for the last time. Mr. Thro was again my helper. We had many good times together, for I had induced him to begin sketching in water color. Mr. Comstock was tired of living alone every July, and {had} decided that I must close this work. I too, thought it best to stop. My classes had been large and appreciative, and I was sorry to say good-bye to Chautauqua.

As soon as the term at Cornell ended we fled to The Hermitage on Cayuga {for a rest}. Ross Marvin[3] went with us to put things in order. It was while we were staying there this summer that we bought it; we had learned to love it so much. The house was up in the woods about fifty feet about the lake and we bought the lake shore for some distance to the south, so that no one should build and disturb the wild beauty of the rocky shore.

In September we went to Otto; my mother had determined to sell her home and live with us permanently. It was a painful experience for us, especially for me, for I had loved this home and its surrounding hills with the passionate devotion of young girlhood which had ripened into the restful devotion of mature years. I shall never forget my mother's courage. We sent her to the home of our friend, {Etta Holbrook}, while we broke up the home. She sat upright and sturdy as they drove away and never turned her head to look at the place in which she had lived 40 years, the happiest years of her life. Meanwhile my cousin Mary King and I sat on the piazza steps and wept. Probably there is no sadder or more wearing experience in life than the breaking up of a home that has been established for many years. A house long lived in has a soul, {I think}, a soul imparted by those who have dwelt in it. {I felt that} on that {fatal day of} September 22, when we left the empty house, that its soul departed also.

We established mother in the study in Fall Creek Cottage, the pleasantest room in the house. Her old bureau and stand and rocker, and pictures made her feel at home and she fell into our ways of living as naturally as if she had always lived with us.

{October 19, 1904, the cornerstone of Goldwin Smith Hall was laid; and Goldwin Smith, himself, laid it. On that same day Mrs. Caldwell passed away and I have never ceased to miss her during all the years since. It has been a

3. Footnote per 1953 edition (p. 213): "After graduation from Cornell, Ross Marvin was drowned, on his homeward journey, after serving as a member of Robert E. Peary's expedition to the North Pole.—R.G.S."

precious privilege to be closely associated with her daughter, Grace Chamberlain, during these later years. Our friend and neighbor, Mrs. Lucien Wait, also died that same week.}

{A student friend whom we had known at Stanford, Carl Thomas, who had graduated and taken a second degree at Cornell, was now married to a charming Stanford girl and called to a professorship in Engineering at Cornell. They lived near us and gave me the use of a room on their third floor where I could get away from the many demands upon me and devote myself to writing.} Doubleday Page and Company had asked me to write a bee book. As I had been associated with Mr. Comstock during all his experience with bees, I {concluded} I could write something that would be of use to beginners. I was also writing a little book for children on the study of wild flowers for the American Book Company. Also, every month I had to get out a lesson leaflet for my large extension class in Nature Study.

{One of our interesting social experiences was a lunch at President White's to meet Baroness von Solter, a Peace Congress delegate. She was a very impressive lady and wore a head dress like that of Mary Queen of Scots. We also had many guests, Ruth Putnam who was trustee of Cornell at the time, L. O. Howard, who came to Ithaca to vote, Alfred Kao-Sze who came to say good bye to us as he was recalled to China, Mr. George T. Powell, leader of the agricultural movement in the States. Of the students who frequented the house this autumn there were Everett Leslie now a professor at Stanford, Vaughn McCaughey, Charles Howard, now in China, E. L. Palmer, now professor at Westtown School, Pa., Effie Reed, now in Washington, D. C., Heloise Abel, Margaret Cook, her friend Alice Simmons who played the violin exquisitely. Also, Harry Law, Mr. Comstock's namesake, who was in the College of Engineering, Will Geer, now of Akron, Ohio, Robert Falkneau, Ross Marvin, and Mr. and Mrs. L. P. Shanks.}

{In November Mrs. Wilder died. She was an exquisite woman, physically and mentally, and we loved her dearly. Her loss was a great sorrow. Soon after, the attractive young daughter of our neighbors, Professor and Mrs. Waterman Hewitt, died. It seemed to us this was a fateful autumn.}

{Mr. Comstock had worked very hard all the autumn and we concluded to go South for the winter. My mother and our cousin Mary King, went with us to Ocean Springs, Mississippi, where we found plain but very comfortable lodgings at the Shananhan Hotel. The table was good, but the breakfast hour was uncertain, as the colored help had to walk five miles to the hotel. We had a large fire-place in our room and as both of us had much writing on hand we arose at six. I made coffee at once by the fireplace and took a cup to my mother and cousin, after which Mr. Comstock and I ate crackers and drank coffee preparatory to several hours work before breakfast. We had delightful walks through the pine woods and around the bayous in addition to many pleasant drives. I also found time to make many sketches. It was my mother's first experience with a southern Christmas and she could not quite get used to celebrating the birth of our Lord with firecrackers and rockets. But she very much enjoyed hearing the birds sing and seeing flowers in bloom on this day.}

{Mr. Comstock and I called on Professor S. M. Tracy, who had a home near, and made the acquaintance of his charming daughter. In January mother suffered an apoplectic shock and we were in despair at first. Through Miss Tracy we were able to get a lovely girl, Miss Sutton, to nurse mother. Mother's recovery was remarkable considering her age, 81, for were able to return to Ithaca early in February.}

I finished the book *How to Keep Bees* and two leaflets. Mr. Comstock was writing on the *Spider Book*, and we both had accomplished much. We regarded the climate at Ocean Springs ideal for winter. It was not warm enough to be enervating and yet was warm enough, so we could enjoy the out-of-doors.

On May 1st, 1905, the ground was broken for the new Agricultural Building [Roberts Hall], an impressive rite. [Former] President White spoke and so did Dean Bailey. The latter plowed the furrow with boys pulling the plow. Then we all spaded the earth and felt that we were entering on a new era of agricultural education.

This Spring Cornell came into the limelight because of the advertised bull fight on our first "Spring Day," which was May 18th, 1905. We had several young men from Cuba, Mexico, and South America and they took for their part of the entertainment the putting on of a bull fight. {They had a tent, and} in their beautiful costumes of matadors they marched in the procession leading the great amiable dehorned bull belonging to the college herd. We paid admission to get into the tent and there saw our gloriously dressed matadors riding sticks with horses' heads carved on them; while the bull was another stick with the bull's head on it. The program was carried through with perfect imitation of a real bull fight and with absolute seriousness. It was a rich performance.

{President} White lunched with us that day, and he declared it the funniest thing he had ever seen. He also brought us his biography, two volumes, very precious to us, both for its contents and its inscription.[4]

4. Footnote from the 1953 edition: "To Prof. and Mrs. J. H. Comstock with the thanks and best wishes of And. D. White, May 1905. —G.W.H."

The newspapers, the length and breadth of the land, gave the news that Cornell was having a bull fight for entertainment and President Schurman was overwhelmed with indignant letters. One, {the worst of all}, was from a person in Mexico who said that they had made great efforts there to stop this brutal sport and felt discouraged when a great University like Cornell countenanced it.

Mr. Comstock's mother, Mrs. Dowell {by a second marriage}, was in {very} poor health and we were greatly worried about her, but it seemed impossible for us to make her a visit for many reasons, one being the expense of the journey. When, however, President Benjamin Ide Wheeler asked me to teach in the Summer School at the University of California we felt that I ought to accept. My {own} mother was feeble and I was not sure she would be with us to welcome me back but I thought of that other mother so far from us, and I made up my mind to go. {I made the best possible arrangements for the care of my own mother, for our friend Margaret Cook was to stay with her, and care for her. Also, Mrs. Margery Smith, who had come to help me by the day for many years, had supervision of the house and the cook, so I knew all would be well.}

When I reached San Francisco, I found Father Dowell awaiting me. I was glad to find Mother Dowell better than I feared. She was not ill but just failing physically and mentally.

I found a pleasant suite of rooms awaiting me at Hillcrest near the campus. I lectured in the Astronomical observatory, which was very pleasant. I had {two classes}—one in Nature Study methods and one in Nature Literature. My daily routine was lecturing in the morning and going to San Francisco to see the family every afternoon {during the week}.

{It was a pleasure to find Mr. G. K. Gilbert in Berkeley. He was working on the debris problem of the American and other rivers where placer mining had been practiced. Another very interesting visitor was Edwin Emerson, Jr. who had just returned from the Russian-Japanese war, where he acted as war correspondent. The Japanese objected to having news of the war given to the world, so they kept Emerson practically imprisoned for some weeks, and used him to break their wild horses, which certainly relieved the tedium of his imprisonment. He gave two public lectures, both thrilling and full of humor, one on "The Campaign in Manchuria" and on "In and Out of Port Arthur," the latter being the story of himself and a fellow correspondent who in a small boat, reached the neighborhood of Port Arthur and somehow smuggled themselves in. When I had seen Edwin last, he had been a charming, irresponsible boy who wondered what "experience" meant. I found him now, a grave man of wide experience, who nevertheless, had retained his humor and his charm.}

{It was a joy to be with President and Mrs. Wheeler again and I saw much of them. Very early in the term, the fact the Fourth of July, Secretary Taft with his party, which included Alice Roosevelt and Nicholas Longworth, passed through on their way to the Philippines. As President Wheeler and Mr. Taft were old friends the latter consented to address the students and faculty of the University. The address was to be given in the beautiful Greek Theater; but the California climate rose up and confounded the proud Californians. The wind changed, and instead of coming in from the ocean, poured in from the sun-baked Sacramento and San Joaquin Valleys; at my house the thermometer stood 118 degrees in the sun and 98 degrees in the shade. The Greek Theater was an oven, and Secretary Taft, with the perspiration streaming over his handsome face, gave an excellent address under the trees on the Campus. The heat continued for a week, and, after that, I wore clothes which I wear in Ithaca all winter and was just comfortable.}

{One weekend I was included with other teachers in the summer school in an invitation to visit Mrs. Phoebe Hearst at her "Hacienda del pozo Verona" on Mount Diablo. Professor William Gardner Haley, an old friend, formerly of Cornell, then of Chicago, Professor and Mrs. Thwaits of Madison [Wisconsin], and Professor [Charles] Seymour of Yale were in our party besides President and Mrs. Wheeler.}

{After leaving the station we drove up into the foothills over a winding road bordered with orchards and vineyards until we reached the gate of the grounds and entered into a paradise of palms and flowers, in the midst of which was a large house of true Mexican architecture,—its walls of white plaster and its flat roofs of red tiles. Part of the house was two stories in height. It was built around a patio in the midst of which was set an exquisite marble basin brought from the garden of an old palace in Verona, hence the name of the Hacienda. The court or patio, except for the drive, was covered with green sod set with gorgeous flower beds. There were colonnades on two sides of the court and many of the pillars were covered with climbing roses. The house was large with great drawing rooms, a library and a billiard room. The gem of the house was the large music room hung with beautiful pictures and tapestries and furnished with many musical instruments, including a pipe organ. The barns were in keeping with the house. The floors, except of the stables, were polished and kept like house floors. I especially remembered the harness room; it was a harness museum, containing trappings of earlier days in Europe as well as the most beautiful harnesses of the present time.}

{The most interesting part of this beautiful home was our hostess, Phoebe Hearst. She was sweet and gentle in manner, very keen intellectually, truly cultured, very sane in her views of life and in her judgment of people. Surrounded by servants she preserved her independence. I was aghast when she insisted on carrying my bag into the house when we arrived. She also brought chairs for her guests, her servants calmly viewing her meanwhile. She confided to me that in her earlier years, when she and her husband were in moderate circumstances, she performed many household tasks. Then after they were able to employ many servants, she was afraid of becoming dependent and had trained her servants to let her alone when they saw her going for a chair or doing like things. She was a rare woman with wide vision, and her devotion to the University of California was made manifest in benefactions that were wisely considered and which will be lasting.}

{Later in the term Professor and Mrs. L. H. Bailey came; he, to give some lectures, and to consider whether he would accept the position of Dean of Agriculture in the University of California. President Wheeler, when he was a Professor of Greek at Cornell, was wont to jeer at the College of Agriculture, but as soon as he became President of the State University of California he appreciated the importance of Agriculture Education, and, also, like the good President he was, tried to get the most valuable man in this department away from Cornell. However, Professor Bailey decided to remain at Cornell, to our great relief.}

Meanwhile the summer class at Cornell was in session. For twenty years Mr. Comstock had had a summer term of ten weeks in entomology with very important results. It had brought to his laboratory many graduates from other institutions who were able in ten weeks to accomplish a term's work toward an advanced degree. Later, when the University established a summer session of six weeks, it was not practicable to demand all the time of a student for entomology, as had been {the case} formerly. Thus, the entomological work was so changed in its nature that Mr. Comstock gave up the ten-week term {and his work} became simply a part of the regular summer school for six weeks and was never quite of the quality of that of the earlier {years}.

{This summer of 1905 he writes me under date of July 5, "This is registration day and I have been kept busy making plans for students until time to go home. Nineteen have registered in the advanced work. Among the advanced students are Dr. Gregory of Wells, Miss Clark and several other of my former students; more than half the class have worked in my laboratory before."}

{He} had begun again to arise early and put the time on the Spider Book. On July 10 he {writes}: "I worked on spiders in the early morning (4:45 to 7);

lectured at 8; went into the field for a reconnaissance from ten to twelve; and took the class into the field from two to five P.M. It would have been a delightful day's work if it had not been so {hot}."

{He} worked with characteristic enthusiasm on the spiders as {the following quotations from his} letters show:

> "My own day has been a successful one. I went to the laboratory at 5 A. M. and except for a little break at breakfast time worked on the *Spider Book* until noon, and the work went well. I wrote up five species which is an unusually large day's work for me. Today I have finished threshing out a table of the genera of the *Theridiidae*, the cob-web weavers, upon which I have been at work for three weeks. It is one of the jobs I have been dreading, as no one has written a table that will work, and these spiders are very common, so I *had* to have a table. We have tables by Simon, Keyserling, Cambridge, and Banks, and in each case one of the principal divisions was "males with stridulating organs" and "males without stridulating organs." As females do not have stridulating organs, and as three out of four specimens collected are females, these table are of little use; so, I have had to find a new set of characters. None of these authors is a teacher; if they had tried their tables on students I think they would have modified them. This forenoon I spent in the field. We went up along Fall Creek and found many interesting spiders. This afternoon I have been photographing some of them; a big *Dolomedes* and her egg-sac; and a *Lycosa* with her back covered with young. Both were trying subjects as neither would stay posed; but I think I got good negatives of both at last."

{A momentous change in our household occurred during my absence, although it was planned before I left. Mrs. Margery Smith, who had been a day helper in the home for twelve years, came to the house to live, bringing with her youngest child, Norman, a young boy. Forced by illness and death of her husband, from comfortable circumstances to work by the day to support her family; she was heroic in her bravery and achievement. She was an Englishwoman of refinement and ability; her personality was pleasing, and she had a dignity that no one infringed upon. She came into our home knowing that I was teaching and writing and had less and less time for household cares, and she was ready to assume the responsibility of running the house. She remained with us nearly seventeen years, an efficient, conscientious housekeeper, as devoted to our interests as if they had been her own;—a sympathetic companion and the treasured friend which she remains to this day.}

{Mr. Comstock's letters gave news of the social life; of Margaret Cook and her devotion to mother; of Alice Simmons who came to make music with her "fiddle brown"; of the chipping sparrows that built in the vine directly over the entrance to the porch; of William A. Riley and his winsome bride; of the joke on Dr. Riley, who chanced to overtake one of our former students and walking along with her, when they met Mrs. Gage, who said; "I suppose this is the new Madam Riley," at which Little Billie, utterly confused, stammered; "I am sorry to say it is not." Mr. Comstock also wrote, "Ross Marvin came this morning to say Good-bye; he is going with Lieut. Peary and they sail next week. He is very happy because he has secured the best possible position he could hope for. He is to be a member of Lieut. Peary's personal party, which included only eight people. Marvin's function is that of observer, astronomical, meteorological, and biological. He receives at least $50.00 a month and expenses.}

{My work at Berkeley was finished August 4th. On the whole, it had been satisfactory, although I was handicapped with lack of knowledge of the natural environment. However, names of plants and animals were not so important. When I took a volunteer class into the field we studied the habits of plants until we knew their secrets before we learned their names. I found my class in Nature Literature knew nothing of the poems or writings of Bret Harte or Joaquin Miller, although both, especially the former, had written exquisitely of plants and animals.}

{The Californians so resented the pictures of their early history as shown in Bret Harte's stories that they would have none of him. I think I showed them their mistake. One woman who attended my classes attracted me greatly, Mrs. Florence Halstead of Los Angeles, who has since endowed so liberally the chairs of Zoology and Botany at Pomona College. She is a rare woman with deep sympathy for nature, and the friendship established between us then, has continued unbroken.}

{Before I left Ithaca, Mrs. Schurman, who had been in Japan the year before, asked me to find a Japanese butler for her. None of my California friends advised taking a Japanese servant east. They said he would prove unreliable. By chance, I met a Japanese student who spoke excellent English and who wished to enter an eastern college. He was willing to work a year to earn money. So, I started east with Ogata, and with a charming young heiress who was entrusted to my care, a strange combination, but it worked all right.}

{Ogata served the Schurmans a year and then entered Cornell, where he made an excellent; and now holds a fine position in Japan. He confided to me at the end of his service at the Schurmans, "It is well, Mrs. Comstock, that you brought a student instead of a Japanese servant to President Schurman's for, if a real Japanese servant had come, he would have killed their Irish cook."}

{I found mother quite as well as when I left her, thanks to the devoted care of Margaret Cook. The latter was to teach at a nearby rural school to carry out some of our Nature Study experiments for us. Vernon Kellogg made us a short visit soon after my return and also Mr. and Mrs. P. L. Windsor of the University of Illinois. In September we took mother to Otto for a last visit to her friends and neighbors. We stayed in the old Allen home with Etta Holbrook.}

{This autumn was made happy for us by the marriage of our lifelong friend Albert W. Smith to Ruby Green Bell. We were very glad to have them near us.}

{The student habitués of the house on Sunday nights were Alice Simmons, Joe Kellogg, a brother of Vernon, Christian Bues, Heloise Abel, Will Geer, Emma Venable, Lee Hawley, Harry Law, Ortis de Zevallos, Pierre Pochet, and our cousin Alice Graves, who was studying at Cornell. Our Sunday nights were very attractive musically this year, as Alice Simmons played the violin and Joe Kellogg accompanied her on the piano.}

{Mr. Comstock} was planning a short visit to his mother in California when December 16th, 1905, we received the news of her death. Her failing health and strength had left her little pleasure in life, but her courage was unfailing. Her cheerful outlook, her integrity, {her loving devotion to us all}, and her happy way of making most of the pleasant things of life, combined to make a stronger character and a lovable woman. Her death was a great sorrow to both of us. {Mr. Comstock} had always held for her a deep love and tender devotion.

On January 2, 1906, William Smith spent the day with us and I took him to the photographer for the only authentic picture of him in possession of the college which he founded. I also took him in the afternoon to see Professor Corson and, as both were ardent spiritualists, they enjoyed each other greatly.

{On Mr. Comstock's 57th birthday he gave a very clear and impressive lecture before Sibley College.}

For years after my long illness of 1884 I found it difficult to go to sleep at the scheduled time. To weary myself into sleepiness, I would write in my "Journal Intime" my reactions from the experiences of the day. These comments finally came to be more or less philosophical, but I never dreamed of giving them publicity. The habit continued, however, and I finally began to fashion a story in the nineties for my own amusement. {I strung on the thread of rather stumbling plot the comments from these several volumes of my journal.} Wilhelm Miller[5] had given me a little Japanese figure cut in teakwood which gave me the motif of my story "Confessions to a Heathen Idol." {Mr. Comstock} was aware of this late-hour occupation of mine {but was not interested}. He was too busy with his own work to be diverted by anything so unrelated.

To my great surprise I finished the tale in 1906, {typed it and sent a copy to George Tansy. He was not very enthusiastic but advised me to send it to a publisher.} Then I went to my husband and said, "Harry, you will just have to read it. I shall not send it to a publisher until you do." So, I {brought} it to him one night then retired upstairs leaning over the banister my heart in my mouth until I heard him laugh. Then I felt better. His judgment was absolutely correct:—"For people who want this sort of thing, it is just what they want." It is a book that has meant much to some, and nothing to others. I sent the manuscript to Doubleday, Page [and] Company and it was accepted within four days; naturally I was jubilant. I felt that it would be scandalous for a scientific woman to write a novel, so I insisted upon the nom de plume, Marian Lee. Of course, this was a futile gesture,—{I think my friend, Mary Hill}, guessed the name of the author within a short time.

Early in April my cousin Eliza Little McCutcheon and her daughter Bertha Bard from Gowanda visited us at my earnest request. Bertha was a beautiful woman just verging on forty and I wished to use photographs of her to illustrate "Confessions to a Heathen Idol." Meanwhile I had made an enlarged replica of the little teakwood image in plaster, so it could be used in the photographs. These illustrations were very successful and received many compliments from reviewers.

Mr. Comstock became interested in the organization of the Cosmopolitan Club at Cornell. He was well acquainted with the two men who were the chief factors in starting it, especially with Christian Bues, who was one of our Sunday night {coterie}. These young men felt that they had no opportunity to know {the native students} in the University and each racial group persisted in keeping by itself socially.

One of the fundamental articles in the constitution of the Club required that one-half of the membership should consist of students from the United States. The Club has had a successful career at Cornell and similar Cosmopolitan Clubs have been established in other American universities.

---

5. Footnote from the 1953 edition (p. 217): "Wilhelm Miller was a Cornellian and a writer, editor, and teacher of horticulture. His wife, Mary Rogers Miller, also a Cornellian and dear friend of the Comstocks, did much noteworthy work in nature study in New York State. —G.W.H."

{In June our French boy Pierre Pochet left us to go back to France to serve his time in the army as demanded of young Frenchmen. He was a boy of high ideals, puritanical morals and hated war. Little either of us dreamed that he would ever be on a battlefield.}

{In June we attended the charming Quaker wedding of Mary Whitson and Professor George Warren at Professor [Frank A.] Fetter's home, Mrs. Fetter being a sister of the bride.}

{On June 10th, 1906, Goldwin Smith Hall was dedicated, and Goldwin Smith came to take part in the ceremony. He said to me: "This is I believe, the happiest day of my life." His interest in Cornell was so genuine that this new University was a part of his life and he gave to it in his will, his books and all that he had to give. He was a Regius Professor of History at Oxford, and the college was deeply hurt because he left it no money, we were told at Oxford later. The Oxford authorities could not understand how a man like Goldwin Smith could become so infatuated with a crude institution of learning in a foreign land. It was difficult to explain how the ideal of Ezra Cornell made actual by Andrew D. White of "An Institution where any person can find instruction in any study," had appealed to him.}

{It was June 3rd, 1906 that Robert Collyer, then 83 years old, preached for the last time in the chapel. He and George Burr took tea with us. I found I must prepare something simple for his meal and Mr. Comstock said to him "Never mind if you don't get much to eat; there is a cigar coming afterwards," at which he said, with his charming smile, "I was wondering." His personality was one of the greatest and most beautiful that I have ever known.}

{The last of June (1906) the A. A. A. S. met in Ithaca, which meant much activity on the part of the Science Faculty at Cornell and of which we took our share. We had many guests, among them Edward Franklin, the husband of Effie Scott and father of Anna Comstock Franklin, Professor J. C. Branner, L. O. Howard, H. E. Summers, Dr. J. G. Needham, and others.}

{Our cousins Glenn and Nannie Herrick and their two young sons, Marvin and Stephen, came to Ithaca for the summer. They had a house near us and their presence was a delight to all of us.}

{My cousin's daughter, Alice Graves, came for the summer school of 1906. She was a graduate of Lake Forest and had been a special student of Dr. Needham's. She was planning to take graduate work in biology for a year, In August, she came down with typhoid fever and was in the hospital three weeks before we could bring her to our own home. She recovered in time to enter the University in October.}

{July 13 was mother's 83rd birthday and we were to have a family party. The night before, Mr. Comstock undertook the task of making a large ring of plaster of Paris to hold the 83 candles which were to encircle the cake. It was something of a task and while he was at it Dean Ernest Huffcut called. He insisted on helping and entered into the task with a boyish enthusiasm that has always lingered in our memory. Around the birthday cake were seven candles of different color which were Marvin Herrick's part of the celebration as he had just passed his seventh birthday. None of us will ever forget the expression of wonder on the beautiful face of my mother or the joy radiating from the face of the seven-year old when the cake came in, all candles lighted.}

{This is a place to tell of the way we had to manage with so many guests in a small house. Mother and the nurse had the study on the second floor. Mr. Comstock had a small bedroom on that floor but his hours for sleeping and working were so different from mine, that I could not sleep in his room without disturbing him seriously. On the same floor was our one guest room. On the third floor was a large room which was Mrs. Smith's. Her son, Norman, had a cot in the hall on that floor. There was a small attic room, on the east side, used as a store room. I put yellow paper on the walls and hung white and yellow cretonne to hide the unsightly nooks, and to cover the packing boxes which I made into a dressing table; it was a sunshiny little nest and I felt happy to have a refuge of my own that no one else wanted. But while Father Dowell was with us in the guest room, Alice Graves came home from the hospital and nowhere to put her except in my eyrie, as I called it. Margaret Cook came also, and she and I camped in the parlor on the sofas.}

September 27th, [1906], the "Confessions of a Heathen Idol" was published and I was breathless with excitement and delight. It received many interesting and agreeable reviews, the best of all by Marion Reedy in the *St. Louis Mirror*. The book was well received and a second edition, under my own name, was published.

I was called to Geneva for a meeting of the William Smith trustees and President Stewardson of Hobart College. There were at the meeting Professor Nathaniel Schmidt, Felix Adler, Henry Graves, and myself, representing William Smith, and President Stewardson and Professor Turk, representing Hobart. The plans were then made for William Smith College. It was left with me to decide whether it should be co-educational or co-ordinate; I decided on the latter because, with an old institution like Hobart, I felt co-education would so change it as to alienate the alumni body. I had always been, and shall always be, a believer in co-education. But circumstances alter cases and I am sure my decision in the case of William Smith College was wise. President Stewardson, {who was a remarkably wise man}, saw no end of trouble with two boards of trustees and so combined them.

On December 14, 1906, I was elected a trustee of Hobart College, {an honor still continued after 26 years of service}.

My election as trustee of Hobart was a great source of amusement to President White; he had spent his freshman year at Hobart and was greatly impressed by the ecclesiastical and dignified trustees of Hobart at that time, all of them Bishops or noted churchmen. Mr. White said: "The world does move. The idea of a woman being elected a trustee of Hobart and of all things such a woman as you, Mrs. Comstock, born and reared a Hicksite Quaker and now a Unitarian!" and he laughed long and heartily. {However}, I found the trustees of Hobart a group of devoted, able business men with whom it was a pleasure to be associated. I am sure I showed more respect for the wishes of {our aged Bishop Walker} than did my colleagues. {His successor, Bishop Brent, has been a joy to us all and our Suffragan Bishop has been the life of the meetings and is as dear to the Unitarian member as to the orthodox ones. Always on November 7th we went to President White to congratulate him upon his birthday. This year we had a particularly happy call. He was 78.}

All during the fall of 1906 we were making the Hermitage habitable. {Mr. Glanister, of whom we bought the place, was a host in himself in making the place over.} We put a large window in the living room which gave us a wide view of the lake. The room was given a hardwood floor and ceiled to make it warm. We set up the wood stove that was in my mother's parlor when I was a child. It had a grate, and, in the evenings, we opened its two front doors which made it as cheerful as a fireplace. Mr. Comstock and I spent weekends there and on each trip, he would walk from Taughannock Station the mile and a half to the Hermitage, carrying on his back a pack-basket filled with materials for fixing the house.

The labor Mr. Comstock performed in and about this place was something remarkable. {He always loved to work along the line of his enthusiasms.} He added paths and built a fine wharf and a double-decked boat house, in the upper part of which we swung our hammocks, and from which we enjoyed the glory of many sunsets. {It} was always a place where work was play; we dumped our cares at the Ithaca station when we left, but they were always waiting to jump at us on our return.

On April 26th, 1907, there was a great celebration of Ezra Cornell's 100th birthday, and the next day [Roberts Hall], the New York State College of Agriculture was dedicated with imposing ceremonies. There was a large reception at the College in the evening. We entered into these ceremonies only half-heartedly for my mother was ill and we were filled with anxiety {for} her.

{I shall never forget the days that followed. She} always smiled at us with her face alight as she greeted us. Dr. [Eugene] Baker was sick and sent Dr. Floyd Wright, then a young man, in his place. Mother thought he was some friendly boy and patted his hand when he felt of her pulse. Doctor Wright was greatly impressed by her beauty; white wavy hair framed her face, her cheeks were pink, and her eyes, violet blue, were shining and he said to me, "I have never seen anyone so beautiful." {Her} last thoughts were of love and happiness for us. She {passed away} May 1st a beneficent, lovable presence during her life, a dear and vital memory since her death.

{Her love of the beautiful in nature and her love of poetry had permeated her life on the farm and made the work there something outside of drudgery. The old English Reader, rich in the poetry of the 17th and 18th centuries, was a joy to her always. During the last months of her life, when her memory of recent events failed, she remembered pages of poetry that she had forgotten in her busy years, but which now came back to her.}

We had a simple ceremony at the house. Mr. Heizer spoke, and Edna Mertz sang "Crossing the Bar" {and we took her to Otto for burial. As the hearse drove out of the grounds}, a chickadee followed us calling "Phoebe-Phoebe-Phoebe" her name which she always loved to hear the chickadee repeat. It was as if he were calling goodbye.

{Our friend, Etta Holbrook, welcomed us to the Allen Homestead and there was a ceremony for the Otto friends and relatives. It was a comfort to them and to us all to see her face so beautiful and sweet, her dear form clad in the gray and lavender that she loved and the gray casket which was covered with violets from the meadows and hill whose beauty was a conscious part of her life for years. Through the May sunshine and with the sweet sad songs of the meadow larks for funeral hymn, we laid her beside father in the North Otto Cemetery.}

{My mother's cousin, Mary King, who had lived with her since my father's death now came to live with us. She was a woman of strong character, exquisitely neat and dainty, very active, positive and ambitious. She had never married; her fiancée had been killed in the Civil War and she remained true to him all her life.}

{On May 27, Mr. Comstock began moving his laboratory from White Hall to the new College of Agriculture where the third floor was given to him. This was a difficult undertaking and required constant care and supervision. I find this note in my diary for June 5. "Dr. [E. P.] Felt dined with us tonight. Harry had been laboratory truck to the college all day and was dead tired and lay on the sofa and snored, and all my vivacity failed to cover up his delinquency."}

{All this spring we spent our weekends at the Hermitage and I believe the rest there saved our lives.}

{On June 18, 1907 I went to Geneva to see William Smith lay the cornerstone of his college. He was over ninety years old; he went to Rochester on business in the morning, returned, laid the cornerstone in the afternoon without apparent fatigue.}

{After the term closed, Mr. Comstock and I went to Hilltop and then for a delightful three days in Geneseo with Mr. and Mrs. Austin Wadsworth, where we made the acquaintance of the little son, William Perkins Wadsworth. Never, I am sure, had a son been more welcome than this one.}

{Mr. Grove Karl Gilbert had planned a wonderful trip for us in the high Sierras, a real geological field trip. Our party of five, Mr. Gilbert, his sister, Mrs. Emma Loomis, Miss Alice Eastwood, the botanist of the California Academy of Science, Mr. Comstock and myself, assembled at Oakland and on July 30th, we started by train for Chinese, whence, by stage, we arrived at Crocker's, high in the mountains among the sugar pines and incense cedars. Here we found saddle horses for ourselves, three experienced mounted guides, and eight pack horses for carrying food and camp equipment. Then followed wonderful days and nights; days that began in the early dawn with breakfast before the sun had a chance to warm us and then the excitement of seeing the horses brought in by Fred from the outlying meadows. He seemed to us to ride like a centaur and he would always bring up the fifteen horses and range them against the barrier rope like a class of children toeing the mark.}

{After all was in readiness and the camp fire absolutely extinguished, we fared forth on the road which was often apparently but a trail through forests of stately yellow and sugar pines, cedars and Douglas spruce, many of them magnificent trees from two to three hundred feet high; past aspen glades; traversing mountain meadows purple with lupine, white with "pussy tail" or coral gilia; across swift streams; along level stretches which showed bear tracks in the dust; then around the shores of mountain lakes, coming out on heights which revealed to the far horizon a chaos of cold, gray granite and snow. Then perhaps there was luncheon by some wayside spring, a rest, a chapter from John Muir's "California Mountains" and then on to camp whither the pack train had preceded us.}

{We enjoyed sleeping on the ground each making his own bed in the afternoon when the sun was still shining. The process is as follows: the ground is cleared of twigs with a shovel for a space of 6 by 3 feet; after it is smoothed and leveled, a shovelful of earth is removed to make a shallow transverse trench about midway of the bed:—this trench is the "hip hole" and, if properly made, adds greatly to the comfort of the bed; a rubber blanket is then spread over the ground and on this a square of canvas is laid so that one-half covers the prepared couch; blankets are then spread in a similar fashion and the sleeping bag put in place on them; the pillows are then added and the blankets folded across the sleeping bag and fastened with safety pins; the free half of the protecting canvas is thrown over the whole and the bed is made.}

{We thought Tenaya Lake Camp was, perhaps, the most interesting of all our stops for this Lake is set in great rock domes with Cathedral Peak rising 2000 feet above it. Tenaya, itself, is 8146 feet above the sea and is a beautiful sheet of water. We climbed to Cathedral Peak and found at the top a little lake, a gem of ultramarine blue, with borders of olive green where the water is shallow. The rocks were white, tinted with red, and extending to the water's edge were patches of huckleberry, exquisitely green.}

{The Tuolumne Meadows are probably the most beautiful mountain meadows in the world,—broad and long, they border the river with craggy peaks and gray domes all around with Mount Gibb and Mount Dada in the distance. The meadows were a Persian tapestry of color made by patches of spring flowers. The fishing here was a delight to Mr. Comstock, but the mosquitoes were villainous.}

{Our next camp, Mono Pass, was 10600 feet above the sea and it seemed as though we were on the ridgepole of the world with great bare rocks hemming us in on two sides. The following night at Tioga Lake, we were in a beautiful amphitheater, a circular meadow of fifteen acres surrounded by majestic mountains. On our return we passed again through the Tuolumne Meadows and camped again at Tenaya Lake. We stayed two days at Eagle Meadow Camp from which we climbed to El Capitan where we found ourselves in the midst of a terrific thunder and lightning snowstorm. It lasted but a short time, however, and then we had a wondrous view of the Yosemite Valley. The next day, Mr. Comstock and I left the party and climbed down the zigzag trail, 3300 feet, to the Valley where we spent two days. After leaving Yosemite we took two days to reach Crocker's where we bade goodbye to our faithful helpers and to our beloved horses. I had named my faithful mount, Demi Tasse, because he was small and black and always after a dinner, and when I bade him farewell I dropped a tear into his lovely pink nostril.}

{We returned from this wonderful mountain trip direct to our home at Ithaca. After settling the house, I had to move my office to the fourth floor of Roberts Hall and soon I had to go to Bedford and Mt. Kisco to farmers' meetings. I was entertained at the latter place at the home of a Friend, James

Wood, and there made the acquaintance of his daughter, Lena, who after the war did such notable work in feeding the children in Germany.}

{One of my enterprises, as a member of a committee of Cornell Alumnae was to establish a house where students could live and do part of the work in order to lessen the expense of their college course. We did our part and kept the house going seven years, but the savings to the students were not commensurate with the labor and responsibility of carrying the project on.}

{The Entomological Department was so luxuriously housed in Roberts Hall that we concluded to add a social half-hour to the Jugatae meeting. Mrs. Riley and I bought the cups, and plates and these teas were a feature, giving us all a chance to become acquainted until my own teaching and work became so absorbing that I could no longer spare the energy to keep them up. Professor Bateson of England, was a guest at one of these teas this Fall, and also a guest at our home.}

{Among our student friends was Mr. J. T. Lloyd, whose destiny had been partly due to Mr. Comstock who had several years before met Dr. Uri Lloyd of Cincinnati at the Cosmos Club in Washington. Dr. Lloyd asked advice about his young son who was interested only in entomology and Mr. Comstock advised grounding him in modern languages first and then sending him to Cornell. In 1905, Dr. Lloyd appeared and said, "Professor Comstock, I followed your advice and sent Tom to Europe to learn languages; he is here now ready for work." Dr. Uri Lloyd is one of the most interesting men we ever knew, an author of stories, a drug chemist, a man of broad culture and experience and of wide vision. The acquaintance with him and his wife and our long and intimate association with Tom Lloyd have enriched our lives.}

{Dr. James G. Needham had come to Cornell as a research worker in Limnology. Mr. Comstock had asked Mr. Jared T. Newman, to grant enough land at Renwick for a limnological laboratory, a request generously granted. The laboratory, a frame building, was put up and became a place for study and research in many lines. Cornell had had the first Insectary in the world and now it had the first laboratory in limnology in the world with a great scientist at the head of it.}

{The fall was very full of things to do for both of us and it was a great relief to leave it all and go abroad for the first Sabbatical year Mr. Comstock had ever taken although there were three due him.}

{We sailed from New York, December 7, 1907, on the S. S. "Frederick der Grosse," bound for Naples. Mary Austin was in our special care for this trip and a very interesting companion she proved to be. In the cabin next to ours was a man of good appearance. There were also two rather striking demimondaines as passengers. We learned, after landing in Naples, that these three had separated a man from his wife in Genoa and getting him drunk, had induced him to cash his entire letter of credit, $10,000, which they made off with leaving him to sober up and explain matters to his family. I had conversed with the gentleman occasionally who said he had travelled extensively in South America. When I asked his business, he said he "dealt in hides." In view of his late swindling performance, I wonder if he was also a humorist.}

John Henry Comstock on a camel during their trip to Egypt.

CHAPTER XII

A Sabbatical Year Abroad—Egypt and Greece

In Mrs. Comstock's manuscript, this is Chapter XII, and it is forty-four pages in length. Approximately seven of these pages are included in the 1953 book as Chapter 14. During my archival research, a displaced page, marked "Special Page" at its top, was included at the very end of the Chapter XII manuscript folder. No page number was assigned; however, through careful comparison with other manuscript pages, it was discerned to be a duplicate of page 13–10 in Mrs. Comstock's manuscript (Chapter XIII). This found page, in the folder of manuscript Chapter XII, was the *only page* from manuscript Chapter XIII that was used to conclude Chapter 14 in the 1953 book.[1]

{It was toward evening of December 19, 1907 that we came to anchor in the Bay of Naples. In the sunset light the sea was dull blue and rose; Ischia and Capri and the Italian shore were deeper blue and seemed swimming in the tender light of reflected clouds in the calm sea. Later, appeared Naples with

1. A partial summation of these pages was offset at the beginning of Chapter 14 (p. 220) by Glenn Washington Herrick: "[In 1907–1908, Professor Comstock was granted his first sabbatic leave from Cornell. With Mrs. Comstock he visited Egypt, Greece, Italy, Switzerland, and France. Most of the trip was like that of other tourists, but the visits to the homes of dragomen, in Alexandria, were unusual and diverting experiences. The attendance of the Comstocks at the wedding of Professor Vernon Kellogg of Stanford University, in Florence, Italy, was also not a typical tourist experience. —G.W.H.]" —KSt.

its lights and Vesuvius looming dark against the sky. Boats with musicians swarmed around our ship as we dropped anchor, and guitar, violin and sweet voices filled the air with music. It was like a beautiful dream.}

{We settled comfortably in Pension Millar, kept exceedingly well by a German. We were lulled to sleep nights by violin and song below our windows after we had thrown centimes to the street. The sights of Naples interested us greatly, but we could not say much of the smells. The ornate donkeys, the colorful streets, the picturesque people, the flocks of goats (each climbing the outdoor stairway to an upper story where dwelt its owner) all made us feel that we were surely in a different world.}

{We hastened to the Aquarium and spent hours studying the sea life there; but witnessing the feeding of the devil fish with raw meat gave material for nightmares. At the Aquarium we met Dr. John S. Kingsley, who was in Naples with his family, all of them delightful folk; their presence added much to our happiness in Naples.}

{However, we were pestered by all sorts of folk that lived off the tourists. The cabmen followed us shouting, the guides grasped us by the arms insisting we go with them. The street vendors entreated us to buy and the news-boys and boot-blacks made Mr. Comstock's life miserable. We had a characteristic experience trying to go to an advertised performance of Carmen at the great Teatro Bellini, the largest opera house in Europe at that time. Our concierge told us our tickets would be 8 1/2 lire apiece. He also bargained with the cab driver to take us there for one lire; after we had driven several blocks our cabby insisted that the fare was one lire apiece; we were helpless, so we agreed. When we arrived, we tipped an usher to take us up a few steps to the ticket office, and we paid 8 1/2 lire for seats. When we entered the auditorium, another usher sold us programs and, to cap the climax, another brought me a foot-stool and insisted that I take it, although the Lord gave me sufficient length of leg that footstools are superfluous and annoying to me. We tipped them all and waited for the performance to begin. Only a few people had assembled, and, after a time, it was announced that the artists refused to sing for so small an audience. Then we had to fee some more attendants to get out; we took our tickets to the office and they would refund only 7 lire for what we paid 8 1/2 for a half hour before; by this time, we were in a gale of laughter, the whole performance was so outrageous that it was funny. We bargained with the cabman to take us to our Pension for one lire and fee and we speculated on how he would raise his price; we nearly fainted when at the pension we asked him how much and he said one lire and fee. Mr. Comstock was so pleased to find an honest cabman that he gave him two lire.}

{Christmas at our German Pension was characteristically celebrated with a great dinner and a Christmas tree for the children of the guests. Among the latter was a Colonel of an Italian cavalry unit and his wife and small daughter. The Colonel was big, ornate and with a gloomy, embittered countenance which was emphasized by his pointed mustache. His wife was tall and rather handsome; the child was a beautiful creature with dark curly hair. She was full of mischief and coquetry as a miss of seven could possibly be, and she held the whip hand over her dumpling of a nurse and also over her sombre [*sic*] father who, it is safe to say, could command his regiment better than he could that small sprite.}

{A complication of the Christmas party was another couple that interested me. The man had a round face, shorn head and looked like a Russian. She had a strikingly ugly face, long and fascinating, and framed in dark hair that was combed down over her ears. Her eyes were dark and flashing. She dressed artistically and devoted all her charms to the enchantment of her companion. It seems that she was a Moroccan dancer and he was a sculptor and the two were living together without benefit of clergy. The virtuous German Frauen, who were guests, objected to having the couple at the dinner and our host asked me how I felt about it. I told him I thought it was a poor way to celebrate Christ's birth by putting sinners out in the cold and I voted to have them.}

{It rained so constantly while we were in Naples that we could not make many excursions, but one day we made the ascent of Vesuvius. A cable car took us up the mountain for some distance where guides met us. Two were allotted to me and they "snaked" me up the trail at a rapid rate, one pushing and one pulling. After a half hour I sat down by a hole in the ground out of which the steam was pouring, and I asked what was to be seen in the crater, "Vapore!" Vapore, Steam!" was the excited answer.}

{"I can see steam pouring out over the top and I can see steam here at this hole: I shall go no further!"}

{"Have courage!" exhorted my guide.}

{"I have courage of my convictions! I stay here;" I declared.}

{Mr. Comstock toiled on through ashes up to his knees and at the rim could not see twenty feet down the crater because of the steam, and when he returned he said I was a wise woman; meanwhile I had been gazing out over the great billows of hardened lava, a picture of desolation that made me realize what a volcano means.}

{We spent one day at the R. Scuola Superiore d'Agriculture which was housed in a grand old marble palace at Portici. The stone stairs were worn by the footsteps of centuries. We visited the entomologists Sylvestri and Leonardo and found them very pleasant. They took us to the roof to show us the magnificent view of Naples and the Bay on one side, Vesuvius on the other, and nearby, the school forest and botanic gardens.}

{On January 1st, 1908, we boarded the Italian steamer "Perseo," bound for Alexandria. It was a cordial kindly ship, not too clean, but very comfortable. We made the acquaintance of Signor and Signora Debenditti of Milan and found them charming companions for many days thereafter.}

{We arouse early January 5 to see our ship make the beautiful harbor of Alexandria; the throng on the wharf was worth coming from America to see. We went to the Grand Hotel des Voyageurs where we were given a room "as big as a barn" and about as attractive. Our chambermaid was a} Frenchman of impressive moustache and dignified presence, and whose services rendered me speechless with embarrassment. I find the following note in my diary.

{"We arrived here this morning after a tranquil voyage of four days on the brusque blue Mediterranean. Here we are in the city of Euclid and Cleopatra! A pomegranate is on the table in front of me; Harry is counting his money in piastres; a surge of queer sounds come in through our tall casement windows from the out-door café' below, where some forty tables are set on the sidewalk and in the public square; these are filled with every kind of folk God ever made and some of whom he must have lost the pattern,—Italian, French, English, German, Greeks, Russians, Egyptians, Arabs, Sudanese, everything. The only things in common to them all are the tables and chairs, for each group has its own kind of food, and hawkers of strange dietary curiosities move about in the crowd, offering gently to sell."}

At Alexandria we fell into the hands of a beguiling dragoman, Alexander Mustafa, called Alex. He spoke English well, as he had been in the employ of an English officer. He took us first through the solid, handsome streets of New Alexandria and then through the native bazaars and where, in the narrow streets, stalwart men of every shade dressed in baggy trousers or long night-gown-like-robes, their heads covered with turbans, or red fezzes, jostled each other. There were Egyptian women in black, whose eyes looked out on the world above their black veils; Turkish women with white veils over the lower face, some of them thin enough to show the features, while the Bedouin women swung along with a second upper black skirt over their heads, their unveiled faces swarthy and purposeful. But of what ever nationality, the woman carried her small child astride one shoulder, one little leg down its mother's back and one on her breast, where she could hold it firm when necessary, and its little arms clasped around her covered head.

The native boys were amusing—all in nightie-like garments reaching almost to their heels. But they were as full of pranks as any properly breeched American boy. They played ball and they caught on behind carriages; they wrestled and ran and were full of mischief.

Alex took me shopping and his finesse as a buyer was something worth remembering. He took me to a native restaurant and treated me to a cup of Egyptian coffee; I asked:

"Alex, are you married?"

"Yes, madam."

"Have you children?"

"No madam, not yet, I have been married only six months. I have also my mother and sisters to support."

"Cannot they find some employment to help themselves?" I questioned, at which he answered scornfully:

"Any man who would allow his mother and sisters to work for money, would be contemptible." I meekly held my peace.

"Would you like to visit my home?" I was delighted to have this chance and thanked him.

We went to the Egyptian Quarter, a narrow, crooked street through houses which were standing in Cleopatra's time and containing all of the smells which since her time, had been hoarded there. {We} finally came to an open doorway into a tiny hall where there was a man and woman working, pounding something in a mortar. The hall was so narrow {we had to make} them get up before we could enter. We went up a flight of solid but {much} battered winding stairs and came into another tiny hallway. There was a scampering of women and I was ushered into a tiny front room, one complete side of which was taken with a huge four-poster bed with white spread and {quite} immaculate curtains. The window of the room was the finely carved mashrabiya [*sic*] common to harems. Under the window was a red plush sofa covered with white; in front of the sofa a marble-top table; at the other corner of the room was a wardrobe. Mrs. Alex was a buxom woman with olive complexion and languishing dark eyes, and was most impressive when her soft, black silk shawl was brought around to cover her lower face; {but} she was not pretty with her veil off as her teeth were rather prominent. She welcomed me with both small hands, hurried out to make coffee and brought it in in tiny gilt cups on a silver server. It was delicious with a bit of spice in it. She unlocked the wardrobe, took out a plate of pie-crusty cakes with holes in their middle, which were the Mohammedan Christmas cakes, and urged me to take them with the coffee. She had a gold bangle in the middle of her forehead, gold bracelets on her small wrists, pretty slippers on her tiny feet and silver bands about her ankles. Her dress was of calico, and she told me in sign language that she had been working and was so sorry that she was not dressed up.

Occasionally she came over and patted me and kissed me on both cheeks. She asked her husband to invite me to stay all night and sleep in the bed with her; I was obliged to decline. She was very voluble and laughed excitedly.

When she in a moment of thoughtlessness dropped her veil, her husband dropped his eyes, and never looking at her at all, soon went out of the room. When he came back she hastily put up her veil. She examined my dress then with much joyous laughter showed me a beautiful ecru broadcloth dress braided with white which was her wedding garment. Then she took down a dozen or more gay flowered dresses made after the usual loose nightdress fashion of the East. These made up her trousseau and her husband said they cost much money. He had told me {at an earlier period} that it cost him $105 to get married, $25 of which was for the wedding breakfast, and as she was an orphan she had no fortune. When I came away she crossed herself and blessed me. All during my visit a rather handsome man-servant came in and out smoking cigarettes, took a cup of coffee in the hallway and looked at her as much as he wanted to, indicated a rather democratic relationship between mistress and servant. She did not seem to worry any when she unveiled before the servant, but before her husband it was another matter.

Alex {himself} was a dignified and courteous man while I was his guest, his dignity contrasting strongly with her excitement and chattering. Alex said he paid his servant $4.00 a month and food and clothing. I asked him what the servant did, and he said, "He sweeps out the house, gets up early, makes coffee for me, goes out on the street and buys things for the household, as the women do not go out." Alex took punctilious care of me on the street, assisting me at every step, and shooing everybody out of my way; the joke of it was everybody took him seriously, and if I had been the Queen of Sheba I could not have had the street made clearer for me, unless traffic were entirely stopped.

{When we left Cairo, Alex tried to make us promise to let him know when we returned, and we said, if we needed a dragoman, we would do so. If we had done as he requested, we would have been spared a harrowing experience later. The ride from Alexandria to Cairo was full of interest to us; there was a changing panorama of villages of mud huts with here and there a taller one like a queen bee's cell, acres of cotton, fields of maize now cut and drying, men plowing with buffaloes and camels, here and there irrigation ditches where the water was raised by means of the screw of Archimedes.}

{We went to the Hotel Metropole, as it had been recommended by Signor Debenditti. We had a charming room opening out on a balcony overlooking the garden and the table was better than at Shepheards, so people who knew the two told us. As we entered our room I saw a card on the door:}

{Ring once for Arab
Ring twice for maid
Ring three times for head waiter.}

{I was so interested in these directions that I hastened to ring once for the Arab; he appeared suddenly from nowhere, tall, lithe, dignified, his each cheek ornamented with three transverse scars, his tribal mark. He wore a white turban and a long, white, striped gown. I looked at him and gasped: "Hot water." He looked pensive and shook his head. I tried pantomime, thrusting my hand in the pitcher and then flirting it and assuming an agonized look as if it were burned. His visage became more sombre and he strode off to find the maid, and doubtless told her there was a lunatic in No. 14 that needed looking after. The maid was an Austrian and talked German and Arabic but no French or English, so by means of my half-forgotten German, through her ministrations, we attained a business basis with "Mohammet," who served us well and faithfully. Rarely through some studied act of mine I could make him smile which wrought a wonderful transformation, changing his expression of utter gloom to cheerfulness; his teeth were white and perfect. Through the maid I learned he was a member of a Dervish tribe of the Soudan, that he slept on a bare floor, never ate meat and never drank wine. He had come to Cairo to earn money for his family.}

{Our dinners were a never-ending source of interest to us. The dining room was very long with the kitchen at one end. The waiters were all tall, athletic Arabs, dressed in long white "nighties," that had shirt "flaps at the heels to allow for strides, broad red sashes secured with safety pins under the arms, red fezzes with black tassels on the heads, and red or white slippers on the feet (usually no stockings), all making a striking uniform very becoming to the swarthy complexions. Our waiter Hassam was nervous, high-strung and alert, black enough to be a negro, but too alert for that race. Hassam had a wild and wary air that always reminded me of a hairy woodpecker. He would speed down the vast dining room with long free, silent strides that made me think of wide spaces, deserts, camels and Bedouins. Our dinners consisted always of at least six courses and would have been tedious except for our interest in watching the waiters. The change of courses was indicated by the ringing of a bell; the moment it sounded, the troop would seem to fly down the long dining room, so silently did they move. Then back they would come in single file in long undulating strides bringing platters of meat, boiled chestnuts, baskets of fruit, and finally small cups of delicious Turkish coffee.}

{These first days in Cairo were the most interesting that we have ever experienced for we had never been in an Oriental country before. We wandered through the Ezbekieh Gardens and admired the palms and studied the hooded crows; they were a new species to us, but they acted crow-like even if their heads were gray. We saw sauntering there sometimes, hand in hand, a Turk and an Arab holding intimate converse. We were told that the Arab was the confidential servant and was treated with great consideration. We never tired of a walk through the Muski, the street which is the artery of the bazaars and the little shops where natives were carrying on their trades all open to the streets; some of these artisans were quadrumanous, using their toes to hold objects on which they were working. There, at a certain place, stood an old Arab with a goat skin of Nile water, genuine and unfiltered, which he gave to those who thirsted, and occasionally gained a piastre for his service. How anyone could drink unfiltered Nile water and live was beyond our comprehension. Our dragoman once told us that he who drank of this would be sick only once and that when he died. We took a train to Old Cairo where the strange architecture and the picturesque inhabitants made a scene for an artist to paint. We went with the Debenedetti to the citadel, where we gained a view of the city and the Nile that made us feel we were a part of an "Arabian Night's Entertainment." We visited the "Superb Mosque" built in 1356 and thence to the Mosque made of Alabaster. The exquisite architecture of the Mosques is, in my mind, the chief benefit that the followers of the Prophet have given to the world.}

{We took the train out to the Pyramids, a beautiful way under the lebbakh trees. But the first view of the Pyramids is as disappointing as the first view of Niagara. One has to get acquainted with them to appreciate their size and beauty. We were also disappointed to find the Sphinx in a hole, when we had always imagined it on a level with Cheops; but later we came to a true appreciation of these grand monuments. We went with our Italian friends to the Barrage of the Nile and admired the mighty weir which regulates the flow of the river. Here Mr. Comstock got a snapshot of a blind beggar and his daughter that has been greatly admired. The girl, unveiled and a little puzzled at Mr. Comstock's performance, had an expression on her face that was mysterious, sad and wistful.}

{We joined Cook's excursions to Memphis and the Step Pyramid, the tombs of Ti and the Sacred Bulls. It was a short ride on the little steamer. We took donkeys from the landing (each donkey being afflicted with a donkey boy) and rode past a tent village of Bedouins, then through the narrow streets of a mud village thronged with interesting looking Arabs, on and out through a palm grove to see the colossal statues. One of granite brought from Assuan, the other cut from limestone, both figures of Ramses II. It was our first face-to-face acquaintance with Ramses II and we paid enthusiastic tribute to his beauty and the smile that was his "trade mark." We then went on a road about twenty feet above the surrounding country; the view from it was enchanting. At the left, close by, were ponds bordered with blue-green rushes; further away, were fields of vivid green wheat with rows of palms beyond and as a background the warm, golden-gray of the desert hills and the stately pyramids on the horizon. At our right there were also ponds, green wheat, and palms, and beyond these the gleaming Nile.}

{One of our most interesting experiences in Cairo was a visit to the University which is held in the Mosque of Gamai el-Azhar. To get there one had to go through the bazaar of the bookseller where, in booths, all sorts of books, mostly small, were piled high, one atop of the other, clear to the ceiling. These were dignified booksellers and did not vocally offer their wares for sale. A crooked dirty main street brought us to one of them mosque gates, the gate of the barbers (because students used to have their heads shaved here). We were met at the door by a man in a turban who asked for our tickets which we then bought, and he tried to keep the change. Then a servant in a white turban and blue dress came with straw slippers which he tied on to our feet before we could enter. (We saw students take off their shoes and go in with them in hand).}

{We were taken to the library, a large room, very high, with ceiling in Moorish design, and with walls ornamented with ancient mosaics, brought from Mecca, the guide said. Here in glass cases were the books. One section was devoted to the Koran grammars and all the others were filled with copies of the Koran. Many of these are Mss. [manuscripts]. Some of them, exhibited under glass, are magnificent books on vellum, illustrated. It seems that when some great man wanted to do something grand and pious he had a new copy of the Koran made. There were thousands of copies of the Koran in this library. The room was carpeted with a dark red plush carpet.}

{Returning to the University we entered first the courtyard. There on the ground were sitting hundreds of men-kind; most of them were studying aloud and weaving back and forth as they did so. Some were writing on paper or on tin slates. Old professors in rather gigantic turbans here and there were listening to pupils recite. I estimated that there was a teacher for every thirty or forty pupils. When a pupil recited he drew near and opposite to this teacher, both sitting on the floor, and repeated aloud what he had learned. Sometimes it seemed as if the teacher repeated in concert with the pupil, but I could not tell. Under one arcade were children just learning to write and read; some of them were giggly little boys just like any school boy.}

{We went on into the liwans, or the covered arcades, and here were pupils of all ages, from old men to young children. I saw one mite of a creature not more than four years, cuddled down by a big man, both studying, and the little one had a tin slate. It was almost noon when we were there, and some were eating a frugal lunch; sometimes two or three sat together, smiling but not talking much. And some were tired and had gone to sleep, simply stretching out on the floor and pulling the long black garment over the head. A few, more luxurious than the rest, had Angora goat skins or rugs on which to sit or lie. Occasionally there would be one saying his prayers, facing toward Mecca. All around the great court and liwans were lockers, each with its own key, and each would hold nearly as much as a steamer trunk. Each student, or perhaps two or three together, had a locker in which clothes, books, in fact all student belongings, were kept. At one end of the court were great rooms, the floors covered with matting and with lockers at the side; each of these was a dormitory for a geographical division of students; Turks, Syrians, Algerians, Sudanese, those living in Mecca and several others, all had separate quarters. In coming out through the court we had to take care not to step on pupils, they were so thick. The noise of so many studying aloud was not a roar, but a humming sound that permeated everywhere. The picture of so many sitting on the floor, all studying and weaving the body to and fro, was one of the most remarkable sights we had ever beheld.}

My interest in a new country is chiefly human, and the magnificent dragomen arrayed in beautiful and becoming garments, their handsome clear-cut features and expressive eyes all made their appeal to my artistic sense, an attitude which they were quick to discover. On the other hand, Mr. Comstock was bored beyond expression by them, because they always wanted to take us somewhere, or do something that had a price, and he would have none of them, an attitude that they at once discovered. So, one of the sights on the streets of Cairo that winter was myself walking along with two or three dragomen in close attendance and my husband staking on gloomily ahead of the procession.

The night we arrived in Cairo a young man followed us to our room and had a fight with some of the servants on the way up. His beautiful dove-colored gown was torn, and he was breathing hard; I so admired his prowess that I promised him if we had a guide in Cairo it should be he and he gave me his card. However, we never employed a dragoman in Cairo, but this young man often met us and my talks with him were most enlightening to me. His name was Abduhl Lamia; he was a tall handsome Arab with gray complexion, intelligent, quiet eyes and beautiful teeth. He was an Algerian and instead of a fez or turban he wore a little cap of striped silk and a long, black outer garment (Ah-by-yah) and under that a dove-colored Yelleck [sic] with wide flowing sleeves and under that a pale yellow, silken garment that I only saw at the neck and at the wrist where it falls over the hand. He had a beautiful silken girdle wound around his waist. He invited me to visit his harem and we had an interesting walk and talk across to Mena village where he lived. He told me that his mother and a married sister were living with him and that he was to be married the next summer to a very pretty and sweet girl. Abduhl's home consisted of two parts, one house above the other, like two huge steps up the side of a hill where was formerly a city, now in ruins. The house was whitewashed and with blue Venetian blinds. We ascended the steps and he threw open a door and ushered me into the parlor. It was a fair sized, high walled apartment with a brilliant, reflowered Brussels carpet on the floor. There were no chairs, but around the edges of the floor on all sides and set up against the walls were cushions, a foot thick and three feet long, rather flat and hard looking covered with bright and varied cotton material. Two or three chairs were brought into the room in my honor. The walls were white with pale blue dado and the timbers overhead were painted pale blue and the ceiling white. From the open door we looked up at the great pyramid almost about us.

Finally, Abduhl's mother appeared, pushing two small boys ahead of her, and carrying a bright but delicate baby of a year or so on her arm. They were all her daughter's children, and her daughter was then sixteen years old. She was a handsome woman with a fine dignity of carriage, full face, healthy colored complexion, cheeks and lips painted red, eyelids touched with black pencil, a blue tattoo on her chin, teeth very white, her nails stained with henna, and her small hands well shaped. Her ear-rings were of long strings of bead-like stones and she wore many strings of beads to match with a green bracelet on one arm and a silver one on the other. Abduhl brought in the coffee which he had prepared and gave me a cup, which I passed to her. The baby {wished it and got it all} and another cup later. {The Madam was dressed in black with a black shawl around her head and about her forehead in true Egyptian style, so as to show the ear rings.} Abduhl left the room and we each talked our own language, neither understanding a word the other said, but we understood each other's attitude and smiles and when we bade each other good-bye we made many bows and amicable salaams. I gave her a bunch of violets and she thanked me by putting her folded hands to the side of her head and bowing. She was evidently a woman of character and Abduhl told me that she lived with him because his father had married a young wife. He said that he should build her another house when he himself was married.

Abduhl and I had a discussion of the marriage {question}. He said that he would marry and if he were happy he would not take another wife. I told him if he was not happy with one he would be twice as unhappy with two. He looked puzzled at my logic. I explained to him that in America the father of the girl paid all the expenses of the wedding. He smiled a brilliant smile and said if he were an American he should then get married very often, for it costs a young man very much to get married here. I said if he were in America he would get married only once and asked him if he knew why and he said:

"Yes, when American marries two wives they hang him by the neck until he is dead." I said to him:

"If a Mohammedan has two wives and they quarrel what does he do," and he answered seriously,

"Then the husband goes in with a stick and makes peace."

However, I noticed that his mother would not live in the house with the second wife, despite sticks. Abduhl said his father and mother had made a pilgrimage to Mecca together and had taken him because he cried to go when he was ten years old. It took them a month only. He said many women went to Mecca but, of course, they were not allowed to enter the temple. I asked Abduhl if he thought a woman had a soul and he said: "Oh yes, I know it—" and then I asked the age of his fiancé.

"Fourteen."

"Too young," said I.

"No, just the right age for marriage," he maintained and asked:

"How old were you when you were married."

"Twenty-four."

"How did you manage to get a husband if you were as old as that," he asked in astonishment.

"How do you know your sweetheart is pretty and sweet? You surely have not seen her face," I asked. He gave me a knowing look out of the corners of his expressive eyes.

"I have seen her, I was not going to put my head in a bag," which showed Abduhl was a modernist, as did the following conversation when he asked:

"Tell me what they teach in the University where your husband is Professor."

"Literature, Law, Medicine, Engineering and Agriculture," I answered, and he asked eagerly:

"Do they really teach engineering there?" "Yes!"

"Then if I were in your country I should go to that University. I think it a waste of time to spend years in learning the Koran."

Abduhl was a real friend, he did us many favors, and offered to do more without pay. All he ever got from us was a box of cigarettes which Mr. Comstock bestowed upon him and which he took reluctantly. After our return to Ithaca he sent me a snapshot of his mother and wife, and the latter really was sweet and pretty.

{It was the 17th of January that found us on the Cook Express boat, the "Queen Hatsoo," bound for Assuan. There were plenty of excursions personally conducted, moving up and down the Nile in the fine excursion steamers, but we wished to see this famous river in a quieter way. This boat accommodated only about 20 first class passengers and, to my great joy, the lower deck was given over to transporting the natives. We found a very congenial group among the passengers—Mr. and Mrs. Rankin, Americans and cousins of a friend of ours, Mr. and Mrs. Walters of Brighton, England, and a charming young Englishman, Mr. Percy Herbert of the family of the poet. There was also a Turkish gentleman and his young brother and an Arab servant. We learned later that the young man was wild and very bad, and his elder brother was taking him on this trip to divert him from the ways of wickedness. They ate in their own cabin and we were always amused to see the Turk buy articles for himself, his brother and less elegant ones for his servant,—a gold-headed cane for the two gentlemen, a silver-headed cane for the Arab.}

{All that first day our pretty steamer, the *Queen Hatsoo*, steamed against the swift current of the Nile, which checked her speed sufficiently to give us plenty of time to gaze at the great flat-topped mountains which flank the great Egyptian river, their steep sides carved into great flying buttresses by the wind. Here and there were openings in this mountain wall which gave us glimpses of the great desert beyond, beset with more flat mountains. The Nile landscape has always for a background the desert and these mountains which take on heavenly tints of rose and purple in the morning and evening lights; for the foreground there is ever the strip of vivid green of the irrigated crops of the river rim, dotted with mud villages and their groves of date palms; and, in the immediate foreground, always the native sail boats with their tall, curved sails and high prows, like great, graceful water birds flitting up and down the opalescent waters.}

{Since these native boats carry no lights it is necessary for the steamers to tie up at night lest there be collisions and consequent bad feeling, which would prove a dangerous asset for a steamship company. This first night we tied up at Esh-Sheikh-Fadhl, which is a village of only 1800 inhabitants, but is made important now because in its midst is a great sugar factory. Times have changed, for once on the site of this very town was the ancient city of Cynopolis where dogs were regarded as sacred, and many dog mummies have been unearthed here.}

{We stopped at Benihanas to visit an ancient tomb out in the rocky cliffs. It was a perturbing donkey ride we had, getting from the landing up to the tombs, but the result was worth the effort. The columns carved out of the "living" rock were very beautiful, each representing 4 lotus stems with the buds for the capitals. Spirited pictures of hunting scenes were painted on the walls. There were excellent pictures of many birds and one of a long-horned antelope browsing on a bush. The tombs were made approximately 2350 B. C.}

{That night the sunset was glorious. The wide still waters of the Nile reflected the gold and rose and pale green of the clouds and sky. On the high bank was a road and silhouetted against the sky were palms, camels, men, buffaloes, and donkeys.}

{These days on the Nile were full of interest. The wide stretches of the river were like inland seas. The high cliffs (buttes) on the Eastern side were always a joy to our eyes. At close range they are gray and pale yellow but, in the morning and evening light, they took on exquisite rose and gold tints with purple shadows.}

{We were immensely interested in the manner of irrigating the land. Near Cairo where the banks of the Nile were low the sakyeh was used,—buckets on an endless chain, geared to a wheel, the latter turned by a bullock or camel blindfolded. It seemed to me this turning of the wheel by walking around and around hour after hour blindfolded was the uttermost depth of monotony. It made me shiver to watch the poor beasts. As the banks of the Nile became too high for this method the shaduf was used. This is like the old-fashioned well sweep in operation. The long pole was weighted heavily at one end and was supported in the middle by two posts made of bundles of cane cemented with mud. The buckets were rather shallow, made of goat skin with rims of wood. The work of the men consisted of pulling the pole down until the bucket was submerged then letting the weight lift it so they could empty it into an irrigating ditch. However, as the banks became higher and higher, it was necessary to have one shaduf above another, each emptying into reservoirs. We saw one place where the water was thus lifted four times before it reached the level of the land. Sometimes there were two men at each shaduf. They were usually dressed in white with white turbans, but one hot day they were naked and the movement of their muscles, as they stooped and lifted, would have delighted a sculptor.}

{The mud villages with their groups of date palms were always picturesque, especially those with pigeon houses. We thought at first these were the temples or perhaps the palaces of the rich as they were always higher than the surrounding houses and quite ornate, having crenulated cornices and bands of different colored clay about the structures themselves, which were rectangular, tapering toward the top. On the nearer view we could see the openings for the pigeons along the sides with a branch of some shrub set primly in cement below each entrance for the pigeons to alight upon. These dove cotes added much to the beauty of the villages. The droppings from the pigeons are the only manure available in this region, as the camel and cow dung is dried and used for fuel.}

{We saw many birds. The "wagtail," a graceful bird with long tail edged with white and a black locket on its white breast, often came on deck. The ubiquitous English sparrow was also on deck quite often and as quarrelsome as ever.}

{The great gray herons appeared in small flocks and stood around picturesquely in shallow pools. Resting on the sands were yellow billed kites and large black and white vultures. There were many flocks of ducks and there were beautiful metallic blue swallows with red brown breasts which skimmed over the waters in true swallow fashion.}

{The boats of the Nile were a constant joy to us. Their tall curved masts and slender graceful sails and high prows made them the most picturesque sail boats we had ever seen. Their cargoes interested us also. We met many loaded with earthen pots or jars. Some boats had panniers of rope on each side, so as to carry more pots. After seeing these we did not wonder that in excavating the old cities, strata of potsherds were found. We saw many boats loaded with grain and some sort of hay. One had a load of donkeys. Once, as we approached a bend of the river, we heard terrifying roars and groans and could not imagine what wild beasts were waiting to attack us. What we found were some men loading camels on a boat. One after another each beast with feet tied and lying on its belly was pushed down an inclined plane into the boat, meanwhile making the welkin ring with anguished bellowings.}

{We wondered how sailors in long gowns could climb a mast. We found it was managed by lifting the gown and fastening it at the waist so that the white trousered legs and bare feet were free. The men went up the tall masts like squirrels.}

{Our boat halted so that we could visit the ancient temple of Dendera. We found donkeys and good donkey boys awaiting us and we rode for a half hour over a raised road that was in the midst of fields planted with wheat and a legume that had purple flowers. We saw in these fields the crested lark and heard its sweet little song. The temple itself was most impressive. Its vestibule had columns eleven feet through with beautiful floral capitals and at the base of each was a particularly lovely conventionalized lotus consisting of three lotus flowers set erect on stems fan-shaped and at each side a lotus bud with stem bent midway at a sharp angle. The view from the roof was magnificent. Outside, on the rear wall of the temple, was a picture of Cleopatra and many other pictures also, which were being obliterated by the nests of a mason bee. Mr. Comstock took a photograph of the wall with its covering of bee nests and later published an account of his observations. The excavations of these temples had cost great sums and here were the inscriptions and the pictures being obliterated by the cement nests of a little insect.}

{The life along the banks of the great river was always picturesque. There were flocks of reddish brown or blackish sheep that had wide fat tails which tapered or curled at the ends. These would be grazing near the cultivated fields watched by boys in blue robes and close white caps. There were buffaloes, standing out in the river or perhaps lying down so that only the head and a little of the back were out of water. There were camels laden with onions in great rope panniers on either side and others laden with sugar cane. There were donkeys laden with clover until all you could see was a heap of hay trotting along on four slender legs. But the human element was always the most interesting. The women of the fellaheen, or peasant farmers, wore no veils. We often saw them at the river's edge filling the jars with water which they carried on their heads moving along rhythmically in their flowing robes. Their faces, especially the chins, were often tattooed in greenish blue. The forehead was often marked likewise. They almost invariably wore bracelets and were usually clad in the long loose black gown, although sometimes the gown was in the color with a black shawl worn over the shoulders and head. The children usually wore gay colored cotton gowns and the white skull cap or perhaps the red fez; they were always very dirty and had sore eyes. I saw small children in Cairo with a row of flies around each eye, making them look as if they were wearing goggles. The fez is undoubtedly responsible for much of the eye disease in Egypt, since the sun is blinding, and the fez offers no protection to the eyes. However, two types of conjunctivitis or eye disease are general, and the flies are undoubtedly carriers of both. Mr. Comstock, at one time, in Cairo tried to determine the extent of eye disease; he was able to count up to nine of the people on the street before he found a person with bad eyes and this was in the tourist season.}

{In some of the villages we saw something neatly piled on the roof of the mud houses and was told it consisted of loaves of cow, sheep, and camel dung, put there to dry for fuel. At supper time we often get a whiff of the pungent smoke of this sort of "firewood." We also saw immense jars on the roofs and were told that these were used for storing bread. If the bread is like some biscuit I bought there, I can believe it, for I have had these in a box for 23 years and they are good as ever.}

{We were able to spend several hours in the magnificent temple of Edfu. It was built some two or three centuries B. C. and is in a remarkable state of preservation. This temple gave us our first real understanding of the majesty of these structures and the psychological astuteness of the builders. The great pylons on either side of the entrance are awe-inspiring in their size as are the colossal figures cut upon them. The court, which was for people in general, was a spacious hall surrounded on three sides by roofed colonnades. Then came the Vestibule to which a limited number were admitted. The walls here were decorated with incised figures and the ceiling was said to have once been covered with astronomical representations. Next came the Hypostyle to which only those high in the priesthood were admitted. The roof was supported by twelve columns with beautiful floral capitals. Then there were two vestibules to pass before reaching the Sanctuary surrounded and covered with thick walls with no windows and containing a shrine and an altar. It was a dark cell in which the All Highest went to receive messages from the Gods. The sanctuary was surrounded by a passage off of which openings led into side chambers. Outside of these and the vestibules and Hypostyle was a corridor next to the high outer walls; the most lonely walk I ever took was around this gloomy corridor.}

{Our next stop was at Assuan, the limit of our Nile journey. The first day there we had a great experience. Ahmed Ibrahim, our self-elected dragoman, who saw us at some place down the Nile and declared himself ours, Ahmed Ibrahim, with a beautiful smile, fairly good English, red fez, dark coat and flaming silk gown, the same Ahmed Ibrahim, arranged for our camels and took a modest donkey for his own use to make an expedition to the quarries. Our camels were yellowish white and had peculiarly camelish countenances. They groaned and growled as they knelt for us to get on and snarled when made to get up. I was too confused in getting on to realize what happened, when with a bellow of remonstrance, the camel came up, but I was glad the seat was deep. As I remember, the camel gets up in principle, like a cow, with a heave of its hindquarters first, followed by a mighty lift upward of its front quarters, and then a final heave behind and the creature is up; each move pitching me forward or backward until I was shaken out of my wits. The rider's motion on a walking camel is peculiar, a motion which one performs himself from the waist up, down forward and up backward, a grand movement for reducing obesity, but a walking camel is a slow agent of transportation. Once my camel turned its head around, aided by its accommodating neck, and looked at me with a most supercilious expression that made me feel quite abashed. He looked snippy. At one place where we tied up I discovered we were guarded by three wild-looking men in long black gowns and with immense guns on their shoulders. The Captain told us that the Sheik of this region always provided guards for the

Cook steamers at night. Next to the Khedive in Egypt, was Thomas Cook in the regard of the natives, well earned through his service to them and his respect for their customs.}

{The dogs of the Nile villages were wolfish looking. We often saw them running over the roofs of the houses like cats. They howl and bark like a pack of wolves; in size they resemble coyotes.}

{First, we went through the native part of the town toward the desert. As we passed a mosque a man in a fez was out on a truncate tower, like an unfinished minaret, and was chanting musically. Ahmed said it was a call to prayer. Then we passed a Catholic cemetery, walled in. Then the real desert, just rock, sand and old tombs and the remains of a wall built by the Romans. We came finally to the granite quarries where all the stone used in the temples down the river was quarried. We saw there, half cut, a great obelisk; some old Pharaoh died before the task was finished. Also, there were many huge granite blocks, partly finished, scattered around. Again, we marveled at the engineering skill that had cut these great stones and transported them six hundred miles, more or less, to build the pyramids or to ornament the cities. Mr. Comstock declared the sight of these unused blocks gave him an overwhelming sense of the futility of human ambition and effort.}

{We went farther in the desert and returned through the village of the Nubians and the tents of the Bisharins; these latter were the wildest-looking folk I ever saw. They were black with long hair put up in many tiny greased braids. The children, nearly naked, pleaded for baksheesh, with graceful dramatic gestures.}

{We took the boat trip to Philae with Ahmed Ibrahim for guide and started at nine o'clock. Our boat, a broad sail boat with true Nile sail, was called the "Bedoin." It was painted yellow, red, white, blue, and green. The mast was yellow, blue, and red. The oars were painted round-wise, irregularly in three colors. There was no scheme for painting the boat, but these primitive colors were put on, hit or miss, except along the boat's sides, which were striped lengthwise inside the rail.}

{We had three sailors; two young fellows, very black, in white turbans, black outside garments, long white shirts, yellow vests and bright blue baggy trousers and an older man in black. When the boys became too warm they peeled off their turbans and showed large silver rings in the upper part of each ear; each wore a little white skull cap around which the turban was twisted in various ways.}

{In the river were great granite rocks. The granite itself is a beautiful mottled red, but here the river had colored it black, until it shone as if polished with shoe blacking; the water had also worn it full of curious pot-holes and had made strange sculptures. At time our passage between these rocks was narrow, and our sailors jumped out on the rocks to sheer off our boat going at full tilt. These sailors were amazingly active and dexterous. The passage up to the first lock was one of the most exciting experiences of my mild career. It seemed sometimes as if we must be dashed against the rocks, which we missed by perhaps a yard or so, not only once, but many times. At the first lock, a majestic structure, we took on two more sailors, who helped us on to the great Barrage, the greatest dam, then in the world, one and one-fourth miles long.}

{After we crossed the bridge, we took another boat and another crew of six, and rowed out to the lake, past rocks that bore inscriptions and past half-submerged palm trees, and again were threatened with shipwreck against rocks. But we finally arrived at Philae, a beautiful golden-brown temple rearing its pylons high above the water, its long, half submerged colonnades made beautiful by ornate columns and capitals. The temple is comparatively modern, as it was begun 350 B. C. and completed by the Roman emperors during the first three centuries A. D. The great temple is dedicated to Isis, and her portrait is everywhere. Here lingered the ancient Isis worship long after Theodosius had established the Christian religion.}

{It was so windy we were obliged to descend into a room (uncovered) to eat our luncheon and soon after we had to start on our return. The whole scene as we pulled away was very beautiful; the golden brown temple, and kiosk rising against the blue skies above pale, olive green waters in which were purple shadows, made it a scene to dream of ever after.}

{The pull back was the most difficult experience of the day. The men pulled tremendously hard, threw off their turbans and outer garments, and the sweat poured down their faces. White caps covered the lake, and the wind was dead ahead. As the men neared the shore they shouted in chorus: "Hip-hip-hurray! Hip-hip-hurray! Hip-hip-hurray! Tank-you! Tank-you!"}

{We crossed the barrage as before and found our boat manned by some extra sailors, and we needed them; for, though the current was in our favor, the wind was mostly off our bows and sometimes ahead. At the lock the men produced a tom-tom, made out of a water jar without a bottom; over the opening was stretched a thin skin glued to the edge of the jar. The flat of one hand applied to the center of the drum, and the fingers of the other near the sides gave two quite different sounds. A song began by one man chanting in a minor key. As his voice slid down at the end, the chorus was taken up by all the men; or perhaps it was an answer to the first. And as this ended in a minor wail two or three clapped their hands in unison with the tom-tom beats; that was the interlude. It was very interesting.}

{We left Assuan January 28th, on the express boat, "Amenartas." At one landing we saw boys with birds, frightened fluttering birds tied to sticks, offering to liberate them for money extracted from tender-hearted passengers. An indignant Englishman jumped ashore, liberated the birds and broke the sticks, to our deep satisfaction.}

{We visited the beautiful temple of Kom Ombo. It stood on a terrace in simple majesty high above the Nile. Although the stone of which it was built was pale yellow, it gleamed white in the afternoon sun against the pearly sky; its shadows were slaty purple and its reflection in the pale blue waters of the Nile shot through the streaks of calm as shafts of yellow light.}

{The temple was a late one built under the Ptolemies and finished by the Romans which perhaps accounts for its excellent preservation. It was dedicated to two gods, the crocodile-headed Sobek, and the falcon-headed Haroeris. It seemed strange that this most beautiful temple should be dedicated to such ugly beasts. We stood long in the great Hypostyle Hall looking out between the rows of superb columns, across the shimmering waters of the Nile, to the far shore with its rows of palms, an exquisitely beautiful scene.}

{The next morning, we stopped at Esneh to visit another Ptolemaic temple then but partially excavated. It was impressive, even though a small part was above ground.}

{Our most interesting memory of Esneh is of the Arabic school we visited. It was in a neat looking building covered with yellow plaster, with awkward mud blocks for steps. A fine-looking man met us and explained in good English that it was an Arabic school and took us into the advanced room where were the boys of twelve to sixteen years; most of these wore turbans but some wore the fez. They were making a good deal of noise which the man stopped by saying: "Sh-sh-sh." He then showed us the "slates," which were oblong rectangles of tin or zinc perhaps a foot long; on them in purple ink was very neat Arabic writing which he translated for us. "God is good. He loves you all; He give you your food and clothing and all that you have." Then he introduced to us a very old Arab with a white shawl over his head, who was the teacher. Our English-speaking guide explained that he was a merchant and came only now and then to help; he certainly looked more prosperous than the others. Mr. Comstock gave the old teacher a coin and then we were conducted across a rather wide entrance hall to the primary room. Here were the little ones with shawls over their heads turban-like, sitting on low benches with desks before them. They were all dirty and some of them were half-blind and some looked very stupid. One brought us his tablet of zinc on which was written part of the Arabic alphabet and words of one syllable. The teacher of this room was a young man with rather fine features, who was clad in a blue gown and white turban. He frankly asked us for money. Our friend, the merchant, led us out with a grand air. In both rooms were small blackboards with numerals and sentences written on them in chalk.}

{We left the boat at Luxor for a few days stay at this more interesting place. Its great temple stands almost at the river's edge. One sunny afternoon I sketched this temple. I was at one end of the great court, and the sunshine brought the soft yellow stone of the magnificent columns into strong relief against the blue sky above and the dense shadows. Below. Doves were cooing under cover of one of the wide architraves; and great red-kites were soaring and circling above on even wing. Through a vista of columns and above them I could see the mosque and its minarets, which two or three centuries ago, had been built on the ruins of the temple and still stands there within the great pylons, its foundations resting on buried treasures of art and architecture. And while I was lost in contemplation of all these historic splendors, the blind Muezzin came out on the balcony of the minaret, holding fast to the railing and chanted with magnificent dignity and resonance the Muslim call to prayer, which being translated is "God is greatest; I testify there is no god but God; I testify Mohammed is the apostle of God; come to prayer, come to salvation." And the doves went on cooing under the architraves and the kites whistled overhead, a hoopoe was industriously scratching in the dust of the sun worshipper, but the sun which had shone on all these successive templed religions shone warmly over all.}

{In Luxor we were cared for by a very magnificent dragoman, Mohammed Abdullah. He procured donkeys and boys for us and we made a memorable excursion to the temple of Sethos I and thence along the Khedive's road in and out great desert hills to visit the tombs of the Kings.}

{Our next experience was a visit to the beautiful temple of Deir el-Bahri. It is the most beautiful temple of all, built on three successive terraces marked by enchanting colonnades very different from the usual Egyptian temple. This difference in plan was due to Queen Hatshepsut, in whom we had developed great interest. She lived some 1800 B. C. and had a stormy career, wresting the throne from one brother only to have it wrested from her by another brother some years after. Then again, she won it back. She was a remarkable woman as is shown by the exquisite architecture of her temple, which has certain Grecian characteristics. We left this most interesting temple of all, reluctantly; as we looked back upon it from a distance we felt overwhelmed by the beauty of its golden colonnades set at the base of the abrupt cliffs which, lifted high above it, were rose and purple in the afternoon light. Queen Hatshepsut was a Queen Elizabeth, a Susan B. Anthony and Catherine the Great combined into one.}

{On our way home, we visited the Colossi of Memnon, majestic still, though defaced by enemies and the sand storms of centuries. They stand in a great fertile plain, looking across to the ruined temples beyond the river and the desert hills. The ancient temples in ruins oppressed our spirits and at the same time aroused our admiration, but the more we admired the more futile seemed human endeavor. The Colossi are the embodiment of eternal loneliness; it seemed to us that they were gazing, mournfully at magnificent Thebes crumbling under the heavy hand of Time, while meditating on the theme, "All things shall pass."}

{We spent the next day at Karnak. The mighty columns covered with inscriptions are awe-inspiring. It is the most tremendous temple of all. It was so overpowering that I was glad to go over to the sacred lake and make a sketch of it and the massive pylon beyond while I watched the swallows dart and swoop, the coots at play in the still waters and a tiny sand piper with a white tippet around his neck and a black crescent in front, skittering around the sandy shore.}

{But though I wrote folios describing the grandeur of these temples, it would mean nothing; for, after all, the interest in them is the human interest. One always sees the great courts filled with those people of old, gathered there to worship their animal-headed gods. And in the pictures carved on the walls one sees the development of a great people, from primitive pantheism, when the crocodile, the goat, the jackal, and the falcon were worshipped, up to the man-bodied gods with heads of animals, and then on up to the supreme Ammon Re, the god with human beauty of figure and face who, combined with Re, represented the sun, the one greatest god. We were weary of sightseeing and returned to Luxor where we spent the greater part of a day in the beautiful garden of the Hotel Luxor. Roses, poinsettias, hibiscus, pansies, sage, were all abloom; and we sat in the shade of mimosa, and Lebbakh trees.}

{While we were in the garden we heard the bang of a gun, the stork gave a great hop, the sparrows ceased chattering and the silence was almost shocking. Then we heard a peculiar chanting and went to see what it meant. It was a funeral. Two boys with red banners led, and I think they led the chant too. A few men in white flowing robes and white turbans followed. Then came four men carrying the corpse in a barrow made of unplaned lumber. Over the body was a green pall cloth with fringed ends, a too-many-times used cloth. Behind followed an old man, with sad face, and that was all. It seemed so dreadfully poor, poverty-stricken and tawdry. I questioned a dragoman about it and he said they carried the body to the morgue for the ceremony and then carried it to the cemetery and put it in the ground with no coffin and nothing around it except its clothing.}

{We sat in the garden until late afternoon when the great kites went to roost in the big palm above us. There were fifteen or twenty, some of them lacking one or two wing feathers, as if they had been shot away. They came in twos and threes, but there seemed to be some places in the tree more desirable than others, and often one would push another off, so it was not altogether an amicable bed-going. Before they were settled the bats appeared in great numbers and dashed about in the sunset glow.}

{We left Luxor on another express boat, the "Nefert-ari." I made many sketches. The Arabian mountains at sunset take on heavenly hues of rose, gold, purple and blue, and the sky reflections in the still waters of the Nile rendered the scene enchanting. The Nile journey will remain ever with us a dream of beauty and a period of communion with the remote past.}

{When we reached our hotel at Cairo, Mohammet was cleaning the stairs. When he saw us his grim, sombre face changed its expression miraculously and he welcomed us with a charming smile. He never understood a word we said, nor we a word of his, but when we left the hotel he gave me a beautiful bead necklace decorated with two carnelian hearts, and to Mr. Comstock a little knitted cap and a gorgeous fly brush.}

{We left Cairo on Feb. 19 for Alexandria. When we arrived at our boat, our trunks were not on board and Mr. Comstock shrewdly guessed that the Cook agent had sent them to the wrong steamer. We were in a great dilemma when at the moment of our need our devoted Alexander Mustafa appeared like an angel of rescue. He went with Mr. Comstock to the other boat, which was bound for Naples, and finally located our trunks at the bottom of the pile in the hold and got them over to our steamer just fifteen minutes before the steamer sailed. Alexander Mustafa said reproachfully, "You should have written me you were coming."}

{It was on the *S. S. Osmaniah* that we took passage from Alexandria to Greece. A very interesting German woman, one of the passengers, told me of her visit to Palestine and her landing at Joppa when there was rough sea. There was no pier there then and the passengers were taken off in small boats. The ship was tossing as two of the sailors took her by the hands and let her down over the side of the ship. She said: "The ship she go up and down, the little boat it go up and down, so the men there could not catch me by the legs and I say to myself "Mine Gott it is feenish!"}

{We landed at Piraeus and were greatly amused during our ride to Athens to see great board advertisements, "Lots for sale" in modern Greek. We found comfortable quarters in the Grand Hotel where the table was fair. One day a queer-looking dish was set before us, called Kalamaraki, on the menu card. We asked the waiter, who spoke French, what it was, and he said a "kind of fish." Mr. Comstock looked at it more closely and discovered a sucking disk. Then we knew we were eating squid. The following extracts from my note-books will give a very good account of our experiences in Athens:}

> {"Here we are following after another set of heathen idols! Ammon Re has given place to Olympian Zeus and Isis to Athena. We are studying another type of temple, we are climbing steep heights instead of voyaging on broad rivers. We derive our nourishment from the honey of Hymettus. We listen to children of three years prattling in Greek. We gaze at soldiers arrayed in ballet petticoats with long tassels on their caps, and balls of fuzz on the toes of their slippers.}
>
> {"The drive from Piraeus to Athens was over a beautiful road amid picturesque scenery. But Athens is such a surprise to us! We had always regarded it as an ancient city; on the contrary it is brand new. About seventy-five years ago it consisted of a little village of three hundred houses; now it has more than a hundred thousand population living in houses well built, of stone or cement, and its environs were laid out in lots for sale like any growing city in America}
>
> {"The Acropolis lifting its shattered columns five hundred feet above the city constantly sends the mind back through two and a half thousand years, while every street with its handsome houses and smart shops brings the mind forward again to the ever-present Now. Thus, the workings of the mental shuttle! The ruins of the temples, gates and theaters have no mellow setting like the ruins of Dendera and Thebes. Instead, they are environed in garish modernity. Only the mountains and the sea, in the whole landscape, seem fitting companions for the Parthenon, the Odeon, and the temple of Olympian Zeus. The Greek gods are much more beautiful than the gods of the Egyptians but are not nearly so mysterious; mystery seemed in ancient times to be a god's "long suit."}
>
> {"We have climbed up to the Parthenon every day. It is a majestic temple, and we constantly compare it with the temples of Egypt. It is not so impressive nor so great as the temples of Luxor, but it is far more beautiful. The color, strange to say, is about the same, for the marble has taken on the soft yellow which characterizes the limestone of the Egyptian temples.}
>
> {"The view to the west of the Acropolis is amazingly like the view of the San Francisco Bay from the hills of Berkeley. In fact, all the

mountains are very like the California mountains in contour, but their constituent rock is much darker, and their color is bluer. Both Mr. Comstock and I felt that if we had awakened in Greece without knowing where we were, we should have decided we were in California, until the ruins of architecture convinced us to the contrary. Even the pepper trees that shade the streets and the almond trees in blossom and the olive orchards bespeak the Pacific Coast. The mountains are not nearly as high as in California; Old Hymettus reaches up only three thousand three hundred and seventy feet at its highest point.}

{"Our favorite point in the Acropolis is by that gem of architecture, the Temple of Victory. We sit there by the hour, the Parthenon rising above us at the left, the wide landscape to the south, and the west stretched out before us, shining in the evening light; the Aegina Gulf, the bay of Eleusis, and the bay of Phaleron, and the rocky islands of Salamis, Hydra, and Aegina with Mr. St. Elias rising above and behind. The mountain ranges, beyond which lie Argos, Mycenae Corinth, and Olympia. On the near shore is Piraeus with its great chimneys, and between lies the plain set with olive orchards while quite directly in the fore ground rises the sharp peak crowned with the tomb of Philopappos, and just below are the still-standing arches of Odeon. This is the spot Byron celebrated in the first stanza of Canto III of "The Corsair."}

{"Yesterday at sunset we went to the Stadium, which completely restored in beautiful marble, represents the true magnificence of the old structure. It is set in a natural hollow of the hills which rise high on either side. The vista out through the gates gives a magnificent picture of the city and the Acropolis high against the sunset sky. In the Stadium, Greek youths were practicing running, and in the gymnasium yard, which we passed on the way, a young athlete was throwing the discus. No wonder that act was perpetuated in marble, for never have I seen such beautiful postures. It was a poem of action of the human form.}

{"On our way to the Acropolis, we stopped to study the tower of the winds and the magnificent old Roman market place. We passed a prison where the windows were grated and there was a grated box outside each window. Through these gratings were thrust out sticks with small bags on the end of them, and voices from within pleaded; "Mohoosah! Mohoosah!" and we knew the prisoners were begging for money. But a guard motioned us not to respond. Near the end of February, we went to Mt. Pentelicon [*sic*]. We started at seven thirty. It was a bright sunny morning but cool and pleasant. We met, as we neared the limits of the city, many old women with loads of brush on their backs; some of them drove donkeys loaded with wood packed on a peculiar saddle.

We met many carts filled with water jars; the jars were graceful in shape, about two feet high, of red unglazed earthenware. We met many peasants coming to town in their big two-wheeled carts, and many people bringing in almond blossoms. As we drove out on the great plain the scene was very beautiful; before us, Pentelicon with great scars on its side where the quarries are; to the right, grand old Hymettus and to the left a high range, its tallest peak snow-spotted. The peasants were in the fields busy with their work; some were plowing, others were trimming the grape vines, while others with great hoes, a foot broad, were trenching the vines, or raising embankments of the clay soil about them in rectangles to hold the irrigating water. These embankments were two feet high, and perhaps higher. There were great fields of wheat or barley just coming up and vividly green. There were many olive trees being headed back so there was a callow twig growth on great gnarled old trees, many of them with holds clear through them. There were many very handsome pine trees with very dense masses of foliage yellow-green. There was much land not under cultivation as we commenced to climb the mountain, and this was covered with what looks like the sage brush and greasewood of the American desert. The almond trees were fully in blossom and were pushing their pink bouquets over the garden walls as well as massing them in the orchards.}

{"The farmers apparently live in villages, as there are no isolated farmhouses. We passed through a most picturesque village, where the gates of the walls into the yards were rather imposing, being made of stones like the walls of houses. The houses all had tile roofs. We went by one place where there were goats, big goats, with large twisted horns, that extended backward, half the length of the body. A handsome old man with shining white hair and whiskers seemed in possession of the place. He had on a Greek costume, with tight trousers, white full petticoats, a theatrical-looking cape which came below his skirts, a black cap with tassel, and black hose. Nearby was a man plowing with one horse and a peculiar steel plow. He had on a black cap, a black sleeveless jacket, waist-length, worn over a gray tunic with full skirt that came half way to his knees, very short, tight white trousers and black stockings.}

{"The scene resembled California very much in contour of mountains and plain, in sage brush, vines, olive and almond trees, but it differed greatly in civilization and methods of doing things. Nature made Greece and California from the same pattern, but man has diversified the two.}

{"As we approached the mountain the stone viaduct, down which the marble was brought from the quarries in ancient times, came into view. About twelve hundred feet up the mountain, we came to the monastery of Mendeli built of cream-colored stone; the large, rather modern-looking buildings, had walled-in gardens, above which towered the slender cypresses and over which foamed the pink almond blossoms. Great sycamores of most perfect growth shaded the road and the grounds near it. From a little public house near, we took the owner for a guide. He spoke not a word that we understood, nor we a word that he understood. His bright little son went along. Near the monastery we came to a reservoir of splendid water. Near by was a shepherd with a flock of sheep, their cream-colored fleeces were of long straight fiber, and they had black faces, and slender black legs. The shepherd was in Grecian costume, short skirts, long cape, and low shoes with fuzzy balls on the toes; he had a crook and a smile. We passed a tiny chapel with blue doors and then some brush huts where the quarry men sleep. Then we took the road to the quarries, up, up, a turning and winding and terribly rutty road, every turn giving us a new and wider view of the valley, and a farther glimpse of the Attic plain toward Marathon. Finally, we visited two modern quarries where the men were blocking out perfectly white shining marble; it looked like snow.}

{"After we left these quarries we took a mountain trail. The trail led high over a bridge, then down steeply to a ravine-like valley where there was a tiny stone chapel with doors ajar. Our guide and his son went in and said their prayers to the Virgin and kissed the head of someone's picture. Then we climbed to the crest of another high ridge from where we could see almost to Marathon. Then down into another valley, up another steep ridge, and steep, steep down to an ancient quarry. Then to another ancient quarry out of which opened a great stalactite grotto, at the entrance of which was a tiny chapel, or rather, shrine. We ate our lunch at the mouth of the grotto. The view of Hymettus from this point was especially beautiful, with some rugged, gnarled, old pines in the foreground. Then we started down the way, paved in olden times so that the great marble blocks might be pushed down over it.}

{"When we arrived again at the monastery we had been five hours steadily walking or clambering. Our host gave us coffee and some of the native wine with resin in it, which tasted like "bitters."}

{"Going home was a delightful experience. Spring was in the air—the larks were singin' in the meadows. There was a haze in the atmosphere and the bay of Phaleron was shining like silver. White Lycabettus stood up bravely, a queer high knob on the landscape.}

{"At one place the almond trees were near the road and we stopped, and our stout old coachman got off his seat and gathered us a great bouquet of branches all ablossom. We waited meanwhile, breathing in the soft air, listening to the bees working in the almond blossoms, the workmen talking as they hoed the grape vines, the birds singing in the far meadow. It was a delicious moment, and the climax of the day's experience.}

{"Our goodbye to Greece on March 1 was as perfect as our first greeting. Our drive from Athens gave us the beautiful receding view of the city and grand Pentelikon rising in all its majesty behind it. We went on board the steamer and sailed at four o'clock. As we went out of the bay of Phaleron into the blue, blue Aegean Sea, the sun, low in the west, bathed the whole Athenian picture in a flood of glory."}

When we left home in December 1907, we had but one definite engagement for all the months that we were to be gone, and that was to be in Florence in April to be present at the wedding of Vernon Kellogg to Charlotte Hoffman. The wedding took place immediately after our arrival. Charlotte had been staying in Florence several weeks and had rented the Villa Orchio at Settignano; an ancient village on the hills east of Florence, where Michelangelo was born. {The Villa was owned by the family of Marion Crawford.} Charlotte had put it in order, engaged servants and made it ready for the nuptials. The Villa {was very old and} had a rose arbor and terraced garden with an olive orchard below it and a commanding outlook with the Villa of d'Annunzio and that of Duse in the foreground.

On April 27, 1908, with other friends, we drove up to the Villa. Mary Austin, Professor and Mrs. Gayley, and Mrs. Charles Wheeler of Berkeley were among the guests. The drawing room had a ceiling of inlaid wood and its furniture was of carved oak; now it was a bower of apple blossoms and in it the twain were made one. A noble pair fitted each for the other and both for helping the world, as their subsequent life together demonstrated in so many {undreamed-of} ways. After the wedding the guests left; the honeymoon was to be spent at the Villa, one of the most beautiful spots in the world. During our three weeks stay in Florence we spent three days at the Villa Orchio, charming days with a very unselfish bridal pair who made our intrusions seem like invited pleasure.

"The Chalet, the home of the Comstock Publishing Company," caption beneath in Mrs. Comstock's handwriting.

Chapter XIII

Italy, Switzerland, and Home

As mentioned in the previous chapter introduction, only one page of Mrs. Comstock's Chapter XIII was included in the 1953 edition (at the end of Chapter 12). The paragraphs that were not included are reinstated here in the context in which they were written. Noted for the reader is an abrupt disconnect in this chapter, where Mrs. Comstock's writing ends midsentence.

{We went from Greece to Sicily on the German steamship "Baiern," whose Captain was very pleasant and who was a devoted disciple of Haeckel. We landed at the dock at Messina and reached Taormina on March 8th. It was the most picturesque town we had ever visited, and Aetna seemed to us the most beautiful mountain we had ever seen. Its upper portion was snow-clad most of the time during our stay and we never wearied from watching it sending up to the clouds its filmy wreaths of smoke.}

{We found Taormina a small city plastered against the side of a precipitous mountain, half way up its slope. Its main street follows the contour of the mountain, and from this street numerous narrow streets and alleys diverge, ascending on the one side and descending on the other by steep flights of steps. There are also short irregular streets, more or less parallel with the main street, the Corso Umberto.}

{Taormina was a walled city, and a considerable portion of the walls are well preserved. On entering or leaving the city one passes through the archway of an ancient gate. In fact, there are four gates on the Corso, for the city was double-walled; so that to enter from either direction the central part of the town, the part that communicated with the castle, it was necessary to pass through two gates.}

{This Corso Umberto is the strangest street we had ever seen. Following the contour of the mountain, it is quite level and somewhat crooked. It appears, however, to be very crooked because no building is oriented with reference to any other or to the street. The result is that it varies greatly in width. In one place, near the center of the town, it is only eleven feet in width; in the wider portions it is about twenty-five feet. The streets leading up or down the mountain from the Corso are much narrower. We measured one which was but two feet width.}

{How delightful the memory of those days in Taormina; when we were tired of sight-seeing we settle ourselves in our room with its absurd stove about the size and shape of two lengths of stove pipe. But there was plenty of lightwood in the market and we were most comfortable during the evenings and rainy days; there were many rainy days, although there were usually intervals when the sun conquered the clouds.}

{We roamed around in a leisurely fashion visiting the Greek theater and enjoying at every step the superb panorama spread before us. We were a little tired of ruins and spent more time looking at Aetna and the superb view than we did in studying the ancient theatre.}

{We sauntered up to the old Gothic abbey, the Badia Vecchia. It is a beautiful old ruin, and we found beyond the main portion, in what must have been a great hall, a grassy terrace; we sat on a hospitable stone pile, near a beauteous milk-white goat, and let the view enfold us; Aetna on one side, cloud-veiled, with mountains in the middle distance brought out by mists in "layers" of perspective. In front of us through the broken arches was the green-blue sea, made more lovely by the contrasting foreground of gray wall and the harmonious green spray of the almond trees. The bells in the town below us sent up musical greetings. The bees buzzed homelike around us, and it was all as soothing as enchanting.}

{We were never tired of wandering about the town and out through the picturesque old gates. Mr. Comstock got an excellent photograph of an old shepherd and his sheep, a picture beautifully composed, and another of a stout peasant woman spinning with her distaff in hand. Mr. Comstock later gave her a print of the picture and when she saw it she cried, "Bellissima, bellissima!" We studied with interest the tombs of the Saracens. I asked a passer by whose tombs were these and he answered, "O an ancient people of Taormina." It made us a little dizzy to think of all these ancient peoples of Taormina since it was founded under Dionysius, 396 B. C.—Greeks, Carthaginians, Romans, Saracens, Normans, and others, all ancient peoples of Taormina.}

{We had one steady task. We registered in the Berlitz School for instruction in Italian. Mr. Comstock, after our experience in Naples, quailed at the thought of two months in Italy without knowing the language. Seno Paola Santisse was our teacher and a most excellent one as well as a fine man. He put no end of energy into his teaching and was most dramatic at times. I'll never forget how during our first lesson he took a ruler in his hand and asked with scorn and flashing eyes and in tones of thunder, "E la penna? (Is it a pen?)."}

{It was Sunday night and we went again to the theater—this time to see the play *Cavalleraia Rusticana*, although we thought it was the opera when we took tickets. We sat in a box with a Mrs. Lee, from which we looked down on a tin dress circle and pit. The orchestra was surely in earnest tonight, and the leader stood up while leading. They played very well something from the opera, and someone sang behind the scenes.}

{The Members of the cast acted exceedingly well but had not really learned their parts. This lack was made good by the prompter, who stood below the stage with head and shoulders issuing from a hole in the stage floor. He was supposed to be hidden from the audience by a board set slantwise over him, and for a less efficient individual this might have sufficed. But not for him! He read aloud from a book every word of the play, much of it perfectly audible to us, and after he had read the part the actor would take it up as quick as a flash, repeat it and act it with great vivacity. It was like seeing words electrified, first to hear them in those scarcely muffled tones and then to see the actor suddenly galvanize them into life, and with vivid gestures and flashing eyes give them their fullest meaning. But sometimes an actor was slow in getting his cue, and then the prompter became excited and pointed at him with a vivacious finger attached to a vigorous arm, perfectly visible to us. And the prompter, being Italian, could not restrain himself when things went badly; he would then wave wildly the hand holding the book toward the delinquent on the left side, while the fingers of his other hand snapped vigorously as he tried to bring up the rear guards on his right. He was a hard-working person and his dramatic powers were so great that he should have been wholly on the stage instead of partly under it.}

{From his own box in the second tier the boy—Pietro Terio Barkers—who dances the tarantella in the cares, saw us and came over for a visit. As we understood very little he said, it was a rather lopsided social intercourse. After he and a pretty little boy had danced exceedingly well on the stage he brought the boy around and we had an exchange of compliments, and the little boy sat on my lap because he was "multo stanco."[1] Pietro Terio worked in a barber shop daytimes and danced nights. Seldom have we been honored by association with stars as we were tonight.}

{One of our last delightful days in Taormina we spent climbing Mr. Venere (2800 ft.) from the heights of which we had a view of chaotic mountain ranges and peaks, a long coast line and an exquisitely blue sea. On our way home, we saw circular floors of concrete or stone which at first puzzled us. Then we remembered a description in one of Kipling's stories of the threshing floors in the Himalayas and, sure enough, these too were threshing floors.}

{On March 31st, we bade a cordial farewell to our kindly and helpful hosts of the Victoria Hotel. Naida our maid called me an angel. Senor Santisse bade us God-speed and was delighted at the fluency of our Italian as we thanked him. We had a glorious drive down to the station. Aetna was kind and gave herself wholly to our goodbye gaze. When we reached Messina Mr. Comstock, armed with Senor Santisse's Italian, made a firm, cheap, and successful transfer of ourselves and baggage to the steamship, "Therapie," bound for Naples. That night we had a grand view of the volcano Stromboli, its red fires making the rolling clouds above it glow like a topsy-turvy inferno and all reflected like dropping coals in the inky sea.}

{We tarried not in Naples but hasted to Sorrento where we found comfortable quarters in the Hotel Royal. Our windows gave us a view of Vesuvius, the bay and in the foreground an orange garden with a peach tree in blossom. We found at the hotel the Misses McCall of Bath, N. Y., whose brother was a classmate of mine, and we had interesting visits with them. We went to Capri, wandering along the narrow walled streets, and through a picturesque landscape and gardens to the Villa of Tiberius where we gained a magnificent view of the bay and its environs, and also had the pleasure of being welcomed by a hermit who had sought refuge there.}

{One afternoon we explored the mysterious tunnel that led from the Hotel Royal down through the cliff to the sea. There we found a boatman who had been at Coney Island shooting the chutes and with him we rowed away over the Vesuvian Bay to see the heavenly blue grottos.}

{On April 11, we engaged a driver with carriage drawn by two good horses and journeyed on to Amalfi, one of the most beautiful experiences of our travel year. We went out past the Villa Brooklyn, which an Italian, who had made his money in Brooklyn, N. Y. had built and where he expected to end his days in leisure. But the spirit of the new world was so strong in him that he lived mostly in America; but was very generous to his native village.}

1. Probably a misspelling for "molto stanco," or very tired. —KSt.

{Our road followed in and out the bold indented coast. We were granted a view of the islands of the Sirens, but they too must have emigrated to America as had most of the inhabitants of certain picturesque, deserted villages along the coast. I think Positano was the most decorative village we had ever see; it had terraced gardens and rose-covered arches through which were entrancing views of the sea.}

{We lunched in Amalfi and spent the afternoon wandering about this picturesque town. We went up to Ravello (1227 ft.) for the night and found lodging in the unique Hotel Palumbo, an old episcopal palace, from the balconies and windows and pergolas of which we reveled in enchanting views. The next morning, we visited the cathedral and admired the thirteenth century mosaics; we were hilarious over the two mosaic representations of Jonah being swallowed,—going down head first and then, apparently, after turning a somersault in the whale's tummy, coming out smiling and triumphant head first. The whale was an amazing creature with long convoluted body, a pig's head, wings on his shoulders, and with four long fingers on his front feet. The expression on its face is eager while Jonah is going down but is changed to one of agonized astonishment as Jonah comes up.}

{In the afternoon we drove down to Amalfi and spent the night. We visited the famous Capuchin monastery, now a hotel, and, like good Americans, read again Longfellow's poem which mentions it and enjoyed with the poet this mediaeval town.}

{Mr. Comstock was not feeling well but the next day we drove on from Amalfi to Vietri, around the base of terraced mountains covered with lemon orchards. Mr. Comstock was too ill to visit Paestum, so we drove to Cava dei Tierreni, nestled among the hills.}

{We went on to Pompeii and found accommodations at the Hotel Suisse. There our driver and equipage left us. Mr. Comstock was so ill the next day that we engaged a sedan chair carried by two men to take him around Pompeii. This place gave us a queer feeling. Other ruined cities which we had visited, had gradually fallen into decay, but here was evidence everywhere of the suddenness of the catastrophe. It seemed that it might have happened only last year, and that the owner of these houses might return at any moment. We were astonished at the smallness of the rooms; but this was compensated by the spacious courts and gardens, the great baths, the amphitheater, the forum and the markets. The luxury which dominated this ancient city was evident at every turn. The voluptuousness and licentiousness evident in pictures and decorations shocked us. Such disreputable pictures certainly mean an advanced stage of demoralization. That little window in the dining room of a palace which was called the *vomitorium* where the feasters could disgorge in order to eat more, is something one would like to forget. However, there was so much of beauty everywhere that it, rather than the disagreeable things, remains the lasting impressions of this ash-submerged city.}

{Mr. Comstock's condition was such that we thought best to go on to Naples the next day and from there to Rome. It was an interesting journey over wide fertile valleys and past many cities set on hills. Our travelling companions were pleasant folk, Dr. and Mrs. Shannon of Seattle, who came with us to our Pension Jasselli Owen in Rome.}

{Our home neighbors, the Misses McCall called on us early the next morning and with them we visited the beautiful Church of St. John Lateran and saw the stairs of penance with pilgrims going up on their knees. Later we drove to the Palatine Hill and wandered through its shady walks, listening to the singing of the merles. Then we came down and went through the Forum and the Coliseum, which was as impressive as the temple at Luxor, although different. We went to St. Peter's and heard the Tenebrae sung which was magnificent. Although the ornateness of St. Peter's seems in poor taste yet the dignity of its statuary in a measure compensates.}

{We were haphazard in our sight-seeing in Rome. There was so much to see that we despaired of getting more than glimpses of the greatness. We were interested in the fountains and we pilgrimaged to see them. We felt chummy with Cleopatra's Needle, but the cross grafted on its apex seemed nothing short of scandalous. We called on Marcus Aurelius, seated on his charger, and told him that we read out of his book every day when we were at home. His beard and hair looked as if they were put in curlers nights, but in that respect, he was like others of his time in marble.}

{The picture galleries were my special delight. We spent a morning in the Vatican galleries and I went without lunch so as to stay there in the afternoon. In the room of the Signature in the painting "On Parnassus," I made the acquaintance of Sappho and found her bewitching. Another day we spent in the Raphael Gallery and in the Vatican Library. We went to the Barberini Gallery to see the portrait of Beatrice Cenci and to the church of the Capuchins to see St. Michael and wandered in the Borghese gardens and in the galleries found Carlo Doci's "Madonna." We found "The Aurora" and, in fact, were more interested in finding all these pictures so familiar to us than in seeing new ones.}

{We called on our companion of voyage, Signor Cagaiti, and he reproached us for not letting him know sooner of our visit, so he could have helped us to see Rome. He took us for a long drive showing us much of the beauty of Rome which we should have missed otherwise, and at his behest, the next day we drove to the gardens of Malta to get a view of St. Peter's; then to the cemetery where Shelley and Keats are buried and to the most beautiful church of all, St. Paul's, outside the walls. Thence to the tomb of St. Cecilia and the Catacombs and the baths of Caracalla, the latter modifying our low opinion of that gentleman quite decidedly.}

{An interesting incident occurred in our pension. Dr. Shannon and his wife were to be received by the Pope, and from their American experience with trunks they naturally expected to have these arrive in Rome with themselves. Alas! The trunk containing Dr. Shannon's dress shoes lingered and he came to Mr. Comstock in his dilemma. Luckily the two wore the same size and ever afterwards Mr. Comstock had a great respect for his patent leathers that had been so highly honored. Later, he gave them to a Catholic student who had a true appreciation of their acquired value.}

{Rome is a place where one should stay for a year to have even a casual acquaintance with it. We did not regret that our stay was but a week; a month would have left us just as unsatisfied. As it is, we have always before our eyes the glamor of the Rome that was and the beauty of the Rome that is.}

When we left home in December [1907] we had but one definite engagement for all the months we were to be gone, and that was to be in Florence in April to be present at the wedding of Vernon Kellogg to Charlotte Hoffman. The wedding took place immediately after our arrival. Charlotte had been staying in Florence several weeks and had rented the Villa Orchio at Settignano, an ancient village on the hills east of Florence, where Michelangelo was born. The villa was owned by the family of Marion Crawford. Charlotte had put it in order, engaged servants and made it ready for the nuptials. The villa was very old and had a rose arbor and terraced garden with an olive orchard below it and a commanding outlook with the villa of d'Annunzio and that of Duse in the foreground.

On April 27th, we with other friends, drove up to the villa. Mary Austin, Professor and Mrs. Gayley, and Mrs. Charles Wheeler of Berkeley were among the guests. The drawing room had a ceiling of inlaid wood and its furniture was carved oak; now it was a bower of apple blossoms and in it the twain were made one. A noble pair fitted each for the other and both for helping the world, as their subsequent life together has demonstrated in so many then undreamed-of ways. After the wedding the guests left; the honeymoon was to be spent at the villa, one of the most beautiful spots in the world for this happy period. During our three week's stay in Florence we spent three days at the Villa Orchio, charming days with a very unselfish bridal pair who made our intrusions seem like invited pleasure.

{We found President and Mrs. Andrew D. White in Florence and saw them occasionally. We also saw much of Mary Austin, who was always most interesting, and we made the acquaintance of Professor and Mrs. Harrower of Aberdeen University. So, we had much social life during our stay.}

{As to many Americans, Florence seemed to us the most interesting and delightful city in Italy. We often walked along the Arno, a wide muddy river spanned by the most beautiful bridges in the world, or so they seemed to us. We went to the Palazzo Vecchio first, not because of its grandeur and history, but to see the magnificent room where Vernon and Charlotte had the civil marriage service performed, the morning before the churchly wedding at Villa Orchio. We went to the Duomo and the Baptistery and studied Brunelleschi's dome and Ghiberti's gates. We visited the Medici chapel at San Lorenzo, to see the works of Michael Angelo [*sic*]. Then to the church of Santa Croce to pay tribute to the tomb of the great artist and to the monument to Galileo. One day we went to San Marco to visit the cloister where Fra Angelico painted, and Savonarola preached. We spent a morning at the Academia di Belle Arti and greatly enjoyed the paintings of Fra Filippo Lippi and Botticelli. We visited La Badia to see the pictures of Filippino Lippi and then to the Bargello and found the museum there and the building itself the most interesting in all Florence. We reveled in the Sala di Donatello. No other sculptor has been so beautifully human as he. We haunted the Uffizi to study there the pictures by Raphael, Murillo, del Sarto and Titian. It seemed to us we enjoyed those masters here more than at any other place; the atmosphere of Florence conduces to enjoyment of art. Thanks to the fact that we both had listened to Andrew D. White's lectures on the Renaissance we were familiar with some phases of Florentine history. The Medici and Savonarola were like long-lost friends, met again on their own stamping ground.}

{We made an excursion to Fiesole, up through cherry orchards wreathed in white blossoms. Of course, we visited the church whose treasure is a Madonna by Fra Angelico and the monastery where Fra Angelico and his brother Fra Benedetto lived as monks. Then to Boccaccio's Villa and Villa Landor with gorgeous outlook where Walter Savage Landor passed miserable years. One afternoon Mary Austin took us for a heavenly drive to San Miniato al Monte and to the Torre del Gallo where Galileo got ahead of his oppressors by studying the moon while imprisoned. The view from the tower is superb.}

{We paid a visit to the Entomological Experiment Station and made the acquaintance of the eminent scientist, Signor Berlese, and his charming wife, who was for us her husband's interpreter. We met all the entomologists employed at the Station and had our photographs taken with them. Signor Berlese took us to Galileo's room where all his instruments are kept. Later, Signor and Signora Berlese and Signor Paulo called upon us. Meeting these co-workers in Mr. Comstock's field was one of our memorable experiences abroad. When we left Florence, Signor Berlese and the staff came to the train to see us off.}

{We left Florence reluctantly. We had in our three weeks, seen about as much as could be expected of two people who were diligent in sight-seeing and who read Vasari's *Lives* and [Oliphant's] *The Makers of Florence* on rainy days. We made several visits to the silversmiths, Coppins, a firm four hundred years old, and still in the same family, a visit to it was like one of the old Dutch paintings of interiors; with the workers dressed in smocks, at their bellows seated at long tables, which extended the length of the long, low room. I had always desired a silver comb. I wished it of a certain shape of which I made an outline pattern, which they filled with a Florentine design. It looks delicate, but it has stood constant wear for 21 years and is now as good as new. Certainly, among the charms of Florence are the silversmiths and workers in leather and other fine artistic handiwork. There is an exquisite quality in their products which America may never hope to attain, for it is the result of centuries of workers who have had no regard for the time element, and therefore were} [manuscript ends here abruptly without explanation].

{We left Florence reluctantly, and although our memories of Florence are many and satisfying, I think our outstanding and happiest remembrance will ever be the wedding of Charlotte and Vernon Kellogg in a bower of apple blossoms in the ancient Villa Orchio, at Settignano.}

{When Americans visit Venice, words always fail them in trying to express adequately their experience and emotions. We lost no time after we arrived in taking a gondola and going the length of the Grand Canal and back. Luckily, there were then no motor boats to dash about and shatter the silence with their sputtering. We also made haste to visit the Square of St. Marks' and feed the pigeons. We spent our first evening at Florin's Café listening to the band. After thus paying our respects to the sights we had longed to behold we did the usual things ecstatically.} {We reveled in the art galleries, in the works of Paolo Veronese, Bellini, Tintoretto, Titian, and Carpaccio. We visited the beautiful churches and the Doge's palace; we passed over the Bridge of Sighs and saw the dungeon beyond, which will ever make me shudder when I see a picture of that beautiful structure. We sat on the steps that led to the water of the Riva and read, Hopkinson Smith's *Gondola Days*; and every evening after the first, we spent in a gondola on the Grand Canal; and when weary in the day, we took a gondola and explored the "piccoli canali."}

{Those evenings—we can never forget them—the gondola itself, is a joy to the eye and also to the spirit. It is ease and grace personified and vivified. Our gondolier was always sympathetic and silent. The waters of the canal were always just near enough to calmness to multiply the lights in great, splotchy reflections. The electric lights on the Mole, in groups of threes, sent down great columns of broken light, while the lesser lights of the streets, the red and blue lights of the steamers and docks, the yellow lights of the battle ships, the myriad firefly lights of the swift-moving gondolas, the pyramids of Chinese lanterns on the music barges, all sent their quivering lines of color through the dark water to us. We were the center of all.}

{We watched the full moon rise, and it was the supreme moment of the evening. The great yellow disk moved upward slowly and stately above the towers and campanile of San Giorgio; then suddenly permeated the darkness with a wide path of shimmering light and lifted the domes of St. Maria della Salute from pale twilight and revealed all the silvered glow of its noble architecture.}

{We took a little steamer to the Giudecca and enjoyed keenly the many-colored sails of the fishing boats. We spent an afternoon on the famous Lido Beach and found it very uninteresting and disappointing, although as a place to bathe it was undoubtedly better than the polluted waters of the canals.}

{After our visits to Verona, Turin and Bellagio we were tired and found Locarno a good point for resting. We found comfortable quarters in the Hotel du Lac and, after dinner wandered along the quay watching the reflection of the mountains in the still waters and the signal lights on the mountain shine out through the gathering twilight. The next morning, we took the funicular up to the church, Madonna del Sasso, a thousand feet above the town. We walked on to the Church of the Trinity for the view and there saw San Franciscan brothers sitting around and having a good time. We walked back to the Church of the Madonna where we saw the really beautiful picture of the entombment by Ciseri.}

{One morning we took a tram to Brignasco. The scenery along the route was magnificent, lofty mountains, shining white cascades, a dashing mountain river spanned by arched bridges, wayside shrines, villages of stone cottages, churches with graceful campaniles and vividly green fields. We took our lunch at the Glacier House with eighty boys from Locarno gymnasium who had made an early excursion into the mountains.}

{While Locarno in itself is not especially interesting, the excursions from there are many and worth-while. One morning we went on the 7 o'clock funicular to its terminal and then took a literal "high road" that passes through Orselina, Brione and Contra, little villages of stone houses perched like swallows' nests against the mountain side, and then winds along the sides of abysses to Mergoscia, a little village of charcoal burners. Margoscia [*sic*] is a hamlet of stone houses above and below the highway which, at the end of the village, came to an end itself at a stone wall for the very good reason that it was cut off by a gorge a thousand feet sheer down. A church stood at right angles above the road which ran beneath a stone arch nearby.

We were surprised to see above the keystone of the arch the United States and Italian flags in amicable companionship, carved in the stone. At the side of the arch, inset and under glass, was the photograph of a man with the statement below that he had died in America and left his fortune to this village of his birth.}

{There was a newly built restaurant near at hand, and we went in and in our best Italian asked for refreshments. Our host answered us at once in American vernacular. He, with others and the man who endowed the town, had gone to Santa Rosa, California, and there earned enough money to enable him to come back six years ago, marry and build the restaurant; his wife was postmistress and they had four children. I asked how much money the benefactor had left the town and he said $2,000.00 We suggest that the interest on this was very little to help the village, to which he replied, "The people here live within such narrow margins that every year this sum makes all the difference between suffering and comfort to several old people." When he added, "The people here all love the United States," we felt we had gained a sidelight on international relations.}

{While I was sketching after luncheon, an old man splitting wood near me began to talk to me in American, for he too had been in Santa Rosa. Wishing to make pleasing conversation I said:}

> {"Italians ought to be better than Americans for they have so many beautiful churches and shrines in which to pray."}
>
> {"Yes, Italians have more beautiful churches, but they are no better than Americans. You have very good churches in America. I liked very much a church in Santa Rosa,—the Presbyterian church."}
>
> {"I dropped my brush in amazement and exclaimed, "But there is a fine Catholic Church in Santa Rosa!" to which he answered in quiet scorn:}
>
> {"Yes, *Irish* Catholic; I liked better the Presbyterian." Suddenly I perceived for the first time that in this world there are Catholics—and—Catholics.}

{One morning we took the boat to Brissago and walked on to Cannobio, which we reached in time to join the procession which carried the Host from one church to another. This was what we had come to see, and it was fully as interesting as we had anticipated. The priests wore robes adorned with priceless lace, the people were in gala attire and the procession ended with twenty blue-clad, red-hatted girls from the Industrial School.}

{After the fiesta was over we came upon a group of gypsies, quite as rascally and much more picturesque than those at home. An old woman with a weird face and piercing eyes, persisted in following me around. She had something to tell me and insisted upon it. She spoke a queer Italian, difficult to understand, but I did understand that I was to get a letter telling me that one of my friends was a suicide by hanging, and that he was not quite right in his mind. She touched her temple with her finger and said in sad tone, "Il povero!" Mr. Comstock tore me away, but I certainly was impressed and scared. It was ten days later in Lucerne that I received a letter telling me that a man well beloved in our family had sought an end to mental depression.}

{Although we had taken but few of the possible excursions from Locano, we were satisfied, because we had rested. On the tenth of June we took the train for St. Gotthard tunnel. We had an hour at Bellinzona, and then came the soul-stirring journey up the Ticino valley and the weird experiences in and out the famous tunnels. We left the train at Goschenen and were driven through a great canyon with sharp peaks thousands of feet above us, to Andermatt where we found comfortable quarters in the Hotel St. Gotthard.}

{The next morning early, we took horses, carriage and driver and went up and up on a nicely graded road from which we could see green velvety valleys, slopes dotted with stone barns, and herds of cattle and goats, guarded by herders, following the grass as the snow melted while the sharp peaks above were snow-streaked. There were great ravines, snow-filled, dashing cascades and here and there a snug village nestled against the mountain-side or in a valley. Our objective was the Rhone Glacier, a chaotic mass of ice that made us shiver, but the view down the Rhone valley was superb. We saw plenty of Alpine flowers on our way—crocuses, marsh marigolds, forget-me-nots and vivid blue gentians; but as we approached the glacier we drove through snow-drifts higher than our heads.}

{We spent the next day in idly wandering about Andermatt, a typical Alpine village. We were amused to see the home-coming of the cows belonging to the villagers. The herd came from high up the mountainside, a boy driving them; some of them playfully bounded down over the rocks and steep places as surefooted as goats; with their tails in the air they made an exciting spectacle.}

{The next day we walked from Andermatt to Goschenen, an impressive experience. We there took the train down the magnificent valley of the turbulent River Reuss, and then by steamer went from Fluelen to Lucerne, certainly one of the most scenic lake voyages in the world.}

{We found a pleasant abiding place in Pension Fuller. It was rather warm, and we greatly enjoyed the dense shade of the pollarded horse chestnut trees, along the quay. The ancient bridge, Kapell-Brucke, with triangular pictures painted in the gables, and the Wasserturm remain outstanding impressions of this beautiful city which we enjoyed leisurely for several days. The Lion of Lucerne had been a familiar work of art to us since grammar school days, but on picture can convey any idea of the impressiveness and majesty of the original, a noble monument to the 800 Swiss soldiers that died for duty and not for glory in defending an alien king.}

{On a day, when we felt brave, we took the boat to Alpnachstad and there took a hair-raising rack and pinion road up Mt. Pilatus, 6790 feet to Hotel Pilatus-Kulm. We arrived in time to see the sunset glow on many snowy peaks. The next morning, we climbed to the Esel Peak and gained the widest view of the Alps that we found anywhere. There was range beyond range, peak beyond peak, of snow-capped and snow-streaked mountains and glaciers with heavenly blue lakes curving around as if loving their feet.}

{We were present in Lucerne during a great church procession. We were on hand to view its component parts and then waited hours to see them "process." There were hundreds of little girls in white dresses with white wreaths on their heads and hundreds of small boys in blue or green caps accompanied by benevolent-looking priests, their teachers, who were decked in white lace "pinafores." Then there were the official priests in cloth of gold carrying the Host; altogether this procession made a gorgeous spectacle.}

{Our Wilhelm Tell pilgrimage was quite unexpected and impromptu. It had its incipience in the conversation of an eminent historian who sat with us at table in our Pension Hall. He quite incidentally remarked that there was no historical proof that Wilhelm Tell had ever existed. We were as shocked as if he had said the same of George Washington.}

{In the seclusion of our own room we discussed the matter indignantly. Finally, Mr. Comstock said, "We belong to natural history and we do not have to believe unnatural historians. Let's go and see what the Swiss people think about Wilhelm Tell." And that is what we did.[2]}

{From Lucerne we went to the interesting old city of Bern. On our way we had wide views of the beautiful valleys on either side of the Brunig Pass. We had a charming voyage on Brienz See and then it began to rain so that our views of Interlaken and the beautiful Thun See were more or less veiled in capricious showers.}

{Our first day in Bern was pleasant; we wandered out to the bear pits to pay our respects to the patron bruins of this city. We visited the Minster,

---

2. Footnote inserted in the manuscript, page 13–20, by Herrick: "The Wilhelm Tell reise of the Comstock's was to them, as it must be to everyone who makes it, a memorable experience too long in the telling to include it here. —Editor [G. W. H.]"

which is adorned with the most beautiful wood carvings we had ever seen. We watched breathlessly the remarkable performances of the picturesque Tower Clock and wished that in Ithaca our hours might be marked by a crowing rooster and a procession of bears. That would seem to make our hours and days' worth-while. More than all we enjoyed walking through the miles of low, dark mysterious arcades that flank the streets.}

{From Bern we went to Veytaux on Lake Geneva so that we might visit the Castle of Chillon, made familiar to us in our childhood through Byron's poem. We went through the picturesque old castle in the afternoon and the next morning I sketched it. Surely there was never another turreted castle set in such glorious environment of blue lake and snow-capped mountains. We noted the spiders "in their sullen trade" and knew they must be descendants of the ones with whom the prisoner "had friendship made."}

{We went on to Zermatt and the Matterhorn. When I began to sketch the Matterhorn, I discovered that it looks more like a giant tooth than it does like a mountain. It was while I was sketching it that we noticed little blue flowers dotting the space about us and then discovered that they were the very orchid which Darwin described in his "Insects and Flowers." We amused ourselves by watching the bees "feather their noses" with the pollinia and later we took these interesting bodies off on the point of a pencil, to which they immediately glued themselves fast. We divided our interest that hour between the might and the small and to each paid sincere tribute. We saw acres of alpine roses that day and stem-less gentians and forget-me-nots and large red purple violets, and bosses of a tiny pink peony with foliage like moss.}

{Our next stopping place was Chamonix; the way led first through the grim Rhone Valley and then the less gloomy valley of Chamonix. Our room at the Hotel des Alpes gave us a fine view of Mont Blanc. We spent one day visiting Les Bossons glacier. We took a train to the village, climbed a hot, tiresome zig-zag path up 1000 feet and then down to the grotto in the glacier, which was like a bit of a fairy land. With a guide, we crossed the glacier. The view of this great ice stream above us was magnificent. We realized anew that reading about crevasses could not mean much until these fearsome cracks had been seen.}

{We left Chamonix on July 9, and that day the light was such that the Rhone valley gave us more cheerful scenes. The ride on Lake Geneva was a dream of delight as the sunset colors touched the mountains and were reflected in the waters below.}

{At Geneva we received a lettering telling of the death of Herbert Northrup, the companion of my youth who had always seemed to me like a brother. This made our stay in Geneva a sad one. We wandered up to the

University and to the Cathedral where the man I most detested in all history, John Calvin, preached. We also went dutifully to the chapel where John Knox preached, but the one pleasant memory of Geneva is of the hour we sat on the balcony of our hotel and saw Mr. Blanc bathed in sunset hues, while below us on the street, a blind man played the lute like an angel from a heavenly choir.}

{Our journey to Paris was hot and tiresome; it took us first through rather bleak mountains. The towns were old and had ruined castles on their hills. We passed many cement mills; then through a slightly rolling country, evidently very fertile; there were large fields of grain and many men and women working at the harvest. The fields were fenced with ragged hedges, often of trees. There were few vines and orchards but much of wheat, rye and potatoes. We arrived in Paris at midnight and found it very gay. People were dancing on the pavements and riding in merry-go-rounds. We had struck Paris at a holiday period, with July 14 as its climax.}

{We spent the next day seeing what we could of this beautiful city. We walked the length of the Champs-Elysees and visited the Jardin des Plantes, where Mr. Comstock was unable to find the entomologist he desired to see. That night we went to the Grand Opera and saw *Tristan and Isolde*, given magnificently. Of course, the audience interested us as much as the opera. The next day we made a most interesting call on M. Eugene Simon, an authority on spiders with whom Mr. Comstock had corresponded; he lived in a pretty villa and made a hobby of blue cats, of which he had many; we admired their aristocratic bearing—blue cats,—blue blood, of course.}

{Then followed days of the usual sight-seeing and for me long happy hours in the Louvre. We left for London July 16th.}

{This crossing of the channel was something to forget as soon as possible. After disembarking in a pouring rain, we had to rush up and down long, uncovered platforms in order to find vacant seats in the train. We did not mention it, but we were greatly irritated with what seemed to us, a needless lack of comfort and convenience for the traveller.}

{We settled comfortably in The Hotel Thackery and met there Professor Allerdyce of Stanford, and later Mary Rogers Miller came to see us. We expected to find London interesting, but it took some days to realize how interesting. We were enchanted with the art galleries, where we found wondrous paintings by the old Italian masters whom we thought we had left behind us.}

{Our friends, Mr. and Mrs. Wilhelm Miller, went with us to see the sights of London and one day took us to lunch at the Cheshire Cheese, an experience which every American cherishes.}

{Mr. Comstock went to Kensington and called on the entomologists, Messrs. Hampson and Kirby. We spent three days at Oxford, where Mr. Comstock spent hours with Dr. Poulton looking at collections of insects; he invited us to his house for lunch with his wife and two daughters and a benign African parrot called "Pepper." Oxford was bewildering to us in all its dignity and beauty. We wandered about the Colleges and the gardens and went into the Bodleian Library. We called on a Cornell friend, Dr. Schiller, at Corpus Christi College and he showed us the rooms, dining hall, silver plate and the kitchen of that famous college; it all seemed like a page from some old English volume.}

{From Oxford we went to Cambridge for a day. We visited Jesus and St. John's Colleges, spacious Trinity, and the King's chapel and the grounds of Pembroke; we greatly admired the beautiful lawns called, "The College Backs."}

{On July 25 we went aboard the S. S. Minnetonka and turned our faces toward home. We had for fellow passengers many pleasant folks and saw much of a Congregationalist minister, Mr. Hall, and his wife and son, and also made happy acquaintance with Mr. Jacob Riis. We greatly enjoyed our talks with Mr. Riis, his point of view on our own country both politically and socially was not only enlightening but inspiring. I am sure that we both are better citizens for having this contact with this keen, wise, broad minded man.}

Anna Botsford Comstock, with Liberty Hyde Bailey and the Junior Extension Group of Tompkins County on a school picnic, May 26, 1905.

 CHAPTER XIV

Chapter 15: 1908–1912, Cornell's New Quarters for Entomology and Nature Study

Chapter XIV from the Comstock manuscript is missing. A note from Glenn W. Herrick, written in the shaky hand of his later life and placed at the front of the manuscript folder for Chapter XV, reads: "Chapter XIV: I cannot account for it." Therefore, the following chapter is taken directly from the corresponding chapter [Chapter 15], as edited in the book by Herrick et al.[1] The length of this missing chapter is unknown; however, it could be surmised, based on other book-chapter lengths versus their parallel manuscript-chapter lengths, that this missing Chapter XIV from the manuscript could have been approximately forty pages.[2]

When we returned to Ithaca, August 4, 1908, it was very warm weather, but we were so glad to be at home that we did not mind. The Gages and the entire Entomology Department staff came to welcome us: Professors MacGillivray, Riley, Needham, and Slingerland. In September, I gave the address at the formal opening of William Smith College in Geneva. The founder of the College, Mr. William Smith, had asked me to speak for him, saying: "You

1. Glenn W. Herrick and Ruby Green Bell Smith, eds., *Comstocks of Cornell: Biography and Autobiography of John Henry Comstock and Anna Botsford Comstock* (New York: Comstock Publishing Associates, 1953), 227–35.

2. Karen Penders St. Clair, "Finding Anna: The Archival Search for Anna Botsford Comstock" (PhD dissertation, Cornell University, 2017), footnotes 88 and 89.

know what I would like to say, and I wish you would say it for me." My address is printed in the William Smith Bulletin.

Our new official quarters in Roberts Hall were of great interest to us. At last Mr. Comstock had a large laboratory with ample windows, with no sashes to bring a bar across the field of the microscope. He won this point by showing Emmons Williams, the Treasurer of Cornell, a close friend, that window sashes impede clear vision in the field of the microscope. Mr. Comstock found his office pleasant. From its windows may be seen a broad landscape to the south and east. The insect collections were placed on the same floor as the lecture room, a great convenience. With three large laboratories, a lecture room, a workroom, and four department offices, Mr. Comstock felt richer than Midas.

My experience was not so gratifying. The Nature Study Department was housed in the two west rooms on the fourth floor. The window in my room was so high that one could see out only when standing. However, I had shelves for my books and a roll-top desk, which seemed a luxury. My assistant, Miss Ada Georgia, had an adjoining room in which we kept files. My classes met around a long table in my room. I kept the north room on the second floor of the Insectary as an overflow office, and as a place for speedy retreat, when social life in the house threatened to interfere with official duties.

On January 31, 1909, a great sorrow came to us. The wife of our beloved Cornell Professor George Burr died in giving birth to a son, and the child died also. I cannot describe the effect of this calamity on our Cornell community. Professor Burr had led such a noble and unselfish life, in helping others, that he had not married while young. His wife, Dr. Mattie Martin, was a beautiful woman, very able, an excellent scholar, and endowed with a charming and inspiring personality; we had all rejoiced that the two had found each other and were glad when we knew they expected a child, for George was passionately fond of children. He had too much spiritual strength to succumb to this blow, but we all knew what he was enduring. Soon after his return from the funeral in Virginia, he again took his place at our table, as a member of our family.

It was during the winter of 1909 that I conceived the idea of writing my *Handbook of Nature Study*. I had worked for so long with teachers that I believed I knew how to help them and had already written many lessons in my Extension Service course in Home Nature Study. I consulted some publishers but received no encouragement. Professor L. H. Bailey also seemed to think a nature study book would not be successful financially; and my husband, who had so heartily and generously backed me in my former undertakings, was most discouraging. He said the book would never pay for the printing. I disagreed with the judgment of my friends and family. I believed that the book would pay for itself after several years; and I felt that I could not let all of the hard work I had done for teachers be lost. So I went at my task with defiant courage. I knew that my husband would help me financially with my book, even if he believed it would be a total loss, and so I put in every spare moment writing, although it was hard to find spare moments.

The Cornell Commencement in 1909 marked the thirty-fifth reunion of Mr. Comstock's class. There was no special provision for the class reunions in those days and no place available for a class dinner, but Harry was class secretary and felt that a dinner was his responsibility. We decided that we must take care of it ourselves. Mr. Comstock cleared out his big laboratory and the tables were set there. A smaller room was turned into a temporary pantry where viands could be kept hot. Our efficient housekeeper, Mrs. Margery Smith, cooked the food in Fall Creek Cottage and our student helpers carried it to Roberts Hall. A janitor in Boardman Hall, Lawrence Powers, a handsome, dignified, and reliable man, served the dinner with great éclat. It was pronounced a success.

We fled to The Hermitage as soon as Commencement was over. We were so tired that for two days we did not do much but sleep and listen to the songs of the veery thrush when half awake. Soon Professor Glenn Herrick joined us. He had been called to fill the position made vacant by the untimely death of Mark Slingerland. Glenn had built a fine reputation as a teacher in the State College of Mississippi and had been called at a larger salary to the State Agricultural and Mechanical College of Texas. In considering his call to Cornell, there was only one possible objection, that he was my cousin's son. However, as to reputation and accomplishment he was the best available man and had been elected.

We spent the summer of 1909 at The Hermitage. In the mornings I worked on the lessons for my *Handbook of Nature Study* and Mr. Comstock on his *Spider Book*. During the afternoons we worked on the house and grounds, making them more convenient and beautiful. Every evening at sunset, we went down to the boathouse and from hammocks swung from its upper deck, watched the sky, radiant with sunset colors that were reflected in the shimmering, opaline waters of Cayuga Lake.

In December 1909, we took a step that was to lead to unimagined results. The Comstock Publishing Company had expanded to publish a textbook, General Biology, by Dr. James G. Needham. He had been suddenly called upon to give a course in biology to Cornell Freshmen. This meant large classes. He had part of the text written and wished to write the rest in installments, to keep ahead of the class. Of course, no regular publisher would consider such a proposal, and so Dr. Needham became a part of the Comstock Publishing Company and financed his own book. This added to the work of the Company, which had hitherto been managed by Mr. Comstock, with a student helper. Some work for the Company had been done by William A. Slingerland, a salesman in Ithaca, and he proposed to devote his evening to the work, on a salary. On December 9, 1909, he was installed as manager of the Comstock Publishing Company, which continued to thrive. In April 1912, Mr. Slingerland was given full-time employment, a fortunate decision, for he was resourceful in placing our books before the public. Publishers who knew of our expansion, prophesied a short life for the Comstock Publishing Company that had only four books to sell, but it is still prospering after seventeen years.

Another step in the growth of the Company was our purchase of a new home in 1910. We had bought "The Pinnacle," a forested hill east of Beebe Lake, when we were sure a trolley line from Ithaca to Freeville would pass it; this, we thought, would solve the problem of getting help, at least so far as transportation was concerned. Now we heard disturbing rumors that this line was not to be built. At this juncture, our friend, Mary Fowler, Curator of Cornell's Petrarch Library, said that she wished to sell her house at 123 Roberts Place. I had always liked the inside of the house, but I think the thing that interested Mr. Comstock most was the light, dry, spacious basement. He saw that an office for the Comstock Publishing Company could be finished there, and the laundry used for the storage of books. For this rapidly growing infant industry, a suitable place was a pressing problem.

On November 6, 1910, we bought the house for $10,000. Our next problem was to get the money to pay for it. Mr. Comstock went at once to Comptroller Emmons Williams and found that the University wished to buy our Fall Creek Cottage, on the Cornell Campus. The price agreed upon was $5,000. We were well satisfied. The house had cost $3,000 and we had lived in it thirty-three years, paying ground rent of one dollar a year. Next, we must arrange to sell "The Pinnacle," which Harry had bought for $1,100. I was in a plight, for I had always had a devastating ambition, to keep a cow, an ambition not shared by my husband, who did not wish to add the milking of a cow to his already too numerous professorial and domestic duties. So, without his knowledge, I had bought two lots in the little valley east of "The Pinnacle," for a barn and pasture. George Burr had helped me to make the first payments. I think I paid $450 for the two lots. Now I had to confess to my ownership. Harry forgave me, and we sold my plots, with "The Pinnacle," to the University for $5,555. We had heard severe things said by our professors of political economy about the sin of the "unearned increment," but we waxed jubilant that, without forethought, we had plucked such plums from this forbidden tree.

On February 8, 1911, Mr. Comstock finished the manuscript of The Spider Book. He always finished his manuscripts to the last footnote, and had every illustration ready and numbered, before sending anything to the printer. Long before I had sent the earlier sections of my Handbook of Nature Study to my printer, and I was striving to keep ahead of the printer, a chapter at a time, trusting that I would have health and strength to finish the book.

Harry and I devoted as much time as we could snatch from our manifold activities to the necessary changes in the house that was to be our home. We had asked Cornell's Professor C. A. Martin, the architect who had built it, to help us. We planned to throw two rooms together on the second floor, to make a study for Harry; to add a sleeping porch above the entrance porch, and a bay window to the dining room; and to finish a room in the basement for the Comstock Publishing Company.

We had to purchase new furniture and I longed to go to Grand Rapids where I could select from a wide range of patterns; but that would cost so much that it did not seem worthwhile. At this juncture, I was invited by Miss Mary Wheeler to go to Grand Rapids, to teach a week in her Kindergarten Training School, with my expenses paid and a hundred dollars besides. This seemed a miraculous occurrence. I felt as if my wish had been granted by magic and I almost expected to take the journey on a flying carpet. I went by rail, however, and I never enjoyed a week of work more. It has seemed to me that all of the women I have known in charge of training for kindergarten teaching have been superior in every respect. Miss Wheeler was charming, lovable, and able. Although my week was busy with teaching and social activities, I found time to visit furniture warerooms and to order what we needed; after nineteen years of constant use, it is still in good condition.

In July carpenters began working on our new home. We had named it "The Ledge" because it was set upon a ledge of rock, meagerly covered with soil. In looking up the meaning of "ledge" I found it to be "a shelf on which things may be laid." This made it even more appropriate, for we were both nearing the age when we were to be laid on the shelf.

Both Mr. Comstock and I had long days of teaching and I had my book's proof to read; Harry often found time to help me at this task. Although he believed that my Handbook of Nature Study would lose $5,000, he was kindness and consideration personified in helping me get material and in helping me make up the book; this illustrates well, the kind husband he was. However busy the days, we stole time to go over to The Ledge and note the progress of the carpenters.

Days before we were to move, our dear capable housekeeper, Mrs. Margery Smith, began packing. The hegira occurred August 7, 1911. Mr. Comstock had estimated that there would be three van-loads and there were twelve. Harry was amazed that so small a house as our Fall Creek Cottage could contain so much and said we could never have put it back again if we had tried, but I knew where every piece was stowed. Those first days at The Ledge were chaotic. I had to teach every day and so did Mr. Comstock.

In many ways, it was heart-rending to leave Fall Creek Cottage, the house we had built and in which we had experienced half a lifetime of happiness and sorrow, success and perplexities, and the working out of a life program together. It had been hallowed by precious associations, through the many friends who had sat by its hearth; my mother had lived there for some years and had died there. There were innumerable ties that bound Harry and me to this home. Perhaps it was best that at this time the University was grading off a great section of our lawn and the dust was almost unbearable, so we were not in an atmosphere in which we could indulge in the sentiments natural to the occasion.

Our experience of uprooting from one home to settle in another gave me the feeling that a house has a soul which it attains only after it has become a home. For weeks after our moving, I felt that we were living in a house in which I was an alien; Harry confessed to a similar sensation. It was only after many friends had sat by the new hearth that we felt that we had another home. One of the great advantages of The Ledge was its charming sleeping porch that looks out into the tree tops beside Fall Creek. We slept here summer and winter for many years, until we were commanded by the doctor to come in during very cold weather. Many a morning in zero weather, Harry looked like an Arctic explorer with his mustache iced.

On September 30, 1911, my *Handbook of Nature Study* came from the printer. It certainly was a ponderous volume, printed as it was on glazed paper. I was so glad to have it done that I was not so much elated over the appearance of the volume as I was relieved that it was finished. I looked it through and said to myself, "I am sure it will pay for itself, if it is given time enough." Mr. Comstock, ever practical, spent his spare time for a week wrapping my books to get ready for the day of publication, on October 7, the thirty-third anniversary of our wedding. I knew the book would help teachers, if they wanted help, but I was also aware that many would not desire anything whatever about Nature Study. I certainly did not foresee that teachers all over the United States, fifteen years later, would speak of it as their "Nature Bible."[3]

In November 1911, I went to Geneva to see William Smith, founder of the college that bears his name. He felt himself failing and had sent for me. We

3. Footnote inserted in the 1953 edition (p. 234): "Mrs. Comstock's Handbook of Nature Study, now in its twenty-fourth edition, has proved to be the best seller among books published by Cornell University. Before Mrs. Comstock's death, in 1930, this generously illustrated book of 938 pages had been translated into eight languages and had sold in North and South America, in Asia, and in Europe. —R.G.S."

both thought it would be our last visit. His mind was clear, and he talked as well as ever. I think he wished me to reassure him concerning the life he was soon to enter upon, and was comforted when I spoke to him of Cornell's Professor Hiram Corson and of his belief in messages from the spirit world, and his feeling that it was glorious to be a part of the great scheme of the universe and at one with its underlying power. Mr. Smith declared that a man should do his duty to the world without any thought of reward or fame. He said our friendship would not cease when one of us was gone and asked me to be true to my trust in looking after his college. He was infinitely gentle and lovable and liked to have me hold his hand while we talked, as if he wanted to cling to his earthly friends as long as possible. I think he felt lonely at passing the barrier alone, although his faith told him that loved ones awaited him. I saw him twice after that. He died February 7, 1912 and Harry and I went to his funeral. Seventeen years[4] have passed since then and I have attended every meeting of the Hobart and William Smith trustees since, except two or three, when I was ill. I have done my best to be true to my trust.

On January 13, 1912, Mr. Comstock lectured before Sigma Xi. His subject was spiders. It was a delightful lecture, illustrated with lantern slides of the webs he had photographed with so much skill. It was 16 degrees below zero that night; I noted in my diary: "Getting ready for bed in the sleeping porch, at 16 degrees below zero, is an extended, almost ritualistic performance."

In January 1912, President Schurman asked Mr. Comstock to represent Cornell University at the celebration of the two hundred and fiftieth anniversary of the royal Society of London, the following summer. This was exciting and delightful. Harry had intended to be in Oxford in August to attend the International Congress of Entomologists, and this important London function added to our anticipation.

Cornell's Commencement exercises this June were held out of doors, in the natural amphitheater, west of McGraw Hall, which as a Cornell Freshman, Harry had helped to build. Mr. Comstock, in academic robes, gave the diplomas to the students of the College of Agriculture, as Dean Bailey was away. The students, in their black gowns and mortarboards, with gay tassels, were seated to face a platform on which were seated the University Faculty and Trustees, also in academic dress. It was a beautiful scene, lighted by sunshine and set in the vivid green of the June landscape.

---

4. The aforementioned date, and the note of years passed, puts this portion of the manuscript to have been written in approximately 1929, one year before Anna Comstock's death. —KSt.

John Henry Comstock portrait.

Anna Botsford Comstock portrait.

CHAPTER XV

The Two hundred and Fiftieth-anniversary Celebration of the Royal Society and The International Entomological Congress

The pattern of incongruous chapter numbering continues with what is Chapter 16 in the 1953 edition. The chapter titles were often altered from one copy to another as the focus of a chapter shifted once the edits, and omissions, were complete. For example, the title of this chapter in the 1953 book is, "Summer in England; Plans for Retirement."

{We left home June 24, 1912 and arriving in Boston the next morning we called on C. H. Thurber at the office of Ginn and Company. Then went to Cambridge to call on Mr. Samuel Henshaw and to the West Newton to spend the night with Jennie Fleming Farnham, and her fine family. On June 26 we started on our voyage on the S. S. Parisian. This was a one class boat and a large number of our fellow passengers were Scots, workers in the New England cotton mills going back to visit. They were wholesome people and happy. We did not lack entertainment for, every evening, Scottish ballads and songs were sung in the saloon and now and then there was a Scottish dance. I shall never forget a little lassie about twelve who performed the sword dance for us and the Highland fling.}

The event of the voyage was seeing an iceberg of grand proportions; far enough away so that we could enjoy looking at the gleaming white broken mass with ultra-marine shadows, an impressive sight. One morning we saw whales spouting. The geography of my youth had a picture of a whale spouting, but I somehow never really believed it could be true until I saw it.

{We sighted Ireland on June 5th, a heavenly blue jagged coast which later turned to the vivid green that made us realize why it was called the Emerald Isle. We stopped at Belfast and then on and up the Clyde and lay at anchor at night at Greenock. The next day we were in Glasgow. As soon as we were settled in the Central Station Hotel we took a ride on the top of a bus to Renken Park and to Paisley. The next day we visited the University and the botanic gardens which we found interesting.}

{Our stay in Scotland was very short and it made us feel shallow and cursory merely to glance at places rich in historical and literary association and pass on. We visited Rowardennan on Loch Lomond and the next morning at 4:30 Mr. Comstock began his climb of Ben Lomond. He returned about 9 o'clock pleased and proud of his feat. I recalled the passage in "The Lady of the Lake":}

{"Right up Ben Lomond could he press
And not a sob the toil confess."}

{From Inversnaid we took a coach gay with red paint and drawn by four horses driven by red-coated drivers. We certainly "made a dent" in the blue-gray landscape as we bowled over the fine road amidst the greenest, rockiest, mossiest roads in Great Britain. At Stronachlachar we took a boat down Loch Katrine between Ben Venue and Ben Aran. This was Scott's country and now at last I felt at home and was living the beloved romances of my girlhood when I had committed to memory several cantos of "The Lady of the Lake."}

{We finally arrived at Edinburgh, the ancient and the picturesque. We visited one of my Cornell sorority sisters, Dr. Frances Storrs Johnston, a beautiful, interesting and energetic woman who had married into one of the fine families of Scotland. She and her husband were charming hosts and they guided us in seeing the city from The Castle to Holyrood. The Johnston home had exquisite furniture, very old in pattern, very new in Circassian walnut, and I took the liberty of speaking about it at which my hostess said, "Well Edinburgh has some advantages over Denver, for it has a furniture factory that has been going for four hundred years and which has kept all its old patterns so I had my choice of both pattern and wood."}

{From Edinburgh we went to Melrose and spent some leisurely hours in the beautiful ruin. We bowed our heads where lies the heart of Robert Bruce.}

{We drove out to Abbottsford, a pilgrimage to the home of Sir Walter Scott, the beloved poet of my youth, which we visited with interest and reverence. While on the way I heard the skylarks sing for the first time. I heard the beautiful songs and looked in vain for the bird until I saw one fluttering back to earth from the clouds above, which hid the songsters whose music flowed down and encompassed us.}

{That night we spent in Durham. The next day we visited the castle and then spent hours in the Cathedral. We were fortunate in being able to attend a choral service there. The boy voices were exquisite and while we listened to glorious music we had the chance to feel as well as see, the grandeur of this cathedral.}

In London we stayed at the Russell Hotel, and the first morning after our arrival George Burr and Charles Hull called on us and, a little later, two other Cornell friends, Florence Slater and Clara Meyers, and we all went out to the Kew Gardens and had a joyful day. That evening Mr. Comstock went to the first informal meeting of the delegates to the Royal Society Celebration.

On July 16, at noon, there was an impressive service for us all in Westminster Abbey {conducted by the Dean of the Abbey}. It was an impressive sight; the delegates were all in Academic dress which ranged from the modest Cornell black gown and red and white hood up through gowns of gorgeous reds and purples to the green velvets trimmed with ermine of the Russians.

That evening there was a great dinner in the Guild hall for the delegates.[1] Mr. Comstock was greatly impressed by the beauty of the hall and the magnificence of the function.

{Eleven of the wives of delegates, including myself, were entertained at dinner by Lady Bradford at her home in Manchester Square. We entered and removed our wraps on the first floor then went up stairs to the drawing room where we met our hostess, a vivacious little woman, very good-looking and well dressed and most entertaining. She was full of interest in every subject that happened to be brought into the conversation. We were all very much in love with her and very grateful for her kindness to us.}

The event of the day following was a garden party at Syon House, the home of the Duke and Duchess of Northumberland. It is a great old house full of impressive furniture, beautiful pictures and what seemed to us miles of shelves containing books. Our host and hostess were attractive, dignified elderly people {real folk although they were Duke and Duchess}; they shook hands with us cordially and gave us the liberty of the house. A beautiful lawn extending from the house to the River Thames, {had a tent for refreshments at its center and} was the scene of the social part of the function. As we were passing toward the tent a Hindu in gorgeous apparel approached us and Mr. Comstock presented me to H. R. H. The Maharaja of Jhalipuhr {and it was} for me an exciting moment. {He was very kind and pleasant; Mr. Comstock} had previously related to me the story of making his acquaintance.

---

1. Sentence inserted here by Herrick in the manuscript: "There were 490 guests present at the dinner." —KSt.

It was the evening of the first reception at Guildhall. Mr. Comstock had met a few whom he knew and then wandered around lonely and ill at ease when he saw a Hindu in glorious raiment standing alone and apparently ignored. {Mr. Comstock} had had Hindu students in his classes whom he had tried to keep from being lonesome in America, so he approached the gentleman and by showing his name upon the list of delegates introduced himself. The Maharajah did the same and they had a very interesting conversation. It was only afterwards that Mr. Comstock realized that the reason this Hindu was standing alone was that the Majesty is supposed to be alone unless it makes a sign that it desires company. {Mr. Comstock being a simple citizen of the United States was affected only by the human side and couldn't see why he should not talk to a lonely fellow being. As a matter of fact} the Maharajah was pleased and ever after sought Mr. Comstock in the crowds; since then he has sent a remembrance each Christmas and given us a volume of his travels.

{The evening after the reception at Syon House there was a conversazione at the rooms of the Royal Society to which we were all invited. The crowd was so great one did not find one's friends but looking at the people and guessing their nationality was entertaining.}

The closing {and supreme} event of the celebration was the garden party at Windsor Castle. The delegates were received by their Majesties in the palace and were shown through it afterwards. The King and Queen were very cordial and shook hands with the delegates which act filled the minds of the English {men present} with awe. {They whispered to Mr. Comstock, "Their Majesties are shaking hands with us;" and Mr. Comstock, being unused to Royalty, wondered what else they could do, but kept discreetly silent.}

{Not only were the delegates and their wives invited to the Garden party but about eight thousand others were also commanded. We were out in the great gardens while we waited long for Royalty to appear; and luckily I chanced to be near the place of their entrance. I was surprised to find Queen Mary so much more beautiful than her pictures represent her. Her exquisite complexion and the pleasing expression of her face made her radiantly beautiful. Her costume of pale brown matched her hair and was very artistic and becoming. King George looked exactly like his photographs, a good-looking typical Englishman. Following their majesties were Princess Mary and two princes, nice looking youngsters in their teens.}

{An interesting phase of the royal garden party was witnessing the struggle for refreshments which were served under an awning. Some kind acquaintance made the effort, which resulted in rescuing for me three or four large delicious hot-house grapes, the sole trophy of his exploit and my only portion of Royal viands. We knew we were in the midst of lords and ladies, but they weren't labelled, so we were none the wiser.}

{In the evening we were the guests of Lord Fletcher Moulton and his daughter at dinner. Lord Moulton was charming in manner; he was a man who made you feel more worth while just because he talked to you. The meeting with this eminent man is one of the memories of this celebration that I most cherish.}

{After it was all finished and we had time to think about it, we realized what a great privilege it had been to be permitted to be a part of this 250th anniversary celebration of the Royal Society of London. It was one of the outstanding events of our lives.}

Five of us made a pilgrimage to Selborne. I had always longed to visit the place where Gilbert White[2] lived and wrote. George Burr, Clara Meyers and Florence Slater joined us for the day. We went from London to Farnham by train and took a taxi to Selborne. We motored through lanes where two carriages could not pass, narrow roads between high hedges made up of hawthorn, linden, elm, and many other species.

The approach to Selborne is up hill and down dale, past stone or brick cottages, vine-covered and with gardens ablaze with flowers. The one long street of the village is perhaps as picturesque as any in all England. Gilbert White's house [known as "The Wakes,"] is at the far end of the street and opposite the village green which is called the Plestor. Part of the house borders the street and some of it is slightly back, with an attractive tile and stone fence in front of it. The house is of brick and much has been added since Gilbert White's time. {The garden is protected by a high brick wall and the place was not open to pilgrims.}

The Plestor is on a side hill and is not a spacious park. It has a large tree in it with seats around its trunk even as in White's time. A path across the Plestor to the far corner leads to the church. Near the church is a tremendous old yew tree that arches the path to the church door and around whose massive trunk is a circular seat. The church is a deeply satisfactory stone edifice with mahogany pews and an oak-beamed ceiling. It is light and restful and simple. There is a stone baptismal font by the entrance, and, in the chancel floor, is a dark stone slab with Gilbert White's name; above it on the wall is a tablet stating that he was for forty years fellow of Oriel College [University of Oxford] and historian of his native town. The ancient graveyard in which the church is set is very attractive; its decaying headstones

---

2. Footnote in the 1953 edition (p. 237): "Gilbert White (1720–1793) was the author of *The Natural History and Antiquities of Selborne*, a pioneer work in natural history. —G.W.H."

covered lovingly with rose brambles and tall, graceful grasses, make it a beautiful "garden of sleep."

We visited the Hanger. I had only a vague idea what a Hanger might be, so I was full of interest as we followed a path up a slightly rising meadow and entered the woods on a steep hillside; the trees were beeches but differed from the American species in many ways. The boles were tall and seemingly slender and at the base were bent toward the valley. I wondered if Hanger meant a forest where the trees hung on to the hillside by sheer strength of their roots. The branches were long and pendulous and the leafage luxurious. The bark was greenish, perhaps because of some mossy growth. Looking out through the smooth high boles the atmosphere seemed filled with a pale green mist, so prevalent was the green of the bark and so fully did the leaf canopy shut out the light; it was like a vast cathedral. {Some of the trees were swathed at the base with English ivy. The view of Selborne from the Hanger is very pretty.} It was a day of deep satisfaction to me. For years I made my classes study the writings of this man, who had never travelled and yet who had seen so much and had seen it so well that he had made countless men and women love his Selborne.

{We} left our companions at Farringdon that evening, they to return to London, and we to make another pilgrimage to Winchester where I might see the River Itchen where that other nature lover, Isaac Walton, forgot his troubles in fishing and in companionship with all that the fields and woods could give to one who understood and loved them. We spent a day wandering about this beautiful, quaint old town.

{We climbed a hill which gave us a wide view of the beautiful winding Itchen. How could Walton have found a more beautiful place for his happy pastime!}

We were tired with sight-seeing and Charles Hull had suggested Porlock Weir as a place of rest. It rained almost continually. Finally came a fair day and we took a driver and carriage to Oare and the Doone Valley, a drive of nine miles and a walk of six more. Our road took us zig-zag up the mountainside through a forest of small white oak; some trees not more than six inches through, growing from the old gnarled stump of an ancestor.

After a time, we left the forests and came out upon a moorland of great rounded hills, covered with magenta patches of heath blossoms and lavender patches of heath, both a relief against the almost black background of heath not in bloom.

When we reached the crown of the hill, Oare Valley opened before us, beautifully green and winding among the hills. From here we could see the Dunkery Beacon, on a barren hill seemingly miles away.

A little hamlet, Oareford, of vine-covered cottages, nestled close to the road, and shortly after we left it we came to Oare Village where John Ridd lived [hero of Blackmore's classic *Lorna Doone*]. A fine mansion now stands on the site of his home and the farming lands about it look fertile. The special feature of the Village is the church built in the 13th century, a small but dignified edifice set in a shaded graveyard. We were shown the window through which Lorna Doone was shot by Carver Doone at her wedding. He could have done this easily, from the slope back of the church.

We drove on through narrow hedged lanes which made us nervous for fear we might meet another conveyance and finally reached the place where the Badgeworthy Water meets the Wear and make the River Lynn. Here we left our {vehicle} and walked on up a cart track, a green-hedged corridor, then on an open road skirting a hill where we saw a farmhouse called Lorna's Bower.

The Doone Valley was before us. Stately hills covered richly with heath and bracken sloped steeply down to Badgeworthy Water, a rather wide stream, turbulent where it dashes over rocks, and forming dark pools in the level places. We entered the Valley by a path along the bank of the stream and in a forest of {rather} scraggly white oaks, whose trunks were covered with thick ochre-colored moss.

After a half hour's walk, we reached the "water slide" where the water comes down swiftly over a smooth, steep stream bed. {It was} on the brink of this that Blackmore places Lorna's house. It is a rugged valley much more beautiful than the one where the Doones actually lived. It is dotted with gray rocks and the slopes are rich with {heath}, heather, and bracken; a few gnarled trees were scattered here and there.

The water slide is the most picturesque point in the valley, but we desired to see the haunts of the Doones, so we went on and on over a rocky path, {winding in and out}, along the sides of the hills until we came to a place where two mountain streams joined, {and} we followed the stream that came in at right angles to the main valley. Here we found the ruined foundation of the Doone houses; one, rather large, was covered with heather. This last stronghold at the Doones is in a rather shallow valley. Sheep were feeding peacefully on the hillsides. There was a shepherd's cottage where we bought mineral water for much needed refreshment. Our memory of the spot is that it was bleak and lonely and only redeemed by the limpid, flashing mountain stream.

{Our morning drive to view the mysterious monuments of Stonehenge was made happy by a thousand tinkling songs of skylarks that fell around us as from a heavenly choir. The strange stones formed a mere dot in the great rolling Salisbury plain when we first sighted it. When wandering among the weird stones and burial mounds, one must always try but in vain, to picture the rites that had taken place here before the dawn of history.}

On July 30th we went to Woking to visit Dr. Francis Morice, who was President of the London Entomological Society, and who had {most kindly} invited us to spend a few days in his home. This was a gracious recognition of the honor which had been bestowed on Mr. Comstock the year previous in making him an Honorary Fellow of the Entomological Society of London. There were only twelve men thus honored each representing a foreign country. {Mr. Comstock} represented {America}.

{Dr. Morice was a fellow of Queen's College, Oxford, and had been a teacher at Rugby. He had taken orders but had never preached. He was a gentle, lovable man of broad culture as well as of scientific attainments. His home was roomy with plenty of books and beautiful pictures. The drawing room opened with double glass doors into the pretty garden in which a prized plant was American goldenrod.}

{Miss Morice was staying with her brother at the time; her raiment was of the most casual sort but I forgot this very soon. She was cultured and entertaining and played the piano beautifully. Our host took us for a long drive to old Guildford and its ruined castle, its aged home for the aged and its grammar school founded in 1500. We drove through the village and up a hill where we gained a superb view of all Surrey and part of Hampshire. We saw rounded blue hills along the horizon which we were told were North Downs.}

We found Dr. Morice was very fond of Lowell's poems and had a {curiosity} concerning the pronunciation of those written in dialect. I read "The Courtin" and parts of the *Biglow Papers*, explaining as I read, the "crooknecks" again the "chimbley" and the "ole queen's-arm" and {"sparkles" which were} all {mystery} words to our host. It made me realize anew what we owe to Lowell for preserving to us the words, the thoughts and the intimate environment of our ancestors.

{Those days at Woking and the privilege of knowing more intimately the Rev. Francis D. Morice belong to our happiest memories of England and the prized experiences of our lives.}

This Congress was a new institution.[3] There had been but one meeting previous to this one at Oxford. We came from London, August 4th, and found we were to be entertained {at "Daneholme," the home of Dr. and

---

3. As indicated in the 1953 edition (p. 241): "International Congress of Entomologists . . ."

Mrs. Hoey, who were delightful hosts. Dr. Hoey was an Irishman, cordial, well read, and interested in all the world. Mrs. Hoey was sympathetic and charming, and before we left she was sufficiently informal to let me see her scullery. I had only a vague notion of a room given over to pots and pans until I saw this one in perfect order. A scullery maid was a poor thing, I gathered from English Literature, and since I learned that her duties included the scouring of the cooking utensils, I pitied her more than ever.}

{The youngest son, Trevor Hoey, was a student in Jesus College; he was interested in butterflies and had made a good collection; he appeared now and then in his short, torn and tattered college gown. It seems it was a matter of pride to wear a gown just as dilapidated as possible without being commanded to buy another. He called his college "Jaggers" which, after all seemed less irreverent than to call it "Jesus."}

The first day of the Congress, {August 5th}, was given over to attending different sections and listening to people of whom we had never {seen or} heard. We were with the Kelloggs[4] at lunch in a great tent on the lawn of Wadham College. The next morning Mr. Comstock gave his address on "Spider Silk." I was so excited that I could not judge whether he had "done himself proud" or not; however, people were very complimentary, so I felt satisfied. {We saw much of Dr. and Mrs. W. Morton Wheeler and Dr. Hewitt; Dr. and Mrs. P. P. Oalvert of Philadelphia were invited to dine with us at Daneholme.}

On August 7th Mr. Comstock presided at one of the meetings {and a large number of the delegates, including ourselves, were entertained at Nuneham, the estate of Mr. [Lewis Vernon] Harcourt, then a member of the cabinet. It is a beautiful old place with extensive gardens and grounds bordering the Thames. Our host was very kind; he told me his wife was an American (she was a niece of J. P. Morgan, I believe). He showed us around the gardens which were bewilderingly extensive and elaborate. I remember especially the rose garden which was a great circular bower. I also remember a flamingo that was flopping and ducking around the grounds; this bird, to be truly decorative, needs to stand still. However, the most interesting thing after all was the evident fact that Mr. Harcourt knew and loved every foot of his estate and every flower and vine and tree in his gardens.}

{We were very interested to see tents on the lawn near the river and he told us he had 75 boy scouts camping there; he said he believed it was a great and most beneficial organization.}

4. As indicated in the 1953 edition (p. 241): ". . . the Vernon Kelloggs, of Stanford University . . ."

To us, one of the important events of this Congress was meeting Dr. Anton Handlirsch of Vienna, the greatest of paleo-entomologists. Mr. Comstock had worked hard and long on the venation of insect wings as a means of tracing relationships and as a basis of classification. This had {fallen dead so far} as getting any real understanding or co-operation among systematic entomologists either in Europe or America, until Dr. Handlirsch's great book on *Die Fossilen Insekten und die Phylogenic der Rezenten Formen* appeared. In this he {pays} tribute to this work of {Mr. Comstock} and states that without the article by Comstock and Needham on classification by wing venation, he would not have been able to classify his fossils.

I was so grateful to him for this recognition that I tried to thank him, and he said, with real feeling, that {Mr. Comstock} was his master and himself his student in the study of wings.

{The last day of the Congress at Oxford, Vernon Kellogg gave a fine address, and that evening there was a great banquet in the Hall of Jesus College. I was very happy to be chosen a guest of honor and sat at the high table at the right of Dr. Poulton and at the left of Professor La Meere.}

{On August 10th we were all invited by the sons of Lord Rothschild to visit their museum at Tring. Of course, we went. I had seen these two men often during the week and once had heard them discussing the robber flies in the museum at Jesus College. They were like two boys in their interest and I heard one say "Look at this! This fly is a beast." The elder, the present Lord Rothschild, was large, fair-haired and florid, and decidedly German in appearance. His brother Charles was rather pale and had dark hair and eyes.}

{The house at Tring had been given to Nell Gwynn by King Charles II. The estate had been for many years the property of Lord Rothschild, father of the two scientists. Our interest was in the museum, consisting of large buildings containing priceless collections of insects and also of other members of the animal kingdom. I remember a remarkable collection of turtles. Each entomologist wished to see what the collection held along the line of his own specialty and Dr. [Karl] Jordan, the museum director made it possible to do this. I was especially interested in the collection of tropical butterflies. It showed what scientific ambitions and unlimited means could do in bringing together species from all parts of the globe.}

{In his address of greeting, the elder brother, the present Baron Rothschild, gave all credit to the teacher who had led him in boyhood to become interested in animal life. It was a beautiful and touching tribute which brought home to us the importance of the teacher's influence. A bountiful lunch was served to us in the town hall of the village, which had been built by the Rothschilds. We were personally conducted by the brothers around the grounds. I remember especially the emus in the park.}

{During the day I came frequently in conversation with Mr. Charles Rothschild, who was the world's authority on *Siphonaptera*. He told me he was greatly interested in a possible reservation in England where nature should have its undisturbed sway. He asked me about our nature preserves and I told him all I knew and promised to send him data after my return. This I did and received two letters from him written by his own hand. He seemed to me a man of attractive personality and of high and unselfish ideals, and he had the modesty of the true scientists. His tragic death many years later, must have been due to some physical breakdown, for he was too wholesome and too calm to have committed suicide when in his right mind. He spoke so happily to me of his two children.}

Dr. and Mrs. [Edward B.] Poulton[5] had been kind enough to invite us to their summer home at St. Helen's on the Isle of Wight, and we were {very} glad to accept. Their home was large, set in an intricate garden that was interesting as well as beautiful. {The} two married daughters with their husbands were there also, {both of them} handsome, attractive young women. {Mrs. Walker was the wife of a Cambridge man teaching in the University of Birmingham. Mrs. Garnett was the wife of an Oxford don. The two brother-in-laws were quite different in personality and outlook. The Oxford don, very scholarly and quiet while Professor Walker was athletic, wide-awake and modern. The two were good friends but their conversational skirmishes were clever and sharp. The youngest of the family, Janet, a sweet attractive young girl, and the lusty baby, Pater Garnett, constituted the family present. However, quite important was Tobias, a wire-haired fox terrier, Tim and Jonas, scotch terriers, and Walt, a white caterpillar of a puppy, and above all, Pepper, the parrot grey with a red tail.}

{Dr. Poulton was busy with his scientific work a large part of each day, and we were allowed to follow our own desires to a large extent, which was restful.}

Two incidents remain in my memory. {Mr. Comstock} awakened early in the morning and {at once concluded} to get up and take a walk. I think it was six o'clock when he went down and came tip-toeing back; as he attempted to pass through the drawing room he discovered all the servants there, and Mrs. Poulton was reading prayers. {We had to add this to the already long list of virtues and accomplishments of our kind hostess.} The other incident was

5. Footnote inserted in the 1953 edition (p. 242): "Hope Professor of Zoology in Jesus College, Oxford, and an eminent entomologist. —G. W. H."

a conversation which we four women were having about domestic affairs. Mrs. Poulton said that the thing she could not understand in America was that the maid waited on the breakfast table just when she should be attending to the beds and other housework. {Mrs. Walker} told me how, in England, a house and financial standing of the family were {estimated} by the number of servants kept. Then they asked me how I kept my house and I explained that I had one servant, the cook, and a woman who came for cleaning and washing; and I always had a student to wait table and do some other light work. This dumbfounded my listeners and then one asked:

"What kind of a fellow would it be who would wait table while studying?"

"Oh, any kind of a good ambitious American," I answered. Then she asked:

"Would he perhaps drop his h's?"

"O never!" I cried, chuckling inwardly, "why I once had a relative of Kaiser Wilhelm who waited table for me two years."

This seemed {so} improbable to {them} and, I am afraid, so outrageous that they could not quite {take it in}. How could I explain that one could rake over our proletariat with a fine tooth comb without finding a lad that dropped his h's?

{Our visit was a delightful experience and we felt a real affection for this interesting and altogether fine family. But alas, the bitterness they felt toward America for her lateness in coming into the war, has severed all relations between them and us. In our experiences the Germans, although they declare we won the war for the Allies, are far more forgiving toward Americans than the English.}

Our next International Entomological Congress was to meet in Vienna in 1915 and Dr. Anton Handlirsch was made President. He made us promise to come, and we hoped we might. How impossible to even imagine that this great scientist would experience not only financial ruin but hunger and privation before the next meeting of this Congress, {which took place during the summer of 1926 at Zurich! Of all the terrible losses entailed by this great war, the loss to science is by no means the least.}

After the Congress we visited Rugby because of Mr. Comstock's devotion to "Tom Brown's School Days;" then to Warwick, where we found the most interesting castle of all those we visited in England.

{Stratford} was {altogether} delightful and interesting. There was a Shakespeare celebration going on {with} a large number of {directors and} teachers {of physical education} from Europe as well as Britain {present. They were engaged in reviving the Morris dances which probably were originally ritualistic in nature, although some claim they were brought to England from Spain by John of Gaunt. Troupes of Morris dancers in fantastic dress entertained the aristocracy, dancing in court yards or in the open, during the reign of Henry VIII. The Puritans put an end to this as an entertainment, and the dances became the favorite amusement of the rural population. Now there were left but few of the old people who knew them. Thus, this revival meant much.}

{We had a special interest in the Shakespeare Memorial Theatre since the husband of our Mrs. [Margery] Smith had been the superintendent in its construction. The older Smith children had been baptized in the beautiful old Church of the Holy Trinity, as the family had lived in Stratford during the construction of the theater.}

In an antique shop in Stratford, Mr. Comstock found an old sundial in a heap of {what looked like} junk and purchased it at a small price. It was a perpendicular dial {and not popular, as most Americans prefer[6] the horizontal dials for their gardens. We found a fine Georgian knocker and some candlesticks plated on copper, so we felt rich in mementos of Stratford.}

{From Stratford we went through the Cotswold Hills to Tintern. The Abbey merits all that has been written about it. It is a grand, gray, ivy-clad ruin still showing in places its pristine beauty. We sat for a long time looking at the walls and their mantling ivy; through the broken arches and exquisite window spaces we glimpsed the wooded hills. We had the feeling of worship for God in His world even as did the Christians who reared the walls and made this Abbey a thing of beauty and who cultivated the fertile valley worshipping as they labored.}

{We should have stopped at Shrewsbury to make a Darwin pilgrimage, but the rain was coming down in torrents and we reluctantly gave it up.}

{On our way to the Lake District we were again made painfully aware of the damage done to England that year by rain, hay and grain were rotting in the fields, a sad sight for one interested in farming. We stopped at the Stag's Head Hotel at Bowness where fires in the grates made a welcome sight after a journey in the rain. We found at our table a young man from America whom we liked very much and discovered that his name was Gilkey and that we knew his family in Ithaca very well. Our first day was given to a pilgrimage to Wordsworth's home which we might look at from the outside, as a

6. At the bottom of the Comstock manuscript (p. 15–18) in R.G.S. handwriting: "We later mounted it on the gatepost at the Ledge. The original owner, we judged, was an old royalist who had been a bitter recluse during Cromwell's regime. The inscription, translated, runs as follows: "O happy solitude! O only happiness! To me the city a prison is, and solitude is paradise. God be with us and bless the work of our hands. 1663. Long live Charles II." This sentence is included in the 1953 edition (p. 243). —KSt.

cat might look at a king. However, we were able to see the view on which he gazed from his windows: beyond the lake, the two mountains, the Lion and the Lamb, were rugged and picturesque. We visited his favorite seat on a rock that projects into the tiny lakelet, Rydal, Water, and gave ourselves over to Wordsworth imaginings.}

{Windermere seemed to us very like some of our small lakes in the Adirondacks. Its irregularity, wooded shores and islets made the resemblance strong. It is the largest lake in England and is 10 1/2 miles long and 1/3 mile wide.}

{We dare the dark clouds and took seats in a coach to Coniston and were rewarded by a day with only a few showers to disturb us. Our road was always in the midst of picturesque scenery. We stopped at Hawkshead to visit the school that Wordsworth attended; when we saw his initials neatly carved on his desk (now under glass) we felt a thrill of delight. I had some way always felt that Wordsworth was born a man and never was a boy. Here was delightful evidence that he was a real boy, and probably was castigated for defacing the desk. We also saw his living quarters in a cottage near by and realized keenly something of the stern simplicity of his early life.}

{At Coniston we visited Ruskin's grave and saw his home and that of Tennyson across the lake and spent the rest of the time in the very interesting Ruskin museum. In here were entrancing water color sketches by Turner, who knew more about beautiful combinations and nuances of color than any other man that ever lived. I was greatly surprised to find how exquisitely Ruskin drew birds and twigs.}

My appreciation of Wordsworth was small in my early years. The lack of fire in his poems made them seem commonplace, but I had grown to understand and care for them and often carried with me in my pocket a copy of the "Prelude." It was not until I studied his life that I appreciated him. His generous radical views had obsessed his youth. After {he saw} the results of such views in the French Revolution, disillusioned and suffering, he turned his back on the struggles of man in the political arena and found diversion and healing in the companionship with nature, even as did Isaac Walton. This gave me an insight {which before I had lacked and} for years I had {gloried} in the first poet who had found in Nature the inspiration and the chief field of his art. One of the treasures I brought home was a copy of "Wordsworth's Guide to the Lakes," which is a mine for a nature lover and perhaps the most generally popular book of the author. Matthew Arnold told of a reverend gentleman who naively inquired of Wordsworth if he had written any other books besides this.

We went aboard the *S. S. Haverford* at Liverpool docks, September 4th. {We coasted along Ireland nearly all day.} George Burr was returning with us which added much to our pleasure. {Among the first people with whom we became acquainted were Professor and Mrs. [Henry] Gibbons, he being professor of Latin at the University of Pennsylvania. Mrs. Gibbons was large and had gray hair. We discovered that people thought we were sisters, which brought up the question of family, and we discovered we were both descendants of Nathaniel Foote of Wethersfield, Conn. Which interested us very much. The voyage remains in my mind as outstanding for the phosphorescence on the ocean which made our evenings memorable. Mr. Comstock and I spent our evenings leaning on the rail at the prow wondering at and admiring nature's pyrotechnics.}

{We arrived home September 17 and found Mary King, Cousin Lide, Mr. Cutcheon and Mrs. Smith all very glad to see us and they looked like angels to us. Our terrace was as green as Ireland's coast hills and the hedge was being planted.}

{Cousin Lide's granddaughter, Catherine Bard, came as a freshman to Cornell this fall and Lide remained to see her settled. Catherine was a handsome girl, very reticent and dignified, largely because she was shy. She had been a year at Oberlin studying music, but with characteristic modesty she concluded she was not a great musician and changed her plans in favor of a University education. However, she played the piano with exquisite feeling and gave us a great deal of happiness by her music during her four years at Cornell. We learned to prize her character for its strength and integrity. Above all, she was clear-visioned and was never led astray by show or specious appearance. One of our pleasant social experiences early that fall was dining at President White's where we met Mrs. White's charming stepmother and our old neighbors, Professor and Mrs. [Lucien A.] Wait, who had just returned from a trip around the world. The large library and several other rooms on the south side of the Presidential residence had been added during the summer and President White was very happy to have his study quite away from the social center of the house. He showed us the views from the windows and all his arrangements with the enthusiasm of youth.}

{The alumnae at Cornell had taken a deep interest in the management of Sage College. We, with many outside alumnae, had wished to have a Dean of Women appointed, but to no avail. Finally, Mrs. Gertrude Martin had been made Advisor of Women; she had struggled in vain for certain reforms and we had suffered and failed with her. She finally had accomplished some reforms in Sage College and we hoped for ultimate success. We were trying a good many things these days. Mrs. Albert Smith had started a plan of co-operative buying of household supplies for members of the Campus Club. However, the usual dead weight that always hangs heavy on co-operative enterprises finally killed this.}

{I note that the way we celebrated our 34th anniversary on October 7th was unique. Mr. Comstock took my class into the field to study spiders. This meant a fine afternoon excursion in the midst of a beautiful autumn day. Shortly after this Mr. Comstock was called to Collins by the death of his namesake, Harry Comstock Law, the youngest son of our lifelong friends Mr. and Mrs. Bennie [Benedict] Law.}

{Another sorrow came upon us; my able colleague, known as the Junior Naturalist's Uncle John, was very ill in the Ithaca hospital. He had come to Ithaca for consultation about his work when he was taken ill. We went to see him every day; he was brave and cheery and said to me with fervor "I am going to do some work in the High Schools yet this fall." But the end came October 24th. There was a beautiful service in Sage Chapel for him the next day. Mr. Comstock and Professor Charles Tuck went to Westfield with the body. The death of John Spencer made me sad and depressed. We had stood shoulder to shoulder in our battle to introduce Nature Study in the schools. He had been brave and full of faith and had often supported me when I might have faltered. When I find Nature Study growing in importance in the schools of the United States I find myself saying to Uncle John, "Your soul goes marching on."}

{The loss that affected us most was the death of Mr. Comstock's half-sister, Margaret Dowell Wiseman. We knew she was ill during the summer, but she gave us no idea that she was in danger. The news of her death was a terrible shock to us both. She was a beautiful young woman, gentle and lovable in character and yet with a firm stability under her sweetness. She died at her father's home in Fruitdale, California leaving a husband and father heart-broken and disconsolate.}

{On November 7th, we celebrated President White's 80th birthday and a speech was made that told him how proud we were of him and how dear he was to our hearts. I have a sweet personal memory of that occasion. As I came down after removing my wraps, I met Mr. White and two of the faculty on the stairs. His face lighted as he saw me, and he took both my hands and kissed them. It was a spontaneous greeting that I have remembered with a feeling open to reverence ever since.}

{Meanwhile, all the autumn, Professor [Gorton] Davis with his helper, Mr. Van Kleek, and laborers, had been making our grounds interesting and delightful. The high hedge and a tall juniper set, when half grown, at the corner of the house had completely changed the unfortunate proportions of our house from the Roberts Place side.}

{The old sun dial was mounted on a standard of cement copied from a stone standard in an English garden. This was set close to the gate opening from Roberts Place. The original owner we judged, was an old royalist who had been a bitter recluse during the Cromwell regime. The inscription, translated, is as follows; "O happy solitude! O only happiness! To me the city a prison is, and solitude is paradise. God be with us and bless the work of our hands. 1663. Long live Charles II."}

{We were astonished at the apparent extent of our grounds after Professor Davis was through. Our lot covers a scarce half acre, but the clever landscaping makes it seem four times as extensive. We have always been happy over his work and enjoy it more and more as the years go.}

{We had company aplenty this fall. "Charlemagne" as we always called G. [Grove] K. [Karl] Gilbert, spent several weeks with us. Our Sunday nights were crowded. Harry Knight and Catherine Bard and Fritz Switzer were always there, and the latter two gave us beautiful music. Madeline Avery and Jean Holmes, the charming daughter of our friend, Professor Joseph Holmes, was also with us much, also David Crawford and Harold Morrison. Mr. Comstock's students came often as did many others. On November 8th we entertained the staff and graduate students of the Entomological Department, and fifty or more were present.}

{I found my classes larger than usual this spring semester. However, I was given another room on the fourth floor of Roberts Hall for my laboratory. Both Mr. Comstock and I gave lectures during Farmers' Week.}

{I discovered a new line of art this winter. Harry Knight, who was very artistic, had learned to color lantern slides, and I became his pupil. We had a few of our slides colored but now I became ambitious and colored more than a hundred of the Egyptian slides and many others. Harry Knight had come to Cornell through my interest in him, as his teacher had told me of his interest in nature study and of his excellence as a photographer. He had his way to make and lived in the student room in the Insectary and helped Professor Herrick care for the breeding of insects. This settled his future. He is now an entomologist of excellent standing in Iowa State College of Agriculture.}

{I was busy on} a new enterprise. I had conceived the idea of field note books for children in the public schools. {A series of questions which they should answer from personal observation, and other questions to be looked up in books; something to relieve the teacher and put the responsibility upon the pupils. I began with bird note books.}

{My bronchial cough from the winter had never left me but sometimes it was worse than others. I kept at my teaching, determined not to give up, but early in March I became so much worse that Dr. [Floyd] Wright declared I must have rest and hospital care and sent me to the Sanitarium at Clifton Springs. Mr. Comstock came with me. I did not realize how exhausted I was until I was forced to relax. The bronchitis was so bad that I dreaded to have to speak a word. I think the following extracts from letters I wrote my husband tells the story:}

> {"This morning I watched the dawn come behind the laced branches of the trees in the park, a restful view. A pale nurse with black eyes, came to find what I was to do. Then a stout pink cheeked masseuse came in to give me gentle mauling, a very comforting experience and soothing to the nerves.}
>
> {"Just as one forgets one is in a sanitarium and one's thoughts are far away, a tap at the door and in comes a most business like nurse carrying a tumbler of jingling glass tubes, one of which is evidently mine, for she drops it into my mouth and then snatches at my pulse to discover if my temperature and circulation are equable, but refuses to tell results.}
>
> {"Later when one drifts off into dreamland comes a benign Doctor who inspects one and writes out something which is a billet doux for the nurse, not for me. Then comes a cheerful nurse with a menu for luncheon. One isn't hungry, so one hazards 'cream toast and cocoa' at which nurse smiles encouragingly and says with unction 'O, there are so many nice things to eat, a bit of steak, nut bread, raspberry jelly.' As she mentions these viands her expression is so entirely peaches and cream that one smiles and says: 'Let's have them all.'}
>
> {"One uninitiated imagines that a salt rub is a nice scrub in foaming salt water; not on your life! A husky damsel is slouchy waist and skirt and barefooted puts me in a closet and tells me to undress and put on a bedsheet which she has given me. I come out an imitation spook and she takes me to another closet, zinc lined, and snatching me stark naked sprays me with warm water which gradually becomes hot water until I am done 'rare.' Then she grabs both hands full of coarse salt and proceeds to sandpaper me down to her idea of proper proportions. Finally, when I am finished off, to suit her she turns on a cold spray to wash off the salt, then wraps the sheet around me, takes me back to the closet, dries me with a towel and spanks an anvil chorus over my unprotected physique and laconically says, 'Now dress.'"}

{Mr. Comstock went to the funeral of our friend and colleague, Professor John Craig, held at his home in Abbottsford, beyond Montreal. He and Professor Alvin Beal represented the University at these last rites. Mr. Comstock was able to spend a few hours with me on the way and on his return, which gave me a great comfort. I came home the last of March and began teaching, but gingerly at first.}

{There had been an alley planned at the east of our lot, but this had never been used and Mr. Comstock was able to purchase it which was a real addition and helped in the landscaping. This was good luck and another bit was the news that our herd at Hilltop had come through the T. B.[7] test perfectly.}

{All this spring our grounds were being planted by Mr. Van Kleek, Professor Davis' assistant, and his men. Mr. Comstock got truck-loads of laurel for the woods garden and as with everything he undertakes he worked at this with enthusiasm and competency. It would be difficult to describe our joy and thrills as we daily watched the progress of our planting.}

{We entertained the Stanford Club one evening and Professor Martin Sampson gave a delightful talk about his experiences during the early days at Stanford. We also had a visit in May from Leal [L. O.] Howard and Monsieur Paul Marchal, the eminent French entomologist. We gave a little reception to the two one evening. The staff in Entomology and Zoology and their wives, about fifty in all, came. It was very informal, and Mr. Marchal said "Comme une grande famille." We were brave enough to invite Leal and Mons. Marchal to a Sunday night supper with our student contingent but I had no way of ascertaining just what the Frenchman thought of this performance. The next day, May 26, we had the meeting of the Jugatae at the field Station. The day was beautiful and the affair a real success; and this did make a pleasant impression on our guest.}

On June 4th, 1913, I received notice that I had been given the rank of Assistant Professor. I had been given this rank November 10, 1898, but a year later, was demoted to the rank of Lecturer when the trustees refused to have women professors. However archaic the Faculty of Arts and Sciences, the Faculty of the College of Agriculture was open-minded and progressive; and two years before, Martha Van Rensselaer and Flora Rose had been made professors because of their work in Home Economics. I had never asked for promotion, but Alice McCloskey felt that we were being overlooked and I believe it was through her stand in the matter that I was given the title. My salary was $1500.

7. Tuberculosis.

We were all plunged into gloom by the resignation of Liberty Hyde Bailey as Director of the College of Agriculture. He had been most successful in getting recognition for the College and had built it up in a magical manner. He was an ideal leader; it was a privilege to work under him and we {could not understand} how we could go on without him. {There had been friction between him and President Schurman. The two men were antipodal in character and temperament. That this friction had its influence on Mr. Bailey's decision is undoubtedly true, but the moving reason} was that he wearied with the executive burden {he was forced to bear; the executive grind was wearing him out.}

On June 19, 1913, a meeting of the Faculty of the College of Agriculture was called. We were seated in the faculty room and when {he} came in we all stood. He spoke to us of his desire to live his own life and do the work he loved best. He spoke feelingly of the co-operation he had received from us all. When he finished we, all stood in silence as he went out. Not a word had been said. We were all too stricken to speak, and I look back on it as one of the most dramatic experiences of my lifetime.

{Mr. Comstock and I were so weary and discouraged with it all that we betook ourselves to the Hermitage for two weeks to rest and heal our hurts. The calm beauty of the place had healing powers and we were soon forgetting our perplexities. We gave ourselves over to Mother Nature.}

{On July 6 we received a telegram telling of the sudden death of Father Dowell. It was a shock to us, as we were planning to visit him as soon as possible. But he was ageing fast and was lonely and we could not wish him back. Later we found he had left all his property to Mr. Comstock, whom he loved as if he had been his own son. They say that the test of a man's character is his relations with his own and his wife's family. Certainly, by this test Mr. Comstock was a shining success.}

{We both taught in the summer session. Mr. Comstock had among his students a fine contingent from Mr. Holyoke; Ann Morgan, now professor of Zoology there, Lucy Smith, Miss Noyes, Miss Platt, Emeline Moore and several others. He had also a Carnegie Scholar from England; Mr. Charles William Mason, a fine-appearing young man. When he first arrived, there was some delay in receiving his funds and we invited him to be our guest until the matter was arranged, a week or two later. He had spent two or three years in India and confessed to me that he had hesitated about bringing his bed with him when he came to America but luckily decided to leave it. He said with a laugh; "I had been warned that if I put my shoes outside my door nights at a hotel, I should never see them again, but no one had told me that I need not carry my own bed." Mr. Mason did excellent work; on leaving here he was sent to Nyasaland, British Central Africa, where he died of tropical fever in 1917, a martyr to science and who deserved as great honor as any who died on field of battle.}

{Dr. G. C. Embody was my partner in teaching this summer, and it was a great pleasure to work with him. He was especially interested in birds and fishes and was and still is an excellent teacher. It was a very hot summer and taking the class into the field was like taking them into an oven, but no one had sun stroke.}

{On August 8th I was called to Geneva to attend a special meeting of the Hobart and William Smith trustees to elect Lyman T. Powell president. He was highly recommended, and a committee of the trustees had met him and found him very pleasant personally.}

{The special happy memory of the summer was the long evening on the piazza and on the seats of the terrace, watching the moon rise and seeing our beautiful garden bathed in moonlight. We were both so very happy in our new home and environment.}

{In August we made a visit to Dr. and Mrs. Raymond Turner at Oswego. Dr. Turner was the son of Mr. and Mrs. Henry Turner, who had been like brother and sister to Mr. Comstock in his early life. Our host and hostess were interesting and delightful people and they took us in their car to call on all the Turner relatives as well as to visit their parents. We did not dream on the day we visited Mr. And Mrs. Joel Turner and their brood of youngsters that one of the little girls with yellow hair and blue eyes would sometime be a real daughter to us and spend years in our home.}

{From Oswego we took steamer to Toronto and went on by train to Guelph to attend the 50th anniversary celebration of the Entomological Society of Ontario. We met there many old friends and several of Mr. Comstock's students, Dr. [Alex] McGillivray, Dr. William Lochhead, and President G. C. Creelman, among others in whose home a reception was tendered us. While there I had the great pleasure of making the acquaintance of Mrs. C. Gordon Hewitt, a charming woman of whom I longed to see more, and straightway developed a scheme to bring her and her husband to Ithaca.}

{On September 8th we attended the funeral of our neighbor and friend Professor Lucien Wait. He, with his wife, had been our guests only a few weeks before, and his death was a shock. My memory of him in his classroom was my ideal of a courteous gentleman; he was charming in conversation and a lover of music.}

{During the summer and fall I had completed the second bird note book and the tree note book. Professor Burr had moved in with us and was, as usual, a member of our family although he had his room with Professor and Mrs. George R. Chamberlain on the campus. He was so much a part of us that we could not think what life would be without him.}

{November 14 I was in Geneva attending the inaugurations of Lyman Powell as president of Hobart and William Smith College. There were many eminent men present: William Finlay, then at the head of the Education Department at Albany, Professor Williams, the head of the School of Journalism at Columbia, Augustus Downing and many others. All the speakers praised President Powell almost to fulsomeness and made us feel that we had done a wise thing in finding such a great man for our colleges.}

{On November 24th we made an important addition to our possessions. We purchased the lot opposite ours on Roberts Place with the idea of building on it a house for the Comstock Publishing Company, which was rapidly outgrowing our ground floor at the Ledge. Then, too, we were afraid some one would buy this place and spoil our view. Directly after this I went to New York and visited Dr. William Thro and his sister. I was still working on the *Pet Book* and wished for more knowledge concerning the care of some animals. I spent my days at the Bronx Zoo. Dr. William T. Hornaday was most cordial and helpful. He introduced me to Samuel Stacy who gave me information about birds and to Peter Marberger who told me about the care of small mammals, and to Richard Deckert whose instructions were of the greatest use to me in the feeding and care of reptiles. I have always been deeply grateful to Dr. Hornaday and his assistants for, through them, I was able to make the Pet Book much more useful. My acquaintance with Dr. Hornaday began when I engraved the head of the man-eating tiger which he killed in India and which is in the Cornell Museum.}

December 6, 1913, Mr. Comstock {handing in} his resignation, to take place at the end of the year, as his 65th birthday would occur in February. President Schurman tried to dissuade him and urged him to stay a few years longer, but {Mr. Comstock} was eager to do scientific research and writing which he could not {possibly} do if he retained his active professorship. His time was {all taken} with executive duties and his lectures. He had excellent graduate students this last year, among whom were W. A. Clemens, I. O. Tothill, Harold Morrison and many others, but he had less and less time to give them. He longed for freedom to do the work he loved best.

{In December we had a memorable visit from Professor S. H. Barraclough of the University of Sydney, Australia. He belonged to our student group in 1891. We had always kept in touch with him and were happy to see him once more. As illustrating the rapid growth of the College of Agriculture I took him to the roof of Roberts Hall to see the changes wrought since he was in Cornell. There were three unfinished buildings in sight and he asked what they were about I could not tell him. I had not wandered over the east of Roberts Hall since summer and I had not realized what was happening. Professor Barraclough left us to go to England. He served in the Commissary Department of the English army during the war and was knighted for his eminent service. He is Sir Henry Egerton Barraclough K. B. E. V. D. BE,[8] Mme., Dean of the Engineering Department of the University of Sydney and has one of the most superior and engaging personalities that I have ever known; he will always be to us our beloved Harry Barry.}

{Mrs. [Susanna] Gage had become interested in the poetry of Amelia Josephine Burr whom she had met. She planned to publish her poem, "Afterglow," as a brochure and asked me to make a water color for the outside of the cover which I did. It made a beautiful booklet and we sent it to our friends for a Christmas greeting that year.}

The new year of 1914 found Mr. Comstock struggling with the reorganization of his department when he should leave it. It found me with the {Mss.} [manuscript] for the *Pet Book* nearly completed. It found the Comstock Publishing Company making a little experiment. Our dear friend Mrs. J. E. Creighton, {a woman of} literary ability and artistic feeling, had written some nature songs for children and we published them. Louis [Agassiz] Fuertes and Anna C. Stryke made the illustrations and when the little volume, *Nature Songs for Children*, by Katherine Creighton, appeared we were very proud of it. However, our {machinery} for selling to children {was not as well organized as it should have been to have sold this book far and wide}. We sold many copies but we never did it justice and the experiment taught the Comstock Publishing Company a lesson regarding their field in the book market.

In February, Mr. Comstock was elected Honorary Fellow by the Societe Entomologique de Belgique, Brussels, {which was a great honor and we were happy over it}. I was always more excited than he over honors conferred upon him. He took his honors soberly and hoped he might show by his future work that {he} deserved {them}.

---

8. Knight Commander of The Most Excellent Order of the British Empire (KBE), and the Volunteer Officers' Decoration (VD).

Professor Comstock at his desk.

CHAPTER XVI

The 65th Milestone and Retirement

This chapter represents another example of confusion in following the path of Mrs. Comstock's manuscript. This is Comstock manuscript Chapter XVI, but this detail was crossed through and changed to "Chapter XV." Furthermore, in the 1953 edition, this chapter is labeled "Chapter 17: 1914–1917 Retirement of J. H. Comstock; Research and Writing."

{Mr. Comstock's} 65th birthday, occurred Feb. 24, 1914, {and for once} he was willing to have it celebrated. The day began with a temperature of 23 degrees below zero but that did not cool our ardor. We invited the entomological staff and all the assistants and wives,—sixty came. It was a particularly enjoyable affair for we were, as Dr. Marchal said, "like one family." {Mrs. Smith} had made a gorgeous cake with sixty-five candles on it. I never saw Mr. Comstock in happier mood. To him, it symbolized freedom from executive slavery and unfettered opportunity to do the work he loved best.

{We were feeling rather gay this period of our existence and we gave several dinner parties; at one we had President and Mrs. Schurman and Dr. And Mrs. [Bradford] Titchener, Professor A. B. Faust, and the non-resident Professor Elster. It was a pleasure to have these friends with us. We had lived next door to the Schurmans over twenty years and had always enjoyed the happiest relations with them.}

The principal events in our lives this spring were the retirement of {Mr. Comstock} and the 40th reunion of his class. He was very busy much of the time with correspondence in connection with the reunion and in making arrangements for the entertainment of {the returning members. In addition, he was more or less anxious regarding his part in the exercises in connection with the presentation of the Comstock Memorial Library Fund.}

{He} engaged {the Rites} house on University Avenues for the reunion headquarters of the '74 {men. In all}, twenty-five members of the class were present for the reunion and nine of them brought their wives. The reunion of the class was really a {week-end} house party. {J. C. Brauner of Leland Stanford University and Bennie [Benedict] Law of Collins, N. Y. were our guests during the reunion days.} At the class dinner on {Saturday evening}, June 13, the members presented {Mr. Comstock} with a leather travelling bag and a silver water pitcher in appreciation of his efforts in arranging for the reunion. The exercises in connection with the presentation of the Memorial Library Fund were held in the afternoon previous to the dinner. {The prefatory note from} the report of the exercises afterwards published by the University, {gives an excellent account of the celebration:}

> "On the occasion of the retirement from active service of John Henry Comstock, Professor of Entomology and General Invertebrate Zoology in Cornell University, his former students presented to him a fund ($2,500) for the establishment of a memorial library of Entomology. This fund was then presented by Professor Comstock to Cornell University, to keep in trust and to use its income for the purposes indicated by the donors of the fund.
>
> "The exercises in connection with the presentation of this memorial were held in the Assembly Room, Roberts Hall, Saturday afternoon, June 13, 1914. The Floriculture Department had prepared elaborate decorations; the date '73, when Professor Comstock was made instructor in Entomology, and '14, the year of his retirement, together with a large C, were formed in flowers and hung on the wall back of the stage.
>
> "At the hour set for the meeting, the University chimes were rung in honor of Professor Comstock, and very appropriately, for he was the chime master in 1872–3; and scores that had been arranged by him at that time were played. Some of these scores had been arranged at the special request of Jennie McGraw, the donor of the chimes.
>
> "The exercises were largely attended by former students, colleagues, trustees of the University, and other friends of Professor Comstock. An especially pleasant feature was the presence of many of his college

classmates, who were in Ithaca, it being the fortieth anniversary of the graduation of their class (1874).

"ORDER OF EXERCISES

Ringing of the Chimes. . . . . . . F. O. Ritter

Introductory Remarks by the Chairman. . . . S. H. Gage, '77

Address. . . . . .L. H. Bailey

A Letter from David Starr Jordan. . . . read by Mrs. Ruby G. Smith

Address by a Classmate. . . . W. R. Lazenby

Address by a Former Student. . . . L. O. Howard

(Dr. Howard was detained on Government business, but sent a letter, which was read by G. W. Herrick)

Presentation of the Memorial. . . . J. G. Needham

Acceptance and Presentation to Cornell University. . . . Professor John H. Comstock

Acceptance on Behalf of the University. . . . President J. G. Schurman."

{During this fall I was busy lecturing at Kalamazoo, Michigan, and at Dayton, Ohio. One thing impressed me deeply on this western trip, and that was the further away from the Atlantic coast, the less interest in the war. Mr. Comstock and I, like most of our faculty, were intensely interested in the war's progress. We had maps and marked every advance of the Germans and Allies. The papers in Dayton gave meager news and no one talked of it or seemed interested in it.}

{On my return I found George Tansey with us, as he had come to the Trustees' meeting. President Jordan came a little later. He gave a very interesting address before the University, the "Confessions of a Peace Maker." Dr. Jordan suffered criticism along with all the others who were working to eliminate war from the world. Sentiments and principles which were noble and uplifting in times of peace were sedition in a war-crazed world.}

{The University Club,[1] was well established in Sage College, and there were many dinners and lunches to attend there. I felt it was a great occasion when I gave my first luncheon party there in honor of my childhood friend, Etta Holbrook, who was visiting me. Miss Mary Fowler of the University Library, her sister Agnes, Professor and Mrs. S. H. Gage, and Miss Mary Hill, were guests. It was a dream come true to have a University Club where we could entertain our friends.}

---

1. Bottom note in manuscript (p. 16–4), from Herrick: "The Club, some years later, was confronted with financial difficulties and was obliged to dispose of its furniture and disband its organization. —G. W. H."

{We also were often at the home of President and Mrs. White. Mr. White was greatly depressed by the war. While he condemned Germany for violating Belgium, he had too keen a memory of England's attitude toward us during the Civil War to really take England's side at first. He always hated English Tories but was a great admirer of the Liberals.}

My *Pet Book* was published December 2, 1914. I had written it with the idea of making the lives of all sorts of pets happier and I trust it has done this.

{The Nature Study Society of America had prepared to hold its meetings with the American Association for the Advancement of Science and I felt that I must attend, although Mr. Comstock had given up these meetings as being too fatiguing. The meeting this year was in Philadelphia and we had a very good session. One evening I dined with Mr. and Mrs. Earl Barnes in their interesting home. It was a charming experience. I remember they had in their family, as a companion to their daughter Mary, a daughter of Alma Gluck, giving her wholesome home life.}

{On my return home Dr. Eliot Downing came with me and was our guest for twenty-four hours. He came to make arrangements with the Comstock Publishing Company to print and publish the *Nature Study Review*.}

The Comstock Publishing Company now had enough books to make a display in the Corner Book Store [of Ithaca] windows. In an effort to lead the pupils in the grades to observe for themselves I had written questions for observation of birds, and Louis [Agassiz] Fuertes had made outlines of birds for the pupils to color with crayons or water colors. These outlines, colored, made the exhibition window very attractive. Later, I made lesson outlines for flowers, trees, and the common animals. Dr. Needham added a note book on insects and Dr. [G. C.] Embody one on fishes. {Thus, were laid the foundations for what has turned out, under Mr. Will Slingerland's excellent management, a large business. I note that during the month of January 1915 the Comstock Publishing Company did $1700.00 worth of business which was very encouraging.}

On February 23, 1915, we moved the Comstock Publishing Company to the building which we had erected for its accommodation across Roberts Place from our home. We felt that it was very {beautiful}; its proportions were excellent; it was a true chalet with a second-floor balcony all around and an outside staircase. It was a fire-proof construction, concrete and steel. The casement windows were leaded and across the front was the motto "Through Books to Nature." {From that day to this} the beauty of this building has been a deep satisfaction to us.

We celebrated Mr. Comstock's 66th birthday by spending it in the Chalet settling the Publishing Company's effects and each of us settling his own desk. We had such a wealth of room and light and beauty! We did not dream that, in a decade, the {house} would be so crowded with the business that there would be scarcely standing room for visitors. It was such an expensive {house to build} that {we included} two apartments on the second floor and a bedroom and bath on the third floor for rent, to help meet the overhead of the Publishing Company.

{Mr. Comstock never enjoyed Christmas and Birthdays. He thought it rather indelicate to set a date for receiving or giving presents. That year he had given me a pair of bronze elephant book-ends two weeks *before* Christmas. I note in my diary for February 24th, 1915, the following pregnant remark "I gave Harry a dining room chair with a high back that he can lean his head against and he accepted it without recrimination." It was a warm, spring-like day and the song sparrows, bluebirds and flickers were with us.}

{In March, Ex-President Taft gave lectures before the University. President and Mrs. Schurman gave a reception for him and we had the pleasure of meeting him and talking with him. There are few people in the world who can give so much pleasure to others by just being in their presence as Mr. Taft. It was perfectly understandable why he was so personally popular and that so much fault was found with his administration. The judicial mind is not fitted for executive duties. The judicial and the executive are at opposite poles.}

{We entertained two entomologists at this season, J. R. de la Torre Bueno and J. M. Aldrich. In March we entertained at luncheon Professor and Mrs. Herbert Whetzel and a friend, a Miss Egts, who was a niece of the late Baron [von der] Osten-Sacken, a noted entomologist with whom Mr. Comstock had been personally acquainted and whom we called upon in Heidelberg in 1888. She had inherited his estate in Heidelberg but said she was tired of having the United States slurred, as she had been born and reared here. She said, too, that in Heidelberg she had been closely associated with the military circle there. She affirmed that the officers constantly derided the Kaiser and ridiculed all of his acts and especially his interests in art and music. She said it made her indignant and she told them they should be ashamed to thus treat the head of their army and government, but they laughed at her. This was an interesting side-light on Germany.}

{In late March, President White was ill in bed with a cold and his eyes were so affected that he could not read. He was rather deaf, and Mrs. White and his daughter Karin found it difficult to make him understand. I had had a long experience in reading to my father who was deaf, and I could do it with ease. The secret is in keeping the pitch even. I could do this and still inflect the words. So I had the privilege of reading to Mr. White the daily papers, mostly for a week or more. Articles that I read would awaken memories, and Mr. White's reminiscences and views on many subjects made these readings of the greatest interest and pleasure to me.}

{As the Spring of 1915 opened Mr. Comstock and I were thrilled with our garden and the landscaping of the grounds about the chalet which Professor [Gorton] Davis had in charge. We walked about our domain every morning to see what flowers had blossomed and to enjoy everything together.}

{My classes were so large this year that my room and an adjoining room on the 4th floor of Roberts Hall were quite inadequate. Director Galloway, who was always most considerate of me, took up the question of room and finally a most satisfying arrangement was made. A roof insectary and conservatory had been built in connection with the third floor of Roberts Hall, which housed the Entomological Department, so the old insectary was not used so much, and I was given the first floor office on the north side, and the east greenhouse for a laboratory. In my office were tables for reading. There were shelves for the nature study library. It was large enough to seat fifteen pupils. The green decorations and curtains gave the room a home-y look and made it a part of out-of-doors, for our windows looked into the trees. My pupils loved it. The happiest teaching of my life was done there. The greenhouse was an ideal laboratory for the months of the college year; it was light and our aquaria and vivaria had plenty of room on the side tables covered with gravel. One great advantage was the nearness of the out-doors,—a few rods in any direction took us to the most interesting places for field work.}

{We had great fun furnishing the suites in the chalet. I made all the cushions and curtains and arranged the fittings. Since they were not rented in June we housed our guests there. Mr. and Mrs. Bennie [B. W.] Law were the first. Later, our friend, Vernon Kellogg found one of the suites a very favorable place for retirement and work. He came to us in the middle of May. He had been called to assist Herbert Hoover and awaited directions for sailing while he was with us. He left us to become Director in Brussels of American Relief in Belgium, an overseas position in which he more than made good, until we went into the war. Naturally we received few letters from him while he was in Belgium, but we read with thrilling interest his "Headquarters Nights" published later in the *Atlantic*.}

{At commencement I had the thirtieth reunion class supper of '85 at the Ledge. There were only fifteen of us including several wives,—Mr. and Mrs. E. H. Bostwick, Mr. and Mrs. J. B. French, Judge and Mrs. A. A. Hartzell, Mr. and Mrs. G. B. Penny, Dr. and Mrs. J. G. White, and the Messrs. J. McCall, D. M. Stevens, and J. Van Sickle.}

{George Tansey was our guest at this commencement and we had Edwin Woodruff and Fritz Coville at luncheon with him, a delightful trio to entertain. After commencement we went to the Hermitage.}

{We returned to Ithaca for an important event. On June 30, 1915, Grace Fordyce and Daniel Scott Fox were married in our home. Grace wished to be married in the garden, but it was a rainy day. The house was a bower of syringa blossoms and pink peonies. After the wedding breakfast, the bride and groom went to The Hermitage for their honeymoon, an ideal retreat.}

{On July 14, 1915 occurred the death of Henry B. Lord, our beloved friend. He and his wife had been kind to us in our student days. All our lives since had been lived in close touch with him. When gentle Mrs. Lord passed away, her sister Miss Ellen Reed had been with Mr. Lord and kept the home a place of gracious hospitality. Mr. Lord was a man of wide culture and sound judgment. He and Professor Hiram Corson read Browning together once a week for a period of years. Not long before his death we spent an afternoon with him and, although then over 90 years old, he had his hand on the pulse of the world. On our way home I asked Mr. Comstock, "Where in this city could we have found such delightful and vital conversation and discussion of social and political present day issues as we have heard today?" Mr. Comstock answered, "Nowhere except at President White's."}

{All this summer Mr. Comstock and I followed closely the fortunes of the Allies in the great war. We marked every advance and retreat on our maps. We had frequent auto rides with President White and, after our first discussion of war news, he would turn the conversation to other topics because he said it spoiled his happiness in the drive to think of the war.}

{After Summer School, Mr. Comstock and I went to the Hermitage and, while there, I began the work on this biography. We had a happy time there as ever; the place is always associated in my mind with the happiness of just ourselves.}

Susanna Phelps Gage had been in failing health for some months. I saw her and {Mr. Gage} in their car on October 4, and the next morning she {passed away}. For thirty-five years she had been a dear and intimate friend, {and there had never been even the slightest cloud between us. She was an inspiration to me always}. Although she had never been robust, she had {carried on} a great deal of {excellent} anatomical {investigation} that had won for her a name in the {realms} of science. {At the same time} she had kept a home for her husband and son, a home that was always hospitable and cheery. Hundreds of Cornell students had spent the happiest hours {of their college life there}. It was always a privilege {to us in the faculty} to be invited there to dinner. The spiritual good cheer was only equaled by that of the physical for Mrs. Gage knew how to prepare a good dinner quite as well as she knew how to cut [microscopic] sections. Her laugh was the sweetest I have ever heard. {All through the long years since she left us, her laugh has remained so vivid in my mind that I can hear it now, and I have been grateful for so cheering a memory.} She was one of the most cultured and interesting women ever associated with the Cornell Faculty. {Her funeral occurred on October 7, 1915, the 37th anniversary of our wedding}.

{It was the fall of 1915 that Professor George L. Burr left our board. He had taken his meals with us for six years, since the death of his wife and baby son. We loved him as if he were of our own blood and were lonely when he left us. He had been asked to live at the Telluride House, and the companionship of these superior young men naturally would be most agreeable to him and keep him in touch with the student side of the University. On the other hand, it would mean much to the members of the Association to have with them in their own home a man so lovable and eminent as Professor Burr. It has turned out even better than we anticipated and Professor Burr is still at the Telluride House and a member of that very interesting, important and unique association.}

{On October 19, occurred the death of Alice McCloskey, who was at that time Editor of the Rural School Leaflet. "Uncle" John Spencer had found her teaching in Saratoga and had been so delighted with her that he had brought her to Cornell to help with the Junior Naturalist leaflets in 1899. She had a fine literary sense and was always an inspiring teacher; she had a unique and interesting personality and was very ambitious; she was made Assistant-Professor in 1914. Her work had been most successful. Fortunately for us she had trained her assistant, Mr. Edward M. Tuttle, a young man of exceptional ability, who was able to continue her work as Editor of the Rural School Leaflet successfully. The war took him away from us and temporarily suspended our publications.}

{Although we were both working up to the limit of our strength, Mr. Comstock spending every hour of his day on the investigation of the venation of insect wings, we entertained a good deal and went out often. I remember an especially delightful dinner at the home of Mr. and Mrs. Louis Fuertes where Dean and Mrs. Albert Smith were present. Louis had shot a pair of wild ducks and we were invited to the feast. Louis Fuertes had been a favorite student of Mr. Comstock's and we were both devoted to him and admired his struggles to do the work he loved best. His father, also a dear friend, had determined that Louis should be an engineer, but later allowed him to study architecture, when all the time he was longing to be a naturalist. By some means, he won out, and speedily made a name for himself in the world of science by his drawings of birds.}

{Besides being a great artist, he was always interesting personally and it was a privilege to be with him, while Mrs. Fuertes seemed just the right wife for him with a great charm of her own.}

{This Thanksgiving, and for all the years after, the Herrick family was with us or we with them. Miss Mary E. Hill, whom we all call Hilary, was always in our family group. It was a joy to me to have members of my family with us for this holiday which had always in my childhood meant a family gathering.}

{"The Chalet," as we called our Publishing Company house, is a beautiful structure. This year the Wharton Movie Company was working in Ithaca. Mr. Wharton was charmed with the Chalet and used it extensively in making his pictures. We observed the manner of movie activity from our windows and concluded that it must be very much more difficult than the regular stage. The actors were galvanized into activity for a few moments, then relapsed into bored repose, only to go through the same act again and again. I came home from my class one bitter cold morning in early December and found the actors in the Ledge garden where we have evergreens. The latter were bedecked with artificial flowers, and the hero, in evening clothes was wandering among them. I invited them to come in the house and get warm. The women accepted; among them was Pearl White. I had often seen her driving about in a vivid blue car and her general attitude had been such that my Quaker mother would have called her a "bold piece." However, her daring acting in dangerous situations in the Ithaca gorges had won our admiration; she was afraid of nothing. I was therefore interested in talking with her. To my surprise, she was greatly interested in the wood engravings which cover our walls and she showed true feeling for their delicacy and beauty. In her manner she was rather shy. Once she turned to me, her face alight with enthusiasm, and said; "Isn't it the most wonderful thing in the world to have an art that one loves and must work for?" This quite won my heart and I have watched her subsequent career with personal interest.}

{December 13, I gave the Founder's Day address at William Smith College. I was the guest of our friends, Mr. and Mrs. William McKay, who were always the most interesting hosts.}

{On December 16th Mr. Comstock gave a lecture on spiders before Sigma Xi. It was interesting and greatly appreciated. His screen pictures of spider silk and webs were superb. Whenever I heard my husband lecture I was impressed anew with the clarity of his discourse and the simplicity of his speech. At the same time his winning, personal attitude always made his audience sympathetic listeners.}

{In January, [1916], President White had an attack of la grippe and again his eyes were affected. I went to him every day to read the newspapers and among them always was the *London Spectator*. He was as usual most interesting, and I certainly got more from his comments and reminiscent discourses than he did from my reading.}

{Miss Edith Patch, State Entomologist of Maine, was our guest in January. While with us, she gave a talk on aphids before the Jugatae that pleased Mr. Comstock very much. Miss Patch, as a student, had been a joy to him and he always took a personal pride in her successes. We also had a guest Miss Anne Dudley Blitz, Dean of Williams Smith College. She was a western woman, a graduate of Columbia and a very able and scholarly executive. She is at present Dean of Women in Minnesota State University.}

{On February 1st, 1916, having finished my semester's teaching, we started for a leisurely trip across to California. Our first stop was Urbana, Illinois. We were the house guests of Mr. and Mrs. P. L. Windsor. Mr. Windsor is the Librarian of the State University and Mrs. Windsor is our much beloved Margaret Boynton, a special student of Mr. Comstock and a member of our family for a time.}

{Our friends gave us a reception at the home of the McGillivrays and there were fifty guests, all acquaintances and many of them former Cornellians. It made us feel that the University of Illinois was, indeed, close to Cornell. Mr. Comstock, especially had interesting visits with Professor Stephen A. Forbes, a life-long friend, and with Dr. McGillivray concerning entomological interests.}

{From Urbana we went to St. Louis to spend two days with Mr. and Mrs. George J. Tansey, during which stay we also saw our other friends, Dr. and Mrs. B. F. Duggar, Mr. and Mrs. Edmund Brown, and Mr. and Mrs. Herman von Schrenck. It was a heart-warming experience from first to last.}

{From St. Louis we went to El Paso for a short visit with Marcia Spurr Russell. We had known her and her brilliant husband [Ernest E. Russell] when they were students at Cornell. He was editor of the El Paso paper for many years; he died in 1904. The stay was very enjoyable both in renewing old friendships and in seeing this interesting city. There were many Mexicans living in the region of Mrs. Russell's home. As we left the house for a drive one day, I noticed she did not lock the doors and spoke of it. She said: "We have lived here twenty years and our doors have never been locked day or night and we have never had anything stolen." This seemed rather a wonderful testimony as to the honesty of Mexicans.}

{At Tucson we were the guests of Professor and Mrs. C. T. Vorhies. Professor Vorhies had taught in the Cornell Summer Session one summer while he was on the faculty of the University of Salt Lake City. We found Tucson a very interesting city and the University a strong institution growing in power. Mr. Comstock gave his lecture on Spiders before the University on February 11th. We found the Vorhies charming hosts and their little son Charles an interesting boy.}

{We went on to the home of Mr. and Mrs. Lyman Van Wickle Brown at Riverside. We had not seen Lyman since he was with us at Cornell. We found the Brown home beautiful within and set in a park in which were many trees. We made the acquaintance of the two small daughters. Lyman drove us around the interesting city of Riverside, of which his father was one of the chief founders. We visited our former colleagues, Professor and Mrs. H. J. Webber at the Experiment Station. When we bade goodbye to Lyman we did not dream that he would "go over the Divide" ahead of us. He had just been elected mayor of Riverside when in 1922 he was killed in an auto accident.}

{From Riverside we went to Claremont to visit Pomona College. We called upon Professor and Mrs. W. A. Hilton and their very young daughter born that week. Professor and Mrs. David Crawford took us for a drive and for dinner and in the evening, we dined with President and Mrs. [James A.] Blasdell, and Professor and Mrs. Clarke of Columbia University. Mr. Comstock gave a lecture before the College.}

{We visited my cousin, Mrs. Kate Sprowls in Los Angeles. It was always a joy for us to be with Cousin Kate, a woman of vital and intriguing personality and a born executive.}

{We also visited the San Diego exposition and had a delightful day at Catalina Island with our friend Carlyle Ellis, who was connected at that time with the photographing staff of one of the move companies. He was always refreshing and stimulating as champagne, and there was a child-like quality in him that from the first won our hearts.}

{We had left the war behind us on this journey. We were sizzling with worry and vital interest in it in the East. As we journeyed west, the interest waned and when we reached the coast we found it scarcely a topic of conversation. The Pacific Coast papers gave very little space to it and the attitude everywhere was, "Well it's Europe's war and Europe is always having wars." No where did there seem to be much partisanship for the Allies. All this was a shock to us. We had always found California aloof in matters that seemed important to us in the East, and this seemed another evidence of it. When, later, we heard so many criticisms of Woodrow Wilson because he did not declare war, we at least, realized that he could not have done so with any success. The West would have been solidly against it.}

{In Palo Alto, at No. 200 Kingsley Avenue, was a charming cottage set in a triangular garden. When we took possession of it February 25, 1916, the fruit trees about the house were in bloom and across the way a Japanese plum flaunted its rose-red banners. It was a comfortably furnished house and had a successful fireplace, and what was more important to our minds, there was a sheet-iron stove in the dining room very near our bedroom door. Again, we marveled at the chill of California nights.}

{The great advantage of our abiding place was its proximity to the homes of some of our dearest friends at Stanford, the Guido Marxes, the David Marxes, Irene Hardy, the Charles Wings, the Edward Franklins.}

{Almost every day I spent an hour or more with Irene Hardy. She had become totally blind and lived in her cottage home with a housekeeper. So great was Miss Hardy's spiritual and mental wealth, that I came away ever inspired and uplifted. Instead of being overcome with pity for her, because she could never see again the beautiful world of nature which she so loved, I was always thrilled by the riches of her thought and feeling.}

{In the early days Mr. Comstock and I had often wandered over by the Frenchman's pond and had said to each other, "When we come to Stanford permanently we shall build on this hill where we can see the valley and the mountains." The Kelloggs had just finished their house on this hill and Vernon had been able to enjoy it this winter for the first time. He had returned from his work with Hoover to his duties at Stanford temporarily; he was under promise to return to Europe when called. We were delighted with the new home built in a fashion reminiscent of the Villa Orchia. We also had the privilege of meeting the little daughter, Jean, who had seemed rather mythical to us, despite sundry photographs. We dined with Dr. and Mrs. Kellogg one evening and, later, members of the Entomological Club came for an informal meeting. It was a real pleasure to Mr. Comstock to meet this group of upstanding young men who were specializing in his own field. We also had the pleasure of renewing our acquaintance with Dr. and Mrs. R. W. Doane of the entomological department.}

{Mr. Comstock lectured before the entomological department one afternoon. On one interesting occasion I particularly remember, a Mr. Asheby from Chipping Camden, England, came to Stanford to lecture. I have forgotten the title of his lecture but the gist of it consisted of arguments showing why the United States should enter the war to aid Allies. Later, we met Mr. Asheby at the home of Guido Marx where he submitted to questioning by a number of people interested. I remember Mr. Comstock and I were much more impressed by his arguments than were most of the others, who found him irritating. We were surprised to find Vernon Kellogg cold to his propaganda. Afterwards, he told us he had suffered such criticism and insults in England because we were not in the war that he was savage on the subject. He maintained that the United States knew what it wanted to do or not to do and, as a nation, was quite able to make its own decisions.}

{We were guests at a great dinner of the Stanford Alumni; more than 300 were present and Vernon Kellogg spoke thrillingly of his experiences in Belgium. Later, we were guests of the Cornell Club of Berkeley at a dinner where 49 Cornellians were present.}

{However, in our memories of this interesting winter, the matrix in which all our pleasures were set, were the hours with the Guido Marxes, for whatever else we did, we spent some part of the day with them—often rather late after other social evenings we wound up before their fireplace, perhaps for sandwiches and beer, or perhaps just for the two men to smoke.}

{When we left Palo Alto in April, we went to Berkeley for a two-day visit with President and Mrs. Benjamin Ide Wheeler. There were many heart-to-heart talks with these sincere friends of ours. Mr. Wheeler was later criticized for his German sympathies. He had been a very successful non-resident Professor in Berlin and had received most gratifying marks of appreciation in Germany; the Emperor and Empress had showered favors upon him and Mrs. Wheeler and he was naturally loth to break such friendships. However, Mr. Wheeler, was greatly misunderstood by the public. His attitude at that time was exactly that of President White. He resented the taking of Belgium, but otherwise as between England and Germany his sympathies were with the latter.}

{After leaving Berkeley we stopped at Fresno to visit Professor I. P. Roberts, who was living there with his son Roger. We greatly enjoyed our stay with our dear old neighbor and his son's family. We had a long auto ride and it was a beautiful country at that time. The fields were a mosaic of buttercups, poppies, lupines, shooting stars, and a pink-purple paint brush. There were little burrowing owls on the fence posts, and along the streams hordes of very red-winged blackbirds, and flocks of ducks and geese.}

{We arrived in Ithaca on April 10, 1916 and were glad to find Will Slingerland waiting for us at the station. After our greetings to the home folks, we had a happy little walk about the gardens. Although we had come from a land of gorgeous flowers, our hearts were thrilled with our own hepaticas, trilliums, crocuses, and gorgeous Christmas roses; and no California birds whatever could compete with our own busy pairs of robins, phoebes, bluebirds and chickadees.}

{We had to steal our peaceful and happy hours this springs for the College of Agriculture was seething under Director [B. T.] Galloway's administration and, although Mr. Comstock had retired, he was greatly concerned over the condition of affairs. It was a mistake to put in as Director a man who had for years been in departmental work in Washington. Departmental administration there and the administration of a college are as far apart as the poles.

In addition to this inevitable cause of trouble, Mr. Galloway was in poor health having suffered a nervous breakdown. Personally, we like him and Mrs. Galloway very much, but that did not help matters. Another phase of the upset was President Schurman's determination to keep Mr. Galloway at the head of the College even if all the faculty of that College resigned. Another thing that aggravated the situation was that, after Director Bailey's years of sympathetic and understanding administration, it would have been difficult for any man, however great, to follow him and give satisfaction. Of course, Mr. Comstock and I could see no happiness for the Galloways if they remained as matters had gone too far to be mended.}

{Mr. Comstock buried himself in his work on the wings of insects; I had two classes to teach and the Insectary was isolated from the tense College of Agriculture. So, I took my pupils to study the brook, and filled my laboratory with the life of the spring.}

{After due consideration, we had solved the George Wiseman problem.[2] His only sister and her daughter, a young girl, were in southeast England. Soldiers were quartered on them, and they needed a man to help them with their many difficulties brought on by the war. We knew we had George to support wherever he was, and the money for his room and board would be a real financial help to his sister. Moreover, he was always kind and helpful by nature, so it was determined that he should go to England. He sailed on May 9th. Will Slingerland went with him to New York and put him on the ship. I wish here to pay tribute to my husband's generosity. He had never liked his brother-in-law and greatly disapproved of his lack of thrift. But now that he seemed quite unable to hold any position, Mr. Comstock supported him until his death some years later.}

May 20th was Professor Gage's birthday and, as he had reached the age of sixty-five this year, a banquet was held in Risley [Hall] in his honor. It was a delightful and memorable occasion. A fund of $10,000 for the establishment of a University fellowship in animal biology had been raised by Professor Gage's former students and present admirers, and the presentation of this fund to the University was an important part of the celebration. There was a most appreciative letter from President White and addresses were made by Dr. B. F. Kingsbury, Dr. Abram Kerr, Dr. Theobald Smith, Dr. G. S Hopkins, Dr. P. A. Fish, Dr. Veranus Moore, President Schurman, and Mr. Comstock. {The address of the latter gives so much of the student life of the two together that I have placed it in the appendix.} Professor Gage's

2. Footnote at bottom of manuscript (p. 16–21), by Herrick: "Husband of Prof Comstock's sister, Margaret. —Ed."

charming and interesting personality {has ever} won the love of {those associated with him}; while his devotion to his work and his achievement as a scientist have won the admiration and respect, {not only of his associates, but} of the world. {There is a vital inspiration that even the casual acquaintance experiences when coming in contact with this original, sincere, humorous and genial man.}

{On June 13th, I gave the Commencement Address at William Smith College and that evening was in the reception line at the Senior Ball. The next day the board of Hobart and William Smith trustees had a long and painful session. Our new president did strange things which were perturbing.}

Mr. Comstock had been elected as faculty representative on the Board of Trustees of Cornell University. This {was an} experiment and an innovation in University management and was looked upon by many as a mistake. {Nevertheless, the plan had been inaugurated and Mr. Comstock was the first one to hold office. He} had no vote but was present at meetings on the Board in the advisory capacity. {At the meeting of the Board, June 20th, Mr. Comstock and George Tansey, who was staying with us, were at the meeting from 10 A. M. until 8 P. M. The discussion of the administration of Director Galloway was heated and long. President Schurman was determined to uphold his appointee. Fortunately for all concerned, Director Galloway became disgusted with the whole thing and sent in his resignation and sturdily refused to reconsider it. He went back to Washington to his scientific work and was relieved to be able to do so. It was at this meeting that the Advisor of Women was given professional rank, an achievement of the alumnae after long and heroic effort.}

{We were both worn to a frazzle with all our work and worry, so as soon as possible we fled to the Hermitage. We spent two days in hard labor cleaning up after squirrel, mice and duck hunters, and then settled down to blissful rest. There were plenty of wild strawberries that year and Mr. Comstock was a rapid gatherer of this delicious fruit—moreover, he enjoyed the performance. So, we feasted on strawberries and cream and we spent our evenings in the hammocks on the roof of the boat house and watched the sunset sky, copper, gold, and blue, reflected in the waters of Lake Cayuga, while listening to the veeries singing antiphonally. Although our interest in the devastating war of Europe grew with the months until it became a nightmare. Our French boy, Pierre Pochet, the boy who had been Quaker-like in his pacifism during his stay at Cornell, had been at the front from the first. He was a revelation of what a pacifist does when he turns fighter. There seemed to be no venture too difficult or too dangerous for him to undertake. He wrote that on no another occasion in life could he think so calmly as when in battle.

He never learned to hate; he risked his life to rescue a German soldier, wounded and helpless in no-man's land. He entered the war a corporal; at the end of two years he was second lieutenant. He was cited three times for bravery and was given the "Cross of War with Palms" and several other medals. In these citations occur the following: "He has ever given to all the most beautiful example of coolness and energy and has volunteered to fulfill the most dangerous missions. He is an officer of rare sangfroid and of remarkable calmness. During the fighting on March 6, he, under an attack of liquid fire rallied his entire section intact in the supporting trench, then immediately regained the terrain occupied by the enemy and established a barrage twenty meters from the first line."}

The following are extracts from his letters written to us in the trenches.[3]

> "This terrible war is lasting longer than we and I know of many friends and relatives whom I shall never see again. This was so carefully prepared by the Germans, was such a surprise for France that nobody was prepared for it. I must confess that I had, myself, a strong propensity to overlook the danger of German militarism, so great was my desire for an era of peace and friendship among nations. I even now take as our motto "Above all nations is humanity." But the German aggression has awakened me to the fact that these beautiful dreams cannot be realized as yet.
>
> "May this year bring a victorious ending of the war and lasting peace. If God spares me, I will try to acquire wisdom like Kipling's Kim and will try to do my best to forget the time when I had upon me the terrible duty to kill human beings.
>
> "Now again has begun the tedious life in muddy trenches. Every one in France knows that we shall be victorious but how few will be the families which this war will have spared in all their members! If, however, this terrible war starts a new era of friendship and good will among nations, all this blood will not have been spent in vain.
>
> "Second Lieut. Pierre Pochet, Cornell '08."

{There were four Pochet sons, and all of them in the war. The eldest was killed in battle. I had been in constant correspondence with the mother and a letter from her in July told me Pierre was a prisoner in Germany. Madam Pochet was the embodiment of heroic motherhood; her letters to her sons

3. As per his daily personal journals, Glenn Herrick may have burned not only Mrs. Comstock's diaries but also any correspondence, from anyone (including Pochet), to Mrs. Comstock singularly, or both Comstocks. —KSt.

were full of cheer, hope and vital faith, and gave never a word of her own sufferings and privations. After his return Pierre pinned his "Cross of War" medal on his mother's breast as he said she was the bravest of them all.}

{A great event in our lives occurred} October 5, 1916. We sold Hilltop farm for $15,000, without the herd, which should bring us $2,000 more. {In a way} it was a wrench to our feelings to sell this abiding place {of my family}. It had been in our possession nearly a century. However, the monthly trips to the farm, although not so hurried as when {Mr. Comstock} was teaching, {yet} were exhausting, and the care of so large an investment so far away was wearing him out. I loved the place where I was born, but I loved my husband a great deal more and was glad to have him free from this incubus, free to spend all his energies on his scientific work.

Mr. Comstock was nearing seventy and was working steadily eight or ten hours each day, trying to unravel the tangled skein of the [evolutionary] relations of insects as shown by their wing veins. As soon as he worked one thread free, at one turn of the reel, it would tangle again. Never had he been more vigorous mentally than now, {and never had he more need of all of his faculties and ability to think clearly.} He had no University duties except to be present at Trustee Meetings.

{I had a large class considering my room this autumn. Among others, Elsie Guerdrum, afterwards our valued friend, Mrs. Arthur A. Allen, was one of my pupils. Often this fall Mr. Comstock would come to the Insectary for a picnic lunch with me on Tuesdays and Thursdays when I could not come home. He was full of fun, like a boy, on these occasions, and we both enjoyed the chance to be by ourselves. We went to all the University concerts and to some plays in the Lyceum and these were our special "celebrations" together. Whenever we were able to get away together we always termed it a "celebration."}

{November 7th was election day and very exciting, for [Charles Evans] Hughes and [Woodrow] Wilson were candidates and we all believed they were evenly matched. We went to lunch with President White to celebrate his 84th birthday. Professors George L. Burr, T. F. Crane, and Lane Cooper were there. Mr. White was as delightful and entertaining as ever but seemed to us to lack his usual vigor.}

{I had an experience in November which I shall always remember.} I was invited to speak about trees before the Seventh and Eighth Grades in the Perry School. When I arrived at the school I found 200 of the primary children and 300 of the upper grades all in one room awaiting me. I was at my wits end, for it was very difficult to hold the interest of small wrigglers {and keep them from wriggling} by talking to older pupils. I had an inspiration.

I began by saying I had a pet at home, guess what? Many guesses were made. None of them right. My pet was a scarlet oak tree and I told how its leaves had to prepare its own food and how it lived and breathed and blossomed and how its acorns were scattered. Guess how old my pet tree is? Many guesses—all wrong. It is four hundred years old; and then I told them all it might have seen of Indians and panthers and bears and wolves and deer. {Talk about inspiration! If one is scared enough, inspiration is natural and inevitable.}

{I made note of an interesting Sunday evening at our home. We had fifteen for supper, among them was Mrs. Alfred Emerson St., her two sons, Alfred Jr. and Willard, who were in the University, and her daughter Gertrude, who had just returned from Japan and China and who entertained us delightfully by relating her experiences. Hers is a most interesting personality, all simplicity on the outside and complexity within; she is very attractive and just to come in contact with her is a stirring experience. Later she joined the staff of "Asia" and at present is living in a village in India to acquire wisdom which, through the alchemy of her mind, will be transmuted to stories that will thrill and delight the world.}

{Although the war was affecting our spirits, we went on with our own affairs in America. We had a Natural Resources Conservation meeting at Ithaca in December. Herbert K. Job lectured on Bird preserves at a banquet that evening,—Dr. Needham was happy as a toastmaster. I remember well the entertaining after-dinner speech made by Louis Agassiz Fuertes, who convulsed the company by asserting that "Man was the Creator's last gasp."}

I rewrote an article on the winter aspect of trees, written several years before for the *Country Life of America*, and made it into a booklet called "Trees at Leisure." It was prettily illustrated with photographs {taken for it by Verne Morton}. It was published in time to send to our friends for Christmas. A second edition has been printed.

The year of 1917 began with new duties for me. I had attended the meeting of the A. A. A. S. held in New York during the holidays, and at the meeting of the American Nature Study Society I had been elected Editor of the *Nature Study Review*.[4] I had been writing by Dr. Maurice Bigelow of Columbia. After the Comstock Publishing Company took over the printing of the magazine [in 1915] I had done much [editorial] work on it. Dr. Elliot Downing was weary of the responsibility and the labor; he was {busy with} teaching and had {plenty of} other writing that he was anxious to do.

4. Side note in manuscript (p. 16–28) by Herrick: ". . . for this periodical ever since it was started in 1905."

{Our work for the year began happily. Mr. Comstock was so infatuated with solving the relations of insect families by their wings that he was putting in long periods of hard work each day; and was very happy that his days were free from teaching and executive duties.}

{February 2, 1917, the entry in my diary is significant, "I had a long and tedious journey to Syracuse. People were talking gravely} of the war at every station and on the train." We felt we were being drawn in to the strife. There had been several pacifist lectures at the University. A Dr. Mez of Heidelberg talked at the Cosmopolitan Club on the futility of thinking war would end all disturbance. John Lovejoy Elliott of the Society of Ethical Culture gave us a fierce arraignment of militarism in schools. We loved to hear him talk so eloquently, but we still believed that schools were just where militarism ought to be taught.}

{An incident of this winter remains in my mind. Our Woman's Alliance of the Unitarian Church had asked young Robert E. Treman to tell us of the foreigners in Ithaca. His work for the firm of Treman and King had brought him in contact with their employees and he gave us a remarkable talk. He spoke with sympathy for their ways and described their homes. He made a special plea to have some of us try to be present when these people were made citizens. He said it should be made an occasion and they should be made to feel that it was really an event to become an American citizen. How prophetic his words! We were soon to learn this lesson through sad experience.}

{February was too soon to foresee our entry into the war, and we were extravagant and bought a very fine player piano for Mr. Comstock's 68th birthday. I know of nothing in our home that gave him so much pleasure. He bought rolls of the music he loved best, *Wilhelm Tell*, *Tannhauser*, and many others. He practiced until he played them with much expression. I loved to listen to his playing. We still had University concerts. Percy Grainger, pianist, and Mary Peterson, soloist, gave us pleasure but left us cold. We had attended the University concerts from their beginning and were very grateful that finally Cornell was becoming musical and music-loving.}

{We had the pleasure of having Dr. Wm. Morton Wheeler as a guest in March. He came to deliver a lecture before Sigma Xi. We invited Dr. Bradford Titchener, Dr. [G. S.] Hopkins, and Dean Woodruff, and Professors Needham, Riley, and Kingsbury, to meet him at dinner at our home. We all enjoyed him very much.}

On April 4, President Wilson sent his war message to Congress. Ever since the sinking of the "Lusitania," the fear of German aggression had been {percolating as more recognition at first.} Now it had swollen to a flood of indignant emotion and like a slow wave had moved from the East to the West. {Cornell had a large number on her staff who blamed Wilson for not declaring war earlier and were bitter in their criticisms. Mr. Comstock and I had seen the indifference of the West and we knew Wilson could not have declared war earlier and have had the backing of the entire country.}

{We had at Cornell a strong German department and at its head our very able Professor Albert Faust. He had argued for American neutrality until he had made himself most unpopular at the Town and Gown Club, which was the chief theater for the expression of individual opinion. At the same time, we had staying in Ithaca, Theodore Stanton, the son of the famous equal suffragist, who had lived for years in Paris and had married a French woman. He was quite as strong in his convictions and arguments that the United States should have been in the war two years before and he argued quite as constantly and valiantly as did Professor Faust, and the effect on the Club Members was quite as fatiguing. People did not want to hear arguments; the news of the war was crystallizing their convictions and when war was declared they knew it was inevitable.}

{Yet when the deed was done our hearts were sad}, for we knew many of our young men would never come back from France. We both had vivid memories of the horrors of the Civil War and had no illusions about what war meant. However, when the Germans refused to modify their submarine policy it seemed that we might have to fight them on our own territory if they conquered the Allies. Many of us had been in Germany and had resented the overbearing manner of the German officers and the glorification of the Military. We had objected to getting off the narrow sidewalk, to let an officer pass. A spirited young American girl who was visiting President and Mrs. White in Berlin declared she would not do this again, so one day she stood her ground. She stopped; the officer stopped. She probably looked mutinous, anyway he lifted her by the elbows into the street and passed on. Such incidents as this had made Americans revolt against what seemed a petty tyranny that was dangerous in its possibilities.}

{An indication of the change of attitude under the influence of the war sentiment came under my observation. In my class was a big vigorous young man from Utah. He was a senior and had planned to have his friends come East at his graduation, and he was indignant when war was declared. "Didn't we elect Wilson to keep us out of war?" he demanded when discussing the subject with me. "I do not want war and I shall not go," he declared. Later I received a letter from him saying he was raising wheat in Utah to feed people instead of taking a gun and killing them. After his wheat was harvested he joined the army at San Diego and was detailed to drill soldiers at Palo Alto, and was quite as interested in killing the Germans as anybody.}

{There had been several young men who were with us almost every Sunday Evening during the year. Harry Knight, William Woods, Philip Munz, Alfred Emerson, Jr., often Willard Emerson, and Edward Urband, Robert King and others. They all went to war this spring; quietly, they seemed to us to melt away.}

{Hendrik William van Loon, Lecturer in Modern European History, tells how the boys went:

> They are going.
>
> And there is something very fine about the quiet way in which these boys have taken to their unpleasant task. There has not been any enthusiasm. That was right. A war like this does not ask for words but for silent deeds.
>
> Our boys seem to understand it. At odd moments they drop into the office. There is very little talk.
>
> "Going away?"
>
> "Yes, sir!"
>
> "Army or Navy?"
>
> "I don't know yet. I called up my people on the long distance phone last night. They said it was all right. So, I'm going to new York, tonight, and then home to say good-bye."
>
> "Want to go?"
>
> "Not particularly. But I suppose it is the only thing to do."
>
> And that is all.}
>
> {They are going and many of them never will come back. The pleasant life of mediocre endeavor has come to an end. To be sure we have never looked at them in the light of heroes. They were nice, lovable fellows. Their outlook upon life was simplicity itself. Graduation and a job. Then, after a few years another job, a little higher up. Finally, a home of their own and some nice girl to be their wife and a few babies and a car and two weeks' vacation to go hunting or fishing. Here and there a man with a hobby or the ambition to do, or write, or build, or achieve some particular purpose.}
>
> {To most of them, however, life meant a cheerful gift to be enjoyed as the faithful days came along. There was no searching for hidden motives or for an ulterior purpose. The amiable Divinity of

Things-As-They-Are ruled their realm. They accepted whatever came with a smile, and they did not ask questions.}

{And now, without a word of warning, they have been asked to face the Invisible Mystery. There was no complaint. They packed their trunks and God bless them.}

{They are going.}

{Thus far they have been my students. But now, in a humble fashion I am grateful that I have been their teacher.}

Mrs. Comstock under her garden clock, 65th birthday.

CHAPTER XVII

Florida and Retirement

In Mrs. Comstock's manuscript, Chapter XVII (fifty-five pages) is the third largest chapter after Chapter IV (sixty-six pages) and Chapter VI (fifty-five pages). As with previous chapters, the timeline is muddled because of the extensive removal of manuscript pages, and this chapter corresponds to Chapter 18 in the 1953 edition. As with other Comstock manuscript chapters, most of Chapter XVII has not been included in the 1953 book. Also, page 17–33 is missing from this chapter but the pages continue serially.

On January 2d, 1919 we started south. The packing and starting was as usual, a cataclysm in our establishment. Professor Gage took us to the restaurant in the basement of Sibley College for dinner and he and Jim[1] and Mrs. [Margery] Smith went with us to the train.

{Our first stop was in Richmond, Va. We had never visited this historic city and naturally we found it interesting. We visited the old capitol and admired the solid mahogany seats for the legislators and wondered if perchance they made for solid legislation. We went to the Hollywood Cemetery on the banks of the tawny, flooded River James and paid our respects to the

1. Note at bottom of the manuscript (p. 17–1) by Herrick: "George H. Russell, nickname 'Jim,' lived with the Comstocks for some years and became like a son to them. He is now a successful attorney in Ithaca. —Editor."

last resting places of Presidents Tyler and Monroe, and Jefferson Davis. We walked the length of Monument Avenue and I confess that my placidity was roiled by the inscription on the monument to Jefferson Davis. I had a vivid memory of my exultation when that gentleman was captured. However, Mr. Comstock consoled me by saying that the inscription on the monument was evidently meant to roil Yankees like me, so I calmed down. There were those in the confederated states whom I had always admired like General Lee, but Jefferson Davis was not among these. We visited the dignified Church of St. John where Patrick Henry made his great speech and had a delightful leisurely day of wandering and looking.}

{We went on to Raleigh [North Carolina]. I wonder if people now remember the crowded trains and the discomfort of the war period. We were in a veritable Methuselah of a car. It was heated by a stove and lighted by kerosene lamps and packed to the limit.}

{We stopped at Raleigh to visit the University and particularly to call on Franklin Sherman, who was State Entomologist. We found him as interesting and charming as he had been in the days of his youth. His assistant, R. W. Leiby, was also one of Mr. Comstock's pupils. Mr. Comstock was pleased with the work they were doing. We visited Franklin Sherman in his home and renewed acquaintance with his wife and their fine sons.}

{Dr. Clarence H. Kennedy, who was teaching in the University, came to breakfast with us. We had become much attached to him during his stay at Cornell and were very glad to see him again. We were invited to lunch by Professor and Mrs. Z. P. Metcalf, who showed us the part of the University in which Mr. Comstock was interested.}

{We took a little walk by ourselves and visited the old Capitol and made a pilgrimage to Peace Institute where our beloved Nannie Herrick was educated and where she taught before her marriage to our Cousin Glenn. It was a simple, dignified school and seemed, in some ways, like Chamberlain Institute where I prepared for college.}

{We wished to go to Charleston, S. C. but train connections were poor so we were obliged to stay all night at Hamlet. The hotel here was my supreme experience, for never before or since, have I slept in such a filthy room. Mr. Comstock had had experience in small southern hotels and he was not specially disturbed, so I took it philosophically. The next day we had a journey through cotton fields, pine barrens, cypress swamps and wide marshes, my initiation to the coastal region of South Carolina.}

{We went to the Timrod Inn in Charleston because I had an interest in this Southern poet, Henry Timrod. Our room was very large and rather bare, but we were comfortable, and we could look out directly on the monument to the Poet. Of course, we visited the Magnolia Cemetery and paid Lanier's tribute to the great live oaks. We had the interesting experience of seeing the aeroplanes competing with the buzzards above our heads. We visited the library and art gallery, enjoying the portraits very much. We spent an afternoon wandering among the pines at Somerville. Of course, we visited Ft. Sumter. We both remembered well when it was fired upon and taken, and the thrill of excitement and terror consequent upon it.}

The train {to Savannah was} packed to the limit. Surely travelling under the aegis of McAdoo in those days was an achievement as well as a journey.

{Our stop at Savannah was for the purpose of seeing again Dr. Eugene Corson and family. We experienced genuine pleasure in renewing our acquaintance with this interesting man and his beautiful wife and daughters. His son was with the marines in France at that time. Dr. Corson was one of the martyrs to the introduction and use of the X-ray. One of his hands was hopelessly maimed and he was fortunate to escape with his life.}

The middle of January found us very happily settled in the excellent St. George Hotel in St. Augustine [Florida], for we had {determined} to spend the winter here. I had taken a severe cold and my winter was made miserable {to a greater or less extent} by my {old} enemy bronchitis.

Mr. Comstock had brought along the chapter on Diptera[2] of the *Introduction to Entomology*, and he worked steadily on it mornings and evenings. In the afternoons we wandered about the ancient town and studied its relics of the past. I sketched the picturesque old Fort Marion and we tried to imagine what its grim old cells and torture chambers had seen of human misery. One way to become optimistic concerning the present time is to take a careful look at the past {ages}.

Some afternoons we spent on South Beach. It had its own peculiar charm. The dunes, beset with prickly pear and saw-palmetto each trying to hold the sands in place. The pelicans fishing. The fascinating flocks of sanderlings that followed each receding wave, probing the sands for food, then arising as a flock in retreat before the oncoming billows. We never wearied with watching them.

Sometimes we went to the lighthouse on Anastasia Island where the wind-swept trees take tortured, fantastic shapes; sometimes to North Beach, on the little steamer Pauline and had seafood at the famous Capot's "Local."

{Our hotel was filled with nice quiet folk and among them we found most congenial friends. Mr. and Mrs. Joseph Dart and their friend Mrs. Utley from Buffalo we found charming, and what is more, interesting. Charm often comes from manner and graciousness, but only the mind creates interest.

2. Note at bottom of the manuscript (p. 17–4) by Herrick: "Diptera,—an order of two-winged insects: flies, mosquitoes, gnats, et al. —Ed."

Mr. and Mrs. Dart read and thought about the same things in politics and literature as did we. The friendship with them and Mrs. Utley bore fruit in later years. A beautiful white-haired lady, Mrs. Taylor from New York, Mrs. Fisher from Indianapolis, Mr. and Mrs. Curry from St. Louis, Mrs. Montgomery and her daughter from Columbia, S. C. and others of pleasant memory were guests at the St. George.}

{We shall never forget the story Miss Montgomery told us of her younger brother who was in the army aviation corps then at Miami. I have forgotten the son's name so I will call him "David."}

{The family had an old colored woman servant, Sarah, who took care of David from birth until he no longer needed care. The two were great friends but always argued with each other, that being their chief entertainment. He came up from Miami while his family was in St. Augustine and Sarah was delighted with his grand appearance in his uniform. She cooked him a perfect dinner and stood by to see him enjoy it when they began an argument, in which David got the better of her, at which she looked at him fondly and exclaimed "Law, Mars Dave, you ain't nuffing but jest bref and breeches." "Nuffin but bref and breeches" stayed with us as an apt description of various people we have met since.}

{An account of social experience in St. Augustine would be lacking indeed, if no mention were made of Sister Esther Carlotta. I had taken up the study of Spanish with Jim during the autumn and thought I would continue it if possible. I was sent by our pleasant host to Sister Esther Carlotta. She was a beautiful woman physically with great dignity of manner. She belonged to an Episcopal order which, I gathered, was defunct in America. However, Sister Esther Carlotta was enough to establish and stabilize any order for she was a woman of resources and initiative. She was an excellent teacher of Spanish and I think she also gave piano lessons. I was never tired of studying her, for she dramatized her life every hour; and she had a fine sense of artistic fitness. The severe simplicity of her home, while a matter of necessity financially, she had arranged as a proper background for her own vivid personality. Each glimpse of her past which she granted me was an act in a drama. Her present poverty and inability to guess where her food next month or next week would come from, was an act in the drama, and was never allowed to degenerate into anything mean or ignoble or, above all, commonplace. The costume of her sisterhood was worn regally and was a great help as a stage property.}

{Not for a moment do I think she consciously played a part. Through her keen dramatic sense, she unconsciously was a part; she could not help being a part of a drama. As such, I enjoyed my association with her keenly, and the show was worth what it cost although, in the end, the cost was rather dear, for I saved her piano from a forced sale, or something of the sort. But she has always remained a glowing spot in my memory, and I hope she still has life by the throat; for her, white, beautiful hands can choke hard, and ultimately, she will win.}

{We had a letter from Marion Reedy, Editor of the St. Louis Mirror, stating that his chief assistant, Miss Alma Meyer, was to be in St. Augustine for a few days on her way to Cuba, a trip for a needed rest. We found Miss Meyer an interesting and very individual young woman and much enjoyed having her with us. We took her out to the Fountain of Youth, the fountain that for certain and for sure was the one Ponce de Leon discovered. A keen-faced elderly woman was the owner and the impresario of this miracle spring. The story she told us, of manuscripts and deeds and descriptions in the archives of libraries in Spain, that proved beyond a doubt that this was the water discovered by the explorer, made a breathlessly fascinating tale. I hope it was true, but St. Augustine residents were cruel enough to doubt. Anyway, it would make a good novel and Alma Meyer was very appreciative of its good points as fiction. We drank of the waters and the three of us are still alive and we hope youthful.}

The last February, Jim[3] arrived and then we had plenty of activity. We had to take him to all the places and introduce him to all our friends. {There was a very sweet young girl, Virginia Lee, from Winnipeg, staying at the hotel, and Jim found her a good partner for the numerous dances at the different hotels, so he enjoyed life greatly.}

He went with us on an inland voyage to Daytona, on the little steamer the "Sea Gull." We threaded our way through tropical scenery for sixty-four miles; we were especially interested in the hosts of herons, (at least three species), the ospreys and kingfishers, and the many species of ducks which had taken possession of these waters. We took a tourist's glance at Daytona and Ormond and the magnificent beaches, {and hied [hurried] us home over the same route next day. I remember that Jim thought a big alligator sunning himself on the shore was a stuffed specimen, put there to thrill the tourists.}

{A visit to the alligator farm at St. Augustine remains with me ever as a hideous experience. If I were to picture a real hell I should populate it with alligators, millipedes, and hyenas.}

{We all enjoyed the pelicans. These birds, so ungainly on shore, are magnificent on the wing, and their tactics in fishing intrigued us. Coming home from North Beach one afternoon, we saw some little gulls riding along the

---

3. Note at bottom of the manuscript (p. 17–7) by Herrick: "George Russell, called "Jim" to distinguish him from the other George (Burr) of the household. Mr. Russell lived with the Comstocks for some years and came to [be] looked upon as a son. He is now a very successful attorney. —Editor."

heads of swimming pelicans. If, by chance, the pelican opened its beak to take a lunch of fish from its creel, the gull darted down and shared the feast.}

{We left St. Augustine on March 20, taking the train to Palatka. We were amazed to find ourselves passing through hundreds of acres of Irish potato fields. We remained over night at Palatka and we were greatly impressed by the magnificent St. John's River from this point. It was wide and still, and the water lilies and water hyacinths had taken possession of its shore waters. A wide river with lotus upon it but, someway, not in the least like the Nile.}

{The next day we spent on a tony steamer threading our way up the Ocklawaha and Silver Rivers. Often the stream was so narrow the cypresses and the jungle foliage made an arch above us. We were so near the shore we could see the water moccasins coiled on the bank; we started counting the alligators but became tired of such a monotonous past-time. However, the reptiles were minor incidents, for this inland voyage gives exquisitely beautiful vistas through the tropical forest at every turn. I consider this one of the truly remarkable experiences for the tourist in America.}

{We spent the night at Ocala and visited Silver Springs, perhaps the most copious and beautiful springs in the world. The water is crystal-clear; as we rowed over its surface in a glass-bottomed boat, we could see the pebbles on the bottom sixty feet below us. The Springs pour forth such a volume of water that the river thus formed is navigable at its source.}

{Thence we went to Jacksonville and found passage on the S. S. Arapahoe bound for New York. Jim and I expected to be seasick for we both had suffered on previous voyages, and we both had active imaginations. However, the voyage was remarkably smooth. My chief memory of it was the distinct demarcation made by the Gulf Stream; it was blue, and the Atlantic along the coast was green, and where they joined the line was as sharp as between sea and shore. The temperature was warm, the air balmy while we were in the Gulf Stream, but as soon as we crossed the line, the wind was sharp and the air cold.}

{We reached New York just as a blizzard struck the city.} When we arrived at Ithaca, March 28th, Professor Gage and Will Slingerland met us and brought us up the hill through snow a foot deep, the air filled with sharp blinding flakes. {It was the first hard snow storm of the year. The winter had been a miracle of mildness and our neighbor, Mrs. Ries, had picked blossoming flowers in her garden every month while we were gone.}

{The fact that the College of Agriculture had established four terms a year, allowed me to be absent during the winter. I had a goodly-sized class this Spring, and George [Jim] Russell was appointed my assistant. He was considering taking up forestry as a profession, and took some courses leading to it in addition to helping me. He also helped me in editing the Nature Study Review.}

{Mr. Comstock and I began our daily walks around the garden, and on April 6, we found our hepaticas all in bloom and the brave little Trillium nivea which we both loved, in bloom. These walks together were always the treasure hour of the day.}

{The University Club was serving us in many practical ways. We both took our guests there and were entertained there ourselves. I remember a luncheon given by Martha Van Rensselaer and Flora Rose, at which Mrs. Casper Whitney, Dr. Georgia White, were guests.}

{The last of April, Jim bought a car, an Oakland. He had driven the cars of his brother-in-law for some years and was a skilled driver. We could not afford to buy a car and hire a chauffeur, but we were glad to pay the running expenses and have the advantage of Jim's car. He really bought it on our account, and it gave us great pleasure for years. Mr. Comstock enjoyed auto rides very much when freed from the responsibility of driving, and he always had perfect confidence in Jim's skill.}

In June [1919], Cornell celebrated its semi-centennial, and it was really a great occasion.[4] The big armory was for the first time used for a social function. A dinner was served there on the night of June 20, to 4800 persons. The Department of Domestic Science had charge and it was a great success from every point of view.

Mr. Comstock and I met more of our old student friends on this occasion than ever before, {even at Commencement. Mr. Comstock's} class had a reunion as did mine, and as their dinners occurred on consecutive nights we attended both. {Professor and Mrs. J. C. Branner and Professor Guido Marx of Stanford were our house guests. I think that on Sunday preceding Commencement we had more callers than on any other day of our married life. I counted fifty and then lost count.}

Commencement occurred on June 23rd and both Mr. Comstock and I {attended and} walked together in the procession. It was {Jim's} 21st birthday and the day on which he received his B.S. degree, although he had finished his work in December.

{I began teaching directly after Commencement. Mary Ellen Donahue was my assistant in the regular class in the College of Agriculture. In July the summer session brought me a large class. Jim was one of my assistants and his car was a great help, for we were able to go far afield for flowers

4. Footnote in the 1953 edition (p. 254): "The celebration had been deferred a year on account of the war. —G.W.H."

and other laboratory material. Mrs. Ethel Hausman and Jay Traver were my other assistants. The Brauners were staying for a few weeks at Glenwood on Cayuga Lake and Jim took us to see them and later took them to their train. We found it very nice indeed to have a son of our own who was so glad to do everything for us and our friends. It was interesting to note that he called me "mother" but always called Mr. Comstock, "the Professor." Some one asked him if Mr. Comstock was not his father and he answered, "He is a very kind step-father."}

{I had the pleasure of having Professor W. G. Vinal of the College of Education of Providence, R. I., lecture before my summer class and we had him as guest at the house. A fine man and a fine teacher; we enjoyed him very much. Another guest who gave us great pleasure was Mrs. Ralph Catterall. The death of her gifted husband, the year before, had been a great loss to the University and a personal grief to Mr. Comstock and myself. Mrs. Catterall, while her son was in Harvard, devoted herself to legal historical research, and was working in the Cornell Library.}

On July 31st, I was made a full professor. I regarded it a tribute to my long service, but it also was a tribute to the Department [of Nature Study] which I had {built up}. I was near the retiring age and I was glad {that when I went}, a {full} professor would be called instead of [an assistant professor or] an instructor, to carry on the [nature] work.[5]

{Mrs. Susan Sipe Alburtis conducted a course in School Gardens and her presence was always an inspiration to us all. We had a reception for the summer class as usual and 130 came. The car gave us other social experiences also for, this summer, we were given to picnic suppers at any pretty place within a radius of ten miles, and we always took friends with us. We also spent week-ends at the Hermitage with ease undreamed of before we had the use of the car.}

{After the close of the summer session I was able to get away for four days and Jim took us to Otto where we visited my cousins and the dear friend of my childhood, Etta Holbrook, and many other old friends. We made a picnic with Cousin Nora and her husband to Hilltop Farm and the gorge called Forty, the picnic resort of my childhood now is a state park. The farm did not look so prosperous as it ought and that was a worry. We came home by

---

5. Footnote inserted in the 1953 edition (p. 254): "As an educational pioneer, Anna Botsford Comstock's teaching of nature study led to her appointment as a Cornell Professor and as first head of the University's Nature Study Department. Through her leadership and teaching, her books and other publications, she helped to extend Nature Study, as an academic subject, to the schools and colleges in the United States and in other nations. —R.G.S."

Collins visiting the Bennie Laws. Then I came back to finish teaching in the long term.}

{On September 1st, I was sixty-five years old and felt that it was a turning point. Two of my summer students, {Miss Eve Marian Provost and Miss May Smith}, spent the afternoon with me and photographed me by the sun dial. {The} shadow showed that evening was approaching and that seemed fitting. {Mr. Comstock always liked this picture of me better than any other.} Mary C. Lowe, {who was in Ithaca that summer}, honored my birthday with the following poem.

"To Anna B. Comstock, on her sixty-fifth birthday.
"You show us beauty everywhere,
In flower and bird and tree;
You open windows which look far
Into infinity.
And we who love these things turn back
Today with word of praise
And grateful hearts to wish you joy
For all the onward ways.
And through the greetings, like a bird,
A something sings and sings
A blessing on you every day
Interpreter of Things.
—Mary C. Lowe"

{In the latter part of September, we had a most interesting motor trip with Jim in his car, which we had named "Daisy"—his sister, Avis Johnson, Mr. Comstock and myself. Our first day took us into the Catskills. The season at Woodstock was over, but the hotel was running, after a fashion, and Jim ever after reviled even the name of Woodstock, because he found a piece of soap in his fried potatoes at supper. Our next day took us through the Berkshires where the scenery is very like that in Cattaraugus County, N. Y. where I was born. Our next stop was at Pittsfield [Massachusetts]. From there we took a side trip to Stephentown where Mr. Comstock spent some time in his childhood with his mother's uncle. The house had been burned, but Mr. Comstock identified the location by the marble steps and threshold still standing guard. Thence we went to Mt. Lebanon to see our dear friend, Eldress Amelia Calver, a charming and cultivated woman who has always remained loyal to the Shaker Community, although her family had deserted it one after another. We were all intrigued by the peaceful comfort of the place and we met many of the Brothers and Sisters of this Community, whose high ideals and business integrity had made it respected wherever known. Amelia Calver is a writer and poet. Several of her nature poems are in the Nature Study Review. It was there that we saw the Shaker cloaks in the process of making and I was surprised the next Christmas to get one from Jim, a garment of beauty and infinite usefulness.}

{We went on through North Adams and our next stay was at Concord, Mass. Where we stopped at the old Wright's Tavern, famous in history and of great interest to me, because it was the place frequented by Henry David Thoreau. It seemed to us that there were no two rooms in it with floors on the same level. Its many two steps up and down were a guarantee that Major Pitcairn, Washington and Lafayette were not tipplers otherwise they never could have reached their rooms to go to bed. I looked long at the low ceiled barroom where Thoreau took his mug of cider and gossiped with his neighbors. It was through a drizzling rain that we visited Walden Pond, but we bravely added our stones to the cairn marking the site of Thoreau's cottage. I was surprised to find Walden Pond such a beautiful sheet of water set in high wooded shores for I had heard slighting remarks about it. After seeing it, I could understand Thoreau's feeling for its attractions. I had always held up Thoreau before my classes as the ideal nature student and had required my pupils to study carefully his superb note-books as a pattern and inspiration. This visit to Concord meant much to me.}

{After Concord we visited Lexington and Cambridge and then followed the coast to Kennebunk where we called at the comfortable attractive home of our dear "Hilary," Mary E. Hill. It was a pleasure to meet her sister Julia and her brother Bertram and in Portland we met her other sister Florence. The Hill's are of the best New England traditions, numbering two governors in their ancestry.}

{Thence we went to Portland and to the White Mountains staying at the famous Crawford House, where we saw sunset and sunrise on the most famous mountains of New England. Thence we passed through the Green Mountains to Burlington and thence to Winthrop, N. Y., Jim's [George Russell] home via Wilmington Notch. Neither Mr. Comstock nor I had ever had such an opportunity to see our own mountain scenery. Later we went to Jim's favorite North Woods resort, Joe Indian Lake, an attractive sheet of water in a picturesque wilderness. We stopped at the comfortable primitive hotel "Pinehurst" and rested for a few days. We returned home the last of September refreshed in body and mind.}

{Soon after my return I went to Cortland to speak before the Fortnightly Club, held in the Wickwire mansion. This club was composed of women who were interesting and interested. I spoke on "The Autumn Flowers" as that was the choice of the Nature study section of the club. Later this club gave me a beautiful silver basket which has been a constant and happy reminder of that pleasant afternoon.}

{After an interview with his devoted and careful guardian, Jim concluded to study law, and entered the Cornell Law School this autumn. His work was arranged so that he could help me in my laboratory and field work afternoons. Jim's car[6] continued to give us undreamed-of privileges. He took us to the movies when we felt inclined. He took our friends with us to dinner to Cortland or Freeville and we thus entertained and had an outing ourselves. I went with Jim to the football games played in Ithaca and again became a "fan." Mr. Comstock went seldom for he was not much interested in the game. I remember that in the days when the football field was in the quadrangle we viewed it from the steps of McGraw Hall, Mr. Comstock had threatened never to go again unless I stopped shouting when the game became exciting. I found I had gained in self-control and no longer disgraced my family.}

{In October we gave a reception to the teachers and instructors and assistants in the Departments of Rural Education and Entomology. Seventy came and we enjoyed having them all in our home.}

This autumn [1919] women voted for the first time and I went to the polls with mixed feelings. I never had belonged to the suffrage movement for two reasons. First, I did not think the women's vote would change the state of national politics. I believed in municipal affairs they would be more influential and already this suffrage had been granted quite widely. Second, I felt unequal to voting wisely. Both of these reasons still hold good. {It is true} I had always believed women should have the same political rights as men, as a matter of justice, but I did not feel like taking up the cudgels for the cause. I had been using all my strength to fight narrowness and prejudice and injustice in the curriculum of the common schools and was weary with fighting. {Mr. Comstock} and I had always been in accord in our political views; {I knew} he welcomed my advent as a voter so that I would take a more {vital} part in trying to discover how we ought to vote. We were always independent of parties, sometimes registering in one and sometimes in the other but with no confidence in the platform of either. We {simply} tried to choose the candidate whose record showed that he would do right and represent the people's interests. It was this that made us vote for Al [Alfred E.] Smith for Governor when we were registered Republicans.

6. Footnote by G.W.H. inserted in the manuscript (p. 17–16): "Even in 1919, a car was a luxury to many people and still a marvelous mode of transportation. —Editor."

{The colleges at Cornell now had grown so large, that except for the clubs and the women's faculty club, we never met the members of other colleges faculties than our own, and we had gotten past calling on new members of our own colleges. In fact, the friendly social life was now limited to departments. I remember Mrs. Mann, wife of the Dean of the College of Agriculture, gave a reception to the women and wives of the faculty of that College and her house was packed, there were so many.}

{We shall never forget our Thanksgiving of 1919. We had with us the Herrick family and Miss Hill and Professor Gage. Cousin Glenn asked the blessing and we all felt in our hearts that the Lord heard. It was our first real Thanksgiving after peace had come as a reality. I also remember that we still had war prices and our turkey cost $9.00, and it was not so very large at that.}

{We found that a son living with us in the home was a great asset. When our dear housekeeper Margery Smith had an infection in her ankle Jim dressed the ankle every day and got the breakfast and helped generally in the housework.}

{We had a rather exciting general faculty meeting in December. There were still those in the Arts Faculty and in Law who objected to faculty representatives on the Board of Trustees. Mr. Comstock, who had been one of the representatives from the beginning of the experiment, believed it was a wise and decidedly progressive movement. He made some short but eloquent and telling speeches in its favor and, as usual, his opinion had weight. He believed that this representation brought the faculty and trustees together and would establish a modus operandi for team work, instead of the more or less resentful attitude of the boss and the being bossed. In fact, Mr. Comstock considered the invitation of the trustees to the faculty representatives a remarkably broadminded and generous act. He told me privately that he considered the trustees were enlightened and the faculty narrow and hide-bound and jealous in this whole affair. The objection of Dean Woodruff of the Law School was based on the idea that a person belonging to an organization should not be on the governing board of it. However, as the faculty representatives had no vote and their duties were simply advisory, this did not seem to be a valid objection.}

Mr. Comstock was so enthralled by his writing and research that he felt he did not have the time or energy to attend the [1919] meetings of the American Association for Advancement of Science, which met this year during holiday week in St. Louis. I was obliged to go as I was secretary and editor of the *Nature Study Review* and the American Nature Study Association always met with the A. A. A. S.

{I was entertained at the home of Mr. and Mrs. George J. Tansey. On December 30 occurred our meeting which was very successful. I met there Professor Drushel and Mr. and Mrs. Satterthwaite and James Newton Baskett who had been a pioneer in popularizing science. His "Story of the Fishes" had interested me more in the "finny tribes" than anything I had read.}

The *Nature Study Review* was not paying its expenses and, at this meeting, methods of extending the subscriptions by establishing clubs for Nature Study was {discussed and} decided upon. {Mr. and Mrs. Satterthwaite, charming and cultured Quakers, carried out the plan in their home town, Webster Grove, a club that continues to this day, I believe.}

{Mr. and Mrs. [George J.] Tansey were most kind. They invited Dr. and Mrs. Benjamin Duggar of the Shaw Botanic Gardens and the brilliant Professor Otto Heller of Washington University to dine with me. The Duggars were old and dear friends. Another evening they had our beloved Vernon Kellogg at dinner. It had been one of my happiest experiences at this meeting that Vernon was present.}

{Miss Molly Tansey (the sister of George) took me one afternoon to the home of Mr. and Mrs. Curran, made famous by the messages they received over the Ouija board from Patience Worth. I had been interested in this phenomenon from the beginning through Marion Reedy's account in the St. Louis Mirror, and I was very curious to see Mrs. Curran. I found her a pleasant, intelligent woman, but about as far from Patience Worth as was possible for two personalities to be. Seeing her and talking with her and seeing her take messages over the board convinced me as nothing else could, that Patience Worth was an entity and not the subconscious Mrs. Curran. I believe the Patience Worth literature is the most convincing and monumental evidence we have of the persistence of personality after death. It is a beautiful and noble body of writing and I have read it over and over with the keenest enjoyment.}

{I was very pleased to get a greeting from Patience herself. Mrs. Curran's hands flew over the board with almost lightning rapidity; as the words were spelled, she spoke them, and Mr. Curran recorded them. After this experience I was more than ever convinced of the personality of Patience Worth. Every phrase and thought bore the stamp of individuality, and if she is not a disembodied spirit she is of far more mysterious origin.}

{On New Year's morning [1920] George Tansey went with me to a breakfast given by Mr. and Mrs. Hermann von Schrenk. Hermann was a Cornell graduate, and during his student days had spent much time with us, giving us real pleasure, at least once a week, by playing for us on the violin. Now he was an expert on timbers for railway and bridge and dock construction and had married into a fine St. Louis family. The breakfast was very gay. The house was filled with guests. It was a revelation to me in that it was such a leisurely, joyous companionable social function of a kind which I had believed extinct. Certainly, we had nothing like it in Ithaca.}

{The Tanseys had given me a very happy time. They had sent me hither and yon in their car and were indeed perfect hosts. It proved to be my last visit in their home.}

{Cousin Glenn Herrick was my companion on the return journey. We were late in getting into Buffalo which resulted happily in that we were able to take lunch with our cousins, Dr. and Mrs. Guy McCutcheon at their attractive home in Delaware Avenue. Our journey had been enlivened by witnessing a fight in the dining car between a southerner and a negro waiter which was squelched by an able Irish conductor. After seeing it through, we concluded that a dining car lacked scope as a battling ring.}

{This year I was in charge of buying and distributing the books in the Campus Book Club.[7] This was an institution of many years standing. Usually there were no more than twenty [pairs of] members. We each paid $2.50 a year and auctioned off the books at the end. Thus, we usually had something more than $100 to buy books for the next year. For years Professor T. F. Crane was our auctioneer. His wit and caustic summaries of the books were always great fun. It was worth the price of joining the club to listen to his clever auctioneering.}

In January [1920] the Comstock Publishing Company bought our "How to Know the Butterflies" from the Appletons. They would not reprint the book without putting on it a practically prohibitive price. We have been able to keep this very useful volume in print at a moderate price ever since.

The Comstock Publishing Company this winter published outline drawings of the Zoo animals with the idea of helping teachers of geography. Louis [Agassiz] Fuertes made superb drawings for the set. Strange to say, his publication has never been used as universally as we had believed it would. Teachers of geography {want to teach seaports and products but do not "care a dam" about} the wild animals of the forests and plains, and mountains. Just the things that would interest the children most and fix in their minds the nature of the country {are ignored}.

This was a very cold and stormy winter and Mr. Comstock declared that he could only work at his writing for short intervals between stoking of the furnace. He would never trust the care of the furnace to {any student

7. Note from G.W.H. at bottom of the manuscript page 17–21: "This club is still active (1938) with 18 pairs of members."

or to} anyone else; he knew best how to keep the house warm and the coal bills down. {As a matter of fact}, most of the Cornell professors attended to their own furnaces; few of them were wealthy enough to keep a man, and {student help}, in this particular branch of labor, was often a delusion and a snare {unless the boy lived in the house}. I was {vastly} amused when {once} I visited Dr. and Mrs. Paul Shorey of Chicago to find that this eminent classicist also attended to his own furnace. I had always held him in awe, but this brought him off the pedestal and made him a {sweet blood} brother to other professors in American colleges.

In January Mr. Comstock was re-elected to represent the Faculty on the Board of Trustees. He was surprised at this but felt glad to be trusted in this office which he believed was {per se} most important. It turned out to be even more important than any of us dreamed for, on February 14, President Schurman handed in his resignation. {This was a great shock to us all.} He seemed to be at the height of his success and usefulness. Many of us felt hurt at what seemed to be his desertion, and {the} feeling of injury was greater because this meant we {should} lose Mrs. Schurman also, and our devotion to her {was unlimited}. However, we all had to realize that a man's life was his own, and Mr. Schurman had labored long and ardently for Cornell and the University had flourished mightily under his administration.

{1920}

{Mr. Comstock's 71st birthday, February 24, 1920, was celebrated in a happy manner. Mrs. Will C. Thro, our beloved Alice Simmons, came from New York with her "fiddle brown" and played his best-loved pieces for him, and of course the rest of us listened and enjoyed.}

Mr. Comstock still representing the Faculty on the Board of Trustees, found new duty and interest in trying to find a President for Cornell. Albert W. Smith, Dean of the Engineering Department, had been made Acting President and carried the work most successfully for the two years while the search went on.[8]

{I was busy revising "How to Keep Bees" and editing the *Nature Study Review* I was a member of the Kappa Alpha Theta Alumnae Council and we concluded to purchase the dwelling[9] on Triphammer Road built by Professor Frank Fetter and make it over for the Sorority. It is an interesting fact that at

8. Written in the margin of manuscript page 17–24 by R.G.S. {also Albert W. Smith's wife}: "Eventually Livingston Farrand was chosen."

9. Footnote inserted at bottom of the manuscript page 17–24 by G.W.H.: "Now, in 1937, this dwelling has been torn down and a large, fireproof, concrete-steel house is being erected in its place by the sorority."

Cornell the sororities had not desired dwellings apart but had preferred living in the women's dormitories. However, when there were more girls came to Cornell than could be accommodated in the dormitories, President Schurman had ruled that the sororities must move out. He reasoned that these were organized and could better care for themselves outside than could the girls not affiliated with groups. This worked hardships at first as our sororities had no wealthy alumnae to build houses for them as had the men's fraternities. At first, rented homes ill fitted for sorority use were all that could be afforded. Finally, most of them had bought private dwellings and remodelled them as best they could. However, the housing of the sororities at Cornell has never been so elegant or so luxurious as that of the fraternities. This is perhaps an advantage, for one of the evils of fraternity life at Cornell has been accustoming boys to live in a manner that will surely be beyond the means of most of them, after they leave college.}

{During the last week in March Mr. Comstock's heart was gladdened by the profuse blossoming of his Christmas roses. I shall never forget how he cherished each individual blossom. It seemed so miraculous for flowers to bloom with the snow still on the ground. The first of April he and I had the experience of being alone in the house with each other. We enjoyed a week of it. It was the first and almost the last time we were by ourselves in The Ledge home.}

{On April 14 there was a University Faculty meeting at which it was decided to keep faculty representatives on the Board of Trustees. Mr. Comstock was greatly pleased.}

On April 17th the first part of the *Introduction to Entomology* was published. This deals with the structure and metamorphosis of insects. It was published separately so that it could be used in the Cornell laboratory. We were very glad to have it in print, but I knew {Mr. Comstock}, when looking at it, felt the urge to complete the second part, which meant much more work.

The last of April I went to New York a guest of Dr. and Mrs. Thro. {However}, my business there was giving lectures before the Brooklyn Teachers Training School, the New York Teachers Training School and at the Brooklyn Botanic Garden. {Later I was a guest of Miss Ellen Eddy Shaw.} From New York I went to Providence, R. I., where I lectured before the students of the Rhode Island Normal College and was the guest of Professor and Mrs. W. G. Vinal. {There was a reception for me where I met many interesting people, and it was a joy to be in the Vinal family. It seemed to me that the Vinals were rearing their two children, a boy and a girl, in an ideal manner. Responsibility was the key note to the training and the results were noteworthy.} It was while here that Dr. Vinal talked to me about the value and convenience of loose-leaf notebooks for nature study. I came home enthusiastic over the idea and Will Slingerland[10] thought well of the plan and this was the beginning of our extensive {and various} loose-leaf series, which now are printed in many thousands every year.

{On my return from Providence I stopped at New York to attend the wedding of Winifred Jelliffe to Alfred Emerson. It took place in the evening, at the home of Dr. Smith Ely Jelliffe and was an interesting experience. It was a pleasure to me to see two of my dear youngsters so happy, and the gathering was notable. I remember I had an interesting visit with William Beebe, with whom Alfred and Winifred were to go to the biological station in British Guinea [sic] that summer. It was through this association with Mr. Beebe that Alfred first became interested in termites; he is now a world authority on the group.}

{We were having many pleasant outings this spring in Jim's car and he often took us to the movies. Having him with us gave us many diversions we had never dreamed of before and which we found recuperative as well as pleasant.}

{The last of May President David Starr Jordan was our guest for three days. He did not seem well, but he gave a fine and spirited address at the convocation hour before the whole University. Never had he taken his whole audience with him more wholly than on this occasion.}

{On June 4th there was a "get-together" of the staff and families of the College of Agriculture. There were 500 present, counting the children, who were given a separate and fitting entertainment. I was one of the after-dinner speakers and my subject was "The geological record of the Cornell College of Agriculture," in which I described the different strata in its development. Mr. Comstock said I did "very well," which was high praise from my husband.}

{On June 9th the Campus Club gave a farewell reception to our dear and beautiful Mrs. Schurman. She was given a silver inkstand and scroll on which were inscribed our appreciation of her and the names of all of us. I was asked to make the presentation speech which was not difficult as I had only to speak from my heart.}

{A few days later, the Faculty gave a reception to President and Mrs. Schurman and presented them with a silver service. Mr. Comstock was chosen to make the presentation address. It was a difficult task for Mr. Comstock to make such an address; he always worked long and hard in preparing for

10. Manager of the Comstock Publishing Company.

such occasions. I think this is the reason that he always spoke so well and consequently was invited to speak again, as occasion arose. However, he was glad to speak on this occasion, for perhaps no one else in the Faculty had watched more closely the progress and successes of President Schurman's administration.}

{On June 10th a dinner was given at the Aurora Street Methodist Church attended by women of town and University for the purpose of starting a drive for a Woman's Building which should serve as a Community House, a decided step forward in the social welfare of our city.}

{I remember the June meeting of the Trustees of Hobart and William Smith College as being a very discouraging one. There were deficits past and present that were perplexing and discouraging.}

Mr. Comstock was hard at work on the second part of the *Introduction to Entomology* and I had been writing articles for the *Compton's Young People's Encyclopedia*. Our writing was the thread on which our days were strung despite a thousand interfering activities.

{The Commencement was overshadowed by the imminent departure of the Schurmans. Soon after Commencement Professor Gage took Mr. Comstock and myself in his car to visit Dr. and Mrs. R. C. Turner and his parents, Henry and Mary Turner in Oswego. It was a very pleasant experience. It was especially gratifying to see the tender care which Raymond Comstock Turner lavished on his parents. Dr. Raymond made dentistry an art as well as a profession and it was a pleasure to the two professors to talk with him about the great development of this branch of medical practice. We were very fond of him and his able and beautiful wife.}

{Again I taught in the long summer term. I had among my pupils three ex-soldiers, all suffering more or less shell-shock. Again, I was made to feel keenly the horrors of war when I saw the struggle of these young men to recover the use of their minds and nerves. The fact that they were plucky and uncomplaining made it seem all the harder.}

{Harry Knight came back to Cornell this June and brought his bride with whom we all promptly fell in love. It made us very happy to find that he had chosen so wisely.}

{This summer our dear Margery Smith wanted to vacation, so we boarded with Miss Ada Georgia in the house now owned by the K. K. G. sorority. It was convenient to our home; Miss Georgia always set an attractive and bounteous table and our fellow guests were interesting. It was there that we experienced a new respect for the South African students who were sent to Cornell on scholarships that netted about $1,000 a year. The slump of the pound sterling rendered these scholarships worth just about one third of that amount and the boys found themselves marooned, in a way. They all had the English prejudice against manual labor as a gentleman's activity. However, they had seen plenty of American fellows working their way through college by waiting table, and they discarded their prejudices and helped serve Miss Georgia's guests. They did their work well and we felt they had thus proven their real strength of character and manhood. One of them, a charming youth, confessed to me that he hoped his people at home would never know of it because "they couldn't understand."}

{I had large classes in the summer session and in the middle of the term I was sent to the sanitarium with bronchitis. Luckily Dr. E. Lawrence Palmer was here, and he carried the work for two weeks with the other assistants. It seemed absurd to have bronchitis in the summer.}

{In August}, after the summer term of 1920, Mr. Comstock and I sat for our portraits in Professor [Olaf] Brauner's studio. We had always been appreciative of Professor Brauner's portraits because of excellent likeness as well as artistic rendering. {We had in mind the Comstock Memorial Library, when it should be properly housed, as an eminently proper place for the portrait[11] of the two of us together and the finished picture is thus disposed of in our wills.}

{We had dreaded the monotony of the sittings, but we did not know the habits of the Brauners then. We were never tired or bored. Professor Brauner had mastered the duplex ability to talk of interesting things while carefully putting the paint on canvas. Moreover, every afternoon Mrs. Brauner came usually with a hot or cold concoction to drink, depending on the temperature of the day. We had always found her pleasing socially, but now we appreciated her wit and her charm and originality as never before. Often their friend and guest, Miss Inge, came with Mrs. Brauner or to dispense refreshments in her stead. My friend, Marian Provost, was visiting us, and often she went to the studio and read aloud for the entertainment of painter and painted. Mr. Comstock declared that the whole experience of twenty days was a social affair, delightful and entertaining. We both think the portraits excellent although Mr. Comstock thought I should have worn my glasses instead of carrying them. He also had grave doubt about the propriety of having a cigar in his hand; but to those who know him, that is a most natural touch. Even Professor Gage, who despises tobacco, declared that it made the portrait seem "truly Comstockian" and so he approved.}

---

11. At the time of the publication of the 1953 edition, according to Herrick, the portrait hung in the main reading room of the University library. At the time of the publication of this book the portrait now hangs in the atrium of Comstock Hall. —KSt.

{I never saw Mr. Comstock smoke until after he was forty years old, although he had done so on some special occasions. However, in his latter years he was very dependent on cigars for comfort and happiness. He likes a light cigar (Bobbies, usually) and smoked one after each meal and often an extra one in between. When we were invited to luncheon or dinner where there were no smokers, he suffered from tobacco hunger and always made excuses to get away early. As soon as we were outside the door he would say "Gad! But I want a smoke!" and he would hasten to light a cigar. I had thought it a benefit to him to smoke in moderation; he was high-strung and active, and tobacco soothed him, and I am sure he never suffered injury from its use. Even had it done so, I am sure the comfort of smoking would have compensated many times over for any injury he may have suffered.}

{In September 1920 we had a real vacation. Our dear son took us and Margery Smith in his car for an Eastern trip. We went through the Catskills and these mountains seemed more attractive than ever. We stopped at Wethersfield, Connecticut, long enough for me to visit the library and read about my remote ancestor, Nathaniel Foote and pay my respects to his monument. He came from England about 1630 and was one of the founders of Wethersfield. I was his descendant of the 9th generation. We went on to Providence, R. I., where Mr. Comstock's ancestor, Samuel Comstock settled at about the same period. But Mr. Comstock wasn't a bit interested in his ancestors, so we did not stay to look up his records.}

{I shall never forget the road from Hartford to Providence. It leads through a wilderness practically uninhabited. There were a few cabins that bore every evidence of belonging to pioneers, although they probably did not. There was a desolation in the landscape that was far more depressing than the actual desert.}

{From Providence we drove on to Provincetown and settled ourselves in lodgings for a week. Here we could study this ancient town at our leisure, and every day we visited some point of interest on the famous Cape Cod. When it rained, and evenings, we read aloud from Thoreau's Cape Cod Journal or from Joseph Lincoln's books. One day we had a voyage on the sailboat True Blue, with Captain Lewis. It was enjoyable but rough; I remember that the captain shipped seas down Mrs. Smith's back on one exciting tack.}

{We had rented our quarters for a week but, when our frugal landlady told us that six days made a week in Provincetown, we fared forth on the evening of the sixth and stopped at Chatham a day or two whence we drove out to gaze at Joseph Lincoln's residence. Our landlord had been in school with Lincoln and said that, even as a boy, he wrote stories. We had delightful drives each day around the coast, visiting the old towns until we felt saturated with Cape Cod's natural environment and civilization. The memory of it has been a distinct asset for happiness.}

{On our way home, we stopped by Plymouth and made the pilgrimage proper to Americans who reverence their forebears. Our days were leisurely and very enjoyable. We were equipped to serve excellent lunches from our lunch basket, so we did not have to time ourselves to be at a hotel at any set hour, when meals were served, and this made us carefree. Every day brought interesting experiences. New England scenery has the fascination of intimacy. Each turn in the road brings an attractive view that is near by and your very own.}[12]

{During this autumn we had a renaissance of going to football games in our new stadium, of course, owing to Jim, his car and his influence. Mr. Comstock went only occasionally but I became what Jim termed "a regular fan." I was thrilled with the plays and I always enjoyed the scene; the setting of the stadium is so beautiful.}

{Miss Ruth Putnam was our guest for a time in November. Her presence in our home was always a happiness to us. We were very proud of her achievements in the field of historical research and writing but our affection for her was what made her a welcome guest.}

On November 19th there was a great get-together of the entire faculty and their families in the great armory. This was due to the enterprise of our Acting President and his wife, Mr. and Mrs. Albert Smith. It was a revelation to us all. I am sure none of us had realized how large Cornell had grown. There were 2200 persons present. The psychological effect was marked; a new pride and esprit de corps was engendered by this realization of the bigness of our University and we were all of us grateful to "Albert and Ruby" for giving us this experience. {We all said, "Isn't it just like them to do this!"} I doubt if there had ever been a man connected with Cornell who was loved by so many Cornellians, both students and professors, as Albert Smith. His radiantly beautiful wife, although she had not been with us so long as he, was a joy to our eyes and a treasure socially.[13]

{It was during this December that a violent attack upon co-education was made by certain students, backed by one or two trustees and possibly by some in the faculty. There have always been a few at Cornell who resented the presence of women, and these outbreaks occur now and then. Among other statements was the preposterous assertion that co-education was

12. Mrs. Comstock's manuscript page 17–33 removed at this point. —KSt.

13. This paragraph is out of order chronologically in the 1953 edition and is an example of the muddled time line in the book. —KSt.

a failure in all Western colleges and universities. Mr. Comstock and I had recently visited seven of these where co-education was so perfectly successful that no one thought anything about it. It was during this controversy that I had the pleasure of meeting Mr. Leonard K. Elmhurst, then a student in our College of Agriculture, and who later married the widow of Willard Straight. Mr. Elmhurst was indignant at the attack on the women students and wielded efficient cudgels in the fight. This was especially appreciated from an Englishman and an Oxford man. However, he was an exceptional Englishman as he believed in the worth and dignity of manual labor and practiced his ideals on occasions.}

{Mr. Comstock was working steadily on the second part of the Introduction to Entomology and had to spend much time with his artist, Miss [Mary] Mekeel, getting the right kind of illustrations selected and made; this is always a laborious process.}

{The last Sunday in December before the University closes for the holidays is always crowded with student functions. I note that on December 1920, I attended a reception at the Theta Delta Chi house and later a supper at the Delta Upsilon lodge and later a Christmas party for Kappa Alpha at the beautiful home of Mr. and Mrs. Louis P. Smith, certainly a busy day.}

{The meeting of the American Association for Advancement of Science met this week after Christmas in Chicago. Mr. Comstock could not spare the time and energy to go, so I went with Cousin Glenn Herrick. The Nature Study Society of America met on December 28th and the session was most satisfactory. That evening occurred the dinner of the society at the Atlantic Hotel which was a very enjoyable occasion. Professor Elliott Downing had charge of the affair and that ensured its success.}

{While in Chicago I visited Professor and Mrs. Paul Shorey. Mrs. Shorey had been one of our dear student friends when she was at Cornell. Beautiful, fascinating, and more than all, interesting, this little Quaker mowed a wide swath socially at Cornell. I shall never forget George Burr's amusement when in dulcet tones she exclaimed "Thee bet thy boots!" I found the Shorey home individual and attractive and soon discovered Mrs. Shorey had lost none of her fascinating, complex simplicity, nor her beauty and charm. I had the pleasure of meeting there Professor Mary A. Jordan of Smith College and Mary Hastings Bradley, the novelist. However, I was especially interested in my host whom I had never before chanced to meet. Dr. Paul Shorey, as an eminent scholar of the classics, had firmly refused to be shelved by our modern, hustling, practical civilization. A valiant reactionary with a pungent pen, a penetrating wit and an eloquent tongue, he has done his share in making us stop and think whither we are bound (or rather, bounding). Although small of stature he is in appearance the ideal of a college professor; more or less careless as to the dress, winning and clever in conversation, scathing in his criticisms, he certainly fulfilled my preconceived idea of the man who could win Emma Gilbert. I have been very grateful to him since for his defense of American ideals, as against those who belittle our great men, and sneer at patriotism.}

{There were many meetings of the trustees to decide upon a President for Cornell. As George Tansey was on the Board we saw much of him as he was usually our guest, while he was in Ithaca. He came to a meeting early in January [1921] and I remember well one evening when Dean Edwin Woodruff came to dinner. The two always made the conversation breathlessly interesting.}

{On January 8th Miss Ada Georgia died. She was a remarkable character. She suffered hardships all her life and her indomitable spirit carried on despite them. She was a passionate lover of books, a keen observer of nature, and an indefatigable worker. She had been my greatly prized assistant in conducting the Home Nature Study Course for eight years. Her devotion to the work and loyalty to me had made her an important factor in my life and a valued friend.}

{On January 11, we celebrated Founder's Day with dinners as usual. The Cornell Alumnae had theirs in the Domestic Science Hall and we had the great pleasure and honor of having with us Miss Mary Cornell, the daughter of our Founder. The Alumni had their dinner at Risley Hall. Mr. Comstock and Mr. Gage attended as usual.}

{There had been established by professors and instructors in Science a Research Council. Usually it met at dinner and discussion followed. Mr. Comstock was a member and enjoyed going to the meetings. He found the influence of the Council stimulating and believed that it was a positive asset to the University.}

{We were experiencing some of the after-horrors of the war. We had had as a fellow traveler in Sicily a lady of wealth and culture from Vienna. Now she wrote asking me for food checks, saying that the people who possessed a competency before the war were now suffering for want of food. The poor were fed but the people of the better class went hungry. Of course, we responded. At the same time Mr. Comstock was, with others, contributing to send food checks to that truly great man of science, Dr. Anton Handlirsch, he who was made president of the International Entomological Congress at Oxford in 1912. It was heart-breaking to think of such people suffering for food. Verily we in America knew little of the privations following war.}

{In January we had the pleasure of entertaining at breakfast our friend, Dr. Theobald Smith, who was staying with Professor Gage. In his student days this brilliant scientist was a pianist of skill and feeling. It was a privilege to listen to his interpretation of the best music and also his own rare improvisations. It was with sorrow that we learned that owing to rheumatism he had been compelled to stop playing. However, he has retained all of the beauty of character and spiritual sensitiveness which characterized his youth. Science, if followed worthily, keeps alive all the youthful best in its devotees.}

{It was during 1921 that the Alumni drive for money, to help Cornell finances, was completed. The Cornellian Council had a notable meeting on January 22. The President of the Council, Mr. and Mrs. Walter Cook, of Buffalo, gave a little reception for us at the Forest Home Inn that evening. Mr. and Mrs. J. DuPratt White were there and many others. The Council had been greatly invigorated by the drive and really, from the first, it had been a steadfast help to the University finances.}

On January 27th I gave my last lecture before the class of regular students of Cornell. I gave it in the old Insectary, that place of so much excellent scientific work, and so much happiness of teaching and writing. My class had always been appreciative and teaching, therefore, had been a joy to me. This last day in the dear old place gave me the shock that always comes when one realizes that things end as well as begin in life.

{On January 20th we were invited to the Telluride House to dinner to celebrate Professor George L. Burr's sixty-fourth birthday. It was a gala occasion and there was an immense cake with sixty-four candles on it for dessert. George was much appreciated by the young men of the Telluride and was very happy in their companionship.}

{We had some interesting women who talked to us at Cornell this year. Senora Olivie Rosetti Agresti gave a lecture on her family (Rosettis) and the pre-Raphaelite movement in England. Even more interesting was another talk she gave on the International Institute of Agriculture in Rome and the efforts of the Italians to come back after the war. She praised the Fascisti influences that saved Italy from chaos financially; she did not stress Mussolini, as I remember, at that time, he was simply a leader of his party.}

{Miss Caroline Wood, daughter of that fine Quaker, James Wood, of Mt. Kisco, had been active in the Friends' Relief in feeding the starving children of Germany and Austria. She came to Cornell in February and gave an evening lecture on the work accomplished. She is a fine woman and was most convincing in her talk. She said what was true, "The Quakers will not make war, but they will work hard and long to mend the ravages of war." My mother used to say when people exclaimed, "When will wars cease!" "wars will cease when all peoples become Quakers." Certainly no one might say her nay.}

{During Farmers' Week, Charlotte Kellogg came and gave an eloquent and moving address on conditions following the war, especially in Belgium. She had been the only woman on Hoover's staff and her experiences were with actual situations. She was our guest, but was physically exhausted when she arrived so that I put her to bed at once. She was to pay for her experiences with the famine-stricken peoples by a long illness later. However, I know that if she had known this was coming it would not have deterred her from doing as she did. Charlotte is one of those people who live "up to the hilt" every day and the deeper the experiences the better. She is a beautiful woman, physically and spiritually, and it was always a joy to us that our beloved Vernon had won such a wife, so truly a mate. While she was with us we took her to a large dinner at the University Club where President Schurman found opportunity to make her acquaintance.}

{During this Farmers' Week we had the pleasure of having with us for a little time our dear friend Charles Tuck, who had returned from an interesting agricultural experience in Manchuria.}

{On February 24th occurred Mr. Comstock's 72nd birthday. He felt like celebrating because he that morning finished the chapter on Homoptera[14] for the *Introduction to Entomology*, and a difficult chapter he had found it. Professors Gage and Burr surprised him by coming to dinner and Mrs. Smith had made a cake beset with 72 candles, so that it seemed a real birthday celebration and he was happy all day.}

{I had a class in Nature Study this semester in the Teacher's Training Class in the Ithaca High School. I had carried on this work for some years and had made many pleasant friends through it.}

{The department of Rural Education in Cornell had grown space under the administration of Professor George Works and it was making itself felt in the State. However, I was the only one who worked in the Ithaca Schools, for some mysterious reason. There were so many in the Department now that the faculty wives belonging to it had luncheons together quite often, always at the home of one of us. It has always been an interesting group and I enjoyed belonging to it.}

{On March 22nd I had the honor of giving an address on Henry David Thoreau before the Phi Beta Kappa chapter at Cornell. It was a fine and appreciative audience and I enjoyed talking about this somewhat misunderstood

14. Footnote at bottom of the manuscript (p. 17–41) by Herrick: "Homoptera, an order of insects with 4 clear and similar wings,—aphids, scale bugs, cicadas, et al. —Ed."

naturalist. My thesis was that he was intrinsically a naturalist and his philosophy was incidental to his environment in Concord, that home of transcendentalism.}

{On April 11 came the news of the death of Mrs. Bennie [Benedict] Law. Mr. Comstock went to Collins to attend her funeral and to be of such comfort as possible to his dear classmate. She too had been his intimate friend since her college days, and her passing meant a sorrow and a loss in my husband's life.}

{This Spring, Thornton Burgess came to Ithaca, and making his acquaintance was an event to me. I had been greatly interested in his Bedtime Stories as they dealt wholly with animals and birds and were dramatic and interesting. I found him a man simple, modest, and with charming manners. He told me that, while he made his animals talk, he tried to represent their habits truthfully; and that he had them illustrated as wearing clothes in order to create in the child an interest in the animal as an individual. This showed his understanding of children who are not interested in masses or abstract ideas, but always in the individual. He spoke in one of our theaters in the afternoon and it was packed with children. They listened with breathless interest to his talk and answered his questions vociferously. I said to him afterwards, "Mr. Burgess you are our literary Pied Piper;" and this is true, for he has enthralled the children of the United States with his stories. It is a great asset to the conservation of our natural resources to have the children of our land interested in the wild life in such a chummy and intimate manner.}

{Mr. Comstock broke his vow about lecturing again and spoke before a club in Rochester at the request of friends. However, it was becoming more and more difficult for him to lecture, all his energies being absorbed in his investigations and writings.}

{Our Chinese students in the University gave an interesting performance,—a short play and other stage acts for the benefit of the Chinese famine fund. The attendance was good, the entertainment excellent and a considerable sum was realized.}

{In May we had the pleasure of a little visit from Leland Howard. George Tansey was with us at the time and the two were vastly entertaining guests. We felt a personal pride in Leal Howard's success in the position which Mr. Comstock once held. We realized that his social charm and keen wit had been an important element in his success. All his great staff of employees were devoted to him, enjoying his company as well as respecting his knowledge and ability.}

{Mr. Comstock had to give a good deal of time to the committee meetings that had to do with the election of a president for Cornell. In May he went to Chicago with the committee to interview possible candidates. He found it a discouraging undertaking. College presidential timber of good quality seemed scarce.}

{On May 19 occurred the annual dinner of Sigma Xi. Professor Gage was the toast master and a good one; Mr. Comstock and I were proud of him. He did not speak unless he had something to say that he believed in; he spoke tersely and stopped when he was through, so what he said made an impression.}

{I had become an honorary member of an interesting student girl organization, the L. O. V. Club. The members were the students who were working their way wholly, or mostly, while in college. Their motto: "Labor Omnia Vincit" gave them the name L. O. V. Dr. Edith Matzke, our first regularly appointed woman physician in the college, had initiated the society. It accomplished a good work, for it established an esprit de corps and a feeling of support and companionship among the girls. They also formulated rules and prices for labor in homes, in consultation with some of the women of the faculty. I was happy to have this contact with these students and at least one meeting a year was held at our home. The first time I had the pleasure of entertaining the L. O. V. girls was May 26, 1921. This organization was active for six years and then lapsed for some reason, probably because of Dean Georgia White's plan to establish one of the outside houses as a home for the working students.}

{It was our habit to have a meeting of the Jugatae at our home once or twice a year. We usually had the spring meeting late enough so that our garden would be in bloom. This year's meeting occurred on June 6th, and a Russian, Mr. Boradin, spoke. We always served punch on the piazza as people came in, so that the meeting would start refreshed. Since Mr. Comstock's retirement the Jugatae was almost the only means he had for meeting the students in Entomology and he usually attended the meeting at 4:30 Monday afternoons. He always sat at about the middle of the second row from the front on the south side of the entomological lecture room. Often Dr. Needham sat with him. He always gave close attention to the program and was always pleased when he heard a senior or graduate student give a clear account of his research problems.}

{I find an interesting note in my diary for June 15. It gives a fair idea of the velocity which characterized our life. "I have an attack of bronchitis and to this I owe an experience I have longed for in vain, during the past ten years. I spent the entire day sitting in the garden. The California poppies and the crimson ramblers filled my foreground with color, and the sky was glorious. Many birds came to drink and bathe in the bird fountain. It was a day near to the garden's heart."}

{After Commencement I went to Camp Kiaora on Lake Morey at Fairlee, Vt. where I joined the staff of Dr. Vinal's school for Camp Councillors [sic]. The work lasted for a week and was interesting and valuable. Dr. Vinal knew by experience that Nature Study in summer camps must be conducted as an activity in competition with other camp activities. Just the idea of study of any sort was repellant to children who had been in school during the years. It was an inspiration of Dr. Vinal's to rechristen Nature Study for camps and call it "Nature Lore," an intriguing title. I met interesting people during the week including Mrs. Edward Gulick whose Aloha camp was near by, and Miss Margaret Cornell, a teacher in the Day School at Winnetka, Illinois. Of our teaching staff I especially remember Professor C. P. Sinnott of the Bridgewater, Mass. Normal School and Mr. Carl E. Rankin of Camp Hanoun, Thetford, Vt.}

{A matter of more moment than we suspected at the time} occurred this summer. Mr. Comstock had always kept in touch with the Turner family at Oswego; however, we knew next to nothing of the great grandchildren of "Pa Lewis."

I had received a letter from Margaret, daughter of Joel Turner, Jr., stating that she had graduated from the Oswego Normal and was interested in nature study and asked my advice. I invited her to come to the summer school and live with us, as a daughter in the family. She came, a shy quiet girl, very good-looking with exquisite complexion, perfect teeth and fair hair with a glint of red in it. She was {very} earnest and studious and found her niche in the family life. Her "Uncle Harry," as she always called Mr. Comstock, had been a tradition in her family and she regarded him with loving reverence. Soon there grew up between them a very sweet and beautiful companionship which developed in a matrix of silence. She sat in his room to study or read and would never speak {a word} unless he spoke first. This gave him a sense of having some one near, but who never interrupted his work or thought.

{Mrs. Jennie Farnham came with her three daughters and son again for the summer and as usual added much to our social good times. Mrs. Farnham was matron in the Kappa Alpha Theta Sorority House.}

{Our summer class was very large, and the teaching was strenuous; Jim was one of my assistants as usual. His presence in the house brought us many happy experiences, for he put himself and car at our disposal almost every evening. We had picnic suppers at secluded and beautiful places three or four times a week. We went often to the movies and had a really festive season. Marvin Herrick often joined our party and we often took with us our dear Agnes and Mary Fowler.}

{A great sorrow fell upon us and the community when Colonel Barton died. He was beloved by all and he had accomplished a great work in the R. O. T. C. during and after the war. He was at height of his usefulness and beneficent influence, a man of physical beauty that was transcended by his spiritual beauty.}

On August 12th I gave my last lecture as active Professor in Cornell. It seemed to me then a greater occasion that it really was. My class was most appreciative and presented me with $25.00 in gold "to buy books," a gift I greatly appreciated and used as directed. {Professor Gage, Mrs. Margery Smith, Miss Hill, and Mr. Comstock all came to the lecture, so I was quite excited myself. Mr. Comstock never enjoyed hearing me lecture, he was so on pins and needles for fear I wouldn't do it right. However, on this occasion he was really pleased and that made me happy.}

{In September we had with us as guest Ellen Coit Elliott, wife of Dr. Orrin Leslie Elliott of Stanford. She had always been a delight to me since her girlhood. A poet and an artist with broad vision and an intriguing outlook on life, she is one who makes all the lives in contact with hers more worth while.}

{September 8th was a fateful day for it was the last day that our dear Margery Smith reigned over our household. For seventeen years she had had all the responsibility of running the house and managing the help and the finances devoted to food. For some years her well-to-do children had wished her to stop work and enjoy some leisure, but she loved us and was loyal and said she would stay until I retired from active teaching, and this time had arrived. It was an interesting instance of conditions in America, that long before we were able to own a car, her sons came to take her riding in their limousines. She had been with us until she was woven into the intimate family life. She had rejoiced with us and mourned with us and our interests had been her interests. Her good judgment and sympathetic understanding had made her a valued friend and such she will remain as long as we shall live.}

{To mitigate the parting} we started with Jim for a vacation trip through the Adirondacks to Ticonderoga, where we visited the Ethan Allen museum; for it was to this branch of the Allen family that Mr. Comstock's mother belonged. My mother's family came from Vermont and she knew several tales of Ethan Allen that are not in print. Considering Mr. Comstock's relationship to Ethan {I think I should make note of them}.

Ethan and a comrade were riding through the forest one day when a violent thunder shower occurred, and a tree was struck by lightning, a few rods ahead of them. Ethan exclaimed: "Well done! Now try that old pepperidge." The words were scarcely out of his mouth when the tree indicated was riven by a thunder bolt, at which Ethan came back with: "Now, damn ye—try old Ethan." It was said his companion immediately dropped behind the Colonel a safe distance, but nothing happened.

{It was well known that Ethan's wife made his life miserable by nagging him about his lack of orthodox belief. His so-called atheism was a scandal in the Puritan community and various means were essayed to frighten him into believing. It was known on one occasion that he was to return late at night from a journey on horseback, and a group of his neighbors arrayed themselves in sheets and after he had put his horse in the stable, they appeared before him single file in solemn procession. He stopped and observed them calmly and then said in a clear, firm voice, "Well, who are ye anyway? If ye are angels I am not afraid—for angels would hurt no one; if ye are men I am not afraid for old Ethan is not afraid of men; if ye are devils I invite you in to supper for I married your own sister."}

{From Ticonderoga we went to Burlington and across to Colebrook, N. H. where we called on my dear girlhood friend Etta Holbrook, at the Holbrook homestead. Thence we visited Dixville Notch which Mr. Comstock found almost as impressive as the Yosemite. Thence we went to Quebec. The forty miles from the U. S. Border took us through a rather bleak country where the farm houses were very poor and, but few school houses were in evidence. However, on almost every hill was a Catholic church, some of them ornate; and wayside shrines numerous. No two civilizations could be in greater contrast than that of Puritan New England and French Quebec. However, this day's journey remains in my memory as a picture of vast expanse of thickly wooded, rolling country, undulating to the far horizon flecked with shadows of the purest ultramarine.}

{Notwithstanding the experience we had achieved in visiting ancient cities of Europe, Quebec still seemed to us very old and picturesque. Of course, we drove out to Ste. Anne of Beaupre, and in wonder observed the vast array of old crutches discarded when the miracle of restoration occurred. Jim was skeptical as to Ste. Anne and I told him he had best be careful or he would be punished. On our way back Jim's car, which we had named "Daisy," commenced to toot hysterically and no cajoling would quiet her. It was really very funny but very exasperating to Jim, especially after I suggested it was a form of retribution imposed upon him by Ste. Anne. Certainly, he had to do penance on his knees and flat on his back before he could release a screw to disconnect the horn.}

{We put the auto on the boat that afternoon and took passage for Montreal. There was a full moon and that evening on the majestic river is one we have always remembered. Montreal is such a dignified conservative city that we have always found it interesting and very different from cities in the U. S. We were surprised to find there the very best and the most attractive cafeteria we had ever seen or patronized. Our home trip included a visit at Winthrop at Jim's home and Joe Indian Lake. His sister Mrs. Goodnow had been with us on the trip.}

{On our return home we found no Mrs. Smith to welcome us and take care of us. A student girl came to work and stayed to play—a student boy, now doubtless gaining eminence as a lawyer, waited table and helped with washing the dishes and, as we had Professor Gage with us, I had a family of seven to cook for. I had determined to get a firm hold on running the house before I tried to hire a cook and the only way to do this, was to do the work myself. Mr. Comstock aided and abetted me in effort and, as ever, Jim was a treasure. I found it very hard work, so many of the duties were elusive and I seemed to find getting ready to keep my family alive a permanent diversion.}

{Of course, I had many other things to do besides housework. I still edited the *Nature Study Review* and had many social duties. The worst of all came upon me when I was elected President of the Woman's Alliance of the Unitarian Church. The alliance had been waiting until I retired to elect me to this office, and of course I could not refuse. I had long ago discovered that being president of anything whatever was quite beyond my powers. I detested presiding at meetings and I never could learn parliamentary procedure, nor could I make committees work. I simply suffered all the year and the Alliance suffered with me. That whole year is a nightmare in my memory, even though I did finally master the household management, and had a dinner party every week to prove to myself that I could cook acceptably and, incidentally, to show off my handiwork to my friends. How my muscles ached for the first two months. I could hardly sleep nights I ached so with fatigue. However, this changed as I grew accustomed to the labor.}

{One thing I accomplished, I had established all the labor-saving devices of which I knew in the house. An electric washer, and ironer, became sisters to my electric dishwasher; and I inaugurated all the "saving" steps arrangements in the kitchen that were possible. My kind helper, Mrs. Blanche Leonard, who did the washing, became a friend to lean on in the kitchen when I was under stress. It is quite wonderful that all my life I have had such superior women to help me in my household.}

{On the forty-third anniversary of our wedding, October 7th, Jim took us to the Hermitage for the afternoon and that evening we went to Drinkwater's play, *Abraham Lincoln*, and found it superb so we felt we had celebrated the day in a truly satisfactory manner.}

{On October 20, President Farrand was inaugurated. It was a great day, but a rainy one. The search for a president had been long and arduous and Mr. Comstock had, at times, been thoroughly discouraged, as were others on the committee who had in charge the important duty to select a President for a great university. After Dr. Farrand was found there seemed to be no doubt in the minds of any of the committee that he was the right man, as the years which have followed have abundantly proven.}

{We were among those who dined at Risley, October 19, with the delegates from other institutions who had come to the inauguration. It was a pleasure to meet Dr. Max Farrand again, for we had known him at Cornell and Stanford. The inauguration took place in Bailey Hall, October 20, as rainy a day as ever occurred in Ithaca. The speeches were excellent and many of them to the point. After the exercises, there was a dinner in the old armory. It was impressive to look upon for there were many fine-looking men in academic regalia and there were fine speeches—too long, as usual on such occasions, meanwhile we were slithered o'er by fierce draughts induced by a mighty wind and came home suffering and weary. However, we were sustained and cheered by the fact that we had the very best president of any of the universities.}

{George Tansy was a guest in our home on this occasion and we had Leal Howard with him at dinner one evening. I felt considerable pride in this dinner which I prepared, although my crown roast pointed bony fingers toward all quarters of the heavens in a rather distracting manner.}

{On October 22nd there was a gathering of alumni and a luncheon in the old armory. Dr. Ernest Copeland of the class of '75 and Holand Russell, son of our dear Professor Russell, were there and we were very glad to see them. In the afternoon there was a football game, Colgate versus Cornell, which Cornell won to the great satisfaction of us all, as it would have seemed discouraging to greet our new President with a defeat. My memory of the game was of struggling masses of helmeted men showing against the sun shining over the western hills.}

{On October 26th, the Campus Club, 600 strong, welcomed our new President's wife at Sage College. Mrs. Farrand, we found very good to look at and very interesting to meet. She is tall, strikingly handsome with beautiful complexion and expressive eyes. Her manner is always cordial, and we were happy to have such a woman to preside over the social life of Cornell. She has been quite different from the wives of our former presidents, who gave their time and energies to the entertainment of the faculty and visitors such as special lecturers and exchange professors. She belongs to the new order and, except for one reception a year to the general faculty, has followed her own interests social and otherwise. She was, from the first deeply interested in our hospital in Ithaca and worked for its advancement financially and in other ways. She has developed beautiful gardens about the President's mansion and has been the moving spirit in a very successful garden club of which Mr. Comstock is a member. She has taken also an active interest in the Campus Club. She is brilliant and interesting in conversation, the two not being necessarily the same, for there is a brilliancy that repels.}

{After seven years of this administration I should say that President Farrand has been a wise and most excellent president. He has shown good judgment and has vision and a broad understanding of the needs of the University as a whole, and also of its parts, the faculty and students. In fact, we believe that he is the supreme university president in America today. However, owing to the great size of the University faculty when he came and to his many pressing duties, and also to a certain elusive quality in his personality and, owing to the individualism of Mrs. Farrand, these two have never been close to the hearts of the faculty as were President and Mrs. White and President and Mrs. Schurman. Of course, this was inevitable. Our former presidents and their families were associated with us as neighbors, when we were few in number. Now the University it like a city, and a disconcerting object upon which to place one's affections except as an abstract idea. The elusive quality in President Farrand which I have always felt may have had its origin in shyness, or because he is not physically strong, or it may be the slippery psychological coat of mail which physicians wear to protect themselves from the onslaughts on their feelings and sympathies; whatever its cause, it is effective in holding people at arms' length the while he meets them with charming courtesy and deference. It is undoubtedly an asset to executive efficiency.}

{From the first President Farrand has charmed his audiences with his addresses. His voice is clear, penetrating and most agreeable. He knows instinctively just the best possible things to say on all occasions and says them with perfect diction and in a manner that thrills his hearers, and brings keen satisfaction to the most cultured as well as those less fortunate among his hearers. He always knows just when to stop, to leave the best impression. Many of us have agreed that he is the best speaker we have ever heard and that is saying much.}

{Our home life was varied. Jim took us to the movies very often. Professor Gage took us in his car to Freeville to Sunday dinners. Our beloved Margaret Boynton Windsor spent a week with us. There were numerous dinners and luncheons at the University Club. Mr. Comstock was very sympathetic concerning my household labors. I remember he stopped his precious work and peeled pears for me to preserve and he often lent a helping hand in the most needed place. One of our pleasant social experiences was going to a "real dinner party" given by Dr. and Mrs. James Creighton; President and Mrs. Farrand, Dean and Mrs. F. H. Bosworth, and Mr. and Mrs. Charles Blood were among the guests. We had almost forgotten what a real dinner party was like during the war, so this seemed to seal the pact of peace in our minds.}

{As a specimen of my own days the entry in my line-a-day is illuminating. "An awful day! I did the housework and cooked three fairly eatable meals. I dictated letters for an hour this morning, gave a talk before the South Hill Parent-Teachers' Association this afternoon and later—[15]

---

15. The manuscript chapter ends abruptly at this point. There are no additional pages. —KSt.

Department of Entomology, circa 1913?

CHAPTER XVIII

The Toronto Meeting of the A. A. A. S. 1922. A surprising election and a voyage westward

The title of this manuscript chapter was originally crossed out and replaced, by co-editor Ruby Green Smith, to "The Last of Life" as well as changed to "Chapter XVII." In the 1953 edition of the book, this chapter is portioned by Glenn Herrick to construct "Chapter 19: 1921–1926: Tributes to Two Distinguished Scholars." This chapter is the last one used from the Comstock manuscript as Chapters XIX and XX of the manuscript were not included in the 1953 book. The reader will get a sense that Mrs. Comstock was elaborating on events recorded in her journal, or a datebook. As these documents do not exist, restoring this chapter gives us a close glimpse into her activities. As with the other chapters in this book the grammar and sentence structures are Mrs. Comstock's per her original manuscript.

The last week in December the A. A. A. S. met in Toronto. {There were many Cornellians on the train with us, for this meeting was expected to be particularly interesting. We had our room in Annersley Hall, Victoria College, of the University of Toronto. We had our meals in Burwash Hall, a refectory of the ancient regime, where there were benches on either side of the long tables instead of chairs. I think it must have been easy for the monks of old to contemplate spiritual things they had so few physical comforts to think about.}

{The campus of the university is large and the distance between buildings was such that one had to take a long walk to get anywhere as some one remarked. The buildings are fine and dignified. The meeting was well attended. On December 27th in the evening we went to hear} L. O. Howard's address as retiring President. {It was a fine, strong, memorable address and} we were very proud of him.

{On the evening of} December 28th a great surprise came to Mr. Comstock,—a dinner was given in his honor. It was held in Annersley House and there were sixty-nine present, many of them Mr. Comstock's {old} students and all of them {personal} friends. Dr. P. W. Claassen of Cornell had engineered the affair in a masterly manner, quite characteristic of this able young scientist. Dr. L. O. Howard. Howard presided most happily; his customary brilliancy {was} made cordial as well as scintillating by his love for Mr. Comstock. The speeches were all impromptu and {all} paid heartfelt tribute to my husband; and he, in turn, spoke with much feeling and delightfully. I think {Mr. Comstock} was happier over this absolutely unexpected honor than anything that had happened since his retirement. {The memory of it has always been a happiness to him.}

The entomological meetings were excellent. We listened to the scientific papers by many of our {old} students' and there was one new one among them in whom we took great interest, Miss Grace Griswold of Cornell, who made her first appearance before a scientific gathering on this occasion and did exceedingly well.

We were entertained in many interesting ways. There was a reception for us in the palatial Government house and a conversazione in the magnificent Hart House, the Student's Union of Toronto University. One evening there was a dinner given in the great hall of the Hart House to the women in attendance {at the A. A. A. S.} To my utter dismay I was seated at the table on the platform and was told that I must say something. I was seated next to {Mrs. Cockschutt}, the Governor's wife, {and} Mrs. J. B. Tyrrell, {President}. Lady Falconer made a good speech and so did several others. My heart had sunk to the very heels of my slippers and my mind seemed devoid of ideas. But when I was called upon, help came from above. I spoke of my childhood in Western New York and how Canada has been {ever} a purple line on my horizon beyond Lake Erie, and how I dreamed that it was a land of beauty and I had a happy ambition to visit it some time. {Now} I found it both beautiful and friendly, a sister country, all the conflict of a hundred years ago gone as I could well illustrate in my own family history. At the time of the American Revolution {one} Amos Botsford of my family, was a professor in Yale University, and remained loyal to England and was made the leader of the Tory migration to Canada after the war. For his loyalty, he was knighted, and a coat of arms found for him, a dove upon a shield. My grandfather, who fought in the {foolish} war of 1812, was so angry that a Botsford had thus acted that he disowned him {and his name was to him anathema}. Behold the change! Now the Band of Botsford,—all of whose members are United States citizens {good and} loyal, have proudly put on their stationery, as I have on mine, the dove and shield, the coat of arms won from King George by {their} Tory ancestor. This was greeted with cheers and laughter.

{On the evening of January 11, after our return to Ithaca, the Alumnae had a Founder's Day dinner in the Domestic Science Hall. The snow was deep and the drifts terrible to struggle through; but I was toast-mistress and Jim put his auto through and drove me through. The especial feature of our banquet was the presence of Miss Mary Cornell, daughter of our Founder.}

{After a few weeks more of doing my own housework I considered myself capable of running the house and so hired a cook and felt that again I had time to attend to things which I had neglected.}

{On Mr. Comstock's 73rd birthday he worked gaily all day and at night we celebrated by having the Herricks and Professor Gage for dinner. Mr. Comstock always celebrated holidays by working especially hard.}

{On February 28th we attended the first large reception given by our new President and his wife. The President's House had been changed beyond recognition. The heavy old wood-work had all been painted in light colors and the whole atmosphere transformed. I was glad. It would have seemed a sacrilege to see another man in the place of President White in his own house which was the dignified home of a scholar. Now the house was modern, all its rich tranquility gone,—just another pleasant, cheerful house.}

In March [1922] I was launched as a candidate for Alumni Trustee [of Cornell]. I was {very} reluctant to permit my name to be used for I did not wish to assume the responsibility of the trusteeship. {It seemed to me that} I had retired from active {work} and I wanted freedom from University cares. However, I was over-persuaded, but I was not elected. The next year, 1923, again I was persuaded to be guilty of the same folly, although I knew I would not be elected. The alumnae felt that I was the only woman graduate who stood any chance of election, and so I yielded, only to experience a second defeat but by a small margin. The majority of men graduates was so overwhelming that it seemed hopeless to try to elect another woman to the Board. However, Dr. Mary Crawford {has "gone one better." She was} defeated twice as a candidate and the third time won. {As for myself,} I was indignant that the men were so unfair toward {us} women, but I was {personally devoutly} thankful that I was not elected. I had already planned for some winters away from Ithaca and I did not wish to be tied down to the onerous work of a woman trustee. It was interesting and characteristic that I had the loyal support of the *Cornell Countryman* and the men graduates of the College of Agriculture,—{another instance of the breadth of view and lack of narrow prejudice of the students in this important college. The narrowness, snobbishness, bigotry and selfishness in Cornell have been characteristic only of urban students.}

{A social occasion that seemed important from the College of Agriculture standpoint took place. The Jugatae, which included the instructing staff and all advanced students in Entomology, gave Dr. J. G. Needham a supper in the big biology laboratory. There were about seventy people at the table. There was a huge cake with 54 candles blazing on it, for this March 18 was his 54th birthday. The speeches were witty and the whole affair a delightful one,—it had an influence on the morale of the department. Grace Griswold was the dea ex machine [*sic*] in carrying though the very excellent banquet itself. Mr. Comstock was very much pleased with the evidence of esprit du corps in his beloved department.}

{On March 19th I played a role never before allotted to me. I preached a sermon in the Unitarian church on "The naturalist's approach to God." I had always been associated with scientists who dealt reverently with God's truths and I believed that no one who had not studied some science was fitted to understand the greatness of the Creator. I think I made my point; at least Professor Gage and Jim who listened to me, assured me so.}

{It was during the month of March that my cousin Bertha Sanders, for many years the teacher of art in the Kent school at Summit, N. J., came for a visit, bringing with her many water-color paintings of the flowers of Hawaii. She had spent part of the previous year in these beautiful islands. The Department of Architecture gave us the use of their exhibition rooms and we let the public share with us the enjoyment of these gorgeous flowers. The weather was very bad but many came to the exhibit. This charming cousin's ambition, ideals and attainment in art had ever been a matter of pride to us.}

{On March 29 we gave our first real dinner party since the war, it was in the home of Miss Sanders; Dean and Mrs. F. H. Bosworth and Professor and Mrs. Louis Fuertes were our guests. It seemed like old times to have a dinner party and I am sure we enjoyed it as much as our guests.}

{One of Mrs. Farrand's earliest and energetic and beneficent enterprises was organizing the society of Cornell Dames. There had been a growing number of mothers and sisters and wives of Cornell students, living temporarily in Ithaca, who were at sea socially as they were not in the faculty or town circles. It was a fine idea to bring them together and perfect an organization which has filled a real want. I was asked to speak on Cornell as I had seen it develop, at this first meeting at Mrs. Farrand's. It has been a real pleasure to me to see that the Cornell Dames had frequent meetings and that they still carry on.}

{On April 18th Jim drove me to Geneva to a Hobart-Wm. Smith Trustee meeting. It was a perfect early spring day. The hills were ultramarine and the splotches of sunshine on them royal purple. The blossoms of the red maples were gleaming like rubies against the gray of the branches, and the willows were green and gold. However, the reason for mentioning this trustee meeting is that I had the pleasure of voting with the others to confer an honorary degree upon President Farrand.}

{On April 20–22, I attended the Cornell Alumni meeting in Chicago. I went, because it seemed my duty, considering the fact that I was a candidate for trusteeship. It was an interesting experience in many ways. Mrs. Vaughn Moody entertained the women in attendance at a supper at the Petit Gourmet restaurant and we had a thrilling evening, meeting old friends and talking over prospects. I remembered Mrs. Moody as a girl in college in 1876,—a beautiful girl with a most impressive and elegant manner. I knew something of the despairing struggle she had gone through in her first marriage, and of her happiness in her second marriage, and her devotion to her poet husband during his illness and her consecration to his memory since. She was still a stately woman and charming of manner. Would that youthful beauty might ever develop with such mature strength as hers.} President Farrand addressed us at the banquet {in the evening and pleased everyone. Cornell Alumni certainly know a good speaker when they hear one, and through} his remarkable gift in saying perfectly what he wishes to say, {he won the loyalty of Cornell very soon.}

On the train coming home I had a {remarkable} [talk with] Robert H. Treman, who felt deeply gratified that Cornell had finally acquired such a president. He had been on the committee for selecting a man for this position. Mr. Treman had been a member of my original class in college, 1878. I remember him as a handsome blonde boy very athletic and with a reputation for honest study, {and as an expert in baseball}. I remember well the {delightful} shock I received when {as a bride in Fall Creek Cottage}, he came with a man from his father's hardware store and set up a stove in the room {that was to be Gage's. He} was in working clothes and most business-like, and I {most sincerely} approved of the way he went into his father's business beginning at the bottom. He has certainly made good in whatever enterprise he has undertaken, {and they are many, and we are proud of his high achievements} and profoundly grateful to him for his more than generous efforts to make Ithaca beautiful.

{On May 15 we sold our beloved Hermitage to our cousin Glenn Herrick. We were finding it ever more difficult to spend enough time there to pay for keeping it up. As a matter of fact, since we had come to Roberts Place to live we felt less need for the Hermitage. We found the Ledge was much cooler in summer than was Fall Creek Cottage; as it is set in the edge of the wood and near Fall Creek, we had shade and water always close at hand. The birds too were here. The veery sang for us morning and evening and the wood thrush also; the redstart flitted about our trees, the vireos built their nests in our tiny woodland, and the orioles built in the elms by the road, many birds came for refreshment to our bird bath in the rose garden. Selling the Hermitage to those whom we loved made parting with it much easier.}

{On June 8th occurred the Ag. College annual picnic, which included the families and instructors. There were five hundred and sixty-five present. Professor Bailey talked to us and entertained us greatly with an account of a tragic journey he made to Chicago when he was a young lad. Although Professor Bailey had been away from the college all these years, its loyalty to him never flagged.}

{On June 13, Hobart College celebrated its one hundredth anniversary. It was a very impressive occasion. A hundred years of continued effort to educate the youth of America was surely a proud record.}

{For the Cornell Commencement we had as guests Dr. David Starr Jordan and George J. Tansey, two most delightful persons.}

On June 16th I was initiated into Phi Beta Kappa and was very pleased at the honor. {We} had need of this honorary society, which is broader in its {plan of} elections than Phi Beta Kappa or Sigma Xi, since it chooses its members from the classical, scientific, and vocational colleges. {The next day I was defeated as Alumni Trustee. I bore the defeat with equanimity, for I had expected it.}

{On June 21st, Jim graduated from the law school, a very important event in our family. His sisters and his friend Blanche Noble came to see him get his diploma and were our guests.}

{Directly after Commencement I went to Cape Cod to teach in the Camp Counselor School at Chequesset, the camp of Professor and Mrs. Vinal. It was a very interesting week. Professor E. H. Forbush, the State Ornithologist of Massachusetts, and Schuyler Matthews, the artist and naturalist, a courtly gentleman of the old school, Dr. Lovell of Providence, and Manley Townsend, a Unitarian minister who loved the out-of-doors, were on the instructing staff. It was a very busy week; there was something doing every hour from early morning to late evenings. I came away more convinced than ever of Dr. Vinal's greatness as a teacher and leader.}

{Margaret Turner came to us for the summer session, which gave us pleasure. My teaching this year was in the Forestry Building, Fernow Hall, and I felt like a cat in a strange garret. However, the work was well organized by Dr. E. L. Palmer and I had no laboratory responsibilities or field work. I lectured once a week to the large class and twice a week to my own special class in Nature Literature.}

{Mr. Comstock was working early and late on his *Introduction to Entomology*. On July 28th we entertained at an afternoon reception forty economic entomologists who were visiting Cornell and inspecting the work here. There were many fine young men among the guests as well as some old friends. Mr. Comstock enjoyed meeting them very much and felt encouraged for the future of Entomology.}

{We had a pleasant intimate social circle this summer, for Mrs. Jennie Farnham and her three daughters and son were at the Theta house, and we had frequent supper picnics with them, for the most part, in a field on Cayuga Heights that gave us a fine view of city and lake.}

{My cousin, Alice Graves, was our guest for several weeks, and when we did not go away for supper we took it in the little glade in our garden, with a feeling of living out-of-doors. We also had as a guest for a few days Gerald Stopp, the husband of my cousin, Catherine Bard. He was an actor and we found him altogether charming and lovable and rejoiced that he was a member of our family; he and Alice Graves were old friends.}

On September 4th, 1922, {Jim} began his law work in the office of Jared Newman and son. The fact that Jared Newman, Mr. Comstock's life-long friend, found place in his office for our boy gave us supreme satisfaction. Mr. Newman is a man of charming personality, of absolute integrity and of high ideals. It has meant much to Jim to be associated, at the beginning of his practice of laws, with a man like Jared Newman, {and he has responded sincerely to the influence. Although he has never been a partner in the firm, of Newman and Newman, his office has been in the same suite as theirs now for six years and he is devoted to Mr. Newman and a loyal and understanding friend of the son Charles.}

{The number of Chinese students had increased until now there was a colony of considerable size at Cornell. Early in September there was a convention of Chinese students from all American universities and colleges at Cornell. We attended the reception at Risley Hall and were greatly interested in these fine young men, who surely sometime will be of great use to their country. Mr. Comstock had several students from China in his department and had found their work excellent. Our dear friends, Alfred Sze' and his wife,[1] were attending the convention, and we were very happy to receive a call from them. We found Mrs. Sze a woman of charm and high intelligence; later, they brought their children to call on us, a fine brood which we were to know more intimately.}

1. Note from GWH at bottom of the manuscript page 18–12: "Sao-Ke Alfred Sze, Envoy Extraordinary and Minister Plenipotentiary from China to the United States."

{Just before college opened there occurred an incident quite characteristic of the Comstocks. We had had for many years a student to wait table and help in the house. This year we concluded we could not afford it, for we were living on Mr. Comstock's pension and a stipend from the sale of our books. Then a letter from Miss Ellen Eddy Shaw of the Brooklyn Botanic Gardens came saying she was giving a letter of introduction to us to a pupil of hers who must work his way through college. Suddenly one night just before supper, the boy arrived with no place to go, and evidently expecting to stay with us. We invited him to supper and discovered that he was partially deaf. He was a good-looking lad with perfect manners and, as I discovered, had no idea whatever of what he could do to earn his way. I held consultation with Mr. Comstock and Jim and we concluded it was our duty to keep him. He was with us all or a part of the time during his entire college course. He was very helpful to me in the house and to Mr. Comstock in the garden and we all learned to care for Jack Wille and are proud of his excellent record.}

On October 5th we attended the exercises of unveiling the tablet {that gave} the forestry building the name of Fernow Hall. Professor Ralph Hosmer had felt that this was a {simple} act of justice, but it took him a long time to get those in authority to see it as he did. Professor Fernow was {really} an eminent man and had done {a great work for} forestry in America. Some {of the people} at Cornell could not forget that his disregard of the desires of {some} wealthy people, who had summer homes in the Adirondacks, had cost Cornell the loss of the State College of Forestry. {His forestry was all right, but he was too independent.} He afterwards did a fine work for Canada, {and was at} the head of the Forestry Department at the University of Toronto {when he died}. His death occurred too early for him to know that Cornell had honored his memory. {However,} his wife, a {truly} remarkable woman, and his sons were present at the ceremony.

{This year Margaret Turner was with us taking her time away from teaching for a year of University work. Mr. Comstock was especially glad to have her for she belonged to him by tradition of her family. She gave Mr. Comstock silent companionship. She adored here uncle and loved to be with him and she is more like a daughter to him than any one of the many girls who have sat at his feet and worshipped.}

{This fall we did as much entertaining as Mr. Comstock's work would allow. We had people to dinner at least once a week. I gave a luncheon to the women of the Rural Education faculty; fifteen present. We had the Herrick family and Misses Mary and Agnes Fowler and Mary Hill for Thanksgiving dinner and Mr. Comstock decorated the table with chrysanthemums from his garden. We also had many delightful rides with Jim during the autumn.}

{On November 26th Jim and Gretel Schenck were betrothed; we were glad for we thought highly of her and we believed a young man should get married as soon as he was able to support a wife.}

{Padraic Colum came to lecture at Cornell at the invitation of our Cornell Women's Club. We had the pleasure of meeting him socially in the afternoon, and it seemed incumbent upon me to introduce him to the audience. This I did with simplicity and brevity that should have been an example to any other introducers present. The most tiresome experience in this world is to listen to a long and elaborate introduction of a speaker. We enjoyed this Irish writer very much, personally, he is charming and simple, a lovable man. His lecture was as charming as his personality; it consisted in part, of reading from his own writings.}

{After the middle of December, I suffered an attack of bronchitis which was most perturbing, because I had weighty responsibilities connected with the yearly meeting of the American Nature Study Association, which was to occur during the holidays at the meeting of the A. A. A. S. in Boston. However, on December 26th, Dr. Harry Bull and Mr. Comstock had a conference and I was to be allowed to go to Boston if someone could go with me. Jim was the only one free, so the burden fell on his shoulders and, as usual, he did his duty exceedingly well.}

{The meeting occurred on December 28 and was well attended, and very interesting. Professor Vinal was the deus ex machina and it was a great credit to his personality and executive ability.}

{The event of the meeting for me was a dinner given in my honor at the Belvue. There were fifty-four guests present. Professor Clarence Weed presided; among the speakers were Leal Howard and Vernon Kellogg, both of whom had turned down other invitations to be present at my dinner. Leal spoke in his usual brilliant and delightful manner and what he said of Mr. Comstock and myself made me happy. Vernon Kellogg's tribute to both Mr. Comstock and myself made me almost weep for happiness. This dinner was engineered by Dr. Vinal and I have always been profoundly grateful to him for giving me this pleasure.}

{When we arrived home, Dec. 30th, we found Mr. Comstock had as his guest Alexis Babine, our Russian friend of thirty years standing. After his graduation at Cornell in 1891 Alexis had been Librarian of Indiana University and, later, was assistant-Librarian at Stanford University, and, still later, had charge of the Slavic Section in the Library of Congress. He had been called back to Russia by the fatal illness of his mother and was there when the great war broke out in 1914. He was made Professor of English in the University of Saratov and remained there through the Revolution and all that followed. The Bolshevik authorities made him interpreter to a section of the American Famine Relief. After this work was ended, Professor George L. Burr received a letter from him asking help to get back to the United States. All of his Cornell friends, including Professor Charles Hull and Mr. Comstock, joined in the effort and he finally escaped. A minor position in the library of the Cornell College of Agriculture was offered him and he came to us and remained our guest for two months. He is a man of high ideals, of broad culture with absolute integrity, and has a striking and interesting personality. He had written a two-volume history of the United States in Russian, which had shown so clearly the problems of a republic, that it had been printed uncensored in Russia during the reign of the Czar. This work has been reprinted by the Soviets.}

{Mr. Babine had always kept his manner of living simple while in the United States and had accumulated enough to support himself comfortably in Russia when he went there in 1911. He had lost all his money under the Soviets and had to begin life over again. He was so relieved to get away from Russia, that he was only too glad to have the chance to begin over again. The tales he told us of the horrors of the Bolshevik regime will remain with us as long as we shall live. He was soon advanced to a good position in the Cornell Library but later was called to his old position as head of the Slavic Section in the Library of Congress.}

{I relapsed into bronchitis again after the Boston experience and was worthless as a wife, mother, housekeeper, and hostess for some weeks.}

{Mr. Comstock working steadily at his writing and celebrated his 74th birthday by working longer and harder than ever, a celebration that gave him great satisfaction. His appreciation of gaieties for celebrations of birthdays had never been developed.}

{I note that on March 5th Mr. Comstock brought me a Christmas rose which had budded when covered with snow. He had taken great interest and pride in his small bed of this hardy flower. He loved the flowers of his garden in a personal way that was, to me, most interesting. He said this early flower he thought would help him reach a haven, for he was floundering in an ocean of hymenopterous literature at the time and usually spent eight hours a day at his desk. I think the Christmas roses must have helped him, for he finished ants and turned to saw-flies two weeks later.}

{Whether I had bronchitis or not, I had to prepare copy for the *Nature Study Review,* a task that was inexorable and always at hand. Although my interest in the magazine never lagged, my grit in doing the work sometimes weakened.}

{The middle of April I had a wire from Vernon Kellogg asking me to come to the National Convention of Girl Scouts and as a guest of Mrs. Hoover. I went and had an interesting experience. I never before spoke under such circumstances. I was to stress the nature lore possibilities and advantages when carried on in the Scout camps. There was no place on the regular program for this talk, so when members of the convention went to Mount Vernon I talked to one half of them going, and some one else to the other half. On the return trip we exchanged halves, and really it was quite satisfactory. I greatly enjoy seeing Mt. Vernon again and I found these women altogether delightful.}

{There was a great dinner at Woodman Park hotel on the evening of April 26th. To my great joy I was seated next to Vernon Kellogg. Mrs. Hoover presided, and Mr. Hoover and Mr. Kellogg made very good speeches. It was a great satisfaction to me to see the kind of people who were interested in the girl scout movement.}

{After my return home we had a family celebration when Jim passed his last bar examination and was a full-fledged attorney and councillor at Law. This occurred on May 3, 1923.}

On May 6th {he took me to church and afterward we bought the Sunday edition of the} New York Times. {I opened it casually and as Jim said, I "faded out" with sheer amazement. The Times} said I had been {elected} one of the twelve greatest women in America by the League of Women Voters. I not only declared but believed it was a mistake and that some more famous Comstock woman was meant. {I thought probably Dean Comstock of Smith College was the one, and calmly went my way.}

However, the next day the fact of my election was made clear {and I was thus honored}. I found {later the idea in} the election was to choose women in different fields who had helped and influenced most persons, and I was chosen from the Natural History field. Martha Van Rensselaer was chosen from the Domestic Science field. She was the first one who ever wrote a leaflet from a University to help farmers' wives. {She was} the first to carry the home-making {propaganda} to the place where it was most needed.[2] {The} other women chosen were Jane Addams in philanthropy, Cecilia Beaux in painting, Carrie Chapman Catt in politics, Annie Jump Cannon in astronomy, Minnie Madden Fisk from the stage, Louise Homer in music, Julia Lathrop in child welfare, Florence R. Sabine in anatomy, Martha Carey Thomas in education, Edith Wharton in literature.

---

2. Added at this point in the 1953 edition (p. 263–4): ". . . while in 1898, I was the first professor in the Cornell University Extension Service."

I {fully} expected that the selection of Martha Van Rensselaer and myself would be criticized, {but if this was the case I was unaware of it}. I felt very meek and overwhelmed by the honor. Mr. Comstock reassured me by saying that the forty thousand copies of my *Handbook of Nature Study* had been sold to schools and teachers {and} would probably affect the lives of many children and therefore do much {general} good so I need not feel unworthy of this election. {My husband} always comforted me in my perplexities and crises.

I received many letters of congratulations but was {morally} certain that my friends were as astonished as was I at this honor bestowed on me. The Ithaca Cornell Alumnae Association gave Martha Van Rensselaer and me a dinner to celebrate the elections. {The most interesting event in connection with the distinction, occurred in June, when I was haled to Washington to help celebrate the dedication of the model house called Home Sweet Home. This medium-sized house had been built near the White House grounds. It was attractive inside and out and the furnishings were in excellent taste. Martha Van Rensselaer and I went together to hear President Harding deliver the address. Later we met him and Mrs. Harding, two charming, cordial people interested in better homes and in folks as well. Despite the revelations that have shown Harding's political associates a rotten crew, the fact remains that he and Mrs. Harding were a lovable pair and did their best personally in the position they held. No one will ever know how much the worry over the political intrigue which engulfed him, conduced to the President's untimely death.}

{In May Dr. Carl Eigeman of Indiana University was our guest for several days while attending a Sigma Xi Council meeting at Cornell. He was a unique and vastly interesting man. His work on the blind fishes and other vertebrates living in caves is monumental, to say nothing of his other works on fishes. He had the true German naïveté which was in him quite charming. He spent much time in his room for he was not well. I had filled the bookcase in our guest room with a wide range of literature and when he left us he said, "I have a new idea of luxury, and that is to have a library of books selected by other people—I have so greatly enjoyed reading those in my room while here."}

{In May occurred the picnic with the Entomological Department. There were 75 present which included the children of the Faculty. It was a gay occasion. The youngsters were greatly delighted to find in a tree a bag which Santa Claus had accidently dropped there. These picnics and the occasional general suppers have done much for the morale of the department. The Agassiz Club had been revived and was flourishing this year. I attended some of the meetings and at the special meeting with Dr. and Mrs. E. L. Palmer, I read aloud Dr. Jordan's "Story of a Stone."}

{The Wardens and Senior girls gave a very pretty reception at Sage College, the last of May. There was aesthetic dancing by girl students on the lawn under colored lights, which made the occasion very festive. The reception was for the faculty and was largely attended. I made note of these functions for I had seen their beginning many years before and hope I shall not live to see their ending.}

{The Commence this year (1923) was uneventful except for the fact that George Tansey was our guest and our lifelong friend August Loos, Cornell '77, was also a part-time guest. Mr. Loos had been a friend of us both during our college days. He was an interesting man with a beautiful character. His exquisite playing of the violin had brought us happiness in our student days. He had married a classmate and their home was one of culture and happiness.}

{One event of Commencement was my second defeat as Alumni trustee, but as I had expected it, my poise was not greatly disturbed.}

{In June I went to State College, PA to teach in the Summer School two weeks before the beginning of our session at Cornell. Jim's friend, Mrs. Blanche Noble, came to stay with Mr. Comstock, Jim, and Margaret Turner while I was gone, and all four of them went with me to see me settled satisfactorily. The motor ride was glorious that day, over mountains and along roads bordered by high meadows made gay by buttercups and orange hawk-weed.}

{I found my class at State College a good one. I felt at once the difference between these teachers in the schools of Pennsylvania and those of New York and other states that came to Cornell for summer study. They were less sophisticated and imaginative, and kept their feet more solidly on the ground.}

{This was my first opportunity for becoming acquainted with Professor George Green, a teacher of Forestry, who had charge of the course and, who is a very able man. When Governor Pinchot foolishly refused support to the Department of Forestry of the College, Professor Green, who had given courses to teachers in the study of trees, was transferred to the head of the new Department of Nature Study. He is a fine-looking young man with great enthusiasm for his work and an inspiring teacher. He and his charming wife were very kind to me; I was welcomed to their home and made the acquaintance of their young son and daughter. It was the beginning of a very happy friendship.}

{The summer session at Cornell was satisfactory. I was especially happy to have Dr. Theodosia Hadley of Kalamazoo, Normal College, in my classes.

She was one of the leaders in Nature Study, having received her training under Dr. Elliot Downing. She is a beautiful young woman and I saw much of her this summer, a great privilege.}

{Alice Graves again spent some weeks with us and Mrs. Farnham and her daughters were at the Theta house again and with Margaret Turner and Jim in the home we had plenty of social life, often having picnic suppers in the glade of our garden, or miles away on some hill with a wide view, or on the banks of some stream.}

On September {4th} I received a visit from Mr. Arthur Newton Pack who made an offer to merge the *Nature Study Review* with the *Nature Magazine*. Personally, I felt that I should be glad to be rid of the work of editing the *Review* and also of the financial responsibility connected with it; for it was a lucky year when I did not sink two or three hundred dollars in the enterprise; moreover, the making up and editing took a great amount of time every month. However, {it} was getting along better at this time and seemed likely to pay its expenses for the coming year. As a result of Mr. Pack's offer, I sent a letter embodying the following proposition to all the members of the Council:

> The *Nature Study Review* was to be a unit in each number of the *Nature Magazine* and was still to be the official organ of the American Nature Study Society, and its editor to be elected from that body.

With one or two exceptions the members of the Council agreed, and the December number of the *Nature Study Review* was the last.

{It is in fact that} the *Nature Magazine* did not carry its part of the agreement; {Mr. Arthur N. Pack's authority was apparently set at naught by the Editor, Mr. P. S. Ridsdale. However, Mr. Pack has done many things for the advancement of Nature Study teaching to compensate for this flagrant breaking of the contract which he was apparently forced into.}

{The *Nature Study Review* was started as the organ of the American Study Society in 1906 by Maurice Bigelow of Columbia University and many notable contributions were made to this magazine in those early years. Dr. Bigelow had in mind a dignified, pedagogical publication and succeeded in this. The trouble was the scarcity of Nature-Study teachers to support it.}

{In 1910 Dr. Bigelow finding the task too heavy, Professor Charles of Normal, Illinois, was made editor. He believed that more subject-matter should be given in the Review and changed its character in this respect. However, Professor Charles died within the year, and Dr. Elliott R. Downing of Chicago University was made editor. In his able and experienced hands, the Review became more generally useful but, after six years, he felt the burden too great and in 1917 I was elected editor. At that time the Review had twelve hundred subscribers. In the six years of my editorship we gained subscribers to the number of twenty-five hundred and the future looked promising.}

{In September we took our usual outing with Jim. We had beautiful drives through the Adirondacks and finished with a restful stay at Joe Indian Lake. On our way home, we stopped at Saranac and I called on Mr. Barnet, the editor of the Trotty Veck booklets. We found him pleasant and interesting and a prisoner to high altitude. We had been greatly interested in the work of himself and his friend who died, in trying to alleviate the sadness of the world.}

{As soon as we returned Mr. Comstock began his work with new zest. I had to revise the astronomy part of my Handbook and had an accumulated pile of mail in connection with the *Nature Study Review*. I seemed to have as much to do as when I was teaching.}

Mr. Comstock worked {this year as he did all the years while he was writing}, *The Introduction to Entomology*. He was at his writing by eight-thirty every morning. {He then} took a siesta from twelve o'clock until luncheon at one. After luncheon he smoked and read {the periodicals} until three; occasionally he did some work in the garden in the afternoon, but usually he went back to his desk at four and worked until dinner at six-thirty. After dinner, he smoked and read for a time but went back to his writing by eight and worked steadily until ten-thirty. He rested by changing his position while working. Part of the time he sat at his desk by the west window of his study but usually worked longer at his "stand-up" desk by the north window. When he was tired, he reclined on his sofa, using a writing tablet to support his paper as he wrote. {He always smoked after meals and always had an extra cigar in the middle of his working periods, making six a day. He smoked light cigars, "Bobbies" being his favorites. For a person so high strung as he, smoking was a blessing as long as he did it in moderation. Occasionally, under pressure, he smoked more than his usual allotment and suffered nervously because of it, but always corrected the habit as soon as he realized it was hurting him.}

{In October I went to Pittsburgh for one strenuous day's work. I was a guest of our friends, Alfred and Winifred Emerson. In the morning I addressed Alfred's class in biology, attended a luncheon, and in the afternoon made a short address before 2000 people at a teacher's institute; then to the College Woman's Club[3] where I made a short address and had the great pleasure of meeting again Elsie Singmaster and listening to her read

3. "College Woman's Club" was crossed out by A.B.C. and replaced with "Meeting of the American Association of University Women." —KSt.

one of her charming stories. That evening I spoke to five hundred teachers and nature lovers at the Carnegie museum; attended a reception afterwards and called it a day.}

{On my way home next day, I stopped at Fairport and gave the lecture on Thoreau before the Fairport Historical Society. The next day I had to address the A. A. C. W. and the Agassiz Club. I then went into seclusion for a rest of two days.}

{On November 12th Dr. Douglas Houghton Campbell arrived,—a guest always most welcome. L. O. Howard was also here. Both had come to a meeting of the National Academy of Science held here. We all attended a lecture by Frank Chapman at the meeting of the Academy and later went to a reception given the visitors by President and Mrs. Farrand. There was a banquet at Prudence Risley Hall in the evening and we sat at a table with Mr. and Mrs. Chapman and Mr. and Mrs. Louis Fuertes, and had the jolliest time ever. The next morning, we went to hear Leal Howard speak on European Entomology before our own departmental students, he was interesting as always.}

{November 19th, I went to Detroit and Ann Arbor to speak before teachers. At Detroit I was the guest of Miss Lenore Conover. I spoke before pupils of teachers' college and before the Nature Study Society and also spoke at a banquet at the Twentieth Century Club. On my way home, I stopped at Toledo to see the excellent nature work done in the schools under the supervision of Professor M. R. Van Cleve. I had the pleasure of meeting his family and we were entertained at luncheon at the beautiful home of our old-time friend, Irving Macumber. In the evening there was a dinner given me by the Nature Study Club, a very enjoyable affair.}

{I was introduced at this dinner in such glowing terms that I felt abashed and told the Club I felt that I was in the same situation as the little boy, who was the hero of an imaginative little girl, whose mother heard her telling herself this story: "Once there was a little boy who was sick, and the doctor came and gave him some medicine out of a bottle with a teaspoon and a nurse came to take care of him but he was sicker and sicker and that night he died. The next morning God came and shook him and said: "Wake up, you boob, and see what you've got! You've got wings."}

{December 5th, I went to Washington to speak before the students of the Ormond Wilson Normal College. I was the guest of Mrs. Susan Sipe Albertis and her husband at their restful home at Chevy Chase. One evening she had forty of her pupils there to meet me; it was a delight to see their devotion to their really great teacher. While in Washington I called on Mr. Ridsdale, the editor of the *Nature Magazine*, and came away feeling that the *Nature Study*

Review was dead and buried, despite Mr. Arthur Pack's promises. I had an interview also with Dr. R. W. Shufeldt which confirmed my conclusions.}

{While in Washington I spoke before the teachers in the Washington schools. Once to the white and once to the colored teachers and had lunch with the "Honorables" who had interests and influences in the schools of the capital city.}

{On December 15, I attended a meeting of the Cornellian Council, and that evening we went to the great dinner at Risley when Boldt Hall was formally presented to the University. Mr. Boldt's daughter was present, which added much to the satisfaction of everybody. President White had been greatly impressed with Mr. Boldt's deep interest in Cornell while he was trustee. While he did not have money to give, he made contacts for Cornell that were most valuable. President White really loved him, and all the trustees appreciated him, so it seemed fitting that this first dormitory for men students should bear his name.}

{A plan had been maturing in our minds. The previous winter had been a torture to me because of bronchitis, and the doctor advised a warm climate for this winter. Moreover, Jim and Gretel were very eager to be married, which under the circumstances could hardly be consummated for at least another year. Thus, we proposed to spend the winter away and let the bride and groom have our house to live in until they should build a home on our lot, next to the chalet, a plan which pleased them greatly.}

{I was due to attend the annual meeting of the American Nature Study Society with the A. A. A. S. in Cincinnati during the holidays. This precluded our staying for the wedding, but, since we were to live with the twain the coming summer, we were satisfied. Thus, on Christmas day we started on our journey. We were pleased to find Dr. Charles Hull and his sister, the Slingerland family and several others at the station to see us off.}

{At Cincinnati we and Dr. and Mrs. J. G. Needham, were guests of Dr. and Mrs. John Uri Lloyd in their beautiful home. I think that Dr. Uri Lloyd is one of the most interesting men I have ever known. As a manufacturing druggist he is a scientist of high repute. As a writer he had attained genuine success; his "Stringtown on the Pike" is perhaps the best story written of the Kentuckians of that period. His other volumes of stories also are full of interest. His scientific writings are extensive, and he is a member of many learned societies. However, granting the excellence of his writings and scientific standing, it is, after all, his personality that is of greatest interest. In physique he is of medium height, very active, and wiry. His face, clean-shaven, shows many interesting lines, a face never to be forgotten.

His voice is soft but high keyed; his conversation original, full of humor and wisdom and of pungent description.}

{Mr. Comstock and I attended the meetings of the entomological sections of the A. A. A. S. and met many of our old students and friends, especially Dr. Alex. McGillivray and Dr. William A. Riley. I gave a full day to the Nature Study meeting which was made especially interesting by a talk on French Educational methods by Dr. Elliot R. Downing, who had spent the previous year in France. From Cincinnati we went to Chicago where we visited my cousin, Alice Graves, and our dear friend Karl Schmidt, in the Field Museum where he introduced us to his interesting if not beautiful reptiles. For the years of his University course he was a member of our Sunday night supper parties and seems very near to us.}

{New Year's Day we spent on the Rock Island R. R. looking out over the illimitable, cornstalk-studded fields of Iowa; so cold that all the cattle and horses had snow on their backs. The next day we arrived at Colorado Springs, the guests of Norman Smith who had become a successful business man in this interesting city. His mother, our Margery Smith, was living with him, and being with her again was a great privilege.}

{We had a happy week in their home. Norman was so manifestly happy to have us visit him that he could not do enough for us. It was reassuring to have a man who had lived in our home fourteen years and well acquainted with our faults and foibles to be so truly loving and devoted to us.}

{From Colorado Springs we went to Santa Fe and spent several days in this old town. One day we visited the Tesuka [*sic*] Indian Pueblo, a solid rambling two-story structure, more interesting than attractive. The Indians were rather fine-looking and their dress very picturesque. We witnessed a funny incident,—a squaw came out on the "upper deck" of a pueblo and threw out a pan of water which fell squarely on a large Indian below, wetting him completely. He made no sign of any sort but went on about his business as she went on about hers. We had read that the women of this tribe owned all the property including the crops and they choose their husbands and divorce them; and evidently, they have a right to spill dishwater on them also.}

{At Albuquerque, we hastened to the University to find Helen Murphy, one of our Cornell girls, who was professor of Biology in this institution. We found her in her laboratory with a class of fine looking students bent on unveiling the mysteries of star-fish anatomy. We had her with us that night at dinner at the artistic Alvarado Hotel, and so sandwiched sight-seeing with social pleasure.}

{We stopped at Phoenix and visited the impressive Capitol building and wandered through streets of attractive dwellings. We then went into the library as I wished to get some information about the life-habits of a certain butterfly. Mr. Comstock undertook to get the book for me, and found the entomological shelf contained chiefly Comstock books. The girl who waited on us brought us our book, *How to Know the Butterflies*, but I told her that this did not contain the needed information. She then brought us Mr. Comstock's *Manual* and declared with emphasis, "This book will tell you all about insects." Mr. Comstock said, "No, this hasn't the facts we want," at which she exhorted him to look it through; she **knew** he would find in it what he wanted. He answered: "I **know** it is not in this book for I wrote the book myself." Doubt and amazement struggled for expression in her face and she gasped. "You wrote this book! Well, what do you know about that?"}

{We arrived in Tucson January 19th and found Professor C. T. Vorhies at the station to meet us. He took us to the Santa Rita Hotel where we settled ourselves most comfortably. It is a handsome and excellent tourist hotel with abundant reception rooms, and garden and sun parlor on the roof. The view from the roof is a vast panorama of mountains and desert, with all the varying colors granted by the Arizona atmosphere to make the world beautiful.}

{We found staying at our hotel Professor and Mrs. M. F. Guyer of Wisconsin University who proved to be delightful companions.}

{We had been led to Tucson especially because of our affection for Professor and Mrs. Vorhies and they gave us some of the most interesting experiences of our lives. There were motor trips through the desert where every plant and every living creature interested us. The way each species adapted itself to desert conditions was a never-ending source of wonder to us. Later, we became acquainted with Dr. Walter P. Taylor of the U. S. Biological Survey, who also took us for excursions through deserts and mountains. Both Professor Vorhies and Dr. Taylor were familiar with the flora and fauna of this region and were ideal companions on these trips.}

{We were of the tenderfoot class when it came to knowledge of desert life; but really, the tenderfoot is granted the privilege of appreciating the wonderful things in any country and especially so of Arizona. To the eyes of the newcomer, the most common phenomena of this land of "imperturbable" sunshine and limited rainfall, were glamorous. Even the creosote bushes, covering vast areas with their yellowish-green, varnished foliage, seemed a miracle, so evenly were they planted by the stern hand of necessity, made manifest in scanty supply of moisture, and yet so glistening glorious do they flourish. Then there was the gnarled and sturdy mesquite and many weird and captivating species of cacti. Especially did those green ghost trees, the Palo-verde, hold us in thrall. We learned to have a vast respect for the terrible cholla which seemed able to spear us if we even looked at it; and yet the cactus wren built its nest in it and the desert rats piled up bushels of its fallen masses of barbed needles to make their homes. We never ceased to admire the giant cactus the Seguaro [*sic*]. We were interested to note how many of them had woodpecker nests; and we were amazed when Professor Vorhies showed us how the woodpeckers hardened the walls of their nests, so they remained hard and firm after the cactus had died and rotted away.}

{One day Professor and Mrs. Vorhies and Charles took us for a long drive to the Santa Rita mountains; along the base of these mountains the desert flora is largely Palo-verde and giant cactus. We went up through a cattle range where Professor Vorhies tried out his Studebaker by chasing an antelope rabbit all over the place; we had many good views of this elusive rabbit and the chase was exciting. We camped for dinner by a mountain stream under a live oak. The place was of special interest, for near here Mr. and Mrs. Vernon Bailey had camped when studying the birds of the region.}

{We saw much of Professor and Mrs. Byron Cummings and were greatly interested in his story of excavations in Mexico. We also frequently went to the fine Archeological Museum he had created for the University. My most vivid memory is of a beautiful sand picture made for Professor Cummings by an old Indian for friendship's sake. One thing struck me as wholly admirable was the respectful and sympathetic way Professor Cummings spoke of the Indians. I found later the same attitude among the artists of the city.}

{We found at the University several friends,—Hayward Severance was instructor in chemistry and Ware and Jack Cattell, sons of J. McKeen Cattell, were students there. We also found staying in Tucson, Romayne Hough and his wife. He was an old Cornellian and the author of the great work on trees and sections of woods. We did not realize then that the end was so near, for he seemed fairly well.}

{Our crowning experience in Tucson was the celebration of Mr. Comstock's 75th birthday as planned by Professor and Mrs. Vorhies who drove us to Nogales. It was seventy miles from Tucson to the border, first through desert country, then along a river with water in it and great greening cottonwoods along its banks.}

{We found Nogales, two towns, one quite American in appearance and one quite Mexican with a wire fence dividing the two. This gate was guarded by police of both nations. We had our dinner in the Mexican town at the famous place called "The Cave," because it is a cave, (probably made by miners) in the solid rock. It was rather crowded, but finally we were regaled with venison, as there are no game laws in Mexico. We could have had all kinds of alcoholic beverages had we chosen, but Mr. Vorhies and Mr. Comstock stood firm and we had coffee. However, we judged that a gay party that had the alcove next to us had drunk through the whole wine list and then some by the sounds they emitted.}

{We often drove by the beautiful desert home of Harold Bell Wright. Incidentally we discovered that he is a public-spirited citizen of Tucson. Whenever there is anything doing for the benefit of the city, he is a moving force in it. We saw him often; his thin, strong face shaded by a sombrero is a picture that stays in memory.}

{We left Tucson the last of February and went to Beaumont, California, to visit our friends Mr. and Mrs. William Tyler Miller at their cherry ranch. It was a beautiful spot on the side of a foothill, with a wonderful panorama in front of cultivated orchards and with the snow-streaked peaks of San Jacinto mountain in the background. Here were our friends, he for many years assistant-editor of *Country Life in America* and editor of the *Garden Magazine*, later a professor in University of Illinois, she a writer and teacher and now both working like laborers, but in their own vineyard; they were laboring joyously, finding strength, health and new happiness in their planting and harvesting and their new partnership with nature}.

{We left the Millers reluctantly and went on to Pomona College where two of Mr. Comstock's former students, Dr. Philip A. Munz, head of the Department of Botany, and Dr. W. A. Hilton, head of the Department of Zoology, were teaching and carrying on their work in research.}

{We had been for some years interested in this small but excellent college, and we had been captivated by its physical beauty as well. Even then, the wise and able President was considering the experiment that now is to be tried, enlarging the college by adding other colleges on the Oxford plan.}

{Our three-day stay was very full and very gay. Dr. Munz took us for drives in the region about and entertained us at luncheon. The Hiltons gave us a reception at which we met a lot of interesting folk; among them Wright Pierce, the ornithologist. Next to Cornell and Stanford and William Smith, both Mr. Comstock and I are more devoted to Pomona than to any other American college or university.}

{Grace Fordyce Fox came for us and drove us to Altadena where we were guests of her and her husband and mother for two happy weeks. Scott Fox was teaching Agriculture in the Altadena High School and we found his plan of work most excellent. In this High School we found at the head of the department of biology a pupil of both of us, Miss Mabel Pierson, Cornell 1900. We were proud of her; for biology is taught in this school in an ideal manner, the laboratory work supplementing and clarifying the field work in a region rich in both land and sea forms.}

{Grace had a car of her own and devoted it and her services as chauffeur, to our goings and comings, and we went somewhere every day. We visited Anna C. Stryke, Mr. Comstock's former assistant, artist and friend, who with her mother and sister were living in Pasadena in an attractive home. We had never ceased to regret that she had left Ithaca. She is a charming and gifted woman whose home duties and ill health have thwarted her possible achievements as a scientist and artist, but whose personality has developed in beauty and strength under her responsibilities and burdens.}

{We found many old friends in Pasadena, Mr. and Mrs. Carl Thomas, whom we know as students at Stanford and who later were our neighbors at Cornell when he was professor in the Sibley College. Two as charming folk as ever made a world happier by living in it. We met again at their home, Abbie Waterman, the brilliant daughter of a former governor of California. She had written charming stories published in the *Atlantic Monthly*, but now was developing a cattle ranch in the Mohave [*sic*] desert near Barstow and doing it successfully.}

{We attended a meeting of the Cornell Women's Club in Los Angeles and met many whom we knew. Julia Rogers and her brother, Dr. Thomas Rogers, were there. We went home with them that evening and they showed us Long Beach lighted, a very fine display on the hill covered with derricks.}

{Miss Julia gave a dinner for us at the Country Club where we met other delightful members of the Roberts family including Mary Rogers Miller and her charming daughter Ruth and also Guido Van Dusen Marx, our "little Guido" who had grown up to magnificent young manhood and had found a sweet wife.}

{From Long Beach we went to Los Angeles to visit my cousin Mrs. Kate Sprowls, a delightful and stimulating person whose outlook on life always made us renew our youth. We also visited Judge and Mrs. Walter Bordwell in their beautiful new home and met their daughter and her husband, both Stanford graduates. We found Judge Bordwell in poor health and it proved to be the last visit we had ever had with this brave, just man.}

{Among other happy experiences of our stay with the Fox family was attending a meeting of the Sigma Xi Club of Southern California, at which we were honored guests. Mr. Comstock again broke his vow and made a good speech}.

{Scott Fox took us through devious ways to find Mr. Comstock's old student and friend Professor H. E. Summers, who had built a home on a hill in Pasadena and lived there with his daughters, since his health was broken, and he had to abandon his scientific work. We found him calm and brave and thinking about his flowers and garden rather than of his own broken life.}

{The last of March found us in Palo Alto, guests of the Marxes. We were happy to find there Eleanor, the oldest daughter, and Ashley Browne, her husband of Sacramento. Our hearts were made glad by meeting all our dear Stanford friends again although two of those we had greatly loved were missing. Dr. John Stillman and Dr. John C. Branner had died since our last visit, and we missed them so deeply we could not talk about it.}

{We found the Jordans in their attractive new home on the Stanford Campus and were glad to find them both so well.}

{Guido and Gertrude took us to Carmel for three days. We found many changes in this beautiful spot. It had become popular with artists as well as with others, but Nature still was steadfast in giving visions of picturesque coast and heavenly sea. Professor and Mrs. Charles Wing, and Professor and Mrs. Pearce were at Carmel and we had a picnic day with them.}

{After a beautiful two weeks stay in Palo Alto we went to San Francisco for a few days of visiting with friends.}

{We spent a day in Berkeley with Dr. and Mrs. Benjamin Ide Wheeler. Mr. Wheeler had begun to fail and it was heart-breaking to realize that his splendid mental powers were weakening; but his beautiful spirit was still strong and supreme—again illustrating the difference between mind and soul.}

{We also made a pilgrimage to see Professor Isaac P. Roberts, then living with his daughter Mary Coolidge. It was my first acquaintance with Dane Coolidge, the writer of Western stories. I found him a rather shy man at first, but, after a little, he told me of some of his recent experiences in the Arizona towns, and I realized that he had first-hand knowledge of the places and people of whom he wrote. We found Professor Roberts well and happy and full of entertaining reminiscences of his early days at Cornell.}

{Gertrude Marx came east with us which added special enjoyment to the journey home. She left us at Geneva to visit her sister and we arrived at Ithaca April 14 and found Jim and Gretel and Will Slingerland at the station to meet us.}

{The last of April I attended the convention of the League of Women Voters held in Buffalo. There were 1500 delegates and others present. At the great banquet, Martha Van Rensselaer and I were the only ones, whom the League had honored, who were present to say thank you. This we did fairly successfully, I think. I was much impressed by the women of the League,—they were so alert and so attractive.}

{Gertrude Marx came to us for a week in May. It was a great privilege to have her in our new home and to share with her all our present interests. Her coming also brought a reunion with other old friends whom we see only occasionally; Edwin Woodruff, Charles and Mary Hull, the Chamberlains and the Fowlers and George Burr. It was a red-letter week with us.}

{June 14th occurred the 50th anniversary celebration of the Class of 1874. Mr. Comstock was class secretary and had been very busy making preparations for the event. Mr. Mynderse Van Cleef gave a reception to the class and their guests at his beautiful home in the afternoon. The banquet took place in the evening in Barnes Hall. There were a goodly number present and all seemed happy. I never saw my husband more relieved than he was when he realized that all had gone well and it was over. More and more he dreaded social responsibilities and worried over them.}

{The last week in June, Jim and Gretel and Mr. Comstock and myself went to Lake Winnipesaukee, N. H. to attend a school for Nature counsellors, this time conducted by Mr. Fagan. I gave several lectures and Mr. Comstock took a class in the field. However, we all missed Dr. Vinal, who was ever the leader and the inspiration of these schools.}

{On our return, we had the great pleasure of having Dr. and Mrs. Benjamin Ide Wheeler and their son Webb for our guests,—all three of them so dear to us. While Dr. Wheeler's disease made him slow to think, yet he made an excellent address before the Ithaca Rotary Club, so that no one who heard him would have suspected his brain was weakening. His devoted wife and son did everything in their power to help him and the visit was a happy one. They all enjoyed old friends for, although they had been away from the University more than twenty years, they had held their place in the hearts of us all. We were greatly pleased with Webb's development; he had become a man of broad vision and sympathies and had the simplicity and dignity of his father. Mrs. Wheeler had been for many years an intimate friend of mine, a woman whose honesty, integrity and loyalty had given her a high place in our affection.}

{I had my usual classes in the summer session and we had the usual reception for them at our home. The house, the piazza, the gardens and the Comstock Publishing Company chalet were all at the disposal of the guests, and all seemed to have a pleasant time. Grace Griswold, Jim and Gretel, and Margaret Turner were the *Dei ex machina* and gave me great comfort and relief.}

{In the middle of the session I went to Morristown, N. J. where I was met and entertained by Mrs. Alfred Roberts and her husband and two delightful small boys in their fine old home, which had been the homestead for generations of Roberts. The next day I addressed four hundred teachers and one hundred mothers of the New Jersey Parent-Teachers' Association at Ocean City.}

{I was quite ambitious this summer and in addition to my teaching and running a house and planning meals for a family of nine, I registered for out-of-door sketching with Professor Walter King Stone. It was great fun; Professor Stone is an original and delightful man and an inspiring and companionable teacher. The class was not too large; the afternoons out-of-doors with paint, canvas and brush, and before us a beautiful, uncritical and uncomplaining landscape,—what more could one ask!}

{In August a great sorrow came to us; our dear friend Jennie Fleming Farnham, who was with her family in the Theta House for the summer, died after a brief but painful illness. She was a brave, loyal and charming woman who as a girl had been like a daughter to us during her years of residence in our home. Her death was a crushing blow to her children who were devoted and dependent upon her for courage and cheer.}

{I shall always remember my 70th birthday, September 1, 1924, for it was warm and pleasant. We had our birthday supper in The Glade, as we call the space below the terrace in our garden. All the Herrick family, George Burr and Alexis Babine, Mary and Agnes Fowler, and Professor Gage, were guests. We sat there until dark and the lights came on giving the trees and woods beautiful illuminations. The perfect end of a happy day!}

{The manuscript of the *Introduction to Entomology*: had been sent to the printer early in August, and the first batch of proof arrived August 15th and from that time until the last of September. We both read proof, valiantly; of course, Mr. Comstock had the hardest part of it, but I read to catch the mistakes he missed. We were both in a fever of excitement over finally seeing in print this work over which he had labored so intensely for so many years. We had a struggle with the index; I dubbed it "Index purgatorius," and Mr. Comstock and Gretel said: "Amen."}

November 4th, 1924 was to us one of the great days in our two lives.[4] The *Introduction to Entomology* was published. In this Mr. Comstock had put his best work as a scientist and as a teacher. It has proven a noble and fitting climax to the life work of a man who labored valiantly and intensely in search of truth and of whom Dr. Walter K. Fisher of the Hopkins Marine Laboratory said, "he has been probably the greatest teacher of natural history that America has known."

The book was received enthusiastically by the Entomologists of American and other countries {as well}. Letters of appreciation and praise came pouring in with every mail and brought to Mr. Comstock reassurance and comfort, and to me much happiness. {Mr. Comstock} had worked so long on the book that he was tired and had begun to doubt its value.

We had come to a happy decision for our winter. Professor Gage suggested that we spend it in Hawaii. He had long desired to visit this garden spot of the Pacific, and he invited his sister, Dr. Mary Gage Day of

4. Inserted here in the 1953 edition (p. 265): ". . . for on that day his book of 1,064 pages . . .".

Kingston, to go along as his guest. Our autumn was filled with the excitement of the prospective journey.

{Our Thanksgiving party this year was varied quite fundamentally from our custom. The entire Herrick family, the Russells, Agnes and Mary Fowler, Alexis Babine, Margaret Turner and Mary Hill, had a dinner at the excellent old-fashioned Shaver Hotel at Freeville. The young people went from dinner to Bailey Hall to get the football returns, the others came home with us, and we gathered around a roaring fire in our living room and had a period of real thanksgiving intercourse. It was the last Thanksgiving that we were to have together, but fortunately we did not know it.}

{Mr. Comstock was very tired and gave himself over to the luxury of resting and reading; evenings we had many games of "Rummy," chiefly because this card game was so simple that it made no demands on our minds. I was glad to see Mr. Comstock rest, but there was no rest for me. Almost every day I did something outside of my ordinary duties. My Sunday School class took much time; it consisted of a charming bevy of young girls whom I loved and enjoyed. I spoke before the graduate women; I went to receptions and teas; I attended Alliance meetings in our church and worked for our bazaar; I went to Kappa Alpha Theta lunches and meetings; I was also finishing articles for the *Junior Home Magazine* and, all in all, I was nearly a frantic old lady.}

{I went to New York ahead of the others and with our cousin Gerald Stopp spent a day in Princeton, New Jersey with Mr. and Mrs. Arthur Pack, in their beautiful and interesting home.} On December 11th we, with Professor Gage, {Dr. Mary Day}, and {our} friends {Florence Slater, a Cornellian teaching in Washington Irving School in New York, and Miss Belle Sherman of Ithaca}, went aboard the Dollar Line S. S. "President Hayes." {Gerald Stopp, Mrs. Thro and Dr. John Lovejoy Elliott came to see us off. We sailed at 2 p.m. and found a glassy sea awaiting us. We found the President Hayes a most comfortable boat and the passengers an attractive crowd. Captain Anderson was genial and a fine man in addition to being an excellent skipper. The servants were all Chinese and the crew Phillipinos, which gave us a feeling that we were in the Orient.}

{We made a stop of a day in Havana, Cuba, and had opportunity to see this really beautiful city. Our most interesting experience was going through the Panama Canal. The mechanics of the locks interested Mr. Comstock greatly. Although we had heard so much of it, we were unprepared to find Gatun Lake so beautiful. Its many islands with their palms and bananas gave us the feeling of the tropics. We were allowed several hours at Balboa and drove out through Panama to the ruins of old Panama. In visiting the ruins of a monastery, we were attracted by the long lines of leaf-cutter ants, skittering along their trails, single file, each holding aloft in her jaws a piece of a green leaf. We spent all of our spare time studying them and, later, I wrote up the experience for the *Nature Magazine*. When we returned to Balboa and visited the fine hospital there in its beautiful park, the tragic story of earlier years came to us. The hospital was a nest of yellow fever. If a man came to it with a broken leg he died of yellow fever; naturally, people begged not to be taken there. Later, Gen. Gorgas found the reason; the trees in the park were often defoliated by these same leaf-cutting ants, therefore, a container, filled with water, was placed around the base of each tree to keep the ants from climbing it. In these containers the mosquitoes which carry the yellow fever germs were breeding by the thousands; and as the hospital windows and doors were not screened the insects had ready access to the patients and thus made sure that no one of them escaped this dire disease.}

{We were surprised to find Central America so extensive. We sailed along in sight of beautiful, tree-covered mountains for three days; then along mountains more sharp and bleak as we neared Mexico; then mountains rugged and desolate for six days more.}

{We celebrated Christmas by opening up many packages that we had found awaiting us on the boat. Some of the passengers awoke us in the morning by singing Christmas carols while marching around the deck. At dinner that night the lights were turned out and a procession, headed by little Soy Chong came in, all robed in white and carrying candles while they marched around and sang "Silent Night," a very pretty celebration.}

Professor Gage had thrust upon him a new role. There was no clergyman among the passengers and he was asked to conduct the Sabbath services, which he did with great dignity and success, owing largely to his engaging personality and to his sister's prayer book; she fortunately being a member of the Episcopal Church and having a ritual at hand.

It was after we left Panama on December 3d that I engaged in an enterprise that had far-reaching results. The Chinese lad Soy Chong who passed the bread and biscuits in the dining saloon had attracted {us. He had dignity and} charm of manner and was a relative of the head-waiter. {I found the monotony of the voyage weighing heavily and proposed to the boy, his relatives and Captain Anderson that I teach Soy Chong English during the remainder of the voyage.} All were willing, and I entered upon a new phase of teaching. The boy knew very few English words but had learned in a Chinese school to write English script. I devised an original method of teaching. We began with the blue sky, the blue sea, the white clouds, etc. and finally arrived at furniture, clothing, and the human body. I found him so bright and attractive and Mr. Comstock was so charmed with him that we offered to take him and educate him. The United States immigration laws had much to say about this wholly benevolent plan on our part, and not until February 1928, did Ernest Soy Chong Sze[5] become a member of the family; since then he has been a source of interest and happiness to {both of us}.

{On December 29, we entered the harbor of San Pedro feeling our way among the fleet of grim battleships. At the dock we found Mr. and Mrs. Wilhelm Miller, their daughter Ruth, and her friend Dr. Thompson, Julia Rogers and Mr. and Mrs. Scott D. Fox. We were guests for the night of Mr. and Mrs. Fox, glad again to be with them and their charming daughters.}

{That evening we were taken to the avenue of the Deodars when their magnificent trees were set with myriads of colored lights, like Christmas trees. It was one of the most bewitching sights that had ever met our eyes.}

{The Pacific had been like a mill pond during our entire voyage; but from San Diego to San Francisco we "teetered and tottered" over dead swells the whole day and were glad to reach the calm of San Francisco harbor. On New Year's Day we left our boat in the morning and went to Berkeley to lunch with President and Mrs. Wheeler, a sad visit, for we could see that this distinguished man was beyond recovery. In the afternoon we visited the beautiful Evergreen Cemetery in Oakland, where are the graves of sister Margaret and Father and Mother Dowell. That evening we went to Palo Alto, guests of Guido and Gertrude Marx, a blessed and comforting end of a sorrowful day.}

{The next day we returned to the boat and, as we cast off, the whole dock was a rainbow of paper ribbons, thrown at and by departing voyagers, a gorgeous sight.}

{We had found on the boat soon after leaving New York, Judge and Mrs. Frear of Honolulu, to whom we had letters of introduction. It had been a great pleasure to make the acquaintance of these wonderful people so early. Among our other interesting passengers were Commander C. J. Long of the Navy and his altogether fascinating wife. The two were indefatigable explorers and were bound for Singapore and thence to penetrate some far mysterious region inland in Asia.}

{Never shall I forget Mrs. Long's graphic and humorous account of an incident of a journey she made in China during the war, when she carried out some mission for the U. S. government. She had her own escort of coolies and, as I remember, she rode a horse part of the time. She finally was so weary and

5. Footnote typed at the bottom of the 1953 edition (p. 266): "Ernest Sze lived with the Comstocks several years and made rapid progress in Cascadilla Preparatory School. After the death of the Comstocks, the executors sent him to the Bliss Electrical School in Takoma Park, Maryland. He made an excellent record there and graduated in June 1932. He is now in China as second engineer on a large river boat on the Yangtze River. —G.W.H."

sore that she told her head man, that she must have a bath in the village where she stopped that night. The room to which she was taken was, of course, filthy and vermin-infested. Then appeared four coolies bringing in a great cauldron of water. Each coolie sought a corner and faced the wall. Her servant stretched out his arms and hung a towel over one and turned his back on her and the cauldron. She tried to think what was best to do and waited. Her Oriental towel-rack turned and signed for her to hang her clothes on his arms and take her bath, the floor being a too dangerous place for clothing; she thought of her country and of the brave soldiers in battle and took her bath, her Chinese companions immovable as if hewn from stone, until she was again arrayed. Lady Godiva would have been perfectly safe with them she was sure.}

{The week from San Francisco to Honolulu was passed, coping with dead swells. The ocean looked very calm, but it was full of hills and valleys. The frigate birds followed us on level wings and we never wearied of watching them. On January 10, we came in sight of beautiful Diamond Head and the Mountains. On the tug that came to meet the ship came Mr. S. H. N. Waldron, president of the Cornell Club of Honolulu to meet and welcome us. At the gangplank, while we listened to the Honolulu band playing the heavenly strains of "Aloha," we were greeted by Professor and Mrs. W. J. MacNeil, Mr. William Morgan, Dr. J. F. Illingworth, Mr. E. M. Erhorn, and Mrs. Arthur Andrews, all Cornellians and all glad to see us. However, as we landed I was very sorry to have to say goodbye to Soy Chong Sze and he was also sad, for we were great friends.}

{"Mr. and Mrs. Comstock spent the winter of 1923–24 in a leisurely trip across the continent to San Francisco. They visited their many friends in Cincinnati, Chicago, and Tucson, Mr. and Mrs. William Miller on their ranch at Beaumont, Calif., Dr. W. A. Hilton and Dr. Phillip A. Munz at Pomona, Miss Anna C. Stryke at Pasadena and Prof. and Mrs. Scott Fox at Altadena. At Palo Alto they visited Prof. Guido Marx and Mrs. Marx, and of course Dr. David Starr Jordan and Mrs. Jordan and finally, Pres. Benjamin Ide Wheeler and Mrs. Wheeler at Berkeley. They returned home in April. The winter of 1924–25 was spent in Hawaii and that of 1925–26 in Europe. These years were the happy conclusions of a life of joint activity. A few months after their return to Ithaca occurred the paralytic shock which incapacitated Mr. Comstock for the remainder of his life. Mrs. Comstock describes the tragic event in language affecting in its restraint and simplicity."[6]}

6. An abbreviated version of this last paragraph, written by Glenn Herrick, was included as a second footnote in the 1953 edition, page 266. The manuscript page is unnumbered and added to the back of the archival folder this manuscript chapter was within. —KSt.

Professor and Mrs. Comstock boarding ship to sail home from Hawaii.

CHAPTER XIX

Honolulu and Happiness, a Voyage to Europe

This manuscript chapter (XIX), twenty-six manuscript pages in length, is completely removed from the 1953 book. "Omit all this chapter" is written on the top of the first page, in purple china marker, presumably by Woodford Patterson. No portion of this chapter has ever been in print before this publication so the brackets used in other chapters have been omitted here.

We had made arrangements with Mrs. Gray, who had sent two sons to Cornell, to stay at her family hotel on Waikiki Beach. It was a most fortunate selection. Professor Gage, Dr. Day, Mr. Comstock and myself were given a cottage on the hotel grounds, where we had a living room of our own, which was especially convenient since we had so many callers. The hotel opens out directly on the most beautiful beach we had ever seen; we were never tired of watching the bathers and the surf riders on the ever-changing sea against the background of the noble Diamond Head.

The second day after our arrival, we were invited to lunch at the Globe Hotel as guests of the Pan-Pacific Club. It was an illuminating experience for, at this weekly club dinner, are assembled those who are interested in Pan-Pacific peace, and any visitors who may be available for this great and good propaganda. At this luncheon Mr. Fullard Leo, a citizen of Honolulu, made the offer of the Palmyra Islands as an international home for a Pan-Pacific Union. These islands are about twelve hundred miles south of Hawaii, covered with tropical flora and a home for many species of birds, as well as a resting place for migrants. I was the only one who seemed favorable to this proposition. In imagination I could see a great capitol arise on one of these islands, where the Orient and Occident might meet in the midst of beautiful flowers, and, beguiled by the songs of birds, plan peace for the world.

In the weeks that followed we were taken somewhere for an auto ride every day. There were five of Mr. Comstock's former students who were doing entomological work on the island,—Dr. David Crawford, President of the University, Dr. E. M. Erhorn who was head of the Plant Quarantine, Dr. Wilbur MacNeil, a professor in Punahou School, Dr. J. F. Illingworth, then working in the Museum, and Frederick G. Krauss, Professor of Agriculture in the University, who had studied with Mr. Comstock at Stanford. In addition to these were Dean and Mrs. Arthur Andres, formerly of Cornell, and William Morgan, who had often been at our home during his student days at Cornell, and Professor and Mrs. Arthur R. Kellar, Mrs. Kellar being an Ithaca girl and both Cornell graduates.

All these put themselves and their automobiles at our service in the most generous manner. We were specially indebted to Dr. Illingworth, who not only took us on long trips about the island but carried and fetched us when we attended lectures and social functions. He is a man of wholesome spirit and of a patience that is monumental; perhaps his patience has played a large part in making him so excellent an entomologist.

In addition to these former students we were welcomed by Professor and Mrs. Frederick Newcombe, he having been Professor of Botany at Ann Arbor for many years, Professor and Mrs. C. H. Edmondson, of the University Department of Biology and in charge of the aquarium, Principal Hauck of the Punahou School and his charming wife, Mr. Frederick Muir, Entomologist at the laboratory of the Hawaiian Sugar Planters' Association and his wife, who was a daughter of the eminent English entomologist David Sharp; also O. H. Swezey of the same laboratory and his wife were most kind. And through all and over all Judge and Mrs. Walter Francis Frear added to our happiness.

We soon had to have an engagement calendar to keep our social affairs straight. Our days were chock-full of interesting social experiences. If there are any uninteresting people in Honolulu we did not meet them.

The volcanic origin of Oahu gives its mountains a sharpness and precipitousness almost unbelievable to one who has not seen their jagged outlines against the sky. They are not far away for, all told, Oahu has barely 600 sq. miles, and yet the aerial perspective ever changing is entrancing; all the more so that the veils of rain move across, swaying as if wind-blown, irradiated with rainbows. Wherever you may be in Oahu the mountains form a background for the views inland. However, when one turns one's back to the mountains one always faces the sea, which is as capricious in its color moods as are the mountains, taking on exquisite greens, blues and purples beyond the power to describe or of pigment to portray. The mountains are covered with forests to a considerable extent, the vivid green foliage diversified by the pale greenish-white of the Kukui trees. The trees that shade the city and the trees of the mountains are various of species and many of them gorgeous of blossoms. However, the tree that interested me most is the Algarrobo, first brought to the Islands by a priest, and which spread over the desert, rendering it fit for other plants to follow, changing waste into arable lands.

The hibiscus is ever a part of the landscape. It is planted in hedges and in ornamental groups and the colors of its blossoms are various. More than two hundred varieties of this gorgeous flower are listed in Hawaii. The bougainvillea adds its magenta or orange masses to almost every view and the oleanders, almost trees in size, make beautiful groups along the avenues or about the bungalows. The night blooming cereus has rendered famous the moonlight nights of Honolulu. However, to the Easterner, unused to such tropic grandeur, the humble nasturtium gives one a home feeling as one finds it in almost every garden.

Of the birds we found but few in the country. There were wild doves and a thrush and once we heard a skylark which had been introduced. The English sparrow was common; but the most common of all is the mina, or mynah, this bird of India which outfights the English sparrow and, being larger, has reduced this pest to apologetic silence. A block away from our hotel was a tree chosen by these minas for their night roost. I watched them come in by the hundreds and, as they settled for the night, they made a terrific racket. This could be borne with patience by the people living near; but the birds awake in the early dawn with the same overwhelming noise, and this is hard to bear. However, there seems no way of heading off the minas when they have once made up their minds to roost in a certain tree.

The only mammal that attracted our attention was the rascally mongoose, introduced to fight rats and devoting itself instead to ground birds and poultry. During any of our drives we were certain to see this dark brown, weasley animal running across the road giving us a shivery feeling. There were never any snakes in Hawaii, so the mongoose is decidedly superfluous. The tiny lizards climbing over our window screen were a delight to us. They always rested in such ornamental postures.

We were as surprised as relieved to find no flies and could not understand it. A tropical region minus houseflies seemed an anachronism. We were told that an ant, introduced from some other region, had exterminated the housefly by destroying the larvae which are developed in filth. We were told also of the ravages of the termites which burrow through the timbers of houses rendering them dangerous. We found spiders estimated highly by housewives and encouraged to live behind pictures and in window curtains as they destroy household vermin. The cockroaches are gigantic; the first one we saw skittering away I thought was a mouse. However, Hawaii is not rich from the standard of an entomological collector.

The fruits of Hawaii that we enjoyed most were the luscious pineapples and the papaya. The latter is at first disappointing, because it looks like a cantaloupe and isn't; but we soon became so addicted to it as a breakfast fruit that it added an extra regret at leaving the land where it grows. Taro root made into poi did not attract us, neither did the breadfruit. Perhaps we had not been disciplined sufficiently along to appreciate their virtues.

The native Hawaiians are beautiful physically when they are young. Never had we seen such superb physiques,—not even in the marbles of Greece, as these swimmers and fishermen possessed. We met Hawaiian men and women and found them dignified and kindly. Their history in relation to the whites is unusual; they have not lost caste nor self-respect. Descendants of Hawaiian and white ancestors are among the most charming and desirable people of the islands and also the most exclusive.

We attended the Hawaiian church and heard excellent sermons and heavenly music. The love of these peaceful natives for flowers and music is far-famed and justly so.

The early missionaries were of the high type of New England men and women who brought education as well as Christianity to Hawaii, so that now all natives are Christians, and have attended the schools. The children of the early missionaries have developed the Islands; they have been excellent business men and women and many of them are very wealthy. However, this is the result of New England blood and is not due to the money inherited from their missionary ancestors, all of whom died poor or with small holdings. It seems as if they were developed by a kind Providence for the good of their Islands, for they are devoted to the general welfare and give freely for the public benefit and, more than all, they are sufficiently broad-minded and have the wisdom needed to deal justly with the mixture of races which make up the population of the Islands. Through excellent public schools they are making American citizens out of the children of thousands of aliens, a large portion of whom are Chinese and Japanese. A thoughtful stay in Hawaii is one of the best lessons in world peace and internationalism that this world affords.

It was surely an appropriate place for the Pan-Pacific Union to be established in 1920, just a hundred years after the landing in the Islands of those self-sacrificing wise missionaries from New England. This organization moves on with greater influence and greater prestige every year, and its various meetings are heralded the world over. We often went to gatherings at the Pan-Pacific Home, a private mansion turned over to the cause. We found Mr. Alexander Hume Ford, a very interesting man; the local activities of the Union were motivated by him and he also had great responsibilities in the international meetings. He is a tall, thin, wiry man full of energy and caring nothing for dress or style, devotes all his powers to the cause of peace in the Pacific.

An instance occurred during our stay that revealed to us the public spirit which permeates Honolulu. A drive was made for a building for the Y. W. C. A. Mrs. Andrews was one of the leaders in this and kept us informed. To our surprise the amount called for was $300,000, which seemed very large to us. The drive lasted a week and went over the top with several thousands to spare. The contributions were from all classes, all races, and it seemed to us from all religions, and consisted in thousands from the wealthy, down to a dollar from a Chinese washerwoman. Each group, racially and religiously, were to have the privilege of meeting in the building which is now completed and functioning.

We attended a Y. W. C. A. clinic for underweight children, none of whom were Caucasian apparently. The mothers were in attendance and received instruction for feeding the youngsters, the lady in charge being most tactful and gracious. We also attended a food clinic where the wife of the Chinese Professor in the University translated the instructions to the group of Chinese women, and a young, wealthy Japanese matron, a graduate of the University did a like service to the group of Japanese mothers.

After seeing all these good works and the sweet spirit of tolerance in evidence everywhere, I felt that if Christ dwells anywhere on this earth it is in Honolulu.

Miss Slater and I attended Sunday evening lectures in the Buddhist Temple in Honolulu when the topic was the attitude of Buddhism toward science. The temple is a dignified building and near it is a Young Men's Buddhist Association building; this association is carried on on the lines of the Y. M. C. A. The priest in the temple was a surprise to us. He was a vigorous, middle-aged Irishman, keen and clever. He had been a Catholic Priest before his conversion to Buddhism, and we were sure he brought over with him more than a little of his Roman Catholic outlook. He was rather flowery in his speech—and had Irish wit—and his singing was fine. He certainly had no grasp on the sciences under discussion, but he made one thing very clear, Buddhism is a religion of the spirit; and whatever the ancient ideas of the physical world were or whatever the modern theories and discoveries are, Buddhism is not affected because it is spiritual. We thought some of our Christian theologies might be benefitted by taking this attitude. The hymns were Buddhistic, but the tunes were of our own common church hymns. We were certain that the versatile priest had written the hymns purposely for these tunes. As a Buddhist priest he was an interesting anomaly.

The Mormons add their sect to the many others in the Islands. Mr. Fullard Leo took us to visit the Mormon Temple he had decorated. It is in a quiet, isolated spot many miles from Honolulu and is an impressive structure set high on a hillside, the cream-white stone of the building shining against a background of rugged green mountains. Four terraces below the temple add greatly to its beauty. In the center of each terrace is an oblong pool, with a column of stone on each side set in the water and reflected in the pool. The water is fresh and flows from one pool to another; beautiful flights of stone steps lead from each terrace to the one above. Above the upper pool, and reflected in it, is a graceful bas-relief representing the blessing of motherhood. The landscaping adds greatly to the setting of this most beautiful temple.

The schools and their problems attracted our interest, for the schools make the melting pot begin to boil from the kindergarten, on up. The ideals of U. S. citizenship are presented early and kept constantly before the pupils, the stars and stripes is their flag and they love it. We attended the Friday morning exercises at the Royal School, a grammar school whose principal, Mr. Cyril Smith, is a man of dignity, ability and devotion to his task. The exercises, calisthenics and marching of the pupils in the school yard, showed perfect precision and was a beautiful sight. After this came the raising of the flag by a few pupils, a privilege earned by excellence in studies and behavior. The act was done reverently, a Chinese, a Japanese, and a Portuguese child were among the honored ones. As the flag went up, all the children saluted, and we witnessed it with tears of feeling in our eyes.

Mr. Smith told us that these children were all American in their feelings and ideals. He told as an illustration, of a Japanese mother who had arranged to take her twelve-year-old daughter back to Japan for a month's visit. When they returned the mother told Mr. Smith of her great enjoyment in the visit. Later, when alone with the daughter, he asked her how she found the experience, "Rotten," was the succinct answer.

Pertinent to this feeling of U. S. citizenship is an instance that occurred while we were in Honolulu. The Oxford debating team, on its world trip, stopped at Honolulu and debated with the University team there. The head debater on the home team was a Chinese, brilliant and logical. At a dinner given the two teams, one of the Oxford men made a rather arrogant remark about the possibilities of the United States, at which the Chinese youth remarked with a smile, "You remember how we surprised you and what we did in 1776." Well, why not? No young descendent of the signers of the Declaration of Independence was any more responsible for or prouder of our victory in the Revolutionary War than this young American citizen.

Organizations are many and flourishing in Hawaii. Several of these belong to women. The Out-door Circle includes all women interested in beautifying the Islands, and they have done a great and beneficent work. They had eliminated all the bill-board advertisements except Camel Cigarettes and Wrigley's Gum, and I believe later, these succumbed. They had planted avenues with trees and helped in city planning. They had a flowering plant exchange. They were pushing an extensive park system and the conservation of the natural beauties of the landscape, and they published a yearly report. Nearly 600 women are members of this active and vital organization. I attended two of the meetings and was impressed by the practical business conducted there.

There is a flourishing American University Women's club which staged a pageant and gave a concert which I attended and enjoyed. The D. A. R. also has a fine chapter there. I attended one of the meetings at the beautiful home of Mrs. Westervelt.

I had been honored by election to the Zonta Association in Ithaca and had greatly enjoyed my acquaintance with the business women of my city. I was made welcome by the Zontians in Honolulu and attended several of their weekly luncheons at Young's Hotel.

It is almost a foregone conclusion that the arts should flourish in Hawaii. A very beautiful literature is growing there. Several poets of whom any land might be proud are writing of the physical beauty, and the unique human phenomena that pervades the islands. Mary Dillingham Frear, Jane Comstock, Don Blanding and many others, have written volumes which every lover of Hawaii must needs have in his library. Our shelf of the Islands poetry has been a perennial joy to us.

Painting also has reached early fruition. Howard Hitchcock has made beautiful pictures of the Island scenery. Mrs. Palmer's pastels also are beautiful and full of feeling. Moore has made some wonderful paintings of the sea and shores. Many visiting artists have also made noteworthy pictures. The Cross Roads Studio is often given to exhibitions. We had the pleasure of seeing there Miss Tennant's portraits of Hawaiians, very excellent.

I was privileged to attend the meetings of the literary sections of the College Women's Club, held in the beautiful and hospitable home of Mrs. Frear. We heard lectures on modern Japanese drama by a talented young Japanese woman, Miss Mashemo, and found them truly revealing. A little later we attended a classical Japanese play put on by the University students, some of the chief actors being Chinese. It was staged and played superbly.

Mr. Comstock attended meetings of the College Men's Club and enjoyed them. He was also the guest of Judge Frear at the Social Club where he found the discussions extremely interesting.

We were invited to luncheon at the beautiful home of Mr. and Mrs. Walter Dillingham. It is set on a flank of Diamond Head and commands a glorious view. The house is of Italian architecture built around a court which contains a fountain playing in a bowl of heavenly blue. The furnishings of the house are from both the Orient and Italy and are as interesting as expensive, which is saying much. Our fruit cocktail was served in white jade cups set in silver, and we drank from Venetian glass goblets. Our host and hostess we found very attractive and it was at this luncheon we had the privilege of meeting Judge Sanford B. Dole; whose name is on the most important pages in the history of the Islands. He was over eighty, but his mind was as keen as ever and his conversation delightful. Mr. Walter Dillingham is a brother of Mrs. Frear.

We can never forget the happy hours we spent in the home over which Mary Dillingham Frear presided with such sweetness and simplicity. She is a wonderful woman; there seems no limit to her capacity. She wrote a pageant in a few hours while I was with her at her seaside cottage. It was for the Y. W. C. A. and was as beautiful spiritually as it was historically perfect. Her devotion to her husband and her two adopted daughters is something I love to think of when gray days come, for one of the daughters is a soul in the prison of a helpless body. Mr. Comstock esteemed the knowing of Judge Frear one of the privileges of his lifetime. These two in their hospitality and friendliness brought into our lives the happiness and spiritual uplift that they had brought into the lives of so many others who were fortunate enough to know them.

In April—we sailed away from this entrancing Island and its rare people. Many of our friends came to see us off and we were almost smothered with beautiful leis. Although we had to come away we left our hearts there, for no experience in our lives had been so interesting, so heartening and so beautiful.

We spent a few days at San Francisco visiting friends and calling on President and Mrs. Wheeler at Berkeley.

We then went to Palo Alto to see the Marxes, where we had, again, the opportunity of meeting many of our old friends at Stanford. We arrived home April 17th and found Jim and Will Slingerland at the station to meet us.

We were delighted to find the hepaticas and blood root in blossom in our woods. Mr. Comstock began working in the garden with an enthusiasm which had been lacking during the year of his incessant toil on "The Introduction." We bought a car; during Jim's stay in our household we had

had the use of his car, and now that he had his own family to care for, we needed a car of our own. Bob Farnham, who lived in the chalet, drove for us until we learned to drive for ourselves. I did the cooking and housework with the help of a maid two days per week. However, with our car we often went out for the evening meal, one of our favorite places being the excellent old-fashioned Shaver's Hotel at Freeville. Every week I counted up my gains in going without a cook, and thus I earned enough to buy a new cook stove and a kitchen cabinet.

This was the first time in years that Mr. Comstock and I had been by ourselves in our home and we greatly enjoyed our meals tete-a-tete. We often played Russian Bank evenings, a game which we learned in Hawaii and certainly an excellent game for two.

We had brought colored slides from Hawaii depicting in some measure the beautiful scenery of the Islands. Mr. Comstock gave a brief talk before the Jugatae, showing the slides, then declared he was done. I was not so sensible and gave talks before the Womens' Club, the Parent-Teachers Meeting, the Newman Club, the Trumansburg school, and finally before the students in the summer session.

The last of May Dr. Schurman and Mrs. Schurman came to Ithaca for the first time since their departure. There was a large dinner given to them in Prudence Risley Hall and we were able to see them and speak with them. They had just returned from China and were going to Berlin. We were much interested in Dr. Schurman's after-dinner speech.

The deep hostility toward the Germans which he had held during the war, when his two sons were fighting, had disappeared and a mild charity had taken its place, which was as it should be, since he was to represent the United States in Germany.

Early in June we had as a guest Dr. A. D. Imms of the Rothamsted Experimental Station in England. He proved an interesting guest, very easy to care for. Mr. Comstock gave him a dinner at the Forest Home Inn, inviting the men of the entomological staff. He did not seem at all shocked to find that I prepared his breakfasts and lunches with my own hands. Here was another instance where I found an Englishman agreeable and charming, when once the crust was broken.

June 22nd, 1924, was an important day for the Comstocks for, on that day, Eliza Vantine Northrup came to us as housekeeper. She had lived with us three years at the beginning of the century. Exquisitely neat, an excellent cook, a loyal and devoted heart and a high ideal of duty characterized her. How many times in the hard months and years since then, we have returned thanks that she was vouchsafed to us.

Margaret Turner came to us for the summer session, as usual. We were always glad when she came and sorry when she went away. I had a fine large class and, as ever, I enjoyed teaching. There were many interesting activities during this session. The Dramatic Club gave plays every week. One night we experienced great pleasure in seeing our Marvin Herrick act the chief part in "The Soul of a Professor," an exquisitely humorous play by Professor Martin Sampson.

An incident showing Mr. Comstock's devotion to Jim and Gretel made me smile. He had always objected to dogs and refused to have one around. However, the Russells "just had to have a dog." When they went away for their vacation, it was amusing to see Mr. Comstock leading their dog around for exercise and feeding it carefully. I do not think he ever made a greater concession to anyone.

One of the social events of the session was a dinner given by Professor and Mrs. George Works to the faculty in Rural Education. The dinner was held at the George Junior Republic Inn and gave us opportunity to make the acquaintance of the lecturers who had come to Cornell from other institutions. The social relations in the Department of Rural Education were always delightful and owed much to Professor and Mrs. Works.

The last of August, Cousin Nora Taft, Mr. Comstock, Marvin Herrick and I started on a pilgrimage to the homes of our ancestors. We had a glorious trip through the Catskills and across the Bear Mountain bridge. Our first objective was New Milford, where we gazed at the inscription of the names of our ancestors,—"Henry Botsford and Elizabeth, his wife," on the beautiful memorial bridge; and then we went to the Botsford homestead. From Milford we went to Wethersfield to pay tribute to Nathaniel Foote, our ancestor on Grandmother's side. We looked with pride on his monument. Then to Bristol where our grandparents had lived, before their hegira to western New York in 1823. On our way home, we spent our last night in Cherry Valley, a place we had heard much about in our childhood, when Grandfather told of the fights with the Indians, which were contemporary with his boyhood. Soon after our return Nora left us and later we all went to the station to see Marvin Herrick off for Ames, Iowa, where this young man was to be Professor of Dramatics.

In late September we had a visit from Mr. Tatsudo Ogata, now in a lucrative and important position in Japan, where he has charge of a herd of cows whose ancestry is monumental. He showed us photographs of his milk-house and dairy, all the walls tiled in porcelain. He was on his way to Europe to buy more blooded stock. This successful man was the same Ogata that I brought from California in 1905 to be Mrs. Schurman's butler. He showed deep and abiding affection for Mr. Comstock and myself and his visit was interesting and inspiring.

In October we gave a reception to the Departments of Biology, Entomology and Zoology in honor of Professor and Mrs. O. A. Johannsen and Professor and Mrs. P. W. Claasen, the former having been away a year in Europe and the latter on leave in China. It happened that this was the last reception, departmental or otherwise, that we ever gave.

Mr. Comstock had been a member of the Heckscher Council from the first and had been vitally interested in the distribution of this fund for scientific research. He had tried to resign before we went to Hawaii on account of the enforced absence from the meetings. However, he was retained. Again, this year he sought to resign because we were planning a winter on the Riviera but he was still retained. It was only after his illness that his resignation was accepted.

It was in October that we went to Bucknell College in Pennsylvania. The occasion for the trip was the everlasting talk on Hawaii, this time to be given by myself before the Women's Club of Lewisburg. We were the guests of Professor and Mrs. N. H. Stewart in their new home. We shall never forget our motor trip to Lewisburg and back. The mountains were spread with Persian tapestries so characteristic of our Autumns, and every turn in the road brought us new and interesting views.

Since buying our car in April we had both taken lessons intermittently in learning to drive. Mr. Comstock had had some lessons with Professor Gage some years ago. He passed his examination in August and the fact filled him with astonishment and consternation, for he did not wish to drive. Driving a horse or an auto bored him excessively; he learned simply because he thought he ought to.

People aware that we were going away [to Europe], entertained us frequently in a happy spirit of loyal friendship. The fatal day of departure came and we both were very tired; I was so exhausted and confused when I finally packed for the journey I could not remember what I had put in the trunks or what I had left out. Finally, on November 25, 1925, Mr. Comstock and the plumber turned off the water in the house, but we still kept on working. We had luncheon with Jim and Gretel and went to the Herricks' for dinner. Mr. Comstock, in getting out of the car in the dark, stepped into a puddle and wet himself to his knees. The mishap so upset him that he came away from the house in his sweater and overcoat, leaving his coat behind and not discovering it until we reached the station. By rushing the car up the hill the coat was retrieved just before the train started. I give this incident to show how very mind-weary Mr. Comstock was at this time. A more methodical man never lived, and to forget to put on his coat after putting on his sweater would have been ordinarily impossible for him.

We arrived in New York Thanksgiving morning and, after settling ourselves as guests of our cousins Catherine and Gerald Stopp in their charming eyrie in Charles Street, we went to the home of Dr. and Mrs. Will C. Thro in Long Island City for dinner. After dinner we had some heavenly music, Mrs. Thro playing the violin and a friend, Mr. Stockman, accompanying on the piano.

On November 28th in the morning we[1] went aboard the *S. S. America*. Many friends were there to see us off.

Our first days were very comfortable, the Atlantic being absolutely calm; then it seemed to remember its wonted devilishness and our two girls were laid low; Margaret Turner, who was with us, declaring her stomach was full of soap suds. Mr. Comstock was comfortable as usual, and I caromed cheerfully up and down the passageways and wished I had as many feet as a millipede to stand on.

At the Sailor's Benefit concert, I read some of John C. Branner's "How and Why Stories" which proved a success. Many of the passengers asked me for the title of the book.

I wonder that no one has written of the wild experiences incident to landing at night at Plymouth and getting a train to London. First of all, we did not know when we were on land, but had to be ready early in the evening and go to the second class dining room. There we waited and waited while boxes and boxes of silver and gold bullion were taken ashore. At midnight we were ferried to the dock, and I do not know what would have happened to us except for the attentions of two courteous and quite delightful Englishmen, Major G. F. Ingham and Mr. A. S. Morris. We had made their acquaintance on the boat and they were guiding angels to us on a dark, perplexing and foreign shore. They saw us through the customs, and after considerable effort, got a first class compartment for Mr. Comstock and myself and saw that the girls were as comfortable as possible in their second class accommodations.

We went to our old Hotel Thackery in London. Fortunately, we were able to get rooms that had coal grates, and for a dollar extra a day, we were able to get enough coal to keep us warm evenings and we were proportionately thankful.

---

1. Footnote at the bottom of the page: "There were four in the party, Mr. and Mrs. Comstock and two young women, Margaret Turner and Mary Ellen Donahue." The note is typed and not signed by editor or author. —KSt.

Then followed ten days of sight-seeing with many glorious hours in the art galleries. Again, I experienced the breathless thrill of the Turners'—especially the sketches. Mr. Comstock and I spent a Sunday in Norfolk visiting The Rev. Allison Osborne and his wife and her mother, the latter being the sister of Margaret Dowell's husband. The fine old rectory set in large grounds, the beautiful little church and the simple, appealing sermon are among our memory pictures. Mr. Osborne, although in delicate health, was a delightful host, full of entertaining stories and a man of fine culture. I shall never forget how he, arrayed in dressing gown and slippers, brought us tea before we arose in the morning and lighted the fire in our grate. The established Church of England is parsimonious in dealing with her lesser clergy and there was small margin for servant hire in this dignified home. The salary was barely a thousand dollars, and the rectory must be kept in repair out of that; and at that time the cost of food in England was quite as great as in America.

Christmas was approaching, and every night there were singers on the street giving to all the beautiful old Christmas Carols. We had two very interesting experiences out of the ordinary in London. After dining at the Cheshire Cheese one day we attended a session of the House of Commons and heard an incisive speech by Sir Alfred Mond on the proposed tariff on cutlery, etc. The members were lounging about, apparently trying to get into easy positions. Those seats must be most uncomfortable. The other experience was attending the three o'clock services at Westminster Abbey. We sat so that we looked towards the Poets' Corner and faced the great rose window that let in pale light of a thousand rich tints. Lights were ablaze in the Chancel. A youth in a radiant red robe placed the books for the choir. The members of the choir wore white robes with red collars. The afternoon light was dim so that the side chapels seemed mysterious and the many monuments shone but palely through the dusk. The priest intoned the service; the choir responded in music to stir the soul; the boy soloists had heavenly voices. It was a most beautiful and impressive service, and we listened to it sitting beneath the outstretched hand of the statue of Peel.

We especially enjoyed showing the Tower of London to our girls, who were greatly impressed with the coats of armor and wished they could see a knight and horse, both big enough and strong enough to carry such an outfit. A tame raven was stalking about near the place where the unfortunate queens were beheaded which seemed mysteriously fitting. We viewed with keen interest the small room where Sir Walter Raleigh was confined for twelve years and where, meanwhile, he wrote his History of the World. It occurred to us that if George Lincoln Burr could only be confined here he would finish his magnum opus which, of course, he will never do while he is loose in a world where so many people need him and his generous ministrations.

We wished we might stay longer in London, but the weather was trying and we longed for the Riviera, so on December 18th we made the crossing on pleasant seas, but this was the only pleasant part. Mr. Comstock nearly suffered nervous prostration getting our many pieces of baggage from the hotel to station and getting it weighed for excess, and then getting it aboard the train. How infinitely easier it is to travel in America where baggage checks take the place of worrying, sweating, human endeavor.

We established ourselves comfortably in Hotel de Louvre in a Chamber of Mirrors and gilt and felt very French-y indeed. Cook sent us a very interesting and able guide, who took us the first day (because it was pleasant) to Versailles. Mr. Comstock ad I had been there before but this time we really saw it because of the excellence of our guide's knowledge. He made very real to us the dramatic picture of the singing of the Versailles treaty, that treaty so widely scorned and yet one of the great events of history.

As we wandered through the great rooms, we experienced a feeling of profound admiration for Louis XIV whose name had always been anathema to us. He "set out" to build the most beautiful and wonderful palace for kings in the world and he accomplished his dream. We had always admired a man who did his job well, so now we paid tribute to Louis XIV.

We went to Malmaison, that most livable of all famous houses. To tell the truth, after inspecting Josephine's own room I lost respect for her. Her walls of mirrors at every angle proved her to be inordinately vain and self-conscious. I promptly stopped being sorry for her, for I think she needed the discipline she surely experienced.

We were especially interested in the Sorbonne, which looked dusty with much learning. The Palace of Justice held our attention for a long time. The regalia of the Judges and lawyers seemed very strange and interesting. We reveled in the stained windows of Saint Chappelle, never anywhere else had we seen such a riot of color. The Louvre was so near us that we went there several times taking in no more than we wanted to digest at one time. I had a whole morning with the Corots, Millets, and Meissoniers, and what tourist could be expected to do more, even though he longed to live a whole lifetime with just one of these pictures.

We were fortunate to secure seats at the Opera, to enjoy a magnificent presentation of Thais. The music was superb and satisfied our souls. Quite different was another evening's entertainment at the Moulin Rouge. We had heard of this place but going to it was born of no desire on our part to have a wild night in Paris. We thought of the Moulin Rouge as vaudeville probably. We were quite unprepared for the display of nude ladies, all the more nude because of their costumes, which did not cover but were enhanced by the gorgeous effects of colored lights.

Mr. Comstock was terribly shocked and ashamed to have brought his women folk to such a place. I was disgusted but our two young ladies took it calmly. They had seen revues on Broadway and apparently could not understand our Victorian resentment. Mr. Comstock said he hoped that none of us would ever tell anybody that he went to such a disgraceful show. He told me that if we were going to stay in Paris he would hire a chaperone to go around to the different theaters and report to him before he would venture to buy tickets.

We spend one memorable day at Rheims, where the great cathedral was being restored. We could still see the devastation wrought and we wondered if this magnificent edifice would ever recover from its wounds and be as it was before. From Rheims, still a shattered city, we drove along the Aisne canal, which was the front line for such a long time. We stopped before reaching Berry au Bac to visit Hill 108, a vast mine crater. Then along the Aisne valley. The Chemin des Dames was a desolate road; skeletons of the trees made desolate the ridge above it. We went to Nesle and saw for the first time a cemetery where American soldiers were buried. We were awed by the vast expanse of white crosses. Joyce Kilmer was buried here, and we carried a flower to his grave. We viewed from afar the tomb of Quentin Roosevelt but were unable to make the pilgrimage to it. We went to Belleau Wood and there again we found a cemetery with its wilderness of crosses, below the poor woods shot to tatters by cruel war, that seemed as hard on trees as on men. Our road led to Chateau Thierry where we visited the monument to the dead soldiers of our Third Division and then sick at heart returned to Paris. The places we had seen were revelations of realities to Mr. Comstock and myself who had studied the maps daily during the war.

We had Christmas in Paris. We had a family celebration by taking the wrappings off of our presents which we had carried along; and by giving to each and receiving from each our little party remembrances. We finished the day by walking through the parks and to the Place de la Concorde and looking at people as well as the scenery. It was all very gay.

Mr. Comstock and I had the special pleasure of dining with Director and Mrs. Albert R. Mann and their family. They had been in Paris all the year as he was visiting educational institutions all over Europe for the Carnegie International Educational Foundation. We were greatly interested in what he told us of his work and it was a joy to be with this charming family again.

On December 28th we left Paris, our girls quite reluctantly. From Paris to Marseilles we had an opportunity to see something of rural France,—well cultivated fields, few farmhouses, picturesque villages and hopeless-looking orchards; meanwhile we were being shaken by a ride over the roughest railroad in our experience. The Saone and Rhone Rivers were on a rampage, and we saw flooded country all the afternoon. We stopped only a night at Marseilles and in the morning took the train for Mentone. It was a ride through the far-famed French Riviera and lived up to its reputation. There were always sharp jagged mountains in sight, and glimpses of the sea through olive trees, often a medieval castle or city crowning a steep hill. It all made me long to delve into history and know more of the turbulent past of this coast.

Professor and Mrs. Comstock sitting on the laurel bench in their garden.

CHAPTER XX

Mentone

This last chapter of the manuscript is thirty-four pages in length. The Comstocks' trip abroad to Mentone in the winter of 1926 was their last major sojourn together before Mr. Comstock was stricken with his first stroke in the summer of that same year. As with the previous chapter, Chapter XX is marked in purple china marker with the following, "Omit all except last page, p. 34." The last paragraphs of manuscript page 20–34 were reworked into a single page (p. 267), for the 1953 edition as "Chapter 20: 1926–1930: The Last of Life . . ."

The entire manuscript, as I have had the privilege to hold and work from, is completely re-keyed in the format originally typed by Mrs. Comstock.

{We were fortunate in finding most satisfactory quarters for the winter in Mentone. It was sheer luck that led us to the Villa Bournabat, presided over by three efficient and most considerate Danish women, the Misses Nevil, one of whom spoke excellent English. The villa was once the private residence of Felix Faure, and later of a wealthy man whose name it bore. Our room was large and, to our delight, was heated with a small stove. Our room on the second floor opened on a balcony that from one side gave us command of the Ave. Felix Faure and on the opposite side, gave us a view of the attractive garden of the Villa, through the gates of which, we could see the Promenade du Midi and the sea. We settled ourselves happily and Mr. Comstock made arrangements to have all the coal he wanted at 25 cents a scuttle-full, so we were ready for a winter in the South.}

{Mentone proved to be a very attractive modern city with an ancient City on a hill in its midst. The ancient city had its ruined castles; its steep narrow streets were beset with high stone houses, often joined overhead, so that they seemed mere tunnels. Through an archway here and there one could glimpse still steeper streets. From the upper windows and on lines across the streets the family wash flaunted its many colors. On the crown of the hill is an ancient cathedral-like church, and on a still higher point is a cemetery set with dark cypresses. A cemetery where the dead did not seem lonesome because they were buried so near to each other that they might hold hands and be comforted. This old city had its beginning in the Middle Ages. Its first statutes show it was a city in 1290 A. D. and in 1348 it was bought for 16,000 gold florins by Charles Grimaldi, Prince of Monaco, and after that its history is mingled with the fortunes and fights of that principality. However, before there was any city whatever there was, in Roman times, a fishing village on the site. The city grew in wealth and strength, and finally in 1850 it, with its neighboring city Roquebrun, separated from Monaco. The two set up a republic and this lasted for some time when these independent people finally chose to join France.}

{Behind Mentone the high and rugged mountains are so near that they seem almost to crowd the city into the sea. Down these mountains dash torrents, bridged picturesquely here and there. A "torrent" we discovered, is a stream that is a raging flood sometimes and sometimes is no stream at all, the dry bed merely a stony gully. The lower reaches of the mountain sides are terraced to an almost unbelievable extent, sometimes the ground gained being scarcely as wide as the wall that holds it, is high. The terraces are set with orange and lemon and olive trees and sometimes with grapes and in some places with flowers, especially carnations.}

{As soon as we were fairly settled in Villa Bournabet our young ladies sought a French teacher, for here was the opportunity to study to some purpose. Through Miss Nevil they engaged Madame Alexandra de Tchahotine, an exile from Russia who spoke a pure French. I also had conversation with her and found her a woman of broad experience, high ideals and possessed of a fortitude that won the admiration of us all.}

{One of our first activities, was a trip to Monte Carlo, an excursion, whether taken on train or in auto or afoot that merits well the overworked term "scenic." Our first experience was the surprise of finding how difficult it is to get into the ornate casino. We had always imagined the doors wide open, a welcome awaiting any who sought to pass within. Before we were through, we felt as if we were passing examination for a position in the diplomatic service. We entered and found a crowd massed around the desks where we were to get tickets. We had to show our passports, tell our ages, and where we were staying and why we were there anyhow, and then sign papers. The clerk who fell to our lot was stupid and slow, and we were tired out by the time we passed into the great hall whose imposing domed ceiling is supported by columns of pinky marble.}

{Then we showed our tickets and passed into the gambling rooms. Since we knew nothing of the games, the performances around the tables were about as intelligible to us as the performances we had witnessed in the Stock Exchange. We watched the people at the table play, and those standing around throwing chips and money on the table and calling out numbers to the croupier who, while we watched, mostly drew in the plunder with his efficient little hoe as the winnings of the table. We saw one man win 2000 franc, but he was a shining exception. We wandered around the spacious, too highly decorated rooms, stopping at tables to look over the players to find our ideal of a real gambler like John Oakhurst, for example.}

{We were doomed to disappointment for no one looked desperate or wicked or debonair or magnificent. All were intent and serious, but a more uninteresting, banal collection of human beings we had never seen anywhere. There were one or two rather fine-looking old men, and one old woman, who, we were sure, was hired by the Casino for people to look at as she so entirely "filled the bill," as an elderly female roué. A fierce wide hat, a thick white lace veil drawn across her highly cosmeticized nose and upper face, her vermilion lips, her high cracked voice, all certainly made a picture to remember. She played every time and was on chummy relations with the croupiers, and she saved the day for us.}

{After looking over the crowd my feeling about Monte Cristo changed. We did not see any people who looked as if they would be of any use in their home society, and we had no pity in our hearts for them if they lost, or if they jumped into the sea afterwards. When we learned that no one could be a citizen of Monaco who gambled or was not entirely a virtuous person, and when we visited the magnificent Oceanographic Museum and Aquarium, our sympathies were all with the principality, the prince and the croupiers. If they could do anything interesting with such an uninteresting lot of folk, they ought to be commended. Moreover, while one cannot but admire the good sportsmanship of Jack Oakhurst and his ilk who lose as calmly as they win, yet I could never understand why one should pity a gambler. I remember one day when on our way to Nice on the train, a woman came into the compartment at Monte Carlo evidently in desperate mental condition. From her murmuring in German we understood she had lost her all at the tables. Mr. Comstock always maintained that to him Monte Carlo was like a movie, and quite unreal.}

{One of our first objectives was a visit to La Turbie, which we had seen from afar, marked by ruins of the marble tower which was reared by Augustus

Caesar, 6 B. C., to celebrate the final victory of the Romans over those hardy mountaineers, the Ligurians. The tower, built on the highest point of the Roman road that extended from Rome to Arles, was a monument to the greatness of Rome. The village was a resting place on this post road, and here came centurions and soldiers, patricians and ladies in sedan chairs carried by slaves, and here came traders from the Orient. However, the grandeur that was Rome faded during the early centuries A. D. During the middle ages the place was made into a fortress, built with the stones fallen from the great tower, and the town was walled from the same source. During the turbulent middle ages La Turbie was taken and retaken by rival European powers and by the Saracens. Now for several centuries, it has lain as it is today, an old, old town, half in ruins with here and there an impertinent new building that emphasizes the destruction of the past. A few years ago two of Caesar's columns, still white and beautiful, were replaced on the half of the tower that still stands. The tower so broken, the two retrieved columns shining in the sunlight, seem to stand in mute protest against the destructive forces of time and man through twenty centuries.}

{On a hill above the tower and built upon the foundation of an old encircling wall is a modern cemetery. It seemed a most fitting place for the dead, where every view brings the conviction that death and destruction are triumphant and human interests and activities are transient.}

{From La Turbie we went on to Eze, that city that has so often been captured and whose streets had been flooded with the blood of the citizens. It is on a steep cliff, 1400 feet above the sea, founded by Phoenicians probably, owned in turn by Romans, Lombards, Saracens, Guelfs, Ghibellines, the Prince of Savory, and finally, betrayed by traitors, was practically destroyed by the pirate Barbarossa in 1543, since which it has ceased to be important. It was the home of famous troubadours in the Middle Ages and in its halls took place competitions of those who wrote their own songs and composed and played their own music. Of all the ancient citadels we saw on the Riviera Eze was the most fascinating and most stimulating to the imagination. That night I wrote the following which, whatever it may be lacking as poetry, represents my reaction to this stronghold perched upon its pinnacle of rock, every stone in its steep streets fairly reeking of mediaeval conflicts.}

{Eze (is)

When the world was born, a might gash upon the mountain side
Was made to form a pinnacle of rugged rocks and gray,
Whose tortured steeps brave trees have clothed. Below, the smiling bay
Extends its azure curves; on high, above its tide
Still stands the wall of Ancient Eze, too might for decay;

Mere token now of power of a splendid bygone day,
The glory of the troubadour, the prize of knightly pride.
Even now there creeps a sluggish life within those narrow walls,
The peasants, few and listless, who climb the stony ways,
Or drive their beasts to stable within those ancient halls,
Where erstwhile knight assembled in armor all ablaze,
And ladyes fayre their guerdons gave. The silence now appalls
The wanderer there who dares to dream of olden, golden days.

Eze (was)

The troubadours were singing six hundred years ago
Within the castle hall above the walls of Eze.
'Tis there that Blacas[1] wins his well earned crown of bays;
"If I were loved as I do love" sings he in sweetest woe!
Then gayly dons his armor, and while the trumpets blow
He sallies forth, with mighty sword and merrily he flays
The enemy who dares to turn his rude and envious gaze
Upon the castle high, meet fate for every foe.
Alas! The day when Barbarossa's pirate fleet
Dropped anchor far below within that azure bay.
A traitor, seeming friendly, led with base deceit
The Turkish hordes far upward through the secret way,
Then carnage piled with dead the every reeking street,
And none were left in Eze to sorrow or to pray.}

{We settled in our comfortable pension to a comfortable routine. There were several English people in the house, among which was Mrs. Helen McAlpin Bacon, an artist and a charming woman.}

{We quite invariably had our coffee with our fellow pensioners in the reception room or parlor and Mr. Comstock smoked happily and deliberately until bedtime. Afternoons we went to the Park to listen to the band which gave excellent music. The crowd there was always eminently respectable and quite uninteresting, except for the magnificent whiskers worn by certain dignified gentlemen. We had forgotten that there was such an adornment for the masculine face. We often walked along the wise Promenade du Midi, one of the most beautiful "board walks" (made of stone) in the world, far more interesting than the one in Nice. On the one side is the beautiful city of Mentone climbing its terraced mountain sides, and cut by its picturesquely

1. Footnote at bottom of the page (source unknown): *Blacas, A troubadour of Eze in the beginning of the 13th century. See Sir Frederick Treves' "The Riviera of the Corniche Road." —KSt.

bridged torrents, and on the other, the Mediterranean, sometimes exquisitely azure, oftimes very dark blue and again gray, its waves dashing up over the rocks by our feet in threatening fountains of spray.}

{One day we went to Roquebrun whose original village and citadel is high on a mountain-side between Mentone and Monte Carlo. It was this city and its rocky estate that united with Mentone to throw off the yoke of Monaco and set up a republic in 1848. We took the tram almost to Monte Carlo, then climbed a well-paved road up the steep hill, new views of the picturesque coast meeting our eyes at almost every step. There was Monte Carlo lifting its towers aggressively toward the sea; a great valley cutting back into the jagged mountain; and houses like bird boxes clinging to the mountain-sides.}

{There was an entomological station in Mentone and we made a pilgrimage to it quite early. We were welcomed by the chief, Raymond Poutier, and shown every courtesy officially. Quite unofficially we were introduced to the beautiful Madame Poutier and the three young sons. We were entertained in their home and had many delightful hours with them; they were more than mere acquaintances to us; we felt for them sincere affection. Mr. Comstock had great respect for Monsieur Poutier's excellent work as an entomologist, accomplished with such limited financial support.}

{We had a great and unexpected pleasure in a visit by our Cornell student friend, Pierre Pochet. He had been an intimate friend of ours while he was in college and had been a revelation to us of the French youth of strict morality and high ideals. I had corresponded with him at intervals since his return to France. He had married and was the owner of an estate on the Riviera. He brought his wife, a gentle young lady of great personal charm, and his eldest child, Marie, to visit us soon after we arrived at Mentone. We found him grown greater in wisdom and spirit and with the old charm of manner, and as modest as ever, and handsomer than when he was a boy.}

{He told us of his experience in German prisons with no criticism or bitterness; he said he was treated as well as could be expected. He had been able to purchase a cello from a fellow-prisoner and was allowed to practice on it which, he said, helped him to pass the weary hours. All that was over now, and he was trying to be a good citizen. He said to me with a smile, "I remember you told me once that it required much patience to be a good citizen of a republic."}

{Later we went one day to the picturesque old city of Biot where he met us with a very lively horse hitched to a good wagon, and we bowled over interesting roads to his home, Villa St. Julian. This was a large handsome villa set in unique grounds. The estate was on a side hill, above and below the villa. It was planted to olives, grapes, and flowers, his specialty being anemones. The latter he raised for the florists in cities, notably in London. His grapes he gathered and spread in the rooms of a long building which, in the days of greatness of the villa, had been used for servants' quarters. By thus keeping the grapes, he sold them at a good price to tourist hotels in the winter. He also cared for a neighboring estate which consisted mostly of orange and lemon orchards. Here he gathered the flowers for the perfume factories at Grasse. He had put in a pump which carried water from the stream below his place to a reservoir on the highest point of his holdings so that he could irrigate his crops.}

{I cannot quite find the words to describe the thrill that the walk about the estate gave us. While among the olive trees and vineyards, we felt as if we were in a scene of a hundred years ago. Every view was someway so ripe in its attractiveness. Luncheon in the villa was memorable, both for company and the menu. We made the acquaintance of petite Marie's two brothers, one a sturdy handsome lad of three years and the other a baby in his carriage. The Pochet family naturally used only a portion of the large house. We told Pierre that, in our old age, we would be glad to take the third story and live there to share his idyllic existence. We were assured we should be welcome and we did not doubt it. This day was one of the sweetest and most satisfying of our winter. Since then we have received many affectionate letters signed; "Your French son and daughter."}

{Two or three times a week we took an auto, or charabanc, excursion in some direction. Whether we followed the road along the sea, or went on the Grand Cormiche,[2] a part of which follows the old Roman road, or whether we followed a winding road up some valley, we always found mediaeval cities perching on pinnacles, cities showing a ruined castle and remnants of the old walls, with the gates often intact.}

{One day we went to such a city, Castellar. The girls walked but Mr. Comstock and I took a voiture with a driver. It was a winding, twisting road all up hill, but our horse was sturdy and sure. We were glad to go slowly and enjoy our changing views of the rugged Mentone valley, enclosed by high peaks. The mountain-sides were terraced almost from the base to the limit of the timber line, and set with orange, lemon and olive trees. We passed groves of ancient olive trees, and if there is a more picturesque tree in its old age than the olive, we have not seen it. As we approached Castellar we had a wide view of the Carei Valley, on the other side of the range, dotted with villages.

---

2. Footnote at bottom of the manuscript (p. 20–11): "The Grand Cormiche is a part of the great military road to Italy constructed by Napoleon in 1806. —Ed. [G.W.H.]."

Finally, we reached the walls of the city more than twelve hundred feet above Mentone. As we entered through a narrow walled road we found ourselves on a little plaza with a great tree at its center and a glorious view all around, of mountain peaks and deep valleys.}

{Castellar is one of the few medieval towns that has preserved the aspect of a feudal fortress. Three narrow streets paved with cobblestones extend the length of the city. The cross streets are narrow, fearsome tunnels entered through low arches under the solidly built and joined houses. There are now 560 men, women and children living in the massive stone houses, the first floors of which are evidently given to the donkeys and goats. Off of a tiny plaza at the far end of the turn is a mellow old church which has in it a painting of St. Sebastian, the city's patron saint, that is beautiful enough to have come from the hand of Raphael. In the church is a tablet to 37 heroes who were killed in the last war, 37 men taken from a community of about 500 souls!}

{I had become much interested in the artist, Mrs. Helen Bacon. Her pictures in water-color were not only beautiful but sincere. I joined her class and thereafter spent my mornings making pictures about Mentone. Her technique was very excellent; she applied plenty of pigment and then removed parts of it. I was too old a dog to learn this new trick, but it was vastly intriguing to me.}

{Mrs. Bacon was a careful critic and knew her technique. Moreover, she was a very worth-while person with whom to work and to play. She gave an exhibition of her work, especially her watercolors of Venice and of the Dolomites. These were superb pictures. She was Scotch, and had a feeling for mountains in their every mood, and the dour, jagged Dolomites proved subjects worthy of her art. I have always been glad I had work with Mrs. Bacon for, although my technique was quite beyond rescuing, I felt decidedly richer for my association with her.}

{During an excursion to the Gorge du Loup, we visited Grasse. Before we were in the streets, the air brought to us the odor of the flowers used in the perfumery factories. We were told that the 36 perfume distilleries in the city use, on an average, 1900 tons of roses, 2300 tons of orange flowers and 1400 tons of jasmine, annually.}

{It is interesting that Grasse made soap for Europe in ancient times. We could not help but consider gleefully how Grasse's industries caught the ancient populace going and coming. If a knight and his lady wished to be clean and have no odor, they could use the soap of Grasse to accomplish this, though when or how they could bathe in a medieval city is beyond our imagination. On the other hand, if they did not wish to wash, they could buy Grasse perfumes and thus go on their way, their natural and inevitable smelliness covered and disguised in the fragrance of orange or jasmine blossoms.}

{We visited the esplanade with its statue of Fragonard, on the spot where thirty worthy people had been beheaded during the Revolution. However, our day in the charabanc is well described in a book by Sir Frederick Treves. "Many hundred day tourists come by charabancs. Their stay in town is very brief, for the excursion to Grasse embraces much in its breathless flight. They are deposited at a scent factory by a not disinterested driver, and they purchase soap as if it were the bread of life." Thus, did we.}

{Early in February Mr. Comstock and I made a pilgrimage to Genoa by autobus. I call it a pilgrimage because the object of our trip was to meet the Dollar *S. S. President Hayes*, at that port and discuss with the head dining-room steward, the plan for taking his small brother-in-law, Soy Chong Sze, to bring up and educate.}

{At the start we were forced to linger on the St. Louis bridge to get through the customs, where no one seemed to be in any hurry. Our road kept close to the sea which was in its more azure mood. It is the most jagged coast in the world, I think; anyway, it was the crookedest road we were ever on. Of the eight hours of our journey it is safe to say that seven were spent on curves, often sharp. There was little auto traffic, but we met or passed scores of two-wheel carts, loaded with stone or vegetables, drawn by tandem teams of mules or horses, usually two in a team, often three. It required expert driving to wait behind such a vehicle until it could pull out of the way, or to meet one rounding a curve.}

{We were hindered in several places at railroad crossings, finding the gates shut; sometimes the gate keeper, keeping in mind safety first, had gone to dinner and we waited until he was haled back to duty. Once we had an amusing obstruction; in going through a narrow village street a midget of a donkey loaded with vegetables stood crosswise the road and refused to budge. Down toward him thundered the giant autobus, tooting horribly, but he switched his tail contemptuously and stood his ground. Finally, our chauffeur climbed down and literally lifted the little rebel out of the way. Often the streets through these ancient villages were so narrow that pedestrians had to flatten themselves against the wall to save themselves. They were very patient, these villagers. We stopped at Alassio for luncheon, a place which had for us special interest, since President and Mrs. White were wont to spend their winter months there while he was Ambassador to Germany. Although it was barely 100 miles from Mentone to Genoa, we were all day on the journey, so crooked were the roads.}

{The next morning, we went through a pouring rain to the dock to see our steward and had a very satisfactory interview. The family would consider it a boon to have the boy educated, and apparently, they were satisfied that we were responsible parties. This off our minds we took a guide, a man who had lived in America, and "did" Genoa after the most approved tourist style.}

{Two memories we shall always keep of Genoa. One, of the municipal palace where two women were honored in monuments,—two who had loved and helped the city; they and the violin of Paganini made the visit to the palace memorable. The other, of the Campo Santo; never could we forget those galleries of statuary. Often there were whole families in marble grouped around the bed of the dying or the dead; veils and dresses of lace were worked out in exquisite detail. In one case, there was a life size statue of a widower, with his handkerchief pressed to his eyes, at the tomb of his wife. Below these galleries of tombs were the ordinary graves of the proletariat, and off at a far corner, possibly outside of consecrated ground, was another cemetery in which, our guide told us in awed tones, the Free Masons buried their dead. Apparently, he regarded that noble order as the embodiment of iniquity. Later he pointed out a showy mansion where he assured us dwelt the greatest Free Mason of all in Italy. We were glad he dwelt near the border for we had been told of Mussolini's antipathy to the order.}

{After we had seen the house in which dwelt the father of Columbus, or what is left of it, and had looked at the vast amount of shipping in the harbor and gazed in admiration on the proud old city with its ancient cathedral, sitting dignified on its steep hills, we felt a new understanding of the discoverer of America. Our journey home on the train was chiefly remembered because we had to wait in Ventimiglia from 1:30 to 5:30 to get through the customs. Mussolini has done much for Italy, but some things are not yet on a business basis.}

{One of our most delightful social experiences in Mentone came through the Poutiers, who were invited with us to lunch at the Palace Carniola by its present owner, Dr. Edward Phelps Allis. He was a rich American, who married a French woman, now dead. His special interest for us lay in his extensive works on the anatomy and development of the heads of fishes.}

{We found him an attractive, gentle-mannered man, modest as are all true scientists. His daughter, who was his housekeeper, had graduated from the Nurses Training School in Geneva, Switzerland, and was deeply interested in social work in Mentone. I think she had established a clinic.}

{The Palace Carniola is a large, stone house covered with pale yellow stucco, with a cornice of garlands in relief. The grounds around it are spacious and the planting luxurious. Mr. Allis had bought it of The Grimaldi, thirty years ago when the Prince was very unpopular in Mentone. We entered a wide hall which opened into a large room which in turn opened out into the garden. The floors were inlaid, and the staircase was of marble. Our host met us in the hall and took us upstairs where the family lived. Two ancestral portraits of the Grimaldi were still on the walls of the reception room; one, a cardinal, was very ornamental. This room had high frescoed ceilings and a beautiful inlaid table was in front of the fire which blazed cheerily under a mantel supported by the two giants carved in wood. There were on either side, two tall cabinets richly carved in medallions, with portrait heads at the center.}

{Soon our hostess came in, just home from the dispensary where she had worked all the morning. She was a striking looking young woman with rather long face, dark hair and eyes, and with sweet simple manners. Intelligence and capability showed in her every movement. We were ushered into the dining room, a large opening out on a balcony that commanded a view of the garden and grounds; a delicious luncheon was served, and we went back to the reception room for coffee, liqueur and cigarettes. Later we were taken through the other rooms on the second floor. The drawing room walls and ceilings were frescoed with much gilt ornamentation which our host said was a hundred years old. The furniture was of old English periods but with chairs of Louis XIV and XVI periods. In the center of the room was a large table inlaid with lapis lazuli. The room adjoining this was our host's study and every piece of furniture in it had its history. Mr. Allis had had a Japanese artist of great skill illustrate his scientific works. The original drawings he kept in a long, ancient sideboard.}

{Beyond the study was the library, the shelves filled with books in exquisite bindings. One of these volumes in tooled leather would have given us joy for a lifetime if we had possessed it. In a windowed alcove off the library was a couch, a most interesting spot for reading. Opening from the library was a guest room in which was a mantel and two tables which Josephine had used in Malmaison; scattered through the rooms were beautiful cabinets containing fans and carvings in ivory and wood of exquisite workmanship. There were also clocks of great beauty and age.}

{Later we went through the gardens and grounds and then visited the laboratories and the scientific library. These were in a long building that had probably housed the servants of the Grimaldi. To us this was quite as interesting as the palace, for it was where our host had carried on his investigations and it was perfectly equipped.}

{The most beautiful part of our first experience as guests in a palace was the feeling of genuine admiration for our host and hostess. Both had kept busy doing their full share of work for benefitting the world. Would that all palaces might have such noble inmates! We were grieved over the failing eyes of Mr. Allis, a calamity that he was bearing bravely. He was centering his interests in his son who was evidently making a place for himself in physics at Harvard.}

{On Mr. Comstock's 77th birthday we joined an automobile party to Tenda in the Italian Apennines. Our road took us first to Sospel and then struck off through the mountains in a northeast direction. On the lower levels were many olive trees, but above, the mountains were bleak with much bare rock and only here and there small areas of pines.}

{Every turn of the road gave us new mountain vistas. Here and there was a solitary dwelling of a sheep herder, or perhaps a house set in a sheltered nook; grass was evidently grown on some of the steep fields. After a time, we descended into the valley of the Roja River and found it walled by rocks more rugged than those of the Carei. As we sped up the valley we were amazed at the skill in engineering as shown in aqueducts and railroads and electrical transmission structures. Such grand arches and massive supporting walls along steep mountain sides we had never seen before. Surely Mussolini is looking after his frontiers.}

{The valley narrowed as we ascended; against a steep mountain side was plastered the gray-walled city of Saorge with its churches and beautiful towers 800 feet above us, and the mountains behind must have been a thousand feet higher.}

{Old Tenda, a dour ancient city, was partly on the river plain and partly on the mountain side. It is gray, supremely gray. The clock tower of the ruined Castello di Beatrice stands out boldly on its heights, a monument to the fact that "we go, time lasts." We wished we might know the story of Beatrice who built a castle above the River Roja.}

{On our return, we followed the River Roja down its entire length of Ventimiglia. We passed the frontier three times during the day, showing our passports each time. A cheerful young chauffeur at one station, enlivened the young ladies of our autobus by exercising his English, which consisted of three words "yes," "no," "give-me-a-kiss". We stopped at Ventimiglia for afternoon tea, which exasperated Mr. Comstock, who did not want tea but wanted to get home. So, we wandered about the town and stumbled upon the flower market which was extensive and altogether a fine display of color. We drove back along the coast through the falling evening shadows,—the placid sea below us glorious in sunset reflections; and thus, ended the last real birthday celebration granted to Mr. Comstock.}

{One day we had a guest, Mr. Baldensperger, the high authority of Europe on Bees and Beekeeping. We found him a charming and entertaining man. He told us of his really dangerous adventures in getting a very desirable species of honey bee from their homes in the cliffs in Northern Africa.}

{On March 1st, Glenn and Nannie Herrick and their daughter, Ann, my namesake, came to Villa Bournabat and life took on a still more interesting phase. We took them on excursions to La Turbie, Eze and Cap Ferrat. Also, Monte Carlo, where Ancie was not allowed to go into the gambling rooms because she was a minor.}

{We spent a day in Sospel. The road to this inland town follows up the valley of the River Carei to a high pass; at first it leads along the levels above Mentone. There are frequent shallow dams across the river, where the women go to wash their clothes; and often there are clotheslines filled with flapping garments attached to trees along the banks. Soon we begin to zig-zag up the heights, now giving us a charming picture of Mentone clustered about the torrent delta and the blue sea beyond, then a view of the spires of the church at Monti clinging to the mountain-side, and a little further on beautiful Castillon on a pinnacle high up on our horizon, its houses gleaming white in the sunshine or gray in the shade. Terraces up the mountain-side supported orchards of orange, olive and peach trees. The latter were in bloom showing exquisitely against the gray stone background of terrace walls.}

{On the steep mountain-side, above the far bank of the river, we saw a cave which is said to have been occupied during the Middle Ages by a pious hermit. He would seem to have needed wings or a miracle to get into his domicile, and what he could have found for subsistence after he got there is a mystery. Perhaps he was one of the prayer and fasting sort. As we ascended, we reached forests of scattered pines and passed over a gulf on a great trestle on arches, coiled out into the valley to afford a turn for the train.}

{Soon we reached the new city of Castillon, the ancient, earthquake-shaken city perched on the crown of sheer rock far above. Our view now was of the valley of the river Bevera and our road led downward along one of its tributaries. It was a broad valley dotted with olive trees, and on the horizon were the Italian Apennines covered with snow. On our left was an isolated peak with a fort on its summit. It is here that the famous French Chasseurs are drilled in mountain climbing. We had met a company of them in their gray uniforms and strange, slouching Tam-caps. These have ever been the best soldiers in the French army and were put into the most dangerous positions during the last war, this accounts for the long death lists in such small towns as Castellar and Roquebrun.}

{The terraces up this valley were so old that their walls were almost hidden in vegetation. Some of the olive trees were purple with ripe fruit, and we saw people gathering it; a canvas was spread beneath the tree on which the fruit falls. We tasted a ripe olive and why any creature, let alone a human being, ever came to think of the raw olive as edible, remains to us a profound mystery.}

{Sospel is a pretty city when seen from the hills above. It is on the plain of the River Bevera and surrounded by steep mountains on both sides. It contains many old houses, some of them dating from Roman times. The houses are piled together on either side of the river; many of the streets are arched over. But the pride of Sospel and the joy of artists is the old bridge across the Bevera with a picturesque tower at its middle. The bridge with its tower was built in the fourteenth or fifteenth century and must have been an efficient point of defense when the weapons of war were swords, spears and crossbows.}

{We had luncheon at a café on a platform built out over the river that gave us a view on the one side of the bridge with its two ancient and unequal arches and strange tower beyond this, and on the far side the Plaza St. Michel and its old church with its very old stone campanile. It was this square that in the sixteenth century heretics were burned, bound hand and foot and thrown into the flames. While looking the other way, we could see the golf links that now connect this town with the winter visitors and is one of its chief means of subsistence. While looking at the links stretching away along the banks of the Bevera, we could not help meditating on what this city had been when it was an important outpost of the Roman Empire; or as a flourishing walled city in the Middle Ages with many thousand inhabitants. Its glory lasted during the seventeenth and eighteenth centuries when it had a cathedral and twenty churches and chapels, fifteen squares, many convents and monasteries, an academy and a college for lawyers; now there are barely four thousand inhabitants.}

{The charm of Mentone is that each excursion gives new and different views of this fascinating region. I remember our visit to Gorbio took us through different country from that we had seen before. The valley of the river Gorno is very narrow and we were brought in to close association with the terraces, so beautiful just then, in their spring verdure and the fruit trees all abloom. We passed charming villas and many little stone houses and the picturesque mills for grinding olives, their great water wheels turned by currents through small and artistically attractive canals. Up and up our road led around hillsides, now above the terraces that a few moments ago were above us, often shaded by rows of olives, and occasionally affording a glimpse of the city on a rounded hill which was our objective.}

{We finally arrived and spent several hours exploring the steep streets, often arched over, and always paved with immortal cobblestones which the traffic of eight hundred years had failed to wear down. We visited the old church whose spire makes beautiful the view of the city from afar. Through a maze of narrow alleys, we finally reached the small square, the only level place in the city. From the fountain in the square the peasant citizens now get their water as they have done for centuries. Gorbio was a Saracen city before the tenth century.}

{However, our greatest excursion with the Herricks was to Peille. We started out on the Grand Corniche, past Roquebrun clinging to the mountain side, past La Turbie and its shattered monument of Roman victory, past gallows hill, with its grim pillar, past ever changing views of the sea and rocky valley to Laghet, an old monastery surrounded by tree-covered hills, where we stopped long enough to wonder at the pictures on the walls showing the remarkable cures wrought here by the Virgin, who seems to have her own sweet way with the unfortunates who seek her healing here.}

{From Laghet we followed down a narrow valley made by a tributary to the River Paillon. The terraces here and the houses were made of yellowish stone, a relief from the eternal gray of the region, and offered a satisfying background for the pink of the peach and the almond and white of the cherry blossoms.}

{The river, Paillon, we found was a broad river bed of sand and gravel with rivulets flowing through it. We ascended the broad valley to the base of a sharp cliff on which is perched the old gray city of Paillon with sheer cliffs below it and jagged mountain peaks above it. Here we turned and ascended a mountain that was completely planted with olives on terraces. We zigzagged and some of the corners were so sharp our autobus had to stop and back in order to negotiate them. We had dissolving views of Mont Agel and its companion peaks and of the Maritime Alps, even to the Italian snow-covered range. We finally sighted our goal, the city of Peille, a great gray town just on the near side of the pass. We arrived at its gates, and leaving our autobus, climbed up through the covered streets of the city. It was the climax of ancient cities in our experience. It, like Sospel, was once a Roman stronghold and had, apparently, not changed much since. We clambered up the tunnel-like streets, with branching tunnels leading off to mysterious heights or depths. Mrs. Herrick exclaimed to the guide "Why this city is like just one great house." We finally emerged on a plaza with the ruins of an old castle above us, and in front of us, a remarkable living fountain carved out of the rock in situ. On our right we saw a small level place that was labelled "Mary Garden Play Ground." It seems that Mary Garden is the guardian saint of Peille. She has a villa here and has built a road around the mountain to connect the city with the Grand Corniche at La Turbie, a good and most glorious road skirting gray mountain peaks, and our shortest way back to Mentone.}

{It was strange, or perhaps not strange, but each of these ancient citadels we had visited had its own striking individuality and could never be confused in our minds with any other. The one we did not visit, St. Agnes, was the one that all tourists visit first. The girls went, but someway we felt it a too obvious excursion, as St. Agnes gleamed whitely down upon us every time we stepped out on the streets of Mentone.}

{On March 19th we left Mentone with regret. Our stay there had been pleasant beyond our dreams. We felt that we were leaving real friends in the Misses Nevil. Mrs. Bacon and Madam Tchahotine came to the station to see us off, two women of high character and staunch courage. Our hearts went out especially to Madam Tchahotine, brought up in luxury and now penniless except for the small amount she was able to earn teaching French to very transient tourists. She was nearing three score years and ten in age, and had nothing on her horizon to hope for, yet she looked each day in the face bravely.}

{We stopped at Hyeres to visit the U. S. Entomological Station where parasites are studied with the idea of introducing enemies of the corn-borer into America. Dr. William Thompson, a former student of Mr. Comstock, was in charge. We spent a happy day with Dr. and Mrs. Thompson at the Villa on the hillside that overlooked the city and the valley. The upper floors had been made into laboratories and the family lived below. Mr. Comstock was greatly interested in the work of the station and we enjoyed meeting Dr. Thompson's able assistant, Mr. H. L. Parker.}

{We went on to Avignon and spent a morning at the Pope's Palace, which is really a fortified castle, and wandered about the great rooms built "hit or miss," and we rejoiced that we were just American citizens at the present day and that fate had not willed that we should be Popes or Princes of six hundred years ago.}

{More impressive than the haphazard old palace were the ramparts. We drove slowly around the three miles of tremendous wall with its massive towers and machicolated battlements. When we realized that each opening in the machicolated battlements on the Pope's Palace and the ramparts was for the purpose of protecting a soldier while still allowing him to fight, we had a fair idea of the ecclesiastical hazards of the 14th century. The Seven Popes of Avignon evidently were of the opinion that safety first was a good plan.}

{In the afternoon we dutifully danced on what was left of the Pont St. Benezet just to prove that we belonged to "tout le monde." Evidently, they all danced the Charleston, or something more vigorous, in those days, for the bridge has been in ruins for two hundred and fifty years.}

{We spent two days in Nimes. Perhaps the most striking structures we saw during the winter were the Roman Arena, and the Pont du Gard. We spent hours clambering around the almost perfectly preserved arena made of solid limestone; the 34 tiers of seats were impressive. We sat first in the section reserved for nobles, low down and very directly above the stage, so to speak; next above, we sat in the seats reserved for knights; still above, we tried the seats for the Plebian; and around the periphery, highest of all, were the seats for the slaves. We unhesitatingly declared the slaves had the best seats, for every inch of the floor could be seen perfectly. After this experience we felt less sorry for the Roman slaves than had been our wont.}

{We were delighted with the Maison Carrere, a beautiful, rather small Roman temple with its thirty-nine Corinthian columns thirty feet high. It and the arena were built in the 1st and 2nd centuries A. D. The museum of antiques within it would have interested us more if we had known more—so often our experience in museums. We went on to the beautiful Jardin de la Fontaine, a park where the clear water from the perennial fountain flows through three ornate pools, guarded by stone railing ornamented with vases. The pools were there in Roman times and beyond them is the Temple of Diana in a state of interesting ruin.}

{We took a taxi at Nimes and drove several miles through a region set with olive orchards to the famous Pont du Gard, the Roman aqueduct and bridge across the river Gard. We were awed by its three tiers of arches; in the lowest one the arches are very broad, in the next narrower and in the upper, which hold the aqueduct, much smaller. It is the most majestic of all the Roman aqueducts left to us. We marveled at the workmanship, which set these stones so perfectly without mortar, that they still stand staunch and firm after two thousand years.}

{From Nimes we went to Marseilles and went aboard our steamer, the "President Garfield" of the Dollar Line. Our voyage was without notable incident. We had for table mate the mother of our Cornell friend, Kate Gleason, the engineer, and found her an attractive woman, very companionable. Our other table mate was Mr. George Hamilton Cunningham, a most interesting man, who had just completed a guide book of London streets giving the history of each and telling of the people who had dwelt there. He had had many interesting experiences abroad and at home. Early in the voyage he confided to me that he always avoided contact with intellectual women "because they always get their learning so wopsed around their ego." I felt relieved and cheered that he never classed me with the intellectuals. He was enthusiastic over the kind of passengers on our ship. "The women are all middle-aged and solid. Just take a look at them and at once you vision white painted homes, green blinds, and grape arbors."}

{When we docked in New York we found Mrs. Thro and Margaret's brother Bob Turner waiting for us. We had supper with Mrs. Thro and Gerald and Catherine Stopp and came home to find Jim waiting for us at the station. When we reached the house, we found Eliza had a real American breakfast ready for us.}

{On April 12th a daughter, Eleanor May, was born to Jim and Gretel, a matter of rejoicing in our family. It was thrilling to have a baby of our own; however, later I suffered the fate of other grandmothers of this day, I was not allowed to hold her or even sit with her when her parents were out, for fear if she cried I would take her up and comfort her instead of steadily listening to her wails; I had to wait until she was grown up enough to come visiting, really to enjoy her.}

{Dr. R. A. Millikan was lecturing at [Cornell] when we returned, and Mr. Comstock and I listened to him not too intelligently I fear. The story of the electrons hopping about in different orbits in the atom was too large a contract of our undisciplined imagination. Surely the physicists are the dreamers of this century.}

{As usual, I was called upon for brief speeches at various semi-social meetings. We attended one especially pleasant function, a dinner at the Ithaca Hotel, given by the citizens of Ithaca to William O. Kerr, for twenty-five years the efficient city clerk. We had regarded Mr. and Mrs. Kerr among our most esteemed friends. Back when Mr. Comstock was Instructor he had worked hard to quash an injustice that threatened Mr. Kerr and some of his fellow students.}

{The faculty had been misinformed and it required all of Mr. Comstock's force of character to inform that body. He was then cautioned by an older professor against getting a reputation for defending students. However, to the end, Mr. Comstock was a human being as well as a professor and he always championed the rights of students whom he believed would justify it.}

{On May 28th Mr. Comstock was a guest at the Bell Telephone dinner celebrating its fiftieth birthday. All the original subscribers, still living and in Ithaca were invited. Mr. Comstock felt that it was a notable celebration; his interest in the telephone had never waned, owing I think, to his interest in physics developed under Professor W. A. Anthony during his undergraduate years.}

{The last of May we went with Mr. and Mrs. Will Slingerland to Otto. The days were heavenly, and the hills were decked in all shades of green and pink and brown, the colors of the new leaves. Every apple orchard was in bloom and we thought New York was more beautiful than the Riviera. We visited Cousin Nora and on Decoration Day we went to the North Otto cemetery where seven generations of Botsfords are buried and placed flowers on the graves of our father and mother. It was a scene I shall not forget. The brook prattled and the bobolinks "twanged their silver lyres," and the blue-purple cloud-shadows swept over the valleys and the hills.}

{Early in June our dear friend, Georgia White, Dean of Women, gave a farewell dinner to her closest friends among the faculty and trustees. We all greatly regretted her decision to leave Cornell, but she was tired under the strain of the exacting duties, and also of certain handicaps which seemed inherent in the position. The trustees did all in their power to keep her, and her salary was larger than that of most of the full professors. However, she had been so long in this special harness that she needed to get away to let the galled places heal. The dinner was in Willard Straight Hall and there were twenty of us. Our hostess was charming and looked regal, as she always did in evening attire. Her great height,—she was nearly six feet tall,—her gracious manner, high color and very blue eyes, all combined to make her a handsome and impressive woman.}

{I had a little party of my own, a lawn party and supper for the girls of my Sunday School class. It was a gay party and a noisy one, for the youngsters were full of good spirits and threw off restraint in a most gratifying manner. I enjoyed seeing them act perfectly natural.}

{Stephen Herrick was with us much of this spring. His parents were in Europe, so we were all the family he had. He has a very strong individuality, a keen mind, a keen sense of humor, and to him clothes were merely an uninteresting necessity. His attitude toward life was wholesome and sensible and his character a fine combination of integrity and lovableness. It was a pleasure to have him with us enough to make his more intimate acquaintance. As a matter of fact, we grown-ups have a very limited acquaintance with the children of our friends and relatives since we see them only in the family circle when the conversation is general.}

{An interesting function occurred on June 11; it was a dinner given in honor of Dr. Benjamin F. Kingsbury when his portrait was presented to the University to hang in Stimson Hall. He is a man of gentle manners, a thorough and inspiring teacher, a genuine scholar, and he has done great work for Cornell. His modesty was such that it was difficult to express to him our appreciation in ordinary life. This was an occasion when he had to listen to our opinion of him and his accomplishments. Professor Gage, who knew him best of all, was able to express the appreciation and admiration which we all felt.}

{Soon after Commencement we had the happiness of entertaining Professor and Mrs. Charles Wing of Stanford and Professor and Mrs. Henry Wing for dinner. Mr. Comstock had always held in greatest regard Charles Wing, and we were much depressed when he told us of the change in the Engineering Departments at Stanford under Chancellor Wilbur's administration. The fine esprit de corps which had always characterized the engineering faculty was evidently utterly destroyed.}

{The last of June found me in Philadelphia attending the summer meeting of the National Educational Association. My address was titled The Paths of Nature Study and it was well received.}

{On my way home, I went to New York to see President and Mrs. Benjamin Ide Wheeler, and their son, Webb, who were on the point of sailing for Europe. Webb was to study for a doctorate under a historian in Vienna and his parents were to be with him.}

{In July I began teaching in the Summer Session. Dr. E. L. Palmer was away, detained by sickness in his family; consequently, I had his class and mine for the first weeks of the term.}

{A special happiness came to us this summer because Sao-Ke Alfred Sze[3] brought his family to Ithaca for the summer and lived in the Phi Delta Theta lodge near us. We had kept in touch with him since his student days. His keen mind, high ideals, integrity, and the unquenchable sweetness of his character had endeared him to us and we highly prized his friendship. We found his wife a noble and charming woman with keen insight and good judgment. The six children were each interesting and very individual. Mamie, the eldest girl, was ready to enter Wellesley. Szeming, the eldest boy, was studying medicine in Cambridge, England, and the younger boy was in an English school. Julia, a girl of twelve, was very bright, while little Betty and the baby were charming; the children were a joy to us.}

---

3. Footnote at bottom of the manuscript page (p. 20–32): "Sao-Ke Alfred Sze, among other services to his country, was minister from China to Great Britain from 1914 to 1921 and Envoy Extraordinary and Minister Plenipotentiary from China to the United States from 1921 for several years. —Ed. [G.W.H.]."

{I had learned to drive the car, but Mr. Comstock always accompanied me and sat with me. I felt safer and, although he did not like to drive, he liked to help me drive. I drove to my lectures and he went with me, taking a book to read while he stayed in the car and waited until I finished. We had some drives together about the country. We had some interesting trips planned for September, never dreaming what would happen before then.}

{On July 27th came a telegram telling of the death of our beloved George Tansey. It was a terrible shock to both of us. He was one of our favorite students as a freshman when he entered in 1884. Since his graduation the friendship had ripened into new richness with each year. During the thirty-six years since his graduation I doubt if there was a fortnight passed without some reminder from him to us, to show that he remembered and cared. Life could never be the same for us with him away.}

August 4th [1926],[4] was a very hot day but Mr. Comstock had become much interested in the garden and grounds and he had mowed the lawn for exercise, as our lawn is not large. However, this morning the heat was so great that he felt ill from the effects of it, {and when} he went with me {to my lecture, he said he would take no book but} would rest [in the car]. The next day {he} still felt seedy but {we had invited the entire Sze family to supper and} he had looked forward to this pleasure for a week; he dressed for dinner, but he did not act natural. We gave the children some of our books and when {he} signed his name I was shocked to see how his hand shook and how wavy were the lines.

The next morning, he was still worse, and we sent for Dr. Harry Bull. {Dr. Harry Bull} had not only administered for many years to our physical infirmities but had been a loyal friend sharing in our joys with pleasure {equal to ours} and in our perplexities with cheering words of comfort and encouragement. Dr. Bull found no very marked symptoms but the next day we knew that Mr. Comstock had suffered a hemorrhage of the brain.

There are no words to describe his bravery and patience and cheerfulness after this calamity which, for us, ended life. All that came after was merely existence.

---

4. Here begin the few final paragraphs, from page 20–34 of the manuscript, which were reworked into Chapter 20 of the 1953 edition. The page is cut with the top half pasted to the bottom. Omitted sections are placed in scripted brackets. —KSt.

Last known photo of Mrs. Comstock, spring/summer 1930.

Editor's Epilogue

The historical restoration project of Mrs. Comstock's autobiographical manuscript was a long process that evolved into a work of dedication to restore her voice to her own work. I was dissatisfied with the conclusion of the 1953 edition, which ended with resignation to fate. As editor of this twenty-first-century edition, I felt it necessary to include, for the reader and researcher, a more comprehensive picture of the last two years of the Comstocks' lives.

Mrs. Comstock closed her autobiography shortly after the couple's last trip overseas, to Mentone and surrounding countryside. In the 1953 edition of their biography, the last chapter ends abruptly with the onset of her husband's paralysis, and the ending phrase, "All that came after was merely existence." My further investigation through the Division of Rare and Manuscript Collections at Cornell University uncovered a small paper trail of letters between mutual friends of the Comstocks, meeting minutes from Comstock Publishing Company, and a day ledger itemizing medical care for Mr. Comstock after his wife's death. Together, all of these documents tell the story of the Comstocks' last months, giving us a better sense of Mrs. Comstock's haunting last phrase.

The summer after their return from Mentone, Mrs. Comstock amended her will, on July 2, 1926, to bequeath some special provisions to family friend

William A. Slingerland, then Comstock Publishing Company (CPC) manager. Mr. Slingerland and his family originally came to Ithaca, New York, in approximately 1909, shortly after the death of his uncle, the late Professor Mark V. Slingerland—beloved student, colleague, and friend of Mr. Comstock. Both Professor and Mrs. Comstock pressed the younger Slingerland, a postman from Michigan, to join in their publishing business to honor their friend's memory and to provide the nephew with an opportunity for a successful career. The Comstock Publishing Company was slated for reorganization in 1928, as part of the specifications from Professor Comstock's will, and Mrs. Comstock began making her preparations early to ensure Slingerland's success in the future.

Slingerland's eventual inheritance, and the transference of rights, from the arrangement included the copyrights of the notebooks known as the Nature Note Book Series (except the *Insect Note Book*, which is the property of James G. Needham); also the copyrights of the loose-leaf plates of birds, animals, fishes, and flowers published by the CPC; the electrotypes and photo-engravings from which the notebooks and plates were printed; and the stock of notebooks on hand at the time of her death.[1]

Almost one month after the amendment to Mrs. Comstock's will, in the late summer of 1926, Professor Comstock suffered his first paralytic shock. He was affected on his right side, and initially, his center of speech remained untouched and his mind remained clear. Mrs. Comstock called the event "a bolt out of the blue."[2] In a letter to President William Peirce of Kenyon College, Mrs. Comstock declined an invitation to the dedication of the Samuel Mather Science Hall, on their behalf, where Mr. Comstock was also to receive an honorary degree. She expressed to Peirce that her husband was in good health during their trips abroad, to Hawaii and the French Riviera in the immediate previous years, without "even a hint of high blood pressure."[3] Mr. Comstock had a partial recovery from this first stroke. Professor Simon Gage, in a letter to his son, Phelps, reported that Mr. Comstock took little walks to the Gage home, aided by Mrs. Comstock.

Little is found about the Comstocks in the interim year, 1927, of the professor's stroke and before the reorganization of the Comstock Publishing Company. Their closest friends kept a sharp eye on both Comstocks. Professor Simon Gage wrote in a letter to W. A. Riley, October 28, 1927,

---

1. Simon Henry Gage and Clara Starrett Gage, "A Half-Century of the Comstock Publishing Company; 1893–1943," 65.

2. Anna Botsford Comstock to Clara Keopka Trump, May 8, 1929. Letter. Clara Keopka Trump Papers, 1909–1986. Division of Rare and Manuscript Collections, Cornell University.

3. Anna Botsford to William F. Peirce, September 15, 1926. Letter. John Henry and Anna Botsford Comstock Papers. Division of Rare and Manuscript Collections, Cornell University.

that Mrs. Comstock was "fairly well,"[4] taught summer school that year, and was working on illustrating some articles for herself. Gage speaks of how Mrs. Comstock was "on hand every minute for Prof. C."[5] Despite these personal increasing hardships for Mrs. Comstock, 1927 would prove to be a calm before the storm of the following year.

On July 1, 1928, the board of the CPC convened for its reorganization endeavors. First, the reorganization of CPC consisted of establishing a copartnership between John Henry Comstock, president (an honorary appointment regardless of his incapacitation); Simon H. Gage, first vice president and acting president; Anna Botsford Comstock, second vice president; Glenn W. Herrick was elected secretary; and William A. Slingerland was appointed manager. As the manager of Comstock Publishing Company, Slingerland was to give a full report of all sales, allocating to each book the amount it brought when sold, including commission.

Second, with the reorganization, Mrs. Comstock officially transferred her rights of the Loose Leaf business to William Slingerland, as instructed per revisions of her will in 1926. According to Gage's notes, the bequest did not wait until her death, but rather, after constant solicitation from Slingerland, become effective on the reorganization date of July 1, 1928. Transferred to Slingerland, for the 1928 sum of $1, were all rights, title, and interest of the above described publications in Mrs. Comstock's will. It was also agreed that both Comstocks (or the surviving spouse should either succumb first), *with* Mr. Slingerland, would equally divide the net income of the Loose Leaf business. The transfer initiated the beginning of the Slingerland-Comstock Publishing Company.

The windfall that landed upon Mr. Slingerland was staggering. The sales of the Loose Leaf portion of Comstock Publishing accounted for almost *half* of the Company's sales in August 1928 at $2,655 [$39,196 in 2018 dollars[6]]. As it stood, the other sales of Anna Comstock's books, John Henry Comstock's books, and Simon Gage's books brought in an additional $2,792 [$41,210 in 2018 dollars]. Mrs. Comstock's sales *alone* accounted for $2,655 [$39,196 in 2018 dollars] of the latter total. Plus, along with the formation of Slingerland-Comstock Publishing, Slingerland received a 20 percent commission on all sales for his managing of the Comstock Publishing Company, had the privilege of selling the Company's books, received a 40 percent discount on any book purchases he made, *and* earned a salary.

---

4. Simon Henry Gage to W. A. Riley, October 28, 1927. Letter. Simon Henry Gage 1880–1957 #14-26-533. Division of Rare and Manuscript Collections, Cornell University.

5. Ibid.

6. All monetary conversions in this Editor's Epilogue section were obtained from www.usinflationcalculator.com. —KSt.

Following the CPC reorganization, trouble began almost immediately and continued month after month,. Several letters were sent by Simon Gage, in late August, to various Cornell University professors (who were clients of CPC) about the reorganization of the Comstock Publishing Company, and of the addressed individual's publication(s) being transferred for marketing to the Slingerland-Comstock Company. Professor Gage sought approval from these clients for the new transfer and also inquired of any royalties due to the addressee. The first flag of concern was raised as reciprocal correspondence to Gage, from all clients, revealed that no royalties had been paid. It seems that Slingerland had kept clients in the dark about their books by either not sending statements of copies printed-to-date nor obtaining settlement of payment. Slingerland also removed books from the Comstock Publishing Company property, without permission, and then sold some of the books himself.

According to the September 3, 1928, CPC board meeting minutes, Slingerland attended only to report on the financial ledger and skirted issues of the non-payment of royalties to the Cornell professors. The university authors, who had their books published at CPC, still received no finite financial statement concerning the number of their publications sold and of the royalties due them. Acting President Gage also pressed Slingerland for accountability of checks not paid to six publishing companies (Little Brown & Company, A. J. Grant, Doubleday Doran, G. P. Putnam Sons, and T. G. Miller & Sons for a total due of $652 [$9,624 in 2018 dollars]) and the sixth, Plimpton Press. In particular, the amount owed to Plimpton Press ($3,220 [$47,535 in 2018 dollars]) was for the reprint of the last edition of Mrs. Comstock's *Handbook of Nature Study*. This was a huge embarrassment to the Comstock Publishing Company. In letters to Plimpton Press, Gage attributed the lack of payment to the Comstocks' health and that "many things have gone unattended."[7]

To add insult to injury, Mr. and Mrs. Comstock were also not issued their monthly rent check from Slingerland for CPC's use of the publishing house ($50 [$738 in 2018 dollars]). Last, at this September meeting, Slingerland was given a scathing letter stating that an audit he rendered through fiscal year July 1, 1928–29 was not acceptable to the CPC board because he took *an additional salary* of $75 a week for himself from the profits. Per the original agreement, Slingerland was to pay 50 percent of the net profits therefrom to Mrs. Comstock as long as she lived, and to Professor Comstock as long as he lived, or to the survivor of them. It was the intent and understanding of the agreement that the 50 percent of the net profits should be Slingerland's profit, *including his services*, and not above them.

7. Simon Henry Gage, 1880–1957, #14-26-480. Division of Rare and Manuscript Collections, Cornell University.

Professor Gage wrote Mr. Slingerland a succinct letter that he was to have ready for the October 1928 monthly meeting, the monthly report of business and the reports concerning each interest for which the CPC has been selling books. What Gage and the others of the board discovered was that royalties of $930 [$13,724 in 2018 dollars], which were paid by a check to Comstock Publishing Company, were charged as an expense by Slingerland in the 1928–1929 Loose Leaf business, and hence reduced the net income of the company. The money that Slingerland should have been using to pay the royalties, before the July 1928 reorganization, had apparently been withheld to supply funds for getting a large stock of publications for his newly formed Loose Leaf business. Gage further surmised that Mrs. Comstock would have had to have paid half of those back-royalties, and that Slingerland received *that* half, plus the entire amount of the Loose Leaf royalties from previous years, to build his business.

Gage must have moved swiftly in November for the Plimpton debt was paid off by the December 3, 1928, meeting of the CPC board. Also, by the following year (1929), the Comstocks were once again receiving their regular monthly check from Comstock Publishing ($550 [$8,119 in 2018 dollars]) as well as the $50 for rental of the Chalet for the publishing business.

Mrs. Comstock probably expressed doubt of any nefarious intentions on Slingerland's behalf. The history between her family, the Botsfords, the Slingerland family and, ironically, the Herrick family was rooted deeply in their collective connection to the hearth and homestead of their childhoods in Otto, New York. True, Mrs. Comstock did sign every letter of protest that Gage and the other board members initiated toward William Slingerland, but her feelings toward him were different from those of the others. The entire affair must have been incredulous to Gage and the many others close to the Comstocks who knew of the swindle. The medical suffering that Mr. and Mrs. Comstock incurred in their last years was alleviated only by the financial support the royalties from what their life's work gave them, particularly the *Handbook of Nature Study*. Comstock Publishing Company records at the time show that Mrs. Comstock's published books were selling at a rate of 3:1 over her husband's. The tampering of this last financial support for them, by one whom they took into their own circle, is appalling.

Ironically, it was not until after Mr. Comstock's death in February 1931 that William A. Slingerland was dissolved of any association with Comstock Publishing Company. Mr. Slingerland was terminated from his position as manager of the Comstock Publishing Company on May 4, 1931, months after the deaths of both Comstocks and the transfer of their interests to Cornell University. Gage was incensed by Slingerland's actions and the financial hardship he placed on the elderly Comstocks. Despite Slingerland's own early demise in 1938, Professor Gage diligently worked up until eight months before his

Last known photo of Professor Comstock, circa 1926.

own death, in 1944, to remove Slingerland's name from any nature-study literature and connection to the Comstock legacy.[8]

As the publishing company's scandal roiled in the background of her life, through 1928 into 1929, Mrs. Comstock continued the daily care of her husband and facilitated her nature study work. A letter to her former assistant, Clara Keopka Trump, gives us a glimpse into the professor's health. In May 1929, Mrs. Comstock described that he had had "two periods of what the Doctor terms 'blood seepage' into the brain."[9] Mr. Comstock lost strength after each episode, but still enjoyed three cigars a day, managing perfectly with his left hand, as well as with Professor Burr helping him. This hemorrhage affected Mr. Comstock's ability to speak. His calm expression reassured his loved ones that he did not suffer pain. It was conveyed that although Mr. Comstock could not talk, he did seem to understand all that was said to him, and Gage maintained the conviction that his friend did not suffer, as he mentioned in an earlier letter to Riley, "the mental agony that might come if the full consciousness of his condition were known. Blessed Nature, she is good to us even if she cannot always protect us from disaster."[10]

Mrs. Comstock does mention her own health to Trump, and what her doctor calls her "damned heart,"[11] but she continued to teach in the Cornell Summer School, refusing to give up "until one has to."[12] The May 1929 letter to Trump seemed to spark a meeting of the friends in the later summer months. Trump mentions in a memoir that her last visit with Mrs. Comstock was in 1929, the year before her death. "The Professor was then a bed-ridden invalid, and could barely speak to greet me. She laid her head on my shoulder, weeping, and said she hoped she could care for him as long as he lived."[13] Mrs. Comstock, by her own admission, was quite ill the past February and again in early spring, and she expressed her concern of not knowing what was wrong with her.

---

8. On July 1, 1932, the value of the inventory of Comstock Publishing Company, one year after the death of the Comstocks, was recorded at $18,910 ($349,063 in 2018 dollars). Simon Henry Gage and Clara Starrett Gage, "A Half-Century of the Comstock Publishing Company; 1893–1943," 91.

9. Anna Botsford Comstock to Clara Keopka Trump, May 8, 1929. Letter. Clara Keopka Trump Papers, 1909–1986, #4266. Division of Rare and Manuscript Collections, Cornell University.

10. Simon Henry Gage to W. A. Riley, October 28, 1927. Letter. Simon Henry Gage 1880–1957 #14-26-533. Division of Rare and Manuscript Collections, Cornell University.

11. Anna Botsford Comstock to Clara Keopka Trump, May 8, 1929. Letter. Clara Keopka Trump Papers, 1909–1986, #4266. Division of Rare and Manuscript Collections, Cornell University.

12. Ibid.

13. Anna Botsford Comstock to Clara Keopka Trump, May 8, 1929. Letter. Clara Keopka Trump Papers, 1909–1986, #4266. Division of Rare and Manuscript Collections, Cornell University.

Professor George Burr, away in Washington, D.C., for an extended period of time (in late 1929 to early 1930), elicited the help of A. B. Martin, who sent monthly rent checks to Burr and reported to him about the Comstocks' well-being. Burr sent a Christmas pudding to all and, in return, Martin's letters gave snippets of the frailty of both Comstocks. One letter described Mrs. Comstock as growing stronger while Mr. Comstock was failing, yet cheerful, in another. Toward the spring (when Mrs. Comstock first mentioned the concern of her own health to Trump), Martin wrote that his "invalids"[14] health had not changed, but he was beginning to think that Mr. Comstock would only minimally last another autumn. Martin's attendance of Mr. Comstock allowed Mrs. Comstock to go to the spa at Clifton Springs to rest, and seemingly it was believed, made wholly well again by her week away. Her friends and caretaker hoped the coming spring would put her on her feet again. After all, she still insisted on teaching her nature study coursework.

Small details are found here and there in the Division of Rare and Manuscript Collections at Cornell University of Mrs. Comstock's final months. Her respite at Clifton Springs revealed a lung carcinoma, the result of which was not shared with the patient but only with her personal doctor, who in turn told Martin and Gage. In April she sold Mr. Comstock's player piano and its music to Professor Gage for $1. In May, the Comstocks' close friend Alexis Babine succumbed from an inoperable carcinoma. It was Burr, already in Washington, who brought Babine's crematory urn back to Ithaca and placed it in the Comstock burial plot, with Mrs. Comstock's permission. Both Mr. and Mrs. Comstock long regarded Babine as a member of their household, almost of their family, and it gave "them satisfaction that his ashes should rest where theirs would someday."[15]

Mrs. Comstock taught her last course the summer of 1930. On the final day of class, August 15, her students went to her home for their final lesson. Martin described in a letter to Burr that from her last class until three hours before her death nine days later,

> . . . she was fully herself. I have never known her brighter, despite pain and weakness, than the day before her going; and, when the final struggle came, she died, thanks to the anodynes, as one who falls asleep. To

14. A. B. Martin to George Lincoln Burr, February 28, 1930. Letter. George Lincoln Burr Papers, #14-17-22. Division of Rare and Manuscript Collections, Cornell University.

15. Charles H. Hull to Dr. Herbert Putnam, Librarian of Congress, May 13, 1930. Letter. George Lincoln Burr Papers, #14-17-22. Division of Rare and Manuscript Collections, Cornell University.

> the end, too, she took only to her couch. True, her cough became continuous and her breath very short, and she undoubtedly suffered more than she ever let us know.[16]

Mrs. Comstock died on August 24, a Sunday morning, in her home. The week was warm and sunny for late August in Ithaca, and that may have influenced, in part, the funeral services being held on the following Tuesday morning, the 26th, in Sage Chapel on the Cornell campus. The pastor, Reverend Frank Gredler, of the Unitarian Church where Anna was a member since 1911, officiated the service. Both Professor Simon Gage and Liberty Hyde Bailey eulogized their personal sorrow, and it is from their grief that we glean the insights into Mrs. Comstock's character we have come to appreciate today. Her "breadth of human sympathy,"[17] and her moral compass in the statement, "Mrs. Comstock saw the good in everybody. Hers was a pure, straight, human friendliness"[18] were the descriptors from Gage. Bailey offered the infamous insight, "Her life was a poem,"[19] that has been repeated so often since he first spoke the words. An editorial in the *Ithaca Daily Journal*, on the day of her burial, described her life as a balance of achievements attributed by her intellectual interests and her artistic perceptions. After the funeral, Mrs. Comstock's body was taken to Rochester, New York, for cremation. She was laid to rest some days later, near Alexis Babine, in a private service at the Comstock family plot at Lakeview Cemetery in Ithaca, New York.

News of Mrs. Comstock's death reverberated through Ithaca and among her friends almost immediately. Professor Burr must have been sent a telegram by Martin, for he was still in Washington. Given the date of return correspondence (from the RMC archives), the day after Burr received the news of Mrs. Comstock's death, he quickly telegraphed many Comstock friends and associates. A friend described the situation as "pathos"[20] and

---

16. A. B. Martin to George Lincoln Burr, August 30, 1930. Letter. George Lincoln Burr Papers, #14-17-22. Division of Rare and Manuscript Collections, Cornell University.

17. "Mrs. Comstock Dies; Famous Many Years As Teacher, Artist." Newspaper clipping. John Henry and Anna Botsford Comstock Papers, 1833–1955, #21-23-25. Division of Rare and Manuscript Collections, Cornell University.

18. Ibid.

19. Bailey, Liberty Hyde Bailey Papers, 1854–2004, 1870–1958. Division of Rare and Manuscript Collections, Cornell University.

20. Charles Thurber to George Lincoln Burr, September 25, 1930. Letter. George Lincoln Burr Papers, #14-17-22. Division of Rare and Manuscript Collections, Cornell University.

as a "tragedy in the end of this family who have given so much to their friends."[21] Another spoke of Mrs. Comstock's friendship:

> She was altogether lovely and "blessed us all". Her friendship was one of my most precious possessions, and one of my greatest joys of anticipation was the thought of seeing her and being with her again. Mr. Comstock will be very tenderly cared for, I know, and perhaps in his present condition does not realize his loss.[22]

The concern over the surviving Comstock was repeated consistently through their friends' letters. There were expressions of concern for Mr. Comstock after Anna's death, wondering if he knew, or in the least, understood her absence. It wasn't until after the interment of Mrs. Comstock's ashes that Mr. Comstock was told of his wife's death. A. B. Martin wrote to Professor Burr, August 30, 1930:

> And we laid her to rest on a lovely knoll in the Lake-view Cemetery overlooking lake and hills. Not till then did we tell Harry, though I think he divined it all. He bears it with the stoical courage that was his always, and our fear that both might go together is for the moment dispelled. He is in good hands, his two nurses devoted to him, and we hope to prevent any interruption in his routine.[23]

The concern of distant friends would be eased by the tenderness of close friends in their care of the ailing professor. Glenn Herrick kept a small financial booklet, "Expenses of Comstock Household,"[24] from September 1, 1930, days after Mrs. Comstock's death, until Mr. Comstock's death in March of 1931. This small notebook gives us the last look into the window of their home at 123 Roberts Place, and of the care administered there, to such an admired man. Monthly bills for laundry, electricity, gas, coal, and oil for the furnace (and its repair) were recorded. Also on the list were payments for water and ice delivery, milk delivery, the telephone bill, new night shirts and medical supplies for Professor Comstock. Added, for his comfort, were flowers, favorite cigars, and a *Reader's Digest* subscription (presumably to be read to Mr. Comstock) in September. Flowers were also purchased again

21. Ibid.

22. Katherine Creighton to Glenn Herrick, September 28, 1930. Letter. Glenn Washington Herrick Papers, 1872–1963, #21-23-844. Division of Rare and Manuscript Collections, Cornell University.

23. A. B. Martin to George Lincoln Burr, August 30, 1930. Letter. George Lincoln Burr Papers, #14-17-22. Division of Rare and Manuscript Collections, Cornell University.

24. Glenn Washington Herrick Papers. Division of Rare and Manuscript Collections, Cornell University.

in October and November, as Herrick purchased flowers every month, for himself or others, up until his own last recorded entry in his personal diary of 1963.

Mr. Comstock had round-the-clock care by five people who rotated in weekly shifts. Eliza Northrup ($12 per week [$182 in 2018 dollars]) for seven months; Minnie Wetzel ($35 per week [$530 in 2018 dollars]) at two-week intervals for seven months; Harriet Turner and Lida A. Reynolds ($28 per week [$424 in 2018 dollars]) in two-week rotations; Stanley Schaefer ($20 per week [$303 in 2018 dollars]) came every week. Herrick also included what he called, "Provisions for Table," and "Cash for the house," for the caretakers.[25] The Comstocks' physician, Dr. Bull, was paid accordingly, as was the plumber and labor about the house and grounds. Herrick also handled the taxes and interest on the Comstocks' mortgage and paid the federal income tax due ($87 [$1,451 in 2018 dollars]) from this pool of finances. Herrick continued to document monies paid after Mr. Comstock's death, including the cost of Comstock's mourning cards, up until August of 1931. George Lincoln Burr "never failed to visit [Mr. Comstock] for an hour every afternoon to play phonograph records. . . . Never would [Burr] accept an invitation outside of Ithaca if it would keep him from that hour."[26]

Mr. Comstock passed away March 20, on a clear Friday afternoon, when the temperatures of winter began to loosen their grip to make way for a new spring to bud forth. As with his wife, the passing of John Henry Comstock brought forth accolades and emotions. The *Ithaca Journal News* featured a six-column article in the evening paper the day of his death. Comstock's closest friends paid personal tribute to the man they were proud to call brother and friend.

Professor Burr said, in part, of Comstock that,

> His trained eye could see in the field and stream a world of life that others blindly passed, and the determination that mastered in boyhood his early stammering leveled in later life every obstacle that seemed at first to hem his way. I never knew, I think, so masculine a man. Yet tender he could be as well, helpful always at whatever cost, and generous to the core in purse and soul. He was a man to follow and to love.[27]

---

25. Glenn Washington Herrick Papers. Division of Rare and Manuscript Collections, Cornell University.

26. Bainton, *George Lincoln Burr: His Life and Selections from His Writings*, p. 141.

27. "J. H. Comstock Dead; Cornell Educator, 82, Famed Entomologist." Newspaper clipping. John Henry and Anna Botsford Comstock Papers, 1833–1955, #21-23-25. Division of Rare and Manuscript Collections, Cornell University.

Professor Simon Gage, in part:

> The watch word that guided his own life was, "Be sure you are right, then look again." This spirit he passed on to the multitude of men he trained by his writings and by his personal instruction or by both; and they have also become leaders, leaders in every country in the world.[28] Gage also added that ever-present in the Comstock home was "the glowing hearth-fire of human kindness."[29]

Professor Gage saw to every detail, and he along with Professor Burr, George "Jim" Russell, and Professor Herrick held as their greatest concern that Mr. Comstock's service "should all be done unassuringly as the Professor would want it."[30] As with Mrs. Comstock, the professor's funeral was held in Sage Chapel and duplicated as close as possible with her service. Reverend Frank Gredler, of the Unitarian Church in Ithaca, once again conducted services for the last Comstock in a Sunday afternoon ceremony. Cornell president Livingston Farrand, one of the many speakers at the funeral, said of John Henry Comstock's passing that his death "removes one of the monumental figures in Cornell's history."[31] Farrand added that "Professor Comstock's scientific achievements are recognized everywhere but it is here in Ithaca that his friendly, lovable, sympathetic personality found its home. He will be sadly missed."[32]

As with his wife, Mr. Comstock was cremated and interred shortly after his funeral. In his final eulogy for his dear friend, Professor Gage remarked that, "the hardest and greatest thing one could do for a friend was to do the last services."[33]

The last professional accolades bestowed upon the Comstocks came from the university in which they entrenched so much of their hard work, determination, and spirit. The following excerpts of each Memorial Statement summarizes the impact of the life, and the sorrow at the death, of both Professor John Henry and Anna Botsford Comstock.

---

28. Ibid.

29. Ibid.

30. Minnie Whetzel to Grace Fordyce Fox, no date. Letter. Grace Fordyce Fox Papers: 1914–1931, #21-23-3574. Division of Rare and Manuscript Collections, Cornell University.

31. "J. H. Comstock Dead; Cornell Educator, 82, Famed Entomologist." Newspaper clipping. John Henry and Anna Botsford Comstock Papers, 1833–1955, #21-23-25. Division of Rare and Manuscript Collections, Cornell University.

32. "Comstock Rites 3 P. M. Sunday Sage Chapel." Newspaper clipping. John Henry and Anna Botsford Comstock Papers, 1833–1955, #21-23-25. Division of Rare and Manuscript Collections, Cornell University.

33. Minnie Whetzel to Grace Fordyce Fox, no date. Letter. Grace Fordyce Fox Papers: 1914–1931, #21-23-3574. Division of Rare and Manuscript Collections, Cornell University.

In summation of the life of John Henry Comstock,

> Professor Comstock was one of the earliest teachers of entomology in the United States; and his ideals and standards have exerted a profound influence on the teaching of entomology in this country. His early struggles in self-education undoubtedly begot in him the habit of clear, precise, logical arrangement in his own mind of the problem in which he was interested. As a result, his lectures were models of simplicity, clearness, and conciseness. This logical quality of mind, together with his infectious enthusiasm and his personal interest in his students, made him a great teacher, and this characteristic, together with his experience as a teacher, lay at the root of his success as a writer of text-books. His greatest service to the University and to the world may but be expressed in this brief sentence: He was a trainer and inspirer of men.[34]

In summation of the life of Anna Botsford Comstock, as offered by Cornell University Trustees,

> In an eminent degree Mrs. Comstock possessed the quality of warm and helpful friendship. Her long life in this community attached her to a remarkably wide circle of friends, all of whom became admirers. Her personality enriched her work as well as her relationships. Her interests were greatly varied and she touched life at many diverse points with the skill of the artist, the warmth of rich enthusiasms, and the emotions of the poet. To all her associates in Cornell University her memory will remain a blessed experience, and to generations of students she will continue to be an inspiring example. We are all conscious that a great soul has passed.[35]

By the high moral standards they held for themselves, their work, and their legacy, John Henry and Anna Botsford Comstock might say that they were *most* successful in the affability and stewardship which they gave to their friends and colleagues. The fulfilment their own hearts received, mirrored in eulogy at their demise, was the result of their dedication to the people they loved, unconditionally, during the whole of their lives.

---

34. Cornell University, Office of the Dean of the University Faculty, https://ecommons.cornell.edu/handle/1813/18147.

35. Cornell University, Office of the Dean of the University Faculty, https://ecommons.cornell.edu/handle/1813/17912.

Professor and Mrs. Comstock at the gate of their Comstock Publishing Company, circa 1926.

Appendix A

Original Preface for *The Comstocks of Cornell*

Written by Simon Henry Gage in 1938

Men and women, or outstanding individuals, such as those in this autobiography are most often met with in a new land where opportunity is practically unlimited for brave hearts and clear heads. However, as one reads through the fascinating pages it becomes clear that in any land and at any time people like the Comstocks and the Botsfords must become leaders, and their difficulties, instead of crushing them, act as agents to bring out their capabilities. Certainly these difficulties had that effect.

From close association with them for over fifty years it is no mystery to me that they accomplished what they did. They believed with all their hearts that what they were trying to do was worth while, and no labor was too great to accomplish it. They developed with the growth of a great university, and for any one interested in the history of Cornell the intimate picture of the early days of the university, of its founders, faculty and students gives precious information that only those on the ground could supply.

In their human relations the Comstocks followed the Golden Rule. When their 'dream children' did not come to them in flesh and blood they opened their hearts wide to the children of all races, and their home became the haven to which many went both in happiness and in distress, and none left without a lighter heart and firmer faith in life.

This autobiography was written by Mrs. Comstock while carrying on the strenuous duties of life, and before there was time and strength to revise it carefully, illness came and the long sleep. Their friend and colleague, Glenn W. Herrick, tried to do for them what they had to leave undone. We who knew them best feel grateful to him for his sympathetic editing, and the Comstock Publishing Company, which they did so much to make successful, is publishing the book for their friends and old pupils with the hope that many may read it and find their aspirations for a noble life justified and strengthened.

Simon Henry Gage

Appendix B

Original Foreword for *The Comstocks of Cornell*

Written by Glenn W. Herrick for the 1953 Edition

JOHN HENRY COMSTOCK was determined to get an education. He came to Cornell University because it offered him an opportunity to earn his living while pursuing his studies. Anna Botsford came to Cornell because women were admitted on an equality with men. She approved of coeducation. These two young people, each born on a farm and reared in a rural environment, had kindred sympathies and like ambitions. It was inevitable that they should gravitate toward each other and that Anna Botsford should become Anna Botsford Comstock. Happily, their pathway in life continued at the University through many years of gracious companionship and enduring achievement.

The Comstocks worked out their life program together and developed along with Cornell University. They shared the trials and struggles of the University during its early years and, with it, labored on to days of splendid fruition. From these early associations and mutual strivings, the Comstocks came to have an abiding love for Cornell and an unswerving loyalty to its ideals. It seemed to be the chief ambition of each of them to achieve something to the glory and honor of their Alma Mater.

Some months before her death, Mrs. Comstock completed a narrative of the lives of her husband and herself. The account was written during intervals of a busy life, the latter part of it during the year of the author's last illness. Anyone interested in Cornell will find much in the narrative concerning the University. Mrs. Comstock had intended to publish the account before her death but the end came before she was aware of its approach.

Although the manuscript left by Mrs. Comstock was long, it was difficult for one who had worked with the Comstocks for thirty years to omit a single page, no matter how irrelevant it might seem to a stranger. I asked Dr. Francis Wormuth, with his more impersonal attitude, to assist in the arrangement of the manuscript material. Dr. Wormuth's experience in editing has been most helpful. I am most indebted to Dr. Ruby Green Smith (Mrs. Albert W. Smith) who, out of her love for the Comstocks and her devotion to their memory, put aside the writing of one of her own books to go over the manuscript with great care, make many constructive criticisms, and consent to become coeditor; also to Mr. George H. Russell, for his personal efforts in aid of the publication of this book; and to the late Professors Simon H. Gage and George Lincoln Burr for kindly criticism and advice.

GLENN W. HERRICK
Ithaca, New York
October 1951

Appendix C

An Epilogue Written by Glenn W. Herrick for the 1953 Edition

Sunset and Evening Star

It remains to record the slow-moving events of the final years of The Comstocks of Cornell.

On August 5, 1926, Professor Comstock had a strange sickness. The next day the "cruel blow" became evident,—he was paralyzed on his left side. The attack, more serious than at first realized, was the prelude to successive hemorrhages of the brain during the next four and one-half years which affected him in a progressively vital manner. After the first shock had spent itself, he rallied sufficiently to leave his bed and with the aid of a nurse to walk about his room and to take short rides, on propitious days.

Early in 1927 he became worse, and in June was again confined to his bed in a sleepy, listless condition. Following this shock, he lost the faculty of speech and became practically helpless. Nevertheless, he remained alert mentally and seemed to understand what was said to him. He did not seem to suffer pain. This condition continued during the next four years, until the final shock that quickly resulted in his death, on the morning March 20, 1931.

In Mrs. Comstock's diary in July, 1926, she spoke for the first time of her "fibrillating heart." Thereafter, she frequently spoke of being tired and languid. Early in 1927, she felt worse and her blood pressure became abnormally high, but she "must be doing," she "cannot sit still and think." She confided to her diary, "Strange days these,—the struggle on my part to self-control." Through all of the next three and one-half years of her husband's invalidism she maintained her round of activities, attending functions, often speaking in public and teaching in the Cornell University Summer Sessions. However, she grew slowly worse and through 1929 and 1930 was obliged to spend many hours in bed.

On June, 1930, Hobart College honored her with the degree of Doctor of Humane Letters. By reason of her indomitable will, and in spite of her physical condition, she made the trip to Geneva to be present at the conferring of the degree. She did not improve as the days wore on, yet she managed to guide her husband's care, to interpret his wishes, to give him her inspiring companionship, and to carry her work of teaching through the Summer Session of 1930. She even received her class in her home, at the close of the term, about the middle of August. Less than two weeks thereafter, on Sunday morning, August 24, 1930, she died as bravely as she had lived.

The ashes of each rest in Lakeview Cemetery, in Ithaca, beneath some fine oaks on a high knoll facing west. The site overlooks the valley below with Lake Cayuga winding away to the horizon, a scene they had loved and enjoyed together through all of their years at Cornell.

Glenn W. Herrick

Appendix D

Memorial Statements for Anna Botsford Comstock Issued by Cornell University and *Ithaca Daily Journal News*

Anna Botsford Comstock

Professor of Nature Study—August 24, 1930

Anna Botsford Comstock, born on a farm in western New York, spent her childhood years among the fields and woods of a beautiful countryside. Here she learned the haunts and habits of the native wild life, came to love and foster domestic animals of the farm, and grew in sympathetic understanding of the problems of farm life. She was always intensely interested in men and women, and particularly in the welfare and education of children.

Entering Cornell University almost at its beginning she began the long period of devoted service that closed with a lecture to her summer class in Nature Literature only nine days before her death. She early began the study of the art of wood engraving in order to illustrate the entomological textbooks of her husband, John Henry Comstock, and achieved marked distinction as an artist, especially in her work representing the delicate texture of the bodies and wings of butterflies. She had a large share in the early extension movement in nature study and agriculture and undertook the leadership of the work in nature study in the University at its beginning. Among her varied and rich interests nature study became the chief field of her activity as writer, lecturer, editor, and teacher of teachers.

Mrs. Comstock became endeared to a wide circle of friends beyond the possibilities of merely professional contacts through the hospitality of the home which for half a century was a rendezvous for her students and those of her husband. Here she received and entertained with that gracious sympathy and understanding that made every guest a real participant in the life of a lovely home.

In an eminent degree Mrs. Comstock possessed the quality of warm and helpful friendship. Her long life in this community attached her to a remarkably wide circle of friends, all of whom became admirers. Her personality enriched her work as well as her relationships. Her interests were greatly varied and she touched life at many diverse points with the skill of the artist, the warmth of rich enthusiasms, and the emotions of the poet. To all her associates in Cornell University her memory will remain a blessed experience, and to generations of students she will continue to be an inspiring example. We are all conscious that a great soul has passed.

As a mark of profound respect, we, her colleagues of the University Faculty wish to place in permanent form upon their minutes this tribute to a life of service to the State, the Nation, and the University.

[Fac. Rec. p. 1657 Resolutions of the Trustees and Faculty of Cornell University, December, Nineteen Hundred and Thirty. Retired: June 1922 Cornell University Faculty Memorial Statement, http://ecommons.library.cornell.edu/handle/1813/17813.]

Anna Botsford Comstock

Editorial, *Ithaca Daily Journal News*, August 26th, 1930

A strong feeling for the significance of nature in all its moods and phases, and an equally intense love of humanity were the dominating emotions of the great personality which has left the material world with the death of Anna Botsford Comstock, dean of American Nature Study.

Mrs. Comstock's life was a balanced achievement. Her intellectual interests were many and growing ones, and her artistic perceptions so fine as to enable her to represent the texture of a butterfly's wing. Both her character and her career were well-rounded. There were no stunted branches on this tree.

Admitted as a peer of the most eminent scientists in this and other countries, Mrs. Comstock might have specialized in any one of many different fields, but she wisely chose to emphasize the importance of nature study as a whole, and of the out-door life, in an era which was rapidly becoming hampered by artificialities. Her affection for boys and girls, her understanding of young people, to which she brought the aid of a ready humor, and her friendly approach to all, served to point the way for a back-to-nature movement, for an elevation of the rural community, the importance of which no one now living can estimate.

Both Mrs. Comstock and her distinguished husband entered Cornell almost at the beginning, and together they caught the spirit of a new development in higher education, and added to that spirit impetus of their own. Their lives are built irrevocably into that of the University which is so proud to claim the distinction of having fostered their early careers.

The extension department of the Agricultural College was one of the several important channels through which Mrs. Comstock's personality flowed to enrich the lives of thousands of farm boys and girls.

Her own books were another great source of influence and so were those of her husband, most of which were illustrated by the woman who first learned the art of wood engraving because no artist sufficiently skilled in the use of the microscope could be found at a time of emergency. This achievement was characteristic of one whose enthusiasms remained fresh to the end.

It would be difficult to say whether Anna Botsford Comstock was better known as an author (her "Handbook of Nature Study" is constantly used in the schools of half a dozen countries), as a teacher, or as an artist. She earned distinction in all three fields. There can be no question, however, of her genius for friendship.

When the Comstock Memorial Library Fund was presented to Professor Comstock at the time of his retirement in 1914 the exercises included the reading of a letter from David Starr Jordan, then president of Stanford University. It closed with the following paragraph:

'No Comstock eulogy is complete without a reference to Comstock's home. His marriage intensified his influence in every way. His home became the center of Nature-Study and of human friendliness. Scores of youth of promise of Cornell have owed as much to the personal sympathy of the Comstocks as to anything anybody taught them in the school. No one of all of them—men or women—but renders grateful tribute today, not to Comstock alone, but equally to the gifted and big hearted colleague, who as helpmate has kept full step with him through all these years.'

Appendix E

Memorial Statements for John Henry Comstock Issued by Cornell University

John Henry Comstock

Professor of Entomology—March 20, 1931

In the death of Professor John Henry Comstock on March 20, 1931, Cornell University has lost the scholar who perhaps more than any other embodied the aims of her founder and the spirit of her earliest years. Fatherless from his infancy and reared mainly by strangers, he spent his youth largely as a sailor on the Great Lakes with but winters for schooling, and his higher education had to be won without financial aid from others. Thus he built up the self-reliance, the tireless energy, the concentration, and efficiency so characteristic of his whole career; and thus there came to him, as to few men, power of observation, skill of touch, boundless persistence, and a rare union of quickness, even impatience, with sympathetic insight and considerate helpfulness.

Already while a sailor he had found spare time for the study of plants and of insects, and he came to the young University a ripe student in these fields. Here, under the encouragement of Dr. Wilder, then in charge of biology at Cornell, he developed so swiftly that he was but half through his undergraduate years when at the request of his fellow students he was set at giving a course on insects. This was but the beginning of a professional career which later assumed world-wide significance. His work as an investigator began to express itself in published papers as early as 1871, and his ability and enthusiasm in research grew with the years. This is indicated by his papers on the Coccidae (1880, 1883), his essays on The Descent of the Lepidoptera (1892), and on Evolution and Taxonomy (1893), and by his papers in collaboration with J. G. Needham on the wings of insects (1899). Subsequent papers embodying the results of researches on spiders appeared regularly during his later years. These culminated in the publication of "The Spider Book" (1912). Following his retirement in 1914 he devoted the remaining years to the rounding out of his life's work. The results of his long years of research on the wings of insects were finally brought together in the form of a book, "The Wings of Insects" (1918), probably his chief contribution of pure research. His last years were devoted to the writing of his final work, "An Introduction to Entomology." Happily this was completed before his last illness.

Professor Comstock never engaged in controversy nor did he criticize the work of others. He did his own work as well as he knew how, and with faith in it he let all adverse criticism pass in silence. On the other hand, no one was franker to acknowledge a mistake than he, for accuracy was almost a fetish with him. Moreover he never appropriated the work of others.

[Cornell University Faculty Memorial Statement, http://ecommons.library.cornell.edu/handle/1813/17813]

John Henry Comstock

Faculty Records, September 1931

Professor Comstock was one of the earliest teachers of entomology in the United States; and his ideals and standards have exerted a profound influence on the teaching of entomology in this country. His early struggles in self-education undoubtedly begot in him the habit of clear, precise, logical arrangement in his own mind of the problem in which he was interested. As a result, his lectures were models of simplicity, clearness, and conciseness. This logical quality of mind, together with his infectious enthusiasm and his personal interest in his students, made him a great teacher, and this characteristic, together with his experience as a teacher, lay at the root of his success as a writer of text-books. His greatest service to the University and to the world may but be expressed in this brief sentence: He was a trainer and inspirer of men.

[Faculty Records, pps. 636, 1690 Resolutions of the Trustees and Faculty of Cornell University, September, Nineteen Hundred And Thirty-One]

Bibliography

Bailey, L. H. (Liberty Hyde). Liberty Hyde Bailey Papers, 1854–2004, 1870–1958, # 21-2-3342. Box 34. Division of Rare and Manuscript Collections, Cornell University. Carl A. Kroch Library.

Bainton, Roland H. *George Lincoln Burr: His Life and Selections from His Writings*. Edited by Lois Oliphant Gibbons. Ithaca, NY: Cornell University Press, 1943.

Burr, George Lincoln. 1857–1938. George Lincoln Burr Papers, #14-17-22. Box 17. Annex. Division of Rare and Manuscript Collections, Cornell University. Carl A. Kroch Library.

Comstock, Anna Botsford, and John Henry Comstock. John Henry and Anna Botsford Comstock Papers, #21-23-25. Box 6. Division of Rare and Manuscript Collections, Cornell University. Carl A. Kroch Library.

"Comstock Rites 3 P. M. Sunday Sage Chapel." *Ithaca Journal News*, March 21, 1931. John Henry and Anna Botsford Comstock Collection #21-23-25. Box 6. Division of Rare and Manuscript Collections, Cornell University. Carl A. Kroch Library.

Cornell University and Office of the Dean of the University Faculty. "Comstock, Anna Botsford," 1930. http://ecommons.cornell.edu/handle/1813/17912.

Cornell University, Trustees and Faculty of Cornell University. "Comstock, John Henry," September 1931. https://ecommons.cornell.edu/bitstream/handle/1813/18147/Comstock_John_Henry_1931.pdf?sequence=2&isAllowed=y.

Fox, Grace Fordyce. Grace Fordyce Fox Papers: 1914–1931, #21-23-3574. Box 1, Folder 3. Division of Rare and Manuscript Collections, Cornell University. Carl A. Kroch Library.

Gage, Simon Henry. Simon Henry Gage 1880–1957 #14-26-533. Box 2, Folder 3. Division of Rare and Manuscript Collections, Cornell University. Carl A. Kroch Library.

Gage, Simon Henry. Simon Henry Gage 1880–1957 #14-26-480. Box 8. Division of Rare and Manuscript Collections, Cornell University. Carl A. Kroch Library.

Gage, Simon Henry. Simon Henry Gage 1880–1957 #14-26-480. Box 12. Division of Rare and Manuscript Collections, Cornell University. Carl A. Kroch Library.

Gage, Simon Henry, and Clara Starrett Gage. "A Half-Century of the Comstock Publishing Company; 1893–1943." Ithaca, NY: Comstock Publishing Company, 1944. Unpublished. Simon Henry Gage papers 1880–1957, #14-26-480. Division of Rare and Manuscript Collections, Cornell University. Carl A. Kroch Library.

Herrick, Glenn W. (Glenn Washington). Glenn Washington Herrick Papers, 1872–1963, #21-23-844. Box 15. Division of Rare and Manuscript Collections, Cornell University. Carl A. Kroch Library.

"J. H. Comstock Dead; Cornell Educator, 82, Famed Entomologist." *Ithaca Journal News*, March 20, 1931, Friday Evening edition. John Henry and Anna Botsford Comstock Collection #21-23-25. Box 6 Division of Rare and Manuscript Collections, Cornell University. Carl A. Kroch Library.

"Mrs. Comstock Dies; Famous Many Years As Teacher, Artist." *Ithaca Journal News*, August 23, 1930. John Henry and Anna Botsford Comstock Collection #21-23-25. Box 6. Division of Rare and Manuscript Collections, Cornell University. Carl A. Kroch Library.

Trump, Clara Keopka. Clara Keopka Trump Papers, 1909–1986, #4266. Box 1, Folder 2. Division of Rare and Manuscript Collections, Cornell University. Carl A. Kroch Library.

INDEX